Public Life and the
Propertied Englishman
1689–1798

Public Life and the Propertied Englishman
1689–1798

The Ford Lectures
Delivered in the University of Oxford
1990

PAUL LANGFORD

CLARENDON PRESS · OXFORD
1991

Oxford University Press, Walton Street, Oxford OX2 6DP

Oxford New York Toronto
Delhi Bombay Calcutta Madras Karachi
Petaling Jaya Singapore Hong Kong Tokyo
Nairobi Dar es Salaam Cape Town
Melbourne Auckland
and associated companies in
Berlin Ibadan

Oxford is a trade mark of Oxford University Press

Published in the United States
by Oxford University Press, New York

British Library Cataloguing in Publication Data
Langford, Paul
Public life and the propertied Englishman 1689-1798.
1. England. Landowners: Aristocracy, history
I. Title
305.52320942

ISBN 0-19-820149-4

Library of Congress Cataloging in Publication Data
Langford, Paul
Public life and the propertied Englishman, 1689-1798/Paul Langford
p. cm.
Includes bibliographical references and index.
ISBN 0-19-820149-4
1. Great Britain—Politics and government—18th century. 2. Great
Britain—Politics and government—1689-1702. 3. Middle classes—
England—Political activity—History—18th century. 4. Middle
classes—England—Political activity—History—17th century.
I. Title
DA480.L27 1991
941.07—dc20
90-41689

CIP

Typeset by Butler & Tanner Ltd, Frome and London
Printed and bound in
Great Britain by Bookcraft Ltd,
Midsomer Norton, Bath

Preface

THIS book results from an invitation to give the 1990 Ford Lectures in English History, an honour of which, in my own university I am deeply aware. But the work on which it is based started a good many years ago, with research into the relationship between politics at Westminster and Whitehall on the one hand, and the wider community implied by appeals to 'public opinion' and the 'political nation' on the other. In the lectures, and much more fully in this book, my aim has been to describe some of the ways in which that relationship evolved between the revolution of the rights of Englishmen in 1688 and the revolution of the rights of man a century later.

No student of eighteenth-century life can safely ignore the immense changes which affected it, or contemporary awareness of those changes. The political processes set in motion by the defeat of Stuart absolutism, the strategic and commercial implications of competition for trade and empire, the social consequences of demographic growth, urbanization, and industrialization, and the intellectual strains imposed by the impact of scientific enlightenment on conventional patterns of belief, all contributed to the sense of a society in turmoil. Yet the resulting transformation had to be accommodated by a mentality instinctively hostile to the concept of evolution, let alone revolution, in its modern, progressive sense, and thoroughly self-conscious about its veneration for the past. This veneration involved certain assumptions about the theory and practice of politics, which, however determinedly challenged, were not superseded until much later. One of these assumptions was a hierarchical concept of civil rights and duties, rendering most Englishmen the pawns of their social superiors, bestowing severely limited responsibilities in a parochial setting on men of modest means, and reserving a full part in the business of government and legislation to a narrow élite. With this assumption went another, whose attractions were positively enhanced by the defeat of divine right monarchy in 1688, and which made property the sole, rightful basis of authority. This was a radical doctrine, more radical than many of those who subscribed to it liked to admit. Property could come to men and women who did not accept traditional views of the use to which they should put it, let alone traditional notions about the kind of State they supported. More important still, property itself could be defined in diverse ways, some of them potentially subversive of established authority. Above all, rapid economic growth and diversification ensured that instability of this kind would increase rather than diminish.

Uncovering the motors of historical change and revealing the make-up of historical structures requires as much as anything else a sense of balance about the relative importance of forces which are difficult to compare and evaluate. Most of the differences about eighteenth-century politics, and at least since Namier wrote there have been many such, result from a natural tendency to exaggerate some forces at the expense of others. It is all too easy to claim that the answer offered to a particular question will do as an answer to all kinds of other questions, or to assert that one question is more 'important' and its solution therefore more 'significant' than others. What constitutes historical importance and significance is, of course, itself a highly subjective matter, affected by fashionable ideas, cultural context, and individual idiosyncrasies. It is all the more necessary, then, to specify the question being asked. My own question is this: how did propertied society respond to the demands made by economic growth, commercial competition, and social change, in respect of the exercise of public responsi-bilities and powers? I have used the expression 'public life' to describe the latter partly because it is a neutral term with much the same meaning today as it had in the eighteenth century, partly because it was itself effectively a creation of that century. Like its sister 'public opinion' it had sometimes been used earlier but did not achieve common currency until about 1750.[1] It was employed both to distinguish the individual's public role from his private affairs, and to describe numerous concerns beyond, but often including, the activities of the Crown, the government and the State in the narrow sense in which these were generally defined. Many of these concerns were carried on under chartered or statutory authority, others merely by means of voluntary association. What they had in common was the ambition of some public good, usually of a kind covered by that most characteristic of eighteenth-century commendations, 'improvement'. Public life also comprehended the relationships which linked propertied people involved in these activities with the central organs of government, especially as they affected parliamentary legislation, the evolution of local institutions, the levying of taxation, and the maintenance of order.

Concentration on this forum of opinion and arena of activity carries obvious dangers. It neglects the central ground of much ministerial and some parliamentary politics, for politics in this very broad, often local sense was something for which governments and parliaments had limited enthusiasm. To that extent it underplays the aristocratic control and oligarchical influence which many have seen as typical of the age. On the other hand, I hope in some measure to have provided a corrective to the view that Georgian politics was overwhelmingly controlled by its

[1] J. A. W. Gunn, *Beyond Liberty and Property: The Process of Self-Recognition in Eighteenth-Century Political Thought* (Kingston, 1983), ch. 7.

aristocracy, as conventionally defined. If this was indeed an oligarchy, it was one which operated within a restricted framework and on a consensual basis; it accepted the priorities of a broadly bourgeois society. A second danger is that in stressing the middle-class drive to social control and political pre-eminence that public life displayed, it is easy to ignore the politics of protest, the resistance of those who lacked property and who did not always acquiesce in what was handed down by their masters. But again I have sought to show that fears of such resistance, however exaggerated, were themselves a powerful stimulus to consensus politics. A third danger is that in emphasizing what propertied people had in common when they pursued their personal and collective ambitions, I may have paid insufficient attention to the forces, ideas, or interests which divided them. Here too, my aim has been to rectify what seems to me an imbalance in the literature, one which makes it easy to neglect how much united bourgeois Englishmen even when they differed. In short, I do mean to argue that our perception of eighteenth-century life has been dictated rather too much by the patronage preoccupations of the gentry, by the retrospective appeal of plebeian revolt, and by the long-standing English obsession with party politics. But I do not mean to argue that these should be ignored, let alone that the relatively open, self-consciously tolerant political community which I seek to describe was one without hypocrisy and a strong sense of the potential for social conflict.

The presentation and organization of the argument are determined by my decision to concentrate on the sources and implications of change. The first, introductory chapter expounds the views of property which were entertained by ordinary Britons, often in a homely setting and with little regard for logic or consistency. The emphasis is on the ways in which commercial development complicated definitions of property and the political priorities which were supposed to flow from respect for property. Chapter 2 examines the growing reluctance to conceive of the State in terms which could impede the accumulation of property and the competition of propertied interests, especially in relation to religious allegiance and party politics. The three following chapters display the resulting imperatives. In Chapter 3 Parliament is transformed from the heroic defender of individual rights and liberties into the pawn of interest-groups, not so much imposing its legislative will as providing its legislative services. In Chapter 4 legislators are revealed employing the favourite safeguard of the age, the property qualification, to expand the governing class while restricting the rights of the governed class, in the process giving free play to the vested interests of business and professional people. Chapter 5 focuses on the accommodations made by the gentry, in terms of the governing responsibility, tax liability, and distinctive economic interests of the landowning class. Chapters 6 and 7 examine, respectively in a rural and urban setting, the response of propertied people to what they considered their social duties, especially as they bore on the exercise of authority and as they involved the participation of newcomers to active political life. Chapter 8 finds a seemingly powerful aristocracy adapting itself to a society in which even inherited rank and title were expected to submit to the requirements of the propertied classes at large.

I have tried not to presuppose knowledge of the major themes, partly because existing coverage of much of my subject-matter is so patchy. On many of the topics discussed there is very little systematic research from which to generalize. Even where there are substantial studies, they are often concerned with rather different questions from that which I have posed. The colossal labours of the Webbs loom large over what they called local government, but their perspective was that of the Fabian archaeologist disinterring a bizarre and irrational structure, rather than the historian recapturing the spirit of a once flourishing organism. Eighteenth-century Parliaments are as well known as any in terms of their personnel and the means by which they were elected. Yet research into Parliament as a legislative institution is in its infancy. The municipal corporations of the eighteenth century, which have left very rich materials, have been the subject of few detailed studies, despite the emergence of a vigorous school of urban history. Even the county community, so long the preoccupation of seventeenth-century historians, has featured only erratically in eighteenth-century studies, and then primarily with reference to electoral politics or to the social policies which were to become so controversial in the nineteenth century. And on major questions concerning the way that central politics related to local communities, including the incidence of taxation and the use of statute to bestow powers on propertied élites, suggestive hints have yet to be followed up by intensive study.

In the following pages I have endeavoured to give full credit to what *has* been written on such subjects, much of it in local and antiquarian journals. But the deficiencies of the secondary literature have largely to be supplied from primary sources. Some of these consist of printed materials, like the *Commons Journals*, which have been used surprisingly little for this kind of purpose. But the great majority are manuscript records preserved principally in the archives of local authorities. They vary hugely in character, abundance, and arrangement. My main attention has been concentrated where contemporary polemic and comment suggest a significant awareness of change, with due caution for the possibility that such comment can be both partial and misleading. I have also followed where the adventitious survival of certain categories of archive dictates; when the materials are particularly rich, I have employed some elementary sampling techniques. I am conscious that this strategy is open to obvious methodological objections. But to answer these conclusively across the range of questions considered in this book would require several lifetimes of research, not the twelve years over which I have conducted it. If my temerity in suggesting answers on the basis of selected evidence stimulates more scientific probing on a narrower front it will have a sufficient justification.

Writing a work of this kind, it is impossible not to be aware of the diversity and vitality of eighteenth-century studies, whatever the gaps that remain. As a political historian concerned primarily with relationships of power and influence, with the ways in which individuals and groups obtained and exercised authority, I know how much I owe to social historians who often illuminate such relationships even when they least suspect that they are doing so. Much research into the eighteenth century has been driven by a desire to place the social relations of the period in the context of longer-term class relations, but in the process a great deal that is uncovered says as much about the peculiar character of Georgian society as about the concepts and constructs employed in modern historiography. In recent years it has sometimes seemed that political history would be left stranded by the flow of research into other, newer channels. In desperation some have fled to the lower reaches of popular politics, others have sought to shore up the defences of 'high politics'. My own belief is that the study of politics in its fullest and authentically 'highest' sense, as the means by which communities organize themselves for what they perceive to be the public good, is enriched rather than threatened by the diversification of modern historical scholarship. I certainly know how much the research that has gone into this book has gained by it.

I also owe a considerable debt of gratitude to individuals who have given freely of their advice and assistance. Joanna Innes has been an invariably stimulating source both of constructive criticism and detailed advice; Susan Brigden with characteristic generosity read and criticized the book in its lecture form. Friends and colleagues who have made valuable suggestions include Jonathan Barry, Christopher Cunliffe, David Eastwood, Austin Gee, Peter Ghosh, Lionel Glassey, John Spurr, Patrick O'Brien, and John Walsh. John Styles and John Cookson kindly allowed me to read unpublished papers.

This book has taken me to many libraries and archives. I am grateful not only for the use of their facilities but also for the advice which I have frequently sought and obtained from their staff. They include the Bodleian Library, the British Library, Cambridge University Library, the Huntington Library at San Marino, the Guildhall Library, London, and York Minster Library, and the following county record offices: Berkshire, Bristol, Buckinghamshire, Cambridgeshire (Cambridge and Huntingdon), Derbyshire, Devon (Exeter and Plymouth), Dorset, Essex, Gloucestershire, Hampshire, Hereford and Worcester, Hertfordshire, Lancashire, Leicestershire, Lincolnshire, Norfolk, Northamptonshire, Northumberland, Oxfordshire, Shropshire, Somerset, Staffordshire, Suffolk (Bury St Edmunds and Ipswich), Surrey (Kingston and Guildford), East and West Sussex, Warwickshire, Wiltshire, North Yorkshire.

P.L.
Lincoln College, Oxford
April 1990

Contents

1 THE PROPERTIED MIND   1

   The Grand Enchantress   1

   An Endeavour to Appropriate   14

   A Carnal and Propertied World   28

   Securing the Property of the Subject   35

   The Power that Naturally Attends Property   51

   A Sort of Property   58

2 PRIOR ALLEGIANCE   71

   Rather Disgustful than Inconvenient   71

   The Attributes of Fanaticism   84

   The Farce of State Oaths   98

   Ignorant and Profane Swearers   107

   The Spirit of Party   118

   Our Social Happiness   131

3 PARLIAMENTARY SERVICE   139

   A Remarkable Alteration   139

   The Supreme Power   148

   Particular Improvements   156

   A Parliamentary Interposition   166

   A Clashing of Interests   176

   The Happiness and Glory of a Representative   186

   Interest and Influence   196

4 QUALIFIED RULE   207

   A More Numerous and More Powerful Club   207

   Strait Wastecoats   214

   Full Authority   222

   Poor Middling People   232

   Interested Persons   243

   Dangerous and Expensive Jobs   256

A Qualification Easily Attained 264

A Parcel of Mean Fellows 278

5 REAL AND PERSONAL 288

The Privilege of Becoming a Legislator 288

Unqualified Officers 295

A Natural Antipathy 305

The Landlords of This Great Empire 315

The Landed Interest 326

An Absolute Land Tax 339

The Real Property of Individuals 350

6 RURAL DUTIES 367

A Scene of Desolation 367

Little Sovereigns 377

The Guardian Magistrate 390

Zeal or Property 398

Priest and Justice 410

Qualified for a Reformer 420

7 JUST AUTHORITY 437

Special Jurisdictions 437

Polluted Cities 448

Supporters of Society 455

Sedition and Tumult 464

The Middle State 477

Friends and Benefactors 490

The Fifth Commandment 500

8 PERSONAL NOBILITY 510

Childish Titles 510

Commoners with Coronets on Their Coats of Arms 523

An Overbearing Tyrannizing Oligarchy 529

Varnished Vices 540

Engaging Condescension 548

The Properest of All Men 558

Virtue Confers the Coronet 569

CONCLUSION 582

INDEX 588

Illustrations

BETWEEN PAGES 306 AND 307

1 (*a*). The Liberty of the Subject
  (*b*). Old England, Great Britain

2 (*a*). Special Pleaders in the Court of Requests
  (*b*). The Country Justice

3. The Inside of a Newly Reformed Workhouse with the Abuses Removed

4 (*a*). Tax on Receipts
  (*b*). The Income Tax

5 (*a*). Public Influence or a Scramble for Coronets
  (*b*). The New Peerage

6 (*a*). The Couch of Adultery
  (*b*). The Two Patriotic Duchesses

7. The Noble Sans Culotte

8. Vices overlooked in the New Proclamation

I

The Propertied Mind

A WORLD without property was almost inconceivable to eighteenth-century Englishmen. The most diverse thinkers shared the assumption that law and government alike must be based on propertied foundations. There was a notable tendency to remove all evidence of alternative ways of looking at social and political relations. The spiritual purposes of religion, for example, were frequently subordinated to the propertied priorities of ecclesiastical life. It became almost impossible to conceive of rights and liberties except in terms which implied individual proprietorship. Any notion that the State should limit or control the operations of property, let alone determine its distribution, was scouted. Yet there were contradictions at the heart of the theory of propertied politics which complicated its application. The widely accepted Harringtonian principle that property determined power concealed uncertainties about the precise nature of the relationship between the two and the proper role of government. It also neglected the questions raised by the striking diversification of property which occurred in the course of the eighteenth century. Commercial growth and the enthusiasm of the age for 'improvement' suggested not the unchanging dependability of a landed polity but the chronic instability of a commercial society. Clashes of interest and the legal security granted to forms of property which assumed reliance on credit made nonsense of simple appeals to the landed proprietor against the moneyed man. Even where landowners were concerned, the complexity of tenures and the impact of economic expansion made for confusion and conflict. If eighteenth-century politics was ultimately about the interests of property, it had as much to do with change and competition within propertied society itself as with the assertion of proprietorial power over largely unpropertied inferiors.

THE GRAND ENCHANTRESS

The respect which attended property was a striking feature of the mental landscape of the eighteenth century. Some of the most questioning minds and critical temperaments held it in awe. John Jebb, a rebel against his church and a reformer at odds with his society, knew its menace yet felt its fascination. It was, he remarked, 'the grand enchantress of the world'.[1] Like some others of his generation, the generation which grew to manhood in the 1760s and 1770s, Jebb sought to bind himself against its charms, while recognizing its fatal attraction for many of his contemporaries. He had friends, indeed, hardy enough to deny the magic of its spell. One of them, Joseph Priestley, insisted that property had no special status among the rights traditionally claimed by men: 'Nothing is properly a *man's own*, but what general rules, which have for their object the good of the whole, give to him.' Priestley had something of saint as well as sage about him. His enraptured pupil Anna Aikin contrasted his intellectual riches with his wordly penury. 'A map of every country known, With not a foot of land his own'.[2] Emulating him would have not have been easy. Thomas Percival, a distinguished Unitarian physician, and himself a product of the War-rington Academy shortly before Priestley became a tutor there, did not share his co-religionist's unorthodoxy in this respect. His 'Inquiry into the Principles and Limits of Taxation', written in opposition to the younger Pitt's tax on Manchester cottons in 1784, justified property as a natural right, with its origin in divine injunction. His friend Richard Watson was shocked into reminding him that property was 'very much the creature of civil society' and the supreme magistrate 'authorised to apply the whole of the property of every individual for the preservation of the whole community'.[3] It was one of the very few subjects on which two fearless reformers evidently did not think alike.

The difficulty which the most redoubtable thinkers got into on this topic is well illustrated by the case of Richard Price. In his *Observations on the Nature of Civil Liberty* of 1776, Price prudently avoided discussing the origin of property. He repeatedly referred to it as the mark of a free state, exploiting its rhetorical effect without explaining its logical force.[4] Price was not known for dodging difficult questions, but his dilemma and consequent confusion were shared by many. His friend Andrew Kippis ws quite content to celebrate 1688 on the grounds that it had been not merely a bloodless revolution but one which involved no loss of property.[5] A century earlier Revolution radicals themselves had displayed similar caution. Real Whigs and Commonwealthmen were reviled for their religious heterodoxy and feared for their republican subversiveness. Yet

[1] J. Disney, *The Works Theological, Medical, Political, and Miscellaneous, of John Jebb* (3 vols., London, 1787), iii. 412.
[2] *An Essay on the First Principles of Government, and on the Nature of Political, Civil, and Religious Liberty* (London, 1768), p. 41; L. Aikin, *The Works of Anna Laetitia Barbauld* (2 vols., London, 1825), i. 55: 'An Inventory of the Furniture in Dr Priestley's Study'.
[3] *The Works of Thomas Percival* (new edn., 4 vols., 1807), iv. 231; iii, p. cliii.
[4] (2nd edn., London, 1776), Part II, *passim*.
[5] *Whitehall Evening-Post*, 6 Nov. 1788.

they whispered no words of heresy when it came to worshipping property.[6] Even millenarians of that age did not always think it wise to deny earthly values in this respect. In Thomas Burnet's apocalyptic vision of destruction succeeded by the establishment of paradise on earth, 'the conflagration of the world, and the new heavens and Earth that are to succeed', room was found for the assurance that there would not necessarily be any alteration in the prevailing distribution of property.[7]

Certain priorities governed the debate about property, its origins, and its implications. One was the need to bring the entire known world beneath its sway. 'Whatever ... hath a *Value* is the Subject of Property', observed William Blackstone. His colleague both at the Bar and later as a judge, Joseph Yates, sought desperately to give some sensual comprehensiveness to the concept: 'It should be something, that may be seen, felt, given, delivered, lost or stolen, in order to constitute the Subject of Property.'[8] A second was the attempt to give it precedence over all other values. There were various means of achieving this, some of them mutually incompatible. One was to posit human acquisitiveness as the natural foundation of other, clearly desirable, sentiments and drives. 'Property begets Affection', Defoe flatly declared.[9] Alternatively, the sheer power of property might overwhelm all other claims on the human spirit. A cynical marriage market made this seem all too plausible. In his diatribe against the Marriage Act of 1753 John Shebbeare had his Earl of Wormeaton describe marriage as 'taking Money with the Mortgage of a Wife to pay off a Mortgage on an Estate'.[10] The anxiety of sentimental novelists to satirize the notion that property could act as a substitute for love is itself testimony to its influence. Sarah Fielding had her Cynthia wooed by a country gentleman who boasted 'I am none of those nonsensical Fools that can whine and make romantick love, I leave that to younger Brothers, let my Estate speak for me.' Cynthia rejected his offer as 'Prostitution'.[11] It was believed that estates and the calculating mentality which went with them got in the way of marriage. As Robert Bage put it, 'here is a great deal of difficulty in this country, to bring two people together, who are unfortunate enough to have property'. Statistical support came from the demographer John Howlett, who noted that in rural areas labourers outnumbered their betters three to one; yet lower-class marriages exceeded those of the middle and upper classes by a ratio of six to one. The reason was simple: a propertied upbringing

[6] J. Duke-Evans, 'The Political Theory and Practice of the English Commonwealthsman' (Oxford Univ. D.Phil thesis, 1980), p. 237.

[7] M. C. Jacob, *The Newtonians and the English Revolution, 1689–1720* (Hassocks, 1976), pp. 112, 116.

[8] 1 Black. W. 322, 338–9: *Tonson v. Collins* (1762).

[9] *Defoe's Review in 22 Facsimile Books* (New York, 1938), viii. 554: 9 Feb. 1712.

[10] *The Marriage Act* (2 vols., London, 1754), i. 93.

[11] *The Adventures of David Simple*, ed. M. Kelsall (London, 1969), p. 109.

promoted an undue apprehension of the risks of an injudicious union, 'checking the impulses of nature'.[12]

Liberty, like love, was a timeless human value supposedly subjected to the hegemony of property. The hackneyed slogan, 'Liberty and Property', suggested an equal partnership, but in practice the latter usually took precedence. While the struggle against the Stuart prerogative was recalled it was possible to argue that property had a subversive, even a seditious potential, which needed careful control if it were to contribute to constitutional progress.[13] But in time it seemed better to forget this aspect of the Revolution Settlement and dwell on property as a stabilizing, conservative force. As Vicesimus Knox noted, 'Liberty has few votaries in comparison with property.'[14] Property was plainly a jealous God, for another commentator was moved to employ a similar analogy. '*Liberty* was our *Dulcinea*, but *Property* our Deity.'[15] Certainly the venerable laws of England seemed to favour the latter at the expense of the former, not least in their treatment of debtors. An Englishman could readily be imprisoned for debt, yet his real estate could not legally be made liable for his debts even in the event of his death. Samuel Romilly conducted a long campaign to rectify this anomaly at least to the extent of rendering land liable to the same extent as personal estate. The larger question of the debtor's loss of personal liberty was to remain a subject of acute concern even longer.[16]

One tactic was to argue that liberty was the means, property the end. 'Pray, what is Liberty—but a Freedom to possess Property, a Liberty to enjoy it, and a Right to defend it.'[17] The poet John Dyer spoke of liberty even more depressingly as a duty indistinguishable from industry, 'whose Hand benign, Teaches unwearied Toil to cloath the Fields, And on his various Fruits inscribes the Name, of Property'.[18] It was a platitudinous observation that liberty on its own was of limited value in the real world, however esteemed in popular rhetoric. The good master would not only free his slave but also make him a gift of property; the one without the other, was, as the clerical author James Ridley put it, 'but an Obligation to change, perhaps, a good Master for a worse'.[19]

Property is a way of looking at the world, as well as a means of sharing

[12] Robert Bage, *Hermsprong; Or, Man As He Is Not* (3 vols., London, 1796), ii. 197; John Howlett, *An Examination of Dr. Price's Essay on the Population of England and Wales* (Maidstone, 1781), p. 28.

[13] 'A Charge Given by Hugh Hare, Esq., J.P., at the General Quarter Sessions for the County of Surrey, Holden at Dorking, 5th April, 1692', *Surrey Arch. Colls.* 12 (1894–5), 110.

[14] *The Works of Vicesimus Knox* (7 vols., London, 1824), v. 191.

[15] *London Magazine* (1742), 449.

[16] *Memoirs of the Life of Sir Samuel Romilly, Written by Himself; With a Selection from His Correspondence* (3 vols., London, 1840), iii. 123.

[17] *Defoe's Review*, v. 632: 31 Mar. 1709.

[18] *The Ruins of Rome* (London, 1740), p. 13.

[19] *The Tales of the Genii* (4 vols., London, 1764), vol. i, p. xvii.

it out. As a metaphor it had many attractions. Theological argument sometimes relied on it to reinforce the authority of the Deity. What Wesley called 'Jesus's property' was a common way of referring to the souls of the Methodist faithful.[20] God as the supreme, ultimately the only freeholder, Lord of a Manor in which all other tenures were subordinate to his will, made obvious sense to a propertied society. The Bishop of St Davids, addressing the subscribers to the London Hospital in 1765, fearlessly reminded them that God was the 'only absolute proprietary'.[21] By an enterprising and theologically alarming leap in this argument, Daniel Defoe made Providence itself subject to the iron law of property: 'Even God himself holds by this Tenure; his Right to rule over us, is founded upon his Property in us.'[22] Such a God was quite capable of considering the special needs of aristocratic estate management. Thomas Manningham, a Hampshire clergyman on his way to the Deanery of Windsor and the Bishopric of Chichester, made this point in an obituary sermon in 1703. His subject, Lady Dorothy Norton, who had long administered the lands of her deceased husband, was described as 'having a Soul compleatly made for Providence to intrust with the *intire Management* of a *great Estate*'. For a woman to be thus equipped must surely be a sign of a special dispensation.[23]

Specific appeals could be directed to divine proprietorship when need dictated. Sabbatarians reminded those who refused to respect the Sabbath that they were trespassers; Sunday was God's own property.[24] Profane as well as sacred speculations profited by such analogies. Suicide was defended on the grounds that one's life was one's own, a consequence of the Lockian definition of property which Locke had not foreseen.[25] This logic was embarrassing for Whigs, since the strongest counter-argument, that a man's life belonged in part to his family, his society, even those set over him, had obvious Tory antecedents. It also had the sanction of English law, which punished suicide by confiscating the offender's estate. Some lives seemed more dispensable when treated as someone else's property. Sending his unfortunate troops into battle in 1777, General Burgoyne reminded them that 'the life of the Soldier is the property of the King'.[26] In the nature of

---

[20] L. Tyerman, *The Life and Times of the Rev. John Wesley* (3 vols., London, 1870–1), iii. 128.

[21] *A Sermon Preached at St Lawrence Jewry, on Thursday, March 28, 1765* (London, 1765), p. 12.

[22] *Defoe's Review* iii. 33: 13 July 1706.

[23] *A Sermon at the Funeral of the Lady Dorothy Norton* (London, 1703), p. 23.

[24] Henry Piers, *Thanksgiving for a Plentiful Harvest* (London, 1760), p. 22. Piers, Vicar of Bexley, had got into trouble in 1742 for his 'Methodistical' views; see *A Sermon Preached (in Part) before the Right Worshipful the Dean of the Arches, and the Reverend the Clergy of the Deanery of Shoreham* (London, 1742).

[25] *Old Whig*, 25 Aug. 1737. Perhaps significantly, this article was not printed in the collected edition. See also S. E. Sprott, *The English Debate on Suicide from Donne to Hume* (La Salle, Ill., 1961), pp. 103–4.

[26] H. Rogers, ed., *Hadden's Journal and Orderly Books* (Albany, NY, 1884), p. 160.

the eighteenth-century State it was the vast mass of men who had *only* a property in their lives who were expected to place it at risk. Those who possessed a more extensive estate and a share in worldly riches were rarely called upon to sacrifice them in the common cause.

John Cleland skilfully employed the figurative richness of property to illuminate the nature of contemporary sexuality. Political theorists asserted that every free human being, however lowly his status and destitute his circumstances, had a property in his own person. The surest way to dehumanize him was to deprive him of it. Cleland made the plight of prostitutes seem peculiarly wretched by pointing out that a woman in the power of London's notorious 'cock-bawds' lacked even this fundamental attribute: 'nothing, no, not her own Person, is her Property, or at her own Disposal'.[27] Marriage itself could readily be viewed as a property transaction, not merely in the obvious sense that it was for people of wealth a highly commercial business, in which the legal details of settlements, dowries, and jointures were apt to obscure the emotional implications of the human relationship thus entered upon, but also as an act of appropriation by the lords of creation. In his tale of a girl lured into a bagnio by her father's enemy, and rescued by a generous-spirited nobleman, Cleland posed a dilemma for his hero, the Earl of Veramore. Veramore's initial intentions were strictly honourable, but his discovery of his beloved in a bawdy-house compelled him to modify them. Disgusted though he was at her depravity, he resolved to purchase her services and enjoy her beauty as 'right of common'. Fortunately she cleared her reputation, and duly made herself available for marital enclosure.[28] Cleland's contemporary Richard Owen Cambridge was also prompted, by the passage of the Marriage Act and a Game Preservation Act in the same parliamentary session of 1753, to use agricultural property as a metaphor. Maidens and hares were alike the prey of the booby squire 'with a crack'd constitution and mortgaged estate'.[29] The legal rights of females were a subject of inexhaustible interest, especially in the later eighteenth century, but when Cleland and Cambridge treated women themselves as a form of property the irony was painfully thin. The instinctive tendency of the age was to express any relationship of unequals in terms which equated power over people with possession of things.

It was not only complacent defenders of the status quo who portrayed personal and political relations in this way. The Dissenting schoolmaster James Burgh, whose *Political Disquisitions* of 1774-5 constituted a treasury of arguments for early parliamentary reformers, based his plea for a wide

---

[27] *The Case of the Unfortunate Bosavern Penlez* (London, 1749), p. 9.
[28] *The Surprises of Love* (2nd edn., London, 1765), p. 109.
[29] G. O. Cambridge, *The Works of Richard Owen Cambridge, Esq.* (London, 1803), p. 302: 'Verses Occasioned by the Marriage and Game Act, Both Passed the Same Session'.

franchise in part on the assertion that even the poorest male members of society had a property in their wives and daughters.[30] The premiss was unoriginal, however novel the use made of it. It had support from fashionable philosophers, including Montesquieu. 'The family is a kind of property.'[31] Anthropologists were well versed in the application of the principle to the early history of human society. It was also thought to have linguistic evidence on its side. The antiquarian Lewis Morris pointed out that the Welsh for marriage (*priodas*) meant making a woman one's own; in his native North Wales the common expression 'y wraig eiddo fi' was literally to be translated 'the wife my property'.[32]

The law which gave men a financial interest in the chastity of their wives and daughters clearly buttressed this mentality, though not all women were equally valuable in this respect. At the time that Burgh was writing, the newspapers were reporting widely varying verdicts. Lord Grosvenor sought £100,000 and obtained £10,000 by way of damages for the Duke of Cumberland's criminal conversation with his wife. Yet a watchmaker prosecuting an attorney's agent on similar grounds was rewarded with only £300.[33] But doubts were beginning to be raised about this species of property. One of the obsolescent statutes which reformers sought to repeal when capital punishment was under consideration in 1772 provided for the execution of a seducer who forcibly married his victim. At issue was a father's right to dispose of his daughter's hand. It was said that 'the act absurdly provided for the security of what could not reasonably be called property'.[34] Feminists were less temperate in their rejection of such thinking but they were familiar with the logic. Mary Wollstonecraft, ironically befriended by Burgh's widow when she set up school at Newington Green, understood the realities of family life. But she neatly turned the tables on sons and daughters who accepted the dictatorship of their fathers by pointing out that in doing so they were in reality merely displaying a 'selfish respect for property' and staking their own claim to a share in it. Fathers were obeyed 'from motives that degrade the human character'.[35]

In the great debate about slavery, it was the slave-owners who were sometimes driven to abandon the argument from proprietorship, relying instead on the innate inferiority of Blacks and the paternalism of the plantation system. Their critics felt no embarrassment in resorting to propertied rights to justify the liberation of slaves, any more than they

---

[30] (3 vols., London, 1774–5), i. 37.
[31] *The Spirit of the Laws*, ed. T. Nugent (2 vols., London, 1949), ii. 3.
[32] H. Owen, ed., *Additional Letters of the Morrises of Anglesey (1735–1786)* (2 vols., London, 1947–9), i. 299.
[33] *London Magazine* (1770), 382; 1772, p. 394.
[34] Ibid. (1772), 352.
[35] *A Vindication of the Rights of Women*, ed. C. H. Paston (New York, 1975), p. 197.

would in denouncing the advantages of monopoly companies. There was no contradiction here. If acquisitiveness is the first, almost the defining characteristic of human beings as social animals, there could be no greater injustice than to deprive them of it by making them a form of property. In this sense slavery was truly a lost cause. A similar logic governed the extension of religious toleration. Within six years of Somersett's case in 1772, the judicial decision which, for all its ambivalence, was hailed by abolitionists as a crucial ruling against slavery within England and Wales, the first substantial measure of relief for Roman Catholics was passed. One of its provisions was to revoke the restrictions on Catholic ownership of land. As John Dunning put it in the Commons debate, a law which 'debars a man from the honest acquisition of property ... needed only to be mentioned in order to excite the indignation of the House'.[36] Granting Roman Catholics, and indeed Protestant Dissenters, full civil rights proved a more protracted business. The minimal basis of rights required by the propertied mentality was precisely the freedom in principle to own what one acquired.

Expansive definitions of property were deeply entrenched. An election tract in 1681 reminded voters of their 'Right and Title to your own Lives, Liberties and Estates: in this every man is a sort of little Sovereign to himself'.[37] Philosophers provided a sophisticated framework of argument for the support of this contention. But few men or women troubled to explore the theoretical basis of their claims to property; speculations about the right which they had to their own bodies and their own labour would have seemed ridiculous. If a great scholar like Locke slipped readily into discussing property in its everyday sense of physical possessions, lesser mortals could be forgiven for thinking for the most part in similarly mundane terms. In doing so they were more likely to be struck by the unequal distribution of property than its indicativeness of a natural equality. Englishmen were not squeamish about the massive disparity of rich and poor. If property was a good thing, it was difficult to have too much of it. Men who were appalled by the thought of owning slaves, or even participating in a trade which permitted others to own them, were completely unembarrassed at their own plenty in a world of poverty, where many of their fellow creatures were so destitute that they were hardly better off than slaves. Indeed they were prone to consider their own community a triumph of social engineering. Frances Brooke lavishly praised the English system of government in this respect, especially what she called 'the democratic freedom and equal distribution of property'. But she was quick to put a gloss on this description. 'When I mention equal distribution of

---

[36] *Parliamentary Register*, ix. 198: 14 May 1778.
[37] *England's Great Interest in the Choice of the New Parliament.*

property, I would not be understood to mean such an equality as never existed, nor can exist but in idea; but that general, that comparative equality, which leaves to every man the absolute and safe possession of the fruits of his labours; which softens offensive distinctions, and curbs pride, by leaving every order of men in some degree dependent on the other.'[38] The egalitarianism on which the British prided themselves held no terrors for the accumulator of property.

Short of having an unequal share of property, it was vital to appear to have it. Eighteenth-century England was an endlessly snobbish society; as foreign visitors liked to remark, nothing distinguished it more than the unceasing struggle of all ranks to emulate those above them. In theory the most powerful weapon in the social war was politeness, a code of manners, not a register of possessions. But the practice was very different. However much moralists insisted on virtue, whether in a Christian or a secular version, as the basis of the code, its dependence on the possession of wealth was all too obvious. 'Property in every country where it is an object of importance, and where is it not such? discovers itself in spite of every counterfeiting.' This was the view of a much-read student of manners, Samuel Jackson Pratt.[39] Some would have urged the superior effect of breeding, which did not always go with property. But this was not very convincing. Contempt for the bourgeois gentleman who did not grasp the difference between the trappings of gentility which he had purchased, and its true spirit, of which he knew nothing, was the standard tactic of an aristocratic élite in retreat, if not yet routed. In practical terms it is better evidence of the threat represented by bourgeois values than of successful resistance to them. Certainly in eighteenth-century Britain it was misleading. The acquisition of wealth was the route to social acceptance and political power at all levels of society. Genteel sniggering was the perpetual prerogative of rank, but it presented no very serious obstacle to the social climber. Those who met the nabob turned country gentleman, Richard Barwell, in the 1780s, inevitably found that 'the mogul prevails strongly ... in his way of life and conversation'.[40] But Barwell, like many other returned East India adventurers, quickly established himself in county society.

Barwell was one of the wealthiest men of his age, and owed his position in Sussex to the purchase of a great aristocratic estate, Stansted Park, formerly the seat of the Earls of Halifax. But comparable gains could be registered somewhat lower down the scale. In the everyday social warfare of middle-class life, the strategy of impressing inferiors and superiors alike

[38] *The History of Emily Montague* (4 vols., London, 1769), iii. 20–1.
[39] *Gleanings in England* (2nd edn., 3 vols., London, 1801–3), i. 86.
[40] Sir L. Namier and J. Brooke, *The History of Parliament: The House of Commons 1754–1790* (3 vols., London, 1964), ii. 61.

depended on less spectacular consumption, but on consumption none the less. This is not to say that commercial society in the eighteenth century can be fully assimilated to the model of consumer society in the twentieth century. Living standards varied enormously and the taxation levied by the State did nothing to reduce the gap between the disposable income of rich and poor. There was a radical difference between the goods consumed by the masses and the goods displayed by propertied people, of kind rather than degree. The list of articles which one censorious calculator considered particularly suitable for punitive taxation in 1733 was a primitive inventory of middle- and upper-class living: gold and silver lace, plate, carpets, ribbons, wine, foreign lace and calico, coaches, and most of the 'enter-tainments' available in London beyond the facilities of an ordinary tavern, especially masquerades, ridottos, and plays.[41] Many of the purchases of people of property were remote indeed from the 'throw-away' products of an age concerned both to create new consumer tastes and to ensure that nothing lasts too long. The quality goods required to make a middle-class home were expensive and were made to last. Porcelain was less expensive than plate, but it was not cheap at several pounds for a modest service; wallpaper at four or five guineas a roll was a permanent investment, as its survival in Georgian country houses testifies; mahogany furniture was vastly more expensive than its home-grown competitors; a silk mantua was treasured for generations; a commonplace portrait by a tolerably fashionable painter, at twenty or twenty-five guineas, was bought with posterity in mind; a carriage was a costly item in itself and involved a continuing drain on income in that it required the maintenance of horses. Items of these kinds were not consumer goods in the modern sense, they were themselves valuable property. It was common to censure the passion of the lower classes for so-called luxuries; but a growing taste for tea and trinkets hardly represented wholesale conversion to middle-class materialism. The clergyman who pronounced luxury permissible when 'confined solely to those, whose rank and fortune allow them to yield to its suggestions' may have been distressingly complacent, but he knew well the difference between propertied life and poverty.[42]

In a modern consumer society, things are cheap, people are expensive. In the eighteenth century, the reverse was true. Employment of a servant was one of the basic criteria of something approaching middle-class status. There is a sense in which it signified the fundamental social division of the day. Haves were employers, have-nots were employees. Yet service represented an inexpensive investment compared with other luxuries.

---

[41] *Fog's Weekly Journal*, 3 Mar. 1733.
[42] Walter Kerrick, *A Sermon, Preached at the Cathedral Church of Sarum, on Wednesday, February 21, 1781* (Salisbury, 1781), p. 14.

Around 1700 a living-in servant might be paid no more than £2 or £3 per annum; in the 1760s the interest on the money needed to buy a Romney portrait would comfortably have paid for a maid; even in the 1780s, it was reckoned that a metropolitan middle-class family in comfortable but not opulent circumstances, would reckon to pay only £14. 10s. a year (including tax) for two maid-servants. This was less than one-quarter of the family's clothes bill, half the charge for keeping a horse in stable and straw, one-tenth of the expense of maintaining a four-wheeled carriage with two horses.[43] The great majority of families could not afford a maid, but still less could they afford more costly commodities. Consumption as a metaphor does not completely express the attitude of the day to the possession of wealth and what it brought. The overwhelming emphasis was on adornment and ostentation. Tax experts understood this well. The beauty of systematic taxation of luxuries, it was pointed out, was precisely that all luxuries were purchased with a view as much to impressing others as to pleasing oneself. Vanity required that such purchases be highly visible, and visibility meant that tax evasion was impracticable. It was impossible to conceive of consumption in complete privacy, for without display, what was the purpose of consumption?[44] Part of the eccentricity of a wealthy eccentric like John Elwes, the most notorious miser of his age, was his anxiety actually to be thought poor. To appear among his fellow MPs without servants, without equipage, without any signs of his wealth, was surely the mark of a deranged mind.[45]

Display might be of very different kinds. Propertied people trailed their possessions before the gaze, fascinated, awed, resentful, of the unpropertied people who were their employees, servants, or merely spectators. They also flaunted them in the face of their own kind, anxiously measuring them against the visible assets of their competitors. Houses, furniture, clothes, jewels, carriages, servants, these were the manifest signs of success. Chancellors of the Exchequer taxed them, with such duties as the plate tax, the carriage tax, and the servant tax, in the knowledge that it was much easier to assess the outward impedimenta of propertied life than the income on which it depended. Some of the advantages of politeness, indeed, were seemingly less a matter of money. But in practice, most of them were bought and sold like any other commodity; travel, education, the mass instruction made available through the press, were all obtainable for cash. Forcing middle-class families to choose between a mother's carriage and a daughter's fashionable education might produce an agonizing dilemma; but in point of the family's social success, the choice was strictly a choice

[43] John Trusler, *The London Adviser and Guide* (London, 1786), pp. 168–71.
[44] Josiah Tucker, *A Brief Essay on the Advantages and Disadvantages, Which Respectively Attend France and Great Britain, with Regard to Trade* (London, 1753), pp. 50–2.
[45] *Whitehall Evening-Post*, 2 Jan. 1790.

between comparable commodities, all ultimately designed to advance their possessors by impressing others. To some this seemed peculiarly a pre-occupation of the times. It was seriously argued at the end of the century that the Revolutionary War was having a purifying effect in this respect. Before 1793 'men regulated their expenses not by what they could afford to expend, but by what they wished others to believe of the state of their circumstances'. Now, the burden of wartime taxation had purged them of their pretentiousness and forced them to buy only what they needed.[46]

The social psychology of this obsession with display was something more than a matter of keeping up with the Joneses. Through the marriage market, and through an infinite variety of business and professional relationships, property was a means of acquiring further property, and therefore further status. Much, if not all its magnetic effect depended on showing it off, even on pretending to wealth which one did not really have. The fact that display itself could be expensive and therefore wasteful of property did not necessarily diminish its value, though it did occasionally lend it a somewhat desperate quality, akin to the gambler's last throw. It also complicated the evaluation of property: judging the reality behind ostentation became a skill of undoubted importance. At the highest levels perhaps only certified rent-rolls and sworn statements counted. But not many families operated at the highest levels, and in any case an open society and a fluid marriage market left much of the preliminary skirmishing to all too human sensibilities and miscalculations. In romantic novels, a misreading of one's potential partner's fortune, based on a deceptive display of wealth, was a commonplace cause of marital disaster. It also became a consideration in the everyday judgement of human frailties. When the colourful Lady Craven was caught misbehaving with the French ambassador in 1783, aristocratic opinion was quick to condemn, notwithstanding her husband's similar indiscretions, 'he having married her with a very small fortune, tho' he possesses a very ample one'.[47] In this there was no double standard. It applied equally to men and women. The Lincolnshire country gentleman Charles Burrell Massingberd, having taken a liking to a chambermaid, was described as using his wife 'extremely ill, which to say the truth is very ungrateful as she brought him so great a fortune'.[48]

The falsity of much ostentation was the tribute which acquisitive vice paid to proprietorial virtue. Successive generations of architects and landscape gardeners attended to the need felt even by the greatest magnates to appear more 'acred' than they really were. The triumph of English land-

---

[46] *A Remonstrance Addressed to the Rev. Richard Warner, on the Subject of His Fast Sermon: May 27, 1804* (Bath, 1804), p. 47.

[47] A. M. Broadley and L. Melville, *The Beautiful Lady Craven* (2 vols., London, 1914), i, p. xvi.

[48] M. Elwin, ed., *The Noels and the Milbankes: Their Letters for Twenty-five Years 1767–1792* (London, 1967), p. 248.

scape gardening had much to do with this demand. The poet William Shenstone defended the gardeners in his ode *Rural Elegance* by appealing to the liberality of the poetic muse: 'Her lavish charter, taste, appropriates all we see.'[49] The gardeners themselves concentrated on pleasing proprietors. Humphry Repton developed this art into a regular system, designing churches to resemble the mansions near which they lay, and adorning market-houses or mere milestones with family arms to create the illusion of property far beyond the manor-house gate. 'The first essential of greatness in a place, is the appearance of united or uninterrupted property.' By the 1790s this preoccupation with 'the air of being appropriated to the peculiar use and pleasure of the proprietor' had become excessive. Repton's antagonists in the 'picturesque controversy', Richard Payne Knight and Uvedale Price, criticized it as pandering to the 'foolish vanity' of owners.[50] But they were not instantly successful in dispersing this illusion of the vain. Repton was obsessed with the quality of 'greatness'. No doubt he had a shrewd appreciation of the business which it brought him in a country, as he immodestly remarked to one of his customers, the Earl of Winchilsea, 'so large a portion of whose scenery has been committed to my direction'.[51]

Humbler but not essentially dissimilar deceptions were practised lower down the social scale. Many of the frauds listed in guides to the criminal life of the metropolis were perpetrated by confidence tricksters whose art lay in conveying the impression that they were men or women of wealth.[52] Less culpable, but not more candid, were businessmen who lived in debt to inspire the confidence of customers, doctors who kept a carriage which they could not afford so as to attract fashionable patients, army officers who pretended to an aristocratic life-style for the sake of preferment. The acquisition of prestige, the assertion of power, the attraction of patronage, all could be achieved by a suitably misleading appearance. They were often linked and always part of the same social rhetoric. A complex society has a variety of such rhetorics at its command; in the eighteenth century the richest and strongest was that provided by property and its related values.

A modern rhetoric, unlike its classical predecessors, is not required to have a rational structure, nor even a consistent set of definitions. Part of its utility lies in its uncertainties, ambiguities, and even inconsistencies. At bottom, however, it requires some ideal, some model which can be applied in everyday situations and which, in a crisis, can be used by way of

---

[49] *The Poetical Works of William Shenstone*, ed. G. Gilfillan (Edinburgh, 1854), p. 128; see also M. R. Brownell, *Alexander Pope and the Art of Gardening* (Oxford, 1978), p. 241.

[50] G. Carter, P. Goode, and K. Laurie, *Humphry Repton: Landscape Gardener, 1752–1818* (Norwich, 1982), pp. 34–5.

[51] P. Finch, *History of Burley-on-the-Hill, Rutland* (2 vols., London, 1901), i. 112.

[52] *The Swindler Detected* (London, 1781).

inspiration and exhortation. For such a model there were some minimal definitional requirements. Property had to be manifestly disposable: even judges, who had a positive mania for parcelling out the physical world which they confronted, admitted that it contained some things not disposable by any human agency. It had to be absolutely at the command of its proprietor, and not contingent on the will of another. Above all, it had to be held unconditionally, without the attachment of any duties whatever. It is important to remember that this is a prescriptive model, not a descriptive analysis. A high proportion of property, especially much of what was most esteemed, real property, would have had difficulty meeting these criteria in a legal sense, and would also have completely failed to meet them in a practical sense. But the concern to apply the criteria, and the desire to subject all forms of ownership to them wherever possible, were characteristic of the eighteenth century and had a strong bearing on the political values of the age. The effectiveness of this process is best viewed in relation to one of its greatest triumphs, the subjection of religion to its priorities, and also in relation to one of its most significant defeats, the failure to extend the law of copyright. In each the desire to push a fashionable concept to the limit of what inherited assumptions would bear, and even beyond, was marked. In each, too, the power and adaptability of the propertied mentality were evident.

AN ENDEAVOUR TO APPROPRIATE

The Church of England was nothing if not a propertied institution, yet it was in principle highly resistant to the prevailing ethic. Virtually none of the property held for the Church by individuals or corporations could be treated in the way laymen treated their property. The system of church leases, normally let to laymen on lives, was notorious in this respect. It ensured that individual churchmen had no interest beyond fat renewal fines and the realization of immediate profits. A candid clerical correspondence of the day, such as that of John Butler, successively Prebendary of Winchester, Bishop of Oxford, and Bishop of Hereford, displays an entirely healthy interest in mortality, not merely the prospective mortality of superiors occupying desirable preferment, but also that of laymen on whose 'lives' beneficial leases depended.[53] It also tended to prevent the Church as a whole from benefiting by agricultural improvement at a time when lay landlords were abandoning beneficial leases in favour of tenancies at will and frequent rent reviews. Most Church property of this kind was held by 'dignified' clergy either in their own right, like many bishops and prebendaries, or in a collective capacity, as in the case of colleges. But even

[53] Surrey RO (Guildford), Onslow MSS, Butler to Onslow, 29 Dec. 1778, 5 Oct. 1779.

the parochial incumbent, invested with glebe and tithe, wanted the first privilege of an ordinary freeholder, the right to alienate it. As one Norfolk parson adroitly put it, he had the 'property not the perpetuity' of his glebe.[54] Moreover, all Church property was held as a sacred trust, an eternal commitment to the maintenance of godliness and good learning. Most of it was directed to specific uses, parochial, collegiate, capitular, charitable; all of it, however improperly used, was ultimately dedicated to the saving of souls.

In practice Church property was subject to the will and whim of ordinary men. The Victorian belief that the eighteenth-century Church was uniquely worldly, even corrupt, is not intrinsically very plausible, and most of what was found wanting in it can be traced back to the origins of the English establishment in the sixteenth century. More credible is the claim that it had become peculiarly secular in its outlook, with the gradual subjugation of the Church and its endowments to the propertied mentality of the period. Certain tendencies made themselves obvious time and again. One was the readiness of the clergy to treat their material resources exactly as if they were themselves laymen; a second was the vulnerability of the Church to strictly commercial exploitation by clergy and laymen alike.

The legal status of tithes was a matter of continuing controversy. Defenders of the clergy took their stand on the immemorial right which made the very notion of absolute lay proprietorship of land untenable. 'No *Layman*, as a Layman, by the Laws of our Country, can have a greater Property than in Nine Parts of the Lands he by any Means possesses.'[55] The principle was not disputed, but interpreting it was a complicated matter. Church courts had long since ceased to adjudicate tithe disputes except at preliminary hearings or in cases involving trivial sums. Rectorial tithes were often owned by laymen; so, in some cases, were vicarial tithes. In the lowest form of parochial cure, the 'mere donative', the corporate contribution to the upkeep of religion had been totally diverted to the private profit of a lay rector, whose control of the minister (assuming he bothered to appoint one) was complete, and virtually immune to episcopal interference. It was difficult to conceive of the tithe as a sacred tenth when it was often farmed on a commercial basis. Crucial judicial determinations in the 1730s removed the lingering supposition that lay rectors should be treated less favourably than the ordinary clergyman when in dispute with tithe-payers.[56] Regardless of ownership, there was also a notable readiness to have the tithe assimilated to ordinary property. The Church made little protest at this state of affairs. Distinguished churchmen, including

---

[54] P. Millican, *History of Horstead and Stanninghall, Norfolk* (Norwich, 1937), p. 59.

[55] *A Letter to a Member of Parliament* in Durham RO, Strathmore MSS.

[56] Bunbury 325, 345: *Lady Charlton* v. *Sir Blunden Charlton* (1733), *The Corporation of Bury* v. *Evans* (1739).

Archbishop Tillotson and Archbishop Sharp after the Revolution, specifically denied that divine right made any part of the clerical entitlement to
tithe, as did the clergy who opposed the Quaker Tithe Bill of 1736.[57]
Individual incumbents argued, pragmatically, that 'Tithes are a part of
Rent which if not paid to an Ecclesiatical would be claimed by a Temporal
Landlord'.[58] As was pointed out on their behalf, the fact that tithe-free
land sold for more than tithable land and the readiness of landlords to
'allow' their tenants sums paid by way of tithe, were clear evidence of the
extent to which it had become incorporated in the ordinary practice of
agriculture and the intrinsic value of land.[59]

It is easy to see why the Church assented to the process of legal
assimilation. Common lawyers were hostile to ecclesiastical jurisdiction but
not to ecclesiastical property. This mattered a great deal when the clergy
sought to claim their share of the improved agricultural profits available
after 1750. John Rayner's summary of tithe judgements, published in 1783,
revealed the high rate of success enjoyed by clergy who took their claims
to law.[60] A series of important cases, attracting much public interest, was
decided in the 1770s, almost all of them to the advantage of tithe-owners.
What was operating was plainly the readiness of the judiciary to accept
what the Church was now content to argue, that tithes were like any other
propertied right, and subject to similar arguments. Even Quakers, known
for their resistance to payment, increasingly complied in an atmosphere
which made it easy to confuse such obligations with those which had no
spiritual implications. Strict Quakers like the celebrated John Griffith spent
much energy lecturing them on the impropriety of this reasoning.[61] When
they did have the temerity to pursue their case before the law courts, they
confronted the incredulity of the eighteenth century rather than the bigotry
of the seventeenth. Judges found it difficult to believe that any civilized
person could connect the payment of tithes with the state of his soul. One
Dorset Quaker thus reported his experience in the Court of Exchequer in
1768: 'The Judges were very mild, and seemed desirous of convincing us
of the propriety of the law; that Jure Divino was now disclaimed, and that
tithes being now claimed only by the law of the land, it was right to pay
them.'[62]

The clergy were understandably prone to want the best of both worlds,
or at least the best of both concepts of property in this world. When it

---

[57] T. Newcome, ed., *The Life of John Sharp* (2 vols., London, 1825), ii. 12–16; *London Magazine* (1736), 656.
[58] Millican, *History of Horstead*, p. 59.
[59] *London Magazine* (1761), 474.
[60] J. Rayner, *Cases at Large Concerning Tithes* (3 vols., London, 1783), vol. i, p. cxxxvi.
[61] *A Journal of the Life, Travels, and Labours in the Work of the Ministry, of John Griffith* (London, 1779), p. 231.
[62] E. W. Watson, *Ashmore Co Dorset, A History of the Parish* (Gloucester, 1890), p. 23.

suited them, they exploited the close correlation between their own wealth and that of laymen. Defending his claim to every species of revenue arising from ordinary worship in his parish, Henry Sacheverell, as Rector of St Andrews, Holborn, appealed not to those high-flying doctrines with which his name was associated but to the 'Properties of the Subject in General'. His friend Joseph Trapp pointed out that the rights of a parish minister were fully entitled to the protection of 'the *Liberty-and-Property* language of the free People of *England*'.[63] At the same time the clergy continued to speak as if they were the true heirs of primitive Christianity. Every form of clerical income, from the miserable surplice fees on which many country curates depended, to the 'pursy' rectorships and 'golden' prebends which kept the wolf from the door of their dignified superiors, was sanctified under the heading of 'church property'. The radical historian Gravenor Henson listed twenty-two kinds of profit entitled to this description.[64] Since some of them were of recent origin, and others, like the fee charged for reading of marriage banns under the Marriage Act of 1753, had been generously bestowed by Parliament, it is hardly surprising that they offended many of those who contributed to them.

The element of hypocrisy was perhaps as irritating as the imposition itself. However much they appealed to biblical authority and sacred custom in defence of their possessions, the clergy tended to treat them as if they were the ordinary possessions of propertied gentlemen. All kinds of forces were consolidating the place of clergymen in lay society in the reign of George III, and it is hardly surprising that their standing as lay proprietors was to the taste of many of them. They served on the land tax commission and on the magistrate's bench, and engaged in squirearchical pursuits such as fox-hunting and old-fashioned paternalism. Enclosure and tithe commutation notoriously enhanced this tendency, helping to transform the clergyman from tax-collector into landlord. One such clerical squire, Pulter Forester of Cosgrove in Northamptonshire, boasted, in the manner, if not quite with the grandeur of the landed magnate, that thanks to the determination of the enclosure commissioners for his parish, 'he could now walk a mile from the River by Wolverton to Furtho on his own Glebe'.[65] All that Forester lacked was the incentive of the landowning layman to maintain and improve his property for future generations. But even this could be rectified. A clergyman able to buy an advowson was well placed to found a dynasty. Rules about a patron's presentation of himself could readily be circumvented, and elder sons were guaranteed orders when they had the sure prospect of preferment. Tithe and glebe, in the hands of an

[63] *The Case of the Patron and Rector of St Andrew's, Holborn* (London, 1722), pp. 10, 30.
[64] S. D. Chapman, ed., *Henson's History of the Framework Knitters* (Newton Abbot, 1970), pp. 247–8.
[65] F. G. Stokes, ed., *The Blecheley Diary of the Rev. William Cole, 1765–67* (London, 1931), p. 271.

incumbent occupying his own living, constituted an agricultural estate much like the patrimonial estates of country squires. Clerical ownership of advowsons was common; so were clerical dynasties. One Norfolk clergyman not in this happy situation had the temerity, under pressure from his bishop, publicly to urge his want of prospects as the reason for his refusal to serve either of his two cures. 'My family had no interest in either of the Livings beyond the term of my life, and the annual profits of them would not admit of my sinking upon them any part of my private fortune.'[66]

Commercial dealing in advowsons, by no means new but increasingly common, was itself a cause of scandal. The great majority of those which found their way on to the market had originally been attached to manorial property. Manors were often completely divorced from the major land-holdings of a parish; even when they were not, it was sometimes convenient for their owners to dispose of their ecclesiastical responsibilities. They were advertised, bargained for, and conveyed exactly like other forms of property. Their value partly depended on the age of the existing incumbent; sale of a vacant benefice was technically unlawful and certainly perilous unless adroitly managed, since it risked forfeiting the nomination to the bishop or the Crown. Either the advowson itself or the right of next presentation could be sold; the difference in value was not large since the acquisition of rights to a second and third presentation was a distinctly speculative investment once the first presentation had installed a young and potentially long-lived minister in office. Livings, appropriately so-named in this respect at least, somewhat resembled leases for lives in the uncertainty which attended the realization of assets, and were treated for commercial purposes on a similar basis. An advertisement for three Devon advowsons in 1779 offered two with one life (that of the incumbent), the other with two lives, because the vendor had already promised the next presentation.[67] Purchasers had the assistance of elaborate actuarial calculations in valuing potential purchases. John Richards's publication of 1739, *Annuities on Lives, and for Limited Terms of Years, Considered*, included a substantial section on advowsons. On a specimen living yielding £200 per annum, with an incumbent aged 60, Richards reckoned that the purchase of the first presentation was worth £790, the second £268, the third £64, and the fourth (a very wild gamble on successive clerical deaths) £10, a grand total of £1,132.[68] Such computations were often rendered more intricate, though not less precise, by the need to take into account parochial customs, and by the ingenuity of the commercially minded, for

---

[66] *The Case of the Rev. C. Le Grice* [1788], p. 4. It is possible that there was an element of victimization in episcopal harrying of Le Grice. He was an associate of the republican Capel Lofft and a supporter of the repeal of the Test and Corporation Acts.

[67] *A Survey and Particulars of the Manor of Otterton* ... (Exeter, [1779]), p. 17.

[68] (London), pp. 102–4.

example granting leases for lives on tithe and glebe. The value of advowsons rose markedly in the late eighteenth century in line with agricultural rents. It was also enhanced by the growing candour which accompanied the transactions involved. Advertisers did not hesitate to specify 'immediate resignation' by the incumbent, a stipulation which smacked of simony but made any bargain much more attractive to the purchaser.[69]

This trafficking in cures of souls exposed the Church to damaging criticism. It was intensified by the expedients employed to maximize profitability. Since an incumbent was tenant for life, and it was impossible to keep an incumbency open without forfeiting the right of presentation, it was common to install caretaking clergy who undertook to resign as soon as the intended beneficiary, usually a relation of the patron, was of age and ordained. The resignation bond required of such clergy was legally enforceable, like any other commercial contract. One of the more telling arguments against the practice was that it turned the parson's freehold into something quite different, 'the lowest of every species of property, an estate at will'.[70] It was also incompatible with the spirit, and probably the letter of canon law. Such bonds were commonplace. Bishop Bagot of Norwich accurately described them in 1784 as 'converting that into property, which is in its nature, no other than a confidential trust for the Public'.[71] He did so in a context of growing episcopal concern on this score. Robert Lowth as Bishop of London conducted a fierce campaign against resignation bonds. In the celebrated Fytche Case, he met with determined opposition from judges and lay peers, eventually securing victory in the House of Lords by only one vote.[72] Even this was but a partial success since it concerned only 'general' bonds, which placed the incumbent totally at the mercy of his patron. Bonds which required their signatories to resign when a patron's son came of age, for instance, were considered unobjectionable. In effect patrons were still able to treat their right of nomination as part of their estate. Moreover, worse horrors presented themselves. The practice of purchasing a living and simultaneously taking a lease of the tithe and glebe for ninety-nine years at a peppercorn rent circumvented the rule against direct purchase with immediate possession. Its eradication was the particular ambition of Lowth's colleague and successor, Bishop Porteus.[73]

Perhaps no aspect of the Church was more difficult to defend. Surprisingly, the Evangelical Samuel Walker vindicated the sale of advowsons on the grounds that 'the right of presenting a worthy minister is a valuable

[69] *Whitehall Evening-Post*, 2 Jan. 1790.

[70] *Thoughts on Bonds of Resignation* (London, 1783), p. 27.

[71] Lewis Bagot, *A Charge Delivered to the Clergy* (Norwich, 1784), pp. 30–1.

[72] Cobbett's *Parliamentary History*, xxiii. 876.

[73] R. Hodgson, *The Life of the Right Reverend Beilby Porteus DD* (2nd edn., London, 1811), pp. 142–5.

and desirable thing'.[74] He doubtless presumed high-mindedness on the part of the purchaser. But even a high-minded man like Walker's friend Thomas Haweis could find himself entrapped in the mesh of legal and commercial considerations which governed Church livings. Haweis believed that he had accepted the Vicarage of Aldwincle in Northamptonshire without conditions; his patron took a quite different view and plunged him into an embarrassing public controversy.[75] The demoralizing effect on the clergy themselves is not difficult to imagine, and must surely have had a bearing on the political cynicism often identified as the besetting sin of the eighteenth-century Church. The careerism which marked the progress of ecclesiastical placemen could readily be related to the procedure which went with their initial admission to the Church. William Dodd was widely censured for his attempt to bribe the Lord Chancellor into nominating him to the wealthy living of St George's, Hanover Square. He also thereby ruined his reputation with the King and probably destroyed his prospects of obtaining that royal pardon which he so confidently expected when he was convicted of forgery in 1777. But if his offence was essentially simony, it is not easy to see what made it morally different from the practices commonly pursued in the disposal of livings.

It was not only parochial cures which were bought and sold as if they were commodities. Regimental chaplaincies were bartered much as officers' commissions were. Army agents offered them on similar terms. In wartime they paid the same attention to the seniority of the regiment in question and its prospects of surviving demobilization when peace was made. In 1796 one such chaplaincy, in a regiment below the fiftieth, and therefore guaranteed a place on the peace establishment, was hawked about for £800, a sum which would have bought a small parish.[76] This was considered a saleable property in the strictest possible sense, and often treated by purchasers as if it were an ordinary incumbency. In the Seven Years War the chaplain to the British garrison at Emden succeeded in absenting himself for a year before he was compelled to resign. Thirty-five years later, during the war against revolutionary France, the War Office was reduced to offering an annuity to those who preferred resignation to residence. The prospect of a station in the West Indies, sharing the hazards of military life with his flock, was too much for one chaplain, who penned a furious riposte to the *Gentleman's Magazine*. 'Sir, what a privation of property, purchased under the sanction of 50 years usage, with the right of selling again.'[77]

[74] G. C. B. Davies, *The Early Cornish Evangelicals, 1735–60: A Study of Walker of Truro* (London, 1951), p. 142.

[75] A. S. Wood, *Thomas Haweis 1734–1820* (London, 1957), pp. 104–9, 126–41.

[76] Lincolnshire Archives Office, Tennyson MSS, 2. 10. 16: J. Kemp to S. Turner, 28 June 1796.

[77] William Hood to War Office, 7 June 1763, in *Notes and Queries for Somerset and Dorset*, 16 (1918–20), 11–13; *Gentleman's Magazine* (1796), 918.

Commercialism was not restricted to the arrangements by which the clergy entered into their famous freehold. Pew rents made a seat in church subject to the same laws of market economics as all other privileges. The rules by which seats descended or changed hands were part of the ancient custom of parishes. In rural areas they were commonly annexed to individual dwellings, not, as Richard Gough, the laborious historian of his parish in Shropshire, noted, to persons or lands.[78] This doctrine came under increasing pressure in the course of the eighteenth century, as proprietors sought to impose their personal control, exclusive of tenants and the parish at large. The case of *Partington versus the Rector and Churchwardens of Barnes* in 1754 was revealing in this respect. Mrs Partington was a humble lodger in a gardener's house, when she went to law for her right to a pew in the parish church. But she also owned a substantial freehold property, which she rented out. It was on the grounds of her standing as a proprietor that the judge, Sir George Lee, found for her. 'Though she did not live in her own house, yet as she had an estate in the parish, I thought that not material.'[79] In 1767 the Master of the Free Grammar School at Leicester pressed a still more controversial claim to a pew which he had once enjoyed in Sutton Coldfield, though he no longer maintained a residence in the parish.[80] The trend was away from a tradition which sought to accommodate local inhabitants towards a convention which put a place below the pulpit, like a place in it, at the disposal of proprietors. Coke of Norfolk even suggested a tax on what was evidently a species of property and arguably a form of luxury.[81]

In many places, even in parish churches, pews became mere objects of trade, bought and sold by means of a standard legal conveyance.[82] In new or rebuilt churches, where pew rents contributed both to capital costs and the maintenance of a minister, it was important to realize the maximum return from a saleable seat in church. When Hawkshead church was repewed attempts to fund the work by traditional means of rating and voluntary contribution repeatedly failed: in the end the new pews were simply sold.[83] In urban areas anything but straightforward sale seemed eccentric. Not to have a seat of one's own was unthinkable for propertied people. The wife of the sculptor Joseph Nollekens was considered both penny-pinching and ridiculous for her refusal to purchase a pew and her habit of glaring at her tenants until one of them made room for her.[84]

[78] *The History of Myddle*, ed. D. Hay (London, 1981), p. 77.
[79] 2 Lee 345–56: *Partington v. Rector and Churchwardens of Barnes.*
[80] W. K. Riland Bedford, *Three Hundred Years of a Family Living, Being a History of the Rilands of Sutton Coldfield* (Birmingham, 1889), p. 47.
[81] A. M. W. Stirling, *Coke of Norfolk and His Friends* (2 vols., London, 1907), i. 187.
[82] An example of a conveyance, of a pew in Faringdon church, is at Berkshire RO, D/EX/351/1.
[83] H. S. Cowper, *Hawkshead* (London, 1899), pp. 444–50.
[84] J. T. Smith, *Nollekens and His Times*, ed. W. Whitton (2 vols., London, 1920), i. 67.

The allocation of seating frequently gave rise to unchristian reflections, particularly on churchwardens responsible for supervising the arrangements. William Hutton of Birmingham was furious when offered a pew of three sittings for one guinea in Withall Chapel, King's Norton, in 1777, only to find himself sitting in a stair hole.[85] A clerical visitor to South Shields in 1788 was impressed when he saw the parish church but had little faith in the eirenic effect of its refurbishment. 'The improvements of the Church shew the wealth and religious zeal of the Inhabitants and I fear the rising disputes for Seats will shew their want of Christian Charity.'[86]

New chapels were particularly productive of such disputes. They were also perilously close to being commercial enterprises. Mrs Bennett's story of a builder who sought to adorn a new housing development with a chapel built as a speculation, the pew rents and burial charges being divided between himself and the minister, was meant to incur the censure of readers, but can hardly have shocked them.[87] The minister in this case was a cynical Methodist, but he had counterparts in the established Church who exploited the mercenary opportunities offered by middle-class congregations. The actor Samuel Ryley told a similar tale of a clergyman who, passing through Birmingham, was impressed by its potential, and suggested, with disarming precision, that for a sum of £4,059.5s.6d., suitably supported by subscription, 'something handsome' might be built.[88] In London the famous preacher Rowland Hill was accused of running the Surrey Chapel as a business operation, to sustain his own career, and to secure his principal backer, a Southwark gauze-man, a generous return on his contribution to the building costs. A shortage of seats in the local parish church of St George's, Southwark, gave him an ideal opportunity to attract hearers at half a crown a quarter.[89] Officially, the Church maintained a certain circumspection about ecclesiastical buildings in private ownership. But for this caution the opulent parish of St George's, Hanover Square, would today be known as Holy Trinity. Archbishop Tenison designed Trinity Chapel, fashionably situated in Conduit Street and much attended by the genteel in the late seventeenth century, as a new parish, to be separated from the mother church of St Martin-in-the-Fields. But the chapel was leasehold property and Tenison's plan had to be abandoned in favour of building St George's on freehold land. Perhaps there was wisdom in this. By the reign of George III Trinity Chapel was in the hands of a

[85] C. H. Beale, *Catherine Hutton and Her Friends* (Birmingham, 1895), p. 121.
[86] Gloucestershire RO, D 2227/30: Journals of Revd Samuel Viner.
[87] A. M. Bennett, *Anna; Or, Memoirs of a Welch Heiress* (4 vols., London, 1785), i. 19.
[88] S. W. Ryley, *The Itinerant* (9 vols., London, 1808-27), ii. 107-8.
[89] William Woolley, *A Cure for Canting; Or, The Grand Imposture of St Stephen's and Surrey Chapels Unmasked: In a Letter to Sir Richard Hill, Bart.* (London, 1794).

bookseller and subject to unseemly squabbles about liability to the poor rate.[90]

Even reputable priests could not afford to be too squeamish in such matters. Richard Cecil was a pious and admired Evangelical; yet he accepted the charge of Bedford Row Chapel, the largest private chapel in London in the early 1780s, only after careful calculation, bolstered by the aid of an aunt of William Wilberforce's and a loan from a friendly lawyer. Though he was determined not to exclude the poor from his church, making it clear that 'any inattention to the established economy of the Chapel was grievous to him', he gradually created what might be generously described as a sound financial base for his pastoral work.[91] The question of free admission was particularly important. At an unprofitable Hampstead chapel in 1796, the pew opener had instructions to welcome strangers at first attendance. But if they presented themselves a second time, he was required to request the annual fee, a minimum of 10s.6d.[92] Benevolent laymen also found it difficult to resist the entrepreneurial implications of church accommodation. When one of Aylesbury's wealthiest citizens, Hugh Barker Bell, purchased pews in the parish church, in 1755, for the use of the parishioners at large, he included travellers among the beneficiaries, but only those staying at his own inn, the White Hart.[93] There is little suggestion in contemporary literature of concern or embarrassment at the manner in which the House of God was virtually auctioned off to his worshippers, though pew warfare sometimes provoked scandal. One warrior at Market Harborough in 1760, who 'took Possession of this Pew (*where he had never sat before*) devoutly and religiously disposed to exclude all Invaders', was plainly not considered a credit to his congregation.[94] His reward for three years' litigation was excommunication with costs against him. But for the most part appropriation in church was accepted in much the same spirit that it was allowed free operation in many other places.

Commercial enterprise in spiritual matters was most distressingly exemplified in the highest ranks of society. One of the privileges of a peer or peeress, enjoyed by impoverished Scottish aristocrats as well as hereditary members of the House of Lords, was the right to appoint a number of chaplains, pro rata according to rank, for his (or her) private household. These 'scarves' entitled their holders to partial exemption from the rules against pluralities, and were thereby valuable commodities. Thus, with

[90] G. Smith and F. Benger, *The Oldest Bookshop: A History of Two Hundred Years* (London, 1928), pp. 31–3.

[91] J. Pratt, *The Works of the Rev. Richard Cecil* (4 vols., London, 1811), i, pp. xix–xxiii.

[92] A. W. Rumney, ed., *From the Old South-Sea House Being Thomas Rumney's Letter Book 1796–1798* (London, 1914), p. 40.

[93] Oxford Diocesan Archive, Archdeaconry of Buckingham, Faculties.

[94] *An Appeal to Reason Concerning a Prosecution in the Arch-Deacon's Court of Leicester* (Market Harborough, 1765), p. 11.

such dispensation in mind for his brother, the North Country landowner William Chaytor cheerfully trawled his aristocratic contacts in 1761. The Duke of Cleveland, the Earl of Huntingdon, and the Earl of Darlington were all possibilities. Chaytor was told that provided he wanted a chaplaincy for a short time to qualify his brother as a pluralist, there would be little difficulty, and Darlington duly obliged.[95] This form of patronage was generally employed by peers to reward their clerical friends and dependants: college tutors of noble undergraduates were virtually guaranteed a scarf. But some were sold for cash, the going rate varying between ten and twenty guineas in the early part of George III's reign. The Bluestocking, Elizabeth Carter, found the practice shocking. 'Would one, in speculation, conceive that persons of noble birth, high rank, and liberal education, should be so contemptibly dirty!'[96]

In the twentieth century the established Church remains a propertied institution in a propertied society. It does not always succeed in escaping controversy when its duty to preserve clerical income and its ethical standards come into collision. But tithes have long since vanished, advowsons are no longer sold, presentations no longer bought, resignation bonds no longer given, pews no longer rented, and chaplaincies no longer auctioned to the highest bidder.[97] The tolerance, indeed encouragement given to such practices in the eighteenth century, is a clear indication of the extent to which the propertied mentality had gained a hold on the contemporary mind.

Somewhat less successful was a more audacious enterprise, to assert property in the products of the mind itself. This campaign was a logical extension of attempts to secure a variety of notional properties which did not fit into the traditional categories of the lawyers. A range of commercial securities and transactions acquired legal definition and the protection of the courts, in an age when the expansion of credit made judicial innovation in this respect seem highly desirable. In effect the paper promise became itself a valuable form of property.[98] Lord Mansfield, from 1756 to 1788 Lord Chief Justice of the King's Bench, has been given a large share of the credit for judgements which made this possible. For Mansfield himself, there is no doubt that this was a congenial task. Even property rights of a lowly kind benefited by his imaginative approach to their interpretation. 'Every subject had a right to secure his property in the best manner he

[95] North Yorkshire RO, Chaytor Papers, 2 QH 11/1/63.

[96] *Letters from Mrs Elizabeth Carter, to Mrs Montagu, between the Years 1755 and 1800* (3 vols., London, 1817), i. 306.

[97] It should be said that the Faversham case of 1988 has none the less confirmed entrenched rights in proprietary pews; see N. Yates, 'The Mayoral and Corporation Seats', *Archaeologiana Cantiana*, 106 (1988), 37–43.

[98] P. R. Atiyah, *The Rise and Fall of Freedom of Contract* (Oxford, 1979), p. 102.

could, whether lottery tickets or not', he observed in 1773, in a case which aroused much interest.[99] It is notable that he had far less success in his attempts to modernize land law. The extreme conservatism of English lawyers in preserving the intricate mass of precedents which constituted the law of real property, while bowing to the need for revision of commercial law, forms one of the most striking and also most characteristic contrasts of the eighteenth century.

More daring still was the notion that property could be vested in ideas and opinions, what one pamphleteer called 'this fantastick Property', a 'Species of Property in this Country without a Proprietor'.[100] In fact, existing patent law provided some support for this concept, albeit under restrictions which irritated inventors, and frequently made it impracticable to enforce the right thus protected. The usual assumption was that authentic originality was required to justify the acquisition of exclusive rights to exploitation. But as some of those with expert knowledge of trade and manufacturing pointed out, many humbler innovators had a good claim to similar treatment in principle. The Birmingham Court of Requests found itself dealing with the case of a buckle plater who sued for the value of a pattern card which had been sent to South America and produced no order: 'Whatever fate attends a card, like this before us, it is still the property of the operator; he possesses a kind of freehold right.'[101] The profits to be made from pattern cards at a time of rapid industrialization naturally made such questions particularly interesting.

The great expansion of the market for the printed word rendered the question of literary copyright similarly significant. Piracy and plagiarism were increasingly commonplace practices in the publishing and printing trade; it was believed that the flourishing state of publishing in Scotland and Ireland derived from deficiencies in English law. Parliament had granted a copyright to authors and their representatives in 1710, but restricted it to a maximum of twenty-eight years. Whether there was a common law right beyond that period remained unclear. The stakes were very big indeed for London firms which had invested in copyrights. After more than twenty years of inconclusive litigation, an adverse judgement in the House of Lords in 1774 was described in dramatic terms. 'Near £200,000 worth of what was honestly purchased at public sale, and what was yesterday thought property, is now reduced to nothing.'[102] An attempt to extend statutory protection was defeated in Parliament in the same year, with much lamentation about the consequences for authors and their preferred publishers. The debates which accompanied these decisions

[99] *Sentimental Magazine* (1773), 11.
[100] *An Enquiry into the Nature and Origin of Literary Property* (London, 1762), p. 6.
[101] William Hutton, *Courts of Requests* (Birmingham, 1787), p. 372.
[102] *London Magazine* (1774), 101.

found judges and legislators deeply divided, but unusually ready to discuss the fundamentals of property theory. Authors were understandably reluctant to give them full credit in this respect. Joseph Cradock pictured the ordinary MP as an ignorant opponent of copyright, incapable of grasping the interdependence of diverse forms of property. He satirically reported an imagined speech by one such thus: authors 'caused all that abuse on men of property that appeared so frequently in the newspapers, and that the booksellers were a pack of bloodhounds that set them on; that he therefore hoped neither of them would have any relief under *this here* bill'.[103] This was hardly fair. The debate on the copyright question was searching and sophisticated, forcing those involved to examine their basic assumptions about the nature of property. The failure of the attempt to extend the law of copyright was not inevitable; the Court of Common Pleas supported it, in statutory form it passed the House of Commons, and it was defeated only narrowly in the Lords.

Quite what explains the outcome is uncertain. Some blamed the vested interest of the interloping publishers, especially the Scottish firms which specialized in large-scale production of cheap editions of staple English works. The success of the bill in the Lower House may well have owed something to the strident nationalism of London publishers and their supporters. In Parliament as a whole there was a certain reluctance to have the legislature interfere in what was a peculiarly difficult legal question, with much to be said on both sides, in point of equity as well as law. But above all there was an appreciation of the difficulty of defining a form of property which was uniquely intangible, and which, indeed, could not be protected without potentially restricting the natural rights of readers. Just where liberty and property lay in the copyright debate was a complicated question, one which exposed some of the underlying awkwardnesses in contemporary worship of property. Authors, like clergymen, were for the most part content to rest their case on the analogy with ordinary property. Defoe spoke, in the year before the Copyright Act of 8 Anne, of 'daily Invasions of Property equal in Villany, to robbing a House, or plundering a Hospital'.[104] The artist John Gwynn, referring to the position of the copperplate engraver, whose plight was even worse than that of the author, observed that he 'must be contented with the gleanings of the field when he had an undoubted right to the whole crop'.[105] Others sought to link the proposed extension of rights to the requirements of an equal and just society. The republican historian Catherine Macaulay pointed out that

---

[103] *Village Memoirs* (London, 1774), pp. 119–20; in the third edition of 1775, 'Corrected and Enlarged', Cradock omitted this passage and substituted a more general discussion of the House of Commons as a representative body.

[104] *Defoe's Review*, vi. 363: 3 Nov. 1709.

[105] *London and Westminster Improved, Illustrated by Plans* (London, 1766), p. 50.

without legal protection for authors, only the tools of aristocratic patrons had a real incentive to publish. 'If literary property becomes common, we can have but two kinds of authors, men in opulence, and men in dependence.'[106]

Against these contentions it could be argued that copyright was not the assertion of a writer's property in his labour but an attempt to monopolize what naturally belonged to all. The most logical answer to this was offered by Blackstone. He saw no difficulty in assimilating property in the products of the mind to a body of law which traditionally comprehended diverse forms of property such as options, advowsons, and rights of common, all under the heading of 'incorporeal rights'. He took head on the charge of monopoly. All property was by definition a form of monopoly. 'What is a monopoly? An Endeavour to appropriate to private Use what before belonged to all the World in Common?'[107] The mentality of the eighteenth century could not cope with logical rigour of this order. In common parlance, monopoly was invariably a term of abuse, the less acceptable face of property, which champions of propertied values did their best to conceal. Enthusiasts for free and fair trade spoke as if monopoly inhibited the freedom to acquire property; but as Blackstone insisted, all property did that, by its very nature. The real debate, one which kept breaking through, was about the limits to which the propertied claims of individuals and interest-groups could be pushed. Implied was a profound and necessary contradiction in the logic of appropriation. It could not be resolved without discomfort to particular interests, nor without damage to the residual sense of the public domain which even a highly individualistic age retained.

Where there was uncertainty about the forms that property might take, or the extent to which it might be pressed, conflict was unavoidable. It appeared in many varieties, and social historians have understandably been intrigued by those which reveal the propertied and the propertyless in a primitive kind of class struggle. But a common theme unites otherwise disparate contests. Rural communities which struggled to preserve their belief that wild animals were the property of no individual, and cottagers who defended the concept of common rights against enclosing landowners, belong in the same framework as churchmen who were shocked that the cure of souls could be treated as commercial transactions, and authors who were dismayed at the pirating of their writings. All were asserting one definition of property against another. It was this that made disputes more embarrassing than a frontal attack on the ideology of property itself, such as was rarely witnessed before the 1790s. The conflicts themselves permit no tidy or simple conclusion. What determined the event in each instance

---

[106] *A Modest Plea for the Property of Copyright* (London, 1774), p. 37.
[107] 1 Black. W. 340–2: *Tonson* v. *Collins* (1762).

was very much a matter of circumstance. There could not be one principle
for application in all cases, because property was an assertion of ownership
that could not always be vindicated without compromising an alternative
concept of ownership or offending another, and no less powerful owner.
When the concept was common ownership and the owner an entire community, or even society at large, the resulting struggles were positively
heroic. It was, of course, a sign of the hegemony of the propertied mentality
that so many of the contentions which brought individuals into conflict
with wider groups and communities were conceived within propertied
terms of reference and conducted with constant recourse to the rhetoric of
property.

A CARNAL AND PROPERTIED WORLD

It is tempting to suppose that confidence in the moral and political superiority of property rested on an ideological foundation peculiar to the period.
But the impression gained from contemporary debate is that any ideology
would do provided it did not challenge the hegemony of property. The
thrust of argument was not upwards from some universally accepted
principle, but rather downwards, from a practical acceptance of the primacy
of property and its associated values, to whatever theoretical grounding
might best support its varied manifestations.

One obvious expedient, almost universally approved in the early eighteenth century, was to make property both chronologically and logically
prior to the State. This premiss proved sufficient to sustain some lamentably
weak arguments. The Whig cleric Thomas Burnet, a protégé of Bishop
Burnet, relied on it for the kind of circular thinking which characterized a
good deal of the debate about government and property. 'The Determination of Property must necessarily have been before the settlement of
Government; this being only a Means for the securing of Property, and by
consequence Government could not be founded in any *Primary* Law of
Nature, if Property itself was not.'[108] Most such reasoning assumed a
contractual basis for civil organization. Those forms of contract theory
which appealed most to Englishmen removed property from the realm of
government by stating it as a right preceding the formation of civil society.
If Hobbes had employed his ingenuity to buttress the individual's right to
property rather than undermine it, he would doubtless have proved less
objectionable, however heterodox his theological opinions. Locke offered
the most compelling version of theories which entrenched property firmly
before the advent of the social compact, and gained corresponding

----

[108] *An Essay upon Government* (2nd edn., London, 1726), p. 21.

respect.[109] But the means by which he did so were of less interest. Though his emphasis on labour as the basis of property has excited modern analysts, it did not notably affect the broad sweep of propertied argument in the eighteenth century. In fact, that biblical patriarchalism which was the main target of Locke's speculations, and which seemed to many Whigs to make property the plaything of princes, was ironically as secure a foundation for subsequent thought as more innovative secularism.

Confused thinkers are often as useful a guide to contemporary needs as more rigorous minds. Defoe was certainly neither lucid nor Lockian; he saw no difficulty in admitting that God had bestowed unlimited property rights on his first human creation, and with them full political authority. What mattered was the crucial assertion that the one preceded the other. 'The Right of Possession always had the Right of Government, which is the Band and Guard of that Possession.' Even irreverent Englishmen must accept this. 'In this Right of Property, the *English* Government is establish'd, and its Original is certainly divine.'[110] Lowering the level of debate in this manner demonstrates at least that it was possible to subscribe to the central place of property in political theory without sharing the robust Whiggism of its more innovative champions. Generations of clerical sermonizers in the eighteenth century gratefully subscribed to a theory of the State which left the right to possession of earthly things divinely ordained, while denying an equally divinely ordained government unlimited power over the individual's share of them.

Contract theory, in any case, had a limited future. If respect for the theoretical credentials of property had depended on it, such respect would soon have foundered. The most influential writings of the mid-eighteenth century leave little room for doubt on this point. Montesquieu's *Esprit des Lois* dealt a double blow to those convinced of the contrary. Property was no more or less than the creation of civil law. It was also fundamentally distinct from those civil rights on which Englishmen so prided themselves. In this sense Liberty and Property were neither intrinsically linked nor part of the citizen's pre-social inheritance.[111] Hume included a devastating critique of contractarians in his *Treatise of Human Nature*. Possessions arose naturally from the operation of the passions. In a civilized state the stability of possessions was the product not of contract but of social convention. Its foundation was the evident need to control the disruptive forces associated with the pursuit of material well-being. The tracing of property in origin to primitive man's labour was neither plausible nor

---

[109] It has been suggested that Locke did not argue for property as a feature of a pre-social state; see J. Tulley, *A Discourse on Property: John Locke and his Adversaries* (Cambridge, 1980), chs. 5–7. This is certainly not how 18th-cent. interpreters understood him.

[110] *Defoe's Review*, iii. 334, 335: 13 July 1706.

[111] *The Spirit of the Laws*, ii. 72–3.

pertinent to its social regulation.[112] Locke did not vanish from sight, of course. Indeed, Josiah Tucker's onslaught on Lockian politics in 1781 provoked an acrimonious debate which testified to their continuing relevance.[113] But the centre-piece of this debate was consent, not property. Tucker had no difficulty quoting latter-day Lockians against each other on the subject of property. What really divided him from his opponents was his attack on natural rights (which might or might not include an absolute right to property) in favour of prescriptive governments, laws, and practices. The debate about property itself had long since moved on.

The historical and anthropological scholarship of the mid-eighteenth century not only took Montesquieu and Hume in its stride but drew from the new accounts a veneration for property no less striking than that of the contractarians. Few of the natural law school had been foolish enough to claim strict historicity for their contracts; none the less the historical flimsiness of contract theory had always been one of its more vulnerable features. The views on offer by the third quarter of the century seemed more compelling. A combination of growing knowledge about primitive societies and intelligent guesswork about the past provided plausible accounts of human progress. One of the advantages of the new thinking was that it made more comprehensible the process by which savage man moved from unsystematic appropriation towards the more organized structure required by an agrarian economy. It also provided a more convincing account of political maturation than the agreeable but unlikely picture of propertied republicans rationally debating their civil requirements. The widely accepted notion that primitive political organization was monarchical rather than republican was quite compatible with a view which envisaged martial leaders who had organized communal defence, and evolved into granters and arbitrators of property. The resulting model of social advance, as presented, for example, in John Millar's elegant and lucid *Observations Concerning the Distinction of Ranks in Society* in 1771, had obvious advantages over its predecessors.[114]

Contract had made property defensible, provided property was itself accepted as one of those natural rights which preceded the social compact. The historical sophistication of the mid-eighteenth century did better. It made property the mark of human advancement, a natural, benign force, which needed no defence and indeed could not be held back. Property,

---

[112] Ed. A. D. Lindsay (repr. London, 1977), ii. 193–6.

[113] *A Treatise on Civil Government, in Three Parts* (London, 1781); see also J. G. A. Pocock, 'Josiah Tucker on Burke, Locke, and Price: A Study in the Varieties of Eighteenth-Century Conservatism', in *Virtue, Commerce, and History: Essays on Political Thought and History, Chiefly in the Eighteenth Century* (Cambridge, 1985).

[114] Ch. 3; also, see R. L. Meek, *Social Science and the Ignoble Savage* (Cambridge, 1976), pp. 123–4.

Adam Ferguson bluntly insisted, 'is a matter of progress'.[115] This assurance became commonplace in Ferguson's lifetime. It had always been flattering to observe visitors from remote parts of the world 'exceedingly astonished', as John Evelyn reported of the Bantam ambassadors in 1682, 'how our law gave us propriety in our estates, and so thinking we were all kings'.[116] In the late eighteenth century there was more information about the deficiencies of undeveloped societies in this respect. By the 1770s travellers beyond Europe were equipped with suitable sentiments for delivery when confronted by what they had been taught to expect. John Stedman, whose account of conditions in Dutch Guiana horrified the first generation of abolitionists, was unsurprised to find no division of property among the Indians there: 'All barbarous and uneducated people have indistinct notions of property.'[117] Even in India it was possible to note the absence of 'that security of descendable property, a want of which ... has prevented the people of Asia from improving their agriculture and mechanical arts'.[118] Closer to home, cultured tourists remarked on the association between wild country and primitive ideas of property. Dr Johnson pronounced, on the basis of his experience in the Highlands, that the inhabitants of mountainous regions lost that 'reverence for property, by which the whole of civil life is preserved'.[119] Such reflections certainly did not lessen that complacency about the operations of property which is so marked a feature of the period.

The complacency was never complete so far as most of the theorists themselves were concerned, however. The same historical insight which rooted property in the age of agriculture and its political organization in the growth of early kingship, also traced its burgeoning importance in the more complex and morally disturbing development of commercial society, of which Britain and France were the outstanding examples. Commerce and its ugly sister, luxury, were at the centre of a long-standing debate about the social trends of the eighteenth century, extending to political values as well as economic developments and moral tendencies. The benignity of the commercial revolution which accompanied and explained the triumph of Western European civilization, in a cultural as much as imperial sense, was endlessly disputed. In the thought of the Bolingbroke school, this produced a notable pessimism, which in suitably gloomy circumstances

---

[115] *An Essay on the History of Civil Society, 1767*, ed. D. Forbes (Edinburgh, 1966), p. 82.

[116] W. Bray, ed., *The Diary of John Evelyn* (2 vols., London, 1908), ii. 172.

[117] *Narrative of a Five Years' Expedition, Against the Revolted Negroes of Surinam, In Guiana, on the Wild Coast of South America; From the Year 1772, to 1777* (2nd edn., 2 vols., London, 1813), i. 398; ii. 277.

[118] G. Cannon, ed., *The Letters of Sir William Jones* (2 vols., Oxford, 1970), ii. 714.

[119] R. W. Chapman, ed., *Johnson's Journey to the Western Islands of Scotland and Boswell's Journal of a Tour to the Hebrides with Samuel Johnson, LL.D.* (Oxford, 1970), p. 40.

could be influential.[120] Perhaps the last Cassandra in this tradition to achieve widespread popularity was John Brown, whose *Estimate of the Manners and Principles of the Times* was published in the first, disastrous phase of the Seven Years War. But the essential defeatism which he exemplified lived on in other forms and found its way into both political economy and radical politics in the early nineteenth century.

Not only followers of Bolingbroke or John Brown were worried about the enervating and corrosive effect of commercialism in an age when property and patriotism seemed no longer to be synonymous terms. Even optimists, on the whole more representative of the trends of the second half of the century, were well aware of the less desirable aspects of commerce: the greed and acquisitiveness which it promoted, the potential irresponsibility and vice which it generated. More importantly, they accepted its intimate relationship with the evolution of property itself. 'In proportion, ... as mankind advance in refinement, the objects of property are multiplied, the difficulty of acquiring them augmented, and the pain of losing them increased.'[121] This was the observation of a writer in one of the monthly magazines, the kind of literature readily accessible to a vast middle-class readership. It was emphatically not necessary to be well-read to grasp its significance.

Responses to the perplexing nature of a commitment to propertied values varied. A few of those who sought to influence public attitudes cast back to an older Christian tradition, treating property as the mark of a fallen creation. One of these was the poet and novelist Henry Brooke, whose rambling metaphysics attracted the approval of other eccentric critics of conventional morality, including John Wesley. Brooke had good theological grounds for his condemnation of a 'carnal and propertied world':

As the goods of this world are subject to appropriation; as they are capable of division, distinction, assumption, and enclosure; they are become the baneful and deadly roots of every species of evil, that hath arisen, spread, and propagated throughout the earth. Hence, avarice, envy, hatred, rancour, rapine, murder, and all the direful train of atrocious malignities that have turned the world, from the beginning, into a wide 'Aseldane', a field of blood and carnage.[122]

At the very least it was possible for churchmen to worry about the cumulative consequences of the multiplication of wealth. As Philip Skelton put it, 'private property hath so increased, that all sorts of people could

---

[120] I. Kramnick, *Bolingbroke and His Circle: The Politics of Nostalgia in the Age of Walpole* (Cambridge, Mass., 1968), esp. ch. 3.

[121] *London Magazine* (1776), 477.

[122] *The Fool of Quality*, ed. E. A. Baker (London, 1906), p. 262; *Juliet Grenville; Or, the History of the Human Heart* (3 vols., London, 1774), ii. 57–8.

afford to be wicked.'[123] Against this, indeed at the opposite extreme, was the readiness of some to glory in the process of appropriation, even to give the scramble for goods a heroic quality. The self-made businessman and first historian of Birmingham, William Hutton, positively revelled in the inevitability of human competition and avarice. 'This property, in ten thousand forms, is coveted by every human being. The grand struggle of life is to grasp it. All have too little. Those who have none, desire it; those who *have*, want more.'[124]

A more intellectually respectable if not necessarily more honest note was struck by those commentators who sought middle ground in the debate about the moral credentials of property. It was possible to accept the ultimate necessity for property while explaining civil society itself as the means of limiting the evils which arose when the pursuit of material goods was unrestrained. Any imperfections which could be discerned in commercial society were slight by comparison with the anarchy which must have reigned in a natural state allowed to evolve into premature, unsocial commercialism. The Dissenting educationist John Ash stressed the nastiness of life in a world which knew property, or rather, he might have said, possessiveness, but not law. Appropriation was uncontroversial where there was ample for all and when many were content to hold 'in common'. But then, as competition intensified, oppression, robbery, violence, and starvation ensued. 'Affrighted Nature shuddered at her own depravity, weakness, and misery; and was soon obliged to seek her security and accommodation in the various regulations of political or civil life.'[125] This was a crude combination of Locke's logic and Hobbes's pessimism. One of the attractions of Locke's theory had been its relatively genteel state of nature, in which competition was more likely to give rise to inconvenience than barbarism, and which might, indeed, seem far superior to the state of affairs in many contemporary societies. A century later it seemed less necessary to hark back to the comparative advantages of a pre-social state. Improvement, not revolution, was the object of mid-Georgian England. In this there was no inconsistency. It was a maxim of the philosophers that law had its origins in disputes over property. 'The desire of lucre is the great motive to injuries: law therefore has a principal reference to property.'[126] The way ahead, for those distressed by the operations of property, was to modify and refine law, not threaten property as a principle. The logical conclusion was reached in the early, classic texts of utili-

---

[123] *A Discourse Preached at St Andrew's Church, Dublin: On Friday the 13th of December, 1776* (Dublin, 1776).

[124] *Courts of Requests*, pp. 2–3.

[125] John Ash, *Sentiments on Education, Collected from the Best Writers* (2 vols., London, 1777), ii. 115.

[126] Adam Ferguson, *An Essay on the History of Civil Society* (Edinburgh, 1767), p. 238.

tarianism. William Paley offered a full-blooded defence of property, but not on the grounds suggested by previous generations. Neither contract nor history was called in testimony. Property could be justified solely in terms of its social value, as the only way in which men could rationally regulate their relations and enhance their environment. It increased the produce of the earth, prevented debilitating contests, and improved 'conveniency of living'. The poorest member of a propertied society was better off than anyone in a world where everything was held in common.[127]

This emphasis on function rather than right was characteristic of the late eighteenth century. It was the argument which William Godwin, pressing his claim that property in the commonly understood sense was synonymous with injustice, found most difficult to dismiss. He dealt with it principally by admitting that his own visionary system of equality would work only in the wake of a change in human nature, or as he preferred to put it, 'great intellectual improvements'.[128] At the opposite extreme of political opinion, judges, the high priests of propertied justice, relied increasingly on it when explaining its mysteries to congregations of the ignorant. As Lord Chief Baron MacDowell expressed it to a Leicestershire Grand Jury in 1794, property was the parent of industry and ingenuity. Alexander Wedderburn, Lord Chancellor in an age of revolutionary turmoil between 1793 and 1801, pushed the argument to its limit, recklessly sweeping aside questions of prior legitimacy. 'Different Originals are assigned of the Right of Property. All agree, that it's final Cause is to promote the Industry of Individuals. Property at first continued only as long as Possession; then, was extended for Life; then, was transmissible to Representatives; lastly, was refined into the Multiplicity of Rights we now experience.'[129] The rights in question did not suffer for want of a foundation in consent, tacit or otherwise. Nor were they purely theoretical. Confronted with a propertied mentality which presupposed a different set of assumptions, the British were capable of radical action. The famous 'permanent settlement' which the East India Company imposed on Bengal in 1793 was designed to introduce clear rights of landownership where there had been none, creating a pseudo-European relationship of landlord and tenant, and thereby promoting improvement and industry on the Western model.[130]

---

[127] *Paley's Works* (London, 1860), 'Moral and Political Philosophy', pp. 34–8.
[128] *Enquiry Concerning Political Justice*, ed. I. Kramnick (London, 1976), p. 744.
[129] *Whitehall Evening-Post*, 6 Sept. 1794; 1 Black. W. 302: *Tonson* v. *Collins* (1761).
[130] P. J. Marshall, *The New Cambridge History of India*, vol. ii, part 2: *Bengal: The British Bridgehead: Eastern India 1740–1828* (Cambridge, 1988), pp. 118–24.

SECURING THE PROPERTY OF THE SUBJECT

Law had to do with property above all else. Even in respect of an uncertain
and unenforceable international law, Englishmen who generally pursued
the right to prize and plunder with patriotic unconcern were occasionally
moved to doubt. Seizure of Dutch property on the captured island of St
Eustatius during the American War was strongly criticized.[131] At home,
there was no doubt that the main function of law was to regulate and
supervise the operations of property. In some circumstances this might
involve diminishing and even destroying property. But most were silent on
this topic. Richard Price at least considered the attractions of communism,
finding them 'in speculation pleasing' if not very practicable.[132] Thomas
Spence's radical proposals of 1775 for the redistribution of land were to
arouse the interest of posterity, but drew little attention at the time.[133]
It was left to religious enthusiasts to attempt practical experience. The
communism of the tiny Sandemanian sect contributed to Godwin's thinking, but attracted few followers.[134] Conventional churchmen were unflinch-
ing in their attachment to the cause of property, as indeed the Thirty-Nine
Articles required them to be. The Unitarian clergyman John Jebb could
not resist a sarcastic reflection on the thirty-eighth article, which condemned the doctrine that the goods of men might be held in common.[135]
His less irreverent brethren found it not in the least discomforting. Thomas
Percy, royal chaplain and editor of the *Reliques of Ancient English Poetry*,
assured the Sons of the Clergy in 1769 that communism was incompatible
with civil society.[136] This truth was not exclusively entrusted to a future
bishop alarmed by the possibility that the orphans of the clergy might
doubt the advantages of a propertied world which excluded them from
property. The interest of Methodist societies in the sharing of their worldly
possessions provoked outrage from Wesley's fellow ministers in the established Church. One of them, Alexander Jephson, Rector of Craike in
County Durham, accused him of misleading people of little or no property.
He calculated that the poor outnumbered the rich forty to one. If every
estate were seized and broken up it would benefit the poor not a jot.[137]

---

[131] *Thoughts on the Present War* (London, 1783), pp. 44–5.

[132] *Observations on the Importance of the American Revolution, and the Means of Making it a Benefit to the World* (London, 1785), p. 70.

[133] P. M. Ashraf, *The Life and Times of Thomas Spence* (Newcastle, 1983), pp. 146–50; M. Chase, *'The People's Farm': English Radical Agrarianism 1775–1840* (Oxford, 1988), ch. 2.

[134] B. R. Pollin, *Education and Enlightenment in the Works of William Godwin* (New York, 1962), p. x.

[135] *Works of John Jebb*, vol. i, appendix (separately paginated), 179.

[136] *A Sermon Preached Before the Sons of the Clergy ... On Thursday, May 11, 1769* (London, 1769), p. 5.

[137] *A Friendly and Compassionate Address to All Serious and Well Disposed Methodists* (London, 1760), pp. 33–4.

For practical purposes the debate about the social regulation of property concerned the creation of a more equitable division, not its outright abolition. Price, like many others, took the view that it was the middle order of proprietors, the hardy and independent yeomanry, who needed strengthening. In Britain there were too many high and low: too much 'scum' and too many 'dregs'.[138] The romantic connotations of the term 'yeoman' and its use for purposes of State propaganda to describe volunteer county cavalry from the 1790s suggest the perceived urgency of the need to bolster the rural middle class. But increasing their numbers by remodelling property law was more controversial. The critic John Hawkesworth, reviewing Goldsmith's *Deserted Village*, predicted that an equal division of property would not last ten years; more extravagantly, the novelist Robert Bage thought it would not endure a day.[139] Such scepticism was commonplace. Defoe, as cheerful a defender of the existing distribution of property as he was of its divine origins, had admitted that if the land were divided into small subsistence parcels, it would support not only the entire existing population but as many as four million more. However, 'this levelling Project can never be put in Practice, the World being quite off that original Way of living'. Moreover, even if practicable, egalitarianism was dangerous. It was vital that the majority of mankind should lack landed property, for without it they would have no incentive to labour for others. In other words the commercial stage of civilized evolution would not be possible at all. Defoe positively rhapsodized about the glories of inequality:

There will be rich and poor; the Diligent will improve, and the Slothful will decay; the Sluggard will be clothed in Rags, and the Good-Wife will be array'd in Purple; the Waster will Starve, and the Good Husband will be rich. This is what we call Industry; and this Industry, as in private Affairs, so in publick, is still bless'd; this makes Nations populous, Kingdoms powerful, great Towns rise, others decay; brings Crowds to this Place, and leaves that bare of Inhabitants, as Opportunities present themselves to encourage and imploy the Hands of those that seek it. This is the Foundation of Commerce.[140]

For those none the less determined to modify the existing pattern of proprietorship, the obvious point of purchase was the English law of inheritance. The most immovable defenders of property as a natural right could hardly deny that rules of inheritance in society as they found it were in some measure artificial, and therefore liable to amendment without violating the fundamental rights of individuals. The relative ease with which the law could be manipulated to redistribute property in future without hurting any existing proprietor might have stimulated some modest

---

[138] *Observations on the Importance of the American Revolution*, p. 72.
[139] *Monthly Review*, xlii. 443; Bage, *Hermsprong*, iii. 19.
[140] *Defoe's Review*, iv. 19: 20 Feb. 1707.

legislation on these lines. In 1767 an anti-Catholic writer who wanted
popish power broken by a law dividing papist estates equally among
children and cousins did not believe that such a regulation would in 'any
way border on the spirit of persecution'.[141] But not many of his compatriots
were enthusiasts for legal reform of this kind, nor did they accept the fiscal
desirability and moral defensibility of taxing dead men's estates. Pitt's
modest legacy duty of 1796 provoked strong opposition and its author was
accused of making England 'a country fit to live in, but not to die in'.[142]

There existed a rich tradition of classical thought with which to combat
the effects of primogeniture. It was pointed out that in England the
evolution of the strict settlement and the readiness of the courts to protect
entails had reinforced the process of concentration and consolidation. The
actual operation of the strict settlement in maintaining the integrity of
estates is open to debate, but its perceived importance was undeniable.[143]
The solution usually suggested was the prohibition of entails and primogeniture altogether, at least for large landowners, in the hope that the
reapportionment of land among younger sons would in time create estates
of middling size. The appeal of this prescription is demonstrated by the
diverse minds which accepted it. For example, Josiah Tucker, the critic of
Locke, was poles apart in political sympathies from the Wilkesite republican
Catherine Macaulay, yet both agreed on the need to uproot the tradition
of primogeniture.[144] There were indeed obvious grounds on which political
economists and evangelical reformers could join with civic humanists when
such matters were under discussion. The moral and economic ramifications
of large landholdings went well beyond the diminished patriotic virtue of
those who owned them. It was claimed, for instance, that the labourers
who worked for small yeomen and farmers were superior in point of religion
and personal morality and therefore in industry to those employed in larger
concerns.[145]

There was little likelihood that a legislature dominated by great property-
owners would accept the logic of an 'agrarian law' to restrict the size of
landholdings. But this is not to say that unthinking acceptance of a rigid
property structure was universal. On the contrary there was considerable
agreement that in a sophisticated society a degree of flexibility, even
instability, was unavoidable and even desirable. Dr Johnson remarked that
it was the natural effect of money to break property into small parts.[146]

[141] *A Warning against Papal Doctrines* (London, 1767), pp. 85–6.

[142] *Gentleman's Magazine* (1796), 839.

[143] L. Bonfield, *Marriage Settlements, 1601–1740: The Adoption of the Strict Settlement* (Cambridge, 1983), ch. 6.

[144] *The Elements of Commerce, and Theory of Taxes* (1753), pp. 44–7; *London Magazine* (1767), 249: 'A Sketch of a Democratical Form of Government'.

[145] Pratt, *Gleanings*, ii. 317.

[146] Chapman, ed., *Johnson's Journey to the Western Islands of Scotland*, p. 92.

One of the arguments employed in favour of the Mortmain Act of 1736 was the healthy uncertainty which attended the property of laymen compared with that of the Church. 'As the Securing the *Property of the Subject*, is, or ought to be, the main *Intention* of every *Government*; so the *fixing Property to Perpetuity* is, at once contrary to the *Rules of Society*, and the *Laws of Nature*; to the Rules of Society, because it discourages *Industry*; to the Laws of Nature, which render all *sublunary Things Mutable*, and which therefore the Schemes of Men ought not to *contradict*.'[147] In due course good churchmen saw the force of this argument. That apostle of reaction, Samuel Horsley, argued that such uncertainties rendered the immense influence of men of great property acceptable as nothing else could. He feared 'the accumulation of power in the higher ranks, were they secure against the chances of life and the shocks of fortune'.[148] Quite apart from the moral and political arguments there were also commercial considerations, urged strongly by the political economists. New proprietors brought new ideas and new investment. The traditionally minded disliked admitting this, but sometimes found it difficult to deny. The rapid turnover of landownership found by antiquarians when they recorded the manorial history of their localities was doubtless matter for sentimental regret. But there was always the cheering consolation that it brought continual injections of new blood to the community and new cash for investment. In 1777 the historian of Stirlingshire, William Nimmo, complacently reflected that 'the face of the county improved, as each new purchaser ordinarily performs something in the way of melioration'.[149]

'Estates', lamented the poet William Cowper, 'are landscapes, gaz'd upon a while, Then advertiz'd, and auctioneer'd away.'[150] The rise and fall of great properties and families was a subject of endless fascination. Trustees of public corporations were well placed to observe the consequences. One such in the York Buildings Company remarked that 'nothing could show the instability and vicissitudes of human affairs more than the different situations of the persons originally holding the company's bonds and their representatives; he says, the administrators of knights and esquires have come in rags for their shares of the money, and the kinsmen of rich merchants have been unable at first to pay the proctor's fees'.[151] The spectacular windfalls of fiscal fortune were similarly the subject of public interest. A lottery prize which enabled its winner to purchase a great property was likely to be long remembered. Hurley Priory, bought out of

---

[147] *London Journal*, 4 Sept. 1736.
[148] *A Sermon Preached to the Anniversary Meeting of the Sons of the Clergy ... May 18, 1786* (London, [1786]), p. 10.
[149] *A General History of Stirlingshire* (Edinburgh, 1777), p. 487.
[150] H. S. Milford, ed., *Cowper: Poetical Works* (4th edn., London, 1967), p. 180.
[151] Cannon, ed., *The Letters of Sir William Jones*, i. 347.

winnings of £20,500, took many years to lose its fascination on this account.[152] Litigation in which the stakes were high aroused similar interest. The case of *Annesley versus Anglesea* in 1743 concerned the disposal of a famous aristocratic estate. The jury included eleven MPs and was reckoned itself to be worth a million pounds. The case was won by James Annesley, who proved himself the legitimate son of Lord Altham and thereby heir to the Anglesea property. After the verdict, 'in less than a Quarter of an Hour all the Streets seem'd to be in a Blaze, and People of all Conditions and Degrees ran up and down congratulating each other as upon a publick Victory'.[153] Local loyalties added zest to these celebrations. In 1792 the *Ipswich Journal* reported the extraordinary 'joy of all ranks' in Brandeston when the Revett family won back the Braham estate.[154]

The turnover of landed property caused much concern. It is easily documented, especially for the early eighteenth century. In the case of Glamorgan it has been calculated that of 31 great estates in the county in 1700, only 10 were held by direct male descendents by 1750.[155] In Buckinghamshire the survival rate of substantial gentry families was rather more impressive, but still disturbing for lovers of continuity. Of the hundred largest estates in the county in 1700, 37 had changed hands by 1750, and another 17 by 1780. The transfer of lands by marriage, often with an appropriate change of name by the beneficiary so as to preserve the illusion of continuous descent, was commonplace. Even so, the extent of selling in the first half of the century remains striking. Twenty-one large Buckinghamshire estates, more than a fifth, were sold between 1700 and 1750. In retrospect it is obvious that demography had a considerable bearing on this instability. Failure of heirs and even heiresses greatly complicated the task of gentry and aristocrats intent on transmitting their names and estates to their posterity.[156] But contemporaries preferred to blame human agency. There were also many, in every age, who, regardless of the statistics, deplored the latest incursion of new men and new money. In Berkshire, at the end of the seventeenth century, there was much anxiety about the threat to the old families and the county community as traditionally conceived. A hundred years later the same concern was still

---

[152] E. J. Climenson, ed., *Passages from the Diaries of Mrs Philip Lybbe Powys of Hardwick House, Oxon. A.D. 1756 to 1808* (London, 1899), p. 175.

[153] *London Magazine* (1743), 618.

[154] 11 Feb. 1792.

[155] P. Jenkins, *The Making of a Ruling Class: The Glamorgan Gentry 1640–1790* (Cambridge, 1983), ch. 2.

[156] The precise value of estates is, of course, impossible to estimate. I have based my figures on manorial descents traced in the Victoria County History and on various materials in Buckinghamshire RO, including land tax assessments, pollbooks, and quarter sessions records; see also Bonfield, *Marriage Settlements, 1601–1740*; L. Stone and J. C. F. Stone, *An Open Elite? England 1540–1880* (Oxford, 1984), chs. 3–5.

being expressed. A Berkshire landowner somewhat extravagantly claimed
that 'one half of our nobility and gentry are poorer than the poor, or
owe a wretched existence to places or pensions unworthy their birth or
sentiments; and we see some of the finest and prettiest places in England
possessed by nabobs, bankers, and merchants'.[157] The theme is the most
hackneyed in the history of landed society.

Land itself was an unpredictable investment. Urban growth might
transform its value. This was a truth well known to families which owned
rural acres subject to metropolitan encroachment in Westminster. It came
home more forcibly to the City of London in 1743 when it was discovered
that the rents of its Conduit Mead estate had risen in the space of less
than half a century from £8 to £14,240.15s. There followed a prolonged
controversy about the best means of exploiting windfall profits on this
scale. The resulting plan was to seem imprudent in the long term, but at
the time it saved the City from bankruptcy.[158] Naturally, the logic of
London's changing social geography could impoverish as well as enrich.
Squares which had risen dramatically in value in the late seventeenth
century were falling as rapidly in the late eighteenth. A house which looked
like a safe investment its owner's youth might be an encumbrance by the
time he reached middle age and a dead loss when he retired. Fashion, it
was bitterly observed by the daughter of the magistrate and musicologist
Sir John Hawkins, 'blasts the value of property'. Recording the social
descent of the Hatton estate, on which she had lived as a child, and
observing the flight of 'persons of fashion and figure' before milliners and
tradesmen, she gloomily observed that 'this is not in the spirit of that solid
liberty of which our nation so boasts'.[159] It was not only embattled country
squires of ancient lineage and uncommercial mentality who had cause to
lament the progress of 'improvement'.

The mutability of landed property narrowed the gap between landed
and business families. Even in those forms of commercial activity which
were highly regarded, such as overseas trade, the unpredictability of success
and failure was well known. A Dublin clergyman visiting London in 1748
was astonished by the equanimity with which it was regarded. 'It was
pleasant, he observed, to see merchants, many of whom had the whole, or
at least the greater part of their property at sea, liable to the mercy of the
winds and waves, relaxing themselves in private with as much ease and

---

[157] Broadley and Melville, *The Beautiful Lady Craven*, ii. 102.

[158] [Thomas Nash], *An Examination of the Conduct of Several Comptrollers of the City of London*
(London, 1743), pp. 5 ff.; see also I. G. Doolittle, 'The City's West End Estate: A "Remarkable
Omission"', *London Journal*, 7 (1981), 15–27, and 'The City's Estate in Conduit Mead and the
Authority of *The City Secret*', *Guildhall Studies in London History*, 2 (1970), 125–35.

[159] *Memoirs, Anecdotes, Facts, and Opinions, Collected and Preserved by Laetitia-Matilda Hawkins* (2
vols., London, 1824), i. 315–16.

complacency, as if they had not a ship exposed to the fickle elements.'[160] The uncertainties of business life featured both in conventional homilies and imaginative literature, reminders at once of the moral and sentimental dangers of worldly pursuits. The emphasis was on the sufferings and sinfulness of individuals. But sophisticated commentators understood that the inscrutable forces of economic change also operated to reallocate resources on a broader scale. John Horne Tooke pointed out that the currency depreciation brought about in America by the War of Independence and in Britain by the Revolutionary Wars constituted a kind of 'loi agraire' in the way it displaced property and restructured society.[161] The socially differentiated effects of price inflation in general were obvious. From the 1750s rising prices began to arouse much anxious debate. Laments on behalf of groups on fixed incomes, such as stipendiary clergy, or officers and men in the armed forces, were common. So were worries about the living standards of employees, particularly in agriculture and declining manufactures, where wages inevitably lagged behind prices. They were matched by distaste at the way many middle-class business and professional men were able to keep up with rising prices and even profit by them.

In theory land was less vulnerable to the winds of economic change than other forms of wealth. Its attraction as an investment was its security; its appeal as the repository of political virtue was its stability. This should have made primogeniture and strict settlements more controversial still, since they tended to the monopoly of a desirable commodity in oligarchical hands. The objections to mortmain were in some measure applicable to the devices by which landed families ensured the long-term security of their estates. There is no doubt that preserving a unified estate was a high priority for the gentry. William Lowndes, a famous Secretary to the Treasury under William III, Anne, and George I, was thought quixotic in the extreme to have divided the estate which he accumulated into several parcels, apportioned among his sons, 'rather than making his eldest a great Gentleman with the whole of his Fortune'.[162] But matters were a good deal more complicated than this. The law of entails was a continuing struggle with the unpredictability of human mortality and vanity, not a flawless piece of oligarchical machinery. The land market of the eighteenth century was vigorous; it was disturbed only by periods of exceptional recession, mainly during wartime. Some authorities even considered that the settlements and entails which governed the descent of so much landed property

---

[160] R. Lynam, ed., *The Complete Works of the Late Rev. Philip Skelton* (6 vols., London, 1824), i, p. lxii.

[161] A. Stephens, *Memoirs of John Horne Tooke* (2 vols., London, 1813), ii. 393.

[162] F. G. Stokes, ed., *A Journal of My Journey to Paris in the Year 1765, by the Rev. William Cole* (London, 1931), pp. 381–2.

represented the ideal balance between competing propertied interests in a
commercial society.

Every intelligent person must consider with admiration, how completely a marriage
settlement or a will, when it is properly prepared, confers the beneficial ownership
on the temporary possessor, for every legitimate purpose, while his abuse of it is
prevented. He must also admire the good sense, with which the present system of
entailing property has been formed; which, while it provides for the perpetuation
of a numerous and respectable aristocracy, leaves a sufficient proportion of land
in commerce, to answer the demands of individuals, and to effectuate the general
object of the national policy, that the owners of personal property should both
have opportunities of realizing it, and be allured to its realization by the superior
stability of landed property, and the importance which the ownership of it
confers.[163]

Moreover, attitudes towards the social utility of land were governed by a
consensus of opinion which had emerged in the late seventeenth century
and which had effectively been consolidated by the middle of the eighteenth.
Davenant had shown conclusively that between 1600 and 1688 the value
of land had risen in response to the expansion of trade and manufactures.[164]
This became part of the received wisdom of the following century. The
close relationship between land prices and other commercial indices was
obvious. The great disaster of the South Sea year, 1720, could be put down
to the folly of naïve landowners in investing their rents and mortgages in
hopeless speculations. But the most prudent proprietor found himself
affected by subsequent fiscal crises. The disastrous collapse in land values
which occurred during the later stages of the American War of Independence was taken as clear evidence of the dependence of agriculture on
commercial conditions. Significantly the relationship did not work in
reverse. Commercial growth occurred for much of George II's reign
regardless of relatively depressed conditions in agriculture. When 'improvement' became the vogue in the 1760s, the propagandists of the new
farming practices did their best to prove that productivity could be
increased regardless of what was happening in other forms of enterprise.
Arthur Young made much of the fact that East Anglian agriculture was
booming at a time when the historic textile manufactures of the region
were in manifest decline.[165] Such contentions were not very convincing. In
what was increasingly a national market, regional farming flourished in
step with the economy as a whole. Moreover, even in a narrowly local
context, the vulnerability of landed property to commercial change was
obvious. Bishop Hildesley of Sodor and Man was appalled by the collapse

---

[163] *Reminiscences of Charles Butler, Esq., of Lincoln's Inn* (3rd edn., 2 vols., London, 1822), i. 60–1.
[164] *Discourses on the Publick Revenues, and on the Trade of England. Which More Immediately Treat
of the Foreign Traffick of this Kingdom, Part II* (London, 1698).
[165] *The Farmer's Tour through the East of England* (4 vols., London, 1771), iv. 361–2.

of land values which occurred in the Isle of Man when the feudal rights of the Dukes of Atholl were transferred to the Crown in 1765, raising fears that smuggling would be suppressed and the island's 'trade' thereby ruined.[166]

In a parliamentary age the attitude of Parliament to property was crucial. By the reign of George III it was being hailed as a legislative giant of unprecedented and unparalleled power. The best-known result was the conflict with the American colonies. The question of taxation without representation was specifically a dispute about the constitutional status of property. 'Why', enquired the American Congress in 1774, 'are the proprietors of the soil of America less Lords of their property than you are of yours?'[167] The question was not unfair. Parliament never relished the taxation of its constituents' property. New taxes in peacetime were invariably controversial. Walpole's excise scheme of 1733 aroused a storm of opposition which forced him to drop his proposals and permanently weakened his regime. The cider excise of 1763 was repealed within three years. In the 1780s a whole series of impositions meant to balance the books at the end of the American War was contested, and several of them were withdrawn within a short time of their passing. Most new taxes were imposed in wartime when patriotic sacrifice could be urged on taxpayers. Even then, some of them proved highly unpopular. The excises introduced during the wars which followed the Revolution of 1688 provoked intense opposition; the plate tax of 1756, paid only by families of some wealth, was sufficiently controversial to provoke repeated reviews and eventual repeal; the beer tax of 1760, required to finance the elder Pitt's profligate war expenditure, met with riotous opposition on the streets of London. If there were no authentic tax revolts in eighteenth-century England, this was because Parliament would never have let such a thing occur without taking rapid remedial action. Even the protests of America were for the most part met with concession. The stamp tax of 1765 was cancelled within a year; all but one of the Townshend duties passed in 1767 were repealed after three years. The colonial demand in point of principle was another matter altogether. Taxation at home was not seriously objected to on the grounds that Parliament had not the *right* to levy it.

Parliament had a horror of invading property rights. Even accidental infringements were quickly corrected. When the hundred of Kirton in Lincolnshire requested and obtained a local act establishing a court of requests for the trial of small debt cases in 1777, the legislature had no notion that it was potentially violating the rights of any individual. But in 1778, when the Earl of Exeter complained that his rights as lord of a court

[166] Weedon Butler, *Memoirs of Mark Hildesley, D.D.* (London, 1799), p. 518.
[167] *London Magazine* (1774), 628.

baron had been diminished, the act was repealed. Exeter's argument was not impressive. His court had not been held for twenty years and the only excuse that he could give for this manifest neglect of the local community's needs was that his steward had been 'extremely ill' for some years.[168] None the less Kirton lost its court of requests.

Lord Thurlow expressed the conventional wisdom of both Houses on this point: 'that private Property should be held sacred.—That no whim, no scheme, no measure what so ever ought to be sanctioned by Parliament, which took away the right of any man without making him full compensation for the loss.'[169] The qualification was obviously important. Occasionally doubts were raised whether any State could properly deprive its citizens of their property, even where compensation was provided. It was argued in the context of the canal mania in 1793 that compulsory purchase by statutory authority was nothing less than 'a power to invade private properties'.[170] But this seemed to be going too far for most. As was said in the Lords in 1747, 'the Maxim, that a Subject may be compelled to sell his Property to the Publick, when it becomes necessary for the publick Good, is a Maxim that has been allowed and established ever since we had a Constitution; yet it was never thought, that by this Maxim the Property of any Man in the Kingdom was rendered precarious'.[171] Moreover, it was argued that juries summoned to decide compulsory purchase terms generally rated the property in question at the highest reasonable rate, and not infrequently took into account the additional inconvenience which its owner might suffer by being forced to sell.[172]

Much trickier were the problems which arose when Parliament prejudiced the use rather than the ownership of property. A bill of 1773 designed, in the wake of a credit crisis, to regulate banking transactions, was resisted on the grounds that it deprived bankers of 'the Right which every Member of the Community has of employing his Fortune in such a Manner as he shall judge most conducive to his Interest'.[173] Rather more startling was the opposition to the Gunpowder Bill of 1772, which followed some horrifying examples of unsupervised manufacturing, and gave JPs the power to prohibit gunpowder making where there was an obvious danger to the general public. It was defeated by the objection that this conflicted with the owner's right to do what he wished with his property, whatever the consequences to his unfortunate neighbours. Defenders of this proposition

---

[168] *Commons Journals*, xxxvi. 640–1, 725–6.
[169] M. W. McCahill, *Order and Equipoise: The Peerage and the House of Lords, 1783–1806* (London, 1978), p. 98.
[170] *A Letter to a Member of Parliament from a Land Owner, on the Proposed Line of Canal from Braunston to Brentford* (London, 1793), p. 19.
[171] *London Magazine* (1748), 4.
[172] Ibid. (1763), 122.
[173] *Commons Journals*, xxxiv. 341.

pointed out that Parliament was 'in general very tender of injuring private property by an act'.[174] Such logic did not always prevail, but the most necessary of public causes could be criticized for its effect on private interests. When Parliament suspended the corn laws and authorized grain imports in order to fend off famine in 1767, one friend of the farmers threatened a Lockian appeal to Heaven. 'So heavy and so unlimited an invasion of property, as is the necessary consequence of such an importation, is contrary to one of the first designs of man entering into society, which is a reciprocal security of property.'[175] Not only the interested parties took this view of their rights. At the end of the century the younger Pitt, as Prime Minister, objected even to an enquiry into the grain stocks held by monopolistic farmers as an invasion of their property. It did not go without notice that he did so at a time when he was urging Parliament to abolish the rights of combining labourers.[176] No doubt there was political wisdom in this. Pitt owed his establishment in power to his defence of the East India Company against Fox's reform proposals in 1783 and knew well the dangers of encroaching on proprietary monopolies. The Company derived its privileges from Parliament, yet Parliament's right to regulate it had long been denied. Statutory controls placed on East India dividends in 1767 and 1773 had been opposed on the grounds that they invaded the sacred rights of proprietors. In 1783–4, horror at Fox's 'rapacious invasion and seizure of private property, so repugnant to the genius of the English Government' played a crucial part in the defeat of the Fox–North Coalition and the electoral victory of George III and Pitt.[177]

Eighteenth-century Parliaments were less squeamish about invading common rights to establish individual property. Statutory enclosure and game legislation are well-known examples. Both were controversial, but both succeeded in part because they drew on a stock of assumptions and arguments which put critics at a severe disadvantage. Although the embattled defenders of small proprietors and cottagers did not always lose out in particular cases, the prejudice in favour of agrarian improvement made their cause in general a difficult one. The protection of game rights was less straightforward, partly because its victims were often respectable and even opulent farmers, partly because the gains to society as a whole were less obvious. Even so, an authority as impartial and enlightened as the *Encyclopaedia Britannica* unhesitatingly supported it on familiar grounds. 'Thus our legislature has universally promoted the grand ends of

[174] *London Magazine* (1772), 611–12.
[175] *The Farmers Address to Their Representatives* (London, 1768), p. 15.
[176] J. S. Girdler, *Observations on the Pernicious Consequences of Forestalling, Regrating, and Ingrossing, with a List of the Statutes, etc.* (London, 1800), p. 57.
[177] N. W. Wraxall, *A Short Review of the Political State of Great Britain, at the Commencement of the Year 1787* (London, 1787), p. 8.

civil society, the peace and security of individuals, by steadily pursuing that wise and orderly maxim of assigning to every thing capable of ownership a legal and determinate owner.'[178]

Some legislation was designed to 'free' the individual proprietor from supposedly outdated encumbrances. The act of 1693 abolishing the custom of York, by which widows and children received fixed proportions of estates, 'even contrary to a man's own will', as it was indignantly remarked in Parliament, was a case of 'constructive' intervention of this kind.[179] So was the statute of 1724 regulating the custom of London.[180] The moral objection, that the consequence was to put mistresses before wives, was swept aside in favour of the overriding sovereignty of the ordinary male property-owner.[181] Paradoxically, securing this sovereignty could involve defining its limits. In 1798 there was controversy concerning the will of a wealthy businessman, Peter Thelusson. Thelusson had left £5,000 in landed income and a personal estate of £600,000 for the establishment of a novel kind of trust. The trust was to accumulate for at least two generations and would revert to Thelusson's descendants only under certain conditions. This was predictably unpopular with the family, but also provoked wider criticism. In essence Thelusson had engaged in a kind of secular mortmain. Its dangers were described in colourful detail by Jean Louis De Lolme. He foresaw the creation of a vast propertied corporation which in time would resemble a palatine county and threaten the integrity and independence of the State itself.[182] The resulting debate was complicated by a clause in the will which in certain circumstances made it possible for the eventual product of the estate to be directed to the reduction of the National Debt. Parliament was unimpressed by this form of bribery, and by a statute of 1800 outlawed such arrangements for the future.[183] MPs who lived to see the end of this story, in 1856, when Thelusson's trust was terminated under the provisions of his will, might have concluded that their fears had been imaginary. Thanks to a combination of protracted litigation, injudicious investment, and falling interest rates, little of the original fortune remained to be distributed to the beneficiaries. But in 1800 the paradoxical priority seemed clear. The rights of proprietors could only be protected if the rules of accumulation were not artificially distorted by cheating posterity of its chance of appropriation. Tested to its limit this logic could have been embarrassing. But few testators were as perverse or

---

[178] (2nd edn., 10 vols., 1778–83), ix. 6506.

[179] H. Horwitz, ed., *The Parliamentary Diary of Narcissus Luttrell, 1691–1693* (Oxford, 1972), p. 293.

[180] C. Carlton, *The Court of Orphans* (Leicester, 1974), p. 100.

[181] *A Letter from a Citizen to a Member of Parliament* (London, 1725), p. 60.

[182] *General Observations on the Power of Individuals, to Prescribe, by Testamentary Dispositions, the Particular Future Uses to be Made of Their Property* (London, 1798).

[183] 39, 40 Geo. III, c. 98.

as ingenious as Thelusson and the potential contradictions of this doctrine remained largely concealed from view.

One of the worries in the Thelusson case was its implication for landed estates. Provided the effect was not to distort the land market, Parliament was quick to legislate where the requirements of great landowners were concerned. The Wills Act of 1752 was hurriedly devised to clarify the legal rules governing the witnessing of wills, after doubts had been raised concerning the Earl of Derby's estate. It was controversial, not least because it was made retrospective in its effect. Even so, it was passed with astonishing speed. The House of Commons received it from the Lords on 29 January, and was able to send it back, passed and unamended, on 7 February.[184]

Very occasionally, Parliament engaged in grander experiments. Viewed merely as a response to the menace of the Forty-Five, the Scottish legislation of the succeeding years can be considered a means of uprooting and exterminating disaffection. But its planners had in mind a radical remedy to the supposed deficiencies of Highland society, one which promised to substitute the civilizing virtues of property for the treacherous vices of feudal organization. Lord Hardwicke, as Lord Chancellor and principal promoter of the legislation, and Lord Milton as the most influential Scottish agent of the Whig government, had a clear vision of what they were doing. As Milton put it, 'The Foundation upon which the success of our Scheme depends is the great power that naturally and necessarily attends Property.'[185] He envisaged an expensive undertaking which would make the Crown a major landowner in Scotland and introduce the Highland clans to the benefits of agricultural tenancy. This never materialized. What was achieved was the destructive part of the programme. The statute of 1747 abolishing heritable jurisdictions was the eighteenth century's most spectacular act of expropriation in Britain. It was preceded by a memorable debate, which pitted modern against outmoded concepts of property. Owners of heritable jurisdictions were lectured on the subject of their obsolescence. 'The Property of hanging a Man, or the Property of cutting off his Ears, seem to me a very odd Sort of Property. I therefore must suppose, that they looked upon all our People living within their Jurisdiction, as our Planters in the *West-Indies* do upon their Negroes.'[186]

Evidently when Parliament did feel emboldened to interfere with established rights, it was in the cause of progress. Property in the approved sense had a positive function, that of dissolving the bonds of superstition.

---

[184] A. L. Cust, *Chronicles of Erthig on the Dyke* (2 vols., London, 1914), i. 321; see 25 Geo. III, c. 6.

[185] C. S. Terry, *The Albemarle Papers* (2 vols., Aberdeen, 1902), ii. 479; see J. S. Shaw, *The Management of Scottish Society* (Edinburgh, 1983), pp. 172 ff.

[186] *London Magazine* (1748), 4.

It was not only Highland society which was expected to bow before the combined force of Parliament and property. The Draconian laws which hindered Catholic inheritance of land in Ireland were justified on similar grounds. Landownership was so manifestly attractive that it could be used by an enlightened legislature to promote the triumph of Protestantism over 'superstitious bigotry'. Robert Nugent, himself a converted Catholic, used this argument to justify the naturalization of Jews in 1753.[187] Old-fashioned Tories were horrified by the idea that the landed patrimony of the gentlemen of England might be invaded and overwhelmed by the children of Israel. Their bolder Whig opponents argued precisely that a proprietary interest would transform the Jews into models of English gentility, reinforcing rather than subverting its essential values. Here was a considerable paradox. It was the Tories who had sanctified the land. Yet it was left to Whigs to urge its transforming potential, not merely in a strictly commercial sense, but also in a moral and cultural sense.

Deliberate remodelling of property was, none the less, a most untypical paraliamentary activity. The same legislature which made the eighteenth century notorious for the creation of a complex criminal code, overwhelmingly concerned with the need to protect property, showed little interest in rationalizing the law of property, even when the interests of property-owners suggested its desirability. The working of land law was a case in point. The silence of Parliament on this subject has been attributed to satisfaction with 'just and flexible rules ... Till the end of the eighteenth century, this system met the needs of different classes of landowners'.[188] Yet propertied society seems not to have taken so complacent a view of its legal inheritance. Most of those satisfied were lawyers, not landowners. The law itself, the machinery which applied it, and the profession which operated it, were bitterly criticized. The tangled mass of rules and precedents that constituted the common law doctrine of real estate were denounced for their irrational and gratuitous complexity. There was endless complaining about the bizarre language and often extended proceedings which seemed essential to the most commonplace transactions. The matching eccentricities of Chancery, responsible for a vast body of property litigation, were scarcely less despised and execrated.

These complaints were conveyed in some of the most widely read literature of the day. They reflected a generally held view of the deficiencies of the law in what should have been its greatest glory, the protection of landed property. Gulliver's lecture to the Houyhnhnms on the subject was

---

[187] *London Magazine* (1753), 305–6.
[188] W. S. Holdsworth, *A History of English Law* (3rd edn., 16 vols., London, 1922–66), vii. 399. On the confidence of 18th-cent. lawyers about the virtues of their inheritance and the defects of parliamentary intervention, see D. Lieberman, *The Province of Legislation Determined* (Cambridge, 1989), Introduction and ch. 1.

a devastating indictment, and culminated in a much quoted remark that 'it will take thirty years to decide whether the field left me by my ancestors for six generations belong to me or a stranger three hundred miles off'.[189] Swift's countryman, Henry Brooke, observed that 'English property, when once debated, is merely a carcase of contention, upon which interposing lawyers fall as customary prizes and prey during the combat of the claimants'.[190] George Lyttelton spoke in similar terms. He observed the paradox which prevented a King of England from forcing an acre of land from his subjects without their consent, yet permitted a knavish attorney to take away a whole estate by exploiting laws designed for its security.[191]

Lawyers and law were in principle amenable to parliamentary correction. But lawyers were well represented in the Commons and their influence exceeded their numbers. In the Upper House, the law lords, reinforced by the advice of the judges, were in a position to block any bill which was thought objectionable on legal grounds. Even so, the inactivity of Parliament in what was in other respects an heroic age of legislation, doubling and redoubling the size of the statute book in a matter of decades, remains remarkable. At the core of land law, the doctrine of seisin and possession and the process of ejectment were virtually untouched by the hand of legislators. It was left to the judicial ingenuity of Mansfield, unaided by his colleagues among the judges, to attempt reform of the law of conveyancing. He was defeated by more conventional lawyers, and derided for his ignorance of the arcane mysteries of the common law.[192] The outer layer of law controlled by Chancery, the law of settlements and trusts, was similarly immune. Minor changes were made, for instance in the relationship of landlord and tenant. But parliamentary enactments were few and tended to modify previous statutes, rather than tackling the central problems exposed in the ordinary course of the law. Perhaps it was for this reason that the Statute of Frauds of Charles II was amended by the most extensive of all such legislative interference in legal procedure, in 1706, and by the act affecting common recoveries of 1741.[193] Regulation of individual courts was occasionally attempted in response to worries about expense and inefficiency. The scandals associated with the appointment of Masters in Chancery not only brought about the sensational impeachment of Lord Chancellor Macclesfield in 1725 but provoked a number of regulatory statutes thereafter. Where fees were concerned and the whiff of corruption detected the legislature was sometimes quick to act. The Chancery Act of 1764 was pushed through both Houses, against some determined

---

[189] *Gulliver's Travels* (Oxford, 1966), p. 310.
[190] *The Fool of Quality*, p. 150.
[191] *Letters from a Persian in England, to His Friend at Ispahan* (4th edn., Dublin, 1735), p. 19.
[192] C. H. S. Fifoot, *Lord Mansfield* (Oxford, 1936), ch. 6.
[193] 4, 5 Anne, c. 16; 14 Geo. II, c. 20.

opposition, with notable vigour. But like other such statutes its object was
to ensure that the men responsible for enforcing the law were paid enough
to deter them from abusing their trust. The absurdities of the laws which
they administered were unaffected.[194]

Some problems cried out for a legislative solution. The complexity of
conveyancing made for uncertainty, expense, and fraud. Paradoxically, this
was peculiarly the case with freehold property. Copyhold estates were, by
their very nature, susceptible to the publicity and review which attended
the proceedings of manorial courts. By contrast, transactions concerning
freeholds often went unrecorded on the deeds and 'writings' which were
taken by laymen to be incontrovertible evidence of ownership. Legislation
of Henry VIII technically required enrolment of conveyances; but in
practice most were made by a legal device associated with the name of the
Jacobean conveyancer, Sir Francis Moore, who had found a relatively
simple means of evading enrolment.[195] It became a common assertion that
clandestine transfers and mortgages interfered with the normal processes
of property exchange. This was the complaint which stimulated demands
to improve the operation of the Statute of Frauds, and which also produced
petitions for land registration. In Surrey in 1729, for instance, it was
stated that purchasers investing the accumulated savings of a lifetime were
'undone' when they purchased land as unencumbered freehold or lent on
mortgage only to find their security burdened with 'prior secret Conveyances and Incumbrances'.[196]

In a few instances Parliament took action. Middlesex obtained a registry
in 1708. Yorkshire was also successful, the West Riding in 1703, the
East in 1707, the North in 1735. Significantly, the courts were less than
enthusiastic about this legislation. Hardwicke's ruling that registration did
not bestow a superior title unless a purchaser could be shown to be unaware
of a prior, unregistered title, deprived it of much of its force; even reforming
lawyers who approved it, such as Samuel Romilly, thought it grossly
deficient in the form that it had passed.[197] Further proposals of this kind
were defeated. An apparently well-supported bill which would have covered
the country as a whole in 1758 got no further than the committee stage in
the Commons.[198] Behind such failures lay an ineradicable conviction that
any change was dangerous, however unsatisfactory the existing state of the
law. One of the earliest registry bills, that of 1678, provoked an apocalyptic

---

[194] 4 Geo. III, c. 28.

[195] Holdsworth, *History of English Law*, vii. 361.

[196] *Commons Journals*, xxi. 244.

[197] See the note by Charles Butler in Sir Edward Coke, *The First Part of the Institutes of the Laws
of England*, ed. F. Hargrave and C. Butler (13th edn., London, 1788), p. 290a, and also Holdsworth,
History of English Law, xi. 587, 8; *Memoirs of the Life of Sir Samuel Romilly*, ii. 175–6.

[198] *Commons Journals*, xxviii. 235.

response from William Williams, MP for Chester: 'This Bill will shake the ancient inheritance of England.'[199] His remark says more about the propertied mentality of the period than it does about the likely consequences of the proposed legislation. It also suggests the sense that property trans-actions constituted a kind of mystery which it was inappropriate to lay bare. Proprietors feared the misuse that might be made of public registers, not just by the State but by interested parties. When the estates of papists were required to be registered by law in 1715 the resulting information was exploited by Tyneside coal-mining concerns able to benefit by detailed knowledge of the debts and mortgages encumbering them. Perhaps this did as much as anything to purge the landowners involved of their Jacobi-tism.[200] In any event the following decades saw no progress in this respect. A legislature which cheerfully assented, for example, to public registration of shipowning shares, a complex, constantly changing business, proved incapable of devising an acceptable means of recording land transactions.[201]

THE POWER THAT NATURALLY ATTENDS PROPERTY

Not many people expected the State to leave its mark on property. Almost everyone expected property to leave its mark on the State. The maxim that property determined power was deemed so incontrovertible that its relatively recent discovery, at least in the Harringtonian form which it took in the eighteenth century, seemed astonishing. Thus reflected Francis Lockier, friend of Dryden and Dean of Peterborough: 'It is strange that Harrington (so little a while ago) should be the first man to find out so evident and demonstrable a truth as that of property being the true basis and measure of power.'[202] The logic of the connection was rarely contested, certainly not by those who favoured redistributing property. They accepted it, of course, in much the same spirit that Harrington had offered it, in order to emphasize that property regulation was the proper, indeed the only effectual means of creating a healthy polity. Harrington's concern had been with the 'balance of property', a phrase which was the source of some confusion to his later readers. This balance was 'the efficient cause of government'. Unfixed, it must produce inconstant and floating government. Forming an enduring system must 'be first by fixation of the balance, and next by erecting such superstructures as to the nature thereof are necessary. Fixation of the balance of property is not to be provided for but by laws;

[199] *Debates of the House of Commons, from the Year 1667 to the Year 1694: Collected by the Honourable Anchitell Grey, Esq.* (10 vols., London, 1769), v. 146: 11 Feb. 1678.

[200] P. Cramar, 'The Coal Industry on Tyneside, 1715–1750', *Northern History*, 14 (1978), 196.

[201] 26 Geo. III, c. 60; see R. Davis, *The Rise of the English Shipping Industry in the Seventeenth and Eighteenth Centuries* (London, 1962), p. 109.

[202] J. M. Osborn, ed., *Joseph Spence: Observations, Anecdotes, and Characters of Books and Men* (2 vols., Oxford, 1966), i. 273.

and the laws whereby such provision is made are commonly called agrarian laws.'[203]

Demands to curtail the accumulation of great estates were generally based on this doctrine. In a book published in 1765, developing further the diagnosis of contemporary ills which his famous *Estimate* had offered in 1757, John Brown noted that it was 'generally acknowledged, that Power follows Property', and went on to propose curbing 'exorbitant Property in Individuals' as a means of recreating a balanced polity and a virtuous society.[204] An understanding of Harringtonian theory helped stimulate the radical impulse of George III's reign. In 1775 John Topham introduced his edition of Glanville's account of disputed parliamentary elections under James I with a description of 'power, the inseparable attendant upon property', particularly in so far as changes in landownership in the sixteenth century had altered the relationship between the House of Commons and the communities which it represented.[205] Topham had a lawyer's training and an antiquarian's interests. His concern was to alert contemporary opinion to the inroads made on the ancient constitution by the progress of oligarchy; the need was for action to restore the balance which had permitted both the English yeoman and his liberty to flourish in a happier age.

There were various ways of taking the sting out of Harrington. His historical account of the progress of property in England was readily usable to remind Englishmen of their peculiar felicity. In the sixteenth century, the death wish of the feudal aristocracy and the expropriation of the Church had made possible a thorough revision of the balance of property, to the benefit of the 'commons'. Many Harringtonians considered the sixteenth century a lost golden age; there were others who argued that it was by no means lost. Samuel Squire, starting from the same staunchly Whig premisses shared by many of those who sought to reform the Hanoverian constitution, showed, as he thought, the desirability of leaving it untouched. His own version of English history differed from Harrington's only in minor respects and he cheerfully accepted that 'In whatever hands the overbalance of national property lies, there the great weight of national power will always be found'.[206]

One of the most thorough expositions of Harrington's doctrine from a historical standpoint was that essayed by a Cambridge divine, Thomas

[203] J. G. A. Pocock, ed., *The Political Works of James Harrington* (Cambridge, 1977), p. 609.

[204] *Thoughts on Civil Liberty, on Licentiousness, and Faction* (Newcastle, 1765), p. 149.

[205] *Reports of Certain Cases, Determined and Adjudged by the Commons in Parliament, in the Twenty-first and Twenty-second Years of the Reign of King James the First, Collected by John Glanville, Esq.* (London, 1775), p. iv.

[206] See R. Browning, *Political and Constitutional Ideas of the Court Whigs* (Baton Rouge, La., 1982), p. 142.

Balguy. The lectures which he composed while Fellow of St John's College explained the history of England from 1066 to the Revolution of 1688 exclusively in terms of what was happening to property. They display the intellectual contortions induced by the need to apply a fashionable doctrine to a recalcitrant body of evidence. Balguy maintained his case partly by ignoring what was inconvenient, partly by relegating major historical forces to the lowly status of 'accidental causes'. Interestingly, in the scholarly speculations of a cleric, many of the latter related to religion. King John's quarrels with the Church, like 'enthusiasm' and anti-popery under the Stuarts, were accidents in this sense. He also had to admit that the balance of property sometimes needed time to take effect. Richard I apparently suffered little as a result of the diminution of Crown property in the twelfth century, 'but the reign was short; and the effect arising from a change of property can never be *instantaneous. Habits* of subjection will prevail for a time; and *some* space is required for men to *feel* the alteration.'[207] Balguy's lectures were published long after his death, in 1831, on the eve of the Great Reform Act. Their author seems not to have seen them as arguments for reform. Despite his Whig background and Hoadly's patronage (he was made Prebendary of Winchester in 1758), Balguy was a profoundly conservative clergyman. Like many other latitudinarians he opted unreservedly for authority and tradition within the Church, without ever resorting to High Church principles.

The eighteenth century contrived many authoritarian variations on the basic theme of property and power, some of which were hardly compatible with its Harringtonian origins. To the clerical essayist John Moir, it seemed that commercial development had made the proposition truer than ever. 'The universal degeneracy and selfishness of modern times renders power and property almost inseparable.'[208] A cynical defender of Walpole considered it one of the obvious arguments against an equal distribution of property. 'It is *incompatible* with Society, that *every* Member should have Power, *every* Man Wealth.'[209] A society without inequality of income was a society without political subordination; it was impossible logically to have one without the other. In 1752 the Dean of Lincoln, William George, explained to the citizens of Lincoln that this was quite sufficient to justify seemingly unjust inequalities. 'A larger Proportion of Property gives a superior Weight, and Dignity, and Authority.'[210] It is not difficult to see

---

[207] *The Maxim 'That Power Follows Property' Applied to the History of the English Constitution* (London, 1831), p. 24.

[208] John Moir, *Obedience the Best Charter; Or, Law the Only Sanction of Liberty* (London, 1776), p. 13.

[209] *The Popularity of Modern Patriotism Examined* (London, 1731), p. 7.

[210] *A Sermon Preach'd at the Parish Church of St Peter's at the Arches in the City of Lincoln, September 18, 1752* (Lincoln, 1752), p. 5.

what made Harrington's doctrine so attractive to defenders of the status quo. If an agrarian law was either impossible, or impossibly dangerous in its conceivable consequences, there seemed no alternative to letting property have its way. Moreover there was at the very centre of the doctrine a large element of ambiguity and uncertainty, at least as the eighteenth century received it. A number of questions presented themselves. Was it prescriptive or descriptive? Did property automatically determine constitutional change, or was it the duty of clear-sighted politicians so to arrange the constitution that the operations of property were unimpeded? Was wholesale regulation of property possible, and if it was not, was judicious tinkering in order? As with other ideologies based on a deductive principle expressed through a historical process, the proper role of statesmen was far from clear.

The concept of a balance of property also left much room for argument about the alleged imbalances to be detected in Britain. Harrington had talked, unguardedly, of the 'state of property' as if it were the same as the balance. Certainly it was easy in a later age to assume that the two were identical. Political rectitude could be ascertained simply by discovering what a preponderance of property favoured. In the House of Commons, divisions were determined by simple majority, but even there it was common to point to the relative balance of property indicated by the make-up of ministerial and opposition votes. Walpole boasted that his supporters represented property as his opponents did not; the latter responded in kind, calculating that the 232 votes cast against the Convention of Pardo in 1739 represented thirty times '*the worth*' of the 260 voters who supported it.[211] One reason why the support of the knights of the shire was so valued was precisely that they were for the most part men of great landed estates. This assumption was embodied in the provision of the Qualification Act of 1711 which required county MPs to have landed income of at least £600 compared with £300 for their borough colleagues. When both Houses of Parliament were involved, each with an equal voice in legislation, it was similarly tempting to compare the property involved. The Peerage Bill of 1719, which threatened permanently to alter the relationship between the two chambers, provoked elaborate calculations of their respective weight. Everything depended in such a comparison on whether the Commons was considered in its representative capacity or in terms of its mere membership. It was reckoned that peers were worth £1,175,500 against £446,400 owned by MPs. But if the electors of the latter were taken into account the

---

[211] W. Coxe, *Memoirs of the Life and Administration of Sir Robert Walpole, Earl of Orford* (3 vols., London, 1798), i. 659; B. Victor, *Original Letters, Dramatic Pieces, and Poems* (3 vols., London, 1776), i. 38.

preponderance was heavily in their favour.[212] Even the Crown could be placed in the scales of property. When Edmund Burke brought forward his scheme for reforming the Civil List and establishing parliamentary control of Crown estates in 1780, he was reminded that 'coronal property' played an important part in the balance of the constitution.[213]

Beyond Parliament, such considerations were still more weighty. County polls were settled by a majority of humble freeholders; but experienced canvassers made their preliminary calculations in terms of the block votes identified with magnate property. The balance of forces could be depicted diagrammatically or pictorially, by displaying the great families and houses, as usefully as by summarizing predicted votes. A map of Norfolk drawn by Humphry Repton in 1780 did just this, with notable accuracy.[214] Some of those who wielded such power preferred not to have it described too crudely. Bishop Bathurst denied that one of those who appeared on Repton's map, Thomas Coke, owed his influence to his 'very large property'.[215] In practice all county elections, and not a few others, were in the first instance contests between men of property. Only at the next stage were other considerations and less propertied contenders permitted to play a part. Where property was united, a poll was pointless. Berkshire, in 1768, was subjected to the indignity of a contest which the great majority of the county's gentry had sought to avoid, the aspiring knight of the shire being compelled to nominate himself at the preliminary county meeting, and finding no seconder. At the poll he attracted support from a gratifying number of small, independent freeholders. But the outcome was the same, an ignominious defeat in which his voters were heavily outnumbered.[216] It was hardly surprising that for practical purposes parliamentary candidates counted the heads of propertied families long before they counted the noses of freeholders. Proposals for reform sometimes took account of this fundamental reality. A plan to restructure Scottish county elections in 1775 included a sliding scale by which substantial landowners would enjoy a plurality of votes in proportion to their holding. 'How can it be reasonable or just, that one who contributes to a fund only £5, should have as much power in the management of that fund, as he who contributes to it £100?'[217]

---

[212] J. F. Naylor, *The British Aristocracy and the Peerage Bill of 1719* (New York, 1968), pp. 204, 223. The notion that property represented could be placed in the scales with property owned was scorned by some: see Steele's *The Plebeian* (6th edn., London, 1719), p. 38.

[213] *The Constitution; Or, a Full Answer to Mr Edmund Burke's Anti Constitutional Plan of Reform* (London, 1781).

[214] Carter *et al.*, *Humphry Repton*, p. 110.

[215] Stirling, *Coke of Norfolk and His Friends*, ii. 75.

[216] Namier and Brooke, *History of Parliament*, i. 208.

[217] William Robertson, *Remarks on the Bill Which Was Intended to be Brought into Parliament in 1775* (Edinburgh, 1782), p. 16.

Public petitioning inevitably led to disputes about the relative propertied worth of those involved. This was as true of the convulsions associated with the 'radical' upsurge of the 1760s and 1770s as it had been in earlier confrontations. In the parliamentary debates which followed the petitioning movement of 1769, on behalf of the Middlesex electors, the landed wealth of those involved was as much disputed as the numbers of signatures.[218] Six years later, when the American War provoked a domestic war between conciliatory petitions and coercive addresses, similar significance was attached to the quality and weight of the names. In Berkshire opponents of the ministry had to emphasize the numbers of freeholders opposing the war, because the gentry overwhelmingly supported it.[219] But when the petitions in favour of reform in 1779 and 1780 produced a positive response from the county communities, they naturally reverted to arguments which stressed the weight of property. Sir George Savile boasted on behalf of his native county that at the great reform meeting at York in 1779 more property was represented than within the walls of the House of Commons.[220]

So complete was the association between property and patriotism that a patriot who wanted property seemed as worthy a charitable cause as a school or a hospital. The elder Pitt acquired a substantial Somerset estate under the will of Sir William Pynsent in 1765 in this way, and the intended beneficiary, Lord North, forfeited it on account of his parliamentary vote for general warrants. Pitt was used to such recognition of his merit. He had received £10,000 from the Duchess of Marlborough by virtue of his opposition to Walpole, and had been promised a large fortune by her grandson John Spencer. When, in old age, he cultivated the companionship of the childless republican Thomas Hollis and discovered a mysterious affection for Hollis's favourite haunt of Lyme Regis, it was assumed in Dorset that he hoped to reap yet a further reward for his principles.[221] For rhetorical purposes, an individual's property was an essential part of his political persona. Candidates for election dwelt much on their credentials in this respect, as did others seeking to impress public opinion. Americans found it difficult to convince their transatlantic fellow subjects that their property rights were at issue in the War of American Independence. But this did not inhibit them from continuing to press it as the crucial argument, nor from using it in individual instances. George Washington's poetic champion, Charles Wharton, emphasized his standing as the greatest American proprietor, with the exception of the chartered proprietors of Maryland and Pennsylvania. He went to some lengths to make Wash-

---

[218] *London Magazine* (1770), 33–4.
[219] *Jackson's Oxford Journal*, 11, 18, 25 Nov. 1775.
[220] *London Magazine* (1780), 122.
[221] 'Thomas Hollis of Corscombe', *Notes and Queries for Somerset and Dorset*, 23 (1939–42), 65, 90.

ington's estate comprehensible to an Englishman, calculating its worth at £4,000 per annum saleable at forty years purchase.[222]

Perhaps the furthest point from Harrington was reached by some of those who basically accepted his logic. If property was omnipotent, good government might consist not in adapting to the views and needs of propertied people, but rather in gently modifying the operations of a force of such immense and almost uncontrollable power. Diverse points of view could be sustained with this argument. The ministerial Whig Antony Ellys, Bishop of St David's, suggested in 1754 that the Crown needed artificially strengthening precisely because, by the reign of George II, property was all on the side of the people. A balanced constitution must not be permitted to reflect the balance of property too faithfully.[223] In this there was no harm to the interests of property; if, indeed, it was all-powerful, it could be safely left to have its influence without the necessity for constitutional draftsmanship. This was the view of the Manchester manufacturer and reformer, George Philips: 'Property, wherever it exists, will always have sufficient influence. Its splendour dazzles the weak, awes the timid, abashes the modest, and corrupts the interested ... Government, instead of making the ascendancy of the rich still greater, ought rather to check their exorbitant authority.'[224] It was a short step from this position to questioning the ultimate political value of property. One of the Yorkshire Associators took this step in 1782. 'There is a prevailing opinion, but a very erroneous one, that our interest in the preservation of the constitution is proportional to the property we possess. The reverse is, perhaps, the truth; for the wealthy have a protector in their riches, that will shelter them from oppression in the worst of governments; but what friendly mediator have the indigent to stand between them and personal slavery.'[225] Doubts of this kind went well beyond those which assailed Harringtonians who worried about the concentration of land in the hands of great magnates. Reformers sought not the redistribution of property but resistance to it. They were concerned not so much to proportion its might as to question its right. Many changes could be rung on Harrington's bells, not all of them pleasing to the ears of his followers.

[222] *A Poetical Epistle to his Excellency George Washington* (Annapolis, Md., 1779, repr. London, 1780), pp. 20–1.

[223] *A Sermon Preached before the House of Lords, In the Abbey-Church of Westminster, On Wednesday, January 30, 1754* (London, 1754), p. 31. This passage belonged in a section of the sermon omitted during delivery because of the 'very sharp Weather' which prevailed at the time; it was printed in full in the published version.

[224] L. S. Marshall, *Development of Public Opinion in Manchester, 1780–1820* (Syracuse, NY, 1946), p. 112.

[225] *A Letter to the Rev. Christopher Wyvill, Chairman of the Committee of the Yorkshire Association* (London, 1782), p. 14.

A SORT OF PROPERTY

When discussion took place of the relationship between property and
power, most people had in mind one particular form of property—land.
But they could hardly ignore the fact that for practical purposes the State
itself had succumbed to the power of paper. Accounts of the constitution
customarily included an analysis of the role of the Bank of England. The
National Debt, whether viewed as the bane or the beauty of the British
political system, was an obvious expression of the political influence of
cash and credit. It was a truism, appropriately summarized by a future
Archbishop of Canterbury, John Moore, in 1782, that 'The Stocks are the
great Political barometer'.[226] The force of the truism perhaps came home
during the last stages of the American War because land values had
collapsed and showed little sign of reviving on receipt of better news,
whereas stock prices recovered quickly. Another cleric, more gifted but
less liked than Moore, William Mason, remarked on the dangerous political
implications. Parliament itself enjoyed less power than the moneylenders.
'No vote of a House of Commons will ever be regarded while a loan can
be negotiated.'[227] Like the truism, the lament was far from new. It belonged
in a recurrent debate which never seemed to lose its relevance, even if,
from time to time, particular events heightened its intensity.

Harrington had admitted that wealth in some societies might consist
largely of goods and money. But he had stressed that this was true only of
small states, and for the most part had avoided discussing its implications.[228]
Subsequent economic development made it obvious that this was a major
oversight. The notorious 'monied interest' spawned by a combination of
commercial growth and fiscal innovation posed an undeniable, perhaps
even an insurmountable challenge to the defenders of the land. Its appearance was identified in the famous issue of Swift's *Examiner* of 2 November
1710: 'the Wealth of the Nation, that used to be reckoned by the Value of
Land, is now computed by the Rise and Fall of Stocks: ... So that *Power*,
which according to the old Maxim, was us'd to follow *Land*, is now gone
over to *Money*.'[229] The new property was portrayed as an illegitimate,
counterfeit pretender to the title and authority properly enjoyed only by
land. Two generations of politicians, the Tories under Queen Anne, and
'country' opponents of the Hanoverian regime, continued to assert the
superior political virtues of landownership. In retrospect this is seen as an
essentially conservative creed, consciously casting back to the values and

[226] BL, Add. MS 61670, John Moore to Duchess of Marlborough, 29 Nov. 1782.
[227] E. W. Harcourt, ed., *The Harcourt Papers* (14 vols., Oxford, 1876–1905), vii. 74.
[228] Pocock, ed., *The Political Works of James Harrington*, p. 406; see also pp. 60–1.
[229] H. Davis, ed., *The Examiner and Other Pieces Written in 1710–11* (Oxford, 1940), pp. 6–7; see
also H. T. Dickinson, ed., 'The Letters of Henry St John to the Earl of Orrery, 1709–11', in *Camden
Miscellany*, 26 (1975), 146.

outlook of earlier generations, in contradiction of the new-fangled commercialism and vulgar materialism of Whig oligarchy. Yet it retained some vitality, even after 1760, when growing economic diversification and changed political circumstances had done much to diminish its relevance.

Celebrations of the land as the repository of patriotic values continued to be commonplace. At moments of crisis, especially during the American and Revolutionary Wars, the old arguments were remembered and used against particularly objectionable forms of mercenary politics. Moreover, the manifold threats to established authority in the age of the American and French Revolutions found many of its defenders speaking in terms which would have been platitudinous a century earlier. The portability of some forms of property was a favourite argument of earlier generations, giving rise to a variety of metaphors. Bolingbroke employed a familiar one in distinguishing between landed men as the 'true owners of our political vessel' and moneyed men as 'no more than passengers in it'.[230] In 1793, Lord Braxfield, the merciless judge in the Edinburgh treason trials, used a different metaphor but to similar effect. 'A government in every country should be just like a corporation, and in this country it is made up of the landed interest, which alone has the right to be represented. As for the rabble who have nothing but personal property, what hold has the nation on them? ... They might pick up all their property on their backs and leave the country in the twinkling of an eye, but landed property cannot be removed.'[231] Fanciful images were made possible by the legal arrangements which attended the ownership of land. Riches could take wing and fly away; land was encumbered with a 'tail' in order to prevent its flight.[232] In this residual sense that land was a unique and irreplaceable form of stake in one's country, the old conviction that it must be granted a special place in whatever constitutional arrangements sustained the State remained defensible. The rhetorical requirements of a beleaguered landed interest in the early nineteenth century brought it renewed significance, and not merely among dyed in the wool Ultras. Lord Palmerston justified the Reform Act on the grounds that it made due allowance for the counties. 'Without meaning to disparage the manufacturing or commercial interests, he must say that he considered the soil to be the country itself.'[233]

The fact that commercial property, indeed almost every form of personal estate, was inherently movable and therefore undependable, was an obvious difficulty for those who thought that its pretensions should be supported against the weight of the landowner. Montesquieu not only offered support

---

[230] 'Some Reflections on the Political State of the Nation', 1749, *The Works of Lord Bolingbroke* (4 vols., London, 1844), ii. 458.

[231] Quoted by W. C. Lehmann, *John Millar of Glasgow, 1735–1801* (Cambridge, 1960), p. 70.

[232] Robert Bage, *Mount Henneth* (2 vols., repr. New York, 1979, orig. 1782), i. 15.

[233] Quoted by N. Gash, *Politics in the Age of Peel* (2nd edn., Hassocks, 1977), p. 14.

for this belief but argued that such property created an entirely separate
loyalty from the State. Movables belonged to the 'whole world in general;
in this respect, it is composed of but one single state, of which all the
societies upon earth are members'.[234] These were not merely the reflections
of a philosopher. There was much anxiety about the tendency of some
investors to move their resources from one country to another, speculating
wherever they could to obtain the best return, and causing chaos in the
money markets when they withdrew funds on which landed property as
well as stock market values had come to depend. The Dutch share in the
British National Debt was a continuing cause of concern, especially in
wartime. Inevitably it was greatly exaggerated.[235]

It was difficult to prevent wealthy individuals from enjoying ill-gotten
gains abroad. States might express their readiness to co-operate for the
purpose of bringing criminals to justice in their own country, but in practice
they could not resist making collaboration conditional. The fraudulent
broker, John Rice, who fled to the Continent in 1763, found himself a
pawn in just such a diplomatic game between the courts of Britain and
France.[236] Not infrequently such malefactors got off scot-free. Perhaps the
most notorious case was that of Robert Knight, cashier to the South Sea
Company. Fleeing to the Austrian Netherlands, he defied all attempts to
bring him home, and made a lucrative second career for himself in France.
His son became an MP and Irish peer, and eventually secured his pardon,
principally on the ground that much of his wealth, invested in Bank of
England stock, had been confiscated by the State after his flight, and
Knight's debt to society thereby redeemed. His plight hardly compared
with that of many landowners to whom the Bubble had brought permanent
ruin. Nor did it remove the obvious contrast with real estate. Men with
property in land were tied to their country. If their patriotism faltered, they
paid a high price indeed. Forfeiture of land was the ultimate humiliation for
a landowner, and attainder the most complete form of incapacitation which
the State could inflict. It might, as a number of Jacobite families discovered,
destroy the inheritance of an entire family, and its effects lasted beyond
the bitterness which provoked it. Such drastic action was increasingly
repugnant to the eighteenth-century mind. There were cases, like that at
Conswick near Kendal, where the local community ensured that at auction
confiscated lands would be sold at far below their market value to an agent
acting for the dispossessed family.[237] Many Jacobite estates gradually

[234] *The Spirit of the Laws*, i. 328.

[235] C. Wilson, *Anglo-Dutch Commerce and Finance in the Eighteenth Century* (Cambridge, 1941),
pp. 150–7; A. C. Carter, *Getting, Spending and Investing in Early Modern Times* (Assen, 1975), p. 22.

[236] *A True, Genuine and Authentic Account of the Behaviour, Conduct and Transactions of John Rice,
The Broker* (London, 1763).

[237] J. J. Cartwright, ed., *The Travels through England of Dr Pococke*, ii (Camden Soc. 44,
1888), 3.

returned to their original owners and in 1784 Parliament legislated for the restoration of those which had not. The MP Sir James Johnstone expressed the prevailing view when he urged 'the hardship of withholding the property of any family, on account of the conduct of their ancestors in a cause with which they had no concern'.[238]

Yet the civic superiority of land was by no means a satisfactory premiss on which to take a stand. Land was part of a complex economic structure. Individual landowners needed little reminding of their dependence on the market for agricultural produce created by a commercially diverse and growing nation. Many, too, derived profits, either directly or indirectly, from mining, manufacturing, or government securities. The concern of men who had made their money in something other than land to sink the proceeds of their enterprise in a landed estate is an enduring feature of English history. It showed no sign of letting up with industrial growth. One of the main functions of the manufacturing cities, as contemporaries were well aware, was to manufacture propertied gentlemen for export to rural neighbourhoods and metropolitan life-styles. As Hutton said of Birmingham. 'Gentlemen, as well as buttons, have been stamped here; but, like them, when finished, are moved off.'[239]

Moving off was not necessary. The tendency for businessmen to buy land without sacrificing all their other interests was very marked in the eighteenth century. Whether they considered themselves country gentlemen with a continuing investment in business, or businessmen with a stake in the country, was very much a matter of personal taste and circumstance. Most, but by no means all the Hull merchants who bought land did so without forsaking their trade.[240] The same was true of merchants engaged in a very different line, at Leeds.[241] Those who did clearly wish to announce their arrival in landed society did not necessarily confine their investments to land. The Bowles family of Mark Lane, in London, was a standing example of adaptability in this respect. Five generations, comprising thirty-four children who lived to survive their fathers, were sustained by the profits of the Vauxhall Glass Works started by the founder of the family fortunes, John Bowles, in 1667, and subsequently extended to Ratcliff. Different branches of the family established themselves in three counties, the most important of them at Burford on the Shropshire and Worcestershire border. There the Bowles were a family of the first conse-

---

[238] 24 Geo. III, c. 57; *Whitehall Evening-Post*, 3 June 1788. For a defence of the principle of property confiscation, see Philip Yorke, *Some Considerations on the Law of Forfeiture, for High Treason* (3rd edn., London, 1748).

[239] *An History of Birmingham* (3rd edn., Birmingham, 1795), p. 31.

[240] G. Jackson, *Hull in the Eighteenth Century* (Oxford, 1977), pp. 114–15.

[241] R. G. Wilson, *Gentlemen Merchants: The Merchant Community in Leeds 1700–1830* (Manchester, 1971), pp. 228–9, and 'Merchants and Land: The Ibbetsons of Leeds and Denton, 1650–1850', *Northern History*, 22 (1988), 75–100.

quence, with a rent-roll under George II exceeding £3,000, and a parliamentary interest which maintained two MPs in the Pelham era and
remained an important consideration in local politics thereafter. For most
of the eighteenth century they retained control of their famous glass
manufactory. At no point were they embarrassed or inconvenienced by the
source of their profits.[242] Nor were the Fullers of Brightling Park in Sussex.
John Fuller was to all appearances a thoroughgoing country squire. In
1754 he bragged of having used his influence in Whitehall to prevent a cut
in the corn bounty, a notable victory for the landed interest and a not
implausible boast for a friend of the Prime Minister Henry Pelham. Yet
he was much more than a well-connected landowner. In 1760 he drew
£2,270 from sugar plantations in Jamaica, £2,200 from ironworks in
Sussex, and £1,200 from diverse investments, compared with only £1,780
from his landed estate.[243] Historians of the local economy are apt to consider
men like Fuller untypical, but they were numerous and noticeable enough
in polite society to affect contemporary assumptions about the nature of
upper-class wealth.

To the extent that landowners withdrew from active involvement in
business life, it was not snobbery that decided them but the specialized
nature of industrial development. For Derbyshire landowners lead-mining
and smelting remained a respectable form of investment, but they could
not easily compete with men whose lives were devoted to the management
of a complex industry in a period of rapid technological change.[244] Mining
generally is well known as a contributor to the income of many landed
families. In Northumberland and Durham it was a crucial part of the
genteel economy. The Montagus and Wortley Montagus certainly derived
great wealth from it; if it amused the Bluestocking, Mrs Montagu, to joke
about the necessity of visiting 'the delectable *agrément* of a coal mine', she
had no hesitation in recommending its 'great advantages'.[245] Such a sense
of incongruity combined with an appreciation of the profits was not
uncommon. The diary of Caroline Girle records a visit to the Yorkshire
estate of the Birt family, the rebuilders of Wenvo castle in Glamorgan.
The diarist was startled to find a village surrounded by coal yards; 'but as
the sinking these pits raised Wenvo castle, neither Mr Birt or his family, I
dare say, think them odious'.[246] Landowners in newly developing minefields
competed eagerly for control of so valuable an asset. In Nottinghamshire

[242] W. H. Bowles, *Records of the Bowles Family* (1918).
[243] R. V. Saville, 'Gentry Wealth on the Weald in the Eighteenth Century: The Fullers of Brightling
Park', *Sussex Arch. Colls.* 121 (1987), 129–47.
[244] L. Willies, 'The Barker Family and the Eighteenth Century Lead Business', *Derbys. Arch. Jnl.*
92 (1972), 69.
[245] *Letters from Mrs Elizabeth Carter, to Mrs Montagu*, i. 346.
[246] *Passages from the Diaries of Mrs Philip Lybbe Powys*, p. 20.

in 1784 the wealthy landowner George Gregory was approached by a peer, Lord Midleton, for his mining rights, but had no doubt that it would be 'better for me to work them myself'.[247] Some of the most successful families of the eighteenth century, the Lowthers and Bowes, for example, owed their rise to rocketing demand for coal, and rightly thought of agricultural land as a secondary investment. 'Coal estates' were acknowledged to be unpredictable, but their very uncertainty made them peculiarly suitable as a form of diversification for landowners, except at times of exceptional recession, for instance during the American War, when it looked as if 'both *Land* and *Coals* will be ruined'.[248] Economic historians remain acutely unsure of the precise contribution which the landowner made to commercial and industrial investment. But in one sense this does not very much matter. What counted was the variety of investment opportunities and the flexibility with which they might be exploited.

The ownership of land was in itself a more complicated business than it sometimes seemed. In principle, a landed proprietor who derived his income entirely from his rent-roll was the very embodiment of the independent gentlemen, the personification of that civic virtue beloved of classical republicans. But political theorists rarely took into account the extent to which lending on the security of land had altered his outlook. By the eighteenth century the mortgage was essential to the landed family's comfort, perhaps to its survival. Upon it depended the life-style of many families who found temporary exigencies too pressing to be met from ordinary revenue. Upon it too there rose the great burden represented by increasingly generous provision for wives, sons, and daughters. Marriage settlements, portions, the whole paraphernalia of dynastic planning, owed much to the capacity of the great estates to support a mounting load of debt. The rising value of land, especially after 1750, ensured that this process would continue without more than occasional interruptions. It was partly offset, of course, by the rising price of conspicuous consumption and the matching increase in the cost of a good marriage. But the reluctance of the State to tax the capital value of land, or even, in the second half of the century, to lay a proportionate levy on landed income, made it all the easier for land to develop its full potential as a source of credit. The tendency was not restricted to aristocratic landowners and great estates. Yeomen and small gentry were infected by the same process, in their efforts to maintain the status of their families and the prospects of their progeny. Marriage settlements and elaborate portioning arrangements featured in

[247] Lincolnshire Archives Office, 2 PG 12. 14. 20: George Gregory to W. G. Williams, 25 Mar. 1784.

[248] J. V. Beckett, *Coal and Tobacco: The Lowthers and the Economic Development of West Cumberland 1660–1760* (Cambridge, 1981); Elwin, ed., *The Noels and The Milbankes*, p. 183.

middle-class life as in upper.[249] Like other patterns of conduct shared with
the landed gentry they were themselves an indication of social standing. A
man who could record of his wife's family that 'The father was a yeoman,
who owned his own estate, and the mother had a settlement', was laying
claim to a modest but telling gentility.[250]

Parliament and politicians in London, and rural communities in the
provinces, continued to behave as if the landed proprietor was all-powerful
in his own domain. But even a great estate might depend on mortgagees
who drew their interest from the land without contributing to its political
management, or accepting any responsibility for its well-being. Some rural
empires rose on foundations of paper. Lord Verney, in the 1780s, was the
third largest landowner in Buckinghamshire. His family contested the
control of the county with its mighty neighbours, the Temples of Stowe.
But Verney beggared himself by lavish house-building, imprudent speculation, and electoral over-ambitiousness. For all his numerous landholdings
he was effectively bankrupt. When he lost his seat in the Commons and
thereby his parliamentary immunity in 1784, he was forced to flee abroad.
This was hardly the vaunted superiority of the landed proprietor, a rural
paternalist beholden to none and proudly exercising his independence as
the true representative of ancient English values. Not surprisingly there
were demands for the parliamentary qualification to be regulated so that
only estates clearly free of mortgages and other encumbrances would
qualify.[251]

Even land which was undeniably the exclusive possession of its nominal
proprietor rarely presented the model of propertied independence beloved
of theorists. One effect of the strict settlement, with its emphasis on the
future prospects of the family rather than the present wealth of the
individual, was to make the heir to many great estates merely a life tenant.
Sons were often resentful of their father's desire to make them their tools,
at least until it came to their turn to do the same for their own sons. The
young Thomas Pitt of Boconnoc, whose father was notoriously capricious,
was warned not to go abroad during a crisis in the family's affairs in 1754,
lest he 'make a property of me in time to my own ruin as well as that of
such as were after me in the entail'.[252] Primogeniture seemed a mixed
blessing to some of its beneficiaries. Lord Finch, son of the Earl of

[249] M. K. Ashby, *The Changing English Village: A History of Bledington, Gloucestershire, 1066–1914*
(Kineton, 1914), p. 225.
[250] L. Jewitt, *The Life of William Hutton, and the History of the Hutton Family* (London, 1872),
p. 168.
[251] *The Works of the Right Reverend Thomas Newton, D.D.* (3 vols., London, 1782), vol. i, App. iii,
'A Letter to the New Parliament' (not paginated).
[252] M. Wyndham, *Chronicles of the Eighteenth Century* (2 vols., London, 1924), ii. 24.

Nottingham, remarked in 1723 that he looked on himself 'as being the eldest, to be the slave of the family'.[253]

Dynastic restraints were among a number of complications which rendered proprietorship less simple than it seemed. Radicals enthused about the 'absolute estate' enjoyed by Anglo-Saxons before the Norman Yoke had descended, but in truth the very notion of an absolute right was an innovation of the early seventeenth century, and continued to jostle with definitions emphasizing the relative nature of all rights.[254] English lawyers enjoyed explaining to the ignorant that their law was primarily about tenure, about possession, not about proprietorship. They had to admit that freehold land, once liberated from its feudal subjection to the Crown in 1641, came as near as English law could contrive to an uninhibited and exclusive propertied interest. Its peculiar combination of historical legitimacy and legal pre-eminence conferred a unique sanctity. In the conflict with America it was accorded 'a radical judicative authority' with which even colonial freeholders, whose rights were rooted in a grant by the Crown, could not compete.[255] Yet in England itself the search for a truly independent proprietor was not straightforward. In some places freeholders continued to have certain obligations specified by local custom; though usually fixed, they were not always so negligible as not to warrant enforcement.[256]

By no means all landowners were freeholders. It was reckoned in 1696 that a third of all property was held by copyhold tenure.[257] Copyhold estates could be devised, sold, and exchanged with great freedom. In some places there was said to be a preference for copyhold.[258] Certainly its transfer could be a simpler matter than a freehold transaction. On the other hand the obligations which attended copyholds made them more troublesome in other respects. Such obligations were governed by the custom of the manor, which varied from region to region, and indeed from manor to manor. The more ludicrous survivals were collected by Thomas Blount in 1679 and republished for the amusement of a wider audience in 1784 and 1815.[259] But Blount's 'jocular tenures' belonged in a body of law which created serious problems. In fact the result of the tenurial chaos which actually represented the legal state of English landed property was largely to vitiate generalizations about the freedom with which landowners could act. In the West Country, leaseholds for lives, comparable to ecclesi-

---

[253] Finch, *Burley-on-the-Hill, Rutland*, i. 277.
[254] G. E. Aylmer, 'The Meaning and Definition of "Property" in Seventeenth-Century England', *Past and Present*, 86 (1980), 87–97.
[255] *London Magazine* (1766), 78.
[256] Watson, *Ashmore*, p. 38.
[257] *Lex Customaria; Or, a Treatise of Copyhold Estates* (London, 1696).
[258] Gough, *The History of Myddle*, p. 140.
[259] W. C. Hazlitt, *Tenures of Land and Customs of Manors* (London, 1874).

astical leases, were so entrenched that they virtually amounted to a kind of copyhold, though the eighteenth century witnessed a growing tendency on the part of landlords to attempt their conversion to simple leaseholds and eventually rack-rented tenancies. In Devon, it was noted in an agricultural report of 1794 that this tenure seemed to amount to 'a species of independent property'.[260] In the north-west, eccentric military tenures, notably the celebrated 'border tenure', created a form of proprietorship short of genuine ownership yet extremely resistant to exploitation from above.[261] Catherine Cappe, brought up in Craven in the 1740s, subsequently tried to bring home to readers unfamiliar with these customs the extraordinary nature of feudal leases, which, as she claimed, amounted to small freeholds. The 'Statesmen' of Craven, she emphasized, were fiercely independent and endlessly litigious. Whatever statesmen of another kind might imagine, they did not think of themselves as in any way inferior to the English freeholder who figured so much in political literature and electoral propaganda.[262]

The value of such property rights could be considerable. Manorial lordship was often divorced from the main freehold interest in the manors to which it pertained; none the less, it might carry valuable privileges, including ecclesiastical advowsons, mining royalties, game rights, and control of unenclosed waste. Agricultural improvers were dismayed by superannuated tenures. William Donaldson called copyhold a 'kind of provincial empire ... the last remains of feudal tenure'.[263] It was a matter of common observation that manorial lords went to great pains to inhibit the growth of the healthy plant of freehold tenure. Thomas Somerville was shocked on a visit to Buxton in 1793 to find the Cavendishes of Chatsworth harrying the primitive cave-dwellers of the Peak district. The Duke of Devonshire's steward, he discovered, insisted on collecting a rent, 'to prevent the prescription of the property of the caves, created by the toilsome labour of their wretched inhabitants'.[264] But it was not necessary to be a grandee to exploit obsolescent rights. Attorneys were adept at digging up old customs which might profit landlords and themselves. The account by one such, John Andrews, of the revival of Ermington Hundred

---

[260] Robert Fraser, *General View of the County of Devon* (London, 1794), p. 16.

[261] A. McFarlane, *The Origins of English Individualism* (Oxford, 1978), pp. 89–90; N. Gregson, 'Tawney Revisited: Custom and the Emergence of Capitalist Class Relations in North-East Cumbria, 1600–1830', *Econ. Hist. Rev.*, 2nd ser 42 (1989), 18–42.

[262] *Memoirs of the Life of the Late Mrs Catherine Cappe* (London, 1822), pp. 6–7 ff. The usage of this term in Craven seems to predate its common application in Cumbria, with which it became associated in the early 19th cent.; see J. D. Marshall, ' "Statesmen" in Cumbria: The Vicissitudes of an Expression', *Trans. Cumbs. and Westmor. Ant. and Arch. Soc.*, NS 72 (1972), 248–73.

[263] William Donaldson, *Agriculture Considered as a Moral and Political Duty* (London, 1775), p. 199.

[264] *My Own Life and Times 1741–1814* (Edinburgh, 1861), p. 281.

Court in south Devon in 1773 reveals the process involved. Initially there was little business: Andrews remarked that it might be called Ermington Club rather than Ermington Court, and on one occasion he and some friends took along their musical instruments and employed the session for 'a small Concert'. But there were rules to settle, services to offer, and business to attract, and Andrews was not averse to experimenting with his powers, as in August 1775, when he 'ran the Venture of granting a Replevin in Ermington Court'.[265] Agricultural improvement combined with traditional litigiousness to make such enterprises well worth undertaking. The risks were slight, and the returns, if small, eminently acceptable.

The ideal of the age was a compact estate, in which authority went with outright ownership. It featured a splendid house, a picturesque park, and a contented community of tenant farmers. But not all estates were of this kind, and few proprietors resisted the temptation to exploit the commercial value of less conventional holdings. As a parliamentary lobbyist put it in 1712, 'Every Man esteems his *Property in Markets, Fairs,* Fisheries in Navigable Rivers and Creeks, *Wrecks on the Sea Coasts, Felons Goods,* etc. *derived by Grants under the Crown,* equal to his Property in his Freehold Lands, and defends it zealously.'[266] The surveyor Thomas Browne, one of the most respected of his profession and accustomed to dealing with freehold estates in the south of England, found himself almost at a loss when confronted with the Duke of Montagu's holding in Lancashire in 1767. It was, he reported, 'the most extraordinary estate I ever valued'. It had no demesne to speak of, and 'no owner of this Estate nor indeed any Gentleman would scarce live upon it'. Yet he recorded 'great profits that arise from Quit Rents, Fines, Profits of Courts, Wrecks and Iron Ore'.[267] What Browne was confronting was the peculiar tenurial tradition of the north. Southerners found it baffling. When the Earl of Suffolk acquired an estate near Kendal from his wife's family, his assumption that his tenants were in essence copyholders earned him a contemptuous correction from his steward. 'Copyhold and our Customary Lands is as much different Customs as Black is from White.'[268] Yet even more familiar manorial rights gave rise to complicated disputes when the rights themselves were uncertain. One of the most famous of eighteenth-century property suits, pursued by Lord Pomfret, concerned a lead-mining franchise. It involved five years of litigation, three appeals to the House of Lords, and costs for each side in excess of £10,000.[269]

[265] Devon RO (Plymouth), 535/11.

[266] Bodleian Library, Bromley's Parliamentary Papers, iii. 69: 'Property Derived under the Crown, Not Inferior To Property, derived under the Subject'.

[267] Lancashire RO, DP 424, Duke of Montagu's Estate, 1767.

[268] O. R. Bagot, 'Some Eighteenth-Century Documents at Levens Hall', *Trans. Cumbs. and Westmor. Ant. and Arch. Soc.*, NS 81 (1981), 81: 27 June 1754.

[269] *London Magazine* (1772), 603.

So complex a structure of landed property had significant political implications. One was the constant temptation to employ the political process to alter the status of tenures. Men who indignantly denied the right of the legislature to redistribute property as a matter of principle, cheerfully sought to employ it for their own purposes. Contentions between major propertied interests, often with distinctive tenurial claims, inevitably had an impact on local politics. The war waged by the great copyholders of Durham against their ecclesiastical superior, the Bishop of Durham, provides a small treasury of ways in which the rhetoric of property rights could be exploited to advance vested interests at the expense of ancient rights, in this instance described as 'restrictions and badges of vassalage'.[270] The project to disfranchise Cranborne Chase in 1787 found the owner of the rights of 'free-chase', Lord Rivers, pitted against a powerful group of landlords, including the Duke of Bolton, the Marquis of Buckingham, the Earl of Uxbridge, the Earl of Shaftesbury, and Lord Arundell. They took their stand partly on high moral ground—the poaching and smuggling encouraged by the existence of a large, open chase, partly on the first principles of property. 'No private property ought to exist so prejudicial to the community at large.' The rights in question, they also pointed out, were themselves 'detrimental to private property'.[271] What constituted legitimate private property plainly depended on the propertied interests of those defining it. Controversies of this sort have an obvious interest for social historians, especially when they provide examples of popular revolt and class conflict. They are no less interesting for what they reveal of conflicts within the ruling class.

Simple propositions based on the freehold model of ownership were manifestly inadequate to cope with the realities of propertied life. The result was a continuing and sometimes acerbic debate about the proper application of traditional arguments. Mary Burnell, a lady of the manor in Nottinghamshire, appealed to the public in 1775 for support to revive the jurisdiction of manorial courts against the power of JPs and constables. In such a case identifying the landowner in fee simple, a favourite solution, did nothing to resolve disputes.[272] Estates held by customary rights were themselves a constant source of political controversy. A copyholder was not dependent in the sense that a tenant was; but neither did he enjoy the independence of the freeholder. Men like William Goodwin of Earl Soham, who renewed his estate in 1786 for a low fine 'from the friendship and moderation of the Steward', understood well the need to conciliate their

---

[270] J. and G. Spearman, *An Enquiry into the Ancient and Present State of the County Palatine of Durham* (1729).

[271] *A Letter to the Noblemen, and Gentlemen, Proprietors of Lands in Cranbourne Chase* (London, 1791), pp. 7, 23.

[272] *The Extraordinary Ill Usage I Have Had ...* [*c*.1775], pp. 18–23.

manorial lord.[273] Copyholders were often freeholders in respect of other property and thereby vulnerable to electoral pressure. Even those who were not sometimes possessed a vote. Their rights were supported by parliamentary reformers and in some places they were permitted by custom to vote along with freeholders. The famous Oxfordshire election of 1754 provoked a statute designed to terminate this practice, and a prolonged debate about copyholders' privileges. It was complicated by the fact that their status was not only unclear, but also unfixed. Some lords of the manor, like Lord Dudley in Staffordshire, pursued a deliberate policy of enfranchising copyholds, essentially for financial reasons.[274] The effect was to turn their possessors into fully-fledged electors.

Adjudicating between freeholders and copyholders as politically responsible classes was an awkward enough task, but it was simple compared with the difficulties which attended the distinction between real property in general and other forms of property. English law had always provided separately for personal estate, the movable possessions and stock which made up so much of the worldly goods of ordinary men and women, and which, in the case of merchants and manufacturers, were of crucial importance not merely to them but to their country's commerce. Economic expansion multiplied and diversified property of this kind. Moreover, by an appropriate paradox, the readiness of eighteenth-century courts to bestow legal protection on new forms of property complicated the task of determining what political significance should be given them. The weight to be attached to a holding of government stock and a share in the National Debt was a subject of continual controversy. But virtually all kinds of personal and paper property produced comparable disputes. Legal definitions had very little to do with these uncertainties. A businessman who chose to employ his assets for electoral purposes could hardly be ignored simply because they did not include real estate. 'The power which property always carries with it, and above all others pecuniary property in a commercial town', was identified in Great Yarmouth as the critical determinant of the local balance of power.[275] The easiest answer to such assertions was, of course, to deny the legitimacy of such power. It was often claimed on behalf of landowners that their 'interest' and 'influence' were acceptable, while the matching use of commercial assets was 'corrupt'. Here was a whole arena of debate which brought into contention incompatible conceptions of propertied politics. Here, too, was a profound challenge to the constitution, one which was never far away from everyday politics. The

---

[273] Suffolk RO (Ipswich), HD 365/2: diary of William Goodwin, 4 Apr. 1786.

[274] T. J. Raybould, *The Economic Emergence of the Black Country* (Newton Abbot, 1973), pp. 38–44.

[275] I. R. Christie, 'Great Yarmouth and the Yorkshire Reform Movement 1782–4', *Norfolk Archaeology*, 32 (1958–61), 106.

political system was threatened less by the revolutionary assault on property than by the divisions and diversities of property itself.

2

Prior Allegiance

THERE was a growing tendency in the eighteenth century to view the rights of individuals in terms of their property and public affairs as an expression of propertied interests. Competing with it there was also an older tradition that made relations between the citizen and the community a matter of ideology, even theology, properly regulated by State-imposed oaths and tests. The theory behind this tradition came to seem increasingly anachronistic. It was also steadily eroded by practice. Protestant Dissenters and Catholic Recusants enjoyed privileges which far exceeded their legal rights, and even their formal status was progressively improved. Many churchmen accepted such liberalization, notwithstanding the demands of a High Church party for a more restrictive policy. Only the threat of revolution and the prejudices of George III prevented wholesale abolition of the code of legal discrimination. With this process went widespread agreement that the use of oaths to enforce the individual's allegiance was inappropriate and imprudent. It was strengthened by concern at the extended use of oaths for purposes of law enforcement and tax collection, and also by genteel reluctance to incur the risks attendant on binding obligation. A second, distinct threat to the primacy and unity of property was the inherited loyalty to political parties. There was general recognition that the party strife which had prevailed in the Augustan age could not coexist with commercial growth and social progress. As far as possible the new forms of association and institution which developed to meet the manifold demands for 'improvement' were designed to be free of the taint of party. Party did not disappear but it was increasingly despised and also increasingly confused. When it revived as a coherent force at the end of the century, it was in a form more compatible with the propertied consensus on which Georgian society had come to rest.

RATHER DISGUSTFUL THAN INCONVENIENT

In a society dominated by property nothing could be more inimical to prevailing values than distinctions unconnected with property. This was the plight of English society after the Revolution of 1688, and superficially at least for a long time afterwards. The Test and Corporation Acts appeared to provide a statutory basis for an entire system of discrimination on religious grounds which was not to be abandoned until the second quarter

of the nineteenth century. The circumstances of 1688 made the status of
this system perplexing. On the one hand the Revolution was brought about
by men who objected to the Test and Corporation Acts as to prerogative
rule, popish government, and arbitary taxation, the bugbears of Stuart
absolutism. On the other hand the fact that the acts had had in a Catholic
king their principal anatagonist made it more difficult than ever to revise
them. This dilemma remained for many years; and by the time it seemed
less baffling they had hardened into a forbiddingly solid system. Prescription lent legitimacy to a structure which had been put in place for
reasons of expediency. Its practical consequences were, however, less than
clear.

If ever there was a debate about apprehensions rather than realities it was
the debate about the civil disabilities of Dissenters. When the Dissenting
Deputies published their account of attempts to interfere with the liberty
of Nonconformists between 1737 and 1767 what was revealed was a
succession of petty disputes, many of them concerning unlicensed schools,
and almost all resolved to the satisfaction of the aggrieved party.[1] Burke,
who was long in favour of repealing the Test and Corporation Acts, and
changed his mind only as a result of what he considered the treachery
of Dissenters, described the laws in question as 'rather disgustful than
inconvenient'.[2] Even their disgustfulness was arguably a novel development. As late as 1783 it was being confidently asserted that the Test Acts,
so contentious under Charles II, had ceased to be a 'subject of complaint'.
The author thought this an argument for parliamentary reform; it demonstrated that what might appear as an innovation would in time be
accepted even by those who had expected to suffer by it.[3]

There were somewhat desperate attempts to find real cause for complaint.
It was pointed out that the law brought significant disadvantages to a
Dissenter. He was prohibited from suing in a court of law or equity,
disabled from acting as an executor or even receiving a legacy, and permanently prevented from holding office.[4] For men of property, profession,
or business, these were intimidating terrors, to be compared only with
those faced by papists. They were, however, quite unreal. Much industry
went into discovering victims of intolerance but the fact was that there
were none. The penalties were those attending conviction under the law,
and conviction was virtually unknown. The sting of the Corporation Act
was carried in the provision which required a sacramental test of all officers
and members of municipal corporations *in advance of* their election. The

---

[1] *A Short Account of Some of the Proceedings of the Deputies and Committee, Appointed to the Care
of the Civil Affairs of the Dissenters* (n.d.).
[2] *The Works of the Right Honourable Edmund Burke* (Bohn's edn., 8 vols., London, 1854), iii. 314.
[3] *The Inadequacy of Parliamentary Representation Fully Stated* (London, 1783), p. 41.
[4] *An Appeal to the Candor, Magnanimity, and Justice of Those in Power* (London, 1787), pp. 4–5.

effect of the famous Indemnity Acts, passed recurrently on an annual basis, was to draw this sting. Although they did not nullify the requirement that municipal governors join in communion with the Church, what they did do was to extend the period in which one thus unqualified might qualify himself. Moreover the Corporation Act, as explained by the Relief Act of 1719, could not be employed once a period of six months had lapsed. Mansfield's judgement in *Crawford* v. *Powell* in 1760 decisively confirmed this point.

Depending on the calendar and one's opponents' planning there still remained the possibility of a prosecution for continuing failure to qualify. It could, however, be eliminated by late, or 'occasional conformity', the practice which contributed so much to Tory rage under Queen Anne, and was outlawed between 1711 and 1718. Occasional conformity was not a flawless solution. There were Nonconformists who could not conscientiously take the sacramental test. But those principally affected, Baptists and Quakers, formed relatively insular communities which gloried in their exclusion from public life. In the case of the Baptists, their wealth and standing were rarely compatible with a prominent part in civic affairs. Presbyterians and Independents were less likely to have conscientious objections to the test and more disposed to claim their share of self-government. The same logic worked for county commissions of the peace. Some celebrated Birmingham Dissenters took their place on the Warwickshire bench, leading Priestley himself to pronounce that the Test Act was '*a cobweb*, which any fly may break through'.[5] Together indemnity and occasional conformity ensured that generations of such Dissenters were untouched by the law.

Frequent elections to corporate bodies would have made the protection afforded by this somewhat tortuous system more doubtful, especially for those whose notion of occasional conformity was excessively occasional. But the great majority of corporations being perpetual, there was little danger of a Dissenter having to present himself repeatedly for election and qualification. Only mayors and sheriffs in effect had to requalify, an exception which permitted threats of prosecution, as at Nottingham in 1789. Even in this instance it was the refusal of the mayor in question to make the token gesture of conformity which rendered him vulnerable. In the course of the previous century a succession of Dissenters had occupied the mayoralty of Nottingham, most of them associated with the famous High Pavement chapel, and seemingly untroubled by the requirements of the law.[6] Under George II the Indemnity Act sometimes went unrenewed,

[5] *Familiar Letters, Addressed to the Inhabitants of the Town of Birmingham* (Birmingham, [1790]), letter iv.8.

[6] M. I. Thomis, *Politics and Society in Nottingham 1785–1835* (Oxford, 1969), p. 117. For details of Nottingham mayors, see A. B. Clarke, 'Notes on the Mayors of Nottingham, 1660–1775: II', *Trans. Thoroton Soc.* 42 (1939), 105–20.

presumably by oversight. But after 1757 it was passed every year until 1867. It proved sufficient to parry occasional campaigns by the ecclesiastical authorities for the enforcement of the law, rendering the issue of writs and the commencement of proceedings so much wasted time and expense.[7] In 1747, for example, a particularly threatening manoeuvre by the Chancellor of Bangor was rebuffed by this means.[8] Not surprisingly such attacks had ceased altogether by the 1760s. There was consequently some complacency on the part of Nonconformist congregations about the so-called 'rights' which they enjoyed, however complicated the legal technicalities. In Suffolk in 1790 it was observed of Dissenters that 'not one in a thousand of them knew anything of the nature of the *Test Acts*, or indeed that there were any such Laws in being—How they should be oppressed, and not feel it, is a paradox not easy to be solved'.[9]

This sense of security partly rested on faith in the judiciary. Dissenters used the courts without fear and generally found them supportive. One of their leaders, Benjamin Avery, remarked in 1751 that the Establishment had learned from Sir Robert Walpole to enforce the Act of Toleration strictly and fairly, not beyond what it offered Dissenters, but 'by a fair Construction'.[10] Sectarian bias was rarely alleged against the courts. In a local context this could be crucial. At Hitchin in 1750 an attempt at the subversion of the local Free School by a hatter turned schoolmaster who sought to discourage Dissenting children was defeated by this means. The Baptist minister who resisted him, Samuel James, was a redoubtable defender of what he conceived to be rectitude, not least in his struggle to ban the hymns of Isaac Watts from his chapel. The outcome was an order from Baptist arbitrators that the hymns might be sung, though always to the same tune. His onslaught on the schoolmaster was more successful. The Lord Chancellor decreed that Dissenters must not be barred, and that the Trustees should be more representative of the community which supported the school.[11]

Propagandists on either side of the debate about the legal status of Nonconformity naturally emphasized its rigidity, whether as matter for triumph or regret. But this was not the universal perception. Enlightened churchmen of all kinds saw their society marching steadily towards an ever

---

[7] See K. R. M. Short, 'The English Indemnity Acts 1726–1867', *Church History*, 42 (1973), 366–76.

[8] G. F. Nuttall, ed., *Calendar of the Correspondence of Philip Doddridge, D.D. (1702–1751)* (Northants. Rec. Soc. 29, 1979), p. 259.

[9] *Observations on the Cause, Conduct, and Effects, of the Late Contested Election, for the County of Suffolk* (Ipswich, 1790), p. 17.

[10] Nuttall, ed., *Calendar of the Correspondence of Philip Doddridge*, p. 355.

[11] G. E. Evans, *Come Wind, Come Weather: Chronicles of Tilehouse Street Baptist Church 1669–1969* (London, 1969), pp. 19–21, 28.

more tolerant, more relaxed, more progressive future. How was it possible
to sustain this view?

It is often forgotten that the Test and Corporation Acts applied only
to a minority of public trusts and offices. Attempts to argue that they bore
not merely on office-holders and the members of municipal governing
bodies, but on all those who enjoyed corporate privileges were quashed in
the courts.[12] Moreover, many institutions of great importance in local
context were unaffected by them. So-called manorial government was a
case in point. In Birmingham the Dissenters had no difficulty monopolizing
the office of Low Bailiff and therefore management of the Court Leet,
which performed most of the functions of a corporation.[13] School boards
could also be powerful bodies. They controlled valuable patronage and
their supervision of the education of middle- and lower-class children made
them both feared and respected. They were by no means necessarily
Church monopolies, for all the traditional association of the clergy with
education and their frequently restrictive charters. Rivington Grammar
School in Lancashire was managed by a Board of Dissenting governors
throughout the eighteenth century, though it was required to teach Church
doctrine and its masters were sometimes clergy. The Commissioners who
reported on it in 1828 were dismayed that such an endowment could have
fallen into the hands of Unitarians, but admitted that they had not abused
the trust.[14]

Some institutions were consciously protected by Parliament or the local
community. Statutory commissions, which multiplied prodigiously in the
second half of the century, were immune, as were a vast and growing range
of bodies sustained by voluntary association and subscription. No doubt the
fact that Dissenters and even Catholics could administer canals, turnpikes,
paving and lighting schemes, hospitals, dispensaries, and all kinds of
philanthropic activity funded by the public at large, made the Test and
Corporation Acts even less defensible to many. But it also made the debate
about their force somewhat unreal. This was very much the achievement
of the eighteenth century. In the years after the Revolution there had been
a real danger that sectarian conflict would be extended to every arena of
political combat and administrative activity. The Corporation Act did not
automatically apply to new institutions which were not dependent on the
Crown, its charters, or its commissions. Nor did the Test Act cover offices
held under such bodies, though there seem to have been fears that it might
be construed as doing so. But Parliament was quite capable of extending

---

[12] 2 Strange 828.

[13] W. H. Ryland, ed., *Reminiscences of Thomas Henry Ryland* (Birmingham, 1904), p. 3.

[14] M. M. Kay, *The History of Rivington and Blackrod Grammar School* (Manchester, 1931), pp. 87,
102–3.

the scope of these statutes, and in particular cases had ample opportunity to do so without risking a general law.

It was at Bristol, the country's second city, that this possibility was faced. Officers appointed by the Bristol Poor Law Guardians, under an act of 1696, were specifically exempted from a religious test. But in 1714 Bristol churchmen had their revenge, when they obtained an act requiring both guardians and officers to take the sacraments according to the Corporation Act. It was controversial and attracted large divisions for a local bill, 138 to 83 on third reading in the Commons.[15] It was also the work of a high-flying Tory Parliament, the same that passed the Schism Act for the destruction of Dissenting education. This represented an intensification of sectarian warfare even on the part of the High Church party. Significantly, three years earlier, when Norwich had applied for workhouse legislation it included no clause of this kind.[16] The Bristol Act of 1714 gave a clear signal as to what would ensue under a prolonged Tory hegemony. In the event it was Whig hegemony that followed and with it a different policy. In 1718 a new Bristol Act was approved, removing all religious tests. It was the subject of a protest in the Lords by four bishops, including the Jacobite Francis Atterbury and George Smalridge, the Bishop of Bristol, and nine Tory peers. They foresaw the establishment of poor law incorporations open to 'all Persons without Discrimination' and dominated by papists and Jews as well as Protestant Nonconformists.[17] The case acquired more than local significance because it stimulated Whig churchmen to demand revision of the Corporation Act as a whole and thereby facilitated the repeal of the Occasional Conformity Act.[18]

The nightmare of what had occurred at Bristol did not vanish immediately. At Manchester it was disputes about the share of power to be accorded different religious groups which wrecked the campaign for a workhouse bill in 1731. High Churchmen were brought eventually to oppose legislation on the grounds that it might entrust extensive powers to 'Quakers, Independents, Muggletonians, or Jews'.[19] In this instance it was the statutory establishment of Dissent that was at issue, but the underlying problem was the same. The maintenance of this mentality in

[15] 7 and 8 Will. III, c. 32; 13 Anne, c. 32; *Commons Journals*, xviii. 729. On the political context, see J. Barry, 'The Parish in Civil Life: Bristol and its Churches 1640–1750', in S. Wright, ed., *Parish, Church and People: Local Studies in Lay Religion, 1350–1750* (London, 1988), p. 169.

[16] 10 Anne, c. 15.

[17] C. Jones and G. Holmes, eds., *The London Diary of William Nicolson Bishop of Carlisle 1702–1718* (Oxford, 1985), p.670; *Lord Journals*, xx.655–6.

[18] On the wearing down of episcopal opposition to repeal of the Occasional Conformity Act, see G. M. Townend, 'Religious Radicalism and Conservatism in the Whig Party under George I: The Repeal of the Occasional Conformity and Schism Acts', *Parliamentary History*, 7 (1988), 24–44.

[19] A. Redford and I. S. Russell, *The History of Local Government in Manchester* (2 vols., London, 1939–40), i. 195; K. Kondo, 'The Workhouse Issue at Manchester: Selected Documents, 1729–35, Part One', *Bulletin of Faculty of Letters, Nagoya University*, 33 (1987), 70.

the mid-eighteenth century when whole new classes of public body were in process of creation would have been profoundly damaging. A notable feature of early eighteenth-century urban life was the tendency of alienated groups to entrench themselves in institutions which might rival if they could not break down the power of corporate bodies. In Plymouth the dominance of the corporation by Dissenters provoked Tory churchmen to exert matching control of the charitable, educational, and religious societies which played a no less important part in town life. At Taunton, when the corporation was Tory, it was the Dissenters who were compelled to focus their activities elsewhere.[20]

This malign incubus of sectarian and social conflict was not exorcised overnight. But the spirit which inspired the voluntary bodies of the mid-eighteenth century was profoundly hostile to it. Hospitals never formally adopted religious distinctions. To have done so would have been disastrous. Their finances were unsteady enough without risking the loss of Dissenting subscriptions. The accusation made against charity schools under Queen Anne and George I, that they were the agents of ecclesiastical or sectarian oppression, was rarely made against the medical charities.[21] Any possibility of this kind was ruled out at an early stage, by Parliament as well as public opinion. Because the Foundling Hospital was founded by Crown charter, in 1739, its governors were arguably subject to the sacramental test. But the act of Parliament which in 1740 conferred statutory powers on the Hospital specifically forbade oaths and sacraments.[22] Statutory bodies themselves were exempt, with important consequences in places where access to power for Nonconformists was a sensitive question. The effect was to narrow the arena in which sectarian rivalries could work. At Manchester there was a revival of the old religious animosities in the 1780s and 1790s. But by then successive acts of Parliament, in 1765, 1776, and 1792, had provided for town government without reference to religious distinctions. 1731 had suggested that there was no meeting ground on which Dissenters and churchmen could join. Fifty years later they in effect agreed to differ only within specific boundaries. The distinction was crucial.

The transformation in terms of mass psychology was more important still than the change in institutional procedure. Practices which had once appeared unchallengeable came to seem outrageous in the 1760s and 1770s. The prison reformer John Howard boasted of acting as High Sheriff of Bedfordshire without qualifying under the Test Act and without provoking criticism. He was to achieve a still greater triumph posthumously when in

[20] J. M. Triffitt, 'Politics and the Urban Community: Parliamentary Boroughs in the South West of England 1710–1730' (Oxford Univ. D.Phil thesis, 1985), pp. 47–51.

[21] William Hendley, *A Defence of the Charity-Schools* (London, 1725), pp. 47–51.

[22] R. K. McClure, *Coram's Children: The London Foundling Hospital in the Eighteenth Century* (New Haven, 1981), p. 39.

1794 he became the first subject of a statuary monument in St Paul's Cathedral. In London itself the position of Dissenters changed dramatically, as the judgement in the famous case of Allen Evans in 1768 revealed. Appointing Dissenters to offices which they could not conscientiously hold in order to extort fines from them had long been conventional in the City. The process of 'going a-birding' for Dissenting sheriffs was the subject of controversy after the Revolution and when carried to new heights for the financing of the new Mansion House under George II aroused intense hostility.[23] Mansfield significantly described the practice as a deliberate assault on the Toleration Act and a 'power to make every Dissenter pay a fine of six hundred pounds, or any sum they please'.[24] The fact that the condemnation came from a judge who was already being identified with constitutionally sinister tendencies made such liberalism at the heart of the judicial system all the more satisfying and striking. Nor was it merely the understanding of a Scotsman who was well aware that within the British Isles there were two faiths established by law, quite apart from faiths tolerated by law. Mansfield's resort to strict, even pedantic legal technicalities to defeat the activities of papist hunters in the 1760s was not less marked than his readiness to protect Protestant Dissenters.[25] There was no doubt that the men he protected were Roman Catholic priests, but his insistence on the most exacting proof of their priestly activities, proof which in the nature of things Protestant informers could not easily provide, demonstrated that the persecuting mentality which sustained old laws no longer had the support of authority.

Catholics were obvious beneficiaries of the marked, and in retrospect quite sudden change in attitudes towards religious dissent.[26] As late as 1766 it was still possible for a clergyman who prided himself on his liberal principles to observe that 'in propriety of speech, Catholics are not Englishmen; they are scarce to be called members of the same community with ourselves'.[27] But fashionable notions of equality and tolerance, combined with the civilizing requirements of business and recreation, made this once commonplace assumption obsolescent. The Catholic gentry had for practical purposes long been protected from the severity of the laws where their property rights and transactions were concerned, and the politeness which went increasingly with all kinds of property ensured that middle-class men and women were not far behind landed families in their somewhat

[23] G. S. De Krey, *A Fractured Society: The Politics of London in the First Age of Party, 1688–1715* (Oxford, 1985), pp. 181 ff.

[24] *Gentleman's Magazine* (1771), 69.

[25] J. M. Innes, 'William Payne' in *Inferior Politics: Social Problems and Social Policies in Eighteenth-Century Britain* (Oxford, forthcoming).

[26] C. M. Haydon, 'Anti-Catholicism in Eighteenth-Century England c. 1714–c. 1780' (Oxford Univ. D.Phil. thesis, 1985).

[27] Thomas Balguy, *Discourses on Various Subjects: and Charges Delivered to the Clergy of the Archdeaconry of Winchester*, ed. James Drake (2 vols., Cambridge, 1822), i. 194.

patronizing but none the less principled complaisance in this respect. It was this which made the formal admission of papists to professional vocations so important in the agitation for Catholic relief. Catholics mixed freely with their countrymen of all sects. Those most eagerly seeking reform were the most enthusiastic mixers. The Catholic publicist Joseph Berington counted Joseph Priestley a friend, and cultivated many Dissenting acquaintances in Birmingham. Mrs Schimmelpenninck recalled how in her childhood her Quaker parents had made a point of providing fish on Wednesdays, Fridays, and Saturdays so that middle-class Catholics in Birmingham would feel able to visit them.[28] Charles Butler, the best known of Catholic lawyers in the Emancipation era, was a vigorous promoter of reform and boasted numerous Protestant friends.

Public office for papists was a far more sensitive question that it was for Protestant Dissenters. Nobody seriously doubted the loyalty of the latter to the Hanoverian family and the Revolution Settlement. Catholics repeatedly asserted that they were not less loyal, but there was too much history to be forgotten before such assertions could be easily accepted and the dynastic threat of the Stuarts remained plausible for long enough to make mass amnesia on this scale unlikely. Moreover, occasional conformity was out of the question for Catholics. On the other hand, once the collective bigotry of propertied Protestants began to lift in the new climate of the 1760s it was possible for practical concessions to be made far beyond what the law technically allowed. Especially was this so where the concession was convenient for those who made it and something of a mixed blessing for the supposed beneficiaries. The ease with which Roman Catholics came to be accepted in parish offices, including that of overseer of the poor, was a case in point. Beilby Porteus, whose diocesan concerns as Bishop of Chester compelled him to take a particular interest in popery, thought this 'surely very singular, and irregular, a very improper appointment'.[29] His predecessors would have been startled that it was happening at all.

By the end of the century this process had indeed proceeded far. Just how far could sometimes surprise the Catholics who experienced it. Charles Browne Mostyn, a Gloucestershire landowner and papist, was almost dismayed to be appointed to numerous commissions, as the full burden of equality was made clear to him. Not only was he commissioner of taxes, but his son was a yeomanry captain and he himself a Deputy-Lieutenant and Lieutenant-Colonel of Volunteers. As Deputy-Lieutenant he was an active attender at militia meetings.[30] Catholics were prominent in the volunteer movement at all levels. Wherever commanding officers were

[28] C. C. Hankin, ed., *Life of Mary Anne Schimmelpenninck* (2 vols., London, 1858), i. 44–5.

[29] *A Letter to the Clergy of the Diocese of Chester* (London, 1782), p. 14.

[30] Leicestershire RO, Turville Constable Maxwell MSS, 1604: to F. F. Turville, 9 Nov. 1803.

prepared to connive at the granting of commissions, Catholic gentlemen could be found in the uniform of an officer.[31] Given the variable enthusiasm of Protestant gentlemen for military service, the importance of mobilizing Catholic tenants and labourers who could be influenced by squire and priest, and the ease with which Protestant and papist mixed in county society, this was not very surprising. But it represented a transformation in the policy of the English governing class, in a matter, the active defence of the State, of supreme importance. The very notion that a Roman Catholic could be a militia officer would have seemed extraordinary to Mostyn's father and grandfather, not to say their Protestant countrymen. In the militia of the early eighteenth century almost the only function of a deputy-lieutenant had been to join in harrying his Catholic neighbours at times of dynastic crisis or civil disorder.

Statutory change helped diminish the intolerance of the State. The act of 1779, which abandoned the requirement that Dissenting ministers subscribe to the Thirty-Nine Articles, was seen as a major concession by those who opposed it. Samuel Horsley later blamed it for inaugurating 'schools of Jacobinical religion, and of Jacobinical politics'.[32] He was doubtless exaggerating its practical significance, if only because subscription had rarely been enforced before 1779. Of more consequence was the fact that it registered the State's formal recognition of the right of the Church's enemies to spread their own doctrines. It suited agitators for the complete repeal of the Test and Corporation Acts to treat it as an inadequate, even damaging compromise. But this perception was a product of novel conditions. Samuel Chandler, the famous Dissenting leader of the 1740s and 1750s, had always considered subscription the last obstacle to genuine equality, and in 1759, at the end of George II's long reign, had prophesied that before very long it would be eliminated.[33] From his standpoint the act of 1779 would have completed the process begun in 1689. With the Act of Toleration and the Indemnity Acts it placed Nonconformists of most persuasions in a position as privileged as members of the Church of England. The 'establishment' of Dissent was complete. Dissenters who did not accept this were making new assumptions about the relationship between personal belief and allegiance to the State. This did not necessarily make their intellectual position less defensible, but it did affect the credibility of their claim to be pressing the historic rights of Dissenters. It was a common belief by the last years of the century that these men were not Dissenters at all in the traditional sense. What seemed conclusive evidence in this respect was provided by the publication in 1791

---

[31] M. D. Leys, *Catholicism in England 1559–1829: A Social History* (London, 1961), pp. 204–5.
[32] *The Speeches in Parliament of Samuel Horsley* (Dundee, 1813), p. 355.
[33] *The Signs of the Times: A Sermon Preached at the Old-Jury, Feb. 16, 1759* (London, [1759]), p. 43.

of a sermon which Richard Price, advocate of reform, friend of both the American and French Revolutions, and antagonist of Burke, had published in 1759.[34] The sermon emphasized the liberty and tolerance of English society, in terms which Chandler could have echoed. It seemed reasonable to suppose that Price rather than the liberty and tolerance had changed.

Chandler's generation was relatively unconcerned by the Test and Corporation Acts, but it is difficult not to believe that if his attitude had remained the prevailing one, the acts would have been repealed. As it was, in 1789, the majority in the House of Commons against repeal fell to only twenty votes. What prevented further progress was the suspicion that what was being sought was not civic rights for Dissenters, but the rights of man and the rights of heathen man at that. Anxieties about the theology of Presbyterianism in its Unitarian phase were commonplace in the early years of George III's reign, not least because the Church itself seemed to have been infiltrated by an Arian fifth column. A new image of what Dissent was about was presented for public viewing. In many ways it was misleading, but the activities of the Rational Dissenters gave it additional impact. Chance seemed to be working in the same direction. There was no essential reason for the Wilkesite movement, for instance, to be associated in the public mind with the Nonconformist tradition. But Wilkes was by birth a Presbyterian, and his enemies were quick to exploit the fact. Samuel Johnson did so with some adroitness, identifying the Wilkesite cause as that of 'the sectaries, the natural fomentors of sedition, and confederates of the rabble'.[35] Wilkes himself was prone to make matters worse. His own views might kindly be described as deistic, and it was, after all, he who said publicly in 1779 'that for his own part, he should wish to see pagodas, mosques, and temples of the sun, rising in the neighbourhood of our finest gothic cathedrals'.[36] Fears thus planted in the public mind could not easily be uprooted. Nor did all Dissenters seem to want to uproot them. The impression given in 1790 was of a revolutionary movement which threatened ruin to a society calling itself Christian and worshipping property. Price's political activities and Priestley's theological speculations seemed to provide all the evidence that was needed of such a conspiracy, and probably did not a little to shift parliamentary opinion away from repeal of the Test and Corporation Acts.[37]

There is no mistaking the distaste with which even some Dissenters came to view their supposed champions. In the agitation for relief in the

[34] *Britain's Happiness, and Its Full Possession of Civil and Religious Liberty, Briefly Stated and Proved* (London, 1791).

[35] D. J. Greene, ed., *Samuel Johnson: Political Writings* (New Haven, 1777), p. 344.

[36] R. Hodgson, *The Life of the Right Reverend Beilby Porteus DD* (2nd edn., London, 1811), p. 57.

[37] R. Watson, *Anecdotes of the Life of Richard Watson, Bishop of Llandaff* (London, 1817), p. 163.

1770s there were many Dissenters, moderates of the old kind, or Evangelicals of the new, who were deeply disturbed by the demands of some of their brethren for the complete abolition of tests. The petitions which the Calvinistic Baptists organized against the toleration bill of 1773 played a large part in its defeat. When it did pass in 1779, the declaration in favour of scriptural Christianity on which government insisted was for such men a welcome safeguard against the dangerous speculations of Unitarians and Socinians. For them, too, the Test and Corporation Acts, as they operated with the loophole exploited by occasional conformists, were not to be considered devices for the protection of High Church prejudices but rather the guarantees that England would remain in a Christian commonwealth. In 1790 John Martin argued that Dissent had no interest in the 'endless contest for civil rights', and quoted some eminent authorities in support of the claim that it would suffer rather than gain by the abolition of sacramental tests.[38]

Similar points could be made in relation to the Catholics. Catholics were at pains to stress that they sought toleration not power, the more conservative distancing themselves from the claims of the Rational Dissenters in this respect.[39] Some had grave doubts about the wisdom of changing their legal status at all. Catholic bishops dreaded the effects of integrating their flock in Protestant life. Bishop Talbot confessed: 'if we are asking for privileges, detrimental to Religion, such as serving in the Army, Navy etc. a refusal might be a blessing'.[40] Successive Catholic committees found themselves embroiled in disputes which divided laity and clergy, and each from each other, culminating in the bitter controversy accompanying the Relief Act of 1791. None the less, the inexorable process eroding legal distinctions between people of property took effect. The Relief Act of 1778 made impossible the use of the law against Catholic priests and congregations, and repealed the offensive legislation limiting a papist's rights in his property. More was to follow. Pitt's liberalism, where the Catholics were concerned, would have startled any minister before the reign of George III. 'He seemed to hint at their being put on a foot with the dissenters.'[41] In fact the Relief Act of 1791 did not go quite as far as that but it did permit Catholics to worship publicly without stigma, and to practise at the Bar, in a legalistic society a mark of equality hardly less significant than a share in the political process. There remained only the Test and Corporation Acts themselves and it seemed reasonable to suppose

---

[38] G. M. Ditchfield, 'The Subscription Issue in British Parliamentary Politics, 1772–79', *Parliamentary History*, 7 (1988), 58; John Martin, *A Speech on the Repeal of Such Parts of the Test and Corporation Acts as Affect Conscientious Dissenters* (London, 1790), pp. 5 ff.

[39] Durham RO, Salvin MSS, M. Tunstall to W. Salvin, 12 Mar. 1790.

[40] Dorset RO, Weld MSS, R 8: Talbot to T. Weld, n.d.

[41] Durham RO, Salvin MSS, M. Tunstall to W. Salvin, 14 June 1788.

that their disappearance would not be long delayed. The extent of support for Emancipation was much wider than it suited its opponents to pretend. William Windham was genuinely puzzled by the belief which he found at Oxford that it was inconsistent to defend the constitution against revolution while urging the abolition of religious discrimination. He had, after all, powerful evidence for his case in 'Mr Burke, who has rendered more service to the Church and the Monarchy than all the Politicians of our time put together, and who yet was at all times and to the last moment the most strenuous advocate for the repeal of the Catholic Laws'.[42]

There remained the King, who had the power, as it turned out, to make Catholic Emancipation a touchstone of loyalism, something it certainly need not have been. He had approved the Irish Relief Act of 1778, the Quebec Act of 1774, the Relief Acts of 1778 and 1791, the Irish Freeholders Act of 1793. He was personally on excellent terms with Roman Catholics. He even made a point of visiting popish gentry in their homes, a startling departure for a Revolution monarch. In 1778, after reviewing the militia at Warley camp he visited Lord Petre's house at Thorndon in some state. Just thirty-five years earlier, in December 1745, Petre's mother had been the victim of a much publicized raid by the Surrey magistrates on her own house at Cheam.[43] Similar memories were stirred in 1789 when the King, on holiday at Weymouth, condescended to call on the Welds at Lulworth Castle, inspecting the new chapel there. The head of the family, Thomas Weld, who arranged to have a chorus of children singing God Save the King in the chapel at the time, considered this visit 'a kind of sanction'.[44] There were certain ironies, or, as Fanny Burney put it, 'singular circumstances'. Weld's brother had been the first husband of Mrs Fitzherbert, who had subsequently and illegally married the Prince of Wales. In 1745 his father Edward had been accused of treason and hauled to London for examination by Privy Councillors.[45]

All seemed set for an emotional reunion of English Catholics with an English king. In 1778 the vicars apostolic ordered prayers for the royal family, as final a repudiation of Pius V's bull of 1570 as could be imagined. Yet George III declined to act out his part. When it was he decided that repeal of the Test and Corporation Acts was incompatible with his coronation oath is far from clear. He had ample advice which would have made escape from his self-imposed dilemma easy. There was an obvious distinction between his role as supreme governor of the Church and his

---

[42] *The Windham Papers* (2 vols., London, 1913), ii.262.

[43] M. D. Petre, *The Ninth Lord Petre or Pioneer of Roman Catholic Emancipation* (London, 1928), chap. 4; *London Magazine* (1745), 622.

[44] J. Berkeley, *Lulworth and the Welds* (Gillingham, 1971), p. 170.

[45] C. Barrett, ed., *Diary and Letters of Madame D'Arblay* (4 vols., London, 1876), iii. 201; M. F. Heathcote, *Lulworth and Its Neighbourhood* (Winchester, 1906), pp. 20–1.

function as one branch of the legislature. His oath to maintain the State religion as by law established left ample room for acceptance of a solemn parliamentary decision to grant Catholics full civil rights. Such reasoning, some of it from advisers whom he respected, he dismissed as 'not a point for Scotch metaphysics'.[46] The consequences were momentous and out of line with half a century of reform and relaxation of the laws.

THE ATTRIBUTES OF FANATICISM

Assimilation was not achieved without difficulty. The language employed in debating the significance of the Test and Corporation Acts sometimes made the controversies of the seventeenth century seem as relevant as ever. In the intellectual turmoil of the 1790s it suited both revolutionaries and reactionaries to claim that little or nothing had changed in this respect since the Restoration and the imposition of the Clarendon Code. Rational Dissenters compared their plight with the victims of Strafford, Clarendon, and Danby. High Churchmen spoke as if the horrors of civil war and regicide were about to recur. 'The Oliverian and Republican spirit is gone forth, and religion is a mere pretence for subverting the Government and destroying the Constitution'.[47] The men who joined issue on this congenial battleground shared a similar sense of what was at stake, and in many respects were of a matching cast of mind. It is not altogether coincidence that the two most redoubtable antagonists of all, Joseph Priestley and Bishop Horsley, were one time colleagues in the Royal Society, of which Horsley served as Secretary. In scientific matters there was no doubt where the advantage lay. In the matter of polemic the rivalry was a less unequal one. But in temperament they were not unalike. It suited Horsley to portray Priestley as an enemy of all authority. Yet his own activities in the Royal Society had given him a name for factiousness. The antiquarian Michael Lort described him as an instance of the 'levelling spirit and impatience of all government which infects the present age'.[48]

Dissenters of the mid-eighteenth century would have been startled by the vehemence of the debate about their rights and privileges in the 1790s, and equally puzzled by both Priestley and Horsley. They believed that they had always been entitled to the amity of the churchmen. As they pointed out, the Corporation Act itself had been passed before the Act of Uniformity, at a time when their forebears had still been loyal to the

[46] F. Bickley, ed., *The Diaries of Sylvester Douglas (Lord Glenbervie)* (2 vols., London, 1928), i. 280.

[47] Charles Burney, 11 May 1780, in R. Twining, ed., *Rev. T. Twining: Recreations and Studies of a Country Clergyman of the Eighteenth Century* (London, 1882), p. 84.

[48] C. R. Weld, *A History of the Royal Society* (2 vols., London, 1848), ii. 169.

Church. It could not have been intended to outlaw them.[49] If any doubt remained on this point it had been resolved by the Act of Toleration in 1789. They argued that the act had 'established' Protestant Dissent as completely as the Acts of Supremacy and Uniformity had 'established' the Church of England. They could point out, with the aid of Bishop Burnet's history, that at the Revolution the oath of allegiance had, in draft form, included a declaration of loyalty to the principle of toleration. According to Burnet this provision had been dropped only because churchmen thought it 'reasonable to oblige the Dissenters to use their liberty modestly, by keeping them under the apprehension of having it taken away'.[50]

These claims were irritating to High Churchmen, for whom the Test and Corporation Acts were as much a part of the constitution as Magna Carta and the Petition of Right.[51] Tory propaganda of Anne's reign provided them with useful ammunition in this respect. In his Chapel Royal sermon of 1707 Francis Higgins had objected to the very term 'Toleration Act' on the grounds that 'there is not one Word of *Toleration* in the Statute, tho' we are sensible of its Effects, and Consequences to that purpose'. He had also denied that it 'in the least Repeals, or Weakens one Tittle of the *Act of Uniformity* which God be praised is *Yet* in Force'.[52] It was for this sermon that Higgins, the 'Irish Sacheverell', had been prosecuted by the Whig ministry. Sixty years later Blackstone's incautious remarks on the subject in his *Commentaries* revealed how sensitive this question remained. His own position was that the statute of 1689 had suspended the penalties attaching to Nonconformist worship but that 'care must be taken not to carry this indulgence into such extremes as may endanger the national church: there is always a difference between toleration and establishment'.[53] Others found it less easy to regard the act as a minor breach in an otherwise imposingly monolithic structure. Its legislative effects were considerable. In 1736 the *Daily Gazetteer* listed a total of ten statutes from the 23 Elizabeth to the 22 Charles II which it abrogated or suspended.[54] Parliament had plainly used to some effect that suspending power which it denied to the monarch. No less a personage than Lord Mansfield differed with Blackstone on this subject. He asserted flatly that the Dissenters' 'way of worship' was 'not only exempted from punishment, but rendered innocent and lawful: it is established, it is put under the protection, and is not merely under the connivance of the law'.[55]

---

[49] Moses Lowman, *A Defence of the Protestant Dissenters* (London, 1718), pp. 32–3.

[50] *Bishop Burnet's History of His Own Times* (2 vols., London, 1734), ii. 299.

[51] *The Weekly Miscellany* (2 vols., London, 1738), ii. 249–57.

[52] *A Sermon Preach'd at The Royal Chappel at White-Hall; On Ash-Wednesday, Feb. 26, 1707* (London, 1707), p. 14.

[53] W. Blackstone, *Commentaries on the Laws of England* (4 vols., London, 1765–9), iv. 51.

[54] 19 Mar. 1736.

[55] *Gentleman's Magazine* (1771), 66.

Mansfield's view was shared by many loyal members of the Church of England. Some of them would have pushed it further. In the early and mid-eighteenth century there were clergy who supported a relaxation of the Test and Corporation Acts, some of them by no means of latitudinarian tendency. Bishop Gibson, a Whig but also a redoubtable High Churchman and reviled as a neo-Laudian by many other Whigs, cheerfully contemplated repealing the acts so far as they applied to corporations, and removing the sacramental test for other officers.[56] Even in the revolutionary era when some Dissenters were vulnerable to the charge of Unitarianism and Socianism it was possible to point to substantial support for their position from Church of England clergy. In 1790 there was a Church in Danger campaign which made considerable inroads into clerical sympathy with Nonconformists. Yet it was not wiped out. In Suffolk the clergy who stated their support for the Test and Corporation Acts left no doubt of their commitment to toleration, and Capel Lofft was able to cite a significant body who denied that toleration was an adequate basis for the rights of Protestant Dissenters. One of those he listed was Thomas Kerrich, a well-known figure, later Librarian of Cambridge University.[57] He represented a liberal strand of churchmanship which did not appeal either to Tractarians or Evangelicals in the nineteenth century and which was accordingly under-represented in the 'lives' and 'works' conveying Victorian perceptions of the eighteenth-century Church.

This tolerance and sense of mutual communion remained in sometimes trying circumstances. It affected some of the most conventional of minds. John Sturge's *Considerations on the Present State of the Church Establishment* of 1779 was a case in point. Sturges addressed his work to the Bishop of London, Robert Lowth, a notably firm Oxonian; he did so at a time when the position of both Catholics and Protestant Dissenters was a subject of much controversy in Parliament and beyond. Yet his work was remarkable for its moderation, even for its 'candor and benevolence towards the adversaries of the Church of England', as reviewers observed.[58] In the same year the Archdeacon of Rochester, John Law, took the unusual step of employing his charge to the clergy of his archdeaconry to defend the relief granted by Parliament to Catholics in 1778 and Protestants in 1779.[59]

If there was a shift of clerical opinion it was perhaps most marked at the highest levels. The bishops of George II's reign had been considered notably sympathetic to men whom their predecessors had harried and persecuted. Archbishop Herring had gloried in becoming Archbishop at a 'time when spite, and rancour, and narrowness of spirit are out of coun-

---

[56] Jones and Holmes, eds., *The London Diaries of William Nicolson*, pp. 668–9.

[57] *A Vindication of the Short History of the Corporation and Test Acts* (London, 1790), p. 35.

[58] (London, 1779); *Critical Review*, xlvii. 289.

[59] *A Charge Delivered to the Clergy of the Archdeaconry of Rochester, in the Year 1779.*

tenance, when we breathe the benign and comfortable air of liberty and toleration'.[60] Even staunch Whigs sometimes found such complaisance irritating. When William Stukeley dined at Sion College in April 1752, with the Archdeacon of London, and the Bishops of Worcester, Lincoln, and Peterborough, he was taken aback to observe hanging in the parlour a portrait of the Dissenting teacher John Allen, who, it transpired, was the tenant of the house in which they dined, within the precincts of the college: 'so little regard had even to the appearance of our minding ecclesiastical polity! As the government does by papists, so we take in known and determined enemies.'[61]

At some point in George III's reign it came to be believed that a decisive change had taken place in the complexion of the episcopate. In the 1790s the bishops appointed by George III were being hailed as 'very different from the Presbyterian Arians of George the Second and Lord Hardwicke'.[62] Yet it is possible that such opinions had more to do with popular assumptions about the respective religiosity of George II and George III than with informed analysis of episcopal opinion. In the 1790s only George Horne, Bishop of Norwich and a Hutchinsonian friend of William Jones of Nayland, could be placed unequivocally in the non-juring High Church tradition. For him, indeed, the defeat of the Dissenters in 1787 was 'a question which, stripped of flourishes, is plainly this; whether we shall tolerate them, or accept a toleration from them'.[63] Other bishops displayed more relaxed attitudes. John Warren, Horsley's predecessor at St David's, publicly dismissed zeal in religious points, such as had marred the mid-seventeenth century, as of 'little or no consequence'.[64] The famous Bishop of Derry even enquired, on the subject of subscription to the Thirty-Nine Articles, 'Did the Presbyterians ask anything unreasonable when they desired to have *their* nonsense tolerated as well as other nonsense'.[65] Like others on the bench he had no great respect for the means by which his own Church was sustained. John Ross, Bishop of Exeter, told the House of Lords in an official sermon in 1779 that religion did not require the pains and penalties levied by the State for its support. He also praised the excellence of the Toleration Act and looked forward to the season, fast approaching, when it would be possible to complete the work begun in 1689.[66]

[60] C. J. Abbey, *The English Church and Its Bishops 1700–1800* (2 vols., London, 1887), ii.39.

[61] 'The Family Memoirs of the Rev. William Stukeley', *Surtees Soc.* 76 (1883), 376.

[62] *Gentleman's Magazine* (1795), 718.

[63] BL, Althorp Papers, E 37: George Horne to Charles Poyntz, 3 Apr. 1787.

[64] *A Sermon, Preached before the Lords Spiritual and Temporal, in the Abbey-Church, Westminster: on Tuesday, January 30, 1781* (London, 1781), p.22.

[65] M. Betham-Edwards, ed., *The Autobiography of Arthur Young* (London, 1898), p. 130.

[66] *A Sermon Preached before the Lords Spiritual and Temporal, in the Abbey-Church, Westminster; on Saturday, January 30, 1779* (London, 1779), pp. 11–13.

Several bishops of the late eighteenth century, for example Porteus and Buckner, could best be described as Evangelicals with a Low Church cast of mind. Others, like Barrington and Yorke, pressed for reform of the Thirty-Nine Articles. A few, such as Law and Hallifax, would have found the episcopal scepticism of George II's reign congenial. But of authentic High Churchmen in the last four decades of the century there were perhaps only two, Horne and Bagot. Even Horsley was careful not to appear bigoted. He seemed the type of the intolerant High Churchman, and his controversial refusal to ordain men who had been educated in Dissenting Academies certainly contrasted with earlier practice; some famous bishops including Thomas Secker and Joseph Butler would have been denied their clerical career by this policy. Yet he rejected the appellation of High Churchman and thereby denied his attachment to what he described as 'the secular rights of the priesthood'.[67]

Characteristic Church attitudes under George III did not necessarily or even ordinarily imply a persecuting spirit or an atavistic view of ecclesiastical politics. Warburton's tolerant Erastianism fitted the 1790s as thoroughly as it had fitted the 1730s, in some ways more so, for there was no one in the 1790s who took seriously the high view of the Church and its jurisdiction over laymen to which men of Gibson's generation had remained loyal. When there was sometimes a sense of intolerance, it sprang rather from a belief that the existing alliance of Church and State was under threat than from any new crusading confidence on the part of High Churchmen. In 1772 and 1790, two such instances, this was certainly the case. And in each the threat seemed temporal as much as spiritual. Tests and subscriptions could be viewed as the outworks of a fortress whose purpose included the maintenance of tithes as much as the protection of liberty and Protestantism. Until at least the mid-eighteenth century the enthusiasm of laymen for the campaign against tithes had been limited by the possibility that their own propertied rights might be affected. The emotive cry of 'abbey lands' was not entirely devoid of power even in the reign of George II. Under his successor it was possible to suppose that tithes might be reformed without any fundamental disturbance to the structure of squirearchical property. The clergy could not but be aware of mounting pressure on this subject. 1772, the year which saw Dissenters demanding further toleration, also saw a bill to limit the right of the Church to tithes alienated at an earlier period. In the same year there was a bill to reduce the Church's jurisdiction where Quakers were concerned, not to

[67] *A Letter to the Right Reverend Samuel, Lord Bishop of St David's* (London, 1790), p. 25; H. H. Jebb, *A Great Bishop of One Hundred Years Ago, Being a Sketch of the Life of Samuel Horsley, LL. D.* (London, 1909), p. 79. The bishops of the period are briefly described in Abbey, *The English Church and Its Bishops*, ii, ch. 7.

say increased public discussion of the oppressive nature of tithes in an age of agricultural improvement.

There was plainly some deterioriation in relations between the clergy of the sects and the clergy of the Church in the late eighteenth century. Under George II there had been a certain appreciation of the community of interest which bound Protestants of diverse opinions in an era of enlightenment and toleration. In 1748, Philip Doddridge rejoiced that 'a generous and catholic temper has been very much spread in these parts within the 25 years I have spent here in Leicestershire'.[68] After 1760 such confidence was less marked. Partly this was an understandable reaction to the prominence of old-style Tories at the new court. Partly, too, it represented a sober assessment of the King's own predilections. And not least, the long primacy of Lord North, Chancellor of Oxford University and friend of some notable High Churchmen, served to promote suspicions. As a well-known Baptist minister, Posthumus Lloyd, put it in 1775, 'Dissenting Ministers are looked upon with a very jealous eye by Administration and their *Master*'.[69] Yet even in such claims there was surely an element of propaganda. Confronted with reminders that George III had done no more to disturb the privileged position of Nonconformists than his predecessor, it was necessary to take refuge in implausible fears. 'The political second sight of dissenters, may possibly discern a schism bill, or repeal of the toleration in embryo.'[70]

The evidence of alienation was on neither side as strong as it sometimes appeared. Churchmen naturally made the most of Nonconformists who seemed to be reasserting the spirit of their ancestors. When the Baptist mayor of Coventry in 1771 openly toasted the name of Oliver Cromwell along with those of the King and Queen, King William, the Duke of Cumberland, and various Warwickshire noblemen, he provoked a typically synthetic controversy of this kind.[71] Predicting the actual conduct of the Dissenting interest at local level was not easy.[72] From the beginning of his reign George III attracted the loyal support of many Dissenters who did not readily surrender their historic allegiance to the Hanoverian monarchy. High Churchmen who had discovered a new loyalty to the same monarchy could still be taunted with their inconsistency. At Ipswich in 1768 they were offended by their opponents' conduct in parading the royal arms through the streets at election time, 'insinuating thereby, that they were persons disaffected to his Majesty, and his government, because they would

---

[68] Nuttall, ed., *Calendar of the Correspondence of Philip Doddridge*, p. 270.

[69] G. E. Evans, *Lloyd Letters (1754–1796)* (Aberystwyth, 1908), p. 44.

[70] *The Constitution Defended, and Pensioner Exposed: In Remarks on the False Alarm* (London, 1770), p. 31.

[71] Bodleian Library, G. A. Warwicks b 1: William Reader's 'Chronicle of the Times', 163–6.

[72] J. E. Bradley, 'Whigs and Nonconformists: ' "Slumbering Radicalism" in English Politics, 1739–1789', *Eighteenth-Century Studies*, 9 (1975–6), 1–27.

not come under a banner so impolitically raised'.[73] Yet the incongruity was
only in their own minds. The King and his ministers showed no desire to
discriminate against Nonconformists. Quakers such as David Barclay and
John Fothergill were courted, the latter with the exceptional offer to
someone unlikely to come within the Test Act of a post as royal physician.
Bute's most effective pamphleteer in the last stages of the Seven Years War
was a City Dissenter, Israel Mauduit, described by the Archdeacon of
York, Edmund Pyle, as 'one of the first rank in Lord Willoughby's Sunday
night club—of Divines, Philosophers and Scholars at large'.[74] Willoughby,
well-known in the affairs of the Royal Society, the Society of Antiquaries,
the Society of Arts, and the British Museum, and the only English Dissenter
in the Lords, was himself a supporter of the court. Mauduit became a
friend of North and a telling critic of the claims of America.

Such men were in no sense turncoats. Mauduit was a strenuous advocate
of the Dissenters in their struggle for further toleration. Above all he
sought to show what the broad mass of Dissent actually represented, and
to confute those 'well-meaning High Church Country Gentlemen' who
'set us forth as wild Enthusiasts, and Fifth-monarchy Men when People
that died a hundred Years ago, Ancestors of we know not whom, were
raised to Life again, to sit for *our* Pictures, and we were drawn with all the
Attributes of Fanatacism'.[75] This strand of moderate Dissent provided a
link between the old Whiggism and the moderate, non-partisan politics of
George III's reign. North was extremely careful not to sever it. His friends
included some notably stern Dissenters, for example Sir Henry Hoghton,
the head of a well-known Lancashire Presbyterian family. George III
himself enjoyed good relations with such men. To a considerable extent
the perceived conflict of the court and the Dissenting sects was an optical
illusion, a result of the distracting propaganda war waged between the
Rational Dissenters, who were by no means representative of Dissent at
large, and a small group of bishops and senior clergy, who were not
necessarily more representative of the Church as a whole.

Hostility to Dissenters rested largely on contempt for their social origins
and anxiety about their political views. Richard Watson calculated that
Dissenters represented a quarter of the population but only one-fiftieth of
the property of England and Wales. This certainly overestimated their
numbers and perhaps underestimated their wealth.[76] But it reflected a
commonplace assumption about the lowly class of most Dissenters. For

---

[73] T. Green, sen., *Euphrasy* (Ipswich, [1769]), pp. 41–2.

[74] R. Hingston Fox, *Dr John Fothergill and His Friends: Chapters in Eighteenth Century Life* (London,
1919), pp. 25–6; A. Hartshorne, ed., *Memoirs of a Royal Chaplain, 1729–1763* (London, 1905), p. 339.

[75] *The Case of the Dissenting Ministers Addressed to the Lords Spiritual and Temporal* (4th edn.,
London, 1772), p. 51.

[76] *Anecdotes of the Life of Richard Watson*, p. 152.

the rest it was the radical politics of Dissenters which did the damage. This was even more misleading. That many Dissenters were opposed to the American War was true. They were certainly prominent in some places among signatories of the petitions of 1775 favouring conciliation rather than coercion. But it was equally the case that many others supported government.[77] When the eccentric Thomas Prentice, teacher of the San-demanians at Nottingham, attacked Dissenters as 'patrons of rebellion' and 'desirous of revolution' he was reminded that in fact many Dissenters had signed the loyal addresses to the Crown against America.[78] Job Orton reckoned in May 1777 that in his own region of the Welsh borders and indeed in most places outside the great cities Dissenting ministers were overwhelmingly loyal to the Crown and hostile to the pretensions of America. These 'quiet in the land' as he called them naturally attracted little interest or attention. One vociferous Richard Price made a far bigger impact on public attitudes than any number of moderate but silent Dissenters.[79]

Dissenters appeared in numbers to support the Crown at moments of crisis, in 1784 against Fox and North, in 1788 at the time of the Regency crisis, in 1792 when the government appealed for a loyal campaign against seditious writings. In this respect the propaganda of loyalism could be deceptive. It suited loyalists, in places where the language of party remained the old rant about religion, to emphasize the connection between Church and State. Toasts to the 'perpetuity of the Corporation and Test Acts' went with toasts to famous Englishmen, famous English laws, and famous English liberties. This was the case in Yarmouth, and in much of East Anglia, where Dissent was strong, but rarely dominant.[80] But the constitution to which Englishmen were asked to pledge their loyalty was capable of very different interpretations, and government itself was extremely careful to leave room for manoeuvre in this respect. The Royal Proclamation of May 1792, commencing the first campaign against reform and revolution, was adroitly worded. It referred to 'the laws and constitution, civil and religious'. This presented no difficulty to Dissenters who believed that they enjoyed the full protection of the law. Dissenters were prominent in the addressing movement which followed the Proclamation, and some of the corporations which they controlled saw no difficulty in expressing their loyalty.

The result was that Nonconformity gave the same impression of division

[77] J. E. Bradley, *Popular Politics and the American Revolution in England: Petitions, the Crown, and Public Opinion* (Macon, G., 1986), pp. 191–201.

[78] *London Magazine* (1777), 406–7.

[79] *Letters to a Young Clergyman, from the Late Reverend Mr Job Orton* (2nd edn., Shrewsbury, 1800), i. 219.

[80] *Ipswich Journal*, 9 June 1792.

and uncertainty as many other sections of society. In the Midlands, Nottingham refused a loyal address, but Coventry applauded Britain's 'excellent constitution' and expressed its unreserved support.[81] The difference was a matter of politics, not religion. Nottingham, where two celebrated radicals, George Walker and Gilbert Wakefield, featured in the life of the town at this time, was something of a battleground between hardline Dissent, with a bias towards Unitarianism in religion and republicanism in politics, and reactionary loyalism. Coventry's Dissenters were theologically more conservative and politically less cohesive. Some of them even accused the corporation of apostasy.[82] But the protesters were in a minority. The committee set up to express the town's horror of sedition included seven Dissenting Aldermen and received united support from local Baptists and Quakers.[83] It did not suit churchmen to cite Coventry rather than Nottingham when depicting the political attitudes of their opponents, but it is not clear that it was less representative of provincial Nonconformity. At Bridport, for instance, the signatures to the loyal address of 1792 were largely those of the Dissenting interest which dominated the corporation. It was their opponents, so-called Church and King men, who were less noticeable.[84]

The wording of the addresses presented in 1792 varied considerably, but in retrospect their most striking feature is the relative absence of High Church language. Specific references to the Test and Corporation Acts and the Church's political rights were missing. Even Oxford University contented itself with a vague but splenetic denunciation of the 'intemperate Zeal of wild Theorists'. Mentions of 'the Establishment in Church and State', as at Tewkesbury, or of the 'established Government both in Church and State', as at Kidderminster, were uncommon.[85] There was even scope in the addressing procedure for the expression of doubts about the unchanging perfection of British government as understood by the opponents of reform. The rather teasing address of the Llandaff clergy, drafted by its idiosyncratic bishop, Richard Watson, pointed out the constitutional 'improvements' achieved under George III, including the acts of 1778–9 and 1791 on behalf of both Protestant and Catholic Dissenters.[86] This was not what the more enthusiastic champions of Church and King had envisaged as the proper way to celebrate the Englishman's resistance to the doctrines of the French Revolution. Yet it does indicate the latitudinarianism of the loyalist cause, both in ecclesiastical and political terms. In this sense

---

[81] *London Gazette*, 21 June 1792.
[82] William Reader's 'Chronicle', 781, 787.
[83] Ibid. 912, 914, 916.
[84] Dorset RO, B3, H7: Declaration of 19 Dec. 1792.
[85] *London Gazette*, 16 June 1792; 16, 21 June 1792.
[86] *Anecdotes of the Life of Richard Watson*, p. 267.

loyalism was too successful for its own good. Reformers who gathered under its umbrella in the autumn of 1792 helped deprive it of ideological coherence, though when one of them at Chesterfield provocatively burned an effigy of Edmund Burke in public, he was removed from the committee responsible for drafting a loyal address.[87]

Ironically, the Rational Dissenters who provided most of the evidence for the political unreliability of Dissent were in some ways the least representative. Unitarian congregations were characteristically small, opulent, and highly articulate. With many of their Nonconformist brethren they had very little in common. Even among themselves there were differences. The obituarist of the Hinckley Unitarian John Smith in 1795 celebrated him as an upholder of King and Constitution.[88] His was a rare but by no means unique instance. Benjamin Naylor, the Unitarian minister at Sheffield, supported the Volunteer movement for the protection of British liberty and property against the French Revolution in terms which somewhat startled some of his congregation.[89] Timothy Kenrick did adhere to the line taken by Price and Priestley but found through bitter personal experience how reluctant provincial Dissenters might be to follow such a lead. At Exeter his denunciations of the Birmingham rioters, the Proclamation of 1792, and the loyalist movement earned limited sympathy his own congregation. He confessed himself mortified by the numerous Dissenting subscriptions to loyalist associations, and suffered the particular ignominy of having a sermon to the local Unitarian Society stopped by 'one Gentlemen, who has distinguished himself, altho' a dissenter, by his zeal in supporting all the vile measures of a vile Court, and by his antipathy to every species of innovation'.[90] Such examples gave force to the claims of Dissenting spokesmen that their churches had successfully resisted 'French principles'.[91]

How divisive religion was by the late eighteenth century is itself an acutely difficult point to determine. It is arguable that it was political strife which exacerbated sectarian conflict, rather than vice versa. This was the opinion of Thomas Gisborne, a liberal clergyman who decried the horrors of republicanism and revolution, but also gloried in the Toleration Act and what he called 'the extension of the rights of citizens to Roman Catholics'. Gisborne was unimpressed by so-called evidence of religious warfare. 'Religious bigotry has a share in these proceedings; but in most cases they

---

[87] E. Fearn, 'The Derbyshire Reform Societies, 1791–1793', *Derbys. Arch. Jnl.* 88 (1968), 56; see also D. E. Ginter, 'The Loyalist Association Movement of 1792–3 and British Public Opinion', *Hist. Jnl.* 9 (1966), 179–90.

[88] *Gentleman's Magazine* (1795), 1059.

[89] *The Right and Duty of Defensive War* (Sheffield, 1803).

[90] 'The Kenrick Letters', *Trans. Unitarian Soc.* 3 (1923–6), 302.

[91] *The Protestant Dissenter's Magazine*, i (1794), 102.

principally arise from political contests actually existing in the place, or not yet forgotten.'[92]

The use of old war-cries to activate forgotten resentments was certainly a feature of late eighteenth-century electoral life. There was an artifical quality about the way in which religious distinctions were introduced into county contests like that in Hampshire in 1779.[93] The sense that the rhetoric was tired and the conflict theatrical was felt by many independent observers. In Leicestershire in 1775 it was difficult not to conclude that behind the ritual propaganda warfare of Church and Dissent, High Church and Low, Non-Resistance and Revolution, Tory and Whig, there was little more than the desire of landed gentlemen to prevent the Duke of Rutland gaining an ascendancy in the county. When a Dissenting minister at Market Harborough, Stephen Addington, announced his adherence to the Tory candidate John Peachy Hungerford, his brethren in the Rutland interest described it 'as a kind of treason against their establishment'.[94] The fact was that the Harborough district was overwhelmingly tied, by economic interest, sentimental attachment, and sense of community to the Hungerford family. It was a loyalty which overrode the secondary ties between one Dissenter and another. Electoral propaganda seeking to exploit the animosity of Church and Dissent was not evidence of deep-seated religious strife, but of quite the opposite. Territorial and civic loyalties were rarely invoked because their power could be taken for granted. But the possibility of shifting a few votes on the margin by reawakening old anatagonisms was well worth the investment of some printer's ink.

What looked like religious conflict was quite likely to mask a different kind of animosity. Dissent was overwhelmingly urban in character, a fact of some significance to an electorate which comprehended both town and country. A market town in which Dissenters were not numerous was a surprising phenomenon, as the clergyman and antiquarian Joseph Greene remarked in describing such a case, that of his own Stratford-upon-Avon.[95] Small towns and the rural areas in which they were set frequently coexisted in a spirit of mutual dependence and mutual irritation. The cultural gulf created by the relative wealth and sophistication of an urban life-style was sometimes widened by the requirements of law and social policy, for example in the regulation of poor relief and settlement. Questions of

[92] *An Enquiry into the Duties of Men in the Higher and Middle Classes of Society in Great Britain, Resulting from Their Respective Stations, Professions, and Employments* (3rd edn., 2 vols., London, 1795), i. 45, 158.

[93] *A Collection of All the Handbills, Squibs, Songs, Essays, etc. Published during the Late Contested Election for the County of Hampshire* (Winchester, 1780), pp. 120, 122, 124.

[94] *Memoirs of the Late Contested Election for the County of Leicester; Or a New Triumphal Arch Erected in Honor of Victory Obtained from That Contest by the True Old Interest* (Leicester, 1775), p. 21.

[95] L. Fox, ed., *The Correspondence of the Reverend Joseph Greene* (London, 1965), p. 157.

religion were not necessarily involved, but one of the fears of the day was precisely that the toleration and collaboration which marked everyday life would be undermined by the malignancy of politicians intent on reviving sectarian strife. In Suffolk in 1790 electors were reminded that Dissenters and Church folk had no difficulty in co-operating for business and professional purposes. But if electoral mischief-making induced churchmen to refuse trading with Dissenters the result would be a disturbing social evil.[96]

Corporations were notoriously prone to sectarian squabbling. The natural effect of municipal oligarchy was to concentrate power in the hands of one or other group united by friendship and economic interest. Since Church and chapel life naturally accounted for many such connections it was hardly surprising that it featured in urban politics. Yet the relative unimportance of sectarian warfare even in places with large religious minorities remains remarkable. At Liverpool, the first parliamentary election to generate a collected edition of published broadsheets and squibs, that of 1761, reveals the difficulty of fixing hard and fast lines in this respect. Religion was dragged in only when one of the candidates was accused of Jacobitism and by implication of encouraging popery. Attempts to unite Liverpool Dissent against him proved singularly unsuccessful and merely confused the issue. All the candidates insisted on their devotion to the interests of all their Protestant electors.[97] The fact was that none of them could afford to alienate religious minorities in a large, open constituency where electoral power did not lie with a small corporate body. No doubt it was for the same reason that the tempestuous electoral politics of London and Middlesex focused so rarely on the conflict of Church and Dissent, notwithstanding the prominence of the latter in the life of the capital.

Corporate bodies occasionally altered their religious affiliation. But interpreting these changes of direction was not a simple matter. Sometimes the process seemed oddly inconsequential. When churchmen gained control of King Edward VI School, Birmingham, it was claimed that they had done so because two Dissenting governors had neglected their duties for a fishing trip.[98] At Beverley the exclusion of Dissenters from the corporation in 1790 was attributed to meeting-house factiousness, originating with the admission of illiterate preachers.[99] In such instances it was always possible to discern sinister conspiracies. But the truth was that they indicated

[96] *Observations on the Cause, Conduct, and Effects of the Late Contested Election for the County of Suffolk*, pp. 14–15.

[97] *An Entire and Impartial Collection of All the Papers, etc.* (Liverpool, 1761).

[98] Ryland, ed., *Reminiscences of Thomas Henry Ryland*, p. 55.

[99] George Croft, *The Test Laws Defended: A Sermon Preached at St Phillip's Church in Birmingham, on Sunday, January the 31, 1790* (Birmingham, 1790), p. iv.

the breakdown of hard and fast sectarian distinctions rather than their persistence. Superficially, the success of the Carter family in Portsmouth in 1782, which gave them control of the corporation for some fifty years, seemed a triumph for Unitarian Presbyterianism. But Carter's victory was achieved by an alliance with elements from outside the borough, including landed gentlemen. It could not have succeeded without strong support from churchmen.[100]

Confusion between Church and Dissent was commonplace. In Bridport, one of the most striking examples of a small borough where Dissent seemed to be the Establishment in every sense, the distinction was not straightforward. The corporation was based on one meeting-house, and largely excluded other Nonconformists as well as Churchmen. But the ruling Dissenters themselves were frequently churchwardens, with pews in the parish church. This was not thought eccentric at the time.[101] In Coventry the enmity of true blue against green and yellow, Church against corporation, was as deep as anywhere. Yet by the 1760s such loyalties were proving difficult to maintain. In the parliamentary election of 1768 the strain proved intolerable when the ruling group split between two candidates, supported by rival Whig magnates. The result was the formation of two new camps, each comprising Dissenters as well as churchmen, and 'the destruction of one of the strongest Whig interests in the kingdom'.[102] Similar confusion reigned at Ipswich in 1768. There the hysterical *Euphrasy* letters were written, with dire warnings of the growing power of Dissent in the corporation. But in retrospect the letters are more suggestive of the decline of sectarian conflict than its revival. Their author, Thomas Green, was principally concerned to chastise churchmen and even clergymen who sided with men they knew to be Nonconformists, and to expose Dissenters who had the temerity to attend their parish church. It was the Ipswich townsfolk's neglect of their religious inheritance that shocked him.[103] Similar dismay attended the situation at West Bromwich, where a Nonconformist teacher carried his flock alternately to meeting house and church and on his death was granted the honour of a funeral sermon in each.[104]

Such anxiety about clerical complacency in populous places was significant. Tithes did not tap urban wealth, and parochial livings in towns were by and large poor, especially in old centres which had to support numerous parish churches. Clerical incumbencies could be 'improved' only by pluralism, or by resort to auxiliary remuneration. The best hope was 'some polite place, where the surplice fees were considerable', or where

[100] A. Geddes, *Portsmouth during the Great French Wars 1770–1800* (Portsmouth, 1970), pp. 11–14.
[101] B. Short, *A Respectable Society: Bridport 1593–1835* (Bradford on Avon, 1976), p. 45.
[102] William Reader's 'Chronicle', 157–60.
[103] Green, *Euphrasy*, iv, vi.
[104] Croft, *The Test Laws Defended*, p. iv.

congregations subscribed for the support of their clergy in the same manner as Dissenters.[105] This state of affairs bred a certain tolerance among the clergy. It was not the latitudinarianism of Whig prelates in search of political advancement but of ordinary parsons conscious of the need not to alienate polite congregations. In such circumstances Dissenters who chose to divide their devotions between church and chapel were not lightly to be criticized. Thomas Green's own answer was the only practicable one, to urge subscribers to make their subscription conditional on the compliance of their ministers.[106] But it was not only Nonconformists who preferred to subscribe to a broad church. Many staunch churchmen took a similar view on doctrinal grounds. Many too had a vested interest in the status quo. A High Church parson could be an uncomfortable presence for friends as well as enemies. When Joseph Rann, the Vicar of St Trinity, Coventry, went to law to assert his right to a statutory church rate by an act of Philip and Mary, he was assailed by his own parishioners as well as Dissenters. 'Philip and Mary', as he became known, learned at first hand the practical difficulties of appealing to an ecclesiastical party which barely existed.[107]

Naturally there were clergy who were infuriated by the requirements of polite life. John Moir was shocked by many London chapels and churches, particularly those attracting fashionable congregations; some, associated with charitable institutions, seemed little more than theatres of sentimental religion in which the priest was merely an actor. He pleaded instead for the revival of the parish church and uncompromising clerical leadership. In a sense he was an 'Anglican' before his time. The values which he advanced were eventually to be more widely accepted by the clergy and congregations of the established Church. But in the meantime it was mutual tolerance, compromise, and collaboration which often represented the realities of interdenominational life. In Ipswich Thomas Green came to regret his intemperance, and his son positively gloried in those charitable activities which promoted union in the 1790s. Even the lowly soup-kitchen served to lessen the tensions created by ecclesiastical politics. 'It was gratifying to observe Churchmen, Presbyterians, Independents, Unitarians, Quakers all actively united in the same benevolent design; and warmed, from this circumstance, into complacency and kindness to each other.'[108] In its early stages the Sunday School movement gave rise to similar reflections, including Joshua Toulmin's anticipation of 'that happy day, when Christians will learn to unite together on the plain truths of

---

[105] *London Magazine* (1764), 409.
[106] Green, *Euphrasy*, iv. 14.
[107] William Reader's 'Chronicle', 273 ff.
[108] *Extracts from the Diary of a Lover of Literature* (Ipswich, 1810), p. 188.

their common Christianity'.[109] Here was one vision of a harmonious future, to be set against the almost paranoid sectarianism and suspiciousness of the Horsleys and Priestleys. It was also the vision which most clearly represented the impulses and preferences of propertied society.

THE FARCE OF STATE OATHS

Some very characteristic concerns of the eighteenth century ran through the debate about the religious prescriptions of the State. One was the distinction between levels of political participation and activity. Burke called it the difference between franchise and office.[110] The tendency of natural rights theory was to merge the two, making every form of civic participation the right of every citizen. But this view only slowly gained ground in England and was inherently at odds with assumptions which related hierarchies of rights and duties to quantities of property. In time inferior political rights for religious minorities came to seem outrageous. But this perception was not a common one even in the 1780s and 1790s. Its subsequent popularity can make it difficult to discern the true nature of protest in this period. The term Catholic Emancipation is a case in point. In the 1820s it could be considered the very embodiment of the principle of full civil equality. Yet it had come into use as part of a conscious campaign to induce in Protestants the same compassion which they felt for slaves. Catholics made a point of using the abolitionist emblem, a negro in fetters, to seal their letters.[111] It is not without significance that the principal counsel they initially employed was Francis Hargrave, who was also the forensic choice of the anti-slavers. Some Protestants, indeed, strongly objected to the implied comparison, since the miseries of plantation life hardly seemed on a par with those of genteel papists.[112] On the other hand it made plain that Catholics were not demanding complete civil equality, for abolitionists did not argue in favour of giving negroes a share in the political process.

A second distinction was no less important. It had to do with the enjoyment of privilege by usage, as opposed to legal right. It was not necessary for a usage to be immemorial or even very ancient, for Englishmen to consider it an adequate safeguard of their rights. When Dissenters were told by Lord North in 1779 that those of their number who could not conscientiously take the revised declaration required of them would not be

---

[109] T. W. Laqueur, *Religion and Respectability: Sunday Schools and Working Class Culture 1780–1850* (New Haven, Conn., 1976), p. 66.

[110] *The Works of the Right Honourable Edmund Burke*, iii. 305.

[111] See letters in Leicestershire RO, Turville Constable Maxwell MSS, e.g. C. Dormer to F. F. Turville, 21 May 1791.

[112] Castalia, Countess Granville, ed., *Lord Granville Leveson Gower (First Earl Granville) Private Correspondence 1781 to 1821* (2 vols., London, 1916), i. 293.

prosecuted, it was an assurance which they accepted, mindful as they were that so much of the legal battery directed against them in theory had in practice been largely unemployed for almost a century.[113] Again, this outlook came under pressure in the last years of the century. In an age of revolutionary declarations and constitutions, it was inevitable that the concept of guaranteed rights, clearly expressed and guarded by the law, would gain ground. But it did so only by degrees and left room for dispute. Those who debated whether the Test and Corporation Acts should be viewed as a system of 'national proscription' in the 1790s were in fact arguing about the proper basis for civil rights, rather than the force of the acts themselves.[114] In this as in many other ways the controversies of the late eighteenth century were not a reversion to old arguments about allegiance to the State but rather redefinitions of the nature of the State.

Perhaps nothing indicates more clearly changing attitudes towards allegiance than the vexed question of oaths. It was one of the boasts of Englishmen that when their government discriminated against some of its subjects it did so not because of what they were but because they would not publicly signify their loyalty by taking the prescribed oaths. The tolerance displayed towards worship outside the established Church, by law in the case of Protestant Dissenters, by connivance in the case of Roman Catholics, made this argument even more important. Strict construction of the Act of Uniformity would have required all Englishmen to be 'Anglicans'. But this was not seriously proposed in the eighteenth century, and the debate accordingly revolved around the question of civil obligations as regulated by subscription to the oaths of allegiance and abjuration. The Catholic Relief Acts of 1778 and 1791 made the status of these oaths a peculiarly sensitive question. Significantly the division of opinion which they revealed was not so much a division between Protestant and Catholic as a division between genteel Englishmen of both faiths and the more traditionally minded of their spiritual advisers.

It was a sensational case of property litigation, the Fenwick Case of 1770–2, which did as much as anything to focus attention on the injustice of the laws against Catholics. At issue was an attempt by the Protestant relative of a Roman Catholic heiress to deprive her of her land. The King's Bench decided against him, the Exchequer for him, Chancery and Parliament against him.[115] The effect was to reveal the irritation, even incredulity with which propertied opinion viewed the laws against papists. Catholics themselves were well aware of the change which had occurred in their favour in this respect. It was a change which had transformed polite

---

[113] M. Fitzpatrick, 'Toleration and Truth', *Enlightenment and Dissent*, 1 (1982), 9.

[114] *A Consolatory Letter to the Rev. John Clayton, from Fidelia* (London, 1791), p. 12.

[115] J. A. Lesourd, *Les Catholiques dans la societé anglaise 1765–1865* (Paris, 1978), pp. 226 ff.

attitudes while leaving largely unaffected the prejudice and hostility of popular opinion.[116] The causes were variously identified. The tolerance and enlightenment of an age of reason, the virtual disappearance of a threat to the Protestant Succession, the civilizing effect of the Grand Tour, all were given credit. Joseph Berington, who traced the process with approval, also thought Clement XIV had achieved wonders in this respect. Englishmen of the higher ranks, he observed, had 'dined with Cardinals, and perhaps conversed with the Pope; and had found him to be a good tempered, inoffensive man, without either horns or cloven feet'.[117]

Whatever the cause there seemed no reason to doubt the effect. Protestants and Catholics hastened to find a form of words which would permit the latter to share the legal protection, if not the civic rights, accorded the former. The oaths adopted in Ireland in 1778, and in England in 1778 and 1791, all denied the civil and temporal jurisdiction of Rome. They also repudiated the doctrine that the Pope could dispense Catholics from a secular oath of allegiance and the notion that papists need not keep faith with heretics. The third Catholic Committee of 1787, led by Lord Petre, went further. It suggested the formal adoption of a title for Roman Catholics, the 'Protesting Catholic Dissenters', which seemed to make papists indistinguishable for the purposes of the State from Protestant Nonconformists, and it asserted a decidedly Gallican view of the rights of Rome, specifically denying papal infallibility. The prolonged and acrimonious dispute which this celebrated Protestation commenced was almost exclusively conducted among Catholics.[118] The Catholic bishops had reluctantly endorsed the succession of oaths with which they were presented, but finally rebelled in 1789. At issue for them was the spiritual authority of the Pope, their own influence over their flock, their suspicion that papists who sought all the rights of Englishmen would end by losing their identity and their faith. Not least they were alarmed that good Catholics could treat any oath as if it were simply a matter of civil obligation.[119]

In the end, after a battle which left its scars on the Catholic community for many years, they secured a compromise based on the Irish oath of 1778. But in retrospect it is the order of battle rather than the ground fought over that is intriguing. Lord Petre found himself engaged on two fronts at once, against Samuel Horsley, the self-appointed defender of the established Church, and against his own bishops. 'So it is now Church against

---

[116] *Letter from the Right Honourable Lord Petre, to the Right Reverend Doctor Horsley, Bishop of St David's* (London, 1790), pp. 5–7.

[117] *The State and Behaviour of English Catholics, From the Reformation to the Year 1780* (London, 1780), p. 98.

[118] The best account is in E. Duffy, 'Ecclesiastical Democracy Detected', *Recusant History*, 10 (1969–70), 193–209, 309–31; 13 (1975–6), 123–48.

[119] M. Hasile and E. Bonney, *Life and Letters of John Lingard 1771–1851* (London, [1912]), ch. 3; *An Answer to the Bishop of Comona's Pastoral Letter* (London, 1790), pp. 23 ff.

State', observed a Catholic of this clash.[120] The ironic nature of this conflict was fully realized when, in 1791, the Catholic bishops successfully appealed to Horsley, as a fellow enthusiast for the spiritual power, to block the oath desired by the Catholic Committee and substitute that of 1778. Horsley was no friend of Catholic Emancipation. He likened advising the King of England to enfranchise papists to advising the King of France to enfranchise Protestants in 1787. In the French instance, he claimed, the consequence had been the Revolution.[121] But priestly rights were another matter. Many years later he explained that he had been defending 'the legitimate authority of the priesthood in the administration of what we churchmen call the power of the keys'.[122] Catholics themselves were divided on this point. The famous Protestation of 1789 had a significance for Petre and his friends which went beyond the immediate context. It was, they said, 'an explicit declaration of *their civil and social principles*'. Shortly after the passage of the act of 1791 they deposited the original manuscript in the British Museum where they were gratified to see it placed between Magna Carta and the Solemn League and Covenant. But some of those who had signed the Protestation demanded the erasure of their names, and the clerical critic of the Protestors, John Milner, even denied that the manuscript deposited was the authentic original.[123] This bizarre dispute pointed to a conflict of attitudes which transcended the bickering on the Catholic committee. In the vanguard of progress were propertied men of all faiths who regarded religious disputes as irrelevant to the secular priorities of their age and impediments to the spirit of improvement. Behind them they had left many of those who lacked property and not a few of their priests. The former could only dissent by violent means, as the Gordon Riots of 1780s and the Birmingham Riots of 1791 revealed. The latter kept up a resourceful and not uninfluential campaign with pen and pulpit. But in the last analysis it was the interests of the propertied community that dictated the pace and character of change.

Allegiance was a confusing subject. Political philosophers argued endlessly about the extent to which individuals were bound by the laws under which they lived. Assuming an essentially consensual relationship, what form did the contract take for men who did not have the opportunity of

---

[120] Durham RO, Salvin MSS, M. Tunstall to W. Salvin 21 Dec. 1789.

[121] *The Speeches in Parliament of Samuel Horsley*, p. 494.

[122] Hasile and Bonney, *Life and Letters of John Lingard 1771–1851*, pp.51–2, 376–8; *The Speeches in Parliament of Samuel Horsley*, p. 499.

[123] Duffy, 'Ecclesiastical Democracy Detected', p. 320; Petre, *The Ninth Lord Petre*, pp. 257–64. Thomas Weld was the principal layman who recanted; his correspondence with Charles Butler, as Secretary of the Committee, on this point is in Dorset RO, Weld MSS, R 8: June–July 1791. Weld did not deny that he had signed in good faith and full awareness of what he was doing, but claimed rather that his signature had been conditional on the document being retained by the Committee, as originally suggested by Pitt; depositing it in the British Museum violated this presumed condition.

joining in that mixture of historical fact and philosophical fiction, the original compact? The attainment of majority without signifying a desire to emigrate, and the acknowledged inheritance of property, were favourite answers. But crude contractarianism increasingly gave way to a different concept of the State as an expression of prescriptive practices and evolving interests. Allegiance itself became an uncertain matter, once the succession to the throne ceased to be an issue. Men who could not recall the bitter controversies on the subject of non-juring were more interested in what allegiance signified than the terms on which it might be secured. In this respect the famous oaths of allegiance and abjuration did not bear much examination. As was pointed out, fidelity to George III amounted to no more than recognition of his legal right to the Crown, something which only eccentric Jacobites were still disposed to challenge.[124] The earnestness with which George III himself persisted in interpreting his own equally unspecific coronation oath against the wishes of many of his subjects and most of his ministers further strengthened this sense that oaths were rather hindrances than helps to a rational doctrine of civil obedience.

Yet law and tradition dictated that loyalty to the State be expressed by a solemn, binding oath. The antiquity of the practice made it almost unthinkable to challenge its validity and utility. Oath-taking was part of the fabric of life at the level of local administration as well as in matters of national moment. Parish officers were on oath for the conscientious and impartial administration of their duties. In municipal corporations a range of oaths applied, to those who enjoyed the freedom of the borough, to those who served as councillors and aldermen, and to every kind of official who had a special function in it. The recording of such oaths was a duty not less important than the very preservation of the ancient charters which sustained them.[125] Swearing to obey the Crown and its agents was in this respect only an extension of swearing to observe the customs and obligations of one's own community. It was partly for this reason that false swearing was the gravest possible charge, albeit one which party political disputes during the era of dynastic conflict made all too common.[126] It also embodied a highly contractual view of political life. Membership of any community, from the parish to the nation, might be thought of in organic terms. But membership of a governing body was a matter of individual consent.

The difficulty occurred when swearing was used to defend particular

---

[124] Thomas Gisborne, *An Enquiry into the Duties of Men in the Higher and Middle Classes of Society in Great Britain, Resulting from Their Respective Stations, Professions, and Employments* (3rd edn., 2 vols., London, 1795), i. 93–6.

[125] See, for example, the elaborate procedures followed at Tewkesbury, Gloucestershire RO, TBR A 1/7.

[126] See e.g. I. M. Slocombe, 'A Bridgwater Riot, 1717', *Somerset Arch. and Nat. Hist. Soc. Proc.*, 106 (1961–2), 74–5.

views of what was politically right. The dynastic crisis of 1688 gave rise to endless debate and recrimination on the subject of oaths. For some of the disputants the concept of consent freely given and solemnly avow:d was not essentially at issue. Their worries about the oath of allegiance to William and Mary had to do with the meaning of what was sworn, not the principle of swearing. Non-jurors did not necessarily challenge the practice of requiring oaths, but the particular oaths which were required of them by a Revolutionary regime. The Association oath of 1696, especially in the form first proposed, clearly implying the hereditary right of William III, made matters worse in this respect. As the leading doubter, Sir Edward Seymour, put it, 'he thought it eno' for him to pay his allegiance, and not to specify upon what head it went'.[127] Even the Quakers, who kept up a long and ultimately successful campaign against the imposition of oaths, did not object to being bound in principle. The attestation which they were permitted to make in its stead was for them as binding as the oath accepted by their compatriots.

Against this there were those who denied the very legitimacy of political oath-taking as practised in England. The Association of 1696 began as voluntary subscription but was made compulsory for office-holders by Parliament. The result was bitter disagreement about the propriety of compulsion.[128] The fact that the authorities at local level had their own ways of making the association compulsory even for those who were not office-holders gave this controversy additional point.[129] Churchmen especially found themselves consulted as to the moral and spiritual implications of such oaths.[130] Subsequent succession crises focused further attention on this aspect of subscription and did much to bring State oaths into disrepute. From the Tory standpoint the oaths of allegiance and abjuration were simply weapons of proscription. Increasingly they came to object to the principle as well as the practice. It was said of Thomas Carew, the Somersetshire Tory who promoted the legislation of 1745 against cursing and swearing, that he would have gladly have prohibited all political as well as profane oaths.[131] On the Whig side the seeming readiness of many Jacobites to take oaths which were incompatible with their beliefs provided a useful debating point, but also eroded faith in such oaths.

Sheer repetition of these tests tended to lessen their force. It was an objection to successive oaths of allegiance that they implied the invalidity

---

[127] J. Garrett, *The Triumphs of Providence: The Assassination Plot, 1696* (Cambridge, 1980), p. 142.

[128] *Bishop Burnet's History of His Own Times*, ii. 170.

[129] D. Cressy, *Literacy and the Social Order: Reading and Writing in Tudor and Stuart England* (Cambridge, 1980), pp. 96–103; W. Gandy, ed., *Lancashire Association Oath Rolls AD 1696* (London, 1921).

[130] T. Newcome, ed., *The Life of John Sharp* (2 vols., London, 1825), i. 267.

[131] R. Sedgwick, *History of Parliament: House of Commons, 1715–54* (2 vols., London, 1970), i. 528.

of earlier pledges. Moreover, large-scale swearing of allegiance came to seem anachronistic. Perhaps it was necessary that it should appear ridiculous before it could be denounced as pernicious. On the whole the Revolution regime managed to maintain the gravity of the exercise, notwithstanding the large numbers of oath-takings involved. Even in rural Furness, for example, it took two teams of justices, with three books to each party, an entire day to get through the thousand and more sworn in February 1689.[132] In 1696 the exertions of the authorities were still greater, but it remained possible to be awed by the spectacle of large bodies of men declaring before God their loyalty to their prince. Subsequent attempts to repeat the exercise carried less conviction. In 1723 Walpole's design was to imitate the triumph of 1696. The nation would be seen to repudiate Atterbury in defence of George I as it had earlier repudiated Fenwick in defence of William III. But on this occasion the stimulus to subscribe was still stronger. The statute of 1723 gave the impression that failure to take the oath of allegiance would incur punitive taxation, though in fact it was the intention only to penalize Catholic estates.[133] In any event vast numbers appeared at quarter sessions to have their oath recorded, imposing a considerable burden on magistrates. The Trinity Sessions for Buckinghamshire were held by adjournment at twelve places and the Michaelmas Sessions at thirteen to cater for those presenting themselves.[134] In rural Devon some 27,000 signatures or marks were laboriously enrolled on membranes over a period of six months. In places the entire adult population of a village paraded before the justices, not only men as in 1696, but numerous women.[135]

The experience was chastening for Whig governors, and remained long in their memories. In 1736 the *Grubstreet Journal* recalled the extraordinary sight of people 'marching in troops with the same air and levity, that is generally observed in those who frequent publick shews' and used it to heighten the absurdity of what it called 'the farce of State oaths'.[136] Speaker Onslow had no doubt of the folly of this exercise.

I saw a great deal of it, and it was a strange as well as ridiculous sight to see people crouding to give a testimony of their allegiance to a government, and cursing it at the same time for giving them the trouble of so doing, and for the fright they were put into by it; and I am satisfied more real disaffection to the king and his family arose from it than from any thing which happened in that time.[137]

---

[132] Historical Manuscripts Commission, *Le Fleming MSS* (25), p. 267.

[133] 9 Geo. I, c. 18.

[134] Buckinghamshire RO, Quarter Sessions Minutes.

[135] Devon RO (Exeter), Quarter Sessions records, 17/2/1–7; Cressy, *Literacy and the Social Order*, p. 221.

[136] 8 July 1736

[137] William Coxe, *Memoirs of the Life and Administration of Sir Robert Walpole, Earl of Orford* (3 vols., London, 1798), ii. 555.

Significantly, 1723 was the last instance of its kind. In 1745 there was no attempt to fix the fidelity of the people by oath-taking *en masse*. In 1767, when the former Prime Minister George Grenville suggested a Test Act to ascertain and enforce the loyalty of colonial Americans, he proposed a declaration rather than an oath, and even so met with no encouragement.[138]

A sure sign that oath-taking was becoming difficult to defend was the ardour of time-serving Whig divines to defend it. On an unpromising subject, the martyrdom of Charles I, Francis Lockier ingeniously argued that the most horrifying feature of regicide was 'an irreligious Contempt for the sacred Bond of Oaths, and the making no Account of the horrid Crime of perjury', a contention which allowed him to link the murderers of a Stuart King with the Jacobite opponents of a Hanoverian monarch; 'there are many that pay too little Regard to their Oaths and Abjurations'.[139] Edward Littleton, a royal chaplain, preached on an awkward text: Matthew 5, 34–6: 'But I say unto you, Swear not at all.' Littleton insisted that common swearing was the target, not the employment of oaths for political purposes. He was manifestly embarrassed by Whig generosity to the Quakers: ' a thing, which though the Lenity of our own Government in particular, lest it should wound any tender Conscience, has been pleased to indulge to a wilful Set of People, who would not be content with it'.[140]

Scepticism about the solemnity which attended ordinary oath-taking was increasingly commonplace, though exceptions were urged on behalf of specific groups. In 1750 the Secretary at War, Henry Fox, claimed that army officers took oaths more seriously than civilians. Their concern with personal honour, rooted in the dependence which every fighting man must be able to place on his colleagues, gave them a vested interest in the sanctity of promises and undertakings. This assertion was made in defence of the oath of secrecy exacted from those empannelled on courts martial. But other MPs placed little reliance on the word of an officer and a gentleman when subjected to the blandishments or bullying of a commanding officer.[141] The contemporary assumption was that in dealing with most classes of men, not excluding the clergy, it was wise, when accepting an undertaking on oath, to insist also on a monetary bond or surety.

Perhaps nothing discredited oaths more than the profligacy with which the State required them for fiscal and police purposes. Not only did the incidence of oath-taking increase so as to deprive the process of its solemnity, but the fact that the purpose was the lowly one of enforcing taxation

---

[138] R. G. Simmons and P. D. G. Thomas, eds., *Proceedings and Debates of the British Parliaments Respecting North America 1754–1783* (New York, 1982–), ii. 476–7.

[139] *A Sermon Preach'd before the Honourable House of Commons, at St Margaret's, Westminster, on Monday, January 31, 1725* (London, 1726), pp. 24–5.

[140] *Sermons upon Several Practical Subjects* (2 vols., London, 1735), ii. 81.

[141] *London Magazine* (1751), 9–20: debate of 29 Jan. 1750.

or apprehending minor malefactors helped lessen the gravity of more serious undertakings. Yet there seemed no escape from this dilemma. Without a bureaucratic revolution government had little hope of collecting what Parliament decreed for its support. Self-assessment was widely employed for tax purposes and depended on the sanction of an oath. The fragile means available for enforcement of the law made any device which increased the individual's sense of obligation seem all the more desirable. Reluctance to organize a paid police force required an elaborate system of informers. It was on these grounds that judges and magistrates defended the multiplicity of oaths.[142] But popular dislike of excise officers and common informers was intense, and however necessary their activities, it could not seriously be supposed that they enhanced respect for the law.

One of the standard defences of a system of tests was that it applied only to higher duties and offices. This principle, distinguishing private activities into which the State did not intrude from public functions which it carefully regulated, was frequently defended, even by some Dissenters. But the use of oaths for purposes of ordinary taxation threatened its integrity. Quakers provide an early and striking example because it was they who were principally offended by the public oath at its simplest. Even Catholics could take the oath which was administered in law courts and by way of public testament. But Quakers could not, and when the occasions on which the oath had to be taken were multiplied for fiscal purposes after 1688 they were placed in peculiar difficulties. This was the plight of a well-known Quaker family, the Richardsons of Cleveland. As a tanner, William Richardson found the new leather excise a double burden; but its hurt to his conscience was still greater than its effect on his finances. The affirmation authorized by Parliament in 1696 helped very little since it still invoked the name of God. Repeated refusals to take the affirmation involved Richardson in the loss of a third of his property, until in 1702 the legislature approved a simple affirmation for such purposes.[143] For Quakers the bearing of oaths on their everyday conduct of business affairs mattered much more than their political implications.

Both customs and excise relied on sworn statements, though it was in many instances impossible to dispatch or receive goods without swearing to values of which the swearer could not realistically be expected to have personal knowledge. Some of the most stringent criticisms of oaths resulted. As William Stewardson put it in 1778, 'Custom-house oaths are extremely

---

[142] *The Second Charge of Sir Daniel Dolins, Kt. To the Grand Jury, and Other Juries of the County of Middlesex* (London, 1726), p. 23.

[143] *Records of a Quaker Family: The Richardsons of Cleveland* (London, 1889), p. 8. Even the amended affirmation provoked objections. In London, in 1713, they had to be quelled by the celebrated and long-suffering Quaker, George Whitehead; see E. Howard, *The Eliot Papers: No II. The Eliot Marriages* (Gloucester, 1897), p. 50.

remarkable, being the severest Satire and the greatest reflection upon the religion, honor, honesty, and integrity of the merchants, traders, etc. that the wit of man could possibly invent.'[144] It was, however, businessmen themselves who sometimes argued the merits of oath-taking. Duties laid at the point of sale rather than the point of production were much preferred. But whereas production could be assessed by the excise service, information as to sales depended on the word of the salesman. It was on these grounds that the crown glass manufacturers pleaded to have Henry Pelham's glass tax levied on the basis of sworn declarations. The alternative, paying a duty not much less than the cost of manufacture, on stock which was vulnerable to breakage, seemed particularly onerous.[145] No doubt in such instances there was also an unspoken desire to keep the excise officers out of business premises. There was also, in the war of interests which dominated so much of public life, an appreciation that the imposition of oaths could be a valuable weapon. During their prolonged campaign to control the supply of home-grown wool, the woollen manufacturers attached great importance to a compulsory oath by which a grower would certify the number of fleeces sold.[146] The use of the law to sustain commercial monopolies inevitably brought the practice of swearing into a wide range of business and professional activities. There was an obvious distinction between the contracts which enforced the promises of ordinary individuals to each other and the means by which the State secured obedience to its laws, and equally obvious moral objections to the latter when they affected so many aspects of life. One of the arguments urged in favour of free trade on Adam Smith's principles was that many souls would be saved by eliminating pernicious oaths.[147]

IGNORANT AND PROFANE SWEARERS

It was argued in 1762 that the State was much to blame for the process by which swearing had lost reverence 'among the vulgar of all ranks'. Oaths of loyalty were in their nature 'taken in a more publick, though not a more solemn manner, than any other sort of oaths'.[148] Nor was it unobserved that this, like many other undesirable features of life, resulted from the supremacy of Parliament. Common law made sparing use of oaths. The principle that an alleged offender should not be compelled to incriminate

---

[144] *A Serious Warning to Great Britain* (London, n.d.), p. 29.

[145] Northumberland RO, Ridley MSS, ZRI/25/4: 'Some Reasons Humbly offered'.

[146] *Observations on a Bill, for Explaining, Amending, and Reducing into One Act, the Several Laws Now in Being, for preventing the Exportation of Live Sheep, Wool, and Other Commodities* [1787], pp. 6–13.

[147] Gisborne, *An Enquiry into the Duties of Men in the Higher and Middle Classes of Society in Great Britain*, i. 158.

[148] *London Magazine* (1762), 67.

himself went with the allied principle that he should not be tempted to perjure himself. But the great mass of oaths imposed by Parliament in the eighteenth century applied precisely to men who had an interest in swearing falsely. Such encouragement to imperil one's immortal soul was surely itself a great sin and a disgrace in a Christian society. This was the basis of Thomas Alcock's personal campaign against oaths in 1754. In two successive assize sermons at Exeter he spelled out the spiritual implications of the multiplication of laws and oaths. One of his texts was 'An Oath for Confirmation is to them an End of all Strife'. In England, he argued, the reverse was the case. Oaths merely perpetuated strife. The State seemed capable of surviving only by imposing more of them. As a result the children of Hell were growing ever more numerous. The theological aspect was important. It was not improved by the argument that only the guilty would suffer. As Alcock pointed out, putting a guilty man on oath was inflicting on him a double damnation, the first for his crime, the second for his perjury.[149]

Worries about State oaths could be shared by all. In an age of deism, even atheism, the binding force of an oath in the face of God was debatable. The superior reliability of Protestantism came to seem doubtful. It was argued on behalf of Catholics that their unshaken piety made them more dependable.[150] Cynicism about spiritual guarantees went with a fashionable view of civil association which left little room for moral conviction. Charles Townshend, who rose to be Chancellor of the Exchequer and might have risen still higher but for his premature death in 1767, carried some characteristic attitudes of his generation to their logical conclusion. His concept of politics smacked of Hobbes and Hume. As one of his Norfolk friends observed, he 'professes, fearlessly, a contempt of all tie but that of interest'.[151] Townshend was considered irresponsible but principally for saying openly what others thought. Such views made nonsense of traditional notions of the State as a moral force, an expression of communal values. Men who were joined only by interest could not be governed by appealing to their better instincts and securing their promises. This view was not necessarily attractive to middle-class men and women unversed in Townshend's worldly ways, but it was held by many of his class who helped shape the political order of the mid-century. Politicians of this kind joked about principles which their forebears had taken with deadly seriousness.

---

[149] *The Law Not Made for a Righteous Man: An Assise Sermon Preached in the Cathedral-Church of St. Peter, Exon, on Tuesday, March 19, 1754* (Oxford, 1754); *The Nature and Obligation of Oaths: An Assise Sermon Preached in the Cathedral-Church of St. Peter, Exon, on Wednesday, Aug. 7, 1754* (Oxford, 1755).

[150] BL, Add. MS 9130, fo. 219: 'Considerations upon the most proper method of raising 100000 on the Estates of the English Roman Catholicks'.

[151] Hartshorne, ed., *Memoirs of a Royal Chaplain, 1729–1763*, p. 270.

One such was the former Jacobite and notoriously foul-mouthed Lord
Denbigh, responding to George III's enquiry as to his wife's fidelity to
the non-juring tradition: 'True, please your Majesty; but I swear enough
for myself and her Ladyship likewise.'[152]

Paradoxically, the work begun by cynicism could be carried on by moral
earnestness. The seriousness of mind associated with the evangelical revival
had striking effects on subscription and oath-taking. This was pre-eminently a question of generation, as the subscription controversy itself
revealed. The clergy who revolted against the Thirty-Nine Articles in the
1770s were not confronted with a new dilemma, but rather with one which
their predecessors had approached quite differently. Many latitudinarian
Whigs had had conscientious scruples about subscription, some to the
extent of refusing preferment in the Church rather than suppress them.
But most of them found means of suppressing their doubts, however
uneasily. The famous Samuel Clarke, and John Jackson, Hoadly's defender,
both accepted the mastership of Wigston's Hospital at Leicester, because
it had 'no Athanasian subscription, no Athanasian worship, no Athanasian
creed!'[153] They did not, however, think it necessary to renounce their
allegiance to the Church. A similar case was that of William Hopkins, a
friend of Henry Pelham and by him appointed to the Vicarage of Bolney
in Sussex in 1731. In due course Hopkins, an anti-Trinitarian, came to
regret the five subscriptions which he had made at various times to the
Thirty-Nine Articles, two at Oxford, two at London, one at Chichester.
Yet he did not resign his living, and contented himself with ensuring that
when he was given the post of Master of Cuckfold Grammar School in
1756 it was 'without any further condition than that of taking the oaths to
government'. His conscience he appeased by modifying the liturgical
formulae which he employed in his own church. To retain a living which
he had obtained by what he believed to be a blasphemous declaration was
dangerously close to living a lie. Towards the end of his life he admitted
that it was 'something very shocking to my soul'.[154]

The Unitarian successors of these men, though sympathetic, were unimpressed when they scrutinized their record. John Jortin, author of a
famous life of Erasmus, Vicar of Kensington, Prebendary of St Paul's, and
Archdeacon of London, plainly had not suffered for his principles. In his
posthumously published *Strictures on Articles, Subscriptions, Tests etc.* he
offered a lax interpretation of subscription to explain his adherence to a
code whose tenets he did not accept. When John Disney came to write
Jortin's life in 1792 he could not help pointing out that these arguments

---

[152] Jospeh Cradock, *Literary and Miscellaneous Memoirs* (4 vols., London, 1818), iv. 187.
[153] Francis Wrangham, *The Works of the Rev. Thomas Zouch* (2 vols., York, 1820), ii. 373.
[154] John Disney, *A Short Memoir of the Late William Hopkins* (Leeds, 1815), pp. 11, 20.

in defence of subscription were in reality arguments for its abolition. The most celebrated of the Unitarian defectors of the 1770s, Theophilus Lindsey, perhaps had similar feelings about William Chambers. Chambers accepted the Rectory of Thorpe Achurch in Northamptonshire from his relative the Earl of Exeter but refused promotion because it entailed further subscription. Lindsey could only console himself that Chambers had repudiated the notion that 'in public establishments of religion there is no harm in speculative insincerity'.[155] Not only the articles were at issue. John Hey calculated that to obtain legal enjoyment of an incumbency it was necessary to take a total of ten distinct oaths, 'which no converted man can possibly carry with an easy conscience, or tranquil mind'.[156] This tendency to insist on the utter solemnity of personal avowals, and the literal sense of words subscribed, was increasingly characteristic of the later eighteenth century. The 'candour' of the Rational Dissenters, and the 'feeling' of the sentimental school owed much to it. It was one of the strongest arguments against tests that they positively encouraged insincerity and infidelity. As William Godwin shrewdly pointed out, the French Revolutionaries were great enthusiasts for such tests. In 1791 they had promulgated an oath pledging allegiance to the Crown; a year later they substituted one requiring its repudiation.[157] If this was the moral consequence of binding political creeds, was it wise of loyalists to insist on them?

The Church's involvement in certain aspects of secular life made the less attractive features of the oath-taking process still more discomforting. The Test Act itself could be charged with prostituting the Holy Sacrament. In theory the clergy might refuse to administer it to unworthy supplicants. But civil officers who found themselves rejected and thereby forfeited their office, could sue for damages. A clergyman might not find it easy to prove to the satisfaction of a court what was likely to be a matter of common report and untriable evidence. This was not the only objection. Canon law forbade the admission of strangers to Holy Communion; yet the Test Act specified only that it be taken in 'some parish church' and many clergy found themselves providing what was more in the nature of a casual convenience than a sacred office. Such arguments naturally appealed to Whigs, like the turbulent Kentish priest John Lewis of Margate, who put them with great force to Archbishop Wake in 1716. They placed High Churchmen in the position of seemingly sacrificing their religion to their politics.[158]

---

[155] Memoirs of the Life and Writings of John Jortin, D.D. (London, 1792), p. 305; G. M. Ditchfield, 'The Revd. William Chambers, D.D. (c. 1724–1777)', Enlightenment and Dissent, 4 (1985), 10.
[156] The Important Question Still Under Consideration, But Approaching to a Decision (Bristol, 1801), pp. 38–9.
[157] William Godwin, Enquiry Concerning Political Justice ed. I. Kramnick (London, 1976), p. 585.
[158] J. Shirley, 'John Lewis of Margate', Archaeologiana Cantiana, 64 (1951), 46.

The procedure by which parish officers were held accountable for the discharge of their duties caused equal concern. Episcopal visitations exhibited the absurdity of this procedure with embarrassing clarity. In theory churchwardens might take their oaths in the awesome presence of their bishop. But as described by John Trusler, who aspired to be the literary Hogarth of his age, what happened was more in the nature of a tavern brawl. The bishop was pictured at dinner with his clergy in the upper chamber of a country inn; an open door gave him a nominal view of what was transacting; there the apparitor would be swearing parish officers, with the aid of a stick to keep them in order.

Conceive now, reader, eight or ten awkward farmers, within two or three steps of the landing-place, pushing forward their right hands to take hold of the book, some over the shoulder, others under the arms of those before them; and this oath-monger scarce able, with one hand, to support the weight of holy writ, pressed down by the unhallowed hands of ignorant and profane swearers, and to keep the king's peace with the other.—Conceive his bawling out,—'Mind, what you are about!'—'Come, swear away;'—'Is all well?'—with another, 'Take off your hat,— you clodpate, in the leather-jacket, or I'll knock it off,' and with a third, 'Hand over your presentments—Dy'e hear?'—and all this with such volubility of tongue and rapidity of utterance, that few could understand him.—Conceive, I say, all this, and you will have some idea of a visitation-oath, administered *before*, that is, in the presence of a *Right Reverend* Father in God, with all the *solemn* form of ecclesiastical law.—Can there be a wonder, that an oath so administered and so taken, is little, if ever, attended to?[159]

Many clergy were offended by the implied blasphemy and perjury of this procedure, which applied to offices held at one time or another by very large numbers. 'Almost every man above the rank of a day-labourer in every parish of the kingdom learns to consider the strongest sanction of truth as a nugatory form.'[160] It did not go without notice that one of the churchwarden's duties was to present parishioners who did not attend Church or a meeting house licensed under the Toleration Act. This complicated the clerical view of the oath. High Churchmen would have been glad to see the oath observed. Evangelical and Low Churchmen wanted it abolished. Stanhope was pressed to include its abolition in his bill of 1789, but its disappearance had to wait until 1835.[161]

Like so many sensitivities of the age, this uneasiness about oath-taking had much to do with class. Trusler highlighted the immorality of imposing numerous oaths by pointing out that gentlemen were increasingly reluctant

---

[159] *Memoirs of the Life of the Rev. Dr. Trusler* (Bath, 1806), pp. 139–40.

[160] Gisborne, *An Enquriy into the Duties of Men in the Higher and Middle Classes of Society in Great Britain*, i. 158.

[161] John Moir, *The Parish Church* (London, 1801), pp. 11–12; G. M. Dithfield, 'Lord Stanhope's Bill of 1789', *Jnl. Eccl. Hist.* 29 (1978), 71–2.

to swear, whereas their social inferiors seemed all too ready to do so. Courts of conscience, which, unlike other courts, were overwhelmingly concerned with the legal transactions of the lower class, were 'very cautious in administering oaths, knowing how ready the lower class of men are to take them, without thinking of the consequence'.[162] Stewardson, in his war on custom oaths, treated them as evidence of the cynicism of a ruling class which had good reason to assume the perfidy of those they had corrupted. The same assumption was incorporated in the house tax legislation of 1778. 'Multiplying oaths by authority is a most melancholy proof, that you, my lords and gentlemen, think the morals of the people extremely debased, so far that their words are not to be taken even for a few shillings!'[163] It was not, however, only people of substantial property who were prone to distinguish between their own and plebeian conduct in this way. In the Forty-Five the tradesmen who volunteered at Exeter declined to take the military oath exacted of their townsmen who had agreed to serve for cash, not on the grounds that an oath of martial loyalty was improper but because the purpose of the oath for enlisted men was to prevent them selling their uniforms and equipment.[164] Parliament took a similar view. As late as the Napoleonic Wars, by which time Evangelical unrest at the imposition of oaths was becoming chronic, the Local Militia Act compelled volunteers to swear that the money which enabled them to escape service in the ordinary militia was their own.[165]

Genteel hesitation doubtless signified a sense of the spiritual danger which attended false swearing, but it also reflected a realistic appraisal of the earthly consequences. A conviction for perjury was a serious matter. It seemed wise to avoid exposing gentlemen to the risks which it was assumed their inferiors, with less to lose, would take. When Lord North charged paper manufacturers with swearing to nominal values to cheat the excise, he was careful to insist that it was their servants who actually took the oath.[166] Local legislation which imposed a property qualification generally levied a simple monetary fine on false swearers rather than subject them to the Draconian penalties for perjury. But the legal implications were not the only consideration. The belief that there was something demeaning about oath-taking was strong, and strengthened by recurrent controversy about the peer's privilege of testifying on his honour rather than on oath. The place of oath-taking in outmoded or superstitious ceremonies enhanced this supposition that it belonged with the lowly and the ludicrous. The extreme case of a 'joke' of this kind was the famous

---

[162] *Memoirs of the Life of the Rev. Dr. Trusler*, p. 143.
[163] *A Serious Warning to Great Britain*, p. 30.
[164] *The Disbanded Volunteers Appeal to Their Fellow Citizens* (Exeter, 1746), p. 21.
[165] *Memoirs of the Life of Sir Samuel Romilly*, ii. 242.
[166] *Whitehall Evening-Post*, 20 Mar. 1781.

Highgate Oath, supposedly extracted from newcomers to London since time out of mind, and by the eighteenth century merely a public house prank.[167]

The peculiar corruptions of a parliamentary age had a bearing on these matters. The oaths intended to sustain the integrity of electors did nothing to preserve the purity of elections. Candidates and returning officers used them with gross cynicism. In an extreme case, the notorious Seaford election of 1790, they proved invaluable to a returning officer who wished to spin out the poll for a week. His object was to legalize the vote of twenty-six chalk diggers who had been smuggled on to the electoral register, and whose residence requirement wanted just seven days. By employing every oath which could be administered to an elector and subjecting each to legal cross-examination, he managed to slow the poll to four votes each day. A local reformer, James Russell of Rye, described the process with heavy sarcasm. 'The scene exhibited candidates speaking against time, counsel pleading against law, clergymen abjuring popery, and the immaculate electors of Seaford purging themselves of bribery and corruption.'[168]

In this respect as in others there was no evidence that MPs were any better than their electors. The Pension Bill of 1740 included a provision requiring oaths of those who received pensions from the Crown. But as Lord Hervey remarked, 'If we suppose a Man so abandoned to all Virtue and Honour, as to betray his Country for the Sake of a secret Bribe or his Pension, upon such a Man can we suppose, that an Oath will have any Effect?'[169] The procedures which Parliament imposed on itself were revealing in this respect. The MPs' land qualification, imposed in 1711, was initially the subject of an oath to be taken by candidates at the request of their opponents or electors. An amending act of 1760 was more stringent: it compelled MPs to swear to their qualification before the House of Commons. But the use of collusive transfers or rent charges to qualify men with no land of their own was commonplace, and the arguments used to defend them notoriously disingenuous. The acts had made offences punishable not under the severe Elizabethan perjury statute, but by common law proceedings; this technicality made it possible to deny that any perjury was involved. It was also said that the practice was so widely acknowledged that the oath must be treated as a mere form. But this seemed dangerously self-indulgent on the part of a legislature which expected higher standards of many of its constituents. 'We are now dealing with a system of morals abstruse, impalpable, and dangerous', observed

[167] J. H. Lloyd, *The History, Topography, and Antiquities of Highgate* (Highgate, 1888), pp. 373–87.

[168] J. Russell, *The Ancient Liberties and Privileges of the Cinque Ports and Ancient Towns: To Which is Prefixed an Original Sketch of Constitutional Rights* (London, 1809), p. 167.

[169] *London Magazine* (1741), 145.

one critic.[170] Significantly Curwen's Act of 1809, prohibiting the purchase
of parliamentary seats, passed only when a clause subjecting MPs to an
oath to this effect was struck out.[171]

Behind anxieties about oath-taking lay a new conception of the relationship between property and the State, though in one sense at least the new
was a development from the old, rather than a break with it. An argument
for oaths had always been that they belonged in a libertarian tradition.
Visiting foreigners were content to contrast the mildness of a system of
discrimination by oath with more rigorous forms of exclusiveness practised
elsewhere. Jews were not badged inhabitants of an official ghetto. Catholics
were not persecuted simply because they were Catholics. 'If the Papists
are not admitted into Parliament, it is not because there is any *Law* which
excludes them directly for being Papists; it is only because there are certain
Oaths to be taken which will by no means agree with the Conscience of an
honest Papist.'[172] This was a rather generous view of the laws against
popery, but it did reflect what Englishmen themselves had long believed,
that the protection of the State by oath and subscription minimized
interference with the rights of the individual and signified the voluntary
nature of his participation in its affairs. But by the standards being applied
as the century advanced it was not voluntary enough. Combination for the
purposes of the public good was a matter of individual choice. It could be
ventured and dissolved at will, and carried effect only in so far as it reflected
the weight and commitment of propertied society.

The answer was free association. What the solemn oath was to the
seventeenth century, the signed agreement was to the eighteenth. What
had once been an awesome undertaking in the presence of one's maker,
was now a pleasingly rational commitment to one's fellow beings. Subscription in the new sense implied a financial rather than a fiduciary
pledge. The old notion was not completely abandoned and in the
peculiar ideological stress of the 1790s, it suited both radicals and reactionaries to appeal once again to its authority. But in essence it had
given way to a novel doctrine, one which made the Associators of the
late eighteenth century very different from the Associators who had sworn
their allegiance to the Protestant Succession in 1696. Here again, as in so
many spheres of late Georgian life, was public commitment as a form of
propertied corporation. Even to those who had little or no property
this logic could be applied. The government which outlawed societies
bound by a secret oath in 1799 was the same which had in 1793 promoted

[170] *Remarks upon Certain Illusory Qualifications of Members of the House of Commons* (London, 1818),
p. 32.

[171] *Memoirs of the Life of Sir Samuel Romilly*, ii. 286–7.

[172] John Ozell, trans., *M. Misson's Memoirs and Observations in His Travels over England* (London,
1719), p. 205.

the formation of friendly clubs based on the principle of subscription.

Eventually, the approved concept of association came to be identified especially with reactionary causes.[173] Subscription was a crucial part of counter-revolution in the 1790s. It sustained activities as seemingly trivial as the public burning of Tom Paine's effigy and as important as military volunteering.[174] Dissenters even feared that 'the fashion of forming associations for enforcing the penal laws' against common thieves and felons might extend to the Test and Corporation Acts.[175] But it also applied in contexts which were politically less clear-cut, for instance in attitudes towards taxation. At one extreme was the notion that the State had the right, even the duty, to compel all to accept its tenets, if necessary by invading their property. Actual expropriation of Catholics and non-jurors was rarely attempted. But punitive taxation, which amounted to the same thing, was. It had been thought appropriate for a variety of malefactors in the 1660s, papists, Jews, aliens, and absentees from divine service.[176] The assumption was not seriously challenged after the Revolution of 1688 and in the form of the double land tax on papists it long continued, though it proved difficult to quantify. An attempt to assess the sums involved in 1788 produced the negligible figure of £2,289.[177] This was plainly an underestimate, but Catholics considered its formal abandonment in 1794 a victory of great symbolic significance. In truth its long duration merely reflected the inertia of fiscal policy where direct taxation was concerned. The last minister consciously to use taxation as a weapon of political discrimination was Walpole, who in this as in many other ways looked back to the past. An act of 1715 compelled registration of Catholic estates; there followed in 1723 the £100,000 tax on Catholics, the last attempt to use the fiscal powers of the State to enforce obedience to its creed. It was not liked even by Whigs, as the close divisions on it in the Commons reveal. Nor did it produce much revenue. By 1725 less than half the sum anticipated had been collected.[178] But Walpole's intention had not been to raise money, so much as to identify the enemies of the State. It was already an anachronistic concept.

[173] See E. C. Black, *The Association: British Extra-Parliamentary Organisation, 1769–1793* (Cambridge, Mass., 1963).

[174] Wiltshire RO, Maskelyne MSS, 1390/17: Powerstock parish subscription, 8 Feb. 1793; Sir C. Fortescue-Brickdale, 'Military Volunteers of the County of Somerset for Internal Defence, 1794', *Somerset Arch. and Nat. Hist. Soc. Proc.* 79 (1933), 95–100.

[175] *Monthly Repositary*, 17 (1822), 137.

[176] C. Robbins, ed., *The Diary of John Milward September 1666 to May 1668* (Cambridge, 1938), pp. 49–50, 62, 239.

[177] L. G. Wickham Legg, ed., *Tusmore Papers* (Oxon Rec. Soc. 20, 1939), p. 71.

[178] *Commons Journals*, xx. 63, 208, 431–2; M. Rowlands, 'Staffordshire Papists and the Levy of 1723', *Staffordshire Catholic History*, no. 2 (1962), 33–8; P. S. Fritz, *The English Ministers and Jacobitism between the Rebellions of 1715 and 1745* (Toronto, 1975), p. 175; P. Roebuck, *Yorkshire Baronets 1640–1760: Families, Estates and Fortunes* (Oxford, 1980), p. 184.

At the opposite extreme was a view of the State which made it merely the expression of the propertied will. Taxation on this basis was a regrettable necessity. Ideally it might be replaced by voluntary subscription. Subscription for purposes of public improvement was commonplace, and for purposes of political activity it gained increasing respectability. It was the favoured response to the Forty-Five. Association in 1745 was not so much a question of armed union as of donation to purchase the arms of others. It placed Jacobite Tories in a dilemma, since contributing would be perceived by their friends as collaboration, and withholding could be portrayed by their enemies as disloyalty. Their predicament was not as painful as the oath of association had made it in 1696, but scarcely less embarrassing. On the other hand, supporters of George II sacrificed very little by their gesture. The Jacobite emergency was short-lived, and those who put their hands in their pockets rather than draw their sword from its scabbard were not compelled to delve very deep. In some cases they were not even required to pay what they had promised. In later wars the test was sterner. It was faced first in America, not unnaturally since the American Revolution was a revolt by colonial property-holders on English propertied principles. American loyalists found subscription for the purposes of war deeply objectionable, in effect a form of compulsory self-taxation, exerted under threat of dire retribution at the hands of rebels. This was the complaint of Jonathan Boucher of Maryland.[179] But Boucher's English friends were not long in resorting to this practice, especially when the war against thirteen colonies turned into a war of survival against the Bourbon powers. It proved controversial. When the institution of a war fund was mooted at Norwich in 1778 there were public meetings and difficult debates. In neighbouring Suffolk, during another great crisis, in 1782, similar disagreement attended the county's offer of a ship of the line for the navy. There ensued a paper war between two well-known controversialists, Arthur Young and Capel Lofft.[180] During the Revolutionary War of the 1790s these disputes were revived in still more acute form.

The constitutional objection rested on the parallel with the ancient benevolences, which in practice had amounted to taxation without consent of Parliament. Opponents of subscription believed that there was a coercive element in what was presented as a free contribution. Against this it could be argued that subscribing to a war fund was like subscribing to the National Debt. In every war the alacrity with which government loans were taken up was watched even more closely than the process by which Parliament levied taxes to pay the interest on them. It was the crucial test

---

[179] A. Y. Zimmer, *Jonathan Boucher Loyalist in Exile* (Detroit, 1978), pp. 162–4.
[180] *The Windham Papers*, i. 18–20; *The Autobiography of Arthur Young*, pp. 101–2.

of propertied people's faith in their governors. At moments of exceptional crisis, for instance in 1782 and 1798, this seemingly slender, essentially psychological resource, was what sustained the nerve of ministers and the confidence of the ruling class, sometimes to the astonishment of experts. In February 1782 even the banker Thomas Coutts was startled by the readiness of lenders to come to the rescue: 'they begin to be almost frightened at the Treasury at the amount of the sums offered'.[181]

Opponents of government were naturally the first to express doubts about self-taxation by means of voluntary subscription. But its advantages to the executive were obvious. In 1794 Edmund Burke and Charles James Fox were embarrassed to be reminded that they had, when in office in 1782, contemplated similar measures.[182] Typically, it was Burke who offered the most sophisticated argument against them. Burke believed that self-taxation, in the eyes of many the means by which propertied people retained complete control of their property, was but 'one step to the subversion of all property'. The logic behind this was that property could only be preserved by the authority of the State, and in Burke's view the principle of self-taxation left the State without authority, perhaps without an existence. 'To recur to such aids is, for so much, to dissolve the community, and to return to a state of unconnected nature.'[183] This was begging a crucial question. Burke could not conceive of a community without a government, and in the last analysis he cared more about community than property. But there was another view, one with little sense of society beyond what constituted the interests of propertied individuals, which would cheerfully have reduced the State to the bare minimum required for the continuance of secure living. Volunteer troops in effect subscribed to it when they indignantly repudiated even the offer of equipment from the War Office. As the Dorset Rangers explained, when they turned down the Crown allowance for horses: 'the Government should never be at any expense on their account'.[184]

There was not, of course, much danger of the State being superseded. The money saved by Volunteering was soon spent on expanding the conventional armed forces. The Voluntary Contribution of 1798 was an impressive display of self-sacrifice, and yielded almost as much to the Exchequer as the assessed taxation which it was designed to supplement.[185] But voluntary contributors were concerned that they might be making a contribution which exceeded that of their neighbours, especially their

---

[181] E. H. Coleridge, *The Life of Thomas Coutts Banker* (2 vols., London, 1920), i. 143.

[182] *Whitehall Evening-Post*, 3 Apr. 1794.

[183] *The Works of the Right Honourable Edmund Burke*, v. 315–6.

[184] 'The Dorset Yeomanry', *Notes and Queries for Somerset and Dorset*, 20 (1930–2), 63.

[185] D. G. Vaisey, 'The Pledge of Patriotism: Staffordshire and the Voluntary Contribution, 1798', *Colls. Hist. Staffs.*, 4th ser. 6 (1970), 209–23.

neighbours of different political sentiments, and in any case patriotic ardour could not be sustained at this level for long.[186] The following year Pitt's income tax was introduced, and with it the prospect of bureaucratic expansion on a scale which was to transform the scope of the State's activities, in some respects threatening the very values that the war was supposedly fought to defend. But the readiness to contemplate radically different means of financing the common weal does reveal how far the propertied mind had travelled in the course of the eighteenth century. The Revolution of 1688 had permitted Parliament to claim a monopoly of the tax-levying power, and to use it in ways which imposed a single vision of the State and its interests on the community which it represented. A century later its function was to serve propertied people who considered that their interests and those of the community were identical. The transition from a society bound by allegiance to a corporation united by its capacity to pay was complete.

THE SPIRIT OF PARTY

Loyalties imposed by the State were one impediment to benevolent combination by propertied people. Not less obstructive was another kind of loyalty inherited from the strife-ridden seventeenth century. It was even more difficult to eradicate. Party was perceived as a characteristically English burden. Englishmen themselves kept telling each other that it was so and expected to hear the same from visiting foreigners. Le Blanc, the French echo of so many English commonplaces about life in England, duly obliged with his observation that 'in this country, the children in all conditions of life suck the spirit of party with their milk'.[187] Allegiance to party was the most controversial of all allegiances. There was a rich classical tradition on which those who emphasized its damaging effects could readily draw. There was also a more recent history of bitter party politics, that 'rage of party' denounced by Addison and Steele in the *Spectator*, which provided ample evidence of the dangers of faction in a parliamentary State.[188] The extent to which party could be reconciled with freedom and the maintenance of a constitutional government was one of the most hackneyed of all political questions. It was almost *de rigueur* for political theorists in the early eighteenth century and remained a favourite topic in those debating societies which mushroomed in the late eighteenth century,

---

[186] Castalia Countess Granville, ed., *Lord Granville Leveson Gower Private Correspondence*, i. 186: Lady Stafford to Granville Leveson Gower, 13 Dec. 1797.

[187] *Letters on the English and French Nations* (2 vols., London, 1747), i. 196.

[188] D. F. Bond, ed., *Spectator* (5 vols., Oxford, 1965), esp. i. 509–12; ii. 1–4.

and in which young men of slender means and boundless ambitions aped the oratory of legislators.[189]

It was easiest to condemn the spirit of party when it threatened the interests of property. David Hume believed that in this respect the danger had been kept at bay. 'Private property has been preserved inviolable, by keeping parties from the courts of judicature.'[190] But this optimism was not shared by everyone. The highest court in the land was, after all, a body dominated by political allegiance. In the House of Lords, where property disputes ultimately arrived if the contestants had the money and determination to carry their contention that far, it was not realistic to expect impartiality. In a much noticed case of 1718 a verdict against the Bishop of Durham was attributed to party spirit. The Bishop was the Tory Nathaniel Lord Crew, his opponent the Whig Sir Henry Lyddell. 'Sir Harry is zealous for the government, and the bishop, a good-for-naught fellow, and so they scarce had any difficulty or dispute.'[191] Perhaps it was as well that the episcopal bench was taken over by Whigs in the course of George I's reign. The Church would surely have fared far less well in property cases if its claims had been prosecuted by bishops out of favour with the Hanoverian regime.

The judicial bench also lost any remaining tincture of Toryism in the 1720s. Where there was any question of politics intruding, impartiality could hardly be expected. According to the Tory newspaper, *Fog's Weekly Journal*, in 1733, the extensive powers of Masters of Chancery were systematically used for party advantage. 'All Estates in Litigation in one or more neighbouring Counties are put into the Hands of Men recommended by the M———r who has a Design upon the Borough in the County, who serves the other M———rs upon the like Occasions.'[192] Modern accounts of the injustices perpetrated by the Georgian legal system, in stressing the impressive thoroughness with which it reinforced the defence of property against the unpropertied, have neglected the extent to which contemporary opinion worried about its abuse for more factious purposes. Particularly at local level, where Whig magistrates could be relied upon to outnumber Tories during the Walpole era, and where Whig sheriffs could ensure partisan juries in crucial cases, Tories were unlikely to have much confidence in the even-handedness of the law. At Ipswich in 1755 it was observed in a murder case that 'as this place produces such Jurys, and party Spirit runs near to madness, none is sure what they will not swear

---

[189] See e.g. G. Cannon, ed., *The Letters of Sir William Jones* (2 vols., Oxford, 1970), i. 345–6.

[190] E. C. Mossner, *The Life of David Hume* (London, 1954), p. 144. The attribution to Hume is Mossner's.

[191] 'Six North Country Diaries', *Surtees Society*, 118 (1910), 105: Diary of Rev. John Thomlinson, 16 Feb. 1718.

[192] 1 Sept. 1733.

to'.[193] Fears that the royal prerogative of pardon was used for electoral purposes were also common.

Genteel social life was dominated by party rivalries. Rural sports were frequently party affairs. Typical in this respect was the Old Charlton, a celebrated Sussex hunt which flourished from the late seventeenth to the early nineteenth century. In the 1720s its territory was invaded by the Duke of Somerset, whose Whiggism was, to say the least, distinctive and seemingly compatible with Sussex Toryism, even Jacobitism. The resulting 'Civill warr', commemorated in a poem entitled 'The Charlton Congress', ended with the hunt becoming a more conventionally Whiggish preserve. When the second Duke of Richmond gave it a constitution in 1738 the gentlemen whom he enrolled as members were Whigs to a man.[194] Even in an urban setting, the rule adopted by Ipswich's Monday Night Club when it was founded in 1725, requiring a common position both in religion and politics of all members, seemed prudent.[195]

Entertainments open to women were equally subject to regulation by party. Assembly subscription lists rarely survive, but where they do reveal their highly partisan nature. The Grantham assembly in 1737 featured the names of Whig magnates such as the Duke of Rutland and the Earl of Exeter, Whig MPs, and Whig townsfolk. Tories were systematically excluded. The most famous of all assembly rooms, that designed by Lord Burlington at York in 1731, had a subscription list in which Tories were permitted to appear. But it was dominated by Whigs, who at times of political excitement, for instance during the excise crisis, asserted their supremacy in balloting for directors.[196] At Manchester assemblies contributed to the strife of a town rent in two by the conflict of Whig and Tory, Hanoverian and Jacobite, High Church and Dissent. In 1746 'dancing down' the Hanoverian regime at weekly assemblies attracted more than local interest when it was attacked in print by a Whig pamphleteer. This form of subversion by 'the giddy girls' of Manchester was difficult to combat, and for that reason all the more attractive to proscribed families.[197] It reached its height in 1749 and 1750 when there was a series of clashes between army officers and the organizers of public balls. They are recorded, no doubt partially, in the diaries of John Byrom, who joined in dancing 'Down with the Rump' and 'Sir Watkin's Jig', named after the Jacobite Sir Watkin Williams Wynne. The resulting *brouhaha* brought from Byrom

[193] Lincolnshire Archives Office, Massingberd Mundy MSS, K. Tancred to Mrs Massingberd, 16 Feb. 1755.

[194] Earl of Marchmont, *Records of the Old Charlton Hunt* (London, 1910), pp. 5–6, 14–40.

[195] [James Ford], *The Suffolk Garland* (Ipswich, 1838), p. 182.

[196] Lincolnshire Archives Office, Monson 21/xii/13; York City Archives, Assembly Directors Minute-Book, 21 Oct. 1734.

[197] Edward Lewis, *Mercy and Judgment; Or, Intestine War But Soon Over: Cattle die; But Men Not Oblig'd to Eat Their Carcases* (London, 1747), pp. 19–35.

a facetious enquiry as to the desirability of a 'catalogue of decent and forbidden appellations', and also a warning that 'little unheeded ill treatments of the people are only forerunners of great ones'.[198]

Association for enlightened purposes was endangered in much the same manner as association for recreational purposes. The charity school movement waxed in an age of party struggle but waned all too quickly, in the view of some, because it had been fatally affected by it.[199] Philanthropic care for the poor was also vulnerable to abuse for party ends. Control of public trusts was jealously maintained, often with electoral advantage in view. The apprenticeship charity established in south Derbyshire by German Pole in 1685 was still, in the 1740s, managed exclusively by Tory gentry.[200] Countless local causes were kept in safe hands, as this was, by co-opting politically congenial trustees. It was not so much systematic skulduggery that was involved as the perpetuation of natural affinities. In the Pole case the trustees were bound by family and neighbourhood connections which went back decades if not centuries. But even beyond such local considerations there was a widespread belief that the spirit of party would vitiate the best of philanthropic intentions. It was the complaint of literary men that the project for a Royal Academy fell a sacrifice to the same petty cause. Oliver Goldsmith, who did so much to fix the label 'Augustan' on the reign of Queen Anne, had to admit that its noblest aspiration, to standardize the English language at the peak of its perfection, had been defeated by 'both *Whigs* and *Tories* being ambitious to stand at the head of so great a design'.[201]

In the circumstances of early Hanoverian rule it was inevitable that the campaign against party would be seen as in some degree the work of party men. It suited Whigs to forget their own origins and accuse their opponents of sedition. This was the burden of the sermon addressed by John Conybeare, the Whig Dean of Christ Church, in 1749, to the House of Commons, on the celebration of the Peace of Aix-la-Chapelle. He dismissed criticism of George II's ministers in terms which could have been employed as readily by Tory supporters of Stuart monarchs against their factious Whig enemies.[202] Other Whigs tried to have the best of both worlds by treating Tory appeals to a bipartisan spirit as a stratagem for their own advancement: 'This has always been the Tory method of getting into

---

[198] R. Parkinson, ed., *The Private Journal and Literary Remains of John Byrom: Vol. II. Part 2* (Chetham Soc. 44, 1857), pp. 509–14.

[199] K. Eustace, *Michael Rysbrack Sculptor 1694–1770* (Bristol, 1982), p. 70.

[200] W. G. Briggs, 'Records of an Apprenticeship Charity 1685–1753', *Derbys. Arch. Jnl.* 72 (1952), 43–61.

[201] *Collected Works of Oliver Goldsmith*, ed. A. Friedman (4 vols., London, 1766), i. 503.

[202] *True Patriotism: A Sermon Preach'd before the Honourable House of Commons, at St Margaret's Westminster, on Tuesday, April 25, 1749* (London, 1749), pp. 26–7 ff.

influence; to seem to wish for the extinction of parties.'[203] But the most consistent critics of party government could fairly claim to be moderate Tories, and in their pleadings it is not necessary to see a Machiavellian purpose. Thomas Randolph's sermon to the University of Oxford in January 1752, *Party Zeal Censured*, was not merely an Oxonian's diatribe against Whig proscription and corruption. It was delivered at a time of acute conflict at Oxford and was meant as a rebuke to Tory as well as Whig hotheads. Randolph was a conventional High Churchman, but there is no reason to doubt his sincerity in 'only desiring that nothing I shall say may be understood, as specially levell'd against any particular Party, Persons, or Measures, but in general against all *Divisions*, and *Party-Distinctions* whatsoever'.[204]

That parties had been nurtured by the power of Parliament was a truism which embarrassed Whigs but also worried Tories. Almost nobody saw party as the glory of the constitution; rather it was at best a regrettable necessity. The challenge was to purge the Revolution legacy of this least attractive of bequests. In the late eighteenth century, especially, local historians looked back with horror to the turmoil and bitterness which triennial elections and parliamentary supremacy had inflicted on their communities. Thus the antiquarian John Throsby grimly recorded the factious disputes which accompanied the accession of Queen Anne in his native Leicestershire. 'Every succeeding parliament, lamentable experience shews, imbitters the social consorts, between kindred, neighbours, and friends'.[205]

The flow of feeling against party was fed from various sources. An objection commonly raised at the height of party warfare under Queen Anne had been that the resources, both material and moral, devoted to politics were thereby diverted from more worthy purposes. As Gilbert Burnet, not known for his neutrality, put it in 1711, 'a Profuseness to support a Party may starve not only their Charities, but even their Families'.[206] Half a century later such doubts were reinforced by the sentimental vogue which presupposed the individual's instinctive sense of what was humane and right. Party loyalties were profoundly corrupting in this sense, for they undermined the natural virtues of the man of feeling, friendship, generosity, benevolence.[207] The point was a favourite one with

---

[203] Hartshorne, ed., *Memoirs of a Royal Chaplain, 1729–1763*, p. 334: E. Pyle to S. Kerrich, 25 Dec. 1760.

[204] *Sermon Preach'd before the University of Oxford, at St Mary's on Sunday, January 19, 1752* (Oxford, 1752), p. 5.

[205] *The Memoirs of the Town and County of Leicester* (6 vols., Leicester, 1777), v. 82.

[206] *A Sermon Preach'd at St Bride's before the Lord-Mayor and the Court of Aldermen: On Monday in Easter-Week, 1711* (London, 1711), p. 10.

[207] *The Causes of our Late Discontents: Their Consequences and Their Remedies* (London, [1782]), p. 37.

critics of Britain's part in the War of American Independence. In his passionate denunciation of the horrors of war, especially a civil war, the Dissenting preacher Joshua Toulmin appealed to readers 'whose humanity is not subdued by the sentiments of party'.[208] Parties were prone to corruption not necessarily more than individuals were, but more damagingly so, for they gave a specious legitimacy to interested views: Pope's 'Int'rest, that waves on Party-colour'd wings'.[209] There was also the mounting egalitarianism of the mid-eighteenth century, the tendency to condemn forms of political association which seemed merely to reflect the requirements of oligarchy. Whigs could contribute to this rhetoric as readily as Tories. Sneyd Davies put it into verse:

> Give *party* to the winds! It is a word,
> A phantom-sound, by which the cunning great
> Whistle to their dependants;—a decoy
> To gull th'unwary; where the master stands
> Encouraging his minions, his train'd bands,
> Fed, and caress'd, their species to betray.[210]

This attitude aided George III in his assault on faction in the 1760s. A king who declared war on party could be viewed as a champion of the patronized middle-class against their aristocratic patrons. But part of its wider appeal was its application in different contexts. Religious enthusiasts used it to distinguish faction from godliness, as their secular counterparts distinguished patriotic purity from partiality. 'I am no party-man', John Fletcher told Lady Huntingdon in the midst of the Calvinist controversy which shattered the cause of Methodist unity in 1770. 'But I cannot give up the honour of being connected with my old friends ... if a master is discarded for believing that Christ died for all: then prejudice reigns; charity is cruelly wounded; and party spirit shouts, prevails, and triumphs.' He meant, of course, that he supported Wesley against Lady Huntingdon. But in religion as in politics the superior claim was not to be of a different party, but to be of no party at all.[211]

One function of evangelical religion was to reinforce discipline and authority in a domestic setting. In his tract in favour of Sunday schools Jonas Hanway made a point of condemning party contests for their effect on the cause of virtue and religion, and more particularly for the way they weakened parental authority.[212] It was a common complaint against party

---

[208] *The American War Lamented* (London, 1776), p. 2.

[209] H. Davis, ed., *Pope's Poetical Works* (London, 1966), p. 579: *Dunciad*, iv. 538.

[210] G. Hardinge, *Biographical Memoirs of The Rev. Sneyd Davies* (London, [1816]), p. 37.

[211] A. C. H. Seymour, *The Life and Times of Selina, Countess of Huntingdon* (2 vols., London, 1839), ii. 238.

[212] *A Comprehensive View of Sunday Schools* (London, 1786), p. vii.

that it had percolated through all levels of society, carrying the distressing enmities of the polite classes to plebeians for whom it was a still more dangerous distraction. The antiquarian John Brand condemned the fidelity with which the common people of the north observed the traditional petty warfare of Royal Oak Day, the wearing of oak leaves on the one side, plane-tree leaves on the other, with the attendant reiteration of old taunts and slogans. 'Puerile and low as these Sarcasms may appear, yet they breathe strongly that *Party-Spirit*, which it is the Duty of every good Citizen and *real* Lover of his Country to endeavour to suppress.'[213]

Exorcizing the spirit of party was a high priority in mid-century, and synonymous with a new brand of patriotism on offer. George III, as a fervent advocate of its miraculous qualities, sold this elixir with conviction. His popularity had its origins in his youthful assault on party in the 1760s, and was renewed by his return to the charge in 1784. One controversialist of 1787 rightly insisted on his proven consistency in this respect, denying that it was, as Whigs displaced in 1784 believed, a 'casual fabrication'.[214] Chatham also benefited by the dislike of party, though in his case more cynically; the scourge of Jacobites and Tories was converted to the cant of men not measures in 1757 and made the slogan of his ill-fated but much fêted new ministry of 1766. Only the hardiest souls and most ingenious debaters dared challenge this new orthodoxy. Of these the outstanding example was Edmund Burke, whose *Thoughts on the Cause of the Present Discontents*, in 1770, offered a thoroughgoing justification of party. Burke's temerity was admired but did nothing in the short run to shift the prevailing horror of parties.

The collapse of party politics had as much to do with the social and business priorities of propertied life as with the swings of political and parliamentary fortune. It was a common maxim that politics and sociability went ill together. 'In what club or coffee-house is not politeness and complaisance forgotten or laid aside, in proportion as politics are upper-most?' asked John Moir.[215] One of the advantages of social recreation was precisely that it might be utilized as a weapon in the war on party. '*Faction*, and the Turbulence of Party Division, can have no Enemy more powerful, than Pleasure, and a Disposition to Amusements of Fancy, or Genius.'[216] At the time this plea was made, in Aaron Hill's *Prompter*, in 1735, this was an over-sanguine view, but at least it reflected faith in the solvent effect of pleasure on party. Thirty years later such notions did not seem optimistic at all. A puff for Tunbridge Wells in 1766 assured potential visitors that

---

[213] *Popular Observations on Antiquities* (Newcastle-upon-Tyne, 1777), p. 354.

[214] *Reply to a Short Review of the Political State of Great Britain, at the Commencement of the Year 1787* (3rd edn., London, 1787), p. 15.

[215] John Moir, *Gleanings; Or Fugitive Pieces* (London, 1777), i. 13.

[216] *Prompter*, 4 Apr. 1735.

'every species of party spirit is entirely stripped of those malignant qualities which render it so destructive of the peace of mankind. Here divines and philosophers, deists and christians, whigs and tories, scotch and english, debate without anger, dispute with politeness, and judge with candour.'[217] Part of the fame enjoyed by the celebrated Spalding Society sprang from its success in avoiding party politics, though it had been founded in 1710, when the rage of party was at its height. Its guiding light and first librarian, Maurice Johnson, had no doubt on this point. 'We deal in all the arts and sciences, and exclude nothing from our conversation but politics, which would throw all into confusion and disorder.[218] Politics were also taboo at the Society of Antiquaries to obviate the 'disputes and quarrels that would arise in a Society of gentlemen of all professions and opinions'. Even so, they broke out from time to time. William Stukeley could not resist accusing his rival Charles Parkin of 'party rage' when they publicly disputed the antiquity of an ancient cell at Royston in Hertfordshire.[219]

Book clubs, which proliferated in the 1770s, displayed a bipartisan spirit in the most unpromising circumstances. At Kibworth and Market Harborough, when a new society of about twenty members was founded in 1772 it seemed inevitable that its membership would have a uniform political complexion. The locality was traditionally Tory, and in the contested county election of 1775, when old Whig and Tory loyalties were revived, it displayed its usual colours. In Market Harborough all 77 votes cast went to the Tory candidate, John Peachy Hungerford; in Kibworth his Whig opponent William Pochin gained only four out of thirty-two. Hungerford himself was a subscriber to the club, and the great majority of his fellow subscribers, country gentlemen and local clergy, were naturally his supporters. Yet there was also room for Sir George Robinson, whose family were long-standing rivals of the Hungerfords, and for three other local Whigs who could see no incongruity in dining with their fellow book-lovers, while voting against them in elections. In fact Leicestershire Whiggism was better represented in what was effectively a social club, than it was among the local freeholders.[220]

Part of the case for the abolition of party was the stimulus which would thereby be given to commercial development. The 'Country party' alliances of George II's reign, which sought a fusion of Whigs and Tories in the cause of quelling Hanoverian corruption, gave prominence to this argument. In 1746, for example, much was made of the legislation designed to render

---

[217] T. Benge Burr, *A History of Tunbridge-Wells* (London, 1766), p. 127.

[218] E. M. Sympson, ed., *Memorials of Old Lincolnshire* (London, 1911), p. 325.

[219] J. Evans, *A History of The Society of Antiquaries* (Oxford, 1956), p. 79; Charles Parkin, *A Reply, to the Peavish, Weak, and Malevolent Objections, Brought by Dr Stukeley, in his Origines Roystonianae, No. 2* (Norwich, 1748).

[220] Leicestershire RO, DE 3077/1.

the smuggling of tea and foreign cambricks more difficult.

> Such zeal, how different from the party-rage,
> Which burns the vulgar spirits of our age!

The patriots credited with these triumphs were both opponents of government: Sir John Barnard, the sternly independent Whig MP for London, and Thomas Carew, the quixotic Tory MP for Minehead.[221] The British Fishery, founded in 1750, was a still more determined attempt to associate patriotic spirit with commercial enterprise. Its object was to challenge Dutch and French dominance of the herring fishery, by encouraging public subscriptions to a company enjoying a monopoly by statute. It was not uncontroversial: in the House of Lords a group of Whig peers strongly opposed it. But it eventually received a royal charter. Its Governor was the Prince of Wales, and its Council dominated by his friends. To this extent it looked like an opposition initiative, as once the New East India Company and Bank of England had looked like Whig instruments of economic power and the Old East India Company and the South Sea Company had had the appearance of Tory preserves. But the circumstances of the 1750s were not those of half a century earlier. The Pelham Ministry proved reluctant formally to oppose the Fishery scheme. Its non-partisan credentials were not seriously questioned.[222]

It seemed a fair assumption that commerce and party were mutually hostile. The assumption suited bourgeois views about the political decadence of landed society. Whether commerce swept party out of its path, or party retreated to permit the progress of commerce was uncertain. But that there was a strong correlation seemed undeniable. Manchester and Birmingham, the obvious examples of spectacular growth, both had a history of party factiousness, and both appeared to have lost it with the prosperity of the mid-eighteenth century. The daughter of the businessman William Hutton remarked that by the 1790s 'party spirit had been gradually declining for an age, and seemed totally annihilated in Birmingham, where trade had mingled all its votaries in one mass'.[223] Samuel Hibbert-Ware, historian of Manchester, noted a matching development: 'Party fury was subsiding before the reviving spirit of commercial industry, and wealth and prosperity appeared in the distant perspective.' He also observed the consequence for the Church. 'Commercial industry was revived, and a new era in the annals of Manchester commenced, the happy character of which

[221] J. Lockman, *To the Long-conceal'd First Promoters of the Cambrick and Tea-Bills: an Epistle* (London, 1746), p. 4.

[222] James Solas Dodd, *An Essay towards a Natural History of the Herring* (London, 1752), pp. 154–78.

[223] C. H. Beale, *Reminiscences of a Gentlewoman of the Last Century: Letters of Catherine Hutton* (Birmingham, 1891), p. 87.

was,—The diminished interest which the clergy took in the political affairs of the town. From this time, the annals of the Collegiate Church of Manchester cease in a great measure to be identified with political contest.'[224]

Conscious aid was supplied to this trend by the Society of Arts, founded in 1754. The avowed aim was to encourage British trade, manufacturers, and agriculture, by publicizing progressive methods and rewarding experimental ingenuity. Members expressed the hope that the Society would 'utterly extirpate all Party distinctions, the Bane of Society and Civil Government'. It seemed that a society which could bring together the High Tory Samuel Johnson and the republican Whig Thomas Hollis must hold considerable promise in this respect.[225] But the ultimate challenge for the enemies of party was sterner, to confront the foe where its influence was most complete, and most baneful, wherever public affairs were discussed. This was not primarily a question of ministerial and parliamentary politics. Rather it involved those numerous bodies which stood between the central political process and life in the localities. Here the role of party was more insidious: it corrupted not the doings of king and legislature but the will of the propertied community regulating its own affairs. The point was made with great force by William Gilpin in 1747, in a tract which he published at the age of 23, long before the tours which were to make his name famous. Gilpin's concern, expressed in the wake of the general election of 1747, was not with the effects of party rage on Parliament and government, but rather 'as it affects smaller societies'. He sketched the anti-social and immoral attitudes which went with it, the self-interest of cliques, the ruin of neighbourliness, the unchristian ambitions which it embodied. Its effects on the commonweal were deplorable. 'Public buildings are delayed, public roads neglected, and public offices kept undisposed of, because *a spiteful opposition*, rather than a *difference in opinion*, sways those who are leaders in the management of these affairs.'[226] Parochial and municipal government were notoriously so affected, and by the 1740s and 1750s new public bodies were springing up: voluntary associations, usually with charitable aims and supported by subscription, and statutory commissions, charged with specific projects of 'improvement'. How could these be made immune to the spirit which Gilpin identified? It was a question asked and a priority urged in many anodyne appeals for patriotic harmony.[227]

[224] *History of the Foundations in Manchester* (4 vols., Manchester, 1830–48), i. 145, 96.
[225] D. G. C. Allan, 'The Society of Arts and Government, 1754–1800', *Eighteenth-Century Studies*, 7 (1973–4), 445.
[226] *The Bad Consequences of Dissention and Party-rage Considered: a Sermon Preached at Buckingham on the 5th of July, 1747, the Sunday Following the Election* (London, 1747), pp. 15–16.
[227] Richard Green, *Conscientious Obedience to Governors Recommended: A Sermon Preached before the University of Oxford, on Tuesday June 22, 1756* (London, 1756), p. 20.

Propertied combination was meant to unite rather than divide. The rage for association and improvement coincided with a profound resentment against party politics. Voluntary bodies and their statutory collaborators had similar aims in this respect. Alured Clark, founder of Winchester Hospital and the guiding light in the early provincial hospital movement, rejoiced that 'every Denomination and Party' combined for this purpose.[228] Thomas Sharp, Archdeacon of Northumberland and son of a famous Archbishop of York, boasted at Newcastle in 1751 that the local infirmary had triumphed over party spirit: 'Neighbourly-kindness is of *no Party*'.[229] Charity schools had foundered in the 1720s precisely because they proved so vulnerable to party contentions. But their revival in the 1750s was credited with silencing the 'harsh Voice of Discord'.[230] The improvement commissions expressed the same spirit. In 1771 the Southampton commissioners received generous offers of donations from General Carnac, 'nabob', purchaser of estates in Hampshire, and an ambitious politician. There followed similar proposals from two other MPs. All were rejected.[231] It was in fact common practice for parliamentary candidates to fund public buildings or services, a form of corruption about which there was understandable ambivalence. Since individual electors did not benefit, such bribery seemed preferable to the more usual varieties of improper influence. For an improvement commission to repudiate it was to proclaim unusually high standards of public morality.

New institutions were increasingly supported by all parties. The clearest test case is perhaps that of the infirmaries, since many of them were established in the crucial period when party was visibly fading. Northampton, the model for many of its successors, was founded in 1743, a few years before a notably controversial county election contest in 1748. But there was no hint of party bias. Whig peers and Tory gentry were both prominent amongst the patrons of the hospital. Of subscribers at large who voted in the parliamentary poll, 62 per cent were Tories, but this was precisely the percentage of freeholders who voted Tory.[232] At Leicester Tory peers played a leading part, to the exclusion of the Whig Duke of Rutland, who refused to patronize the infirmary. But among the townsfolk of Leicester and the subscribers of the county Whigs were as prominent

---

[228] *A Sermon Preached in the Cathedral Church of Winchester, before the Governors of the County Hospital* (2nd edn., London, 1737), p. vii.

[229] *A Sermon Preached at St Nicholas's Church in Newcastle, before the Governors of the Infirmary, for the Counties of Durham, Newcastle, and Northumberland, on Thursday May 23, 1751* (Newcastle, [1751]), p. 23.

[230] William Sharp, *A Sermon Preach'd at the Parish-Church of St. Martin in the City of Oxford, on Sunday, Sept. 28. 1755* (Oxford, 1755), pp. 24–5.

[231] Southampton RO, SC/AP/1/1: 4 Feb. 1771.

[232] The subscribers for 1748 are listed with the published sermon on behalf of the charity in Bodleian Library, Gough Northampton 15 (7).

as Tories.[233] At Salisbury in 1766 bipartisanship was equally the order of the day.[234] The same applies to schools, whose governing bodies were all too frequently nominated by one party in the early eighteenth century, with electorally valuable patronage in view. By the reign of George III this was less commonly the case. At Rugby in 1777, at the height of the American War, the Speech Day held on 3 August was attended by trustees who included Lord Denbigh and Lord Craven. Each represented an old Warwickshire family which had produced a succession of royalists and Tories. But by the 1770s they were far apart: Denbigh was an uncompromising supporter of the court, Craven a no less committed member of the parliamentary opposition. They evidently had no difficulty in collaborating for the purpose of governing an important school.[235]

Public improvements were often hailed as triumphs of patriotic unity. At Stockton in 1764 the completion of a great new bridge over the Tees produced enthusiastic celebrations on this theme, with a suitably plebeian tinge.

> Fill then your jovial bumpers round
> Join chorus all in Stockton's glory
> Let us love our native town,
> A fig for patriot, whig, or tory;
> What'er they say, whate'er they do,
> Their aim is but to fleece the nation,
> Let us continue firm and true,
> To honest Stockton's commendation.[236]

In practice, continuing firm and true was not quite so easy. Even the voluntary bodies found it difficult to steer completely clear of party politics. Some of the most noted London charities of George II's reign had a Whiggish air. The London Hospital was patronized by the great Whig families, and was dominated by Whig officers and Whig subscribers.[237] The Foundling and the Magdalen were never narrowly partisan, but they certainly owed more to Whig than Tory patronage when they commenced operations. In the provinces it was also difficult to keep party loyalties under control. A visitor to Shropshire boasted in 1746 of 'the true *Salopian*

[233] Leicestershire RO, 13 D 54/13: list of subscribers, and pollbooks of 1768, for the town, and 1775 for the county.

[234] Wiltshire RO, J 8/100/1: list of benefactors and subscribers, compared with pollbook for county 1772.

[235] W. H. D. Rouse, *A History of Rugby School* (London, 1898), p. 119.

[236] *The Bishopric Garland; Or, Durham Minstrel* (Stockton, 1784), p. 13.

[237] See *A List of the Governors and Contributors to the London-Hospital, or Infirmary* printed with Matthias Mawson, *A Sermon Preached before His Grace Charles Duke of Richmond, Lenox, and Aubigny, President, and the Governors of the London Hospital, or Infirmary* (London, [1750]).

Character; ... not much corrupted or heated with Party Rage'.[238] Given the intensity of political strife in Shropshire, this was an unwise claim. When the celebrated theologian Job Orton became Secretary of the Shrewsbury Infirmary, the most that his friends could boast, for all his saintliness, was that he 'had the happy art of so conciliating matters, that the charity received no essential injury'.[239] This was in the latter part of George II's reign when Shropshire politics were particularly acrimonious, and a bitterly contested election of a new matron even attracted the notice of the national press.[240] But similar animosities affected public charities under his successor. At Shrewsbury itself, in 1777, the friends of concord found it necessary to reprint the sermon which William Adams, Master of Pembroke College, Oxford, had delivered in 1749 on behalf of the infirmary. 'It may reasonably be hoped that societies of charity will be less infected with this evil than any other', he had hopefully but not very convincingly declared.[241] Successive annual reports by the Governors of the Salop Infirmary stressed the need for harmony. A conventional line was that the anniversary meetings held in church were particularly helpful in this respect, as they tended to 'soften those asperities, which Clashing Interests, or jarring Opinions, are apt to excite'.[242]

Shrewsbury was by no means unique. At York William Mason feared that in elections at the York Lunatic Asylum 'the ideas of Whig and Tory, or some similar Party distinctions at the time, may operate more on the minds of the electors with respect to the qualifications of the several candidates than medical skill and antimaniacal science'.[243] At Liverpool it proved impossible to protect the infirmary against the malign influence of parliamentary elections. In 1761 it was claimed that voters had been threatened with exclusion from the benefits of both the Blue-Coat Charity School and the Infirmary. On the other hand the political capital made out of such charges and counter-charges at least revealed a strong belief that charity should be immunized against political infections.[244]

Statutory bodies faced similar difficulties. In theory they were well placed to overcome traditional rivalries. They were not covered by the Test and Corporation Acts, a consideration which permitted them to appeal to Dissenting interests excluded from a share in many corporations. Without an open door of this kind, there was little prospect of a successful application

---

[238] *A Journey to Llandrindod Wells, in Radnorshire* (2nd edn., London, 1746), p. 13.
[239] *Letters to a Young Clergyman, from the Late Reverend Mr Job Orton* (2nd edn., 2 vols., Shrewsbury, 1800), i. 147.
[240] *London Magazine* (1759), 728.
[241] William Adams, *Perseverance in Well-Doing* (2nd edn., Shrewsbury, 1777), p. 26.
[242] Shropshire RO, 3909/6/2: report for 1791.
[243] William Mason, *Animadversions on the Present Government of the York Lunatic Asylum* (York, n.d.) p. 34.
[244] *An Entire and Impartial Collection of All the Papers, etc.*, p. 119.

to Parliament, as the breakdown of Manchester's workhouse scheme had demonstrated in 1731.[245] No doubt this was why Leicester, dominated by a High Church corporation, and torn by sectarian disputes, made such little progress in this respect. On the other hand the establishment of a commission did not invariably resolve these difficulties. At Coventry the improvement commission set up in 1790 was accused of biases matching those of the Dissenting corporation.[246]

It was not only in parliamentary boroughs that such problems existed. Turnpike trusts, many of which were founded at a time, in the 1730s and 1740s, when party strife was still intense, were affected by it in much the same way as the magistracy in county and corporation. Accusations such as that made by Lord Strafford in Northamptonshire in 1739, to the effect that a local turnpike had been 'only a Job ... to Oblige Old Sergeant Hanbury, whom they had a mind to set up as Knight of the Shire', were commonplace in an age when a Whig majority in the Commons could be employed for strictly party purposes.[247] After the middle of the century Parliament was less obliging in this respect. Even so, the tainted inheritance of party politics was difficult to discard altogether. It was observed by an agricultural reporter in Herefordshire in 1794 that the local turnpike trusts had become hopelessly enmeshed in electoral politics.[248] In such cases the very diversity of local practice made for difficulties. In 1749 it was argued by way of objection to a court of conscience in Southwark that it would be peculiarly liable to electoral malpractice, compared with its established rivals in the capital itself. 'The Power of the Court of Conscience also in London is not so likely to be made an Ill use of to influence Elections as in Southwark because the Right of Electing members in London is in the Liverymen and not in the poorer Sort of freemen who are the most frequent Objects of the Jurisdiction, whereas in Southwark the lowest house keepers paying Scot and Lot who will probably be the Objects of this Jurisdiction and Suitors there are likewise Electors of Members of Parliament.'[249]

OUR SOCIAL HAPPINESS

For all the residual power of party, it was becoming difficult, by the 1760s, to comprehend the venom of the old disputes. When the playwright Isaac Bickerstaffe revived Colley Cibber's Non-Juror in 1768 he renamed it *The Hypocrite* and made its target a religious enthusiast rather than a Jacobite

---

[245] J. E. Bailey, *John Byrom's Journal, Letters, etc. 1730–31* (Manchester, 1882), pp. 3–4.
[246] William Reader's 'Chronicle', 896–7 ff.
[247] Northamptonshire RO, Isham MSS, IC 2999: Strafford to Sir Edmund Isham, 9 Mar. 1739.
[248] J. Clark, *General View of the Agriculture of the County of Hereford* (London, 1794), p. 53.
[249] BL, Add. MS 35390, f. 297.

traitor, such was the unsuitability of party propaganda for the stage. There was a growing tendency to want to compartmentalize politics, to separate it off from every other area of life. Garrick inadvertently fell foul of this with his production of *The Clandestine Marriage* at Drury Lane in 1766. The play included a reference to 'Anti-Sejanus', whose diatribes against the Rockingham Ministry were enlivening the newspaper columns of the day. It was common knowledge that they were the work of the clergyman James Scott, who happened to be in the theatre during one performance and thereby occasioned something of a stir when his work was referred to. Garrick feared that such personalities would make the play unpopular with audiences which no longer relished such differences. His friend Joseph Cradock judiciously observed: 'The passage itself should have been omitted. The politics of the day are not properly adapted either to the Pulpit or the Stage.'[250] In the press during the 1760s there was a conscious campaign against the 'unsocial rage' inspired by politics.[251]

Much pride was taken in the taming of party. Pleas for the extension of religious toleration in the 1760s were supported with the claim that 'the violence of party spirit is happily abated'.[252] It was believed that political disagreement had been reduced to the absolute minimum. The storms of an earlier age could be seen in context and the crucial changes of sentiment could be understood for what they were. This was the perspective of the *Encyclopaedia Britannica*.[253] So it was too of the enlightened Bishop of St Asaph, Jonathan Shipley, who told the House of Lords in 1776: 'The dissentions in state have not been kindled for many years by the fury of national parties, but by that ambition and struggle for power, which will ever be inseparable from human nature.'[254] Coming as it did from an opposition politician this claim carried some weight. Shipley's friends in the Rockingham party treated their own differences with the court of George III as a continuation of the historic struggle of Whig and Tory. But Shipley was too clear-sighted and too honest to accept this interpretation. He was not the only bishop so candid, though his colleague Richard Watson put the point more pejoratively. 'There was neither *Whiggism* nor *Toryism* left; excess of riches, and excess of taxes, combined with excess of luxury, had introduced universal *Selfism*.'[255] From this unconventional

---

[250] Cradock, *Literary and Miscellaneous Memoirs*, i. 202.

[251] G. W. Stone, ed., *The London Stage*, Part IV: 1747–1776 (3 vols., Carbondale, Ill., 1962), ii. 1000.

[252] *Considerations on the Penal Laws against Roman Catholics in England, and the New Acquired Colonies in America* (London, 1764), p. 29.

[253] (2nd edn., 10 vols., Edinburgh, 1778–83), ii, *sub* 'Britain', the account of George II's accession.

[254] *A Sermon Preached before the House of Lords, in the Abbey Church of St. Peter, Westminster, on Tuesday, January 30, 1770* (London, 1770), p. 12.

[255] *Anecdotes of the Life of Richard Watson*, p. 194.

standpoint the triumph of commerce over party had been almost too successful.

On the other hand, the terms Whig and Tory continued in common use, though mainly on the tongues of self-proclaimed Whigs and opponents of George III. In the early years of his reign the King was accused of hoisting the banner of Toryism. But considering the number of Pelhamite Whigs who marched beneath this banner it was an unconvincing claim. Later, the onset of the American War made it seem more plausible.[256] Americans themselves used the terms without apology and even in Britain the presentation of the war as an issue of principle seemed at last to provide something like a hard demarcation. But the principle was not always very clear. Some use was made of a rather watered down theory of divine right against America. But it was heavily overladen by Whig assumptions about parliamentary sovereignty, and it was as much on the lips of men with Whig family backgrounds as Tory. What it meant to be a Tory was not certain. The Earl of Abingdon, himself the son of a Tory peer, simplified the task by identifying Toryism with tyranny. 'Tories follow *arbitrary Power*, as *Crows* do *Carrion*, wherever it is to be met with; and are driven in search of it, by the same *blind impulse*, that drives a *Newfoundland Dog* into the Water, after a Stone that he cannot reach.'[257] It was not necessary to be a dyed in the wool Tory of the old school to resent this charge. One of Abingdon's enemies was the Marquis of Granby, heir to a famous Whig family, the Rutlands, and successively a follower of Newcastle and Chatham. But in 1775 he was a supporter of Lord North. 'Though I have found a Tory connexion, Whig principles are too firmly rivetted in me ever to be removed.'[258] What Granby meant by this was that he had no desire to alienate those, particularly in the electoral warfare of the East Midlands, for whom the ancient Whig battle-cry retained its power. In 1775 his father and friends were pressing the Duke of Rutland's claim to one of the county seats for Leicestershire. Rutland rhetoric relied heavily on the old, tired slogans of Queen Anne's reign. On the other hand, among the men with whom Granby voted in the Commons there were representatives of old Tory families. From Granby's standpoint North's ministry had Tory men, but not Tory measures. From Abingdon's it included many old Whig men, but its measures were unquestionably Tory. The truth, of course, was that neither in point of men nor measures was it easy to identify a coherent tendency one way or the other.

Complicated explanations like Granby's and simplistic generalizations like Abingdon's became common responses to the confusion of the 1770s.

---

[256] *The History of the Second Ten Years of the Reign of George the Third* (London, 1782), p. 242.
[257] *Thoughts on the Letter of Edmund Burke, Esq.* (6th edn., Oxford, 1777), p. lii.
[258] *Anecdotes of the Life of Richard Watson*, p. 49.

Some of them would have startled Lord Macaulay. It was claimed in 1781 that 'Tories, or those who are called such, but who ought more properly to be called the children of Tories, are now professed friends to liberty and the constitution'.[259] For Sir Willoughby Aston at Nottingham in 1784 it was said that 'his father firmly stood upon the Tory interest, but the present Sir Willoughby is of Mr Fox's party'.[260] Explaining his own position against that of his two rival candidates before the parliamentary election for Oxford University in 1780 William Jones found himself in some difficulty. There were two professed Whigs, Jones himself and William Scott, against a candidate who repudiated party, Sir William Dolben. The last Jones described as a 'Tory from family-prejudice'. Scott, he decided, was a Tory 'from principle and erroneous reasoning'. 'I am certainly the only Whig candidate.'[261] Friends of government, including Dolben, dismissed language such as Jones's as mere opposition rhetoric. Certainly it was difficult to see that Toryism in the 1770s was much more than a shorthand for describing supporters of Lord North, whatever their beliefs and connections. Opposition propaganda was confronted with real problems in this respect. *Remarks on the Members of the House of Commons* in 1780, which set out to analyse the political loyalty of MPs found itself attributing 'Tory prerogative principles' to an MP like Sir Henry Hoghton, one of very few Presbyterians in the Commons, on the grounds that he supported North, and admitting that John Tempest, a prominent supporter of opposition, was of a 'Tory family', but not of 'Tory principles'. An alternative distinction was that vouchsafed by another opposition pamphleteer, between 'speculative' and 'practical' Whiggism.[262] The truth was that by this time the most profound state of confusion existed as to the meaning of the old party terminology, reinforcing the belief of many that its justification had vanished. The most honest conclusion was that of an earlier analysis of the state of the parties in the Commons, the *Characters* of 1777; it was that except on the question of America the 'creed of the *Modern Tories* and *modern Whigs* seem only to differ in name'.[263]

Even among the committed there was a tendency to want to preserve the essence of Whig and Tory strife, but within a controlled framework, which would exclude extremists. Henry Goodricke made a passionate plea for this position in 1778. Whiggism and Toryism, he insisted, was 'not an heirloom that descends with a name or an estate, and it is an insult to a man's understanding and heart to seek for his political principles in his

---

[259] *Candid Thoughts; Or, an Enquiry into the Causes of National Discontents and Misfortunes since the Commencement of the Present Reign* (London, 1781), p. 14.
[260] Lincolnshire Archives Office, 2 PG 12/14/20: G. Gregory to W. G. Williams, 29 Mar. 1784.
[261] Cannon, ed., *The Letters of Sir William Jones*, i. 377.
[262] *Thoughts on the Present County Petitions* (1780), p. 26.
[263] (London, 1777), p. 20.

family pedigree. But I hope to God the *real Tories* and *Republican Whigs*, those two extremes that always generate each other, may never hold up their heads again in this country.'[264] Goodricke's desire to demonstrate the absurdity of party as an heirloom was shared by many. When the Duke of Richmond reminded the Earl of Rochford in 1772 that Whigs had an inherited duty to take the part of Dissent, Rochford was unimpressed. 'I answered him as descended from the Nassaus, I cou'd not agree with a Descendant of the Stuarts.'[265]

The American War did not establish a lasting structure capable of supporting a revived Augustan concept of party. On the contrary, Fox's coalition with North, and the rallying of Shelburne and the younger Pitt to the court of George III, plunged all into utter confusion. Again it was only the vested interest of a small group of self-proclaimed Whigs which sustained the language of party. Some of these Foxite Whigs looked very odd indeed in point of consistency. North himself was the son of a Tory converted to the cause of Hanoverian Whiggism; Sir Gilbert Elliot was son of a Whig friend of the Earl of Bute. Ironically, during this period families with an ambivalent record were all the more anxious to prove their consistent party credentials, even in matters which might have been thought remote from the concerns of George III's reign. The archives of the Orford and Townshend families were made available to the historian of Queen Anne's reign, Thomas Somerville, only on condition that he would use them to justify Whig rejection of the peace terms of 1707, an offer which he refused.[266]

In the 1790s it seemed that the deep divisions of a revolutionary era reintroduced party with a vengeance. The process was uncomfortable for those who had come to believe that party could be kept under control. When the Whig party itself split in 1793 it was the social consequences, unprecedented in many years, which caused the greatest sensation. William Windham noted that the secession from the Whig Club seemed to have caused more complaint than any difference in voting or speaking.[267] For their part loyalists were particularly anxious to appropriate the moral superiority which went with the denial of party spirit. 'May our political opinions never destroy our social happiness' was the characteristic toast of the Church and King Club of Yarmouth in June 1792.[268] Anyone who advanced the doctrine that parties were the bane of all government was likely to be treated as a 'Tory' by radical Dissenters.[269] It is doubtful

[264] *A Speech on Some Political Topics* (London, 1779). p. 6.
[265] Warwickshire RO, Denbigh MSS, Letter-Book, 334, Rochford to Denbigh, 12 May 1772.
[266] Thomas Somerville, *My Own Life and Times 1741–1814* (Edinburgh, 1861), p. 290.
[267] *The Windham Papers*, i. 120.
[268] *Ipswich Journal*, 9 June 1792.
[269] Robert Bage, *Man As He is* (2nd edn., 4 vols., London, 1796), i. 230.

whether loyalists fully appreciated the implications of their creed in this respect, though a few of them acknowledged that social happiness might involve unpalatable politics. William Wilberforce saw in parliamentary reform the advantage that it would make possible the final disappearance of party connections.[270] The antiquarian and clergyman Thomas Wilson, who carried his conservatism to the extent of unreservedly supporting slavery, found electoral life in the parliamentary borough of Clitheroe personally distressing and professionally embarrassing.[271] But for the most part, the party of the 'Establishment' was not much concerned with the social happiness of those it identified as enemies of the community's harmony. In this there was the same kind of hypocrisy which had characterized early Hanoverian Whiggism. Jacobins like Jacobites could be condemned as subversives. But there was one crucial difference. Whigs of the Walpole era never renounced their Whiggism, nor their faith in the Whig party. A hundred years of civil strife and party politics had gone into their political creed, and they were slow to forget their heritage, however absent-minded they might be in applying it consistently. Loyalism in the 1790s drew on a contrary tradition, one which had strengthened steadily since the 1740s. It was precisely its claim to have vanquished party.

Whigs naturally deplored the tendency to foreswear party in the cause of patriotism for with it went their own *raison d'être*. Burke gave up a promising career to defend it. Fox sustained it at the cost of a disastrous coalition. Coke carried the old cause into a new age and was still boasting, in 1810, that 'From Party this country had derived the glorious Revolution; and from Party, founded on pure principles, he had no doubt that it would receive important future advantages'.[272] But the terms on which party was defended were increasingly confined. It was no longer the necessary means of achieving a patriotic goal, which could be discarded once the objective had been attained. Rather it was a perpetual alternative, making possible a healthy diversity of views. It permitted friends to debate and differ on matters which might otherwise detach and divide them. It had a crucial potential 'to moderate both sides, and lessen that bitter acrimony, that prejudic'd violence, which does so much harm'.[273] This, said by the unreservedly Whiggish Lady Bessborough at the height of the revolutionary controversy of 1794, was coming close indeed to the modern concept of party. It was worlds away from the old fear that party rent the social fabric rather than held it together. But it was not the consequence of the intrinsic

---

[270] R. Coupland, *William Wilberforce: A Narrative* (Oxford, 1923), p. 16.

[271] F. R. Raines, ed., *Miscellanies: Being a Selection from the Poems and Correspondence of the Rev. Thomas Wilson* (Chetham Soc. 45, 1857), p. xxvii.

[272] A. M. W. Stirling, *Coke of Norfolk and His Friends* (2 vols., London, 1907), ii. 90.

[273] Castalia Countess Granville, ed., *Lord Granville Leveson Gower Private Correspondence*, i. 102: Lady Bessborough to Granville Leveson Gower, probably Nov. 1794.

genius of the British constitution, nor the creation of great political thinkers
or philosophers, nor the result of a reformed Parliament learning to cope
with a mass electorate. It was the working out of the process which had
begun in the mid-eighteenth century, the reconciliation of dangerously
opposed forces. It reflected the need to prevent political differences shattering the social and commercial imperatives of a propertied class coping
with improvement, inflation, and industrialization.

If the revival of party had to be accepted, it was in company with an
underlying harmony, which was expected to prevail even in narrowly
electoral politics. The most violent contests had to be prevented from
embittering polite life. At Carlisle in 1769, during the notorious conflict
between the Duke of Portland and Sir James Lowther, the most uninhibited
of its kind in the early years of George III's reign, the traveller William
Hervey was shocked to find party running so high that 'they scarcely visit
each other'.[274] An earlier generation would have been surprised to find
social visits proceeding at all under such circumstances. Activities which
could not be kept free of party politics had to be restricted. Nottingham
waited a long time for its first public subscription library, in part beause
its political feuds were so bitter. When one was finally established in 1815,
the patronage of a Whig MP and Tory Lord Lieutenant were bestowed
only on the understanding that 'it will be in no way political'.[275]

Electoral rhetoric naturally reflected the requirements of an at best
reluctantly partisan public. At the Surrey election of 1780 the defeated
candidate Thomas Onslow publicly stated, 'now, that the contest was at
an end, he hoped also that party and political distinctions would cease,
and that they would live again, as formerly, in good neighbourhood and
friendship'.[276] Onslow represented the leading landed family of Surrey,
county MPs for generations back. He had been humiliated by the alliance
of a radical populist, Sir Joseph Mawbey, and a popular admiral, Augustus
Keppel. His real feelings are unlikely to have been so eirenic. But the
public required such platitudes if only because they veiled more substantial
priorities, those dictated by material interest. MPs went to great lengths
to emphasize their impartiality, especially where their own community was
concerned. Such was the conduct of Charles Anderson Pelham in 1807.
Pelham was a supporter of the Ministry of the Talents, who had the
temerity to stand for Lincolnshire against the background of the King's
struggle with his ministers over Catholic Emancipation. The contest was
bitter and Pelham peculiarly identified with the spirit of party. But he took
the occasion of his speech of thanks to explain 'that he should never suffer

---

[274] *Journals of the Hon. William Hervey, in North America and Europe, from 1755 to 1814* (Suffolk
Green Books, 14, 1906), pp. 219–20.
[275] J. Russell, *A History of the Nottingham Subscription Library* (Nottingham, 1916), p. 19.
[276] *Whitehall Evening-Post*, 30 Sept. 1780.

political differences in opinion to invade his private friendship; that it
would be his endeavour to merit their esteem by a strict attention to their
local interests'.[277] The sentiment was anodyne enough, but a century earlier
it would have aroused incredulity on the part of those to whom it was
addressed. The party rage of Anne's reign was unconfined, out of control.
That of George III's was an altogether less dangerous blaze, and kept
within limits which at least preserved property from its heat.

By the early nineteenth century the new doctrine of party was firmly in
place, acknowledged by those who attacked established values as by those
who accepted them. The radical Robert Bage thought it highly regrettable,
and contrasted the insipidity of English political life with the vigour to be
found in America. There strong opinions were both respected and challenged. In England seeming harmony and tolerance were based on 'polite
hatred for opinion'. Such politeness was bought at too high a price.
Bage was confronting a pervasive mentality which had won a conclusive
victory.[278] So was William Cobbett, who treated it as a monstrous imposition on the people, a means by which the ruling class shared the spoils
of public corruption while justifying its petty feuding to its subjects.
Confronted with the great country houses built by two famous legal
families, the Pratts and the Yorkes, he declaimed: 'In one shape or another,
the families of *both* have, from that day to this, been receiving *great parcels
of the public money*! Beautiful system! The Tories were for *rewarding Yorke*;
the Whigs were for *rewarding Pratt*. The Ministers (all in good time!)
humoured both parties; and the stupid people, divided into *tools of two
factions*, actually applauded, now one part of them, and now the other part
of them, the squandering away of their substance.'[279] Cobbett was himself
a victim of myth. Both the Yorkes and the Pratts had passed through a
tortuous party history, as Whigs under George II and variously supporters
of both opposition and government under George III. They were supreme
examples of the absurdity of party labels, not the reverse. But the very fact
that Cobbett sought to assimilate them to a system which others boasted
as the glory of the British constitution showed how propaganda had
transformed the traditional meaning of party.

[277] *The Speeches Delivered at the County Meeting at Lincoln, held on Friday, May 22, 1807* (Lincoln,
1807), p. 16.
[278] *Hermsprong*, iii. 236–7.
[279] W. Cobbett, *Rural Rides*, ed. G. Woodcock (London, 1967), pp. 177–8.

3

Parliamentary Service

THE parliamentary achievement of the century which followed the Revolution of 1688 is often thought of in terms of constitutional progress, paving the way for cabinet government and parliamentary democracy. It should also be viewed in functional terms, from the standpoint of the broad-based propertied society which it served. Regular and predictable parliamentary sessions facilitated legislation on an unprecedented scale. Growing confidence in the supreme authority of Parliament made statute the obvious source of legal certainty. 'Improvement', the watchword of the middle and late eighteenth century, signifying a multitude of ambitions and activities, relied much on its coercive power, not least in the taxation and regulation of private property, and the invasion of corporate or customary rights. But neither governments nor Parliaments dictated the use of this power. Rather it was deployed in response to the demands of interests, groups and communities, not so much imposing a sovereign will as providing a legal service. The result was the characteristic feature of the Georgian statute-book, a vast quantity of small-scale legislation, most of which would later have been described as local or private, and which would have raised major questions of policy if its assumptions had been embodied in national prescriptions. Rapid commercial change and an intensely competitive culture ensured that the process was not necessarily either orderly or harmonious. But it was the role of Parliament to minimize conflict, policing the preparation of legislation, arbitrating disputes, and resolving conflicts. Representation for this purpose had little to do with the civic rights and electoral justice which preoccupied reformers. Rather it was a matter of ensuring that MPs and peers broadly reflected diverse interests and localities. In this respect the political system which evolved after 1688 proved surprisingly adaptable and serviceable.

A REMARKABLE ALTERATION

Built into properties attitudes was a certain ambivalence about the authority of the State. Much reliance was placed on a system of law which preserved property and restricted the interference of government in it. The common law was valued precisely because it offered immemorial sanction to a great multitude of rights against the intrusion of centralized control. But the acknowledged instability of property in a commercial society and the requirements of economic progress made it necessary to devise means of enforcing change which would reward the enterprise of the propertied without arbitrarily invading their rights. Such enterprise not only affected the unpropertied, a matter of absorbing interest to twentieth-century historians, but also required some form of arbitration between different propertied interests. This depended on the most delicate of balances. Powerful groups must be protected, propertied people respected. Conflicts must be averted, or resolved with a minimum of lasting damage to the politics of consensus. Not least, the contemporary sense of what constituted the 'public interest' had to be served.

Parliament learned to perform these demanding tasks with great success. But the process by which it did so was not the work of a moment. Essentially it rested on four distinct accomplishments. One was the availability of Parliament's services to all who needed them. A second was acknowledgement of its overriding authority. The third was the use of its powers in a manner which avoided or at least minimized accusations of injustice and partiality. Fourth was its capacity to reflect and represent the relative weight and wealth of extremely diverse interests. These functions were not carried out to universal satisfaction, even the universal satisfaction of propertied Englishmen. But on balance the judgement of the late eighteenth century was that all four had been achieved within the limits of what was practicable. That achievement was, of course, comprehensible only in terms of contemporary values. To an earlier age it would have seemed extraordinary. To a later age it was in many respects to seem highly objectionable. At the time its functional effectiveness was rarely challenged and its ideological credentials widely respected. It was a large part of the story of Parliament in the century following the Revolution of 1688.

Availability was much the most straightforward of these objectives. It required only one thing: the predictable sitting of Parliament for a given period at regular intervals. Before 1688 both Parliaments and parliamentary sessions were erratic and unpredictable. After it regular Parliaments were enforced by statute; regular parliamentary sessions by convention. From 1689 Parliament met every year. It did so for long and lengthening sessions, often extending from autumn to summer and invariably including the months of February and March. The significance of the change can hardly be exaggerated and was well understood by contemporaries. It was described by a parliamentary reporter in 1767 as 'a remarkable alteration in our constitution'.[1] From the vantage-point of the early years of George III, it seemed to have modified, and perhaps jeopardized, the ancient balance of the constitution, a favourite point of political analysts. 'Our laying the crown under an absolute necessity of having every year a session

---

[1] *London Magazine* (1767), 440.

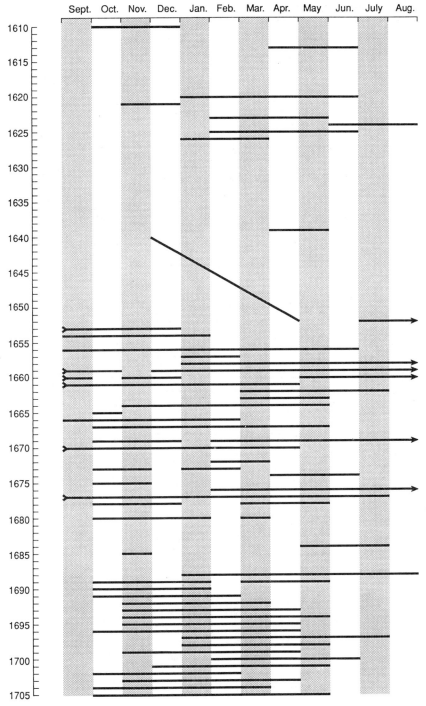

House of Commons Sessions 1610–1800

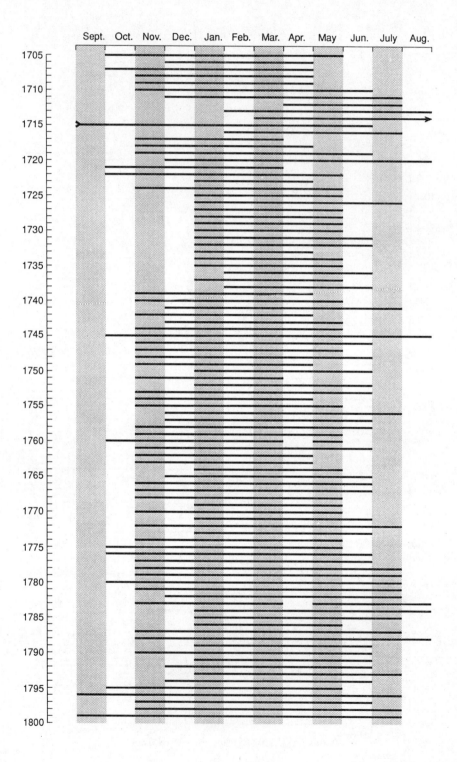

of parliament, may at last throw into our constitution a little too much of the democratical form of government.'[2]

William Paley attributed the change to the restriction which the Bill of Rights had placed upon the Crown's prerogative to raise troops without parliamentary consent. A standing army made necessary a standing Parliament. 'This single reservation has altered the whole frame and quality of the British constitution.'[3] The diminution of the prerogative was certainly important, but constitutional historians have pointed out that Parliament continued sitting at a time, in the late 1690s, when the annual Mutiny Act which authorized the maintenance of troops was not being passed.[4] The true reason for annual sessions was the Crown's need for supply in an era of recurrent, expensive warfare with Continental powers. At the time this did not please all parliamentarians. In 1693 Francis Robartes, knight of the shire for Cornwall, 'thought an annual sessions would be an annual tax upon the people'. His colleague for Westmorland, Sir Christopher Musgrave, also declared his preference for biennial meetings at most.[5] It was, however, the House of Commons which ensured its annual recall by insisting on annual budgets. By 1742 it was a commonplace of constitutional theory that yearly meetings were 'absolutely necessary to keep the Wheels of Government in Motion'.[6] Government would doubtless have preferred less temporary arrangements. The Civil List was guaranteed for a reign at a time. Excise duties were usually authorized on a more or less permanent footing, either to finance the Civil List, or, increasingly, to support the interest charge on the National Debt. These were described as the 'perpetual parts' of the revenue; but there was also a 'temporary part'.[7]

The temporary part consisted principally of two taxes, which peculiarly symbolized the allegiance of the landed classes to the parliamentary constitution inaugurated in 1688. The land tax was passed every year from 1697; though the rate varied, there was no session in which it was not renewed. The malt tax, though an excise, was also approved for a year at a time. It was the custom to pass both early in each session, a kind of ritual reminder that business was proceeding as usual. Opponents of government, in time-honoured fashion, objected to this annual demonstration of confidence in the regime, formally because it amounted to granting money to the Crown without hearing the grievances of its subjects. In 1722 it was suggested that parliamentary candidates should bind themselves to vote

---

[2] Ibid. (1762), 682.

[3] *Paley's Works* (London, 1860), 'Moral and Political Philosophy', p. 142.

[4] J. Carter, 'The Revolution and The Constitution', in G. Holmes, ed., *Britain after the Glorious Revolution, 1689–1714* (London, 1969), p. 44.

[5] H. Horwitz, ed., *The Parliamentary Diary of Narcissus Luttrell, 1691–1693* (Oxford, 1972), pp. 406–7.

[6] *Craftsman*, 7 Aug. 1742.

[7] *London Magazine* (1762), 682.

money bills only at the end of every session.[8] As late as the reign of George III, the timing could be controversial. In 1763 it was argued that the malt and land tax bills should be left until the end of the session so as to maintain an effective parliamentary scrutiny of the executive.[9] In December 1770, during the Falkland Islands crisis, there was an opposition motion to postpone the land tax until after Christmas.[10] The Prime Minister, Lord North, insisted that he was merely following normal procedure. 'With regard to moving the land and malt tax before Christmas, it is what I have always done, unless the parliament happened not to meet till after.'[11]

This controversy was part of an attempt by North's radical opponents to exploit the psychological significance of the land tax. James Townsend refused to pay the sum assessed on his Middlesex property in 1770 on the grounds that Wilkes's incapacitation as MP for Middlesex had removed its legitimacy. Even at the time this seemed a desperate measure. Certainly it failed to impress ministers.[12] Before very long it came to seem absurdly anachronistic. Thomas Percival, in his 1785 essay on taxation, accepted the citizen's ultimate right to resist illegitimate expropriation, but considered Townsend's conduct frivolous. All taxes were equally levied by consent: there was no point in selecting one, even the land tax. 'The bonds of the state are not to be rashly loosened by every temporary error or misconduct of statesmen.'[13] By then, all logical connection between the system of taxation and Parliament's institutional security had lapsed. But the argument had done sterling service over a long period before it was finally rendered redundant.

In the 1780s, even in the 1760s, the land tax was a small proportion of total taxation. But before the wars of the mid-century, its substantive significance, as distinct from its symbolic importance, was undoubted. In the peacetime budgets of the 1720s and 1730s, Walpole's objective was to reduce it to an absolute minimum, thereby relieving the ordinary country gentlemen and providing the ultimate argument for the superiority of Hanoverian government. This was an enticing prospect, but a dangerously uncertain one. Without a land tax what guarantee was there that ministers would continue to consult Parliament at all? Part of the menace of Walpole's excise scheme was that it held out the possibility that the land tax might be eliminated altogether and replaced by excise duties beyond the power of any individual Parliament. 'Nor do they need to be told', observed Lord

---

[8] *Freeholder's Journal*, 14 Mar. 1722, supplement.

[9] *London Magazine* (1763), 463.

[10] *Commons Journals*, xxxiii. 61.

[11] *Sir Henry Cavendish's Debates of the House of Commons*, ed. J. Wright (2 vols., London, 1842), ii. 196.

[12] Warwickshire RO, Denbigh MSS, Letterbook, Rochford to Denbigh, 7 Nov. 1770.

[13] *The Works of Thomas Percival* (new edn., 4 vols., 1807), iv. 246.

Haddington of his fellow parliamentarians, 'when the revenue is so much encreased that Parliaments will be useless.'[14]

It was appropriate that the main reason for the introduction of annual sessions was the need for an acceptable means of taxing property. Regular Parliaments not only had the most profound consequences in terms of the relationship between executive and legislature and the evolution of a parliamentary constitution, but also affected the way in which ordinary property-owners regarded the legislative function. Before 1688 a variety of institutions, judicial, legislative, and executive, provided the means of determining disputes, securing change, and entrenching privileges. After 1688 there was growing recognition that Parliament provided the only sure machinery for achieving all kinds of objectives which would earlier have been sought in any of a number of places. Something of the sort had been glimpsed earlier. In the 1660s schemes for fen drainage had been the subject of parliamentary legislation, principally with a view to obtaining an 'irrefrangible legal title' such as earlier devices, for example Privy Council decree secured after much lobbying at the court of Charles I, had not secured.[15] But under Charles II and James II Parliament's availability was unpredictable. After 1689 the utter certainty of annual sessions removed the one restraint on the development of Westminster as the natural resort of all seeking permanent legality for their designs, though it took a while for the full significance of what had happened to become clear. The regulation of the fens continued to be the subject of judicial as well as legislative guidance into the early eighteenth century.[16] But the effects of the underlying change were noticed very quickly. The enormous growth of private and local legislation could hardly have occurred without regular and dependable access to the legislature. Particularly where property was concerned such certainty was vital: without it other bodies, the Privy Council and the Court of Chancery, for example, both of them permanent institutions with well-established administrative procedures, would surely have been called upon to bear much of the burden which Georgian Englishmen placed upon Parliament.

It is paradoxical that Parliament should have found its *métier* as an institution devoted to the remodelling and revision of property rights. Yet this was the reality of what occurred in 1689. A legislature which represented the resistance of propertied Englishmen to the royal prerogative found itself constantly intervening in the propertied rights and interests of those same Englishmen. This lent a rather perilous air to the rhetoric of parliamentary sovereignty. Daniel Defoe expressed a common assumption

---

[14] Historical Manuscripts Commission, *Polworth MSS*, v. 49.

[15] C. Holmes, *Seventeenth-Century Lincolnshire* (Lincoln, 1980), pp. 227–8.

[16] K. Lindley, *Fenland Riots and the English Revolution* (London, 1892), p. 252.

of the age, when he identified the unique protection afforded property as one of the peculiar blessings of a parliamentary constitution. 'We talk loudly of PROPERTY in *England*, and when we are before Parliament, we should more particularly talk of it—For 'tis the Language of the Place, 'tis the Darling of the *House*.'[17] This was a truism throughout the eighteenth century. Yet it was compatible with a great volume of legislation which removed, reallocated, and, in short, invaded property. As Charles James Fox enquired in 1780, denying that the Crown's Civil List should be treated as sacrosanct, 'in making turnpikes and new roads, was not private property meddled with? and did not Parliament do it every week in the course of the session?'[18]

There was no actual contradiction. The very respect which attended property required that there should be one, and only one means of regulating it. Much of the legislation of the eighteenth century was necessitated by the reluctance of ordinary Englishmen to cede their property or a proportion of it for some purpose required by the supposed interest of the community to which they belonged. Hence the profusion of powers embodied in much fiscal and regulatory legislation, and beyond it, in improvement acts, turnpike acts, canal acts, enclosure acts, and so on. Most provided for some form of rating or taxation. Many permitted outright expropriation in return for compensation. So far as compulsory purchase was concerned, there were some who argued that Parliament was too cautious in bestowing such powers on statutory bodies, especially where houses rather than land were in question. Others thought it had gone far enough: statutory bodies themselves were often anxious not to proceed with the full rigour of the law.[19]

Compulsory purchase attoned for an invasion of property so far as any earthly body could. Yet it left an uncomfortable awareness that after all the victim had not in any real sense agreed to part with his property. Even bills involving only private parties caused concern. The most insignificant estate bill was, by definition, designed to treat property in a manner which diverged from the settled law of the land. And yet it was precisely because Parliament offered legal certainty superior even to a decree in Exchequer or Chancery that statute was so attractive to men of property. There was a rush of family and estate bills in the 1690s. John Evelyn put this down to the extravagance and vice of the age. 'Never were so many private bills passed for unsettling estates, showing the wonderful prodigality and decay of families.'[20] For this view there is seemingly statistical support. There were only 77 acts for the sale of property to meet the demands of creditors

---

[17] *Defoe's Review in 22 Facsimile Books* (New York, 1938), v. 631: 31 Mar. 1709.
[18] *Parliamentary Register*, xvi. 381: 8 Mar. 1780.
[19] John Scott, *Digests of the General Highway and Turnpike Laws* (London, 1778), p. 291.
[20] W. Bray, ed., *The Diary of John Evelyn* (2 vols., London, 1908), ii. 337.

between 1660 and 1688 compared with 260 between 1689 and 1714.[21] But the availability of a new legislative facility was as perhaps as important as the imprudent habits of landowners and their heirs. Under Charles II and James II there were seventeen years without a parliamentary session longer than three months and ten without a session at all. After 1689 landowners were assured of adequate parliamentary time. Some of Evelyn's contemporaries found the trend disturbing. Was it, they asked, legitimate to use the legal power of Parliament in this way? When one such bill reversed a judicial decision concerning a Welsh estate, it was pronounced in the Commons 'a matter of great concern, touching the inheritances and settlements of the subject'. The country MP Paul Foley called it 'a bill to shake the common assurances of the nation, which I hope you will be very cautious in'.[22]

The process by which private estate bills evolved was to be repeated with other kinds of legislation as full awareness of the constructive opportunities offered by regular parliaments dawned. Occasional, experimental applications for statutory powers would lead to more extensive usage, followed by some heart-searchings about the legal and social implications, more or less feeble attempts to restrict the less desirable consequences, and eventual acceptance of the new procedure as a standard feature of parliamentary business. Enclosure bills, one of the more notorious instances of legislative intervention in favour of private enterprise, were an obvious instance. At the beginning of the eighteenth century they were virtually unknown. By its end they constituted one of the most prominent and time-consuming categories of legislation.

Estate and enclosure bills seem small beer compared with the matters government policy and national moment which Parliament was often called upon to debate. Yet there were some resemblances. A feature common to very diverse kinds of legislation was a sense that statutory expropriation was an awesome responsibility for a Parliament obsessed with property rights. The polemic, for example, which accompanied the punishment of the Porteous rioters in 1737 and the Boston tea-party rioters in 1773 involved arguments which applied equally when parliamentary sanction was sought for a bill extinguishing rights of common or breaking an entail. They belonged in a recurrent pattern of uncertainty and tension about the expansive power of parliamentary legislation and the propertied rights of Britons. On a day to day basis this was discernible in the most humdrum business of Lords and Commons. In 1767, for instance, the House of Commons was debating two issues of exceptional importance, the taxation

---

[21] Sir J. Habbakuk, 'The Rise and Fall of English Landed Families, 1600–1800: II', *Trans. Roy. Hist. Soc.*, 5th ser. 30 (1980), 199–221.

[22] *The Parliamentary Diary of Narcissus Luttrell*, p. 451.

of the American colonies and the reduction of the chartered rights of the East India Company. The future of the empire depended on the way in which Parliament tackled these problems. Simultaneously it was considering the fate of two small communities, Castle Sowerby in Cumberland, and Haute Huntre fen in Lincolnshire.[23] Both were threatened by enclosure bills, in each case bitterly contested. Parochial though such matters appeared, they were not in principle different from the great debates on America and India. The very preoccupation of Parliament with propertied life tended to create a sense of moral equivalence between the diverse matters which it was called upon to consider. In 1788 Sir John Thorold, a furious opponent of the woollen manufacturers on behalf of his native Lincolnshire, saw no incongruity in comparing their treatment of the graziers with the crimes of Warren Hastings in India, and the inhumanity of slave-owners in the West Indies.[24] All three were before the legislature in 1788, and all three presented the same essential appearance to Thorold. They concerned the invasion of property.

THE SUPREME POWER

By the 1780s Parliament's overwhelming legislative authority was a commonplace of political debate, and ready to be enshrined in a full-blown theory of law which linked it, ironically, with older, absolutist theories of the State. William Paley, who reduced so many late eighteenth-century notions to their simplest and most defensible form, had no hesitation in identifying the basis of this authority. A system of appeals must necessarily be finite. In every society there is a power from which there can be no appeal, a power 'absolute, omnipotent, uncontrollable, arbitrary, despotic'. The power 'is called the *Sovereign*, or the supreme power of the state. Since to the same power universally appertains the office of establishing public laws, it is also called the *legislature* of the state.'[25]

Sweeping though such claims were, it had taken a long time for full awareness of the revolutionary potential of the Revolution of 1688 to become clear. Opponents of the Robinocracy were aware that in corrupting Westminster, the Hanoverians posed a greater threat to liberty than the royal prerogative of the Stuarts had ever posed. 'A parliamentary Yoke is the worst of all Yokes; and that the said parliamentary Yoke is the only one we have, in Reality, to fear.'[26] It took longer to appreciate what powers Westminster now claimed. Blackstone's famous assertion of Parliament's supremacy in his *Commentaries* was made in 1765: 'It hath sovereign and

[23] *Commons Journals*, xxxi. 184, 200–1, 240–1, 258–9.
[24] Cobbett's *Parliamentary History*, xxvii. 389–90.
[25] *Paley's Works*, 'Moral and Political Philosophy', p. 136.
[26] *Craftsman*, 14 Aug. 1742.

uncontrollable authority in making, confirming, enlarging, restraining, abrogating, repealing, reviving, and expounding of laws, concerning matters of all possible denominations, ecclesiastical, or temporal, civil, military, maritime, or criminal: this being the place where that absolute despotic power, which must in all governments reside somewhere, is entrusted by the constitution of these kingdoms.' Blackstone seems almost to have been shocked by the momentous nature of his discovery. He called the 'omnipotence of parliament' a 'figure rather too bold'. He also criticized Parliament for its recklessness in extending summary jurisidictions at the expense of the common law tradition. Above all, he made plain his belief in the existence of an overriding natural law, though he was not explicit about the means by which the ultimate superiority of this law was to be secured in practice.[27]

The 1760s certainly constituted a watershed in the recognition of parliamentary supremacy, even if the fact itself was by no means new. By comparison the legislative potential of the Crown was considered a feeble thing indeed. Contemporary sensitivity to the changing balance of power was revealed in some bizarre episodes. In 1764 a House of Commons frequently accused of showing too much favour to a prerogative-minded prince none the less went out of its way to condemn Timothy Brecknock's inconsequential and ludicrous plea for royal power, *Droit Le Roi*.[28] The same House of Commons, two years later, was angered by Lord Chatham's use of royal proclamation, between sessions, to impose restrictions on grain exports which technically breached parliamentary supremacy. Chatham and his 'patriot' friends, Camden and Beckford, renowned for their record of anti-prerogative populism, were denounced for imitating the suspending power claimed by the Stuart absolutists, Charles II and James II.[29] A few years later a High Church sermon in celebration of the 'divine virtues' of Charles I, and a historical controversy concerning the alleged treachery of the great Whig Algernon Sidney, provoked the staging of a somewhat theatrical revival of seventeenth-century polemics.[30] In weightier matters, too, Parliament displayed its new-found confidence and aggressiveness. Whether the American colonies and the Middlesex electors were entitled to believe that they were the victims of a parliamentary tyranny, there is no doubt that their predicament was a consequence of Parliament's new pretensions. The Declaratory Act of 1766 was the clearest possible

---

[27] W. Blackstone, *Commentaries on the Laws of England* (4 vols., London, 1765–9), i. 156

[28] *Parliamentary History*, xv. 1418–20.

[29] Ibid., xvi. 245, 251–313.

[30] Thomas Nowell, *A Sermon Preached before the Honourable House of Commons, at St Margaret's, Westminster, on Thursday, January xxx, 1772* (London, 1772), p. 21; Joseph Towers, *A Letter to the Rev. Dr. Nowell* (London, 1772); A. F. Steuart, ed., *The Last Journals of Horace Walpole* (2 vols., London, 1910), i. 271–3.

statement of Westminster's conviction of its own omnipotence. The House of Commons was not less emphatic in confronting its own electorate when it claimed the right in 1769 not merely to disqualify the MP for Middlesex, John Wilkes, but to select in his place a candidate for whom only a small minority of the electors had voted.

One of the features of this period of self-assertiveness on the part of the legislature was the difficulty with which contemporaries brought themselves to challenge its ideological basis. The principle of Westminster's supremacy over the colonies was accepted by the great majority, even of those who thought it unwise to enforce it. The opposition to Wilke's treatment by the House of Commons was extensive but the one argument on which it agreed was the claim that the Lower House had pre-empted the authority of the legislature as a whole. More radical notions, that there were some rights, including those of the electorate, which defied the power of statute, were far more controversial. Increasingly the opponents of government in the first half of George III's reign focused on the corruption of Parliament by the Crown. In doing so they denied the legitimacy of much of what Parliament did. But even when they sought to replace or reform Parliament, they rarely denied the essential concept of unitary sovereignty expressed through a representative assembly, which was what the parliamentary system accomplished in 1688 amounted to.

None the less, there were moments when it seemed possible to offer a more fundamental challenge. The Royal Marriage Act of 1772 was one such. It was criticized by some on the grounds that marriage was an institution of divine origin beyond the power of Parliament to regulate. The reformer John Horne eagerly drew from the resulting debate the conclusion that 'there are acts of parliament which are not laws'.[31] The sources of the claim were numerous and various. But in the eighteenth century they were so many lights lost largely from sight in the superior glare of parliamentary sovereignty. One, the belief of common lawyers that Parliament at best was charged with declaring law, and at worst had no standing in matters where past record and ruling were clear, retained something of its glitter. In the sense that there were large areas of law where Parliament preferred not to intervene it remained unchallenged. On the other hand there is no example of an eighteenth-century statute the force of which was denied in an English court. As early as 1722 electors were warned of the gravity of the change taking place in this respect. 'Now it is worth considering, that the Parliament Law is of such Pre-eminence and Dignity as to control the other, and to overrule all our Judicature, both in the Courts of Law and Equity.'[32] At this point it was still possible

---

[31] A. Stephens, *Memoirs of John Horne Tooke* (2 vols., London, 1813), ii. 69.
[32] *London Mercury*, 31 Mar. 1722.

to argue that offences against statute should be considered venial compared with infringements of the common or natural law. In 1735 an opposition newspaper complained that juries were too easily impressed by the prescriptive power of Parliament, and urged them to remember the independence of the law which they served and sustained.[33] But the underlying trend was clear, and the ultimate supremacy of statute increasingly went unchallenged.

Some churchmen continued to believe in the superior, or at least separate force of canon law. But the suspension of Convocation in 1717 removed the one body capable of asserting the superiority of its jurisdiction. Its experimental revival in 1742–3, during the turmoil accompanying the fall of Walpole, was not a success. The rulers of Whig England concluded that it would be unwise to permit its voice to be heard, after a turbulent priest, Archdeacon Reynolds of Lincoln, justified its claims to independence in unequivocal terms.[34] Moreover, Lord Hardwicke's judgement in the case of *Middleton versus Crofts* in 1738 left little room for hope that the judiciary would grant canon law a status which it seemed bent on denying to common law. Bishop Gibson was enraged by Hardwicke's judgement, and planned a work showing that the laws of the Church might apply to laymen. As his episcopal colleague Francis Hare pointed out, at issue was a simple proposition, one which had acquired overwhelming force since the Revolution, 'that nothing can bind the Subject but an Act of Parliament'. In the event Gibson evidently changed his mind to 'save our sinking jurisdiction'. If any cause was lost under George II, it was his.[35]

Religion none the less armed its adherents with some sceptical arguments as to the extent of Westminster's supremacy. The evangelical Howell Harris denied that Parliament had the right to compel militiamen to exercise on Sundays. In Parliament itself this view was supported by James Erskine, brother of the Jacobite Lord Mar, friend of George Whitefield and a Presbyterian Tory. Erskine told the Commons bluntly that 'none ought to obey such a Law, because the Parliament nor any Power on Earth could abrogate the Law of God'.[36] This was, however, a claim which the clergy of the established Church increasingly found it inconvenient to recall. The clerical response to parliamentary sovereignty was, indeed, one of the clearest indications of the change which occurred in the mid-eighteenth century. In retrospect it seems a delayed response, but time was required to habituate the passing generations to the extraordinary accretion of legislative power which followed the Revolution of 1688. Gibson was no Tory, yet he utterly rejected the claim of a Whig Parliament to behave as

---

[33] *Fog's Weekly Journal*, 1 Nov. 1735.
[34] *A Letter to the Reverend Dr. Lisle, Prolocutor of the Lower House of Convocation* (London, 1742).
[35] Huntington Library, Gibson MSS, Hare to Gibson, 29 Nov. 1739.
[36] G. M. Roberts, ed., *Selected Trevecka Letters (1742–1747)* (Caernarvon, 1956), p. 188.

if it were the only source of legal authority. It was a concern which he shared with many other Whigs. Richard Venn, ancestor of the Evangelical Venns, and a fierce defender of the Hanoverian regime, thought the doctrine of parliamentary omnipotence a dangerous one. He was a friend of Gibson but put the argument in a context broader than that provided by canon law: 'There is doubtless, the same supreme Power in all Nations, but in some Places more of it is contained in the *Society*, in others more of it vested in the Legislature. 'Tis a great Mistake therefore to assert *in Gross*, that the Legislature can do every thing; their *political omnipotence* is restrained by the Law of God, by the Laws of Right and Wrong, by the Nature and End of Government, by the Commissions they may in some Countries receive from their Principals, and always, and every where by their own *Contracts*.'[37]

Fifty years later Venn would surely have taken a very different view. By the reign of George III the ordinary clergyman's acceptance of the supremacy of Parliament, in matters religious as well as secular, was taken for granted. Those few who doubted it were not much respected by the great mass of ordinary churchmen. One such was Richard Watson, who publicly denied the unchallengeable authority of the legislature. But Watson was a radical spirit, a friend of the Rational Dissenters and a thorn in the side of the established Church as well as the government which it supported in the 1770s and 1780s. Where Venn's doubts had sprung from widely entertained views about the limitations of parliamentary power, Watson's derived from a perspective which most of his brother clergy considered at best reprehensible, at worst heretical.[38]

The changing attitudes of the parties in this respect are striking. Many lay Whigs and Tories under George II had entertained doubts about the growing authority of Parliament. This was true even at the highest levels of government. The same Lord Hardwicke who acquiesced in Westminster's triumph over Westminster Hall, and who demolished the last pretensions of the Church to an independent legislative power, was worried, in his last years, by Parliament's claim to supremacy in the colonies.[39] His colleagues among the ministers of George II are not commonly regarded as pawns of royal absolutism, yet they were not entirely negligent of the interests of the Crown in matters of prerogative. In 1754, barely a decade before Blackstone's historic assertion, a Mutiny Act for America, designed to provide a system of military discipline based on parliamentary authority as had been the case in England since 1689, was rejected on the grounds

---

[37] Richard Venn, *Tracts and Sermons on Several Occasions* (London, 1740), p. 123.

[38] *The Principles of the Revolution Vindicated* (Cambridge, 1776), p. 10.

[39] P. Langford, 'Old Whigs, Old Tories, and the American Revolution', in P. Marshall and G. Williams, eds., *The British Atlantic Empire before the American Revolution* (London, 1980), pp. 114–15.

that it must be 'too great an encroachment on the prerogatives of the crown'.[40] Three years later the King and some of his leading ministers defeated a Habeas Corpus bill which seemed to deprive the Crown and its judges of a large element of judicial discretion.[41]

Under George I and George II Tory anxieties on this score were naturally sharper still. Their ideological heritage and their current grievances made them contemptuous of Parliament's pretensions. The ministerial press in the 1730s accused them of leading the populace to deny the legitimacy of statutes such as the Gin Act and Smuggling Act.[42] Certainly there were agitators capable of encouraging such irreverence. The broadsheets which an eccentric non-juror scattered about the law courts in Westminster Hall in 1736, employing an explosive device to do so, specifically denounced the exceptionable statutes of recent years. This was described by a grand jury as 'a wicked, false, infamous and scandalous Libel, highly reflecting upon his Majesty and the Legislative Power of this Kingdom'.[43] Tory arguments continued to question the credentials of a legislature which was not after all their legislature. Perhaps the last Tory to voice them unequivocally was John Shebbeare whose *Letters to the People of England* in the mid-1750s eventually brought down the wrath of the Whig government. Shebbeare argued that there were certain fundamental laws beyond Parliament's power to repeal or amend.[44] He shared this position with many opponents of the Hanoverian regime, Whig and Tory alike, and might have been surprised to find how many ministerial Whigs sneakingly sympathized with it.

After 1760 appearances were very different. Whigs and Tories came together to celebrate unlimited legislative supremacy. George III vindicated his claim to have reconciled them in nothing more than his championship of parliamentary authority in the colonies. Dr Johnson, a Tory, even a Jacobite in the previous reign, pronounced its absolute validity in his tract of 1774 *Taxation No Tyranny*, and Shebbeare joined him in defending the American policies of the King and Lord North on the grounds of unconfined parliamentary right. Their opponents put this down to the continuing influence of divine right theory, albeit in novel form.[45] But the enemies of America included many old Whigs: George Grenville's supporters did not shrink from the legal implications of colonial taxation. 'It is fundamental in the law of nations, that the Sovereign power cannot

---

[40] *Parliamentary History*, xv. 387.
[41] Horace Walpole, *Memoirs of King George III*, ed. J. Brooke (3 vols., New Haven, Conn., 1985), iii. 17–22.
[42] *London Magazine* (1737), 475.
[43] Ibid. 398.
[44] *A Fifth Letter to the People of England* (London, 1757), p. 12.
[45] *Thoughts on the Letter of Edmund Burke Esq.* (6th edn., Oxford, 1777), p. lii.

either limit, or give up its own Supremacy, or the People's Subjection. These two, in all cases, are correlative terms; indivisible things; inseparable ideas.'[46]

It was, naturally, the subjection of the people which worried some of the new, radical Whigs of the 1770s and 1780s, and led them to challenge its premiss. William Jones insisted that 'the Omnipotence of Parliament is a Solecism in Terms'.[47] His friend Granville Sharp, in *A Declaration of the People's Natural Right to Share in the Legislature* of 1774, roundly denounced the notion of omnipotence as a 'kind of *Popery in Politics*'.[48] He fastened on one of the better-known consequences of the doctrine, Parliament's supposed right to regulate elections to the House of Commons. The Septennial Act had been cited by Blackstone as evidence that the legislature could indeed, by prolonging its own life, demonstrate its independence of all other powers. This infuriated Sharp and his friends, as it had Tory opponents of George I and George II. It was precisely legislation like the Septennial Act which convinced many radicals that Parliament in its post-Revolution stage had fatally exceeded its authority. Yet neither Sharp nor his radical collaborators were prepared to place defined limits on parliamentary sovereignty. The thrust of their argument, as of much so-called republican argument later, in the 1790s, was not that Parliament must abandon its power but that its members must be rendered fully accountable for their exercise of it by electoral reform.

There was always, of course, the ultimate alternative of revolution, one which radicals spoke of with some enthusiasm. Bolingbroke had expressed the logical viewpoint of those who basically accepted the principle of parliamentary sovereignty while denying it unlimited right to do ill. 'The legislative is a supreme, and may be called, in one sense, an absolute, but in none an arbitrary power.' If Parliament violated the constitution, he argued, 'the people would return to their original, their natural right, the right of restoring the same constitution, or of making a new one'.[49] This was not a particularly subversive doctrine. The most complacent defender of the constitution as established was bound to admit that there might be circumstances in which the sovereign betrayed its trust and thereby left the subject free to rebel. But increasingly such defenders preferred to treat revolution as an absolutely last resort, one which, given England's happy constitution in Church and State, was virtually unthinkable. Their opponents were correspondingly more and more ready to condemn the corruption and wickedness of the status quo and to appeal to revolutionary means of restoring its virtue. This was not a very satisfactory dialectic.

[46] Huntington Library, Stowe MSS, STG Box 192: R. Mackintosh, undated draft.
[47] G. Cannon, ed., *The Letters of Sir William Jones* (2 vols., Oxford, 1970), i. 258.
[48] (London, 1774), p. xxix.
[49] *The Works of Lord Bolingbroke* (4 vols., London, 1844), ii. 150–1.

Rules which merely reduced the debate to a subjective judgement about the point at which legislators forfeited their delegated authority left much to be desired. It would have been preferable to have some systematic theory of graduated powers, such that the legislature could be held within certain definable bounds, without sacrificing the political value of parliamentary control of the executive.

This need was not felt only by opponents of Parliament and conventional politics. MPs with a vested interest in septennial elections were unlikely to be moved by criticism of the logical justification for the Septennial Act. But there were other uncertainties about their powers which were more perplexing, not least because they raised awkward questions concerning the legislature's treatment of property. One of Richard Venn's contentions was that a legislature must be bound by its own contracts. Perhaps the best known of Parliament's solemn bindings was its undertaking, after the Revolution, not to tax interest payments on the loans which it received from the public. The National Debt was thereby rendered sacrosanct. In the context of the annual budget the status of this 'contract' with the nation's creditors was important, far more so, it might be argued, than other questions raised by constitutional lawyers and parliamentary reformers. The general view was that the faith of Parliament could not be violated. Casting about for a plausible wartime tax in 1748, William Beckford even suggested a 'voluntary' duty on government stock rather than contemplate the possiblity of compulsion.[50] Nor was it only the Debt itself which was affected by such arguments. When Pitt sought to appropriate unclaimed dividends in 1791 he was accused of making 'a proposition to break a solemn Compact entered into between Government and the Public Creditors'.[51] Another Prime Minister, Walpole himself, extended the logic to the Sinking Fund. When he established it in 1717, he announced that the appropriation of duties to the Fund would constitute a kind of 'fundamental law', to be considered unbreakable by future Chancellors of the Exchequer.[52] Ironically he was the first Chancellor to violate this contract, when he transferred surpluses on the Fund to his budgetary account in 1733.

This matter of contract was central to the question of Parliament's capacity to bind itself. Acts which, it was often said, could not be repealed or modified by Parliament, were implied or even expressed contracts: the Bill of Rights of 1689, the Act of Settlement of 1701, and the Scottish Union of 1707, not to say still older enactments, the Petition of Right and Magna Carta. Even the most pragmatically inclined MP could be brought

[50] *London Magazine* (1748), 501.
[51] *Whitehall Evening-Post*, 24 Mar. 1791.
[52] *Parliamentary History*, viii. 1218.

to understand the difficulty when such statutes were compared with the petty legislation which occupied most of an ordinary session. Shebbeare put the point with characteristic force. Fundamental laws must be 'of a Nature more unchangeable and sacred than those which establish a Turn-pike, and not be altered or defeated with the same Ease, as an Act which removes the Fair-Day of a Market Town from *June* to *September*'.[53] This illustration exposed the difficulty very neatly. One of the principal attractions of parliamentary supremacy as it evolved after the Revolution of 1688 was that it made all kinds of seemingly trivial legislation binding and irremovable, short of a further statute, in the same way as the Bill of Rights or the Act of Settlement. If it followed that the Bill of Rights or the Act of Settlement had a legal status no better than that of turnpike acts, then there was no remedy. But the result was a dilemma of considerable proportions.

PARTICULAR IMPROVEMENTS

Employed to penalize individual property-owners, this mighty engine of legislative power would have been devastating. It would also have created the most acute political controversy. This was no part of Parliament's design. It went to extraordinary lengths to avoid invading propertied rights, at any rate in the mass. One result was a characteristic feature of the Georgian statute-book, its propensity to small-scale legislation. Social reformers longed for a limited body of uniform, universal law, providing for the governance of the realm on rational principles. On such firm ground could be built a truly enlightened State. What they got was a great bog of uncoordinated lawmaking, ever expanding but always unplanned. Par-liament was often pressed to adopt general legislation based on clear principles: it repeatedly refused to do so.

The most important single aspect of social policy, the provision of relief for the poor, was typical in this respect. Successive generations of parliamentarians were reminded of the inadequacies and anomalies of the Elizabethan Poor Law and the Caroline Law of Settlements, and urged to revise them *en bloc*. Individual MPs with an interest in the subject, for example William Hay in the 1730s, Richard Lloyd in the 1750s, Thomas Gilbert for a period of some twenty years from the 1760s to the 1780s, sought a complete overhaul of the poor law. Not infrequently they obtained authority to conduct a formal investigation of the problem of poverty and its relief; occasionally they even got the Commons to approve specific changes in principle. But the anticipated legislation was rarely adopted, and then only on a permissive basis. The Workhouse Act of 1723 and

---

[53] *A Fifth Letter to the People of England*, p. 12.

Gilbert's Act of 1782, for example, both gave powers to poor law authorities: neither required them to use them. Gilbert himself remained hopeful that his act would in due course be replaced by a general, mandatory statute.[54] This did not happen. Yet the volume of poor law legislation passed at the request of individual parishes and groups of ratepayers was immense. During the century which followed the Revolution of 1688 nearly 120 such bills were approved, affecting a wide variety of metropolitan, urban and rural communities. In territorial terms the smallest district to acquire its own chapter in the *Statutes at Large* was the liberty of the Old Artillery Ground in London, in 1774: the largest was the union of three hundreds, Hartesmere, Hoxne, and Thredling, in Suffolk, in 1779.[55] This was a time of intense debate about the poor relief in general, and particularly about the value of county workhouses. But only once was there a statute providing for an entire county, and then only for limited purposes, in the case of the Devon Insurance Act of 1769. Significantly, this act was repealed only four years later.[56]

Legislation of limited scope was plainly preferred. There was a certain horror of revising venerable laws, quite apart from the practical difficulty of so doing. Some of those who argued for a general review of poor law legislation argued that they sought only to revive the spirit of the earliest laws on the subject. In 1744 it was proposed 'to go to the very Root; and at the same Time abrogate no fundamental Part of the 43rd of Eliz. but enforce every Part of it to its just Intent and Meaning; such a one as will break through no already-settled Point in Westminster-Hall; but will leave no material Point relating to this Law hereafter to be settled there'.[57] If legislation was meant to meet demands such as this, it is hardly surprising that it was rarely forthcoming. It was much easier to add new, particular laws, than revise all-embracing old ones. It was also easier to plead for exemption rather than reform. Even a new, unpopular piece of legislation, like the Freeholders Registration Act of 1788, which aroused intense opposition and had to be repealed before it took effect in 1789, was treated with caution in this respect. Cheshire, the first county to challenge it, was advised by the county's MPs to apply for relief in point of its peculiar, palatine status, rather than petition for repeal of the act as a whole.[58]

It is arguable that the general legislation which did succeed was adopted precisely because it made available on a wider scale the results of local experiments. The acts of 1723 and 1782 were both preceded by a number

---

[54] Thomas Gilbert, *Considerations on the Bills for the Better Relief and Employment of the Poor* (London, 1787), p. 10.

[55] 14 Geo. III, c. 30; 19 Geo. III, c. 13.

[56] 9 Geo. III, c. 82; 13 Geo. III, c. 18.

[57] *A Short View of the Frauds, Abuses and Impositions of Parish Officers* (London, 1744), Preface.

[58] North Yorkshire RO, QDE (M) 8/16: James Taylor to Joseph Bird, 22 Sept. 1788.

of local acts, in the former instance incorporating workhouse trusts in large cities, in the latter permitting groups of parishes to unite for the establishment of hundred workhouses. The general acts facilitated similar projects without the trouble and expense of private bill legislation. Paradoxically, the accumulation of local statutes gradually brought large areas within the scope of new principles of public policy. By the late 1780s most of the larger parishes on the perimeter of London and Westminster, those subject to rapid population growth and consequent strains on the traditional system of poor relief, had obtained their own act. A similar development occurred in East Anglia, where fifteen poor law unions were established between 1756 and 1779. By a form of legislative contagion, spreading from one neighbourhood to another, substantial portions of Suffolk and Norfolk came under the control of Poor Law guardians administering workhouses in a way which would not have been approved on a county or regional basis. It was customary to model each successive act on its predecessors, with due amendment to suit local circumstances. The Canterbury Workhouse Act of 1728 was recommended as a legislative pattern for towns seeking a union of parishes for poor relief purposes.[59] The resemblance between the East Anglian statutes was very strong. When Whitchurch in Shropshire applied for its own act in 1791 the vestry began by ordering its clerk to obtain copies of all such statutes passed under both George II and George III.[60] There was in fact a succession of acts for Shropshire. Shrewsbury acquired the first in 1784; there followed Oswestry and Ellesmere in 1791, Whitchurch and Atcham in 1792, Montgomery in 1792. In due course they exemplified one of the more striking, if paradoxical features of this process of progressive, imitative legislation. Pitt's proposal for poor law reform in 1796 provoked a meeting of delegates from the poor law incorporations in the region to petition Parliament for exemption from any general legislation.[61]

The Small Debt Acts provide another instance of this form of legislative particularism. The courts of requests which they established were equipped with summary jurisdiction and designed to supersede the cumbersome judicial machinery involved in suits of less than forty shillings. They were a typical example of the eighteenth century acting in a way which would be considered rational, efficient, even arbitrary if it had done so by means of general rather than local legislation. There was, indeed, a series of attempts to introduce legislation which would apply to the country as a whole, in 1730, in 1734, in 1741, 1742, and 1743. The bill of 1741 passed the Commons by narrow majorities, and failed in the Lords. That of 1742

---

[59] *An Account of Several Work-Houses* (2nd edn., London, 1732), p. 124. The advice was taken at Manchester: see J. E. Bailey, *John Byrom's Journal, Letters, etc. 1730–31* (Manchester, 1882), p. 7.

[60] Shropshire RO, 3091/4/5.

[61] Shropshire RO, Shrewsbury Incorporation, 83/1: 23 Jan. 1797.

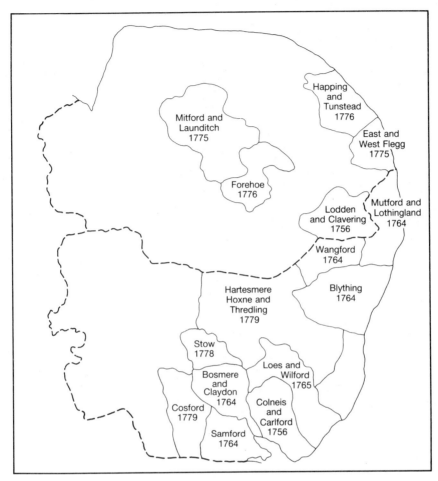

Figure 2

East Anglian Poor Law Incorporations 1756–79

attracted 208 to vote on one division, more than on some questions of first-rate political importance.[62] Even on a county basis such legislation was rejected, except in the case of Middlesex. Somerset's petition for comparable treatment was given a frosty reception.[63] But what Parliament would not accept as a matter of general policy, it was quite prepared to implement piecemeal. By 1800 some fifty acts had been passed: only a

[62] *Commons Journals*, xxiv. 249. For draft bills, see *House of Commons Sessional Papers of the Eighteenth Century*, ed. S. Lambert (Wilmington, Del., 1975–6), vii. 13, 159, 459.

[63] *Commons Journals*, xxi. 323.

Figure 3
Courts of Conscience or Requests 1689–1800

handful of petitions were rejected. In the process large tracts of country
were brought under the courts of requests, larger than was obvious from
the title of the bills in question. Halifax, for instance, included a whole
series of courts in the West Riding of Yorkshire. The Cirencester court
covered one-quarter of Gloucestershire: in combination with the Wiltshire
courts, it ensured that most of the West Country textile region came within
the new jurisdiction. Large portions of Kent and Lincolnshire were also

comprehended. News of the advantages to be derived from a private bill evidently spread rapidly. On the Kent coast there were no courts of conscience until the end of the War of American Independence. Then Rochester in 1782, Dover in 1784, and Sandwich, Deal, and Folkestone in 1786 imposed the new discipline on large numbers of men of Kent.

Some forms of statutory regulation were unthinkable unless introduced in principle for all or none. The criminal law, for example, though it bestowed immense discretionary powers on judges, could hardly be permitted to vary from place to place. Even so it was possible to obtain special local arrangements for its implementation. Cumberland and Northumberland obtained a succession of local acts between 1662 and 1757 in their war on 'moss-troopers'. The peculiar mixture of public policing and private insurance thereby legalized had no precise parallel elsewhere.[64] Moreover, legislation which was unambiguous in its universality was implemented with generous allowance for local preferences. Taxation for the support of government, of its very nature, required a degree of uniformity. Thomas Paine thought it the obvious exception to the essential 'republicanism' (he might have said anarchism) of English government: 'the sense of the Nation is left to govern itself, and does govern itself by magistrates and juries, almost at its own charge, on republican principles, exclusive of the expense of taxes.'[65] Yet even unified taxation was rather misleading. The Land Tax Acts included a clause of beguiling simplicity which laid down the procedures for assessing all kinds of income and property. In practice, of course, this was largely a tax on land, collected not according to the prescribed formula for valuing property but in conformity with quotas fixed by Parliament for each county. Even so the actual process of taxation varied bizarrely from region to region. Counties taxed themselves with little or no reference to the statutory forms, and in some instances employed means which had no parliamentary authority whatever behind them. In the most notorious case, that of Cumberland and Westmorland, ancient forms of taxation were used, including the 'purvey'. Not only was this anomaly known, it was urged as a reason for not assenting to a general revaluation of the land tax in the 1760s, on the grounds that purchasers of land in the north-west had paid a price which assumed continuing underrating by tax assessors. For a while, before the Treasury woke up to the fact in 1713, Westmorland got away with using its rating system to pay the window tax, which was not intended to be assessed on a quota basis at all.[66]

[64] J. L. Kirby, 'Border Service, 1662–1757', *Trans. Cumbs. and Westmor. Ant. and Arch. Soc.*, NS 48 (1949), 125–9.

[65] *Rights of Man*, ed. H. Collins (London, 1969), p. 148. Cf. David Hume's *Essays Moral, Political and Literary* (Oxford, 1963), p. xvi.

[66] J. V. Beckett, 'Local Custom and the "New Taxation" in the Seventeenth and Eighteenth

Even in less remote regions, land tax quotas were payable according to established conventions about the local division of responsibilities rather than anything resembling a realistic assessment of wealth. The Lancashire rating book of 1752 traced tax apportionments back to sixteenth-century subsidies, fifteenths and 'ox lays'. It provided for each hundred, each parish, and each township on these ancient principles. The town of Manchester, for example, paid 30 per cent of what was levied on the parish of Manchester; the parish paid 45.5 per cent of what the Manchester division paid; the division paid 42 per cent of what Salford Hundred paid; the hundred paid 16.5 per cent of the quota for the county as a whole.[67] In theory Parliament was not intended to have cognizance of such procedures. In practice it was well aware of them. In 1705 the Lincolnshire land tax commissioners, presenting evidence to the House of Commons, made no reference to the legal requirement of a pound rate, but gave a lucid account of their 'usual and ancient' method. Lincoln paid one-fifteenth of the county's total apportionment; the parts of Lindsay paid half the rest, Kesteven four-sevenths of what remained, Holland three-sevenths. The Commons solemnly resolved that Kesteven had paid its full proportion.[68] If the law courts had been asked for a verdict on such a system, they could not possibly have ruled it in accordance with the statutes.

Faith in local procedures was deeply entrenched. In Middlesex attempts to standardize county rate assessments provoked protests against 'this equalising system of property, founded on the visionary basis of equity in opposition to the existing and genuine principles of the constitution'.[69] From Parliament itself, especially in matters as sensitive as taxation, there was little danger of interference. It was far more likely to intervene in defence of custom than against it. At Queenborough in Kent poor assessments had traditionally been made, not in accordance with the act of 1601, by which occupant householders were assessed, but according to a local system of rating resident inhabitants. Faced with litigation by a knowledgeable ratepayer, the borough declined to apply the law as it stood. Instead it appealed to Parliament for a bill endorsing its procedure: the result was an act legalizing an illegal departure from an explicit statute.[70] When theorists discussed the merits of centralized, absolute sovereignty, this was not quite the role they envisaged for it. But the mentality involved was so pervasive that it could be modified only with great difficulty. The general thrust of fiscal policy was in the direction of uniformity and

Centuries: the Example of Cumberland', *Northern History*, 12 (1976), 105–26, and 'Westmorland's "Book of Rates"', *Trans. Cumbs. and Westmor. Ant. and Arch. Soc.*, NS 77 (1977), 131.

[67] Lancashire RO, DDX 603: 'A Book of Rates', by James Hardman, 1752.
[68] *Commons Journals*, xiv. 487.
[69] M. D. George, *London Life in the Eighteenth Century* (London, 1966), p. 413.
[70] 7 Geo. III, c. 72; *Commons Journals*, xxxi. 77–8, 150.

universality. But even explicit directives could be interpreted eccentrically where interest dictated. In 1778 the Commissioners of Taxes found themselves having to circulate rural tax assessors on the subject of North's house duty. 'We have been inform'd, an Opinion has prevailed among the Assessors, that the Act was meant chiefly to affect Cities and great Towns, which cannot be so, as no Distinction at all is made therein.'[71] Considering the latitude with which so many statutes were read, enforcing uniformity was to prove an uphill task, often beyond even the most centralized of departments.

In some instances it was possible to proceed in the piecemeal way beloved of eighteenth-century legislators, but difficult to deny the need for a broader approach. Highways present an obvious example. Turnpike trusts were established at the request of particular localities. But in time they created a national road network. By 1770 they covered 15,000 miles of road, administered by more than five hundred separate trusts. Even in an age unworried by local autonomy this gave rise to difficulties. A large amount of traffic, both passenger and freight, was bound either for London or regional capitals, passing constantly from the territory of one trust to another. Regulation of the vehicles involved could hardly be left to the discretion of individual trusts. There were thirty-four 'general' statutes regulating highways or turnpikes between 1714 and 1790, twenty-five of them falling in the forty years which represented the climax of the turnpike mania, between 1740 and 1780. The most important of them, in 1741, 1753, 1755, 1757, 1766, and 1773, were complicated pieces of legislation and involved intricate negotiation with the interested parties beforehand.[72]

These statutes cast much light on the legislature's reluctance to engage in general lawmaking. For even when passed, they quickly produced a hostile response from those adversely affected. The act of 1753, which was intended as a final solution to the problem of road damage caused by over-burdened and inadequately fitted carts, had to be amended within two years of its enactment, when Birmingham complained that it was threatened by 'utter Ruin', Walsall and Dudley protested in similar terms, and the farmers of eighteen Middlesex parishes warned that they would be unable to bring their produce to London unless the act were modified. Subsequent legislation proved equally controversial and occupied an inordinate amount of parliamentary time. The definitive consolidating act of 1773 aroused contempt for its complexity and ambiguity among those who had to implement or observe it. Nor was the subject one of minor consequence. The prolonged war of broad and narrow wheel was a parliamentary conflict of punishing proportions. At its height in 1755 the Tory MP Thomas

---

[71] East Sussex RO, D 472: to acting commissioners of Hastings Rape, 4 Oct. 1778.
[72] W. A. Albert, *The Turnpike Road System in England, 1663–1840* (Cambridge, 1972), pp. 134–8.

Prowse referred to it as 'the Spirit, or rather the Madness, about Broad Wheels'.[73] In terms of its impact at Westminster as well as the public debate to which it gave rise, it deserves to be rated with better-known causes of political strife.

The great majority of legislation was in effect public legislation, at least in the sense that it bore on sections of the public at large. Though often promoted by individuals or interests with private advantages in mind it was generally intended to bind members of the public, not least in that it might tax or take away their property. Parliament had a formula for inclusion in all public acts, requiring them to be 'judicially taken notice of as such by all judges, justices and others, without being specially pleaded'. But judges did not suppose that the absence of this clause precluded them from taking notice of a statute. Nor was Parliament consistent in inserting it. In this respect the distinction between public and private bills was arbitrary and uncertain: it confused, among others, the King's Printer, who was responsible for publishing the statutes in their unabridged form and frequently found himself in difficulties. In 1753 he invented a classification of his own: acts affecting the public at large, private acts for the benefit of individuals or particular groups, public acts which applied in geographically limited areas. The result was that some kinds of legislation, for example, fen drainage schemes, appeared within the space of a few years in all three categories.[74] Only in 1798 was some order brought to this confusion when the categories of 'Public General' and 'Public Local and Personal' were devised. Even after this, the old terminology lingered on. When Yorkshire formally acknowledged the services of William Wilberforce, on his retirement from a county seat in 1812, it thanked him for supervising the 'private business of the county'.[75] In fact the legislation in question was private only in the sense that it was not in the province of the Crown or its ministers and rendered its promoters liable to the payment of fees to the officials of each House of Parliament. In practice many of the acts which paid fees as private legislation were effectively public acts. No doubt, if Parliament had wanted to encourage them further, it could have done so by abolishing or remitting the fees payable. Something of the kind was briefly attempted in 1701 when it was agreed that bills for the better governing of the poor would be passed free of fees. Halifax was one locality which was thereby prompted to apply for workhouse legislation.[76] The

---

[73] *Commons Journals*, xxvii. 119, 138, 149; Somerset RO, Gore MSS, DD GB 148/214: T. Prowse to W. Gore, 25 Feb. 1755.

[74] On the problem of definition, see S. Lambert, *Bills and Acts: Legislative Procedure in Eighteenth-Century England* (Cambridge, 1971), chap. 5, and for examples of the inconsistent treatment of fen bills, see 2 Geo. III, c. 32; 4 Geo. III, c. 21; 7 Geo. III, c. 98.

[75] R. Coupland, *William Wilberforce: A Narrative* (Oxford, 1923), p. 374.

[76] *Commons Journals*, xiii. 273, 597; John Watson, *The History and Antiquities of The Parish of Halifax, in Yorkshire* (London, 1775), p. 629.

experiment was not repeated. Presumably the vested interest of the clerks, the likely burden on the Exchequer, and the reflection that fees at least deterred frivolous applications had their effect.

Loaded with fees or not, statutes of this kind were widely approved. In the jargon of the day they had in common 'improvement', some manifest benefit to the public, even when the object of the promoters was private advantage. In the third edition of Defoe's *Tour*, published in 1742, notice was taken of the use of acts of Parliament to improve 'particular Neighbourhoods'.[77] This association between improvement and particularity was very characteristic of the age: it became almost incontestable in the late eighteenth century, though there were individual doubters who were aware that the process could mask low, ignoble motives. Joseph Ritson's experience as High Bailiff of the Liberty of the Savoy gave him a cynical outlook on these matters. 'Every little dirty parish in the environs of London must have a law for itself. The churchwardens can provide the money, the attorney wants a job, the justice looks forward to the penalties, and the "gemmen of the westry" like authority: an act of parliament is accordingly obtained and being an admirable compound of ignorance and knavery, cannot fail of proving exceedingly beneficial to the community.'[78] Ritson was an eccentric: atheist, antiquarian, animal-lover, simultaneously Jacobite and Jacobin. But his view was shared by others. Specific projects sometimes moved their opponents to question the basis of the system as a whole. One such was the proposed canal linking London with the Midlands in 1793. 'Who takes care of the Public?' asked a protestor. 'Surely this is the province of the Legislature ... Whilst the legislature permits Subscribers to obtain Laws to empower them to do what *they please*, and to divide, amongst themselves, all they are permitted to raise upon the public, it is no wonder that the public interest is made, by these circuitous arrangements, subservient to private advantage.'[79]

These doubts notwithstanding, it was generally assumed that the promotion of improvement was best left to the ordinary citizen. The expectation was that conflicts of interest would be settled locally. Thus a Suffolk onlooker observed philosophically of the Beccles to Ipswich turnpike in 1795: 'It was a long Contest and carried on with violence, Ill manner and Committees, but the Strength and Money laid with Its well Wishers.'[80] Parliament was there as a final court of appeal, but its crippling incapacity to arrive at a policy in such matters ensured that direction from the legislature was unlikely to be forthcoming. Nor was government commonly

---

[77] *A Tour through the Whole Island of Great Britain* (4 vols., London, 1742), vol. i, p. v.

[78] H. A. Burd, *Joseph Ritson: A Critical Biography* (Univ. of Illinois, 1916), p. 34.

[79] *A Letter to a Member of Parliament from a Land Owner, on the Proposed Line of Canal from Braunston to Brentford* (London, 1793), pp. 27, 29.

[80] Suffolk RO (Ipswich), HD 365/2: Diary of William Goodwin of Earl Soham, Dec. 1755.

concerned to take a lead. The nearest thing to ministerial interest in improving legislation was a general injunction such as that contained in the King's Speech to Parliament of 1765, expressing a hope that 'every session of parliament may be distinguished by some plans for the public advantage'.[81] It was not supposed by anyone, least of all the Marquis of Rockingham and his colleagues in government at the time, that a minister would propose such plans, or attempt to ensure that they operated to the public advantage.

A PARLIAMENTARY INTERPOSITION

The result was that the mighty legislative force of Blackstone's omnipotent Parliament resembled nothing so much as a gigantic rubber stamp, confirming local and private enterprise, but rarely undertaking initiatives of its own. Up to a point this followed from Parliament's very success in enforcing its supremacy. Traditionally Parliament was the petitioner on behalf of the people. In the eighteenth century it was itself the redresser in almost all kinds of grievances, certainly those which suggested the need for 'improvement'. The most untutored minds absorbed something of the significance of the transformation. In 1773, Jonas Hanway persuaded a committee of prominent businessmen to remonstrate publicly with the employers of infant chimney-sweeps, on the subject of their conditions of work. The circular letter which they penned carried no official status. But Hanway was struck by the terms in which the beneficiaries described it. 'It was common for these boys, when enquired of, to answer in a pleasing accent, that "since the act of parliament," so they called the *letters*, "our masters have treated us in a better manner than before." '[82] Touching for the King's Evil had perhaps been superior in its mystical appeal, but nobody doubted in late eighteenth-century circumstances that the ultimate remedy was a strictly parliamentary one. Even the poetic muse was summoned up to celebrate its efficacy. Anne Candler's *Stanzas Addressed to the Inhabitants of Yoxford* in 1787 were written to mark their application to Parliament for a weekly market bill.[83] Chartering markets had once been the exclusive prerogative of the Crown.

Not everyone approved the use of statute to short-circuit the traditional procedure. Owners of tithe-free lands at Misterton in Nottinghamshire in 1771, threatened by an enclosure bill, argued that their legal rights were triable only at law. In 1774, when the Inns of Court attempted to entrench their presumed poor rate exemption in statute, thereby pre-empting a decision by the courts, the parishes in dispute with them protested vocifer-

---

[81] *Parliamentary History*, xvi. 2.
[82] *A Sentimental History of Chimney Sweepers, in London and Westminster* (London, 1785), p. 67.
[83] [James Ford], *The Suffolk Garland* (Ipswich, 1838), p. 43.

ously against 'a parliamentary Interposition'.[84] Complaints of this kind
had good historical antecedents. Private bill legislation was based on the
assumption that it righted a wrong which could not be redressed by other
means. When the volume of such legislation had increased under Charles
II, attempts to restrict the flow had been answered with this argument.
'We are not to exclude Property, by Petitions from private persons, that
cannot have remedy in another place.'[85] But parliamentary remedies were
not invariably appreciated by subjects of the Stuarts. In 1649, Lincolnshire
opponents of fen drainage had objected to an act of Parliament regulating
the Great Level on the grounds that a statute could not affect a commoner's
rights.[86] The intellectual and political climate of the late eighteenth century
was deeply hostile to the mentality implied by this claim but it was not
altogether lost from sight. James Ibbetson, an articulate opponent of
enclosure legislation in the 1770s, questioned the doctrine of 'supremacy
of law' implied by parliamentary enclosure.[87] In his argument, the essential
connection between the grand assertion of sovereignty over the empire as
a whole and its seemingly parochial, but no less crushing employment
against small rural communities, is once again clear. However, whereas
adherents of a more traditional concept of sovereignty were numerous in
the American colonies, they were lonely voices in Britain. So strong was
the prejudice in favour of unitary sovereignty that the best hope for
communities which had a choice of arguments was not to object to the
doctrine as such, but to plead a degree of separation from the society which
it governed. Little Guernsey, in 1771, wisely insisted that it was 'a distinct
and separate state from England, and we make no part of the community
of England'.[88] Americans themselves were shortly to grasp that this was
the most logical as well as most practicable position to take.

Parliament, of course, did not see itself as imposing a despotic will. Nor
did it hand down what it thought of as judgement. The Commons had a
strong sense of its own historical status as a court, and the law lords
sometimes confused their judicial and legislative functions. But neither
pretended to match the expertise and impartiality associated with law
courts when they considered petitions for legislation. Petitioners did not
look for these qualities. On the contrary the object was to obtain legislative
sanction of processes of inquiry and arbitration which had already occurred.
This is seen most clearly in instances where a minimum of deliberation

---

[84] Commons Journals, xxxiii. 309; xxxiv. 410.
[85] Debates of the House of Commons, from the Year 1667 to the Year 1694: Collected by the Honourable
Anchitell Grey Esq. (10 vols., London, 1769), iii. 163.
[86] Lindley, Fenland Riots and the English Revolution, p. 170.
[87] Critical Review, xiv. 149.
[88] The Rights and Immunities of the Island of Guernsey, Most Humbly Submitted to the Consideration
of Government (London, 1771), pp. 3, 31.

was required. Boundary disputes, though often seemingly trivial, could occupy generations of litigants, enriching only the lawyers. An act of Parliament provided a simple and definitive means of settling them. This was what was sought to resolve an ancient disagreement between the parish of Tring in Hertfordshire, and the neighbouring hamlet of Betlow in 1749. If Betlow was deemed part of the parish, its farmers, tenants of the Duke of Leeds, would be rated to the poor of Tring; if, as they claimed, it was extra-parochial, it would have no liability for any but its own burdens. There was a wealth of evidence on both sides. By the time Parliament was addressed on the subject, Hertfordshire Quarter Sessions, the Buckingham Assize, and the Court of Common Pleas had all considered it. The result was eventually a compromise formally registered in the Common Pleas. But there remained a fear that no judicial ruling could deter future generations from repeating this harrowing process. Parliament offered nothing by way of debate or determination. What it did offer was the priceless asset of cast-iron legal security, in the form of a statute enshrining the compromise.[89] Similar legislation for Kendal in 1767 followed adjudication at the Cumberland Assize and formal registration in Chancery.[90] But prolonged disputes were not necessary. Local agreements were presented to Parliament for endorsement without reference to any court. At Stanwell in 1771 a deal was done between the Lord of the Manor, Sir John Gibbons, and his parishioners, by which he was permitted to close public footpaths interfering with his view, in return for a bequest to the poor.[91] Parliament by this time was accustomed to being used for parochial purposes.

The language in which legislation was sought reflected the realities of this process. Most legislation had its origin in the procedure of petition for redress. This assumed an identifiable grievance which might be remedied by a paternalistic Parliament. But 'improving legislation' was designed to obviate what at worst was an inconvenience sanctioned by time. Even so those who petitioned for change did their best to give the impression that they were perpetuating the spirit of ancient laws, or at least that only technical defects in existing laws had driven them to seek novel powers. The modifications of language and phraseology which occurred are strikingly suggestive of this process of initial caution evolving into uncompromising innovation. The early street bills were requested in circumspect, even regretful terms. Colchester's petition in 1737 described the dangerous and dirty condition of many of the town's thoroughfares and lamented there 'not being sufficient Power in the Laws now in being effectually to remedy the same'. It cited the inadequacy of the ancient Statute of Winchester,

[89] *Commons Journals*, xxv. 744.
[90] Ibid., xxxi. 302.
[91] Ibid., xxxiii. 119.

which prescribed duties of watch and ward without providing appropriate powers to finance them. In the same session Salisbury petitioned in similar terms.[92] By the 1760s when such legislation no longer seemed unusual, petitioners were less cautious. At St Sepulchre in Middlesex it was asserted in 1763 only that the desired improvements 'would be of great Benefit to the Inhabitants, and of public Utility'. In the same year, at York, they were expected to 'conduce to the Security, Convenience, and Advantage of all Persons residing in, and resorting to the said City', and at Whitby in 1764 'they would tend to the great Ease and Convenience of the Inhabitants'.[93] The benefit and convenience formula became almost standard, as recognition grew of Westminster's readiness to bow to the wishes of local communities without requiring tedious recitals of the omissions in venerable and estimable laws.

A similar process occurred with enclosure bills. Early petitions for enclosure emphasized the unanimity of the parties concerned and the legal difficulties which they faced. The petitions promoted by the Grenville family at Ashendon in 1738 and Wotton Underwood in 1742 claimed that because some of the petitioners were ecclesiastical bodies with limited powers of alienation, and because others were bound by family settlements, 'such Division and Inclosure cannot be made effectual and binding to all Parties interested, without the Authority of Parliament'.[94] Gradually, however, the rehearsal of legal impediments became perfunctory. In due course it was dropped altogether. In 1753 the enclosure petitioners at Welton in Northamptonshire stated merely that 'the Parties concerned have agreed to apply to Parliament, to obtain an Act to inclose, and divide the same into just Allotments and Proportions to and for the several Parties interested therein'.[95] Thereafter the pattern was simply to inform Parliament of what petitioners desired.

This psychology carried over to subsequent proceedings. Parliament's scrutiny of legislation was itself closely scrutinized. When Whitchurch's committee reviewed the progress of its bill before the Commons in April 1792 and discovered that certain amendments had been made, it adopted a lofty tone. In its minutes 'this Committee' rejected the suggestions of the 'House of Commons committee' with some asperity.[96] Parliament's tolerance in such matters was surprisingly extensive, though not unlimited. Occasionally concern was expressed about the quantity of legislation with which it was confronted, as when Somerset put forward a succession of

[92] Ibid., xxii. 789, 738.
[93] Ibid., xxix. 707, 412, 730.
[94] Ibid., xxiii. 64; xxiv. 120.
[95] Ibid., xxvi. 625.
[96] Shropshire RO, 3091/415: 30 Apr. 1792.

turnpike bills in 1753.[97] It was well known that Parliament's readiness to make its services available on payment of fees was not unconditional, but depended on assurances that substantial agreement had been reached beforehand. Lawmaking was in this sense a grass-roots activity, and the place of the legislature in the process optional. When the butter traders of Newcastle examined the case for quality control in 1737, they found that it had been adopted by five towns in Yorkshire. But only two of these relied on statutory regulation; the others had found it possible to exercise similar powers on a voluntary basis.[98] It was agreed at Manchester in 1775 that plans for street improvement by compulsory purchase would be submitted to twelve adjudicators. If this procedure failed, recourse would be had to Parliament.[99] This was the mentality assumed by a Liverpool election tract which referred to a potentially contentious navigation project in 1761. 'The Terms of the *Weaver* Bill were amicably settled by the respective Parties and of Consequence not litigated in Parliament.'[100] Where a bill did not apply to any community but that which sponsored it, Parliament was likely to be interested more in the process which produced it than its essential justice or wisdom. One of the main aims of the opponents of such a bill was to demonstrate that it did not reflect the wishes of those affected. The French visitor De La Rochefoucauld was naïvely impressed by the safeguards which made it difficult for enclosing proprietors to oppress poor commoners.[101] In fact, the only safeguard of consequence was the requirement that at least two-thirds of property-owners affected assent to the legislation. This offered nothing to the poor. It was noticed that when enclosure was controversial, as at Stanwell in 1768, it was because the protesters had money and rank to argue for them.[102]

Along with consent went consultation. MPs were understandably nervous about legislation which had not been carefully prepared. Sir Henry Liddell, MP for Morpeth, advised a Northumbrian friend in 1745 that 'if Gentlemen will please to have this public good talkt over at any public meetings in the County, many difficulties may be removed by that means, which if started at the time this bill is to be begun, may occasion much dispute, and in some particular points a good deal of opposition; I mean where private interests may be concerned'.[103] Local bills frequently gave rise to complaints that the promoters had not given notice of their intention or provided for proper consideration at meetings open to the public. It was

[97] Somerset RO, Dickinson MSS, DD/DN/210: J. H. Coxe to C. Dickinson, 29 Jan. 1753.

[98] Northumberland RO, Delaval MSS, 2/DE/49/1/23.

[99] Mrs Hibbert Ware, *The Life and Correspondence of the Late Samuel Hibbert Ware* (Manchester, 1882), p. 49.

[100] *An Entire and Impartial Collection of All the Papers, etc.* (Liverpool, 1761), p. 24.

[101] J. Marchand, *A Frenchman in England, 1784* (Cambridge, 1933), pp. 208–9.

[102] *London Magazine* (1768), 459.

[103] Northumberland RO, Ridley MSS, ZRI/25/2: to Sir Matthew White Ridley, 14 Feb. 1745.

alleged of Shrewsbury's paving bill in 1755 that it had 'never been printed off and dispersed as it uprightly ought to have been'.[104] At Coventry, in 1791, it was expected that an improvement project of this kind would be advertised in advance by means of a public exhibition displaying drawings as well as printed details of what was involved.[105] Parliament paid close attention to such matters where there was any suggestion of a difference of opinion among the supposed beneficiaries. The enclosure at Bolton in Cumberland in 1778 provoked close questioning by a Commons Committee of witnesses as to the meetings held in advance.[106] The Wareham Road Bill of 1766 had to be revised to take account of a protest from Dorchester, Wareham, and Corfe Castle to the effect that there had been no public meeting.[107]

Accusations of intrigue were taken seriously. When the St James portion of Clerkenwell sought to separate for paving and poor relief purposes from its sister parish of St John in 1774, the latter complained that 'the whole Application has been carried on in a secret Manner, without consulting the Petitioners'.[108] The objectors to the Wakefield Improvement Bill, which granted power to demolish houses obstructing public thoroughfares, alleged that they 'were perfect Strangers to the several Proceedings upon the Bill, and scarce knew how to take the necessary Measures to secure their Property'.[109] Concern was still greater when sharp practice occurred during the parliamentary process. According to the protesters against the Eynsham Enclosure Act in 1782 the statute passed during the previous session contained provisions which breached the original agreement in the parish.[110] This was tantamount to claiming that the local community was the legitimate legislative body, with Parliament merely providing the cloak of final legality.

The defenders of the Birmingham Street Bill of 1769 assured the Commons that they had 'repeatedly taken every Method to obtain the Sense of the Town, which Law and Custom have established in Cases of a like Nature'.[111] Inevitably, in time there was pressure on Parliament to define more clearly what law and custom required. The object of the standing orders for enclosure bills in 1773 was precisely to set minimal standards of public consultation and propertied consent. They laid down a number of requirements regarding the arrangements for preparing

---

[104] Shropshire RO, 177/1a: broadsheet, 20 Dec. 1755.
[105] Bodleian Library, G. A. Warwicks b 1: William Reader's 'Chronicle of the Times', 891.
[106] *Commons Journals*, xxxvi. 1001–4.
[107] Ibid., xxx. 739; 6 Geo. III, c. 92.
[108] *Commons Journals*, xxxiv. 548.
[109] Ibid., xxxiii. 307.
[110] Ibid., xxxviii. 688.
[111] Ibid., xxxii. 373.

enclosure legislation. The effect is open to question, but their promulgation at least indicated the concern which attended such legislation.

No application to Parliament could succeed without some assurance that the fees payable to parliamentary officials would be paid. Even relatively uncontroversial legislation involved considerable expenditure of this kind, and also a good deal of other kinds. The employment of clerks and lawyers was essential to the presentation of business. So, very often, was the marshalling of evidence, the examination of witnesses, and the use of expert advice. All this required money. Sometimes it could be charged against income expected from the legislation in question. This in itself was controversial, and sometimes reinforced the impression that one part of the community was making another part of it pay for its own enslavement. The Halifax Small Debts Bill of 1780 included provision for annuities to be charged on the fees payable in the local court of requests. Considering that the fees had previously gone to bolster the excessive earnings of the clerk of the court this seemed not unreasonable. But in the House of Lords it was condemned as 'holding out a precedent for interested people to be suing for Acts of Parliament on the slightest pretence, seeing they were to be repaid in consequence of the Act'.[112] This was not a bad description of whole categories of local legislation.

Most improvement, whether private, like enclosure, or public, like street paving and lighting, was accompanied by expenditure which might include the costs of obtaining statutory powers. But there had to be some advance provision if only because legislation did not always result. Arrangements for the financing of turnpike trusts, improvement commissions, and canal projects became increasingly complex. Public subscriptions commonly preceded petitions for legislation. Even relatively humble bodies were accustomed to find the funds for an approach to Parliament. When forty-two delegates of Yorkshire friendly societies met at the Bull's Head in Bradford in 1793 to promote an act protecting their legal status, they subscribed two guineas on behalf of each society.[113] Commercial lobbies, like local communities, were accustomed to resort to a well-established machinery for lobbying Parliament. Colonial agents were granted special status by ministers contemplating colonial legislation and heard with respect in Parliament because the colonies lacked formal representation.[114] But their practices were not notably different from places closer to home. The employment of agents and attorneys for the purpose of preparing and promoting parliamentary business was positively commonplace. A whole

[112] *Whitehall Evening-Post*, 29 June 1780.

[113] York Minster Library, Hailstone MSS, H8.

[114] See M. G. Kammen, *A Rope of Sand: The Colonial Agents, British Policy and the American Revolution* (Ithaca, NY, 1968).

class of London-based lawyers flourished on this trade in legislation.[115] Local 'solicitors' were also involved, and sometimes blamed for mishaps. Alexander Fothergill, a highway surveyor whose daily doings are particularly well recorded, was accused by the Lancashire trustees of the Richmond–Lancaster turnpike of neglecting their interests in the preparation of the bill, a charge which he indignantly rejected. None the less, he was dismissed from his post as surveyor for the western portion of the trust.[116] The doings of such agents were closely supervised, with an anxious eye kept on the money that they spent. In 1791, when the Whitchurch Poor Bill reached the relative safety of the Lords, the Shropshire attorney John Gregory was ordered to return home at once without incurring further expense.[117]

The collection of funds had to be carefully organized. At Newcastle there was an established procedure by which the local insurance clubs and friendly societies collaborated to pay the expenses of the town's delegates.[118] Large cities shared the cost of major legislative projects, as Liverpool, Bristol, and Birmingham did in respect of the regulation of American iron production during the Seven Years War.[119] Where the interests involved came from diverse regions, elaborate formulae for local contributions were worked out: the clothiers, for instance, set up a standing administration to account for the considerable sums of money involved. Their application to Parliament in 1790 for a revision of the wool laws was accompanied by printed accounts which reported the expenditure of more than £4,500. Twenty-one distinct regional bodies contributed, ranging from Yorkshire's £1,683 to the £10 given by Kidderminster and Shropshire.[120] The clothiers had a justified reputation for effective lobbying. Their delegates were accustomed to meet in provincial assemblies whose pretensions thoroughly irritated their opponents. That at Exeter in 1786 was jealously described as 'a little senate'.[121]

Perhaps the cheekiest venture into this form of extra-parliamentary representation with taxation was the attempt by Liverpool in 1774 to secure a bill permitting the levy of a local import duty. As the petitioners explained, since the early 1730s the local merchants had voluntarily adopted such a duty on American goods because 'the very great Attention shewn by the House to the Commercial Interests of this Kingdom, renders it frequently

---

[115] J. Brewer, *The Sinews of Power: War, Money and the English State, 1688–1783* (London, 1989), pp. 239ff.
[116] North Yorkshire RO, ZB 1400: Alexander Fothergill's diary, 9 July 1756.
[117] Shropshire RO, 3091/415: 25 May 1797.
[118] *Observations on the Coal-Trade in the Port of Newcastle, etc.* (n.d.), p. 15.
[119] *An Entire and Impartial Collection of All the Papers, etc.* p. 61.
[120] York Minster Library, Hailstone MSS, KK 14: printed accounts for meeting at Bristol, 2 Mar. 1790.
[121] *Parliamentary History*, xxvii. 389.

necessary to send up some of their own Body from that Town to attend, during the Sitting of Parliament, on Matters of Trade'. The bill would have made this duty a legal obligation. The notion of imposing a tax to support the dispatch of parliamentary delegates from a town which elected two MPs of its own was evidently startling: it was overwhelmingly defeated by 122 votes to 21.[122] Yet the very fact that such a request could be made was revealing. MPs who were sometimes offended by the importunities of colonial agents seem never to have objected to this system, no doubt for good electoral reasons.

In the case of towns which did not elect MPs in their own right the machinery was crucial. Manchester regularly sent off delegates to London. When its bells were rung on 10 June 1731, it was not, as some alleged, to celebrate the Pretender's birthday, but to welcome back John Byrom who had succeeded in defeating a controversial workhouse bill, and who denied timing his return with a Jacobite anniversary in mind.[123] In happier times such celebrations were still less inhibited. When the town succeeded in getting Parliament to repeal the fustian duty in 1785, its rejoicings featured a public dinner at the Manchester Hotel for Thomas Stanley as knight of the shire for the county. Stanley was an assiduous campaigner for the manufacturers of Manchester but on this occasion the public honours were shared with Thomas Walker and Thomas Richardson, the two delegates who had been sent to Westminster. No doubt such procedures did something to lessen the apparent injustice of a representative system which left great cities without a voice in theory but in practice well capable of exerting their persuasive power.[124] The MPs for such places grew used to dealing with men who in effect were equally engaged in the business of representing their constituencies or interests in which constituents were involved. There were times when the House as a whole seemed actually to be directed by these unelected representatives. In 1774 a controversial bill for the regulation of hop bag sizes, which had generated conflict between the competing interests of Kent and Essex, was withdrawn when the hop merchants involved, sitting in the stranger's gallery, were openly asked for instructions: 'The members who were friends of the bill then went up into the gallery to the hop merchants, brewers etc. who attended, and consulted with them, whether it would not be better to give up the bill entirely, than to submit to the weight of the bag proposed.'[125] On some occasions, the involvement of spectators was a little too enthu-

---

[122] *Commons Journals*, xxxiv. 510.
[123] R. Parkinson, ed., *The Private Journal and Literary Remains of John Byrom: ii, part 2* (Chetham Soc. 34, 1855), p. 518.
[124] W. E. A. Axon, *The Annals of Manchester* (Manchester, 1886), p. 112.
[125] *London Magazine* (1774), 577.

siastic. In 1791, during a debate on the Kingston Turnpike Bill, the gallery had to be cleared by order of the House.[126]

High priority was attached to avoiding contested legislation. If a bill was controversial it was simpler to reduce its scope than engage in a costly fight to the death. Reviewing the possibilities in 1697, Liverpudlian enthusiasts for a bill regulating fish weirs concluded that it would be wise to restrict their concern to the Mersey, rather than campaign for 'a general Bill against all the Fishweares in the Kingdom'.[127] Bills which were not local when drafted tended to become local in their effects. A hatmakers' protest did not lead to the abandonment of a prohibition on rabbit warrens in the vicinity of sea walls in 1765, it merely succeeded in confining its scope to Lincolnshire, whence the proposal came.[128] In this way the spirit of compromise worked constantly to whittle down the extent of legislation. The penalty was precisely that irrational muddle of laws which later enraged the Benthamites. But at the time there was little resistance to the *ad hoc* character of so much statutory innovation. A rare exception was Parliament's refusal to pass a bill proposed by the City of London in 1763. The bill would have permitted freemen of the City to act as witnesses in cases involving the corporation's property. It failed when it became clear that the same would have to be done, with more objectionable results, for other municipal corporations.[129] Such reasoning did not normally prevail in a legislature which permitted the establishment of countless statutory authorities, with wildly varying composition and powers.

This was not the only sense in which it could be argued that the public interest suffered. Parliament's concessive attitude, its readiness to respond but its refusal to lead, left extensive powers in the hands of vested interests. As the regulatory machinery of the Tudor and Stuart State was allowed to fall into disuse, this became more of a problem. Thus, when the cutting butchers attacked the alleged monopoly of the carcass butchers in 1765, there was widespread interest in the outcome. London meat prices were rising, and it was easy to assume that the consequence would be a price reduction and a better-controlled market. But before legislation found its way on to the statute-book, the butchers made up their differences. 'The contest', wrote one commentator, 'ought not, I think, to have been allowed to be dropt at the pleasure of the contending parties, because it was a contest in which the publick was deeply concerned.'[130]

---

[126] *Whitehall Evening-Post*, 26 May 1791.

[127] T. Heywood, ed., *The Norris Papers* (Chetham Soc. 9, 1846), p. 39: T. Patten to R. Norris, 8 Jan. 1697.

[128] 5 Geo. III, c. 14. The war of hatters and rabbit-wool exporters was recurrent; see the report of the compromise achieved again in 1784 in H. Baring, ed., *The Diary of the Right Hon. William Windham 1784 to 1810* (London, 1866), p. 11.

[129] *Commons Journals*, xxix. 149–50, 152–3, 187, 225.

[130] *London Magazine* (1766), 393.

A CLASHING OF INTERESTS

Parliamentary procedures depended on the assumption that a communal consensus would have been achieved at some preliminary stage. But in many communities there would be minorities which resisted the will of the majority and demanded parliamentary support. In others it might be alleged that a minority had improperly claimed to represent the majority. Most likely of all, in seeking to promote what seemed an indisputable good, it was possible to offend external groups which claimed the right to equivalent treatment. Diverse interests were ever ready to glimpse some threat on the legislative horizon, as the MP James Oglethorpe argued in 1732.

In all Cases where there seems to be a Clashing of Interests, we ought to have no Regard to the partial Interest of any Country, or Set of People; the Good of the Whole should only be considered ... A Petition was once presented to this House by one County, complaining that they were injured in their Trade as to the Sale of Beans by another; and they modestly prayed, that the other County should be prohibited to sell them.[131]

However ludicrous the example, the logic was commonplace. John Shebbeare considered it an incurable condition. 'Northumberland and Newcastle, Cornwall and Penzance, are in England. Are the concerns and interests of the several inhabitants of these districts the same, when the two former are supported by the trade of *coals* and *salmon*, and the latter by that of *tin* and *pilchards?*'[132]

The spirit of competition throve on numberless jealousies and animosities. Parliament's predicament can only be fully understood in the context of a pervasive mentality of conflict. Philosophers identified the processes of regional higgling as one of the guiding principles of a middle-class polity.[133] Politicians were expected to respect the pettiest of provincial rivalries, many of them based on ancient prejudices which had obtained the status of unbreakable law by sheer force of custom. One of the prime functions of the patronage system was to accommodate the pretensions of localities. The Duke of Newcastle was ever attentive to the nuances of parochial rivalry, not least in his own county, where East and West Sussex were united only against outsiders. 'I love Hughes,' he assured the Duke of Richmond, when presented with a powerful claim to an East Sussex living in 1748, 'but Barcomb, being within half a mile of Lewes, can't go

---

[131] Ibid. (1732), 324.

[132] John Shebbeare, *An Essay on the Origin, Progress and Establishment of National Society* (London, 1776), p. 103.

[133] N. Phillipson, 'Adam Smith as Civic Moralist', in I. Hont and M. Ignatieff, *Wealth and Virtue: The Shaping of Political Economy in the Scottish Enlightenment* (Cambridge, 1983), p. 195.

to a Chichester man.'[134] The conflict of close neighbours was a fundamental fact of political life, often overriding every other kind of issue in local politics. Dr Johnson gently mocked the rivalry which he found on a visit to Plymouth. There the town and the dock were continually at odds, in this instance on the subject of the water-supply. 'No, no! I am against the *dockers*; I am a Plymouth-man. Rogues! Let them die of thirst. They shall not have a drop.'[135] Fighting for water was not the commonest form of dispute, but there were many others. Two features of poor relief administration, the rating system and the law of settlements, reinforced the divisions which set parish against parish and township against township. The relative burden of local taxation was a perpetual bone of contention, not least in the north, where large parishes were sometimes subdivided into numerous rating units, and where economic change created glaring injustices out of long-standing conventions. The thirty years war between Bradford and Howarth, which was not fully settled even by a judgement at the West Riding Assizes in 1792, was unusual only in its duration.[136]

The law of settlements was still more productive of friction, and lamented on that account by almost every chronicler and critic of the poor law. 'Ten thousand parishes have been making war upon each other,' declared Edmund Burke.[137] Not only were these battles legitimized by parochial loyalty, but the attitudes which endorsed them were most deeply entrenched at the middling level of yeomen and tenant farmers in the countryside, and the small tradesmen or shopkeepers in the towns. This was pre-eminently the class which staffed local offices, and which, notwithstanding the supervisory power of justices, commissioners, and corporations, possessed an unshakeable hold on much of the political infrastructure of the age. But even the gentry shared some of their prejudices. For Buckinghamshire landowners, a dispute between two neighbouring parishes was not just a matter of conflicting interests, it was 'Winslow law' against 'Claydon law'.[138] It is doubtful whether appeals to the good of the nation as a whole could ever have uprooted these attitudes; rather it was the substitution of still stronger antagonisms, particularly those of class, which were ultimately to make possible a parliamentary attack on them.

The rhetoric of custom and particularism clothed vested interests and restrictive practices as well as authentic local pride and self-reliance. Many

[134] T. J. McCann, ed. *The Correspondence of the Dukes of Richmond and Newcastle, 1724–1750* (Sussex Rec. Soc. 73, 1984), p. 275.

[135] J. L. Clifford, *Dictionary Johnson: Samuel Johnson's Middle Years* (London, 1979), p. 289.

[136] G. Firth, 'The Genesis of the Industrial Revolution in Bradford 1760–1830' (University of Bradford Ph.D. thesis, 1974), ch. 2.

[137] *The Writings and Speeches of Edmund Burke, vol. ii: Party, Parliament and the American Crisis, 1766–74*, ed. P. Langford (Oxford, 1981), p. 403.

[138] M. M. Verney, ed., *Verney Letters of the Eighteenth Century from the MSS, at Claydon House* (2 vols., London, 1930), i. 211.

small towns, and not a few great ones, owed their prosperity to preferential
treatment by the State. The law, for instance, had always provided a source
of livelihood to the towns in which it was dispensed, and the eighteenth
century, with its accumulation of judicial and administrative power, did
nothing to diminish its importance in this respect. Courts brought judges
or justices, barristers and attorneys, sheriffs and bailiffs, as well as those
who sought justice and those who were about to receive it. They also
brought the wives and children, servants and friends of any or all these
individuals. As a form of public subsidy to a town with declining manufactures the administration of the law had a special significance. In the
words of a visitor to Preston, where the Duchy of Lancaster was based, in
1759, it might amount to the 'staple trade'.[139]

There was competition for such subsidies. In counties where quarter
sessions were not invariably held in the county town, magistrates found
themselves burdened with an uncomfortable degree of discretion. When
the Staffordshire justices first met at Wolverhampton it was a tribute to
the town's growing importance.[140] Sometimes, powerful arguments in
favour of temporary change were resisted for fear of their longer-term
implications. In Cambridgeshire in 1757, when the county town was
affected by smallpox, the magistrates were subjected to a barrage of claims
and counter-claims on behalf of Newmarket and Royston.[141] Magistrates
sought to meet local requirements by using their power of adjournment,
transferring their court from place to place without technically convening
it anew. In Lindsay, with four hundred parishes to serve, it was the
practice in mid-century to hold sessions in as many as five places in each
quarter, minimizing inconvenient travel and spreading the incidental profits
of justice. But the jealousies aroused required a formal opinion in 1768
from a distinguished lawyer, Charles Yorke, to quieten them.[142] Suspicions
of gerrymandering were easily awoken, not without reason. In Berkshire
it was customary to ring the changes between Reading, Newbury, and
Abingdon, with occasional removals elsewhere to meet particular needs.
But a series of unprecedented adjournments to New Windsor between
1756 and 1761 gave rise to controversy. Windsor's electoral history was
turbulent, and it was easy to suspect a ploy by one of the magistrates
involved, Lord Vere Beauclerk, with a view to serving the political interests
of his brother, the Duke of St Albans.[143]

Parliament managed to stay out of disputes about quarter sessions. It

[139] B. G. Hutton, 'A Lakeland Journey, 1759', *Trans. Cumbs. and Westmor. Ant. and Arch. Soc.*, NS
61 (1961), 289. The visitor was a Bristol merchant, John Crofts.
[140] G. T. Lawley, *A History of Bilston, in the County of Stafford* (Bilston, 1893), p. 64.
[141] BL, Add. MS 35679, fo. 244: W. Greaves to Hardwicke, 23 Nov. 1757.
[142] BL, Add. MS 36225, fo. 357.
[143] Berkshire RO, Quarter Sessions Minutes.

was less successful in respect of assizes. The twice yearly assize was the climax of county life; particularly in the summer it brought landed society flocking to the town where it was held, and stimulated a variety of social activities, from theatrical and musical entertainments to fairs and horse-races. A good assize week was of inestimable value to traders and the municipal corporations which they sustained. The honour of being an assize town was eagerly contended for. In Sussex, Lewes competed with Chichester, in Cornwall, Launceston with Bodmin, in Norfolk, Norwich with Thetford, in Suffolk, Ipswich with Bury St Edmunds. It was for the Lord Chancellor and the judges to determine where they would hold court, but in a parliamentary age Parliament could not avoid becoming embroiled. The contest between Buckingham and Aylesbury provided the most notorious of all such contests. An act of 1748 asserting Buckingham's right to the summer assizes was seen as electoral rigging at its worst, but if nothing else it demonstrated the importance of such seemingly minor disputes. It was accompanied by a bitter political controversy, which temporarily took priority over matters of pressing national concern.[144] The sequel was also instructive, for the act brought MPs and peers under renewed pressure from other counties. Suffolk appealed to Parliament for its own statute on behalf of Ipswich against Bury St Edmunds in 1749.[145] Cornwall also took a part. The letter which the Duke of Bedford addressed to the Lord Chancellor in 1750 on the subject clearly illustrates the pressures created by parliamentary involvement in local rivalries at a time when electoral interest and the power of patronage provided temptations both for briber and bribed. He regretted his request, he assured Hardwicke, but he was

absolutely forced to it, by the importunities of the People of Launceston. It was in vain for me to alledge over and over again to them, that it was not only improper to urge the request to your Lordship, but that I very much doubted whether it was in your power to comply with it. Nothing I could say could prevail with them ... and I was forced to promise them at last to apply to your Lordship, to know whether what they requested could be complied with or not, and in case of a negative they have agreed to be satisfied with my expending a certain Sum of money, in some publick work for the benefit of the Tòwn in general.[146]

Problems of this kind multiplied as the administrative and judicial business of provincial England expanded in the late eighteenth century. The provision of new court-houses, shire halls, and county gaols naturally stimulated competition for the public spending involved. The contest for a new gaol and shire house in Essex between 1769 and 1772 threatened to rival

---

[144] L. M. Wiggin, *The Faction of Cousins* (New Haven, Conn., 1958), pp. 124–9.

[145] *Commons Journals*, xxv. 725.

[146] BL, Add. MS 35591, fos. 106–7: 22 Aug. 1750. Launceston was seeking to reverse an earlier and very rare parliamentary intervention which had allocated the summer assizes to Bodmin, the winter to Launceston.

that relating to Buckingham in 1748. The report which the House of
Commons compiled on this subject in 1771, after exhaustive examination of
witnesses and documentary evidence, ran to nearly fifty thousand words.[147]
Disputes occurred in the capital itself. Relations between the City of
London and the county of Middlesex were not always easy, despite London's ancient success in appropriating the election of the county sheriffs.
The expense of maintaining Newgate and the respective rights of City and
county in committing prisoners to its custody was a subject of some
acrimony during Sir John Hawkins's tenure as Chairman of the Middlesex
bench.[148] Nor was it only at the relatively lofty level of the county and the
King's justice that such debates took place. The outrage with which the
corporation of Richmond reacted when the officials of the archdeaconry
moved their proceedings and records to Kendal, and then to Lancaster,
deserves its place alongside the indignation of Buckingham. The consistory
court was a judicial midget compared with the giant of an assize, but to a
small Yorkshire town which derived a dependable income from the records
of probate and a bigger one from the suits of testators and inheritors, the
issue was not less important. On behalf of the inhabitants, the Mayor of
Richmond described the removal of the court's archives from the town as
a 'shameless invasion of this Property'.[149]

Against this background it is hardly surprising that the manifold innovations of an age of self-conscious improvement gave rise to conflicts. The
object of local, *ad hoc* legislation was to meet the stated needs of particular
communities. But highly localized legislation could harm the interests of
other communities. In a sense much of it was meant to. Many improvements
were designed to achieve an advantage at the expense of some other locality,
even when they were manifestly of public benefit. Bridges were a particular
passion of the improvers. But the siting of bridges was a matter of great
local consequence and inevitably affected vested interests. Many new
bridges required an act of Parliament to authorize the purchase of land or
the financing of construction. Some epic parliamentary battles resulted,
not least among competing parts of the capital. The building of Westminster
Bridge was bitterly but unavailingly opposed by the City of London. But
the later erection of a third bridge in London, at Blackfriars, caused a
redrawing of battle lines and split the Court of Common Council down
the middle in 1755. Those representing the western portion of the City
had an obvious interest in supporting it, those representing the eastern

---

[147] *Commons Journals*, xxxii. 364; xxxiii. 81, 124, 207, 368–98, 415.

[148] *Memoirs, Anecdotes, Facts, and Opinions, Collected and Preserved by Laetitia-Matilda Hawkins*
(2 vols., London, 1824), i. 325.

[149] *The Case between the Mayor and Corporation of the Town of Richmond, and the Principals and
Officers of The Consistory-Court, of the Archdeaconry of Richmond* (1748), p. 12.

portion an equal interest in protecting the monopoly of London Bridge.[150] The legislation approving each of these undertakings was cumbersome and contentious. This was not merely because they affected powerful interest-groups, but also because financing them aroused intense controversy.

In theory many projects authorized by statute generated revenues for their own maintenance. Canals created new services for which a toll could be charged: on the strength of anticipated tolls the capital needed for construction was raised. Turnpike bills also provided for the levying of tolls on the traveller. They did so, however, on roads which, for all their improvement by the activities of highway trustees, were usually ancient thoroughfares, previously maintained by statute labour and travelled free by all who used them. The tolls were therefore in the nature of a tax, supplementing one form of highway rate with another. It was in this light that they were viewed by many of the poorer sort, as the riotous destruction of turnpike gates in the early years of road improvement reveals.[151] Most of the plans placed before the legislature did not even pretend to be self-financing in this limited sense. Street improvements, water-supplies, poor houses, all required capital expenditure which must either be raised by taxation, or by borrowing secured on taxation. Parliament was remarkably liberal in approving the wishes of the local community in this respect. Certainly it did so without reference to any general principles or national policies. A bewildering variety of rates, tolls, and taxes was approved. This was not controversial at the time. What did cause complaint was the dawning realization in many cases that the incidence of such taxation was unjust. The ideal means of financing improvement was to lay the cost on some body other than the beneficiaries. Since it was often difficult to calculate the relative benefits to different communities of particular projects, there was much room for disagreement.

Bridges were again a case in point. In Lancashire, the Ribble Bridge Bill of 1751 met with great hostility. Lonsdale Hundred in the north of the county described it as 'so unreasonable a Project, founded on local Considerations only'. The bridge was to be financed by a levy on the whole county, yet 'Nine Parts in Ten of the said County Palatine will never have Occasion to pass over it'. This view evidently had wide support. Every Lancashire hundred, with the exception of West Derby, petitioned against the bill; so did a number of individual boroughs and parishes, including Wigan, Bury, Bolton, Clitheroe, Rochdale, Rossendale, and Ashton under Lyne. Rossendale's demand was typical: 'if the intended new Bridge is to be built, it ought to be done at the Expense of such Gentleman as will have

---

[150] J. Entick, *A Continuation of the History and Survey of the Cities of London and Westminster* (London, 1775), pp. 3–4, 8–9.

[151] W. Albert, 'Popular Opposition to Turnpike Trusts in Early Eighteenth-Century England', *Jnl. Transport Hist.* 5 (1979), 1–17.

have an Advantage thereby, and not charged upon the whole County.' The bill had to be recommitted and amended before it was passed.[152] Town and county conflicts were commonplace. The Shrewsbury plan for financing a new bridge in 1771 provoked a protest from the county of Shropshire on the grounds that charging a proportion 'of the Expenses of rebuilding the said Bridge upon the County of *Salop* at large, lays an additional Land Tax upon the Estates of the Petitioners'.[153] Opposition could come from much further afield. When Hull proposed to remodel its harbour with funds raised by duties on all cargoes passing up the Humber in 1767, it met with an impressive array of objections from York, Gainsborough, Leeds, Pontefract, and Halifax.[154] Gloucester was equally impudent. Its bill to repair the bridge over the Severn by levying tolls on river traffic brought hostile petitions not merely from Gloucestershire but from places as far away as Montgomeryshire, Shrewsbury, Wolverhampton, and Bewdley.[155]

Conflicts were numerous in the capital. London and its hinterland had one of the most controversial of all taxes, the duty on sea coal. Its purposes were primarily local, including the financing of new churches. But it proved a lucrative fund, as London's fuel consumption rocketed, and from the time of Walpole it was raided by Chancellors of the Exchequer. On both counts it caused much irritation, from London to the extent that taxes paid by Londoners were devoted to general purposes, and from many consumers in the south-east and in the Thames valley, who obtained their coal via the port of London and objected to subsidizing the 'Ornamental Convenience of the Capital'.[156] Even amongst Londoners it created differences when the duties were partially diverted to improve the environs of Blackfriars Bridge in 1767. It was pointed out that the benefits would accrue almost exclusively to the City. Demands from Westminster and Southwark for a share in the proceeds were accepted by Parliament. But the precedent proved dangerous. As soon as the improvement commissions of Southwark and Westminster had been satisfied, the Middlesex portion of the parish of St Botolph Aldgate applied for a matching share. No doubt every parish within the London area but outside the City strictly defined would have followed suit if the House of Commons had not hastily drawn a line at this point.[157]

It was in the nature of metropolitan improvements that they had endless ramifications. Street paving and lighting schemes from the 1750s onwards

---

[152] *Commons Journals,* xxvi. 129, 138, 146, 149–50, 153, 184, 195.
[153] Ibid., xxxiii. 271.
[154] *London Magazine* (1768), 402–3.
[155] *Commons Journals,* xxxvi. 322–5, 449–50, 471, 475, 484.
[156] David Hardie, *Taxation of Coals* (London, 1792); *Extracts from the Navigation Rolls of the Rivers Thames and Isis* (London, 1772), p. vi.
[157] *London Magazine* (1768), 292–6.

produced many disputes. The most ambitious of these, the Westminster Paving Commission, initiated in 1762, met with protests from Surrey and Kent, whose market gardeners and carriers found themselves subjected to a new duty, the proceeds of which were devoted solely to the welfare of their customers.[158] The City of London's own project on these lines, begun two years earlier, proved almost as contentious when, in 1766, the corporation sought powers to raise money by way of tolls as well as rates. The parishes of Shoreditch and Whitechapel both objected. As the inhabitants of Whitechapel pointed out, 'they will not have it in their Power to go out of their Parish, without paying a Tax, which is, by the said Bill, declared to be for the Purposes of paving *London*, and its Liberties only, although the Petitioners will not have travelled upon any Part of the Pavement of the said City or Liberties.' They went on to add that although they intended to apply for a similar bill of their own, they 'should not presume to desire a Power to tax the Inhabitants of *London* towards the same, unless they shall travel thereupon'. In the light of later events there was a certain irony about this assumption of moral superiority. When Whitechapel applied for its bill in 1769, it was opposed by the freeholders and farmers of Essex, who noted that 'several Tolls are proposed, which will greatly injure the Petitioners, and affect the Trade and Tillage of the said County of Essex'.[159] Economic historians congratulate early industrial England on its freedom from local tolls of the kind which the physiocrats denounced on the Continent, yet Parliament cheerfully consented to their imposition on numerous occasions. When it refused to do so it was generally in response to local opposition. Maidstone lost a clause authorizing tolls to finance street paving in 1791 because neighbouring countrymen made their hostility all too clear.[160]

If the stresses of legislative life had been confined to the conflicts of localities, they might have been kept within bounds. But this was an unrealistic hope. Parliament was as much the adjudicator of interests as it was the arbiter between localities. Interests sometimes coincided with particular regions, sometimes cut across them. They created problems, to which, in theory, contemporary wisdom offered a ready solution. Wherever British interests clashed with those of foreigners, they would be granted the preference which conventional mercantilist principles dictated. Wherever internal interests conflicted, anything which tended to monopoly would be crushed, anything which promoted healthy competition for the good of the public at large would be encouraged.

The realities were more complicated than this simple formula suggested.

---

[158] *Commons Journals*, xxx. 806.
[159] Ibid., xxx. 771; xxxii. 323.
[160] J. M. Russell, *The History of Maidstone* (Maidstone, 1881), p. 239.

Lines of demarcation between the interests of foreign and domestic producers were not always easily identified. Questions of external trade might
turn into questions of internal competition. Special pleading by one or
other group of Britons was almost as much a feature of legislation regulating
overseas commerce, as of legislation relating to home manufacture. One of
the most enduring enmities of the period, that of linen and wool, was
typical in this respect. The linen manufacture was growing vigorously in
Ireland, Scotland, and several parts of England. In Ireland and Scotland
public bodies with strong political support encouraged the development of
the industry. A recurrent demand was for additional protection against
foreign competition, in the form of high import duties on linens imported
from central Europe and the abolition of drawbacks on the re-export of
foreign linens to the British colonies. But Germany and Silesia were not
only exporters of linens to the British empire, they were also importers of
British woollens. The Prussian government made it clear that any measures
against Silesian lawns would be counteracted with measures against English
cloth. Applications to Parliament by the linen manufacturers, in 1745,
1751, and 1774, led to gruelling struggles with the woollen producers.[161]
Parliament, confronted with conflicting demands from two great textile
interests, sought to avoid alienating either by granting the linen manufacturers additional export bounties which could not technically be presented as damaging foreign imports. But these, too, produced problems.
Bounties had to be financed by taxation: the first of those on linen was
raised by levying a duty on foreign cambrics, which duly provoked a
retaliatory duty on British goods exported to Flanders. Moreover, in a
domestic context, even bounties were a form of discrimination. The cotton
manufacturers of Manchester were able, in 1751, to obtain support for
their own trade on the grounds that their products competed directly with
Irish linens, and deserved similar treatment.[162]

Colonial trade created comparable problems. British goods were in
almost all cases guaranteed preferential treatment in colonial markets, and
colonial competitors were treated much like foreigners, as the Hat Act of
1737 and the Iron Act of 1750, both aimed at American manufacturers,
revealed. Economic circumstances made the American and West Indian
colonies weak competitors in point of manufacturing capacity, or the
resulting clashes would have been far worse. But the adverse balance of
trade with the possessions of the East India Company was far less satisfying
in this respect. The struggle between the Company and domestic producers
of the lighter textiles proved bitter. It culminated in the passage of the
Calico Act of 1721, which laid the foundations of an indigenous cotton

---

[161] *Commons Journals* xxiv. 770–1; xxvii. 74–6; *Parliamentary History*, xvii. 110–58.
[162] *Parliamentary History*, xxvi. 74–6, 234–5.

industry and incidentally provoked a parliamentary contest of exceptional intensity. This had considerable ramifications. The Company, for all its negative effect on the balance of trade, imported valuable oriental commodities. It also exported large quantities of British manufactured goods. The guaranteed market which it was required to provide, on uneconomic terms, for woollens, helped prop up the declining West Country cloth industry at a time when it was being overhauled in the home market by the Yorkshire manufacture.[163] Nor could it be seen in isolation. Calicoes and cambrics were a continuing source of dispute because the products of France and the Austrian Netherlands were competitively priced even when burdened with discriminatory duties. It would have seemed absurd to exclude Company goods merely to allow the flooding in of imports from across the Channel. But the consequent duties on cambrics provoked retaliation in Europe and in turn affected the market for home manufactures. The simplest proposition for the defence of native industry had a way of turning into a disorderly mass of contentious arguments.

Parliament was well aware of the way its war on foreign competition could be used to favour vested interests at the expense of domestic rivals. When the lace-makers of Buckinghamshire, Bedfordshire, and Northamptonshire requested not only a higher duty on foreign products, but an actual prohibition on the import of French lace, there was an understandable suspicion that the object of the petitioners was to raise prices at home, not to exclude unfair competition.[164] Nor, in truth, was it necessary to advance the excuse of foreign undercutting. Home industries were quite capable of demanding special treatment against domestic rivals. Such conflicts, often between different branches of the same industry or between different sectors of wholesale and retail trade, usually commenced with a claim of unfair practices on the part of a rival. But accusations of monopoly could well conceal an attempt at monopoly. Much parliamentary time was spent trying to get to the bottom of bickering of this kind, and conscientious MPs were required to struggle with a forbidding body of documentation if they sought to understand it. The destruction of the archives of the House of Commons in the fire of 1834 carried away most of the evidence with which to reconstruct this process of legislative warfare. But where the personal archives of MPs survive, it is possible to glimpse the multiplicity of arguments and interests which assailed ordinary legislators.

William Bromley's papers for the last years of Queen Anne's reign, when he was Speaker of the House of Commons, comprise an extraordinary variety of pleadings, most of them printed, and plainly distributed to MPs

[163] J. de L. Mann, *The Cloth Industry in the West of England from 1640 to 1880* (Oxford, 1971), pp. 43–4.
[164] *Commons Journals*, xxxvii. 185–6, 303.

en masse.[165] Interests lobbying Bromley in 1710 included paper merchants, cocoa-makers, gun-makers, iron and steel manufacturers, glass-makers, innkeepers, leather-sellers, bakers, copper and brass-makers, the Mine-Adventurers, colliers, the Thames and Scottish fisheries, and Hackney-coachmen. In 1711 they included the Royal Africa Company, the Newcastle hoast-men, brick-makers, pasteboard-makers, bookbinders, woollen exporters, brass manufacturers, cocoa importers, clockmakers, calico-printers, parish clerks, dealers in drugs, coffee, and tea, poor gauze-weavers, gold and silver wire manufacturers, Greenwich Hospital, linen manufacturers, the Hudson-Bay Company, holders of Crown leases, leather-sellers, poor paper-makers, copper and brass merchants, starch-makers, the Dutch and French Protestant Churches, linen-drapers, keelmen, hard cake and white soap-makers, silver traders, turpentine importers, and Quakers. This list takes no account of authentically local petitions or petitions concerning electoral disputes: both categories produced a number of papers. The point of such petitions varied hugely. Some were protests by vested interests against taxes or other legislation. They required MPs to balance the interests of the public at large against those of some specific group. Depending on the MP and the interest they might have awkward electoral implications. Others were contests between related but distinct groups. Pasteboard-makers battled with bookbinders, clothiers with wool-card makers. In these cases the only public concern was fair competition, far from easy though it was to secure it. Conflicts of this kind were the stuff of the ordinary legislator's parliamentary life, and resolving them no less important than coping with the competing pressures of Court and Country, Whig and Tory, government and opposition. Bromley, as Speaker, doubtless received more than his share of paper. But any MP who attended his duty in the Commons would have been subject to similar lobbying. The collection of tracts left by George Bowes, knight of the shire for Durham under George II, reveals a similar diversity of concerns.[166]

THE HAPPINESS AND GLORY OF A REPRESENTATIVE

How did Parliament cope with the pressures of a divided, competitive, and vigorous property-owning society, given to commercial combat at every opportunity? However hard it sought to secure harmony by rendering legislation local and particular, and by insisting on the agreement of those primarily affected before legislation proceeded through either House, it was not possible to avoid all conflicts. Resolving and composing them was sometimes beyond the capacity of a body used to absorbing considerable

[165] Bodleian Library, Parliamentary Papers of William Bromley.

[166] Durham RO, Strathmore MSS. Printed 'Cases' gradually gave way to longer presentations in pamphlet literature and to alternative forms of lobbying; see Brewer, *The Sinews of Power*, p. 242.

tension. What mattered most in such cases was that the damage inflicted on Parliament as an institution was limited, and that, as far as possible, those disappointed did not take their disappointment out on the political structure which had failed them. It was not, for the most part, a matter of haves versus have-nots, but of haves versus other haves. Controlling the resulting disputes was of the first importance to the successful working of the constitution, perhaps to its survival. This was the politics of interest, rather than the politics of class, or the politics of faith, though all three were sometimes involved. The way in which Parliament dealt with the demands on it was of supreme importance in this context, for if the eighteenth-century State was not parliamentary, it was nothing.

On the face of it Parliament was not well equipped to meet this challenge. In theory the representative function was fulfilled by an elected House of Commons. But the practice of parliamentary elections was singularly unpromising. The irrationality of the unreformed electoral system is well known. It is a common assumption that the worst injustices which it bred related to the franchise, particularly in so far as it excluded large numbers of Britons from a share in the choice of representatives, and vested it in many places in small, oligarchical minorities, and in some in 'borough-mongering' individuals. This criticism of the parliamentary constitution was voiced frequently at the time, and was central to the critique of contemporary government put by the parliamentary reformers. But the franchise was not the only grievance of those who felt aggrieved. The distribution of constituencies, particularly as it bore on the representation of regional and local interests, was equally disturbing.

Three charges stand out. Only 92 of the 513 English and Welsh MPs were elected for counties, at a time when the most generous estimate of the urban population would not have more than about 30 per cent of English and Welshmen living in towns, and considerably less living in towns with parliamentary seats. This manifestly discriminated against the inhabitants of the countryside. Secondly, although no less than 203 boroughs had MPs of their own, all but five of them two MPs, the historical accidents by which they had been selected for the privilege had created an utterly inconsistent form of municipal representation. The author of *Facts, or a Comparative View of the Population of England and Wales* in 1783, reckoned that there were 112 towns with 400 houses chargeable to the house tax, the minimum criterion for a town of substance. Of these only 60 elected members of the House of Commons.[167] The remaining unrepresented places included some of the most dynamic urban centres, of the age: Birmingham, Manchester, Leeds, Sheffield, Sunderland, Wolverhampton, Stoke, and so on. On the other hand 143 towns which failed

[167] (Doncaster, 1783).

to meet this criterion did have their own parliamentary seats. Even worse, the geographical distribution of the small parliamentary boroughs made a nonsense of any claim to fairness. There were four substantial counties (Cheshire, Derbyshire, Leicestershire, and Cambridgeshire) in which only the county town itself enjoyed the franchise. In these instances the entire population of the county and its constituent boroughs was represented by a total of four MPs. Yet a county which happened to contain a number of parliamentary boroughs was ludicrously over-represented. Cornwall's 44 seats and Wiltshire's 32 were notorious.

Contemporary critics rang the changes on demographic and fiscal comparisons to demonstrate the grotesque effects of the electoral system. The results exposed regional disparities as well as the inequities of county and borough. Two of these anomalies stand out in retrospect as they did at the time. The injustice done to the capital and its immediate environs was extraordinary. Middlesex had a tenth of the population and paid 16 per cent of the land tax throughout the eighteenth century. It contributed 26 per cent of the candle duty in 1756, 40 per cent of the tax on silver plate in 1757. But it had only eight seats in the Commons, less than 2 per cent of the whole.[168] This needed none of the new industrial growth of the late eighteenth century to make it objectionable. In 1742 Sir John Barnard enquired why Middlesex, London, Westminster, and Southwark should support one-fifth of the nation but elect only one-fifty-fifth of the Commons.[169] A 'Middlesexian' in 1762 pointed out that at least a hundred MPs would be needed to provide fair representation for his county.[170] There was little doubt about where the seats should be taken from to meet this demand. The eight south-western counties enjoyed 36 per cent of the parliamentary seats, but sustained only a fifth of the land tax and a fifth of the population. Their privileged position was endlessly analysed and criticized by the parliamentary reformers.

If MPs had been strictly answerable to their electing constituencies the results of these imbalances would have been devastating. Accountability was one of the main demands of late eighteenth-century reformers. It was profoundly unpopular with legislators. Reformers, of course, also wanted radical changes in the representative system itself, so that electoral control of MPs would go naturally with a distribution of seats which corresponded to the distribution of population. Their opponents rightly saw that rejection of popular control and preservation of the existing system went together.

Changes in the terminology of representation were significant in this context. The expression 'Parliament-man' placed an MP alongside other

---

[168] Candle duty returns for 1756 at PRO, Cust. 48.15; plate duty returns at T. 47. 5.
[169] *London Magazine* (1742), 158.
[170] Ibid. (1762), 363.

agents of the community, such as Alderman, Common-Councilman, Tything-man, Convocation-man. It went with an old tradition of paying MPs to reimburse them for the expenses and burdens of representing their electors. It was still commonplace in the early eighteenth century but increasingly fell out of favour in the second half of the century. Its more august successor, Member of Parliament, suggested a dignified club, self-appointed and self-governing, rather than the forum of the people. But the new dignity of a representative appealed even to those who wanted greater accountability. The coronation of George III reminded observers of the peculiar insignificance of the Lower House of Parliament in the rites of the State, at a time when its power was manifestly increasing. 'So many reasons will occur to every Briton, why their Representatives in Parliament, the Protectors of their Liberty, the Dispensers of their Property, ought to act some distinguished part in this ceremony.'[171]

Unfortunately, as it seemed to many, the dignity was exerted at the expense of the people. Just how dignified and club-like the Commons could appear was shown all too clearly when parliamentary privilege was employed against John Wilkes, his publishers, and his electors. The result was a considerable debate about the function of representation. The Wilkes-ites emphasized popular control of MPs, and sought a revival of those forms of 'instruction' which had once been common and which had been used, for instance, against Walpole.[172] In doing so they provoked the most famous defence of the alternative doctrine, that MPs, however elected, owed it to the community as a whole to consult only their own conscience and their own sense of the national good when determining their par-liamentary conduct. Burke's arguments, addressed to his Bristol con-stituents in 1774, were not new. It was, however, unusual for a newly elected MP to put them publicly to his own electors: Burke himself claimed that he was the first ever to have done so. More importantly, he established on an enduring basis a thesis which was eminently acceptable to MPs, and perhaps to most of their electors. The Wilkesites' attempt to secure a nation-wide set of instructions in 1774 was a humiliating failure.[173]

In some respects these controversies were rather misleading. The debate about instructions was partly semantic. For practical purposes most MPs were perfectly used to being instructed by their constituents. But the language in which these instructions were expressed was generally diplo-matic. Among the papers of Sir John Delaval, thrice MP for Berwick, there are numerous 'entreaties' and 'requests' from his electors. When his support

---

[171] *General Evening Post*, 20 Aug. 1761.

[172] P. Kelly, ' "Constituents' " Instructions to Members of Parliament in the Eighteenth Century', in *Party and Management in Parliament, 1660–1784* (Leicester, 1984), p. 189.

[173] I. R. Christie, 'The Wilkesites and the General Election of 1774', in *Myth and Reality in Late Eighteenth-Century Britain and Other Papers* (London, 1970), pp. 244–60.

for the Fox–North coalition in 1784 offended the Berwick corporation, he suddenly found himself the recipient of 'instructions', a shift of terminology whose meaning he well understood.[174] Burke himself was immensely proud of his role as a representative of the empire's second city, and went out of his way to stress that he thought it 'ought to be the happiness and glory of a Representative, to live in the strictest union, the closest correspondence, and the most unreserved communication with his constituents'.[175] He was a dutiful and industrious constituency MP. None the less he had a clear sense of the impropriety of sacrificing the interests of the whole or other parts to those of his electors. In 1780 he refused to oppose Lord Beauchamp's bill to release debtors from gaol on grounds of humanity and principle. Similarly, he declined to follow the commercial principles of his constituents when they conflicted with those of Ireland and the empire as a whole. In these respects he was most unusual. An MP who flouted his electors' views, especially when doing so was not necessary to appease the government of the day, was a rarity. Burke suffered by his defeat at the following election, as any other MP would have, however talented. In Bristol admiration for a parliamentarian of extraordinary gifts was not the same as readiness to let him use them according to his own genius. But his attack on constituency control of MPs had been directed elsewhere, at radical groups which sought to impose a specific line of political conduct on him. In this he was probably not offending more than a tiny minority of his own electors.

How many Bristols were there? In 1800 there were 153 MPs with constituencies which had more than 1,000 voters, 89 representing counties and 64 substantial boroughs. A further 67 sat for constituencies with more than 500 voters, 3 of them counties, the remainder boroughs.[176] These were not in any sense uncorrupted constituencies. Contesting them was extremely expensive. But they were by and large constituencies in which failure to support local interests would be electorally disastrous. Up to a point, this was true even of small constituencies. An MP who ignored the demands of electors in a rotten borough threatened by specific legislation would find that no amount of money could repair the damage. 'The only political tenet to which your St Mawes electors will bind you is the belief that the Pilchard is the best of all possible fish, which, as long as you are not obliged to taste it, you may undertake for their sake to believe,' the Marquis of Buckingham told William Windham in 1801.[177] In fact the

---

[174] Northumberland RO, Delaval MSS, 2DE/49/2; Delaval's labours emerge most clearly from his papers concerning the Tweed Fisheries Bill of 1771 at 2DE/49/3.

[175] *Speech at the Conclusion of the Poll, 3 November 1774* (Bristol, 1774).

[176] R. G. Thorne, *History of Parliament: House of Commons, 1790–1820* (5 vols., London, 1986), ii. 43.

[177] *The Windham Papers* (2 vols., London, 1913), ii. 195.

Cornish fishing industry was not negligible, and MPs were expected to support it without wavering when there was any question of competition with interests elsewhere. But it was true that rotten boroughs were rarely touched by legislation. Nor were they likely to seek compliance with a particular statement of principle or policy. By contrast, substantial towns and counties were often affected by parliamentary business: this amounted to roughly one-third of all MPs. The rest could not be said to represent electors with a real interest in the legislation which they supervised.

The House of Lords was constituted without reference to any public or extra-parliamentary body. Heredity and the patronage considerations of new creations did not suggest any rationale to the selection of an upper chamber that would be useful in terms likely to be understood by those petitioning for legislation. Yet the Lords had all the rights enjoyed by the House of Commons. In some respects its judicial standing gave it superior status where 'private' legislation was concerned. The vetting of bills carried out by the judges and law lords was a searching scrutiny and might amount to a form of veto. Only bills raising taxes on the public were considered the peculiar prerogative of the Lower House. It was broadly accepted that the Lords could not initiate or amend 'money bills'. Yet in respect of local legislation it held the whip hand. Thus in 1791 it ventured to amend the tolls levied by a Sussex Road Bill. The Commons reacted with predictable irritation but the Lords stood their ground. The MP who had sponsored the bill, Thomas Pelham, assured the Lower House that he would rather sacrifice it than concede a constitutional principle. But it was the Upper House which won this tussle. In due course a revised bill was produced and passed.[178]

When 558 MPs and more than 200 peers consulted their conscience, there was nothing to choose between them. But most legislation did not raise fundamental questions of conscience. Moreover, most legislators were likely to have considerations other than Burke's ideal before them. For practical purposes they thought of those who elected, supported, and influenced them. Their constituency, their residence, their property, their connections, and their interests, as well as their relationship with political masters, were all in question.

The need to consult closely with constituents was often emphasized. It was a standard tactic of seventeenth-century MPs to announce their intention of doing so before casting a vote on important matters. Sir Edward Coke's Fourth Institute enshrined this practice of 'conference with their counties'.[179] The recess was considered particularly useful in this respect. As late as 1774 the King's Speech at the start of the session talked of

---

[178] *Whitehall Evening-Post*, 26, 30 May 1791.
[179] *The Fourth Part of the Institutes of the Laws of England* (5th edn., London, 1671), pp. 14, 34.

members having returned from their 'respective counties'.[180] In practice
this assumption that MPs were wont to come into regular contact with
their electors had ceased to be realistic. When Lord Strange demanded an
opportunity to confer with his constituents about the East India Mutiny
Bill in 1754, he plainly feared that he would be thought old-fashioned.
'Though I shall not pretend to set bounds of the power of the legislature,
yet in all such cases I think we should follow the example of our ancestors,
by saying, that before we can consider of any such matter, we must have
a conference with those of our several counties, and places who put us in
trust.'[181] Even if the practice itself had continued it would not have fitted
with the legislative timetable as it was evolving. Improved postal services,
and the financial penalty for delaying legislation, rendered it convenient to
push bills through as quickly as possible. The sheer quantity of legislation
made it difficult to keep track. It was pointed out in 1765 that only as a
result of the *Votes* had it come to the notice of the hatters that a clause
incidentally affecting their trade, but concealed in a bill regulating the
fisheries, was about to pass through Parliament.[182] Samuel Whitbread in
1781 urged the Brewers' Company to peruse the published *Votes* regularly:
'as Bills had often made progress in Parliament and even gone through,
without any attention of Persons who afterwards found themselves hurt by
them'.[183] Even so there remained an expectation that MPs would bring to
the attention of their electors measures which affected them. In 1763, when
a controversial road bill foundered in the Commons, it was remarked that
MPs would be able to return to their constituencies, equipped with printed
copies of the bill, to obtain the instructions for the following session, 'which
is certainly the best way that can be taken for rendering any new law
compleat and perfect'.[184]

The surest guarantee that an MP might represent his electors' interests
would have been provided by residence among them, at least for a portion
of each year. Several statutes of the fifteenth century specifically required
MPs to reside in this way. This highly inconvenient requirement was
flouted in subsequent centuries, ruled irrelevant by the courts, and finally
repealed by Parliament in 1774.[185] It is significant that the act of 1711
which laid down a propertied qualification for MPs did not stipulate that
the property in question be held in any particular place. In the counties such
a provision would have been redundant, since it was almost unthinkable that

---

[180] R. C. Simmons and P. D. G. Thomas, eds., *Proceedings and Debates of the British Parliaments Respecting North America 1754–1783* (New York, 1982–   ), iv. 1.
[181] *London Magazine* (1755), 107.
[182] *Commons Journals*, xxx. 167–8.
[183] P. Mathias, *The Brewing Industry in England 1700–1830* (Cambridge, 1959), p. 222.
[184] *London Magazine* (1764), 180.
[185] 14 Geo. III, c. 58.

a knight of the shire would be elected from outside the county community. But the omission was crucial with regard to boroughs. Many borough representatives were carpet-baggers, men who had made their money in London or overseas. For them residence would have been out of the question. Even country gentlemen seeking a seat in a neighbouring borough would have been loath to reside among the townsmen whose support they sought. One objection to the Qualification Act was precisely that it tended to promote the election of landowners from the neighbouring countryside rather than burgesses of the town. This is not to say that residence was considered irrelevant to representation. A standard response to the invasion of Parliament by nabobs was to insist on it. The Essex antiquarian Peter Muilman, somewhat ironically in view of his own foreign origins, urged the North ministry to adopt as a 'fundamental Rule' the principle that only Essex men should sit for Essex seats.[186] Even the more sophisticated Josiah Tucker, no radical, advocated in 1781 a property qualification to be held within thirty miles of the constituency.

Tucker identified a crucial change in the residential habits of MPs, which radically affected their representative function.

The Complaint usually brought against *Cornwall* and *Wiltshire*, is, that they return too many Members in Proportion to the rest of the Kingdom: Whereas these Counties might justly retort the Accusation, by saying that though they have *Nominally* more Members than *London*, Westminster, and Southwark, yet in *reality* they have fewer. For most of the Members for the *Cornish* and *Wiltshire* Boroughs have their chief Residence in the Metropolis, with Country-Seats perhaps in its Environs:—None of which Villas, generally speaking, are at a greater Distance than 20 or 30 Miles from it:—And what is still worse, most of such Members have not a Foot of Land *in*, or anywhere *near* the Places for which they were elected: So that having no personal Interest in the Premises, they might with much greater Propriety, be stiled the Representative of *London*, *Westminster* and *Southwark*, and of the several Districts in the Neighbourhood (where the Estates and Fortunes are supposed to be) then the Representatives of the Boroughs in *Wiltshire* and *Cornwall* where they have no Property at all.[187]

Tucker's argument is supported by the available evidence of residential habits among MPs. During the preceding hundred years the number of MPs with a residence in the south-western counties had progressively diminished. The eight counties of the region had 185 parliamentary seats, but by 1784 only 106 resident MPs. The eight counties of the south-east, including London, had 104 seats, but 179 resident MPs. Middlesex alone, with its meagre total of 8 seats, had 57 resident MPs.[188] It is not difficult

---

[186] *Trans. Essex Arch. Soc.* 15 (1921), 100.

[187] *A Treatise Concerning Civil Government, in Three Parts*, pp. 280–1, 291–2.

[188] For fuller information see P. Langford, 'Property and "Virtual Representation" in Eighteenth-Century England', *Hist. Jnl.* 31 (1988), 94–5.

to explain this shift from south-west to south-east. Much wealth was invested in the increasingly valuable asset of a parliamentary seat once it became clear, in the years following the Revolution of 1688, that Parliament was a permanence and the monarchy permanently amenable to the influence of parliamentarians. A great deal of the wealth was derived from trades pursued in London and its surroundings; a high proportion of the purchasable parliamentary seats was in the south-west. Moreover, men who made a fortune in overseas trade, in financial speculation, or in service with the East India Company, tended to seek a country residence within reach of London, and a rotten borough in the West Country.

The question of residence was complicated by the fact that legislators did not necessarily reside very much at their 'country seat'. A local connection was an asset for parliamentary candidates in large boroughs. But even in such places a London residence all the year round was not necessarily a disadvantage. On behalf of the Liverpool MP Charles Pole in 1761 it was urged: 'Is it not a great Convenience to you during the recess of parliament, that you have always such an Advocate ready and willing to solicit your various Applications?'[189] In practice the distinction between residents and 'foreigners' was in any case a rather artifical one. By the mid-eighteenth century the overwhelming majority of peers and MPs either owned or rented a residence in London, or more precisely in Westminster. In the 1760s one of the mass-produced diaries, *The Daily Journal*, included in its appendices of useful information the London address of all MPs whose residence it could identify. In 1764 it failed in only ten cases. Seven MPs were said to be abroad on diplomatic or military service, two lived 'chiefly out of town', and one, the Cheshire MP Samuel Egerton, could not be located more exactly than 'near the horse guards'.[190] Even John Elwes, the legendary miser and MP for Berkshire, felt compelled to have a permanent lodging in town, though in his case this involved moving into his nephew's house, an imposition which his nephew tolerated in the mistaken expectation of inheriting his fabulous fortune.[191]

MPs expected to do business at their London address. The Scottish MPs were outraged in 1749 when the Duke of Bedford sent letters requesting their attendance on a turnpike bill, not to their homes but to the British Coffee House.[192] Not so long before this would have been thought standard practice. One consequence of the change in residential habits was that London had an effective form of representation which helped offset its notorious deficiency in this respect. As Baptist Noel Turner pointed out in 1783, when reformers were pressing the case for more metropolitan

---

[189] *An Entire and Impartial Collection of All the Papers, etc.*, p. 18.
[190] p. 158.
[191] *Whitehall Evening-Post*, 2 Jan. 1790.
[192] A. L. Cust, *Chronicles of Erthig on the Dyke* (2 vols., London, 1914), i. 306–7.

MPs, 'every member of both houses has an interest in it thro' his part-residence'.[193] If Middlesex had 57 MPs in 1784 with a permanent residence in the county, it had still more with a regular presence there, probably in excess of 500. Hardly a session passed in the late eighteenth century without specific legislation affecting one or other of the metropolitan parishes. MPs and peers as ratepayers were directly affected by such bills, as were their friends and neighbours. Not surprisingly these bills were closely followed and often gave rise to controversy. MPs who sat for distant constituencies were to be found taking a close interest in their fate, as in the government of Westminster and the urban parishes of Middlesex and Surrey generally. Select vestries included as many peers and MPs as possible for precisely this reason: they were expected to ease the passage of legislation affecting their fellow parishioners. When the parish of St Marylebone was contemplating legislation, it merely instructed the MPs and peers who were members of its select vestry to act as a committee for that purpose.[194] Whether this was genuinely an advantage to the public was another matter. Jonas Hanway doubted it, and told a plausible story of a workman who lamented the impossibility of maintaining paving properly when the waterworks which kept breaking it up in order to repair pipes were mostly owned by MPs.[195]

It was not only residence which created a bond affecting parliamentary conduct. By their property eighteenth-century men were known. Landlords had an obvious interest in the affairs of their locality even when they rarely visited it. They were expected to defend and promote the interest of their tenants, and it was their interest to do so. Rents reflected the totality of local conditions, not the theoretical targets defined by agricultural experts. Landlords who were also legislators were sometimes accused of feathering their own nest, not least where enclosure bills were concerned. Some MPs, like Sir Edward Turner, knight of the shire for Oxford in the last years of George II, went out of their way to avoid attending on bills in which they were interested. Others found it harder to resist the 'temptation to sink the legislator in the landowner'.[196] The reformer John Horne had the temerity publicly to accuse one MP, Thomas De Grey, of what amounted to corruption in such a case.[197] But accusations of this kind hardly begin to touch the web of relationships which governed the landowning MP's response to the requests and importunities of his friends, neighbours, and

---

[193] *The True Alarm* (London, 1783), p. 50.

[194] F. H. W. Sheppard, *Local Government in St Marylebone 1688–1835* (London, 1958), p. 128.

[195] Ibid., p. 75.

[196] W. E. Tate, 'Members of Parliament and Their Personal Relations to Enclosure: A Study with Special Reference to Oxfordshire Enclosures, 1757–1843', *Agric. Hist.* 23 (1949), 213–20.

[197] Stephens, *Memoirs of John Horne Tooke*, i. 422–30. Horne's protest was made on behalf of William Tooke, by whose will he was to benefit, and whose name he therefore took.

dependants. It was difficult to determine motives in such instances. When James Townsend, Wilkesite and MP for West Looe, opposed the Moorfields canal in 1774, some scepticism was expressed about his public-spiritedness. Townsend's home was at Bruce Castle in Middlesex. He admitted that the canal would run close to his kitchen garden, which he had spent some hundreds of pounds fitting up, and also that the £10,000 which he had spent on his estate would be endangered by the canal. But, he ingenuously added, 'he had not taken so warm a part in the affair merely for himself, but for his neighbours'.[198]

There is no means of knowing the precise distribution of the property of MPs or indeed of peers, but the evidence of land tax assessments in the 1780s makes certain broad conclusions possible. One is that the geographical pattern of land-holding among MPs was very different from that of the parliamentary constituencies, and helped compensate for its manifest deficiencies. Counties in the south-east of England which were under-represented in terms of parliamentary seats made up for it in terms of MPs who owned property in the area. Essex, for instance, had only eight MPs, a long-standing source of grievance. Cromwell's short-lived reform had recognized the justice of its claim, as did the proposals of late eighteenth-century reformers.[199] In 1784 it had 19 MPs with a residence in the county, and 51 with property there. Counties in the south-west, with many more elected representatives in the Commons, in practice had fewer of their landowners there. Dorset occupied 20 seats in the Commons, but had only 11 resident MPs and 17 landowning MPs. Peers also helped to boost the representation of otherwise underprivileged areas. Aristocratic land-holdings were notably more prominent in the eastern half of the country than the western, and some of the worst instances of nominal under-representation were in the East Midlands. Derbyshire and Leicestershire were counties which reformers identified as deserving additional representation. They each had four MPs, two for the county, two for the county town. The considerations of residence and property somewhat improved their position. Derbyshire had 8 resident MPs, 12 landowning MPs; Leicestershire only 2 resident MPs but 13 landowning MPs. In the House of Lords they did better still. Derbyshire had 11 peers, Leicestershire 28.

INTEREST AND INFLUENCE

How did the residential and propertied standing of legislators affect the conduct of parliamentary business? In the first place it made it much easier

[198] *London Magazine* (1775), 57–8.
[199] *Grey's Debates*, iv. 2; R. Robinson, *A Political Catechism* (London, 1782).

to obtain the services of a local MP or peer who would introduce and oversee legislation. Many Englishmen were at a distance from any parliamentary borough, but very few were far from property owned by an MP. Essex's three boroughs were all on the coast, leaving the great mass of the county represented only through the county MPs. But the truth was that all twenty-three of Essex's hundreds had at least one MP among their landowners, and all but one of them, Winstree, had a peer as well. The geography of landlord representation created a situation dramatically different from that of electoral representation. The property in question might well be very small. MPs and peers alike characteristically had a substantial block of land in one county, and smaller portions in others. But it was the local connection thus created, not the quantity of property, which mattered. Contemporaries cited it as one of the glories of a parliamentary system, that 'the people of every province, even the most remote, have by our constitution the happiness to have some gentleman in the neighbourhood who has the honour of a seat in our supreme legislature'.[200]

Perhaps even more importantly the honour of a seat could be handed around within a given number of families. Parliamentary dynasties were not unknown, but the common pattern for county families with a political tradition was irregular rather than continuous membership of the Commons.[201] In the process networks of influence and connection could be built up. Looking back in 1779 on the recent history of Whitby, its chronicler Lionel Charlton attributed great importance to a series of statutes providing for the maintenance and improvement of the harbour, in 1702, 1709, 1723, 1735, 1750, and 1766. 'Every one of the before-mentioned acts of parliament', he remarked, 'hath been obtained by the interest and influence of the Cholmondeley family.'[202] In fact the family had sat in Parliament for barely a third of the period, but this was sufficient for the purposes of Whitby. On the other hand, even casual contacts were not to be ignored. When Lord Chatham visited Lyme Regis for his health, the local gentry were inclined to 'make him pay' for it by engaging his support for an improvement project.[203] In this instance they were surely overrating both the influence and the goodwill that they could command, but the attitude was typical of the age.

Some, indeed, thought this too much of a good thing. John Scott of Amwell, an experienced critic of highway legislation, believed that MPs were far too vulnerable to the pressures of the local community, and noticeably wanting in that enlightened public spirit recommended by

---

[200] *London Magazine* (1767), 388.
[201] Sir L. Namier, *The Structure of Politics at the Accession of George III* (2nd edn., London, 1961), pp. 242–3.
[202] *The History of Whitby, and of Whitby Abbey* (York, 1779), p. 332.
[203] Francis Blackburne, *Memoirs of Thomas Hollis* (2 vols., London, 1780), i. 457–8.

Burke. His satirical account of what happened when the consumers of Whalebone and Whipcord met in council at the Blue Boar or Black Lion to put pressure on their landlords highlighted the pettiness and selfishness displayed in such lobbying.[204] But 'landlord representation' certainly provided a useful defence against the parliamentary reformers. As William Combe put it in 1792: 'It may be true that, according to strict, arithmetical calculation, the nation at large is not represented in a fixed, accurate, proportion between the numbers in different districts; but, in effect, has any part of the country, whether inaccurately represented or not, any cause to complain of a want of parliamentary service?'[205] Both Scott and Combe were thinking of the House of Commons but the point applied with equal force in relation to the House of Lords. Particularly in the Midlands, where peers were thicker on the ground than elected MPs, they played a part not through the Commons but in their own right. The lobbying of the West Midlands was a feature of late eighteenth-century Parliaments: it affected matters as diverse as the repeal of the American Stamp Act, the building of the Trent and Mersey canal, and Josiah Wedgwood's patent battle with Richard Champion of Bristol. Peers like the Earl of Dartmouth, the Earl Gower, and Lord Dudley were prominent in it.

Where conflict arose it was often possible to call on legislative resources not revealed by electoral statistics. Contests between unrepresented boroughs and boroughs which had MPs of their own were less uneven than might have been supposed. When Evesham, with its own MPs, sought to steal a march on neighbouring Pershore, in a turnpike bill of 1728, it was quickly brought to terms by the pressure of a Hertfordshire MP who happened to be a substantial landowner near Pershore.[206] But not only a small town like Pershore could call on help of this kind. The same logic worked for great cities. Manchester's want of its own MPs was one of the most notorious instances of the absurdity of the electoral system. Yet in 1784, when it was about to commence its successful assault on the government's fustian tax, it had five MPs who owned property in the parish, including the celebrated Coke of Norfolk, who was a well-known figure in Lancashire.[207] In these circumstances it was easy to forget that the town had no elected representatives. When Lord North opposed the granting of commercial concessions to Ireland in 1779, his hostility was attributed by an ill-informed pamphleteer to his fear of Manchester's MPs:

[204] *Digests of the General Highway and Turnpike Laws* (London, 1778), pp. 278–9.
[205] *A Word in Season, to the Traders and Manufacturers of Great Britain* (London, 1792); see H. W. Hamilton, *Doctor Syntax: A Silhouette of William Combe, Esq. (1742–1823)* (London, 1969), p. 166.
[206] *Commons Journals*, xxi. 67, 78–9, 82, 85, 90, 97, 103–4, 106–7, 130–1, 135, 161, 163.
[207] T. W. Coke (Norfolk), J. W. Egerton (Brackley), Sir Thomas Egerton (Lancashire), T. P. Legh (Newton), Sir George Warren (Beaumaris). In Norfolk the Lancashire connection was used against Coke, and also against his ally and MP for Norwich, Sir Harbord Harbord; see *Memoirs of the Life and Writings of Richard Gardiner* (London, 1782), pp. 194–5.

'A minister, who preferred the preservation of two votes from Manchester, and as many from Lancashire, to the loyal affections and happiness of an entire nation.'[208]

Some old anxieties were eased by the priority which propertied representation acquired over electoral representation. In the Cavalier Parliament of Charles II there were prolonged debates about the relativities of provincial life. Allegations tht some areas were over-taxed and under-represented were frequent.[209] Fears that the block vote of privileged regions would be used to force through legislation which discriminated against less fortunate parts of the country were common in the early eighteenth century. The prolonged battle over legislation to construct the Weaver Navigation, which was spread over two decades between 1699 and 1721, featured a number of worries on these lines. A host of interests found themselves involved in a dispute which at bottom was a conflict between the rock salt and brine salt trades. The parliamentary calculations were complicated by the regional incidence of the industries affected. Opponents of the navigation had a justified belief that fish-curers of the south-western seaboard would support the designs of the Cheshire rock-salt producers, and employ their legislative influence to assist them. The discrepancy between Cornwall's forty-four MPs and Cheshire's four became unusually interesting in such circumstances.[210] At that time Cornwall still had a disproportionate number of authentically local MPs prepared to use their weight on behalf of their county. This force was much feared. When the keelmen of the north-east petitioned Parliament for a bill regulating way-leaves in 1714, Lord Lansdowne pointed out that the value of way-leaves in Cornwall ensured that every Cornish MP must oppose it or 'never think of being chose again'.[211] By the reign of George III Cornish MPs were largely divorced from the local interests of their constituents, and the south-west was regarded primarily as a refuge for Court and Treasury men who had no connection with the region.

It was the colonies, lacking not only delegates of their own, but also any means of exerting real pressure on Westminster, that aroused controversy under George III. British MPs, instinctively sensitive to the susceptibilities of communities in which they themselves resided or owned land, were unsympathetic in dealing with those of a distant society in which hardly any of them had a vested interest as individuals. The argument for virtual representation was plausible in a British context. To use it in America, where conditions were so different, was at best imprudent, at worst cynical.

[208] *A Political Mirror* (London, 1779), p. 60.

[209] *Grey's Debates*, i. 120–1; iv. 1–4.

[210] E. Hughes, *Studies in Administration and Finance 1558–1825* (Manchester, 1934), p. 233.

[211] J. M. Ellis, ed., 'The Letters of Henry Liddell to William Cotesworth', *Surtees Soc.* 197 (1985), 135: 13 May 1714.

John Fletcher sought to persuade the colonists of the absurdity of their position. He reminded them of the 'constitutional rule, by which the members of a Welch borough are appointed to manage the affairs of all England'.[212] But the parallel was not valid. Welsh MPs had a say both in their own particular affairs, and in those of Britain as a whole. Americans had no direct representation of their own, and very little indirect. They could hardly be asked to take the rough with the smooth when the smooth seemed to be enjoyed only by others. None the less, it is easy to see why English MPs found it easy to neglect the voice of America. Ireland, without seats of its own at Westminster, had a powerful lobby there which called on MPs, including a number of Irish peers, and British peers with Irish property. This did not head off the Irish nationalism which developed under the stimulus of the American War, but it worked for much of the eighteenth century, and helped make complaints about the supremacy of Westminster a question of principle rather than practice. Even the West Indies had a voice in the Commons, some argued an excessive one where sugar interests were concerned. America was unique in the disjunction between its strength in terms of wealth and population, and its feebleness as a propertied presence in Parliament.

One consequence of 'landlord representation' was that the traditional distinction between county and borough MPs became less important. Knights of the shire had always enjoyed a special status, and the vigour with which leading families competed for the honour of representing their county in the late eighteenth century reveals its enduring prestige. In 1760 it was even suggested, during a difficult negotiation about the fate of the Weaver Navigation, that the MPs for Cheshire should have the entire property of the Navigation vested in them in perpetuity as a form of public trust, such was faith in their guaranteed integrity.[213] County MPs continued to have special responsibility for the supervision of bills directly affecting their own county. But the weight of local legislation made this an onerous responsibility, especially for a class of men who were frequently more interested in fox-hunting than legislation. Complaints about county MPs were common at election time, in part no doubt because so much was asked of them. But the tendency in the second half of the century was increasingly for borough MPs to play a larger part in everyday legislative life. No doubt it was for this reason that counties grew less concerned to preserve the old conventions by which knights of the shire were drawn from different parts of their county. There were long-standing agreements that the county should be divided into two for this purpose: East and West

[212] *American Patriotism Farther Confronted with Reason, Scripture, and the Constitution* (Shrewsbury, 1776), p. 23.
[213] T. S. Willan, *The Navigation of the River Weaver in the Eighteenth Century* (Chetham Soc., 3rd ser. 3, 1951), pp. 66–8.

Northamptonshire, Chiltern and Vale Buckinghamshire, East and West
Sussex, East and West Kent, and so on. But such concordats were increasingly abandoned in the late eighteenth century.[214] None the less, knights
of the shire had a prodigious load of parliamentary business to bear,
especially where there was a shortage of parliamentary boroughs locally.
Even a caretaker MP like Sir Edmund Cradock Hartopp, brought in by
the Duke of Rutland in 1798 for an eight-year spell in Leicestershire, where
only Leicester itself was separately represented in the Commons, found
himself responsible for a stream of local bills.[215]

Access to roughly equal parliamentary services did not ensure the pain-
less passage of legislation. MPs were sometimes caught between conflicting
groups none of which could be comfortably offended. Sir William Meredith
of Henbury Hall admitted his agony in respect of a Cheshire turnpike bill:
'I hoped every prejudice against it would, on consideration, be removed
and that I might have the unanimous consent of all my friends and
neighbours.' 'Jammed betwixt discordant sentiments', he begged the promoters to approach one of the Derbyshire MPs.[216] But conflict did not end
with the dilemma of individuals. Bills which brought one locality or one
interest into contention with others might generate major debates and suck
in large numbers of MPs. Some of the epic struggles of a parliamentary
age related to canal legislation, which often affected a wide variety of areas
and interests. The Selby–Leeds Canal Bill of 1774 brought into conflict
two sets of waterway entrepreneurs, pitted riding against riding, town
against town, trade against trade. It involved forty-six days of committee
work, eight hundred pages of evidence, and £9,000 in costs.[217] It also
impeded the business of the House of Commons at a time when it was
wrestling with legislation of the first importance, namely North's Coercive
Bills. A few years later, in 1783, the battle over the Birmingham Canal Bill
proved still more bitter. Birmingham's first historian, William Hutton,
described a contest in which none of the towns most immediately affected,
Birmingham itself, Walsall, Wolverhampton, Wednesbury, and West
Bromwich, had MPs of its own. It made little difference. 'Each party
possessed that activity of spirit for which Birmingham is famous, and
seemed to divide between them the legislative strength of the nation; every
corner of the house was ransacked for a vote ... Perhaps at the reading
when both parties had marshalled their forces, there was the fullest House
of Commons ever remembered on a private bill.'[218]

In conflicts of this kind what mattered most was that the outcome should

[214] Thorne, *History of Parliament*, i. 14.
[215] Leicestershire RO, 10 D 72: Cradock Hartopp MSS.
[216] C. S. Davies, *A History of Macclesfield* (Manchester, 1961), p. 161.
[217] *London Magazine* (1774), 521.
[218] William Hutton, *An History of Birmingham* (3rd edn., Birmingham, 1795), p. 409.

be determined so as to minimize lasting damage. A realistic appreciation of the consequences of inflexibility often averted disaster. Parliamentary procedure gave opponents of legislation ample opportunity for obstruction which itself promoted compromise. Petitions, readings, committees, the long-stop presented by the House of Lords, all could be negotiated speedily if the interested parties were agreed. But the process became protracted if there was determined opposition: it did not necessarily have to be numerous opposition. The expense of parliamentary legislation, not merely in respect of fees, where they were payable, but in terms of the cost of mounting a campaign supported by witnesses and lawyers, could be huge. When the Oxford paving commissioners sought to justify the cost of passing their bill in 1774, at more than £1,000, their excuse was that there had been a prolonged dispute in committee.[219] As manager of a Northamptonshire turnpike bill in 1739, the Earl of Strafford constantly emphasized this consideration. Anticipating the Commons committee stage he strongly recommended dropping a controversial clause. Failure to do so would merely mean a battle in the Lords, the possible loss of the bill, and extra expense. When those involved seemed ready to risk a division in committee, he was furious. 'They may Lose their Bill by these tricks.'[220] A bill lost made for completely wasted expenditure, which at best would have to be repeated on a subsequent occasion. Hence the readiness to accept a compromise and the hard bargaining which constantly took place behind the scenes.

If negotiation broke down only a vote in either or each house of Parliament could decide the outcome. When he outlined the duties of upper- and middle-class men in 1795, Thomas Gisborne treated integrity and impartiality with regard to local and private bills as matters of the highest importance for aspiring MPs.[221] The local loyalties of MPs were so widely distributed and the arguments in these cases often so nicely balanced, that the verdict rarely produced an enduring sense of injustice. But there were certain dangers. Such was the intensity of party political conflict in the first half of the eighteenth century, that otherwise uncontroversial legislation could easily be affected. Much of the conflict took place in select committees, where the detailed work of review and amendment was carried out. Packing these committees with political friends whose own localities were not involved was an obvious tactic. They were not even required to

---

[219] *An Attempt to State the Account of Receipt and Expense Relative to the Oxford Paving Act: With Remarks* (Oxford, 1774).

[220] Northamptonshire RO, Isham MSS, IC 2999–3000: Strafford to Sir Edmund Isham, 9 Mar., 12 Apr. 1739.

[221] *An Enquiry into the Duties of Men in the Higher and Middle Classes of Society in Great Britain, Resulting from Their Respective Stations, Professions, and Employments* (3rd edn., 2 vols., London, 1797), i. 157.

undergo the tedium of committee work. Thus John Byrom, testifying against the Manchester Workhouse Bill of 1731, described what he called 'the Committee way—when questions are to be put, Mister Brereton goes and sweeps the out-lying Members in, who not having heard anything of the matter are ready cut and dried for the purpose'.[222] Thomas Brereton, a friend of Walpole and a prominent Liverpudlian Whig, was past master of such techniques. He was also involved in the Stuff Button Bill of 1738, which brought the button weavers of Staffordshire, Cheshire, and Derbyshire into dispute with those of Warwickshire. Some prominent supporters of the Walpole Ministry had electoral interests at Coventry, where the Warwickshire manufacture was based, and in its later stages the bill was plainly the object of straight party-voting.[223] In such circumstances numbers of MPs were likely to find themselves used as lobby fodder. The Cambridge Turnpike Bill of 1730 produced extraordinary divisions in the House of Commons, involving more than 250 MPs. It originated in party strife in Cambridgeshire, which set off a chain reaction in the Commons.[224]

After the mid-1750s, contests of this kind became rare, though personal and party differences sometimes left their mark. In 1765 Lord Sandwich complained that a turnpike bill in which he was interested had been 'warmly contested in the House of Commons and become a mere party affair, the whole opposition, except one or two, voting against me'.[225] But Sandwich was a quite exceptionally provocative figure; controversy and malice followed wherever he went. In general, the balance of property replaced the balance of party as the determining factors in parliamentary contests. As a result the numbers involved in divisions fell markedly. MPs still sought to involve their friends and connections when votes were needed. But it took unusual circumstances to enlist large numbers. The Sandwich Drainage Bill of 1776 was contested because it had the support of barely half the proprietors whom it would affect. Its committee stage in the Commons was carried by only 43 votes to 40, with Kentish MPs deeply divided as to its merits. Inevitably there was a furious search for support from members with no direct interest. When it was eventually passed it produced a division of 111 to 97. But a division of more than 200 or even 100 on a local bill was most unusual.[226] Trivial disputes under George II caused far more bitter disagreements, simply because they activated the chemistry of party.

The attitude of government was an important part of the changing

---

[222] K. Kondo, 'The Workhouse Issue at Manchester: Selected Documents, 1729–35 Part One', *Bulletin of Faculty of Letters, Nagoya University*, 33 (1987), 77.

[223] *Commons Journals*, xxiii. 50, 75–6, 88, 90, 95, 101, 126, 142, 156, 162.

[224] Ibid., xxii. 466, 472, 475, 498, 520, 537, 538–9, 541, 546, 557, 562, 563.

[225] Historical Manuscripts Commission, *Denbigh MSS*, v. 294.

[226] *Commons Journals*, xxxv. 759.

framework which determined parliamentary decisions. The Court and
Treasury party commanded unbeatable voting strength in both Houses.
In the early eighteenth century it was often assumed that ministers could
readily be got to commit their parliamentary following on behalf of private
interests. But such expectations or apprehensions were exaggerated. Walpole's failure to take a hand in the Manchester Workhouse Bill dismayed
his supporters, and was attributed by his enemies only to his preoccupation
with other matters. But it is more likely that his instinct for self-preservation
kept him out of a vituperative controversy in which he was likely to make
new enemies as well as gratifying old friends.[227] It was, in fact, increasingly
rare for ministers to allow themselves to become officially involved in such
combats. The dangers of doing so in terms of embittering electoral politics
and alienating important interests were obvious.

Interest-groups were adept at finding reasons which might induce the
government to support them. Much effort was devoted to presenting a
conflict as one which afected the national interest. The Newcastle coal
industry adroitly opposed inland waterways, which threatened the price
competitiveness of sea-borne coal, on the grounds that the coastal trade in
coal provided the navy with a steady supply of recruits in wartime. Ministers
resisted this reasoning, though it is difficult to believe that they were
convinced by the claim of the Leeds–Liverpool canal promoters that inland
navigations would also prove a nursery of seamen.[228] Only occasionally did
government allow itself to become involved, and then when pressing
arguments of public policy could be adduced. The Framework Knitting
Bills of 1778 and 1779 were designed to achieve a measure of wage
protection for stockingers suffering under the dual strains of the American
War and mechanization. They were supported by many propertied people
in the East Midlands, where the industry was based, including the MPs for
Nottingham. But the employers' argument that conceding wage regulation
would weaken the competitive capacity of British manufacturers in general
evidently convinced Lord North. John Wilkes accurately predicted the
defeat of the bill in terms which nicely caught the particularism that
normally guided such decisions. 'You need not be in such a hurry, Gentlemen, the Cornwall and Devon miners have sunk a new pit for you to fall
into to-night.'[229]

A dispute between employer and employee was significant in this respect
because it was of a kind in which the Crown, through the Privy Council,
had traditionally been involved. But Parliament was reluctant to permit
government to take a formal role in such matters. When, in 1727, the Privy

---

[227] Kondo, 'The Workhouse Issue at Manchester', p. 77.
[228] *Commons Journals*, xxxii. 294.
[229] S. D. Chapman, ed., *Henson's History of the Framework Knitters* (Newton Abbot, 1970), p. 401.

Council seemed prepared to listen to the complaints of weavers, the House of Commons displayed some irritation at its involvement.[230] This was one of the major differences between the seventeenth and eighteenth centuries. As the court tended to confine itself to questions of pressing national policy, especially international relations and fiscal strategy, the legislature was left free to take up almost all other matters. In doing so it succeeded in averting much of the faction and not a little of the friction which had marked the play of interests in an earlier period. Ironically, there ws a greater chance of local interests using their parliamentary strength to put pressure on government, than there was of government deploying its weight to influence Parliament in local matters. One of the more impressive demonstrations of regional unity was the round robin which the Welsh MPs addressed to the Treasury in 1779 when it threatened changes in the management of Crown estates in Wales. Only one of them declined to sign.[231]

Lobbying of ministers certainly did not stop, and under the younger Pitt, who took a close interest in commercial questions, it probably increased. Pitt was a good listener and a great information-gatherer. Newspapers reported his activities in terms which suggest something of modern Prime Ministerial politics. Thus in 1788 it was noticed in the London press that MPs and manufacturers from Lancashire, together with the Lord Advocate of Scotland and Scottish manufacturers, had 'had an interview with the Minister, at his house in Downing Street' to discuss the cotton industry.[232] Provincial newspapers were equally impressed by this accessibility. In February 1793 the *Ipswich Journal* announced that Pitt had agreed to see representatives of the town's trade and shipping interests.[233] But Pitt's enthusiasm for consulting businessmen did not extend to allowing his name to be used for one interest against another, let alone one locality against another. Indeed his object was probably to reinforce the highest priority in the legislative process itself, the tendency to seek compromise rather than confrontation. Part of his legacy was the notion that there were large areas of policy in which ministers and party politicians need not involve themselves. As Lord Liverpool, a shrewd tactician, remarked of a matter, the regulation of the Spitalfields manufacture, which had sometimes engrossed his predecessors, it 'is not a *national*, but a local one between London and the Country'.[234] This definition of 'local' stretched to the limit the eighteenth-century conception of parliamentary impartiality.

Here was a powerful argument against parliamentary reform. What was

---

[230] *Commons Journals*, xx. 746–7.

[231] e.g. ibid., xxxix. 82, 126–7, 149, 176, 191.

[232] *Whitehall Evening-Post*, 15 Apr. 1788.

[233] *Ipswich Journal*, 10 Feb. 1793.

[234] A. B. Hilton, 'The Political Arts of Lord Liverpool', *Trans. Roy. Hist. Soc.*, 5th ser. 38 (1987), 151.

missing from the reform campaign of the early 1780s was the resentment of powerful groups of propertied people. There were considerable petitioning campaigns in favour of change in 1782 and 1783, but they were sustained largely by those who lacked the vote in towns which had seats in Parliament. In 1783 most of the boroughs which petitioned did so in protest against the narrow scope of the municipal franchise.[235] The voice of the great centres of population was missing from this protest. As parliamentary opponents of reform were delighted to observe, Birmingham, Manchester, Sheffield, Leeds, the new manufacturing districts of the north and Midlands, London's circle of suburbs, all ignored the call for action. These places evidently did not consider themselves hard done by. During the decade which preceded the petitions of 1783, sixteen parishes in outer London, all unrepresented except through their counties, had had legislation before Parliament. Among other large centres of population, so had Leeds, Halifax, Keighley, Doncaster, and Otley in Yorkshire, Manchester, Stockport, Bolton, and Workington in the north-west, Stourbridge and Wolverhampton, Brighton and Frome; Birmingham sought no less than five bills during this period. If the test of an effective parliamentary system was its capacity to meet the requirements of the most vigorous creators of wealth, there is not much doubt about the credentials of the eighteenth-century legislature.

[235] *Commons Journals*, xxxix. 82, 126–7, 149, 176, 191.

4

Qualified Rule

THE eighteenth century entertained great faith in the virtues of free association, especially the association of propertied people for purposes of philanthropy and improvement. Such activity was to some extent self-regulating, but where it came into conflict with existing organizations, such as chartered corporations, or where it was necessary for Parliament to establish new institutions, guidelines had to be drawn up. The main device for ensuring adequate standards of competence and probity was the property qualification. Statutory commissions for diverse purposes multiplied rapidly and in effect generated a new ruling class, defined by ownership of property. If this was an élite, it was not, however, a very exclusive élite. Property qualifications were expressed in terms of personal rather than landed estate and were often set at low levels. They enabled middle-class families to participate in the manipulation of their environment and the management of their community. Such people often brought with them a narrow, self-interested view of what constituted the public good. As individuals they benefited both by the financial and business opportunities presented and by the professional and official services required. Their right to direct and control the propertyless was taken for granted. In such a society the main challenge seemed to come from those on the margin of propertied life. In Georgian England there were many small men who could not meet the new property qualifications, but whose inherited electoral rights were extensive and well established. Mass disfranchisement was out of the question, but Parliament did its best to regulate and restrict popular political activity in pursuit of a vision which recognized the civic virtues of the respectable householder at the lower levels of public life but entrenched the power of the authentic property-owner at its upper levels.

A MORE NUMEROUS AND MORE POWERFUL CLUB

It is not usual to think of eighteenth-century Britain as consciously remodelling its ruling class, let alone creating a new one. There were no wholesale Reform Acts to alter the structure of the parliamentary electorate, and no grand designs for the institutions of government, central or local. Yet the power of statute was used radically to revise and expand the membership of Britain's governing body. It was done by a variety of means and mostly in response to *ad hoc* demands. The results were not less important for that. Working out from a landed class which had long represented the ideal embodiment of legitimate authority, the legislature extended important functions of government to a broader but essentially propertied élite. Working in from the potential democracy which survived in some aspects of electoral life, it restricted popular participation in politics to those who at least shared some of the concerns of the same propertied élite. The process was not without its inconsistencies. But it was clear enough to leave little doubt of where the eighteenth century wished to locate political power and executive responsibility.

Most of the new governors of Georgian England were so by virtue of a local or private act of Parliament. In the statutes appointing them they were generally described as commissioners. Their functions were as diverse as the purposes of such legislation. In 1783, if anything a rather light parliamentary session in this respect, around five thousand were so authorized. Forty-five named commissioners were appointed to supervise the improvement of Whitechapel Streets, 71 to manage those of Rotherhithe; 280 trustees were named for the Wetherby–Knaresborough turnpike trust and 108 commissioners, to be elected by the local ratepayers, were invested with the direction of Birmingham's poor relief. Nine were appointed to manage Hull's gaol. In 1783, and in not a few other sessions in the last quarter of the century, a high proportion of those thus dignified with parliamentary power were involved in canal projects. The Stroudwater and Thames Canal Act approved 75 members of the company involved, which included women as well as men, permitted them to nominate further members, and appointed 231 arbitrators to adjudicate disputes arising from the powers of compulsory purchase awarded the company. A similar act for the Trent Navigation sanctioned a company of 88 and appointed 800 commissioners with powers of arbitration. The most sweeping statute concerned the Leeds–Liverpool canal: it gave powers to every owner of property worth £100 per annum in Lancashire and the West Riding of Yorkshire. How many were thereby included is a matter of guesswork. It certainly exceeded 2,000, and may well have approached 4,000.[1]

These figures make no allowance for new powers granted and new commissioners added to existing institutions. A number of bodies created by earlier statutes or charters had their authority extended or renewed in 1783, including commissions of the peace, land tax commissions, commissions of sewers, the Common Council of London, commissions of supply in Scotland, and many turnpike trusts. In the breadth of its concerns the parliamentary session of 1783 was typical, though there were some . chronological variations. Earlier, especially in the years before 1770, new

---

[1] 23 Geo. III, c. 91; 103; 31; 54; 55; 38; 48; 47.

turnpikes figured much more, and navigation projects much less. Moreover, the numbers involved increased consistently, from relatively small annual totals in the first half of the eighteenth century, to very large ones at its end. Parliamentary commissioners multiplied at an ever increasing rate under George III.

It would be wrong to dismiss the powers exercised under statutes of this kind as trivial. They were often extensive and implied functions of government which would be considered part and parcel of the modern State. The eighteenth century had a very limited concept of the State in formal terms. In effect it was synonymous with the King's government, though political theorists and advocates of legal reform were talking of it in a much wider sense by the end of the century. But beyond the State strictly defined there were many public bodies entrusted with significant powers. They included three distinct categories, all of which deserve consideration in any definition of the governing class of the age. One consisted of the public corporations created by Parliament in the manner described above. They had powers of taxation or arbitration which in effect took away the Englishman's property, the severest test in the eighteenth century of any political institution. A second comprised those bodies whose origins or activities were essentially commercial but which depended on the endorsement of the legislature to carry out their ordinary functions. A number of monopoly concerns, once dependent on the chartering pre-rogative of the Crown, but increasingly reliant on parliamentary authority, were in this class, including the East India Company and the Bank of England. A third division was composed of genuinely voluntary insti-tutions, most of them charities, which depended on the subscriptions of their members and were not normally subject to parliamentary scrutiny. Numerous medical and educational trusts were in this class. Each of these categories raised questions of politics, policy, and 'police' in the sense that contemporaries understood these terms.

Attitudes towards political union were ambivalent. Some forms of common action were generally approved. Voluntary associations to promote a manifestly patriotic purpose came under this heading. Hence the appro-priation of the term 'association' for activities such as the defence of the Protestant Succession in 1696 and 1745 and the movement for economical reform in 1780. Other political combinations were highly suspect. For most purposes 'party' was a term of abuse, more or less interchangeable with 'faction'. Many legally unimpugnable bodies were almost as unpopular. Various arguments joined to condemn municipal corporations. Since they had economic functions which stood in the way of market forces, enthusiasts for a progressive view of commercial life considered them barbarous vestiges of a feudal past. 'Corporations, generally speaking, are inimical to the constitution of this kingdom: They are the tattered remains of that

antient system of oppression introduced into this country by the aspiring
Norman bastard; and every one who glories to be called an Englishman,
should be ashamed to be seen in them.—They are barriers to liberty; they
are a fence against honest industry; and they impede the progress of merit.'[2]
This was part of a blistering attack on the self-elected corporation of Bristol
in 1792. Co-opted bodies were naturally open to accusations of corrupt
and conspiratorial self-interestedness. The Jacobite John Byrom described
them as stagnant pools, which needed regular elections to keep them clean
and sweet.[3] As the commercial functions of municipal corporations fell
away this objection ensured that the case against them remained as strong
as ever. It was a standard argument that they were inherently degrading,
turning decent citizens into servants of corruption. The poet William
Cowper took this view.

> Charter'd boroughs are such public plagues,
> And burgers, men immaculate perhaps
> In all their private functions, once combined,
> Become a loathsome body, only fit
> For dissolution, hurtful to the main.[4]

The objection was more fundamental than either commercial or political
malpractice, however. It is notable that the most radical spirits of the age
were particularly horrified by the corporate impulse, as an illicit call on the
loyalty of citizens. John Jebb analysed the mentality which it promoted in
a work significantly entitled 'Every Man His Own Priest'. 'One maxim,
which will be found to predominate, more or less, in the minds of individuals in every corporation, consists, in an overweening opinion and
extravagant zeal for the interest of that body, to which, as it is often
expressed, they "have the honour to belong."' Jebb thought 'this cor-
poration-spirit' most marked in the army, in the East India Company, in
the Society of Jesus, and in the Church of England.[5]

Even Jebb and his friends approved of some forms of association. The
Society of Supporters of the Bill of Rights and the Society for Constitutional
Information, meant to rescue a depraved nation from its awful fate, were
clear instances. There were others too, but the criteria for endorsing them
were rigorous. The first and most indispensable was that membership must
be genuinely open. Such clubs were not only defensible but admirable,

---

[2] *Free Thoughts on the Offices of Mayor, Aldermen and Common Council, of the City of Bristol* (Bristol,
1792), p. 9.
[3] R. Parkinson, ed., *The Private Journal and Literary Remains of John Byrom: Vol. i, Part 2* (Chetham
Soc. 34, 1855), p. 484.
[4] V. Newey, *Cowper's Poetry: A Critical Study and Reassessment* (London, 1982), p. 177.
[5] J. Disney, *The Works Theological, Medical, Political, and Miscellaneous, of John Jebb* (3 vols.,
London, 1787), iii. 170–1.

and provided the true model for the State as many critics of traditional government saw it. The reforming lawyer William Jones observed that 'a free state is only a more numerous and more powerful club'.[6] In this respect there was not much in principle to separate men like Jones from more conventional thinkers. But in practice there was a great deal. Jones assumed that the qualification for membership was the property which every man had in his own life and liberty. Others assumed that it was property in a more confined sense. Current definitions of property were so ambiguous that they left endless room for argument on this point. But when the definition was narrow and the qualification was high, the result was precisely to encourage that corporation spirit which Jebb deplored. Significantly, Lord Braxfield, in his notorious judgement against Muir in 1793, defined the State itself in these terms:

A government in every country should be just like a corporation; and, in this country, it is made up of the landed interest, which alone has a right to be represented; as for the rabble, who have nothing but personal property, what hold has the nation of them? What security for the payment of their taxes? They may pack up all their property on their backs, and leave the country in the twinkling of an eye, but landed property cannot be removed.[7]

It was not necessary to be Lord Braxfield to have a view of the importance of property which rendered association the prerogative of the few. Most forms of subscribing association, including a great variety with charitable purposes, were in principle open to anyone and in practice restricted to those with a certain quantum of wealth.

The object must be laudable. 'Improvement' was a favourite word. It somehow avoided the idea of innovation while suggesting the desirability of change. All shades of opinion felt happy with it. Improvement without innovation was the watchword of many politically conservative figures. Improvement as progress was equally favoured by reformers. Catherine Macaulay's charge against the Revolution 'System' was that it 'was totally void of improvement'.[8] Naturally, charity was the most admirable form of improvement. Associations which were criticized on other grounds hastened to take shelter behind its protective shield. George Smith, in his *Use and Abuse of Free-Masonry* of 1783, emphasized the activities of masons in 'this peculiarly humane and philanthropic aera'. His clerical brother Daniel Turner declared that 'To assist the weak is the glory of humanity, but the duty of a mason'.[9]

In this respect as in many others, a hard and fast line could not be drawn

---

[6] *The Principles of Government, in a Dialogue between a Scholar and a Peasant* (London, 1783), p. 8.

[7] T. B. Howell, ed., *A Complete Collection of State Trials* (London, 1809–26), xxiii. 231.

[8] Catherine Macaulay, *The History of England from the Revolution to the Present Time in a Series of Letters to a Friend* (London, 1778), p. 5.

[9] George Smith, *The Use and Abuse of Free-Masonry* (London, 1783), p. 140.

between voluntary and State ventures. The distinction was more one of means than ends. At Carlisle in 1790 it was agreed to organize an association of citizens for the purpose of maintaining the municipal watch, until an act of Parliament could be obtained to give it compulsory effect.[10] Voluntary association created legitimacy; Parliament merely bestowed legality. Statutes were obtained where the desired legal powers could not be exercised without parliamentary authority, and more especially where powers of taxation were deemed essential. Workhouses were thought to require both. Hospitals were generally assumed to need neither. But it was possible to envisage a workhouse without statutory force behind it, and a hospital which might need public chartering. Moreover the men who managed hospitals were often the same as those who supervised workhouses. The policies which they implemented were likely to be closely related. Above all the underlying mentality which informed their activities would be similar. Given a choice between defining the public domain as that which had to do with the operations of government and Parliament, and that which had to do with the functions of property in an organized, collective sense, there was a growing tendency to prefer the latter. Inevitably, it jostled with older conceptions of the community which treated of law and liberty rather than property. But in the mentality of the eighteenth century it occupied a dominating place. One of its most interesting consequences was the tendency to confuse public activities which to the modern eye would seem quite distinct.

Parliament itself was strongly influenced by this mentality. For instance, in establishing corporations for the administration of poor relief it frequently appointed as poor law guardians not only ratepayers, but also voluntary subscribers and benefactors. Since the object was to ensure that the requirements of social welfare and regulation were met under the supervision of the people who paid for it, whether they were taxpayers or philanthropists, the distinction hardly mattered. The ideal would have been to pass all such activities to voluntary associations. The more visionary philanthropic schemes certainly envisaged such a development. The State would wither away, not because property would cease to be necessary but because property-owners would come to accept their responsibility for the poor. It was one of the complaints about the immense, complex structure of the poor-law system that it had a sinister tendency to subvert and set back this beneficent process. Jeremy Bentham observed that the poor laws 'are daily destroying all natural Subordination and affection—The Master Manufacturer uninterested in the fate of the Hands whom he employs becomes a mere Negro-Driver—while the man of Property loses that political Influence, which it has been a Fundamental Principle of all

---

[10] *Whitehall Evening-Post*, 24 Mar. 1791.

constitutions to suppose attendant on Property, by the Poor being taught upon all occasion to look up to the King's Justices for Relief and I shall not be surpriz'd to see the Poor make as separate an Interest in the State as the Clergy do'.[11] The ultimate object was, so to speak, to de-institutionalize poverty, removing it from the domain of the State. Some looked to principles of unfettered free enterprise and the benevolence of the market to bring this about. Others hoped to achieve it by increasing the quantity and improving the quality of private philanthropy. But these were manifestly long-term aims. In the mean time voluntary subscription left much undone and many property-owners found themselves compelled to pay for what they would not voluntarily support. But at all events they must be protected by a proper system of accountability. Statutory commissions were intended to resemble voluntary associations while accepting the need for a degree of compulsion. Even so, they caused concern. One opponent of poor law incorporations argued precisely that they extended the apparatus of the State. Existing poor relief procedure, he claimed, 'does not mix itself with the *Public* expenses, or funds; nor does it cost the State, as a State, one single Shilling; Whereas, should the proposed method of great Buildings, and numerous Officers take place, it must occasion a *Public Expense*, as large at least as that for maintaining the Army'.[12]

Some bodies are extraordinarily difficult to classify. The constitution of the Bedford Level Corporation was a bizarre muddle of charters, statutes, and prescriptive practices. In origin it was a private corporation like the monopoly trading companies, its members 'adventurers' who owned the minimum voting qualification of 50 acres. By the reign of Charles II it was becoming much more complicated with an elaborate series of property qualifications to determine the different levels of participation in its government, and commissioners appointed to hear disputes and tax landowners. Different parts of the Level came to be subject to different statutes and rules, parish vestries were permitted to elect commissioners, and a whole range of detailed provisions for compulsory purchase, taxation, and tolls was laid down under George II. The result was a curious amalgam of private property and public jurisdiction.[13] Another body whose eccentricities were generated by the needs of a particular locality was the Convocation of the Tinners in Cornwall. This 'Parliament of the Stannaries' claimed extensive

[11] I. R. Christie, ed., *The Correspondence of Jeremy Bentham, vol. iii: 1781–8* (London, 1968), p. 45.

[12] *Further Considerations on the Laws Relating to the Poor* (London, 1760), p. 19.

[13] Charles Nalson Cole, *A Collection of Laws which Form the Constitution of the Bedford Level Corporation* (London, 1761); Webb, S. J. and B. *English Local Government from the Revolution to the Municipal Corporations Act* (9 vols., London, 1906–29), vol. iv: *Statutory Authorities for Special Purposes* (1922), pp. 27–32.

powers of regulation when it was convened by the Prince of Wales for the first time in forty years in 1750.[14]

STRAIT WASTECOATS

Though statutory bodies were only one expression of the mentality of collective improvement under the auspices of propertied people, they exemplified some of its features more clearly than other, less controversial forms. An act of Parliament was usually sought where it was impossible or undesirable to proceed without some degree of compulsion. Rating and compulsory purchase raised delicate questions in an age when power over property was considered the most dangerous power vested in any constitutional body. The life of an ordinary propertied citizen was much more likely to be affected by a statutory commissioner granted local powers than by the State in the sense of central government. Enclosure acts, turnpike acts, and canal acts took away property, albeit with compensation. Improvement acts, poor relief acts, harbour and bridge acts also sometimes did so, and, more particularly, they levied large sums by way of taxation.

The novelty of these statutory powers was recognized at the time. So was the potential conflict which they brought. Municipal corporations were frequently affronted by the threat to their own status and authority. Yet it was the inadequacies of such corporations that made it necessary to create new bodies. In this respect, as in many others, legislators found themselves in a dilemma. They were reluctant to use their authority to diminish ancient rights of any kind. Memories of Stuart meddling were vivid, and the notion that the Revolution Settlement had once for all ruled out an invasion of charters was firmly embedded in the propertied as well as popular mind. Municipal corporations were quick to connect their own liberties with those of other chartered bodies. Not a little of the outrage which greeted Fox's attack on the East India Company in 1783 was prompted by this analogy. The contention of Fox's friend John Lee that 'a charter is nothing more than a piece of parchment with a bit of wax dangling to it' caused fury.[15] At Bath, for example, the implied danger to chartered corporations was seized upon.[16] Considering the preponderance of boroughs among English parliamentary constituencies, it seems likely that Fox's discomfiture in the subsequent general election of 1784 was in large part a consequence of this alarm.

A wholesale onslaught on borough liberties was never envisaged in

---

[14] [Thomas Pitt], *A State of the Proceedings of the Convocation, or Parliament, for the Stannaries of the County of Cornwall* (London, 1751).

[15] E. Sidney, *The Life of Sir Richard Hill* (London, 1839), p. 324.

[16] S. C. Macintyre, 'Towns as Health and Pleasure Resorts: The Development of Bath, Scarborough and Weymouth, 1700–1815' (Oxford University D.Phil. thesis, 1973), pp. 89–90.

the eighteenth century. The importance of many corporate bodies in parliamentary elections made any interference the subject of the most intense suspicion. Corporate practices and privileges came frequently before the courts, but the idea that they should be revised either by the Crown or Parliament was anathema. In 1724 a bill to regulate mayoral elections in corporations was introduced, without success.[17] In 1725 Parliament was persuaded to intervene in the electoral affairs of the City of London itself, action which was regarded as constituting a dangerous precedent. In 1767 the Commons considered legislation to regulate writs of quo warranto.[18] But Parliament could never bring itself to pass a general bill. Nor did the Crown hasten to intervene. A rare attempt by the Whigs in 1708 to alter the charter of Bewdley provoked a Tory protest against 'the arbitrary Attempt of new-modelling Corporations', and revocation of the offending charter.[19] It took a complete breakdown of the machinery of chartered self-government to induce ministers to step in, as they did when Helston and Saltash were eventually granted new charters in 1774. In this instance a succession of political contests and judicial decrees had effectively dissolved the old corporations. Even so it was objected that North's ministry was using the opportunity to enhance the influence of the Crown.[20] It is easy to imagine the indignation which would have followed a serious attempt to reorganize borough government.

It did not follow that much respect was entertained for the manner in which municipal corporations actually conducted themselves. On the contrary, among those who did not have the privilege of belonging to such bodies, disgust and contempt were more likely to be the customary feelings. The graft and corruption inseparable from borough elections to Parliament inevitably fixed obloquy on many corporations. In the second half of the century the power of creating freemen was primarily a device for manufacturing votes in parliamentary elections. As the elaborate machinery of guild, freedom, and apprenticeship ground to a halt, so the public respectability of once venerated restrictions and practices declined. But the case against corporate status was not merely deployed by entrepreneurs anxious to exploit an open market for labour. At Birmingham the alleged unwisdom of seeking incorporation was closely related to a socially responsible commercial policy. Its inhabitants were threatened with the fate of the neighbouring corporation of Sutton Coldfield. Sutton had once been a prosperous town: now it was utterly dwarfed by its unchartered neighbour.

[17] *Commons Journals*, xx. 336, 352, 357, 359, 361–2.

[18] Ibid., xxxi. 359, 362, 380, 386, 397.

[19] Ibid., xvi. 445, 683.

[20] H. S. Toy, *The History of Helston* (London, 1936), chs. 16, 17; Sir L. Namier and J. Brooke, *The History of Parliament: The House of Commons 1754–1790* (3 vols., London, 1964), i. 240; *Commons Journals*, xxxv. 254–6.

'Your corporations d'ye see, are like strait wastecoats, nobody can work in 'em, or get their bread.'[21] The poetic celebrator of Gosport's growth in 1755 also dwelled on its unincorporated state.

> What tho the guilded Court of Magistrates,
> With all the Pageantry of Pomp and Show,
> No Place has there? What tho the wrangling Noise
> Of Lawyers, fright not with their barb'rous Sounds?
> Nor Nonsense, strive to palm for Eloquence;
> Safe from their Arms, in sweet Commercial Arts,
> Her Grandeur springs, the just Pre-eminent.[22]

Corporate privilege was considered synonymous with maladministration. Corporations had few public responsibilities but those they had were frequently treated as opportunities for self-enrichment. The leasing of municipal properties on favourable terms to corporation members was standard practice. It was all too easy to treat the public trust represented by legacies of property in the past as perks for co-opted trustees. Examples abounded, in small boroughs as in great. The borough of Woodstock seems to have been typical in this respect, however petty the practices involved. Its properties were in effect monopolized by its rulers. In 1715 it even inserted a clause in the lease of a cockpit providing that common councilmen of the borough be admitted free to cock-fights. As in many other places there was much back-sliding after virtuous attempts at reform. In 1759 a system of letting meadows to the highest bidder was replaced by a lottery among the common council, with the rider that any member not wishing to take advantage of his good fortune should give one of his colleagues a chance to take the lease before making it available to an outsider. The custom in Woodstock was to vote funds from the common stock 'for the Mayor and gentlemen regaling themselves after a troublesome day's business'; it is difficult not to conclude that the main business was serving themselves.[23] But what was involved was as much a change in public attitudes as in political morality. The elaborate feasting with which all kinds of corporate business were conducted was increasingly subject to public criticism. Ritual self-indulgence, which had once seemed an uncontroversial and perhaps necessary adjunct of privileged authority, was losing its legitimacy.[24]

---

[21] *Very Familiar Letters, Addressed to Dr Priestley* (3rd edn., Birmingham, 1790), p. 20.

[22] Archibald Maxwell, *Portsmouth: A Descriptive Poem, in Two Books* (Portsmouth, 1755), p. 17. It should be added that Maxwell was equally gushing about the governors of Portsmouth, who *were* incorporated.

[23] A. Ballard, *Chronicles of the Royal Borough of Woodstock* (Oxford, 1896), pp. 111–12.

[24] J. M. Triffit, 'Politics and the Urban Community: Parliamentary Boroughs in the South West of England 1710–1730' (Oxford Univ. D. Phil. thesis, 1985), p. 163.

The greed displayed by municipal rulers was a common cause for complaint. It produced particular outrage when the corporation of Worcester sought to profit by the triennial meeting of the Three Choirs, withholding the use of the town's ballroom by the stewards of the music meeting, so that a 'large share of the nett profits would have run into a channel very different from that of Charity'.[25] The ordinary assumption was that if a corporation took an interest in something, it was for reasons of private enrichment rather than the public good. In 1780, when the City of London reasserted its right to nominate governors to the four royal hospitals of Bethlehem and Bridewell, Christ's Hospital, St Bartholomew's, and St Thomas's, the resulting uproar and 'spleen' indicated something of the public cynicism as to its motives.[26] Corporate misuse of patronage for corrupt or political purposes was commonplace. It was inevitable, for example, that contracts for building work, in a large city such as a Norwich, where twenty to thirty contractors were employed annually in mid-century, would become the subject of factional disputes and party manipulation.[27] Select vestries, in many ways analogous to municipal corporations, faced similar charges. The parish of St Botolph without Bishopsgate revolted in 1721, its namesake without Aldersgate in 1733. In each case the accusations against the vestry were similar to those levelled at corporations.[28] They included mismanagement of parochial finances, as well as personal corruption on the part of vestrymen.

Corporate finances were not notable for good husbandry.[29] In 1729, the corporation of Liverpool, a reliable Whig body, none the less found itself prosecuted by a Whig regime for misapplication of its revenues. Liverpool owed its wealth not to efficient management, but rather to the expansion of its port, and the consequent increase in receipts from dock duties from £811 in 1724 to £4,554 in 1772 and £13,243 in 1792.[30] Revenues also rose at Newcastle, from £8,056 in 1700 to £25,699 in 1780, and, less spectacularly, at Exeter, from £2,000 in the early eighteenth century to

[25] C. L. Williams and H. G. Chance, *Origins and Progress of the Meeting of the Three Choirs* (Gloucester, 1895), p. 29.

[26] *London Magazine* (1780), 188, 583.

[27] D. S. O'Sullivan, 'Politics in Norwich, 1701–1835' (University of East Anglia, M.Phil. thesis, 1975), ch.4.

[28] Guildhall Library, MS 4527A: 'The Case of the Inhabitants of Bishopsgate', c.1721; *The Report of the Committee Appointed by a General Vestry of the Inhabitants of the Parish of St Botolph without Aldersgate, London: February 22. 1732* (London, 1733). Dissolving select vestries in Bishopsgate did not put a stop to the accusations; see *A Collection of All the Letters, Papers, Songs. etc.* (London, 1740).

[29] The financial management of corporations is put in context and sympathetically assessed, however, by E. J. Dawson, 'Finance and the Unreformed Borough: A Critical Appraisal of Corporate Finance 1660 to 1835, with Special Reference to the Boroughs of Nottingham, York and Boston' (Hull Univ. Ph.D. thesis, 1978).

[30] 1 Barnardiston, 236–8; William Enfield, *An Essay towards the History of Liverpool* (2nd edn., London, 1774), p. 69; *The History of Liverpool* (London, 1810), p. 280.

more than £6,000 by the 1780s.[31] In each case it was the capacity to tap commercial profits through some form of toll or royalty which was crucial. Few inland corporations were so fortunate. London itself staggered from one expedient to another. The most notorious, the election of Dissenting sheriffs with a view to collecting a handsome fine for non-service and thereby meeting the building costs of the new Mansion House, was terminated by Lord Mansfield in the case of Allen Evans.

There is no doubt about the general view. 'Everyone knows', it was observed in an election tract published at Coventry in 1754, 'that nothing is more common than loud Complaints, and many very just ones, against Corporations in General.'[32] Whether corporations deserved their reputation is less certain. Plainly, there were responsible administrators as well as cynical urban politicians. London's record was not altogether dishonourable.[33] But the public reputation of such bodies remained unfortunate, to say the least. In the second half of the century the very attempts to reform some of the worst practices indicated a general awareness of what was involved. The report in the *London Chronicle* in November 1775 that Doncaster Corporation was underletting municipal lands to its own members clearly assumed that readers would be outraged by a practice which would surely have been utterly unsurprising a few years before, and which was only just beginning to be publicly questioned.[34] In London in the 1770s attempts to curb the well-established custom of selling City offices were largely nullified by the vested interests involved; the principal effect was to provide additional publicity for practices which were increasingly condemned in public but almost ineradicable within the framework of oligarchical corporations.

Mock corporations nicely if unconsciously satirized the less desirable aspects of municipal life. Chichester's Corporation of St Pancras was founded in 1688 and annually commemorated Gunpowder Plot. It was open to 'men of all degree', spawned a regular friendly club, entailed the election of officers and councillors to shadow the official corporation, and was patronized by Lords-Lieutenant and MPs.[35] Manchester had a similar society, though it was not a formally incorporated town.[36] At Liverpool, which was incorporated, the mock rival met at Sefton in summer and in Bootle coffee-house in winter. Though its principal activity was dining and

[31] P. M. Horsley, *Eighteenth-Century Newcastle* (Newcastle, 1971), p. 220; R. Newton, *Eighteenth-Century Exeter* (Exeter, 1984), p. 95.

[32] Bodleian Library, G. A. Warwicks, b 1: William Reader's 'Chronicle of the Times', 57.

[33] I. G. Doolittle, 'The Government of the City of London, 1694–1767' (Oxford Univ. D.Phil. thesis, 1979).

[34] 18 Nov. 1775.

[35] E. E. Street, 'The Mayor and Corporation of St Pancras's, Chichester', *Sussex Arch. Coll.* 24 (1872), 135–8.

[36] W. E. A. Axon, *The Annals of Manchester* (Manchester, 1886), p. 96.

drinking, its customs included many which seemed indistinguishable from those of authentically chartered bodies. It had a variety of offices to bestow, some of which hinted at the realities of Liverpool life—Butler, Window Peeper, Clerk of the Court of Conscience, others merely ludicrous—Translator of the Oriental Languages, Imperial German Ambassador. It had a pew in church, elaborate rituals, and an agreeable distaste for party disputes: in March 1784 Pitt and Fox were simultaneously voted the freedom of the corporation. There were all too many municipal corporations which might have seemed no more useful.[37] Naturally enough, where the mock aldermen also held real office, it was easy to suspect them of politically sinister activities.[38]

Various though the complaints made against corporations might be, it is notable that for most of the period the principal animus did not stem from social envy. By the 1790s when William Blake wandered through each chartered street, by a chartered Thames, and noted in every face marks of weakness, marks of woe, there was no doubt more than a hint of class antagonism towards the great chartered corporations.[39] But before the last years of the century, the complaint was more likely to be that they did not adequately represent the bourgeoisie than that they represented it too well. The tussles at Bristol concerning police rates in the mid-1750s attained the significance of a national issue when Parliament found itself repeatedly debating the oligarchical character of the country's second city. After the mayor and aldermen petitioned for a watch bill in 1754, a substantial body of inhabitants countered with the simple assertion that the 43 members of the corporation were 'in no respect the Representatives of the citizens'.[40] In the subsequent controversies this was the central issue. The argument was imitated elsewhere on numerous occasions. The long struggle to obtain an improvement act for Cambridge, which began in 1768 and was not successful until 1788, centred on the credentials of the local corporation. The corporation's response to criticism was not very convincing. 'It is a matter of Surprise that the Inhabitants should be so unreasonable, as to demand a Power to be placed in their Hands, which, could they divest themselves of Self-Interest, they must see, cannot be attended with either Pleasure or Profit.' Corporations were evidently better fitted to govern. Nor were they to be despised if some of their members were less than opulent. The mayor, Francis Tunwell, argued that if the corporation's own property, held in trust for the public, were taken into account and added to the property which individual aldermen and common councilmen owned,

---

[37] E. Horley, *Sefton* (London, 1893), pp. 140–2, 151–2.

[38] J. Russell, *The Ancient Liberties and Privileges of the Cinque Ports and Ancient Towns: To Which is Prefixed an Original Sketch of Constitutional Rights* (London, 1809), p. 117.

[39] J. Sampson, ed., *The Poetical Works of William Blake* (Oxford, 1905), p. 131.

[40] *Commons Journals*, xxvii. 128.

it was sufficient to qualify any members of the corporation to what would compare with other townsmen.[41]

Corporations, at least those whose rulers were co-opted with tenure for life rather than elected and regularly accountable to their electors, were oligarchies, but they were not invariably oligarchies of the rich. A commentator of 1740 talked of men of 'middling Circumstances, and of ordinary Understanding'.[42] Even when they were rich they were likely to be selected on political, religious, or merely personal grounds. Very often the rich felt positively excluded. Lord Bathurst claimed in 1727 that at Gloucester the corporation consisted of a 'set of mean, corrupt, insignificant fellows' who derived their power from the management of charitable funds, and ruled a city in which the substantial inhabitants were proscribed.[43] One of the attractions of parliamentary reform was that it offered a means of tackling unrepresentative governing bodies. At Launceston in 1782 the petition in favour of reform alleged that the preceding twenty years had seen a catastrophic decline in the respectability of their corporation. Then the mayor and aldermen had been 'Men of very great Property within the Borough, as will appear from the Land and Poor Rates'. Now they paid rates worth £22.4s.4d. out of a total of £172.6s.8d.[44]

It was not only corporations which were liable to this objection. Select vestries, though they often derived their authority from prescription rather than charter, were in much the same position. The battle over vestries in 1742 was essentially a dispute about which form of parochial government better represented property, a bone of contention in numerous places. A bitter pamphlet controversy in 1754 in which such bodies were characterized as 'select Companies of Rogues' centred on the affairs of St Paul Covent Garden.[45] At St Marylebone in 1764 it was debated whether power should be entrusted to a select vestry or an elected committee of parishioners. The latter claimed that it represented more property than the former.[46] In St James's, Westminster, in 1783, the objection made to the vestry was precisely that it did not include adequate representation for propertied people. The petitioners produced a list of vestry members which diverged markedly from the roll of householders rated to the poor at above £50. But their real grievance was the composition of the local paving committee, a subject of long-standing resentment. In 1762 the Westminster Paving Commission had in effect seized control of street improvement from the vestries of Westminster. Subsequently that control had been

---

[41] Bodleian Library, Gough Cambridge 35 (4): handbill dated 16 Feb. 1769, pp. 4, 7.
[42] *The Livery-Man; Or, Plain Thoughts in Publick Affairs* (London, 1740), p. 35.
[43] J. W. Croker, *Letters to and from Henrietta, Countess of Suffolk* (2 vols., London, 1824), i. 279.
[44] *Commons Journals*, xxxix. 82.
[45] Ibid., xxiv. 196–211, 232–44, 250–6; *The Select Vestry Justified* (London, 1754), p. 14.
[46] *Commons Journals*, xxix. 800.

returned to the parishes by means of committees dominated by the vestries. The petitioners in 1783 sought guarantees that for the future the paving committee would include 'Persons who pay a high Proportion of the Taxes, or who have considerable Property in the said Parish'. The vestry counter-claimed, not implausibly, that they had more sense of the interest of the parish as a whole than their antagonists. The petition presented against the vestry was found to have 23 signatures, that in its favour to have more than 1,600. There followed a furious struggle which at one point attracted the votes of more than a hundred MPs on division in the Commons. The formula adopted, like that applied to many corporations, was to create a joint committee: 24 elected by the inhabitants, 12 by the vestry. But even this proved too much. The Lords preferred 25 representatives for the vestry and insisted on amending what could be considered a money bill. The Commons refused to endorse the alteration and the bill was lost.[47]

The significance of the statutory commission was that it offered a new deal in which only lack of property barred a man from a share in the management of his environment. This was sometimes the specific request. In 1744 an analysis of the deficiencies of parochial government suggested that select vestries in London and corporations elsewhere were irre-deemably tainted by the corruption which beset close bodies. With some-what startling precision it reckoned that a town of ten parishes with 2,000 households and 400 freemen could 'gratify' as many as 200 freemen every two years, 80 by rigging the rates, 120 by overcharging for goods supplied. What was needed to purify this system was a property qualification for bodies appointing overseers of the poor and other officers.[48] In effect this was a demand for political reconstruction on a large scale.

Only Parliament was equipped to carry out such reconstruction. It is ironic that the parliamentary process was itself in large part to blame for the decay and demoralization of the traditional organs of urban rule. What united many corporations, and incidentally influenced the single most important function of local government, the relief and management of the poor, was an obsessive preoccupation with parliamentary elections. The rocketing rise in the value of a seat in the Commons after 1688 overwhelmed the integrity of a class of municipal governors for whom the election of MPs had once been in the nature of a tedious and costly chore rather than a valuable perquisite. In a parliamentary borough party politics and personal interest were almost bound to take precedence over other considerations. No doubt it was awareness of the ugly realities of electoral politics which predisposed the House of Commons to grant new powers to less contaminated bodies of propertied citizens.

[47] Ibid. 138, 153, 186–7, 285, 301, 354, 412–13, 466, 470, 478–9, 486, 674, 681, 685, 691, 693–4.
[48] *A Short View of the Frauds, Abuses, and Impositions of Parish Officers* (London, 1744), p. 35.

This was not the only irony in the process of statutory innovation. Not every corporation in the late eighteenth century was despised as Launceston evidently was in 1782. There was a tendency to gentrification in some municipalities which made it difficult to argue that they were hopelessly degenerate. At Shrewsbury, where local gentry had long served as aldermen and mayors, this was not a novelty. Elsewhere the acquisition of politeness and opulence was more recent. But the result was the same. The young Duke of Rutland, visiting Scarborough in 1796, was impressed by the corporation's respectability and could not resist praising it in his account of his travels. Here was 'a body of men, whose situations, and profession in life raise them far above dependence'.[49] But such respectability was gained at a cost. It frequently depended on the introduction of men whose authentically representative function, even where property was concerned, was doubtful. The growing prominence of doctors, lawyers, bankers, even clergy, in corporations, inevitably at the expense of ordinary tradesmen and craftsmen, and frequently exploiting leisure and connections not open to their business colleagues, could create tensions. So could the intrusion of non-resident country gentlemen, whose purpose was the service of a magnate or a share in electoral influence. In the fashionable but somewhat decayed cathedral city of Salisbury elections to the common council became competitions between the local gentry.[50] Genteel non-residence was common, sometimes in violation of charters and by-laws. It was a crucial element in the crisis which beset Durham in the early years of George III's reign, culminating in the voiding of the corporation.[51] From the standpoint of the bourgeois citizen, this state of affairs was not necessarily preferable to the social debasement which afflicted other corporations. Certainly it took nothing from the argument for creating new and more strictly representative institutions when the opportunity for improvement offered.

FULL AUTHORITY

It was inevitable that many corporations would resist attempts to bypass them. But they rarely had the temerity to apply for the desired powers in their own right. At issue, above all else, was the power to tax. In this respect there was a contrast between the practices of town and country. In rural areas pressures to raise and spend money were mounting at the same time that they were elsewhere. But Parliament took quite different views of the two. When the JPs of Middlesex and Buckinghamshire petitioned for clarification of the county bench's power to rate in 1737, the result was eventually a statute which authorized such rating and in due course

---

[49] *Journal of a Tour to the Northern Parts of Great Britain* (London, 1813), p. 86.
[50] Wiltshire RO, 1553/37: letter of Henry Wyndham, 14 May 1767.
[51] Durham RO, DU 1/2/3.

produced a large new category of local expenditure.[52] But there was less enthusiasm for entrusting such powers to corporations and vestries. Municipal powers to rate were uncertain, and when exerted, restricted to specified purposes. An act of 1784 gave borough justices certain powers to rate and borrow for police and gaol expenses.[53] But this was not much utilized, nor was it the same thing as giving powers to the corporation as a whole. The rare exceptions did not constitute happy precedents. The provision in the Bristol Workhouse Act of 1696 which reserved money-raising powers for the mayor and aldermen caused intense controversy.[54] Similar disputes arose at Hull. In 1742 the corporation there had to be specifically deprived of its power to alter assessments other than at quarter sessions in open court.[55]

Some corporations claimed that they had the legal powers to carry out all the services required of an enlightened regime. Liverpool's select committee for improvements, managed by JPs, was active enough to provoke the anger of some of those whose property was thereby affected.[56] Opponents of a bill to improve Gloucester's streets in 1777 argued that the corporation owned sufficient of the property in question to have a clear obligation to bring them to the required standard.[57] Cambridge, too, claimed in 1769 that it only consulted the town 'out of Civility, not Necessity'.[58] Such propositions were highly debatable. The common belief was that neither corporation charters nor the Statute of Winchester provided adequate powers. That there was some degree of obligation was not in doubt. It was for this reason that some corporations supported petitions for a new statutory body which would relieve them of their paving duties. Not infrequently they were prepared to make a financial contribution as a kind of *douceur* to ratepayers. Shrewsbury offered £45 per annum in 1755, and endeavoured to impress the town with its generosity by pointing out that in practice it had spent only £30 in recent years.[59] Plymouth offered £20 per annum in 1772.[60] But obligations did not necessarily imply powers. Many townsmen in such places were content to argue that their rulers

[52] *Commons Journals*, xxii. 769, 776; 12 Geo. II, c. 29.

[53] S. J. and B. Webb, *English Local Government from the Revolution to the Municipal Corporations Act* (9 vols., London, 1906–29), vols. ii and iii: *The Manor and the Borough* (1908), ii. 703–4 n.; 24 Geo. III, c. 54.

[54] J. Tomlinson, *Doncaster* (Doncaster, 1887), p. 278.

[55] John Cary, *An Account of the Corporation of Bristol, in Execution of the Act of Parliament for the Better Employing and Maintaining the Poor of that City* (London, 1700), p. 3.

[56] 15 Geo. II, c. 10.

[57] *Dancing Masteriana; Or, Biographical Sketches for an Inquisitive Public* (London, 1799).

[58] *Commons Journals*, xxxvi. 221–2.

[59] Bodleian Library, Gough Cambridge 35 (4): letter of Mayor and Corporation of Cambridge, 13 Feb. 1769.

[60] Shropshire RO, 177/1c: broadsheet, 10 Jan. 1756.

should provide appropriate services without conceding their right to use powers of compulsion.

Much depended on the nature of the proposed improvement. At Leicester in 1774 the mayor and justices ordered the relocation of the beast market and publicly asserted their legal rights in such matters. Doubts had been raised in advance but in the event they were not challenged.[61] The regulation of markets was well within the prerogative of many chartered corporations. More ambitious projects generally required collaboration with the community at large. In very small towns this was feasible. At Appleby the corporation had sufficient tolls and rents to carry out most of its responsibilities, and in 1756 when more extensive repaving was needed, managed to raise the balance by public subscription.[62] But such acquiescence was unusual in larger places. Corporations which carried out extensive improvements without resort to statutory powers did so by employing their own funds, and usually ran into debt as a result. Doncaster's record in this respect was the boast of its unreformed corporation and was also unusual.[63] When Southampton mounted an opposition to an improvement commission in 1770, the Commons was unimpressed by its claim to have adequate legal powers for street repairs.[64] At issue was a straightforward conflict of jurisdictions which required the establishment of a separate authority. The Plymouth Paving Act of 1770 also aroused the most acute controversy. In 1772 a petition was presented accusing the commissioners of imposing unjust taxation: 'it is apprehended, the Act is a manifest Violation of the Town's Charter; and representing to the House, that, by the ancient Charters granted to the Mayor and Corporation, they have full Authority to put in Execution every necessary and needful Purpose, for the good Government and real Benefit of the Town and Corporation.' A new act was passed, only to produce similar protests two years later.[65] Rather than resting on the defensive argument that they did not need new powers or external assistance, some corporations went on to the attack, denying the representative credentials of those applying to Parliament. Rochester in 1769 alleged that the petitioners for local improvement included people who were not ratepayers. The Commons' answer in such cases was not to refuse a separate commission but to ensure that the corporation was permitted to nominate some of its members.[66]

Major improvements frequently required the granting of powers of

---

[61] Devon RO (Plymouth), 227/6: act of 1772.
[62] James Thompson, *The History of Leicester in the Eighteenth Century* (Leicester, 1871), p. 154.
[63] C. M. L. Bouch, 'Local Government in Appleby in the 17th and 18th Centuries', *Trans. Cumbs. and Westmor. Ant. and Arch. Soc.*, NS 51 (1952), 168.
[64] *Commons Journals*, xxxii. 703–4.
[65] Ibid., xxxiii. 522; xxxiv. 426.
[66] Ibid., xxxii. 203.

compulsory purchase. Ipswich boasted that its paving act of 1792 was 'the most moderate in its principle of any bill of its kind' because it did not include a clause to this effect.[67] Such moderation was certainly unusual. This was a sensitive issue when the improvements seemed to involve judgements of taste and convenience rather than manifest public exigency. In 1824 the memoirist Laetitia-Matilda Hawkins recalled how in her childhood the social life of Hatton Street had been ruined by the resulting disputes. In one instance levelling the paving deprived a genteel householder of the snobbish appeal of a step up to his front door. He never spoke to his neighbours again. 'This unfortunate business of giving to a street then esteemed one of the best in London, the advantage of a good pavement, occasioned such heart-burning and enmity, that it broke up long-standing friendships, and made strangers of those who, before this time, had been in the habit of almost daily intercourse.'[68] It was not only doorsteps that were at stake. In 1763, when improvement bills were becoming numerous, it was enquired 'if the widening of narrow passages, and opening convenient streets, can be deemed sufficient motive by the legislature, for obliging persons to quit their habitations, and dispose of their properties at a price fixed by a jury.'[69] On the whole the answer seems to have been in the affirmative provided the arrangements for representing the general will of the propertied community were thought adequate. But it was still possible to keep a watchful eye on the improvers. In 1774 the paving commissioners of Wapping were successfully prosecuted for unreasonably using their powers to raise footways and thereby block access to certain houses.[70] Costly obstructiveness sometimes made improvers wonder whether their efforts had been worth while. A visitor to Gloucester in 1782 found it 'very much improved by the Removal of large and useless and awkward Gates—by regular Pavements, by Lamps and opening to public View public Buildings—but it is doubtful whether the Commendations or the Complaints are superior—the Opposition of an Individual doubled the Expense'.[71]

The tensions involved were painfully exposed to public view in the case of Southampton by a local physician and antiquarian, John Speed. Speed was a determined opponent of the improvement commission, considering it an outrageous interference in the rights of the corporation and an intolerable financial burden on the town. In a speech to the corporation, of which he was an honorary member, he warned in 1769, 'you will have

[67] *Ipswich Journal*, 27 Apr. 1792.

[68] *Memoirs, Anecdotes, Facts, and Opinions, Collected and Preserved by Laetitia-Matilda Hawkins* (2 vols., London, 1824), i. 15.

[69] *London Magazine* (1763), 141.

[70] 1 Black. W. 924–6.

[71] Gloucestershire RO, D 2227/30: Journal of Revd Samuel Viner.

no reason to be surprised if you should soon dwindle into a meer Cypher, when that happens you may e'en burn your Charter, and make a present of your Maces to the new Commissioners'. He also pointed out that the improvements were to be sustained not by the setting up of a special fund or the levying of a toll, but in effect by direct taxation in the form of a rate which would affect owners only in the short run and occupiers in perpetuity. Those who sought this innovation he considered foreigners: 'some few strangers who had a very few years before come to live in the Town, being seiz'd with the Epidemical Madness of New Paving'.[72] These new settlers, many of them army and navy officers, 'cou'd not brook submitting to the Government of the Magistracy of the Town; but began to look on the Senators, who were most of them men of Business, for Gotham was a trading Town, with great contempt; and, from despising their Persons and Occupations, they came to treat their legal Authority, with much unmannerly Insolence; even to the endeavouring to wrest it out of their hands'.[73] There was also some party animus in the case. In the contested parliamentary election of 1774, the first such contest since 1741, the corporation gave strong support to the two candidates with an established interest, Hans Stanley and John Fleming, but the improvement commissioners appointed outside the corporation showed a greater readiness to support their challenger, the brother of the Duke of Manchester, Lord Charles Montagu.[74]

This suggestion of a social, occupational, and political gulf between town governors and improvement commissioners is none the less misleading. Even Speed's 'strangers' were not necessarily unwelcome. Particularly in the older towns of southern England, where manufactures were suffering by comparison with those of the Midlands and the north, polite immigration held out the possibility of a distinct urban renewal, bringing with it commercial prosperity and cultural vitality. There was a natural association between this immigration and improvement. The first historian of Taunton, Joshua Toulmin, welcomed the local improvement act of 1788 on precisely these grounds: 'The town, by these improvements, now affords, what for many years it wanted, houses for the reception of genteel families out of trade.'[75] Retired business and professional people were a major source of income and a guarantee of social status. It would certainly have been difficult to exclude them from the bodies which supervised improvement,

---

[72] E. R. Aubrey, ed., *The History and Antiquities of Southampton* (Pubs. Southampton Record Society, 1909), pp. 420–1.

[73] Southampton RO, Speed MSS, 'An Account of the ancient Town of Gotham'.

[74] Corporation votes were cast as follows: Stanley and Fleming, 16; Stanley, 1; Montagu, 1. Commissioners voted: Stanley and Fleming, 5; Stanley and Montagu, 4; Montagu, 1.

[75] J. Toulmin, *A History of Taunton* (Taunton, 1791), p. 184.

however much sentimental traditionalists like Speed would have liked to do so.

Corporations were not invariably opposed to new commissions. Senior municipal rulers saw some utility in such bodies. At Whitby the ruling burgesses, whose privileges were not chartered yet seem never to have been challenged, quietly turned themselves into paving commissioners in 1764.[76] Chartered corporations themselves could see the point of wielding wider powers on a collaborative basis. In 1791 Chichester's ruling body loftily declared that it would not object to a commission which involved sharing responsibility with the town. 'In order to avoid increasing the animosities, which are now too prevalent in the City, such right should be waived.'[77] It may have been making a merit of necessity. A similar bill had been defeated in 1782 when the local Guardians of the Poor, since 1753 elected by inhabitants, and beyond the influence of the corporation, had objected to the rating procedure involved.[78] Corporations, in any case, were not homogenous bodies. One of the effects of the growing resort to JPs was the shift of power which it reflected within corporations, strengthening the aldermanic elements, from which magistrates were customarily drawn, at the expense of junior councillors, common councilmen, bailiffs, assistants, and so on. This meant that corporations did not necessarily pull together in support of their corporate rights. As Speed was forced to admit, the ruling body of Southampton was itself split on the issue. He attributed this in part to self-interest. The town clerk and leading municipal champion of improvement, Charles Le Gay, or as Speed called him 'Mr Plausible Catchpenny', was rewarded for his support with the office of clerk to the new commissioners. The rest he treated as unrepresentative renegades, tempted by a share of the new power: 'but the People held them in such contempt, that the very children piss'd upon them, as they went along the Streets'.[79]

Speed's jaundiced account also conceals the extent to which the improvement commission represented a genuine coming together of diverse elements, of whom only a proportion had a share in chartered government. Southampton's common council minutes reveal considerable support for the bill in 1769–70. Both corporation members and commissioners were well represented at meetings of the commission. The first President, Charles Vignoles, was chosen from the non-municipal commissioners, but in the

---

[76] G. Young, *A History of Whitby, and Streoneshalh Abbey* (2 vols., Whitby, 1817), p. 600.

[77] F. H. W. Sheppard, 'Street Administration in Chichester, from the Sixteenth to the Nineteenth Century', *Sussex Arch. Colls.* 90 (1952), 30–1.

[78] 'Chichester Workhouse', *Sussex Arch. Colls.* 74 (1938), 131–67; Alexander Hay, *The History of Chichester* (Chichester, 1804), p. 379.

[79] 'An Account of the ancient Town of Gotham'; common council minutes for 1769–70 in 'Journal 1764–83' in Southampton RO.

early years the chair generally alternated between aldermanic commissioners and others. There is no suggestion in the minutes of clear lines
of demarcation during the first twenty years of the commission's existence.[80]
Differences of opinion seem not to have had any connection with the
privileged position of the corporation. Perhaps the most significant evidence
in this respect is the first paving rate for Southampton in May 1771. Many
of the most substantial ratepayers were men who were not members of the
corporation but had been appointed to the improvement commission.[81]
They were regular attenders at meetings of the latter. The conclusion is
obvious. The propertied community of Southampton was only erratically
represented on its governing body. If significant changes were to be made
and substantial taxes raised, some means had to be found of ensuring
them a voice. Preventing disputes was an important object in municipal
improvement.[82] The statutory commission helped achieve it.

The Southampton formula was widely adopted. Between 1749 and
1796 nineteen towns were granted commissions which included the entire
corporation, together with a number of named individuals. In most cases
the latter were in a majority, marginally at Southampton, massively at
Brecon, where 115 individual members were nominated. An alternative
arrangement was the inclusion of a specified proportion of the corporation,
usually consisting of mayor, recorder, aldermen, and justices.[83] The precise
arrangements reflected local circumstances. But the overall impression is
of co-operation. The very establishment of a statutory commission usually
reflected a measure of agreement among the propertied community. Where
that agreement was lacking the result was the failure to adopt legislation
rather than its entrenchment in the commission. Leicester, deeply riven
by political and sectarian division, made only one abortive attempt to
obtain a bill, in 1750, and had to wait until the nineteenth century for
statutory improvement.[84] But there were many boroughs with potentially
turbulent politics which succeeded in resolving or at least suspending their
feuds for the purposes of improvement. Shrewsbury had a history of party
political warfare at least as impressive as Leicester's, but it achieved an
impressive degree of consensus for the purposes of improvement. The
minutes of five distinct bodies survive for the 1790s: the corporation itself,
the paving commissioners, the directors of the house of industry, the Salop
infirmary, and the trustees for the rebuilding of St Chad's church. They
reveal the existence of a large group of men whose interests and activities

---

[80] Southampton RO, SC/AP/1/1; see also A. T. Patterson, *A History of Southampton 1700–1914*,
vol. i: *An Oligarchy in Decline 1700–1835* (Southampton, 1966), pp. 47–52.
[81] Southampton RO, SC/AP/5/1.
[82] A. McInnes, 'The Emergence of a Leisure Town', *Past and Present*, 119 (May 1988), 71.
[83] F. H. Spencer, *Municipal Origins* (London, 1911), p. 143.
[84] R. W. Greaves, *The Corporation of Leicester 1689–1836* (Leicester, 1970), pp. 32–4.

closely overlapped and who worked together for diverse purposes. This veritable governing class, an élite united by wealth, and composed of landowners, merchants, professional men, and substantial tradesmen, was as prone to dispute and faction as any other oligarchy. But in the last analysis common interest dictated a degree of co-operation, and in founding new institutions for practising such co-operation Shrewsbury was notably successful.[85]

Even sectarianism could be overcome, or at least neutralized for the purposes of propertied rule. At Leeds a corporation well known for its orthodox Toryism and High Churchmanship worked with paving commissioners of much more diverse views.[86] The chairman of the committee which obtained the Derby Street Act of 1792 and thereby made him unpopular with the poorer inhabitants of the town was no dyed in the wool Tory but the Unitarian manufacturer William Strutt.[87] At Bridport in Dorset the borough was ruled by Dissenters, who found no difficulty in obtaining a broader measure of support for a paving commission. There were ample grounds for division in the 1790s but the dominant force at Bridport consisted of moderate Nonconformists, who managed its parliamentary politics, expressed their loyalty to government in the political crisis of 1792–3, and were equally well represented both on the corporation and the improvement commission.[88] Even under stress statutory commissions were capable of glorying in their tolerant ethos. During the Gordon Riots of 1780 the paving commissioners of St Sepulchre, Middlesex, who formed a body called Guardians of the Night to patrol the streets, indignantly rejected a motion to exclude those of their number who were Roman Catholics, and recorded their view that nobody should be prevented from defending the parish 'merely on Account of any Religion which he may Profess'.[89]

In Tewkesbury, a small town in which religious distinctions mattered little, the process of conciliation and co-operation was completely untroubled. The initiative for an improvement bill was said to have come from outside the corporation, but it was readily accepted. The committee which prepared the bill was chaired by an attorney and prominent member of the common council, Neast Havard. He also supervised its passage through the legislature. In the commission which assembled in 1786 townsmen who did not sit on the council were in a substantial majority,

---

[85] These minutes are in Shropshire RO; they do not cover precisely the same periods, but make possible detailed comparison for most of the 1790s.

[86] R. G. Wilson, *Gentlemen Merchants: The Merchant Community in Leeds 1700–1830* (Manchester, 1971), p. 165.

[87] C. L. Hacker, 'William Strutt of Derby (1756–1830)', *Derbys. Arch. Jnl.* 80 (1960), 60.

[88] Dorset RO, Bridport MSS, B3/J1; EF 6; H 7; Bridport Act 25 Geo. III, c. 91; B. Short, *A Respectable Society: Bridport 1593–1835* (Bradford on Avon, 1976), chs. 7, 8.

[89] Guildhall Library, MS 9084/1: paving commission minute-book, 30 June 1780.

though there were no signs of tension between the two elements. In effect the improvement commission installed the natural governing body of Tewkesbury in power. The qualification required £30 per annum in land, or £600 in personal estate. The result was a petty ruling class of some thirty-five tradesmen, shopkeepers, and manufacturers, the top layer of a propertied society which included about 350 ratepayers. The corporation, by contrast, was a highly artificial, self-appointing, and self-perpetuating body which principally concerned itself with the dwindling agenda of market regulations and the more flourishing business of parliamentary elections. It included local gentry with political influence in the borough, and outsiders who were thought useful or were merely connected with members of the common council. Those of them who were also important men of property in the town co-operated cheerfully with commissioners who played no direct part in corporate affairs. Here was a division of functions which was to seem highly objectionable fifty years on, but which in eighteenth-century conditions proved eminently acceptable. The municipal oligarchy was left to its traditional activities. For the important business of reconstructing the town, providing it with civilized, hygienic services, and above all rating and purchasing property, it was necessary to go beyond it.[90]

The nomination of an independent group of propertied men was not the only means of ensuring that an oligarchical corporation was prevented from grasping powers of taxation. A common device, particularly in improvement bills, was the inclusion of electoral machinery. Much of the controversy aroused by the Plymouth bill of 1770 had to do with its absence, an omission which was remedied by the amending act of 1772. Thirty commissioners elected by ratepayers were then added to the nominated governors.[91] At Cambridge this was part of the formula envisaged from the start. Negotiations there were complex, partly because the town itself was divided, partly because the university's interests had to be taken into account. A paving scheme was first proposed in 1769, but it was not until twenty years later that an act of Parliament was obtained and a commission instituted. It included representatives of the university and corporation, and provided for the annual election of parochial representatives. This was an explicit recognition of the unrepresentative credentials of municipal government. It also gave a say in such questions to relatively humble parish vestries. The first election for Holy Trinity parish in 1788 was evidently a considerable affair. Seventy-nine parishioners were present to vote, including eight women. Ten of the voters, three of them women, were unable to sign their names.[92] Those elected were assiduous attenders. At the first

---

[90] Gloucestershire RO, TBR A 1/7; A 7/1.
[91] Devon RO (Plymouth), 291, 227/6: acts of 1770, 1772.
[92] Cambridgeshire RO, P. 22/8/1.

meetings of the Cambridge commission in 1788 and 1789 the university, the county, and the corporation were well represented. But gradually numbers dwindled and parochial commissioners came to dominate proceedings. By 1790 the elected part regularly constituted a clear majority of commissioners and controlled the standing committee which effectively managed the street improvements. This pattern was common. At Bath the elected parochial commissioners were particularly active.[93] It is not difficult to see why. Improvement commissions could have the most dramatic impact on the urban scene. The immense destruction at Canterbury after the improvement act of 1787 was the subject of great controversy. An ordinary parishioner had a considerable stake in such matters. The fact that it was his own shop front that he might be preserving doubtless increased his desire to use his franchise at an election, or to attend meetings if he was himself elected.[94]

TABLE 1. *Attendance Figures of Cambridge Improvement Commissioners 9 June 1788–3 November 1789*[a]

Category	No. of Commissioners	Possible Attendances	Actual Attendances	Percentage
University	16	864	148	17
County, etc.	20[b]	1,084	43	4
Corporation	12	648	229	35
Parishes	14	756	361	48

[a]During this initial period of hectic activity there were 54 meetings. This figure is multiplied by the number of commissioners in each category to produce the maximum possible attendance.
[b]This is the number attending meetings at all, not the number entitled to attend. If it were increased to take account of the latter, the actual attendance would be still more derisory.
Source: improvement commission minute-books in Cambridgeshire RO.

One impression gained from the later history of the commissions is that in some respects they were difficult to distinguish from the corporations. They came to be viewed as lethargic institutions displaying little more vigour than the bodies which they were designed in part to supplant.[95] But the context in which they operated in the mid-nineteenth century was quite different from that in which they had evolved in the mid-eighteenth century. Political rights do not necessarily depend on their constant exercise but on a sense that they are there to be exercised. A corporation which excluded many propertied members of the community was regarded quite differently from a commission which was open to all but for practical

[93] Macintyre, 'Towns as Health and Pleasure Resorts', p. 110.
[94] D. Gardiner, *Canterbury* (London, 1923), pp. 112–14.
[95] Webbs, *Statutory Authorities for Special Purposes*, pp. 345–6.

purposes controlled by those who had the time, energy, and interest to attend it. One of the characteristics of the governing class of eighteenth-century England was precisely that it consisted of those entitled to govern, rather than those who troubled themselves with the actual business of governing. Moreover, when controversy arose or particular exigencies required, those whose participation was minimal had a way of enforcing their views.

In this respect the surviving records of *ad hoc* bodies, whether turnpike trusts in the countryside or one of the diverse commissions given powers in the towns, can be misleading. The crucial period for most such bodies was their inauguration. It was at first setting out that the most contentious decisions had to be taken in terms of policy and the appointment of officers. Major financial questions had to be settled: how much to borrow, from whom to borrow, on what terms to borrow; how much to raise by way of rates and tolls, and on what basis to levy them. These were matters of overwhelming interest, and exactly those which municipal corporations were not trusted to carry out. The early years of a new commission naturally involved a large number of meetings. At Southampton there were 64 in the first year, 1770–1, 33 in 1774–5, 24 in 1779–80, and only 19 in 1784–5. Attendance followed a similar pattern, with more than a third of the total membership regularly present during the early years, and only a handful present during the second decade of the commission's history.[96] Wherever the early records are complete, for instance at Cambridge, Tewkesbury, and Wallingford, a very similar pattern seems to have prevailed.[97]

POOR MIDDLING PEOPLE

Uniting the commissioners who found themselves exercising the power delegated by statute was their property. There was an obvious comparison with voluntary bodies. The men who managed hospitals, dispensaries, and schools were the same men who were entrusted by Parliament with improvement of various kinds. At Shrewsbury in 1755 it was urged as an argument for establishing a paving commission that the promoters were essentially those who had earlier founded the Salop Infirmary.[98] Most statutory improvements began with a subscription which would underwrite the costs of making an application to the legislature and which gave some indication of the propertied community's commitment to the project in

[96] Southampton RO, SC/AP/1/1.

[97] Cambridge improvement commission minutes, commencing 1788, in Cambridgeshire RO; Tewkesbury improvement commission minutes, commencing 1786, in Gloucestershire RO; Wallingford improvement commission minutes, commencing in 1795, in Berkshire RO.

[98] Shropshire RO, 177/1c: broadsheet 10 Jan. 1756.

question. But voluntary subscription, revocable at will, was not an appropriate means of providing for permanent powers, particularly powers which might affect the legal rights of every citizen. The answer was a property qualification.

The property qualification was the crucial safeguard of sound, respectable government. This principle went virtually unchallenged for most of the eighteenth century. It did, however, conceal certain ambiguities and tensions. Some qualifications, including the landed requirements for MPs and JPs, did not claim to be more than safeguards. They presupposed some earlier process of election or selection and did not of themselves empower those who enjoyed them to exercise power. MPs had to be chosen by their constituents, JPs by the Crown. But there was a growing tendency to treat qualification by property as a sufficient rather than a necessary condition. Only radical politicians seem to have resisted it. John Wilkes, mindful, no doubt, of his own deficiency in this respect, denied that the opulent were invariably 'distinguished for knowledge, sagacity, and that attachment to the public cause, which ought to mark a man in public life'.[99] William Godwin denounced what seemed to him an assertion that a man was of less value than his property.[100] The reforming Duke of Richmond also objected to the practice of equating proprietorship with political responsibility. He did so in defence of the corporation of Chichester, arguing that as an elected body its standing was superior to that of commissioners whose only title derived from nomination by statute.[101] Considering that municipal councils like that of Chichester were better described as co-opted than elected, this argument was less than convincing. It was, in any case, largely ignored by Parliament. Sometimes it provided for the election of propertied commissioners, but often it did not. It proceeded frequently by naming those entrusted with authority in the body of the relevant statute. In some instances it simply legislated for all men, and even women, of a given 'quality' in a specified district, to act with statutory powers. And not least it usually bestowed on such trustees further powers of co-option, especially to fill the places of those who died, retired, or removed. The propriety of these procedures was largely taken for granted.

There was much more debate at the time about the kind and quantity of property required. At an early stage it was conceded that land would not do for this purpose. Not only was the strain on the administrative responsibilities of landowners as a class unrealistically high, but in an urban setting the emphasis on landed property would have produced bizarre,

[99] *Kearsley's London Register, Brought down to Michaelmas 1787* (London, 1787), p. 181.
[100] *Enquiry Concerning Political Justice*, p. 626.
[101] Sheppard, 'Street Administration in Chichester', p. 31.

impractical results. Outside the acknowledged preserves of landed qualifications, the county magistracy, the land tax commission, and the militia,
themselves increasingly difficult to defend, a landed requirement was very
rare. Gloucestershire's gaol reform programme in the 1780s was entrusted
to men who had £250 or were already JPs, but gaols were peculiarly the
business of the county magistracy.[102] Almost all statutory qualifications
were expressed by a formula permitting either land or personal property
to qualify, the former as an annual rental value, the latter as a capital sum.
The ratio between the two varied, but the commonest assumption seems
to have been that personal estate to a value about twenty times its equivalent
in landed income should be required. Land bought at twenty years purchase
was decidedly cheap in the late eighteenth century; thirty would have been
more in line with land values. To this extent the formula was loaded in
favour of personal estate. Lower down the social scale, a still more generous
ratio seems to have applied. Under the highway legislation of George
III's reign, the main object was merely to find someone willing to serve.
Surveyors could qualify by owning £10 or occupying £30 worth of real
property, or in desperation, if they were among the 'most reputable' of
their parish.[103]

The actual levels set varied a great deal, though there were attempts to
standardize them in the late eighteenth century. By 1780 practice had come
to vary within reasonably predictable margins. Commissioners of small
debt courts were expected to have £50 from property or personal estate of
£1,000 at Halifax in 1777, but at Oldswinford in the same year the
equivalent sums were £20 or £600. In 1782 it was £20 or £400 at Brosely.
At Shrewsbury in 1783 the matching figures were £30 or £600, at Dover
in 1784 £30 or £500.[104] These differences plainly reflected local conditions.
Brosely and Oldswinford were small districts with a thriving metal industry
but few men of property; Dover, and still more Shrewsbury, were residential towns with numerous bourgeois householders, including men of
professional background; Halifax covered a large area in which there were
numbers of well-qualified merchants, manufacturers, and landowners.
Significantly, when the rural districts of Bolingbroke and Candleshoe in
Lincolnshire obtained a small debt court in 1778, they did not trouble to
specify a qualification, but simply named the local gentlemen who were
suitable to act.[105] The elaborate calculation of personal estate qualifications
was a particular requirement in urban and industrial areas, where it was
impracticable to rely on a landed élite but important to ensure a decently
respectable body of commissioners.

---

[102] J. R. S. Whiting, *Prison Reform in Gloucestershire 1776–1820* (London, 1975), p. 12.
[103] John Scott, *Digests of the General Highway and Turnpike Laws* (London, 1778), p. 1.
[104] 17 Geo. III, c. 15, c. 19; 22 Geo. III, c. 37; 23 Geo. III, c. 73; 24 Geo. III, (I) c. 8.
[105] 18 Geo. III, c. 34.

This range of personal qualifications was similar to those for other statutory bodies. Street improvement commissions possibly set slightly more stringent requirements. £1,000 of personalty was normal for parishes around London and also for many provincial cities, some of them, such as Wolverhampton, by no means resorts of the gentry.[106] In a Westminster parish like St Paul's Covent Garden, it rose to £2,000.[107] But in many smaller towns it sank to £500. Turnpike trusts displayed similar variations. In 1777 seventeen road acts were passed. The qualifications which they listed ranged from £3,000 personalty in County Durham and £2,000 in Oxfordshire and Berkshire, to £800 in Dorset, Sussex, and North Wales.[108] The record was that for Westminster Paving Commissioners, set in 1762 at £300 worth of real property or £10,000 of personal estate. This caused irritation to the tradesmen who helped govern Westminster parishes and fuelled their successful campaign to whittle away the powers of the commissioners.[109] It was also quite untypical. Most personal property qualifications were in the order of £500 to £1,000. There was a tendency to raise the sum stipulated at the end of the century, but it is unlikely that this did more than take account of inflation, perhaps not even that.[110]

What did this level of personal wealth signify? Personalty of £500 to £1,000 was a guarantee of at best modestly middle-class status. One commentator in 1766 characterized possessors of £500 to £2,000 or £3,000 as 'poor middling people of rather small fortunes'.[111] Business and professional men of any substance would easily meet it. The turnpike legislation assumed that it matched landownership of £40 per annum, itself a figure which could easily be achieved by landlords of minimal standing. In the midland counties of Derbyshire, Leicestershire, and Warwickshire in 1784 there were between 250 and 300 landowners with estates of this value, in a smaller county with few large estates, Surrey, over 600, and in a larger county, Essex, as many as 800.[112] Comparisons of this kind are of less value in an urban setting where freehold property was not subject to consistent agrarian values, and where, in any case, it might be a rare commodity. But statutory attempts to find an equivalent of real and personal estate for householders who could not qualify under either heading confirm the

---

[106] 17 Geo. III, c. 25.

[107] 23 Geo. III, c. 42.

[108] 17 Geo. III, c. 110, 105, 103–4, 91, 111; in the King's Printer's enumeration these are c. 109, 104, 102–3, 90, 110.

[109] 2 Geo. III, c. 21; for objections, see the MS petition drawn up by the parishes of St Margaret and St John, Westminster, at Northumberland RO, Delaval MSS, 2DE/49/1/20.

[110] Spencer, *Municipal Origins*, pp. 138–9; the increase is here linked with the growing importance of the role of the Lord Chairman of Committees.

[111] *London Magazine* (1766), 98.

[112] This is based on the land tax assessments in the appropriate county record offices; it assumes a ratio of roughly 1 : 9 between the tax paid and the gross rental.

comparatively lowly status which was aimed at. In the Clerkenwell Poor
Law Act of 1775, the qualification was set at £500 personalty or £20
rateable value for occupiers; at Bermondsey in 1791 the same quantity of
personalty, or a £50 freehold or £10 occupancy were stipulated.[113]

Low qualifications were adopted especially where the administration of
poor relief was concerned, perhaps in recognition of the long-standing
rights of ratepayers. The early workhouse acts were markedly liberal in
this respect. At Norwich in 1712 rate payments of 12d. a year or a £10
occupancy were sufficient.[114] But in this instance it remained for the
corporation to select such householders for service. In other instances all
those with a minimal qualification were empowered to act without previous
selection. At Nottingham in 1762 every £10 householder was entitled to join
the improvement commission. At Worcester in 1770, any £40 freeholder or
possessor of £800 personalty who also occupied a £10 property was
permitted to do so. At Manchester in 1776 all who contributed £20 to the
expenses of the public works were thus enfranchised.[115] These relatively
undemanding provisions looked forward to the household franchise which
came to characterize municipal government in the mid-nineteenth century.
What influenced them was the spirit of inclusiveness. Sometimes the
multiplicity of means by which a qualification might be achieved reflected
the same spirit. At Boston in 1776, commissioners might own a £50
freehold anywhere in Lincolnshire, or be heir to a £100 freehold, or possess
a £10 freehold in the borough, or occupy a £20 tenancy, or possess personal
estate of £500.[116] Plainly the object was to exclude nobody of the requisite,
decidedly modest status.

Complaints about the social standing of bodies protected by such legislation were legion. John Scott was contemptuous of 'the Farce daily made
of Qualification Oaths', and incidentally considered £800 much too low.[117]
He thought even £1,000 would have been inadequate. The figure of £800
had particular significance, having been specified in a general highways act
of 1773 for trusts which did not already have a statutory qualification.[118]
More than any other description of statutory delegation, turnpikes created
social division, even class conflict. Scott's complaint was that the qualification permitted farmers and shopkeepers a share in road government.
Shopkeepers took insufficient interest; farmers took an unduly narrow
interest, preferring bad roads to a higher toll. This was a long-standing
grievance of their landlords and social superiors. A committee of the

---

[113] 15 Geo. III, c. 23; 31 Geo. III, c. 19.
[114] 10 Anne, c. 15.
[115] Spencer, *Municipal Origins*, pp. 159–60.
[116] 16 Geo. III, c. 25.
[117] *Digests of the General Highway and Turnpike Acts*, pp. 246, 245.
[118] 13 Geo. III, c. 84.

Commons in 1752 found extensive evidence of its consequences. The Cranford Bridge to Maidenhead trust revealed maladministration on the part of the 'Farmers, Tradesmen, Maltsters, and Dealers in various Commodities' who managed it. It took the unexpected turn-out of a number of gentlemen with considerable estates in Buckinghamshire and Berkshire to compel commissioners to charge themselves tolls, and put a stop to scandalous misappropriation on the part of a treasurer who had given no security for his office. The committee was also interested in the history of the Basingstoke to Hertford Bridge trust in Hampshire. It identified what it considered the critical stage in its degeneration into the tool of unworthy trustees. It found that

about Five or Six Years ago there were 17 Commissioners, of considerable Estates, assembled in One Room, debating upon the Business of the Trust; and that there were about 30 Tradesmen, who were likewise Commissioners, in another Room; That a Proposal was made in the Room where the Gentlemen were, to re-erect another Turnpike Gate; which had been removed; That the Majority of the Gentlemen were against that Re-erection; upon which the 30 Tradesmen were called in, by those who proposed to erect it; and without hearing any of the Debates, the Question being put, they voted it should be re-erected; That upon this, several of the Gentlemen being disgusted, declined acting any longer in the Trust.[119]

Arthur Young took an indulgent view of such occurrences. If the business were done, he reasoned, what did it matter that farmers and carters did it? He also thought that the objection held 'equally against all public works executed by commissioners'.[120] None the less, turnpikes were peculiarly sensitive as indicators of social tension. They brought the natural rulers of the countryside, the landowners, into conflict with those they deemed their inferiors. In 1822 Parliament even went to the length of abolishing the personal property qualification in order to provide them with some protection in this respect.[121] By that time relations between the landed interest and its competitors had re-entered an era of chronic competition. Perhaps, too, there were sufficient landowners in the 1820s to assert their rights. In the eighteenth century landlords were quick to express their indignation but less ready to shoulder their responsibilities. The organizer of a highway improvement at Ilchester in 1752, J. H. Coxe, was dismayed by the country gentlemen's lack of experience in this respect.[122] If they had been prepared to play their full part in the management of highways, it would not have been necessary to call on others. In the early days of the turnpike trusts JPs had been expected to conduct their business. But this expectation did

[119] *Commons Journals*, xxvi. 491–2.
[120] *The Farmer's Tour through the East of England* (4 vols., London, 1771), ii. 189.
[121] W. A. Albert, *The Turnpike Road System in England, 1663–1840* (Cambridge, 1972), p. 58.
[122] Somerset RO, DD/DN/210: J. H. Coxe to C. Dickinson, 26 Nov. 1752.

not survive the rapid expansion of the turnpike network in the 1730s and 1740s. Once less respectable elements were entrusted with a managerial role, landowners proved still more reluctant to carry out their duties. Just as they fled from the magistracy, the land tax commission, and the militia, when confronted with onerous duties and the company of less genteel governors, so they fled all the faster before the invading forces of the farmers and carriers who had a vested interest in the turnpikes.

It is difficult to form a balanced view of the extent of such problems. Most of the complaints had to do with turnpikes in the metropolitan area or at least in the Home Counties, where the sheer volume of traffic and the profitability of the main freight routes to London created unusual conditions. In rural areas conditions varied a good deal. In Somerset, for example, some of the turnpikes were in highly respectable hands.[123] The roads around Bath were under the management of genteel commissioners in practice as well as in theory. Elsewhere in the county peers and substantial landowners were prominent in the trusts. At Ilminster in 1759 they included Lord North, already a minister and later to become Prime Minister. On the other hand a few miles' distance could make a considerable difference to the social complexion of the management. Around Yeovil there were two distinct trusts. They derived their authority from the same act of 1753, but their administration was separated for all purposes. The roads to the east of the town were entrusted to men with £100 in land or personal estate of £2,000. For those to the west the equivalents were respectively £50 and £1,000. This distinction was preserved in subsequent acts of 1777 and 1800. Only in the later act of 1819 was a new qualification of £100 in land or £4,000 personalty applied to both districts. The assumption that the parishes to the west could not muster the gentility to be found to the east was endorsed by experience. The eastern trust had little difficulty of any kind, and when the act was first renewed in 1777 only five new trustees had to be named. Prominent West Country families, including the Phelips of Montacute, the Fanes, Earls of Westmorland, and the Portmans, appeared regularly among its trustees. In the west, around Chard, it was quite a different story. There the affairs of the turnpike fell into the hands of clothiers, apothecaries, and the like. In 1777 it proved necessary to name 280 additional trustees in order to obtain a quorum for meetings. Two of those who duly presented their qualifications in consequence were unable to sign their names and reduced to using a mark. This was not generally what a property qualification was presumed to entail.

Chard was the centre of a manufacturing area, and its experience was not necessarily typical. In many provincial trusts, the workhorses of the

---

[123] Turnpike records in Somerset RO at D/T/ba, ch, yeo, ilm, ta, sm, for Bath, Chard, Yeovil, Ilminster, Taunton, and Shepton Mallet, and DD/LW/C/134 for Frome.

county benches, clergy and small squires, were left in charge. In others, where the interests of important towns and cities was involved, a high proportion of trustees was respectably mercantile. Of the commissioners appointed to the Markfield trust in 1783, less than half were landowners.[124] The rest were principally drawn from the professional and business class of Leicester. Paradoxically, there was less likelihood of conflict between this class of men and the county gentry than between the latter and their rural inferiors. The élite in town and country shared so much in point both of manners and material interest that they had little difficulty working together.

In an urban setting conflicts between county gentry and other classes were still less likely. This was not because the gentry had everything their own way. Local circumstances often made it essential to give a voice to lowly householders. The Dorchester Paving Act of 1776 appointed 86 trustees in addition to senior members of the corporation. This was in a town with only 200 households rated to the poor. Moreover, as indicated in the parliamentary election of 1774, the political preferences of these

TABLE 2.   *Voting at the 1774 Dorchester Election*

Voters	Candidate		
	William Ewer	John Damer	Anthony Chapman
Total Poll	232	214	145
Resident Voters	120	110	113
Non-Resident Voters	112	114	32
'Esquires'	23	12	3
Trustees	46	47	38

Source: poll is in Dorset RO, 132/33/4; trustees are named in 16 Geo III, c. 27.

trustees were quite different from those of the neighbouring gentry. On the other hand, the latter were by no means excluded from the government of the towns. Improvement commissions frequently included them. No doubt part of the intention in these cases was to ensure that improvement did not incur tolls which would be paid by countrymen more than townsfolk. But aside from this consideration the deferential habits of country towns required due recognition of local landowners. What matters in retrospect is that in practice landed families took little part in such ventures. At Cambridge the minutes of the improvement commission show

[124] 23 Geo. III, c. 107, compared with Leicestershire land tax assessments.

them turning out in force for the inaugural meeting and then disappearing
from sight. At Wallingford they did not put in an appearance at all. In
both cases this may have been in part because they had no desire to consort
with their inferiors.[125] But it also reflected the absence of any fundamental
conflict of interest between country gentlemen and the urban communities
which they patronized. Significantly, landed gentry were most likely to be
found playing a prominent part in improvement where there was no
practicable alternative. Cheltenham acquired a paving commission in 1786.
This was not a question of meeting the requirements of a bustling commercial centre, but rather of providing for polite visitors in what was still
a small, though expanding resort. There was no established borough
machinery, and little more than the nucleus of a respectably propertied
business community. Not surprisingly, the commission was dominated by
gentlemen and clergy, led by the De La Beres, country gentlemen *par
excellence*. They were self-appointed, but indisputably necessary sovereigns
of a newly fashionable town. When royalty itself visited the spa in 1788
'Mr Delabere' was quite content to be described by his august guests as
'chief magistrate of Cheltenham'.[126]

The De La Beres knew the importance of carrying out their local duties.
Such conscientiousness was crucial in determining who ruled Georgian
England. Appointing rulers was easy. Getting them to act was more
problematical. In this respect the fairest test was probably provided by
new poor law authorities. Poor relief was unlike any other form of improvement. In terms of social policy, it was uniquely important. The sums of
money raised to support it far exceeded any other kind of local taxation.
It was governed by an elaborate system of parochial administration which
for all its deficiencies was highly prized by ordinary Englishmen. The
statutory incorporations of the eighteenth century were intended to create
a more cost-effective system of management, principally by establishing
large workhouses which deterred the idle poor from applying for relief and
made profitable use of the labour of those who did. They were simply too
important and too expensive to be left to the support of subscribers and
the goodwill of propertied people, as many other public bodies were.

The incorporations of the decade or so after 1688 all related to large
boroughs with chartered corporations. They were politically controversial
and subject to revision. The Poor Relief Act of 1723, which permitted any
parish to apply a workhouse test, made it unnecessary, for a while at least,
to extend this model. It was not revived until the end of George II's reign,

---

[125] At Cambridge 19 such commissioners attended the first meeting, 4 the second. Thereafter there
were never more than 2 present; minutes in Cambridgeshire RO. For Wallingford, see Berkshire RO,
W/AL 1.

[126] Gloucestershire RO, CBR Box A; C. Barrett, ed., *Diary and Letters of Madame D'Arblay*
(4 vols., London, 1876), ii. 592.

when two MPs, the celebrated Admiral Vernon and the tireless advocate of poor law reform, Sir Richard Lloyd, were credited with providing the necessary impetus. The new authorities all owed their existence to a local act of Parliament. Some were to be found in chartered boroughs. One of them, at Shrewsbury, attracted national interest and was widely regarded as a triumph of enlightened social administration. Others were rural or semi-rural. In two areas, East Anglia and Shropshire, they were numerous, and gave rise to prolonged debate about their merits. They constituted a major political and administrative experiment.[127]

Certain principles united these late eighteenth-century foundations. They all incorporated a body of ratepayers under the name of 'guardians', with the safeguard of a property qualification. They all entrusted special powers to an élite of 'directors' subject to similar or superior conditions, and elected from the wider constituency of guardians. They all included provision for the building of a house of industry on the model beloved of poor law reformers, serving a group of parishes or at least a substantial population, and looking forward to the nineteenth-century unions. They all authorized borrowing from the public at large, on the security of the rates, and they all guaranteed that the rates would not be raised beyond specified levels. Not least they all partially superseded the traditional machinery of poor relief, in some measure bringing parochial officers under their control and displacing the supervisory role of magistrates. What common lessons could be learned from them?

Perhaps the most obvious was that attention to duty could be enforced only up to a point. The workhouse acts generally required the attendance of elected directors and acting guardians, on pain of a fine. Even so, maintaining a quorum proved far from easy. In Suffolk there was an informal procedure by which directors covered for each other. The clergy, as proxy governors of rural England, were in demand for this purpose, standing in for neighbouring gentlemen.[128] At Whitchurch in Shropshire there were acrimonious exchanges on the subject, one of which occurred in 1797 when the directors divided between those who claimed to have observed the hour shown on the workhouse clock, and those who preferred the clock on the parish church. The truth was that getting an adequate number of either to attend was a major undertaking for the clerk. At intervals the delinquent were reminded of their duty. But the fines imposed, of 5s., were invariably revoked once an excuse had been offered. In the Shropshire unions some of those elected as directors argued that their

---

[127] The records of the Suffolk poor law incorporations employed are at Suffolk RO (Ipswich), ADA/7 (Samford), 8 (Stow), 10 (Carlford and Colneis), 11 (Loes and Wilford); I have used land tax assessments for 1799, to establish the landed credentials of directors and guardians. The Shropshire records are at Shropshire RO, 83/1 (Shrewsbury), 3091, 3127 (Whitchurch), 13/5, 904/1 (Atcham).

[128] Suffolk RO (Ipswich), HA 50/19/4.3(1): diary of J. Longe, 5 Apr. 1796, 19 July 1796.

appointment was a parish office, and subject to similar exemptions, including Tyburn tickets. At Whitchurch they succeeded with this plea, after
legal advice had been taken. At Atcham they failed, after counsel's opinion
to the contrary. On the other hand there is no doubt that meetings of the
poor law incorporations were much better attended than those of comparable bodies. At Shrewsbury this was so much the case that the Salop
Infirmary altered its constitution to make possible a similar procedure,
with named directors being chosen for six-month periods on the assumption
that they would act. But Shrewsbury had its own political and admin-·
istrative traditions and a considerable corps of practised governors. Its
experience was of interest only to comparable boroughs.

Who did turn out? In all cases the simplest answer would be those who
came up to the minimum qualification and had either an interest in so
doing, or the inclination and time to engage in an unrewarding form of
public administration, whether out of officiousness or high-mindedness.
In Suffolk the concern seems to have been to ensure that tenant farmers
never found themselves in the driving seat. As acting guardians, charged
with supervision of parochial relief, in effect glorified overseers of the poor,
they were expected to play their part. But they were never allowed to
become directors unless they owned land of their own. On the other hand
the directors themselves were not the county gentry beloved of enthusiasts
for the traditional rural order. Overwhelmingly they were proprietors of
modest standing, or professional men with a small estate. In some instances
they can barely have met the requirement, itself a low one, that they own
£50 of land in the area. In terms of status they often ranked only just above
the farmers whom they directed, and who were required to own £30 or
pay rates on £60. The titles which they claimed in the minutes are not
without significance. Within a year or so of the establishment of most of
the hundred houses of East Anglia, 'Esquire' had largely disappeared, to
be replaced by 'Mr' and 'Rev'. One of the claims made by the champions
of the houses was that the landed rulers of the region had failed in their
duty to superintend the old system of poor relief. This was hotly denied
by representatives of the East Anglian gentry, but the record of the
incorporations scarcely seemed to justify their faith in genteel dutifulness.[129]

In Shropshire the pattern varied. In the county town the directors were
a small body of men, serving in rotation, and as such played their full part
in other local institutions. Their social status was similar to that of the
borough justices who had previously supervised poor relief, with the
difference that the pool from which they were drawn was larger, and the

---

[129] Robert Potter, *Observations on the Poor Laws, and the Present State of the Poor, and on Houses of
Industry* (London, 1775), p. 38; N. J. Abercrombie, 'The Early Life of Charles Butler (1750–83)',
Recusant History, 14 (1977–8), 285.

competing demands on their time accordingly less. But perhaps the most revealing case was that of Whitchurch. There the necessity for action had been thrust on the community by local clergy doubling as county magistrates. A record of niggardly poor relief, dangerously unhygienic workhouse conditions, and generally lax administration compelled the parish vestry to apply for statutory incorporation. But the results can hardly have come up to the expectations of the leading clergyman-justice involved, the Rector of Whitchurch, Francis Egerton. He found that he could be as easily outvoted on a statutory board as in his own vestry. The corporate seal which he had commissioned, displaying his parish church, was eventually rejected, and he found himself selected at the first opportunity for the unwelcome honour of a parish apprentice. The Whitchurch Act included an elaborate procedure for phased election of directors by the vestry, on the assumption that after a year or so of administration by nominated proprietors the ratepayers would be capable of choosing their own governors. But the committee set up to obtain the act had insisted on a property qualification of £20 in land, £75 rating liability, or personal estate of £500. These exceeded what the House of Commons committee had proposed and no doubt their object was to keep parish affairs in safe hands. Elections became a farce managed by those who expected to be elected. The men who directed the Whitchurch House of Industry were the same who had previously run the parish.

INTERESTED PERSONS

Unity was the object of the property qualification but it was unity with a purpose, often a repressive purpose, however dressed up in the rhetoric of improvement. There was a suspicion that so-called reformers brought a depressingly narrow perspective to their work. One of the sharpest tests of their intentions arose in connection with the small debt courts. These were unlike most of the other forms of statutory innovation in that they were not directed to 'improvement' as such. But they certainly suggested the same mentality, and in that they were adopted on a piecemeal basis, according to the expressed requirements of specific localities, they belong rather with 'public and local' legislation, and even with some 'private' legislation, for instance enclosure, than with the regulation of civil and criminal offences in a conventional sense. Their projectors claimed much on their behalf. The old hundred courts, which traditionally dealt with debts of less than forty shillings, were often defunct. When they were not, as at West Derby in Lancashire and the Wirral in Cheshire, they were notoriously liable to abuse.[130] The small debt legislation was presented as

[130] R. Stewart-Brown, *The Wapentake of Wirral* (Liverpool, 1907), pp. 84 ff.

a humane and rational solution to a major social problem. When he penned
his definitive account of the new kind of court in 1787 the Birmingham
businessman, William Hutton, treated it as the perfect model for civilized
litigation in a commercial society: 'Nothing is so necessary, in the whole
system of English jurisprudence, as a concise method of recovering
property, and terminating disputes. This is the great hinge upon which
the welfare of a nation turns.'[131] The courts also succeeded because their
judges were resident, unpaid, and dedicated to maintaining the credit and
morale of their locality. The hundred courts, and the borough courts which
served a similar function in many places, failed on both counts. Without
the benefit of summary jurisdiction, they gave rise to interminable and
expensive suits. Moreover the men who controlled them, exploitative estate
stewards in the country, corrupt municipal officers in the boroughs, were
utterly unsuited to a judicial function. This at least was the theory,
and the creation of special tribunals, supervised by independent men of
property, on principles of equity, the practical solution. Courts of conscience were not in fact new, and in London went back to the sixteenth
century. But in the form desired, they were few in number and unevenly
distributed.

Long before Hutton summarized the case for the defence, petitioners
for legislation had stressed its social utility. There were recurrent demands
for such courts in the late seventeenth and early eighteenth century. They
even featured in the instructions drawn up by the electors of Middlesex in
1722.[132] Such requests were generally grounded on the inadequacies of the
existing law of debt, and especially on the sufferings of small debtors. If
there was a fear it concerned the dangers of summary jurisdiction. It was
argued that the better-off, especially, would be at risk of persecution by
their inferiors. Respectable citizens might be hauled before an arbitrary
court by servants and shoemakers.[133] But when the movement spread in
the middle of the century somewhat different arguments were voiced.
Birmingham and Liverpool applied for courts of requests in 1752 with
appeals to the value of ready credit in vigorous commercial centres. Their
supporters pointed out that the legislation would make possible the dis-
ciplining of anti-social elements. In Liverpool it was said that Irish immigration had expanded local trade but also encouraged 'many dishonest Persons
to presume to run in Debt'. At Birmingham 20,000 artificers and handicraft
people relied on credit but without the legal right to enforce payment the

---

[131] *Courts of Requests* (Birmingham, 1787), p. 9.

[132] *Weekly Journal*, 31 Mar. 1722; on early doubts about the courts of requests, see W. H. D.
Winder, 'The Courts of Requests', *Law Quarterly Review*, 59 (1936), 369–94.

[133] *Reasons against Erecting a Court of Conscience within the City and Liberty of Westminster* (British
Library 816 m 15/8).

whole structure of credit was threatened.[134] Much depended on perspective. In the same session a bill regulating the Tower Hamlets Court of Requests provoked acute controversy. The 'useful poor Manufacturers' of the liberty petitioned against it, urging the injustice of a bill which subjected unemployed workers to the extortionate practices of court clerks, and referring to their loyal support for the Crown during the rebellion of 1745.[135] Hutton himself had his critics, not a few of them among those whose welfare he thought he was safeguarding. According to his daughter, it was because he was known as a commissioner of the local court of requests that he shared the fate of Joseph Priestley in the infamous Birmingham riots of 1791.[136]

As the courts multiplied, the suspicion that they were being used in an oppressive manner grew. In 1780 the report of a Commons committee on the Halifax court, with a large jurisdiction in the industrial West Riding, contained damning evidence. Though the small debt courts had been designed to minimize the use of imprisonment for debt, the committee found that it had been employed in Yorkshire in the most trivial cases. A subterranean room known as 'The Breaking School', in which the most squalid and insanitary conditions obtained, was used to terrorize recalcitrant debtors. There was no fund for the support of the gaol or the relief of sickness in it; commissioners had no power to reduce the fees payable to the court's officers, nor were they permitted to charge plaintiffs a portion of the costs. Above all the qualifications of the commissioners were 'much too low'; they could not be trusted to dispense even-handed justice.[137] The Commons was sufficiently concerned to promote a bill regulating the courts and limiting the use of punishment.

Confronted with this peril the terms in which the courts defended their record are significant. On the borders of Kent and Surrey it was observed of the victims that

the Terror of a Gaol being held out to them, they most commonly submit to the Direction of the Court to pay their Debts by Instalments, which are always proportioned by the Court to the Debtor's Circumstances and weekly Earnings, which Indulgence enables the Sober and Industrious Poor to avoid an Execution, and those who are willing, and by their Industry endeavour to maintain their Families, and pay their Debts, are neither subject to Imprisonment, or any other Hardship under the Process of the said Courts; and that the Poorer Sort of People cannot always support themselves and Families without the Assistance of a small weekly Credit, particularly in Case of Sickness or Want of Employment.[138]

---

[134] *Commons Journals*, xxvi. 368–9.
[135] Ibid. 439.
[136] C. H. Beale, *Reminiscences of a Gentlewoman of the Last Century: Letters of Catherine Hutton* (Birmingham, 1891), p. 89.
[137] *Commons Journals*, xxxvii. 746–7.
[138] Ibid. 759.

Similar arguments came from Exeter.[139] It was repeatedly urged that credit secured by the threat of weekly payments, under pain of imprisonment 'in terrorem', was essential for the local labouring community. In the short run these arguments won. The bill of 1780 for the general reform of courts of requests was lost. But in 1785 its main provisions were carried in a new bill which applied to London, and subsequently extended to the provinces.[140]

It plainly suited small tradesmen to give credit to their poorer neighbours, when by means of a court order they could obtain a prior call on their weekly income. Sometimes the vested interests at stake were clearly visible. Confining the court of requests, it was alleged in Norwich, 'will increase the Poor Rates of the said City (already very burthensome) to a Degree which the middling Ranks of Tradesmen will be totally unable to support'.[141] There was also an obvious connection between the interests of manufacturing employers and the practice of the courts. The Halifax Act, which proved so controversial, had been passed in 1777 and took its place alongside the Worsted Act of the same year. That was essentially designed to reduce the independence of the outworkers with whom the worsted employers dealt, regulating the quality of their product and limiting the time for which they might retain their materials. The court of requests was part of the process by which working practices might be controlled and violations punished. Stockport's initially unsuccessful attempt to obtain a similar tribunal in 1785 was based on the same premiss, that great numbers of people employed in the silk and cotton industries refused to pay their debts.[142] It is no coincidence that many of the early courts of conscience originated in the unincorporated manufacturing districts of the north, the Midlands, and the south-west. Industrial employers had no desire for the inhibiting framework of guild and corporation. They did, however, see the advantage of statutory regulations to control their workforce.

At Halifax the qualification of the judges in the small debts court had been fixed at £20 of real property, or £500 of personalty. It was the contention of those who sought change in 1780 that these stipulations were insufficient. The acting commissioners were 'frequently interested Persons, such as small shop-keepers and retail Dealers'.[143] On behalf of the court it was countered that in fact they were 'Gentlemen, Clergy, and first-rate Persons within the said Parishes and Places'.[144] The reformers sought a

---

[139] Ibid. 762–3.
[140] 25 Geo. III, c. 45; 26 Geo. III, c. 38.
[141] *Commons Journals*, xxxvii. 767.
[142] G. Unwin, *Samuel Oldknow and the Arkwrights* (Manchester, 1924), pp. 37–8.
[143] York Minster Library, Hailstone MSS, KK 6: 'A Summary Account of the Present Application to Parliament'.
[144] *Commons Journals*, xxxvii. 763.

minimum of £60 in land or £1,500 in personalty. Although the Commons supported this proposal, it was thrown out by the Lords. A further suggestion, indicating the extent of concern about the oligarchical nature of the courts, was that all real estate owners of £60 or more should be able to act as small debt commissioners even if they had not been specifically nominated or elected according to the usual machinery. This was evidently too radical a solution. Even in the friendlier atmosphere of the Commons, it was defeated.[145] The level of qualification was crucial in such debates. Almost all improvement legislation was designed to fit a model of improvement which commended itself to genteel or pseudo-genteel elements. The frontier of gentility was itself a subject of endless dispute and uncertainty. What is clear is that it ran through the centre of middle-class life, not so much dividing poor from rich, and lower class from upper, but rather separating small tradesmen and householders from more opulent business and professional men.

Identifying and policing this frontier was a task of great difficulty. In many instances it was believed by the richer classes that it should have been fixed less generously. But the downward pressure proved difficult to resist. When the act of 1786 did finally set a general qualification for courts of conscience, £20 from land or £500 of personal estate was specified. This was just the level at which critics suspected a marked degree of self-serving. It is difficult not to sympathize with their view. In the diary of Matthew Flinders of Donnington in Lincolnshire there is ample evidence to support it. Flinders was a country surgeon of humble origins but modest professional success. He was a subscriber towards the bill establishing the Kirton court of requests in 1777 and proved an assiduous commissioner. The Kirton Act did not specify a qualification at all but it is doubtful whether Flinders would have passed the test established for such courts generally in 1786. There is no doubt, however, of his motives. 'I attended the first court held at the School Chamber, being one of the commissioners; this is an excellent act for our Hundred, I do not in the least regret the money I subscribed towards obtaining the act, as it will bring the never pay villains to a little sense of honesty. It has already brought me I believe more than one bill.'[146]

Flinders did not long enjoy this deterrent for use against his debtors. The Kirton Act was repealed in 1778 not as a result of its commissioners' activities, but because the Earl of Exeter claimed that it had invaded his

---

[145] Ibid. 744.

[146] Lincolnshire Archives Office, diary of Matthew Flinders, surgeon, 1775–1802, 27 June 1777. The diary gives Flinders's estimate of his personal estate for insurance purposes in 1785 at £680. Some real estate, investments, and cash would have raised this somewhat. But in 1777 he was still a struggling country surgeon on the margin of respectability; at that point his accounts suggest a total below £500.

manorial jurisdiction.[147] But Flinders's attitude was doubtless all too typical. It was also understandable. As a French visitor observed, 'England is perhaps a country where the public good is more talk'd of than anywhere else, where in fact private interest is the most pursued.'[148] Men like Flinders did not find it easy to distinguish the two. In Flinders's case, when he did discern the public good, he was given to naïve self-congratulation on his own selflessness. The local Association for Prosecuting Felons he loyally supported; 'being a Member of no great Utility to me but it is worthy of encouragement as a Public Benefit'.[149] The public interest was either one's own as a property-owner, or at the very least it was the interest of other property-owners. It had little to do with concern for the unpropertied.

The argument was not restricted to debt jurisdiction. It was a common complaint against poor law commissioners, for instance, that they represented a class unfit to manage the affairs of the poor, particularly to the extent that they were drawn from ordinary freeholders. 'Surely no body of people would be more unfit. Every acting Magistrate must have often seen how anxious they are to save their own pockets, and, in general, how little compassion they are blessed with.'[150] Even when the social credentials of workhouse guardians were not in question, doubts about their compassion still remained. The Shrewsbury House of Industry, founded in 1784, was considered an outstanding success, 'that noble Institution! which stands forth as a Pattern, worthy the Imitation of every Parish throughout the Kingdom'.[151] But its directors behaved much as might be expected of opulent businessmen whose concern for the labouring poor was not always to the fore. In theory it was their duty to supervise the distribution of relief. But a little experience taught them the disagreeable nature of face-to-face contact with their charges, 'it being found to the hindr'ance of the necessary Business, as well as being very Tedious and Tiresome to the Directors and Officer to admit the Out Poor personally into this House to make their Complaints to the Directors, on Board days'. Subsequently they preferred to work through the overseers of the poor. Humane management of the labour force in the workhouse, or 'factory' as they were calling it by 1788, was meant to be one of their prime objectives. But within four years of the foundation they were bending their own rules and extending the working day for inmates from twelve hours to fourteen.[152] Whether they made better masters than parish contractors was not some-

---

[147] See above, pp. 43–4.
[148] Abbé le Blanc, *Letters on the English and French Nations*, (2 vols., London, 1747), ii. 297–8.
[149] Diary of Matthew Flinders, 1785.
[150] *Remarks upon an Intended Bill for the Relief of the Poor, Now under the Consideration of Parliament* (London, 1777), p. 4.
[151] Shropshire RO, 3909/6/2: printed Salop Infirmary Report, 1787.
[152] Shropshire RO, 83/1: incorporation minute-book.

thing on which the poor themselves were consulted.

Even improvement legislation gave rise to worries of this kind, if only because its purpose was in part fiscal: it authorized the borrowing of money with which capital projects could be funded, and the levying of rates with which recurrent costs, including interest charges, could be financed. In both respects it could be presented as class legislation, though in somewhat different terms from the accusations made against the courts of requests. Taxation was always controversial, especially as it bore on the ordinary householder. At Ipswich in 1792 there was a lively debate about the respective merits of a coal duty and a paving rate. The preference was for a combination of the two, but both could be considered unfair to the poorer members of the community.[153] Richmond's bill for poor relief and street improvement in 1765 was opposed on the grounds that those promoting it were primarily noblemen and gentlemen: 'the Inhabitants of the said Town chiefly consist of Persons who lett Lodgings, deal in Provisions, Household Necessaries, and other Matters, which produce only a bare Maintenance for themselves and Families; and that they are in general already burthened with as many Taxes as they well can bear.'[154] Similar objections were expressed to Shrewsbury's paving project of 1755, as a conspiracy of the rich.[155] It was in towns where the electoral arrangements gave a genuine say to relatively lowly members of municipal society that improvement schemes on the rates were most successfully resisted. Norwich did not get a paving act until 1806, but when it did the results were tumultuous. The city's MPs, earlier charged by their opponents with 'Jacobinism', found themselves arraigned for their support for the bill at the general election of 1806. One of them, the well-known Dissenter William Smith, lost his seat, victim, as he said, 'of an abominable clamour raised about a paving bill'.[156] The other, Robert Fellowes, desperately sought to establish his impartiality on the bill, but saw his poll severely reduced.[157] At issue was the rating burden on poorer residents of the city. They were well represented among the numerous freemen who constituted the parliamentary and municipal electorate of Norwich. Petitions against street improvement schemes often came from the poorer elements or on their behalf. At Nottingham in 1761 it was said that the result would be 'a heavy Burden upon the Town in general, and upon Manufacturers in particular'.[158] At Derby in 1792 the knife was given an extra twist when it was proposed to

[153] *Ipswich Journal*, 16 Mar., 7, 14 July 1792.
[154] *Commons Journals*, xxx. 521.
[155] Shropshire RO, 177/1b: broadsheet 24 Dec. 1755.
[156] R. W. Davis, *Dissent in Politics, 1780–1830: The Political Life of William Smith, M.P.* (London, 1971), p. 127.
[157] *The Norwich Poll-Book* (Norwick, 1806), pp. xiii–xiv.
[158] *Commons Journals*, xxix. 152.

meet the cost of a paving scheme by enclosing the town's commons. In the resulting uproar the injustice wreaked by opulence was a predictable complaint.[159]

Borrowing was as important in the economics of improvement as taxation. Most projects required the raising of a substantial capital sum in the first instance. The process of legislation usually started with local subscriptions designed to defray the costs of applying to Parliament. These subscriptions were in the strictest sense speculations. If an act of Parliament was not forthcoming, for whatever reason, the money was lost: only the clerks and attorneys and other professional agents involved made a profit. But in the event of success, the preliminary subscription could be viewed as a down payment on a bigger and less risky loan, needed to finance the project itself. At Lewes in 1789 the promoters of a new market were at pains to emphasize that they were raising a loan, not making a donation.[160] In many instances the cost of the application was treated as a charge on the project itself, to be met by tolls, rates, or whatever other financial measures were arranged. The process was usually both speedy and profitable; it was also comfortable for those involved. Tewkesbury's experience in 1786 was altogether typical. Its act received the royal assent on 22 March, and the first meeting of the commission was duly held on 3 April. By 9 May a bill of £400.16s.2d. had been presented, and the attorney who had incurred it thanked 'for his very reasonable Charges and for his candid Behaviour in the whole Transaction of obtaining and passing the said Act'. £400 was immediately raised by loans from a maltster and a tanner, both commissioners under the act, with interest payable at 5 per cent and on the security of a paving rate. The attorney, also a commissioner, got his money, and the ratepayers of Tewkesbury were assessed for the first levy under the act. £400 exceeded by £100 the total burden of the poor rate for the previous year. Perhaps it is not surprising that Chancellors of the Exchequer believed, in the face of constant protests about the level of taxation, that ordinary householders could be squeezed harder.[161]

The expense of obtaining a bill was treated as a first call. It was followed by many others. The only significant class of local legislation which did not require large-scale borrowing was the small debt legislation. Almost everything else involved building, engineering, purchase of materials, procurement of services, and labour. The sums involved ranged from the hundreds of thousands required for major canal projects to the few hundreds needed for a lighting scheme or a small workhouse. This process resembled the working of the National Debt. For the investor it meant

---

[159] C. L. Hacker, 'William Strutt of Derby (1756–1830)', *Derbys. Arch. Jnl.* 80 (1960), 60.

[160] V. Smith, ed., *The Town Book of Lewes 1702–1837*, (Sussex Rec. Soc. 69, 1972–3), p. 79.

[161] Gloucestershire RO, TBR A 7/1.

lending on parliamentary security, and receiving regular interest from tolls or rates. Not surprisingly, it was most popular during peacetime when new borrowing on the National Debt ceased and it was necessary to find other forms of investment. For provincial investors it was especially valuable. Holders of government stock were overwhelmingly based in the metropolitan area. Fully four-fifths of the investing class as a whole, more than 90 per cent if foreigners are excluded, lived in London or the home counties.[162] Public projects elsewhere mopped up capital which its owners were either unwilling or unable to place where Londoners placed it. In political terms there were other resemblances. The National Debt was guarded by the elected representatives of a propertied electorate. Local debts similarly depended on a political process acceptable to those who ultimately paid the bill. The arrangements for choosing the men who managed statutory commissions, together with the property qualification guaranteeing their respectability, ensured that the men and women who lent money for public improvements either had a direct say in the way it was used, or at least that those who had such a say would have propertied interests similar to their own. In this respect there was little to distinguish statutory bodies and voluntary associations supported by subscription, though the ethical problems thereby created were more clearly exposed in the case of the latter. They were none the less readily resolved by a society which considered the interests of property and the welfare of the public at large indistinguishable. The early hospital promoters were aware of the argument that donors might be profiteering from alms but dismissed it with little sign of discomfort.[163]

Some improving enthusiasm plainly derived from the desire to find a safe but satisfying investment. Improvements were best supported when alternative channels of investment were wanting. It is unlikely to be coincidence that the workhouse acts of the 1760s and 1770s were most popular, so far as rural areas were concerned, in East Anglia, where a profitable agriculture existed side by side with a declining textile manufacture and a notable absence of potential for waterway improvement. Who would not rather lend money at interest to reduce the cost of poor relief than pay ever higher poor rates to support an unproductive system? Significantly, the one incorporation which did not take effect, that authorized for Hartesmere and Hoxne by an act of 1779, fell victim to high interest rates and depressed conditions at the height of the American War. Lenders simply could not be found. But at more propitious times houses

---

[162] P. G. M. Dickson, *The Financial Revolution in England: A Study of the Development of Public Finance, 1680–1750* (London, 1967), pp. 256–7; A. C. Carter, *Getting, Spending and Investing in Early Modern Times* (Assen, 1975), pp. 67, 137.

[163] Alured Clarke, *A Sermon Preached in the Cathedral Church of Winchester, before the Governors of the County Hospital* (2nd edn., London, 1737), p. x.

of industry proved an attractive investment. The East Anglian workhouses were grand affairs, serving large districts and capable of housing some hundreds of inmates. They were criticized for outdoing country mansions in splendour of design and richness of embellishment. Considerable sums were involved. £4,800 was raised to build the Nacton House of Industry, the least pretentious of its kind, £10,000 for Barkham, £12,500 for Bulcamp. Recurrent expenditure created a continuing opportunity. At Nacton, where the initial investment was made in 1758–9, further loans had to be raised in 1768, 1769, 1774, 1776, 1791, 1794, and 1805. As a result the outstanding debt still stood at £2,400 in 1811.[164]

Projects of this kind did not generally depend on one or two well-heeled subscribers. Manchester was unusual, in 1791, in raising its initial requirement of £4,000 for a new workhouse by means of two loans and four annuities.[165] More typical was the Leeds Waterworks Commission, which in the same year raised £12,200. £2,500 came from eleven men, all of them appointed commissioners by the act. But small investors also had a place. There were 104 mortgagees, many of them holding the minimum of a £100 share.[166] A financial stake in any concern was a stimulus to an active interest in its affairs. Around Leeds seven turnpike trusts were created between 1741 and 1758, each with between 150 and 200 trustees. The funds which sustained them were derived from merchants rather than landowners, and it was merchants who managed them.[167] They needed improvement as much as improvement needed them. Turnpikes, indeed, testified to the diversity of investment patterns. The Petworth trust raised £6,150 in 1764. Only eighteen lenders were involved, and £3,000 was provided by two peers, the Earl of Egremont and Lord Winterton.[168] But peers and peasants could cheerfully mix at least in this company. In 1791 the Swindon, Calne, and Cricklade turnpike in Wiltshire had a list of 59 investors, headed by the Earls of Peterborough, Clarendon, and Radnor. It also included several who described themselves as yeoman with shares descending to £25.[169] Across the county boundary in Somerset, most of the trusts operated on the assumption that subscriptions would come largely from small lenders in £50 or £100 units.[170] Investors were often

---

[164] Arthur Young, *Political Arithmetic: Part II* (London, 1779), pp. 65–76; H. Fearn, 'The Financing of the Poor-Law Incorporation for the Hundreds of Colneis and Carlford in the County of Suffolk, 1758–1820', *Suffolk Archaeology*, 27 (1955–7), 96–111.

[165] G. B. Hindle, *Provision for the Relief of the Poor in Manchester 1754–1831* (Chetham Soc. 22, 1975), p. 34.

[166] R. S. Pepperd, 'The Growth and Development of Leeds Waterworks Undertakings, 1694–1852' (Leeds Univ. M.Phil. thesis, 1973), p. 258.

[167] Wilson, *Gentlemen Merchants*, pp. 145–9.

[168] Lord Leconfield, 'The Minute Book of the Petworth Turnpike Trustees, 1757–1801', *Sussex Arch. Colls.* 95 (1957), 105–15.

[169] Wiltshire RO, 1553/7.

[170] See n. 123 for sources.

tradesmen who treated the trusts as a form of bank; still more commonly they were retired business people or 'genteel poor' for whom the priority was a dependable pension. The immense demand for retirement annuities ensured that there would always be such investors in the market. It was in London, with its enormous concentration of business and professional people, that this source of capital was most extensively tapped. Yet even here it was not only locals who were involved. When the paving commissioners of the parish of St Bartholomew accepted four proposals in 1769, one of them came from as far afield as Totnes in Devon, and only one from within the parish itself.[171] The small saver was a crucial figure in the calculations of improvers and projectors, and thus in the emergence of a genuinely national money market.[172]

Allegations that improvement was undertaken to support the interests of creditors were common. When the Farnhill to Stony Stratford trust sought an extension of its powers in 1736, there was opposition. The opponents attributed the disastrous state of the turnpike's affairs to an act of 1707 which had made the principal creditors trustees. It was said that they had bought up a number of debts cheaply and then used their authority as trustees to award themselves handsome profits at the expense of the upkeep of the road. The public had gained only an obligation to pay tolls on a road which was no better than it had been when maintained by the traditional device of statute labour. For their part, the trustees countered with a claim that heavy wagons were responsible for the deterioration of their road, but the weight of the evidence was against them.[173] Even individual lenders could do much to influence or obstruct improvement. The projectors of a turnpike from Stratford-upon-Avon into Gloucestershire in 1756 had to overcome obstruction from a local gentlemen 'who has a little money on a neighb'ring Gate'.[174] When statutory authority expired creditors were in a position to determine the next step: a renewal of the statute, complete suspension of the trust, or an application for modified powers. In the case of the insolvent Dunstable trust in 1790 it was a joint meeting of creditors and trustees which decided on the last.[175]

Concern about a potential conflict of interest in this respect was rarely expressed as a matter of principle, however irritating individual cases might prove. The likelihood that many forms of public improvement would be managed by men who had invested in them was not only thought defensible

---

[171] Guildhall Library, MS 3995/1: paving commission minutes, 10 May 1769.

[172] B. J. Buchanan, 'The Evolution of the English Turnpike Trusts: Lessons from a Case Study', *Econ. Hist. Rev.*, 2nd ser. 39 (1986), 232 ff.

[173] Buckinghamshire RO, Hartwell MSS, petitions. The dispute was resolved; see *Commons Journals*, xxii. 765, 781–2.

[174] L. Fox, ed., *The Correspondence of the Reverend Joseph Greene* (London, 1965), p. 76.

[175] *Whitehall Evening-Post*, 9 Sept. 1790.

but desirable. Borrowers had a stake in efficient management which often persuaded them to help manage. Moreover, they might well find themselves having to increase their stake rather than risk losing it. Trustees frequently had to make short-term loans to tide their turnpike or workhouse over a cash crisis. So did their official servants, the clerks and attorneys who provided professional administration. Even so, very few projects could rely exclusively on their own managers. Virtually all improvement depended on attracting external funds. It thereby became an exacting exercise in fiscal salesmanship. The scope for fine tuning was restricted. Interest rates were subject to maxima set by the statutes which established such trusts. Trustees had some discretion, especially where the negotiation of annuities was concerned. Officers made by potential life annuitants had to be scrutinized to ensure that they were not younger than they claimed and to achieve an interest rate which reflected prevailing conditions without overburdening the trust. But trustees could not be expected to match every movement of the London market in government securities. During the stability associated with peacetime conditions an assured $4\frac{1}{2}$ per cent, or 8 per cent for elderly annuitants, looked enticing to lenders who liked the idea of putting their money with men they trusted and in causes which were locally supported. But in wartime, with interest rates above 5 per cent, rising to 12 per cent or even 14 per cent on life annuities, the art of raising money was more difficult. It was customary to reassure creditors of their prior claims on assets, and also to promise preferential treatment for loyal savers in the event of interest rate changes. The American War and still more the Revolutionary War were testing in this respect, as the Shropshire Poor Law corporations discovered. Those at Atcham and Whitchurch were established at a time of commercial buoyancy and confidence in 1792. But by the time they were spending and borrowing on any scale war had broken out and disastrously affected the financial prospects. They survived partly by desperate expedients, including, at Atcham, personal appeals to the landowners of the area, partly by relying far more on parish rates than had originally been intended.[176] Such problems beset urban as well as rural areas. The London parish of St Botolph without Bishopsgate obtained a workhouse act in 1795. This was a year of dearth and debt. The commissioners spent an anxious month or so raising money to pay their parliamentary expenses and purchase land on which to build a new poorhouse. They then lapsed into helpless inactivity. Not until 1802 did it become feasible to put the act of 1795 into operation.[177] In these instances at least the dream of a successful social policy financed by the

---

[176] Shropshire RO, 13/5: Atcham incorporation, letter of chairman, H. Jones, 14 July 1794.
[177] Guildhall Library, MS 21131: workhouse trustees minute-book.

enlightened self-interest of the bourgeoisie proved elusive. But faith in public borrowing was not readily dented.

It is unsurprising that men with a professional interest in finance got involved in new ventures. The larger London charities generally employed a number of companies. These accounts were good for business, and no doubt helped stimulate a suitable display of humanity. In the affairs of the London Hospital, the banking families of Minors and Boldero, allied by marriage and business, figured prominently among subscribers and life governors.[178] Provincial banking was less specialized. Even so there is a striking association of names involved in embryo banks and those concerned in the management of improvement schemes. At Birmingham, by a happy coincidence, the famous bank of Lloyd and Taylor was founded in the same year as the hospital; the partners, one of whom coined the memorable slogan 'we do nothing for nothing for nobody', were among the first supporters. Henry Hoare's benefaction to the Salisbury Infirmary, at £200, was on a scale which made it absurd to suppose that his object was to secure custom, though the Governors hastened to pay him the compliment of banking with his London house.[179] No doubt the liberality of smaller men was more in line with the scale of their businesses. Apart from other considerations, the requirements of sound administration made it seem desirable that men of substantial fortune should join in the running of philanthropic and public concerns. The logic applied more particularly to bankers. When John Kidgell, the Treasurer of the Godstone division of the Surrey and Sussex turnpike, decamped with £2,000 in 1764 much of the resulting controversy arose from the revelation that he was both a clergyman and a friend of the Earl of Sandwich. But the problem was familiar. The solution seemed obvious. The Crown required security of some of its own employees, including the receivers of the land tax. Many charities imitated its practice by insisting on sureties from their treasurers. Eventually Parliament saw the wisdom of making a similar stipulation for the employees of statutory bodies. In 1771 the Commons announced a standing order requiring security of the treasurers of all canal or street schemes which made provision for levying tolls or duties on the public.[180] One advantage of a surety was that it avoided the necessity for legal processes which might be embarrassing even when they were successful. Kidgell's effects were sold by the turnpike commissioners to pay off part of what he had owed, but critics pointed out that this put the claims of the

---

[178] The lists of governors and subscribers were printed with the annual sermons for the benefit of the hospital; see Bodleian Library, Gough London 53, and J. J. Muskett, *Suffolk Manorial Families* (Exeter, 1900), i. 187–8.

[179] S. Lloyd, *The Lloyds of Birmingham with Some Account of the Founding of Lloyds Bank* (3rd edn., Birmingham, 1909), p. 56; Wiltshire RO, J 8/100/1: Salisbury Infirmary minutes, 24 Sept. 1766.

[180] *Commons Journals*, xxxiii. 95.

public before those of private creditors, a debatable principle.[181] The
practice of requiring securities also ensured that men with large financial
interests were well placed to exploit the opportunities offered.

DANGEROUS AND EXPENSIVE JOBS

Lower taxation, good housekeeping, and attractive interest rates were not
the only rewards of statutory improvement. The professional and business
middle class often had much to gain. One of the fears expressed by
opponents of statutory bodies was that they would become 'dangerous and
expensive jobs'.[182] Their defenders, on the contrary, argued that they would
be less prone to interested management than the humbler parochial bodies
traditionally entrusted with social welfare. Some critics, like Robert Saunders in his account of what went on at Lewisham, thought it common 'to
see the greatest rivals united at a vestry to vote away the poors money in
jobs'.[183] Poorhouses made heavy demands on the distributive trades. In
this respect the new district establishments were thought to be much more
efficient and economical than their parochial predecessors. As Arthur
Young contemptuously noted, parish officers often bought their provisions
'from the most paltry of all shops' in the locality. Now they could place
large orders in the county town. Similarly, where before they had purchased
fuel by the faggot in a desultory way, now they could advertise for
entire shiploads of coal at highly competitive rates.[184] The advertisements
published in the *Ipswich Journal* bear Young out. For example, on behalf
of the Shipmeadow house of industry in March 1773, nine bulk contracts
for groceries alone were offered for tender: malt, hops, peas, oatmeal,
cheese, butter, salt, soap, and candles.[185] These arguments on behalf
of statutory improvement closely matched what was said of voluntary
associations. Hospitals were awarded high marks for their bulk buying and
rigorous cost-accounting. The scale of business could be considerable and
rose rapidly. Butcher's meat at Gloucester Infirmary cost £105 in 1764,
£237 in 1780. Bread and flour purchases rose in the same period from
£142 to £213.[186] Contracts of this order were attractive. The sufferer, of
course, was the small trader. Whether his suffering saved the public money
in the long run is another matter. It was all too easy for monopolistic
interests and dishonest management to defeat the intentions of subscribers.
In 1747 it was cited as a maxim that '*Parish Business, County business,* and

---

181 *Gentleman's Magazine* (1764), 247, 393.
182 James Nasmith, *The Duties of Overseers of the Poor* (Wisbech, 1799), p. 64.
183 *The Farmer's Tour through the East of England,* ii. 185–6.
184 *Ipswich Journal,* 20 Mar. 1773.
185 *Further Considerations on the Laws Relating to the Poor,* p. 8.
186 *The State of the Glocester Infirmary* (Gloucester, 1764 and 1780).

Kingdom business, is always done at a very dear rate'.[187] By the late eighteenth century there were many other forms of public business of which the same could be said.

One of the attributes of tradesmen was said to be their superior knowledge of everyday life, the prices of necessities and so on, knowledge, in the nature of things, which a gentleman might not have. In an age which prided itself on prizing practical knowledge, this expertise at least qualified businessmen to join their social superiors in public administration.[188] But there were obvious dangers if the motives of such men were mixed. In the Suffolk workhouses whose economy so impressed Arthur Young it was common for public trustees to sell private services to their trusts. At Capdock in 1766 the contractor for both coal and malt was Thomas Alderton, an active director of the workhouse.[189] Eventually attempts were made to stop such practices. The act establishing a house of industry at Stowmarket in 1778 expressly forbade contractors to serve as directors or guardians.[190] Rooting out perks was a continuing preoccupation. Even the incorruptible directors of the Shrewsbury incorporation found it necessary to pass an order prohibiting their number from using the workhouse boat except on official business.[191]

Charities also exhibited some of the more hypocritical aspects of private trading in public business. When Leicester's infirmary was being established in 1766 the trustees found themselves entangled in awkward negotiations. Their first duty was to purchase land on which to place the hospital. One proposal came from Richard Walker, a prominent figure in Leicester, a tradesman-gentleman who liked to be identified as an 'esquire', a common councilman, and himself a governor of the infirmary. He suggested selling a piece of his own property for 500 guineas: 'if accepted, then he offered to give fifty guineas towards building the Infirmary, if that is not agreeable he offers to Subscribe annually three Guineas'. When the trustees authorized a door to door collection for funds, Walker was the only one of them who presented himself for doorstep duty on the day fixed. He was not, however, the only trustee to employ his privileged position in this way, nor the only one to make benevolent gestures of a strictly conditional kind. One of his colleagues, A. J. Keck, offered to lease a building of his own to the hospital, and to subscribe £20 per annum towards the rental. Other trustees developed in due course a similarly philanthropic interest in supplying provisions to the sick. The infirmary's

[187] *Westminster Journal*, 10 Jan. 1747.
[188] *A Candid Address to the Inhabitants of the United Parishes of Saint Andrew Holborn above the Bar, and Saint George the Martyr, 3 April 1767.*
[189] Suffolk RO (Ipswich), ADA 7/AB 1/1: Samford quarterly minute-book, 1766.
[190] Ibid., ADA 8/AB 1/2.
[191] Shropshire RO, 83/1: incorporation minutes, 7 Nov. 1796.

official purveyors of bread, groceries, beef, malt, and candles were all
governors and all regularly attended meetings. Drawing a line between
business and benevolence was and remains acutely difficult. How, for
instance, should the printer of the *Leicester Journal* be regarded? John
Gregory was a conscientious governor and loyal friend of the hospital.
Nothing was more damaging to a public charity than public criticism, and
Gregory earned the commendation of the governors in 1771 when he
refused to print a hostile letter in his newspaper and also promised for the
future to accept no matter relating to the hospital without the signed
approval of the secretary. He also had the contract for providing the
infirmary's printing and publishing needs. His motives were known only
to himself.[192]

Diverse kinds of public business created by Parliament could be rewarding. Enclosure acts generated professional surveying, much of it carried
out by commissioners named in the statutes in question. These commissioners were not public trustees in the same sense as improvement or
turnpike commissioners. They were usually appointed on the recommendation of the principal landowners affected. None the less their
decisions had obvious consequences for the rural community, and their
calibre was a matter of continuing concern. Some were accused of being
'trading Commissioners' in the same way that Middlesex magistrates
were 'trading justices'.[193] Their allowances gave rise to irritation. Even an
enthusiast for enclosure such as Young protested at the 'most precious
piece of delegated despotism', by which commissioners determined their
own reward and expenses.[194] The subject aroused the interest of Parliament
from time to time.[195]

The pickings from public works more narrowly defined were substantial.
One of the reasons for worries about the social standing of turnpike trustees
was the suspicion that men with an interest in road-building would obtain
control of the turnpikes. When the turnpike movement accelerated in the
1720s and 1730s, there were some spectacular examples of maladministration, especially around London where much highway improvement
was concentrated. No less an authority than Alexander Pope was moved
to remark that 'Many of the highways throughout England were hardly
passable, and most of those which were repaired by Turnpikes were made
jobs of for private lucre, and infamously executed, even to the entrances
of London itself'.[196] His friend Bolingbroke linked the frauds uncovered
at Hyde Park Corner with the political scandals associated with monopoly

[192] Leicestershire RO, 13 D 54/1.
[193] *An Answer to the Rev. E. Walls* (Horncastle, *c.* 1795), p. 22.
[194] *A Six Months Tour through the North of England* (2nd edn., 4 vols., London, 1771), i. 226.
[195] See, for example, *Commons Journals*, xxviii. 1069.
[196] M. R. Brownell, *Alexander Pope and the Arts of Georgian England* (Oxford, 1978), p. 302.

companies in the age of Walpole, as evidence of a corrupt mentality which pervaded a whole society.[197] But the problem of corruption remained long after Walpole's fall. A Commons committee on turnpike management in 1764 found ample evidence of mismanagement by trustees interested in works on the highways which they administered. In St Marylebone the 'acting Trustees were most of them Tradesmen and Artificers' with a stake of their own or through their relations in the works.[198] Not only turnpikes gave rise to such difficulties. When the London Building Act was passed in 1774, and the Court of Aldermen was required to appoint surveyors, it weeded out the names of tradesmen, 'not chusing that it should be in the power of any set of men, through a professional pique, to oppress others, or by too strict an adherence to self-interest screen themselves'.[199] Nor was it only tradesmen who were thought liable to a conflict of interest. Attorneys, the most reviled of professions, were active in the business of improvement as they were in every other kind of business. In corporations they were frequently in a crucial position to ease the process by which chartered bodies accepted the partnership of the wider propertied community.[200] In rural areas it was even suggested that they should not be permitted to act as turnpike trustees. Two Yorkshire trusts under consideration in 1755 were subjected to close scrutiny as a result. In each attorneys were excluded, after Commons divisions which attracted the relatively large numbers of 113 and 88 respectively.[201]

Professional men less open to criticism than attorneys had almost as much to gain. Where the medical profession was concerned, private philanthropy and public improvement were equally profitable. Hospitals were often promoted by medical practitioners. There was nothing surprising in this. Their motives were naturally as mixed as those of other men of learning or skill who simultaneously sought their own advantage and the public's improvement. The bookseller who received a salary and room rent when he pioneered a scholarly library at York, and the inventor who was paid secretary and housekeeper to the Bath agricultural society which he instituted, were in much the same position as the Liverpool physician who inspired the foundation of the Liverpool Infirmary, made a substantial donation to its funds, held the ground on which it was eventually built, and then secured election as its first physician.[202] But the philanthropic

---

[197] *The Works of Lord Bolingbroke* (4 vols., London, 1844), ii. 28.

[198] *Commons Journals*, xxix. 1005.

[199] *London Magazine* (1774), 353.

[200] S. D'Cruze, 'The Eighteenth-Century Attorney as Political Broker: The Case of Francis Smythies', *Trans. Essex Arch. Soc.* 19 (1988), 223 ff.

[201] *Commons Journals*, xxvii. 235, 245.

[202] *An Account of the Rise and Progress of the Subscription Library at Kingston-upon-Hull* (Hull, 1810); T. F. Plowman, *Edmund Rack: The Society He Founded and the Company He Kept* (Bath, 1914); G. McLoughlin, *A Short History of the First Liverpool Infirmary 1749–1824* (London, 1978), pp. 13–14.

purpose of hospitals put doctors in a potentially delicate position. In most cases physicians and surgeons were expected to give their services free, where patients did not pay a fee. They were praised in lavish terms for 'voluntarily attending these Houses of Mercy, and, by a virtuous Application of their natural and acquired Powers, freeing their afflicted Brethren from Misery or the Grave'.[203] But the range of medical experience offered by a hospital, and the custom which allowed them to accept pupils for training in such establishments, made election to a hospital post a coveted honour. In the 1780s the going rate for acceptance by a surgeon was twenty-four guineas.[204] Half a dozen such pupils represented a considerable income. Apothecaries benefited similarly, especially when the pharmaceutical materials which they provided were their own.

Workhouses of any size offered interesting possibilities. With a view to the dangers of a local monopoly of medical services, Birmingham's infirmary made a rule that no surgeon of the workhouse might serve as surgeon of the hospital.[205] In cases of this kind there was an awareness that professional competence and private interest could easily become confused. But it was difficult to criticize when the result was presumed to be an overriding public good, as it was, by and large, in the case of medical charities. No doubt it was partly for this reason that more searching scrutiny was directed to the turnpikes, or to other improvements in which the jobbery of specialized professions could be detected. In fen drainage, for example, the novel breed of 'Men stiled Engineers' came to be seen as a force in their own right, competing with those who owned the land and truly the 'vultures of Society that have infested this part of the Country'.[206]

Legal and administrative officers were naturally required to service the new institutions. Nominating officials and fixing their salaries was one of the first duties of a new commission, with due allowance for the scale of operations. In 1766 the London paving commissioners appointed a chief clerk at £100, a first assistant clerk at £60, a junior clerk at £50, a surveyor at £200, and three inspectors at £60. At the opposite extreme, Cheltenham's paving commissioners in 1786 paid their treasurer £6.6s. and their clerk, who was expected to double up as collector of rates, £8.8s.[207] For many of these offices a lawyer's training was desirable and for some essential. The clerk to a court of requests obviously required legal expertise, even though the courts operated on principles of equity. The profits to be derived

[203] George Talbot, *A Sermon Preached in the Cathedral of Glocester at the Opening of the Infirmary, on Thursday, August 14, 1755* (Gloucester, [1755]), p. 19.
[204] Shropshire RO, 587/59: G. Whitfield to R. Whitfield, 30 Oct. 1784.
[205] *The Statutes and Rules for the Government of the General Hospital, Near Birmingham* (Birmingham, 1779), p. 16.
[206] *Observations on the Means of Better Draining the Middle and South Levels of the Fens* (London, 1777), pp. v, 29.
[207] *London Magazine* (1766), 268; Gloucestershire RO, CBR Box A: 26 June 1786.

from the fees payable in the courts could be considerable and offered opportunities for racketeering clerks. Part of the scandal uncovered at Halifax in 1780 was said to consist in the grasping nature of a clerk who sought to maximize his fees by treating the judges to free dinners. Like almost every other argument this strengthened demands for a higher qualification for judges so that they would not be tempted by the bribes at the command of a mere attorney. It also prompted the critics of the Halifax Act of 1777 to suggest paying the clerk a fixed salary of £220 and making him accountable for his fees. If nothing else this gives an idea of the profit which the clerk must have been making.[208]

Turnpike trusts and improvement commissions provided a wealth of work for lawyers. Wherever public administration expanded, opportunities would be available for men with knowledge of the law and a taste for committee work. In this vast and growing industry a recurrent difficulty was to determine what constituted impropriety in a professional sense. At Gloucester in 1782, for example, concern was expressed at the state of the infirmary account. It transpired that the treasurer had sold a substantial holding of government annuities in order to pay what was due to him for his office. But in 1782, at the end of the American War, stock prices were at an unprecedently low level and the result of the sale was a massive loss to the hospital. Within a few weeks of the sale better war news and the prospect of peace saw values rocketing. The governors took the view that the treasurer should not have sold without the consent of their committee, but the point was a moot one and raised in acute form the uncertainties which attended official duties in the new institutions.[209]

It was a common gibe that law and medicine profited by corrupt times. But so did the clergy. Some pressure was exerted to ensure that they were given their share of the rewards of public spirit. When the London Hospital was inaugurated, the Reverend Matthew Audley was asked to read prayers but received nothing more than a surplice for his pains. The Bishop of Oxford demanded regular Sunday services, and after initial opposition from the governors, eventually forced them to appoint Audley their chaplain at a salary of £100 per annum. He gave up his living to carry out his hospital duties and held the office until his death.[210] Entire family economies could be based on the opportunities presented by charities. When the same hospital was electing a matron in 1797, the offer by one of the candidates, Mrs Buckham, to the effect that her husband would resign his post as secretary at £50 per annum and 'retain only the office of Chaplain, with Residence' casts an intriguing light on the petty patronage possibilities of

[208] York Minster Library, Hailstone MSS, KK 6: 'A Summary Account of the Present Application to Parliament'.
[209] Gloucestershire RO, HO 19/5/1.
[210] E. W. Morris, *A History of the London Hospital* (London, 1910), pp. 62–3.

such institutions.[211] Charles Johnstone's satirical account of a great charity in *Chrysal* painted a depressing picture of greed and extortion; the treasurer, steward, secretary, apothecary, cook, and attorney were all on the make at the expense of the patients, and even the governors were too busy feasting to notice; only the chaplain was not 'in the secret'.[212] *Chrysal* belonged to the early years of George III's reign. It is doubtful if its author would have made an honourable exception for the chaplain twenty years later. By then the infamous deeds of William Dodd, Chaplain of the Magdalen, and Francis Kelly Maxwell, Chaplain of the Lambeth Asylum for Orphan Girls, had taken their place in the annals of clerical crime. But even without such roguery there were questions of principle. The stipend for a chaplain in the Suffolk workhouses in the 1760s was £35, £5 less than for a surgeon.[213] Spiritual services of this kind were difficult to value and had implications beyond the immediate concerns of the employer. In this instance the ratepayer was financing a form of clerical job creation for the relief of, or at the expense of the ordinary parish priest who would otherwise be expected to accept pastoral responsibility for the poor. Even without the involvement of taxpayers objections could be put. The High Churchman John Moir argued that the foundation of fashionable chaplaincies at London charities impaired the communal spirit of metropolitan parishes, and reduced the authority of the parochial clergy.[214]

Local office on the traditional model had been much less attractive. An old saw sometimes attributed to James I and rendered into verse by James Bramston reminded the middling freeholder and small squire of his good fortune in this respect: 'Too low in Life to be a *Justice* I, And for a Constable, thank God, too high.'[215] A great many public offices, as distinct from offices dispensed by the court and its political servants, brought neither profit nor honour. Shrievalties and magistracies in the countryside were unpaid and often involved their holders in expenditure and inconvenience. Parochial offices, the burden of the ordinary householder and ratepayer, were expensive at least in the sense that they could consume time otherwise reserved for more remunerative activities. Avoiding jobs of these kinds often stimulated as much ingenuity as did seeking jobs of the profitable sort. Just as the county gentry strove to escape a stint as sheriff, so their humbler borough brethren dreaded a turn in parish offices, especially in large urban parishes, where they might amount to a full-

---

[211] Bodleian Library, Gough London 53: printed circular, 26 Dec. 1797, addressed to Richard Gough.

[212] Ed. E. A. Baker (London, 1908), pp. 134–8.

[213] Suffolk RO (Ipswich), ADA/7/AB 1/1: Samford quarterly minute-book, 30 Sept. 1766; ADA 11/AB 1/1: Loes and Wilford quarterly minute-book, 27 June 1768.

[214] *The Parish Church* (London, 1802), pp. 42–4.

[215] *The Art of Politicks, in Imitation of Horace's Art of Poetry* (London, 1729), p. 30.

time employment. The Tyburn ticket, which rewarded public-spirited prosecution of malefactors with exemption from the burden of parochial office, is perhaps the best-known recognition of the onerous nature of local offices.[216] Fining those who avoided office or service on a municipal corporation was commonplace. It was widely used as a fiscal expedient: the notorious example of London, which systematically elected and fined Dissenters who would not accept the shrievalty, in order to fund the building of the Mansion House, drew public attention to a procedure which was less controversial when shorn of its sectarian implications. Election to office also had its utility as a form of political victimization. Corporations and select vestries were accused of using it to quell opposition and deter criticism.[217]

New offices matched a new model of what was thought publicly defensible. To posterity this is best known from the work of bureaucratic reformers, particularly as they influenced and eventually transformed the operations of central government. The principles of public administration announced in the reports of the Commissioners of Public Accounts between 1780 and 1787 seem in retrospect to look forward to the procedures which were made axiomatic by Victorian government. But the perspective of posterity can be misleading. Most of what the Public Accounts Commissioners recommended was novel only in the clarity and coherence with which it was formulated. Their ideas were already well established, jostling, no doubt, with older concepts of public service, but steadily gaining ground throughout the eighteenth century. Departments of government which expanded rapidly to meet the demands of war and finance, such as the Excise Board and the Navy Office, had done much to implement them.[218] More intriguingly, the new organs of improvement and social policy at local level had long since absorbed them. It is not impossible that they found their way into assumptions about the desirable criteria for public service from this source rather than from the adumbrations of theorists. It would be characteristic of the age for important ideas to work from the locality to the centre rather than the reverse. In 1800 J. S. Girdler argued precisely that the procedures increasingly adopted for the award of parish contracts, workhouse schemes, and lighting and cleaning services should be adopted by government itself, with a view to improving the integrity of public administration.[219]

---

[216] L. Radzinowicz, *A History of English Criminal Law and its Administration from 1750* (3 vols., London, 1948–56), ii. 155–61.

[217] Russell, *The Ancient Liberties and Privileges of the Cinque Ports*, p. 68; Guildhall Library, MS 4527A: 'The case of the Inhabitants of Bishopsgate'.

[218] J. Brewer, *The Sinews of Power: War, Money and the English State, 1688–1783* (London, 1989), p. 102.

[219] *Observations on the Pernicious Consequences of Forestalling, Regrating and Ingrossing, with a List of the Statutes, etc.* (London, 1800), p. 94.

The key arguments concerned appointments to office. It was a standard criticism of parish government that it bestowed authority on 'cabals of ignorant and interested men, who are flattered by the power of appointing Apothecaries, Vestry Clerks, and other parochial Servants'.[220] Men who devoted themselves to the campaign for local reform, such as Thomas Battye of Manchester, who made himself famous as 'an enemy of parochial peculation', were concerned as much with the quality of the personnel as with the defects of the procedures.[221] Both charitable and statutory projects were meant to offer a new deal in this respect. There was no sale of offices or reversions. Appointees were customarily elected by ballot of governors, subscribers, or statutory commissioners. Nor was there tenure for life, delegation of duties, and division of payment, or 'quartering' of pensioned office-holders on their successors. Payment was for the most part by fixed salary rather than by fees and perquisites. Above all, offices were filled at the instance of respectably propertied people. This was one respect in which local offices of the old kind constituted a major problem for those with genteel aspirations. When the employers were of inferior standing or little property, to accept nomination even for the sake of sound administration was humiliating. Remarking on the dearth of surveyors, John Scott observed that 'a Gentleman or reputable Tradesman will scarcely accept a Salary from the Parish'.[222] Accepting a salary from turnpike trustees, hospital subscribers, or improvement commissioners was another matter altogether, and one which might even follow a public advertisement. This was to a considerable extent a matter of status, of dignity. When Hereford Infirmary advertised the relatively humble position of secretary, with a salary of £40, bed, board, and washing, in 1780, it was none the less offering the kind of respectability which no parish vestry could match.[223]

A QUALIFICATION EASILY ATTAINED

Government and administration in the widest and most improved sense belonged with people of property. The property qualification and the elaborate structure which it underpinned were designed to ensure that this remained the case. But this was not the only means by which society was kept safe for the propertied. It was important to disqualify as well as qualify. The attitude which Sidney Smith satirized when he observed that 'it is always considered a piece of impertinence in England if a man of less than two or three thousand a year has any opinions at all on important

---

[220] *Morning Herald*, 7 Feb. 1787.
[221] Hindle, *Provision for the Relief of the Poor in Manchester*, ch. 5.
[222] *Digests of the General Highway and Turnpike Laws*, p. 107.
[223] *British Chronicle*, 27 Jan. 1780.

subjects' had widespread ramifications, even if few would have set the criterion as high as £2,000.[224]

The standard justification for a concept of politics which confined an active part to men with property was that it ensured their independence. A traditional assumption dictated that land was the only absolute guarantee of such independence. By the second half of the eighteenth century this assumption had been massively breached. Personalty and occupation were widely accepted as being of equal validity to real estate and freehold ownership. But there was a good deal of hypocrisy on this point, which suggested that the real concern was more with quantity than quality of property. When obligations and duties were in question the equal status of all Englishmen with a property in their persons and liberty was remembered, whereas when privileges and rights were in question, it was forgotten. Sometimes it was even suggested that the law should in a formal sense take account of property qualifications, granting legal privileges in the same way that Parliament granted political rights. These proposals did not invariably come from the unregenerately oligarchical. Among the reforms proposed on behalf of the Thatched House Society for the relief of poor debtors was one which would have exempted housekeepers of certain rank and all freeholders from personal attachment for debt.[225] The all-pervading sense that property created two completely separate nations even seemed to have enveloped the spiritual life of the Church. One of the most persistent worries of the godly was that communion itself had become a mystery accessible only to gentry, a private rite of property in which the poor did not expect to share.

What sometimes troubled the Church occasionally disturbed the complacency of the State, particularly when older concepts of civic responsibility were recalled. Tories traditionally stressed the injustice of burdening the poorer members of society with duties which rightly belonged with their betters. Sir William Wyndham put the case clearly when opposing Walpole's reimposition of the salt excise in 1732. 'A poor Man, who has no Property, ought not certainly to be charged for the Defence of Property; he has nothing but his Liberty to contend for.'[226] Tory paternalists never completely forgot this argument. It was remembered nearly a century later when Tory votes played a crucial part in the repeal of the salt excise.[227] But increasingly it gave way before a standard Whig argument, emphasizing

---

[224] *A Memoir of the Reverend Sydney Smith: By His Daughter, Lady Holland* (London, [1854]), p. 21.

[225] William Dodd, *An Account of the Rise, Progress, and Present State, of the Society for the Discharge and Relief of Persons Imprisoned for Small Debts* (London, 1774), p. lxi.

[226] *The History and Proceedings of the House of Commons from the Restoration to the Present Time* (11 vols., London, 1742), vii. 170.

[227] E. Hughes, *Studies in Administration and Finance 1558–1825* (Manchester, 1934), p. 495.

the essential equality of all citizens. Men who considered liberty and labour
as a form of property saw no reason for exempting their possessors from a
share in the burdens of the State. Sir John Sinclair, one of the first
systematic historians of public finance, claimed in 1783 that total exemption
for the poor 'in a free state, perhaps would be unjust: for there the poor
have rights to which they are entitled as well as the rich; and they ought
to pay for the privileges they enjoy'.[228]

It is difficult to pinpoint the moment at which this mentality gained the
advantage over older, more hierarchical notions, but the divergence of
reasoning is particularly apparent in the debates accompanying the reform
of the militia in 1757–8. The old militia, virtually defunct by the 1750s,
had made propertied families responsible for contributing men and material
in relation to their wealth. Robert Vyner, knight of the shire for Lincoln,
argued like Wyndham that the poor should be left to labour, and that the
militia should consist of gentlemen, freeholders, and at the lowest levels
farmers and master tradesmen.[229] But the new militia smacked of full-
blooded Whig individualism. Service was determined by a ballot of all
able-bodied males between the ages of 18 and 50, regardless of social
standing. To individualism was added equally characteristic Whig commercialism. Anyone balloted who chose not to serve was permitted to hire
a substitute by private negotiation or to buy exemption for £10. Elaborate
forms of local insurance and risk-sharing sprang up to protect all but the
poor from militia service.

The result seemed wildly unjust at a time when economic growth was
widening the gap between the rich and the poor. The violence of the anti-
militia riots suggested something of the resulting bitterness. In defence of
the rioters it was pointed out that 'what common men desire is men of
estates to hire men for the Militia, as they were formerly; being very fit
that they who have lands will hire men to maintain them'.[230] In effect the
State was using its power to do what a patriarchal landed class had
previously done at its own expense. For labouring men and men of business,
it was pointed out, 'Their Time is their Estate'.[231] Obligatory service was
a form of tax. One opponent in 1763 argued that the essential unfairness
was that property was not made the basis of the militia contribution. Choice
by age and ballot rather than wealth 'obliges the Labourer, not worth a
Shilling, to be upon a Level with his Lord, and those worth Thousands a-
year'.[232] After the next war in which the militia were deployed Thomas

---

[228] *The History of the Public Revenue of the British Empire* (3rd edn., London, 1803), ii. 369.
[229] R. C. Simmons and P. D. G. Thomas, eds., *Proceedings and Debates of the British Parliaments Respecting North America 1754–1783* (New York, 1982–), i. 31.
[230] *General Evening Post*, 7 Mar. 1761.
[231] *London Magazine* (1737), 487.
[232] *A Letter to the Right Hon. Charles Townshend, Secretary at War* (2nd edn., London, 1762), p. 21.

Pennant made a similar observation, pointing out on behalf of the oppressed classes of North Wales that a poor labourer who preferred his daily work to service in the militia had to find exactly the same sum by way of fine as 'the greatest squire in the principality'.[233]

Pennant, best known as a botanist and travel-writer, was also an ingenious critic of the ways in which the law effectively taxed the poor more heavily than the rich even when there was no avowed intention of doing so. Not many of the MPs who approved Pitt's proposal to exempt the new mail coaches from turnpike tolls can have thought they were approving a measure of class discrimination. Yet Pennant claimed that the consequences in his home county of Flint were serious. The toll-free mail coaches replaced a stage-coach service which had existed as long as the North Welsh turnpikes, and which had provided £40 per annum for the Flint trust. Without this revenue the trustees were unable to maintain their road and were compelled to call on neighbouring parishes to provide statute duty. In 1789 they laid fines totalling £1,200 on parishes consisting largely of impoverished labourers. 'Justice can never require that the poor should keep pace with the innovations made for the benefit of commerce or luxury'.[234] Taxes on the propertied were easily seen as taxes on their inferiors. The servant duty in effect taxed servants to the extent that it drew on income which would otherwise have gone towards paying them more or employing additional labour. In this sense, as was observed by the poet Thomas Penrose, 'Each *Footman* is a state-supporter'.[235]

Compelling the unpropertied to take their share of obligations as diverse as the militia and the servant tax did not entitle them to a say in the political process, even at its lower levels. Throughout the eighteenth century there was an ambivalence about the electoral mode of politics which went very deep. Certainly it had more behind it than mere dislike of the popular violence which, for instance, beset some parliamentary elections. One of the central assumptions of the propertied mind was that property protected its possessors against the dangers of corruption. For the propertied therefore, elections were defensible and practicable. But in practice even elections among the respectable had a way of turning into distressingly corrupt affairs. It was parochial elections, based on a franchise that guaranteed the ratepaying householder a say in his local government, which prompted a critic of parish affairs in Holborn to declare 'that the Arrow which sticks in our Side, as a Nation, is the Disorders and evil Practices of Elections'.[236] Municipalities in which popular election rather than co-option determined

[233] *Free Thoughts on the Militia Laws* (London, 1781), p. 7.

[234] *A Letter to a Member of Parliament, on Mail-Coaches* (London, 1792), pp. 2–5, 29.

[235] *Poems by the Rev. Thomas Penrose* (London, 1781), p. 61.

[236] *A Candid Address to the Inhabitants of the United Parishes of Saint Andrew Holborn above the Bar, and Saint George the Martyr*, p. 2.

membership of corporate bodies frequently gave rise to scandal, not least in the capital itself. The extraordinary litigation arising from the election of aldermen and common councilmen in the City of London was calculated to have cost £2,150 between 1711 and 1719, and led to an investigation by the House of Lords.[237] The City Elections Act of 1725, often viewed as mere oligarchy on the part of Walpolian Whigs, was supported on this count by many who were not partisans.[238] It took a radical disrespect for propertied assumptions to maintain faith in popular politics. Joshua Toulmin insisted that a popular constitution such as his own borough of Taunton enjoyed enabled the poorest citizen to 'hold up his head against the insolence of wealth and rank'.[239] This was certainly not the common perception. One of the reasons which had made it necessary to modify the first great experiment in the statutory incorporation of poor law authorities after 1688 had been the horror which greeted the electoral arrangements involved. The rulers of a town such as Gloucester were appalled at the consequences of regular election of guardians by the community at large.[240] In subsequent legislation care was generally taken to entrust the electoral machinery to propertied vestries.

Wherever there were elections, it seemed that there was friction and disharmony at best, corruption and violence at worst. The ludicrous acrimony which attended the electoral practices of a body as august as the College of Physicians in the 1750s provoked disgust as well as merriment.[241] In fact the medical profession generally presented an unedifying spectacle when engaged in supposedly open competition. Elections to hospital posts were cut-throat affairs. They sometimes featured subscription for the purpose of vote-creating, and were even accompanied by charges of bribery; the distinguished physician George Cleghorn spoke of his stomach revolting at the standard practices involved.[242] Ecclesiastical elections could be equally distressing, not least among Dissenters who prided themselves on their democratic traditions. Battles between Presbyterian trustees and congregations led to litigation before the law courts, and raised 'great Animosity, Spirit, and Obstinacy', as at Plymouth in 1762.[243] Some parish livings and many lectureships in the established Church were also subject to election. The resulting conflicts often ended up before the courts. The

---

[237] William Maitland, *The History and Survey of London* (2 vols., London, 1756), i. 521–5.

[238] I. G. Dolittle, 'Walpole's City Elections Act (1725)', *Eng. Hist. Rev.* 97 (1982), 304–29.

[239] *A History of Taunton* (Taunton, 1791), p. 67.

[240] 13 Geo. I, c. 19.

[241] *An Attempt to Reconcile all Differences between the Present Fellows and Licentiates of the Royal College of Physicians* (London, n.d.)

[242] R. Hingston Fox, *Dr John Fothergill and His Friends: Chapters in Eighteenth Century Life* (London, 1919), p. 124; the election process and practices can be followed in Richard Gough's papers at Bodleian Library, Gough London 53.

[243] 3 Burrow 1266: *Rex* v. *Barker et al.* (1762).

choice of a lecturer at Shoreditch was a recurrent cause of disputes, the worst of them in 1796. The result on that occasion was 'a standing mark of indecency and violence in the annals of their parish'; 1,496 votes were cast and one of the churchwardens was nearly killed in the mêlée.[244] It seemed a reasonable supposition that such proceedings must install the worst kind of clergymen. William Moreton of Willenhall, whose notorious drunkenness, lewdness, and indebtedness greatly embarrassed Staffordshire churchmen, occupied an elective incumbency from 1789 to 1834. He won it by openly soliciting votes during divine service, and defended his right to it by litigation.[245]

Authority tended to the view that in such matters the less popular election the better. Bishops were suspicious of procedures which gave the laity an undue share in appointments, especially when the share was exercised by a number rather than individuals. They even objected when it was proposed in 1773 that magistrates be given the right to nominate prison chaplains, on the grounds that it would be 'a matter of disputes, cabal, and debate'.[246] They were not alone in their anxiety. The essayist John Moir published a sermon entitled *Canvassing for Popular Preferment Equally Disparaging to the Gospel and its Ministers* in protest at the practices which prevailed in Southwark elections. For others it was the sheer indignity of the procedure which was worrying. John Trusler denounced 'probation sermons' which exposed candidates for City lectureships to the scrutiny of mere tradesmen and mechanics. To reinforce his point he pictured a cheesemonger-churchwarden instructing an aspiring lecturer in incongruously rhetorical terms: 'I am for *voice* and *action*, so mind your hits.'[247]

Whig judges who by no means shared the perspective of the clergy none the less took a similar view of the dangers of popular election. Lord Hardwicke, despite irregularities in an electoral trust at Leeds in 1748, declared an 'absolute power in the trustees, without any devolution on the parish at large, to prevent the inconveniences of a popular election'.[248] In the case of Clerkenwell's clerical elections under a deed of impropriation dating from 1656, he found himself in a dilemma. The deed granted the right of election to the 'parishioners and inhabitants for ever'. Presented with evidence that housekeepers at large rather than scot and lot payers had traditionally voted, he concluded that they must be permitted to go on doing so. But he strove hard to find arguments the other way. As to the proposition that only ratepayers should be allowed to vote, he remarked,

---

[244] Henry Ellis, *The History and Antiquities of the Parish of St Leonard Shoreditch, and Liberty of Norton Folgate, in the Suburbs of London* (London, 1798), p. 49.

[245] N. W. Tildesley, 'William Moreton of Willenhall', *Colls. Hist. Staffs.*, 4th ser. 6 (1970), 172.

[246] *London Magazine* (1774), 374. The bishops were unsuccessful; see 23 Geo. III, c. 58.

[247] *Modern Times; Or, the Adventures of Gabriel Outcast* (4th edn., 3 vols., London, 1789), i. 157.

[248] Ambler 87–8: *Wilson* v. *Dennison and Others* (1750).

'I cannot say the limitation ... would have been an unreasonable one.' He also dropped an interesting observation about the difference between mid-seventeenth- and mid-eighteenth-century attitudes to elections. 'Consider too the time of the grant; *the independant congregational scheme* prevailed then, and therefore it must be supposed the donor had an intention to make the right of election as liberal as possible.' Hardwicke was a thoroughgoing Whig, and sympathetic towards Dissent, but his relief that liberal election rights were no longer fashionable was obvious.[249]

The view that it was better to have no representation at all than a form which involved public election was widely held, more widely than enthusiasts for parliamentary politics recognized. It was a commonplace assertion that a town which lacked its parliamentary representation was one that lived in peace and prosperity.[250] There was a story told of the famous seventeenth-century lawyer Sir George Treby that the greatest curse he could think of laying on a town which had incurred his wrath was to seek its enfranchisement. This witticism had lost none of its force by the late eighteenth century. In 1783, Baptist Noel Turner, an opponent of parliamentary reform, enquired: 'How many have owed their ruin, or even their deaths, to the misfortune of having a vote? Communities, as well as individuals, may be injured by this circumstance, especially great ones, so that it seems lucky, in this respect, that so many small places are invested with a power of choosing.'[251] Many agreed that commercial and industrial growth was not compatible with the electoral franchise. The Evangelical John Newton pointed out that 'many judicious people' at Birmingham and Manchester preferred not to have parliamentary elections.[252] Such judiciousness was certainly shared by an early historian of Manchester, James Ogden:

nothing could be more fatal to its trading interest, if it should be incorporated, and have representatives in Parliament. For such is the general course of popular contests, that in places where the immediate dependence of the inhabitants is not upon trade, the health and morals of the people are ruined upon those occasions. How much more fatal would the effects be in such a town as this, where, to the above evils, there would be added the interruption of trade, and perpetuation of ill-will between masters and workmen, who were independent; while those who had nothing to depend on but labour, would contract habits of idleness and drunkenness, or fly to other places, where they could be free from the tyrannical restrictions and partial usages which generally prevail in corporations.[253]

[249] 3 Atkyns 576–9: *Attorney-General* v. *Parker, Price and Doughty* (1747).
[250] *Defoe's Review in 22 Facsimile Books* (New York, 1938), v. 143: 19 June 1708.
[251] *The True Alarm* (London, 1783), pp. 52–3.
[252] *The Works of the Rev John Newton* (6 vols., London, 1808), vi. 587: 'Letter on Political Debate', 1793.
[253] W. E. A. Axon, ed., *Manchester A Hundred Years Ago* (Manchester, 1887), pp. 93–4.

Even Joshua Toulmin, for all his liking of popular constitutions, had to admit that there was force in such arguments. He attributed the disastrous decline in the clothing trade at Taunton to a particularly bitter election in 1754. Workers had abandoned their looms for weeks on end and orders unfilled had never been repeated. No businessman could have faith in a politicized workforce.[254]

It was a cherished belief of supporters of the ancient constitution that the county electorate was not liable to the criticisms which could be brought against borough elections. But by the late eighteenth century the effective devaluation of the forty-shilling freehold was giving rise to anomalies. One was the confusion which it bred in respect of naval impressment. The traditional respect accorded the freehold was expressed in the well-established notion that a freeholder was exempt from conscription. But Thomas Thurlow, successively Solicitor-General, Attorney-General, and Lord Chancellor, had grave doubts about the wisdom of admitting it as a criterion. 'It's a qualification easily attained: a single house at Wapping would ship a first-rate man-of-war. If a Freeholder is exempt, *eo nomine*, it will be impossible to go on with the pressing service.'[255] Another comparison was made with the game qualification, which drew from Blackstone his oft-quoted criticism of 'there being fifty times the property required to enable a man to kill a partridge, as to vote for a knight of the shire'.[256] To some it seemed that the freehold was a dangerous privilege, improperly trusted to men who were undeserving of the honour. When it disturbed the natural order of property relations it seemed particularly objectionable. In his disputes with a farmer the Buckinghamshire clergyman William Cole was irritated that he could not get his way. Not only were the farmer and his brethren able to pull strings with their betters on account of their votes in county elections, but a jury of freeholders would invariably stand by its kind.

And this convinced me of the Fallacy of vaunting ourselves of the Blessedness of our English Constitution and the Glory of Juries; when it is well known, that a quarrelsome Neighbour and of an active Spirit, will probably get the better and trample upon one of a more peaceable Temper. In short the Spirit of Liberty among the commonalty is arrived to such a Length, that they may almost do what they please; for the Yeomanry and Freeholders must not be disobliged, as they are the Electors of Members of Parliament; so that what was designed for our Security, is, by the Rage of sitting in that House, become our great Misfortune.[257]

---

[254] *The History of the Town of Taunton*, p. 98.

[255] J. R. Hutchinson, *The Press-Gang Afloat and Ashore* (London, 1913), p. 15.

[256] W. Blackstone, *Commentaries on the Laws of England* (4 vols., London, 1765–9), iv. 175.

[257] F. G. Stokes, ed., *The Blecheley Diary of the Rev. William Cole, 1765–67* (London, 1931), p. 88.

It suited some people to maintain the peculiar respectability of the county franchise. Freeholders as a body had a legendary integrity which it was difficult altogether to forget. Lord Shelburne talked of 'yeomen' as 'almost the only rank of Men yet uncorrupted'.[258] Edmund Burke made still higher claims, in connection with the petitions on behalf of the Middlesex electors in 1770. 'A freeholder is as good a gentleman as any in the kingdom.' He even compared them favourably with JPs appointed by the Crown. 'The gentlemen, it is well known, are much influenced; but the freeholders are above all menace, all fear, all influence.'[259] But Shelburne's remark was made at a county meeting where such rhetoric was guaranteed to go down well with ordinary freeholders, and Burke had political reasons for championing them. Less partisan commentators, including the radical reformer Lord Carysfort, thought the qualification very low.[260]

The extent to which ordinary freeholders could be coaxed or coerced by their betters remains a matter of dispute.[261] What is certain is that contemporaries were well aware of the means by which county voters could be influenced, and discounted their independence accordingly. A country estate was so synonymous with electoral influence that it was almost impossible to divest it of its function in this respect even when the owner sought to do so. There was dismay in 1748 when it was discovered that the steward for an estate which belonged to the Sons of the Clergy at Stowe in Northamptonshire had threatened to eject tenants unless they voted in parliamentary elections as he directed. How could so untainted a cause as the Sons of the Clergy have become enmeshed in such corruption? Simply, it seemed, by owning land. Contrary to a widely held belief the possession of government stock would have been less contaminating.[262]

The devaluation of freeholds was attested by the ease with which they could be manufactured for electoral purposes. The simplest means of achieving this was the granting of annuities secured on land. Particularly in a small county this held out the possibility of commanding a sizeable proportion of the total vote. Huntingdonshire, dominated by two great families, the Dukes of Manchester and Earls of Sandwich, provided such an instance when the possibilities of the annuity as an electoral weapon were first appreciated in the 1760s. Between 1753 and 1763, 5 annuities were recorded in Huntingdonshire, and in 1764–5 a further 17. Then between 1765 and 1767, with a general election approaching and a bitter

---

[258] Huntington Library, Stowe MSS, L 9 D 10: account of meeting 26 Mar. 1780.
[259] *London Magazine* (1770), 34–5.
[260] Lord Carysfort, *Thoughts on the Constitution* (London, 1783).
[261] See F. O'Gorman, 'Electoral Deference in Unreformed England: 1760–1832', *Jnl. Mod. Hist.* 56 (1984), 391–429; R. Hopkinson, 'The Electorate of Cumberland and Westmorland in the Late Seventeenth and Early Eighteenth Centuries', *Northern History*, 15 (1979), 96–116.
[262] E. H. Pearce, *The Sons of the Clergy 1655–1904* (London, 1904), pp. 246–7.

contest in the offing, 154 were created. A statute of 1763 laid down that annuity votes could not be cast unless they had been registered with the clerk of the peace for at least a year. This did nothing to curb the practice. By 1792 there were 492 annuitants out of a total electorate in Huntingdonshire of 1,700.[263] Part of the appeal of freehold-splitting in this form was that it did not permanently alienate property. Another part was the advantage it offered even to small freeholders; their voting power could be multiplied and their political prospects accordingly enhanced. When Sandwich recommended a local man, Stephen Arundel, as Distributor of Stamps in Huntingdon in 1771, he described him as 'an excellent politician, in good circumstances, and a very honest man'. It happened that Arundel had used his slender patrimony to create two annuities for the election of 1768; he was not long in claiming his reward.[264]

There was an analogy between freehold-splitting and the creation of honorary freedoms for non-residents in boroughs. It is no coincidence that the County Annuities Act was passed in the same session as the Durham Act, which sought to restrict the electoral manipulation of the freedom in corporations. Traditionally the freeholder enjoyed a status altogether higher than the freeman, but by the 1760s it was permissible to disparage free-holders as a class in terms which would earlier have seemed faintly shocking. In 1762 the Countess of Northumberland found Samuel Egerton, the Tory knight of the shire for Cheshire, unimpressed by his constituents: 'Ask'd why he did not entertain Freeholders, say'd he did not value them.'[265]

It was not necessary to be as contemptuous of the freeholder as Egerton to be disturbed by the social ordeal involved in presenting oneself as a candidate at a parliamentary election. The personal and social humiliation inseparable from an electoral contest was a familiar theme. Defoe, pre-senting his county election picture of a 'Baronet among the Boors', argued that the consequence was the election of degraded MPs by degenerate electors. The process involved 'stooping to all the meanest, and vilest, and most indecent things imaginable, ... this beastly Doing is enough to show the Gentlemen their own Picture *in little*, when their Interest guides them to seek an Opportunity of getting into a Parliament House. What Men can stoop to this are fit for, when they come there, is a Question admits of a further Enquiry'.[266] This view was even shared by radicals. The reformer Thomas Day considered standing as a parliamentary candidate in the

---

[263] Cambridgeshire County RO (Huntingdon), Hinchingbrooke MSS 8/13, 17, 19: lists of annuities. The contrast with the experience of large counties, where the electoral benefit to be derived from freehold splitting was proportionately slight, is marked; in Northumberland during the same period, between 1763 and 1792, only 46 annuities were registered (Northumberland RO, QRPa).

[264] Ibid. 8/287: Sandwich to Robinson, 26 Feb. 1771.

[265] J. Greig, *The Diaries of a Duchess* (London, 1924), p. 35.

[266] *Defoe's Review*, v. 123–4: 8 June 1708.

turbulent borough of Southwark but withdrew when informed of the
corrupt practices which he would have to employ. There were those who
believed in the majesty of the people without being impressed by the
spectacle of a popular election. In his *Instructions to a Statesman* of 1784
William Godwin stressed the demeaning features of the 'disgustful scene'
of an election: 'It is he, most noble patron, who can swallow the greatest
quantity of porter, who can roar the best catch, and who is the compleatest
bruiser, that will finally carry the day. He must kiss the frost-bitten lips of
the green-grocers. He must smooth the frowzy cheeks of chandlers-shop
women. He must stroke down the infinite belly of a Wapping landlady.'[267]
Godwin's exploitation of the sexual as well as social incongruities of these
occasions could be employed to even greater effect when it was women who
were doing the courting. The growing involvement of women, especially
candidates' wives, in electoral canvassing gave rise to much adverse
comment on this point. A lady compelled by her husband to dance attendance on a pettifogger's wife could only be pitied when she was compelled
to submit herself to the small-mindedness of bourgeois society. She 'often
listens, through sad necessity, to the petulant animadversions of females
affecting independence'.[268]

It was possible to have both aesthetic and moral objections to such a
scene. At the general election of 1761 there was concern about the ribaldry
and obscenity of election gatherings, at a time when a new King was
holding out a new prospect of pure and patriotic politics.[269] No doubt such
anxieties contributed to the indifference or even revulsion with which
middle-class Evangelicals regarded parliamentary elections. But it was the
element of social condescension to which commentators turned time and
again. Foreigners were intrigued by it. The Abbé le Blanc recorded with
amazement the complaisance of the Duke of St Albans and the Duke of
Marlborough before the humble electors of New Windsor in 1738.[270]
Englishmen themselves continued to find it fascinating. John Trusler
designed a play to suit Hogarth's celebrated election series with the emphasis on the necessity of being obsequious to all ranks and degrees: 'fawning
on, kissing and flattering the women all day, smoking, boozing, and licking
the very spittle of the men, all night'.[271] The paradox he observed was 'how
farcical it is, that men who pride themselves on their distinction, should
stand aloof when speaking to one of the lower class of people, and dread
his approach, as if his breath would contaminate them, and yet at elections

---

[267] B. R. Pollard, *Four Early Pamphlets by William Godwin* (Gainesville, Fla., 1966), pp. 130–1.
[268] *Gentleman's Magazine* (1796), 563.
[269] *General Evening Post*, 16 Apr. 1761.
[270] *Letters on the English and French Nations*, ii. 157, 159–60.
[271] *The Country Election: A Farce in Two Acts* (London, 1768), p. 37.

all condescend to hug the greasy rogues, and shake hands with every dirty fellow'.[272]

Personal experience of this paradox was common. When the Honourable Thomas Fitzmaurice, MP for High Wycombe between 1774 and 1780, made his annual visit to cultivate his constituents, it was his custom to take with him a house party which might relieve the *longueurs* of a tedious market town in high summer. Part of the entertainment was the vulgarity of the company which they had to keep. One of his guests, Percival Stockdale, recorded the subtle social revenge to which they were reduced. 'Our time was marked with peculiar, and prominent social characteristics. The elaborate, and grotesque manners; the formal importance that expressed nothing; and the course mirth, and jokes, of the Wycombe burgesses; made very advantageous foils, to the easy, and engaging flow of politeness; and to elegant conversation.' The high point of Stockdale's visit was a meeting with a very old alderman who boasted of having made the famous Duke of Wharton, a vigorous electioneer under George I, take off his boots 'during the universal, and licentious freedom, which the situation of an election gives; or rather during the despotick power which is then arrogated by the little over the great'.[273] Experiences of this kind served to enhance the general sense of a surrender of genteel values: 'the sacrifice of convivial elegance to vulgar feasting, of politeness and decorum to obsequiousness or influence, and of approving friendship to stupid admiration'.[274]

Wycombe was a small parliamentary borough, but there was not much to choose between county and borough elections. No doubt the social horrors which attended a county election, as well as the expense, had something to do with distaste for fighting one. Elaborate conventions and manoeuvres were evolved in order to stave off a real contest; almost as much attention was devoted to the polite preliminaries as to the subsequent canvassing and voting. In this respect late eighteenth-century elections were more mannered, more ritualistic than their predecessors. At the Essex by-election of 1763, which brought to an end almost thirty years of electoral peace in the county, it was noted that 'during this long contested affair, and even after the decision, both the Candidates behaved to each other with the greatest politeness'.[275] The Leicestershire election of 1775, which revived the bitterness of ancient conflicts between the house of Manners and the Tory gentry of the county, involved much attention to the procedural punctilios of making and announcing nominations.[276] In this instance there was little hope of averting a poll. But the concern of both sides to catch

[272] *Modern Times*, iii. 192.
[273] *The Memoirs of the Life and Writings of Percival Stockdale* (2 vols., London, 1809), ii. 143.
[274] *Gentleman's Magazine* (1796) 563.
[275] *Suffolk Notes from the Year 1729* (Ipswich, 1883–4), p. 55.
[276] *Memoirs of the Late Contested Election for the County of Leicester* (Leicester, 1775).

their opponents out in ungentlemanly treatment of the gentry revealed the gap between polite and popular roles in a parliamentary election, and the determination of genteel voters to keep it in being.

A standard technique was to divide freeholders into different classes. The inferior freeholders became a distinct category, to be treated with condescension if not contempt, not least by their immediate superiors. Sir Gerard Vanneck caused fury among the farmers of Suffolk at the election of 1790 when he made a point of treating their poorer neighbours.[277] There was confusion in the middle of the century about the relative fortunes of different ranks of freeholders, compounded by the seeming prosperity of gentlemen farmers who were only incidentally freeholders if at all.[278] But laments about the fate of the old English yeoman had mainly to do with the 'better' freeholder, and the general assumption was that the poorer freeholders had increased in number. Ironically it was often the more respectable freeholder in the countryside who was likely to be a tenant farmer while his less reputable brother might well be a relatively independent, if not incorruptible, tradesman, artisan, or labourer, as likely as not the inhabitant of a market town or a large, undisciplined village. The real complaint against Vanneck in 1790 was that he had courted the impoverished inhabitants of Sudbury, far removed from their rural compatriots in wealth, status, and, not least, religious opinions.

Explaining the political processes which influenced such men needed care. In the Surrey election of 1780 Lord Onslow's episcopal friend John Butler contrasted the 'Noise of Ragamuffins' with solid votes based on his patron's 'natural interest'.[279] This attitude assumed that a tenant could not be bribed by his landlord. When the House of Commons dealt with charges of corruption in the Anglesey election of 1725 it was thought a sufficient defence of many of the voters involved to identify them as 'Tenants to Lord *Bulkeley*, and such as always voted in his Interest'. They were described as men 'whose Character and Circumstances freed them from Suspicion of Bribery'.[280] Later trends if anything reinforced this mentality, as the approved agricultural practice of long leases helped cement relations between landlord and tenant, creating a comforting bond of tenurial harmony. Coke's toast of 'long leases and good tenants' was admired for 'giving him a preponderance of freeholders, and rendering him thereby less dependent on the inferior class of voters, whose favour he is frequently obliged to court, in opposition to his feelings and rank in life'.[281]

---

[277] *Observations on the Cause, Conduct, and Effects, of the Late Contested Election, for the County of Suffolk* (Ipswich, 1790), p. 60.

[278] Malachy Postlethwayt, *The Universal Dictionary of Trade and Commerce* (4th edn., London, 1774), *sub* 'People'.

[279] Surrey RO (Guildford), Onslow MSS, Butler to Onslow, 4 Oct. 1780.

[280] *Commons Journals*, xx. 441.

[281] K. Kissack, *Monmouth: The Making of a County Town* (London, 1973), p. 570.

A case could be made for natural interest as the expression of a true communal sense, resting on a hierarchical conception of society which ultimately ensured the welfare of all. By contrast, bribing the petty freeholder in a county or the ordinary freemen in a borough was a cynical act of seduction, with no implications beyond the immediate outcome. However, the difference could be exaggerated. The much respected knight of the shire for Yorkshire, Sir George Savile, warned his nephew Richard Lumley against relying on his 'natural interest' at Lincoln. Compared with what Savile mockingly called the practice of buying a borough in the 'usual honourable way', it involved its possessor in endless trouble. It was a curse, not a blessing, which frequently entailed its possessor in mortgaging the rest of his estate. 'I don't speak only of the *guineas given*, but of the *tradesmen employed*: (a more decent and well covered kind of bribery indeed and shading off into what one calls *natural Interest* and fair influence of neighbourhood and Property). So far from *such* a Seat *as it has been* being honourable, it is more dirty than a seat in a privy.'[282]

When the campaign against electoral corruption in the era of Wilkes led to demands for disfranchisement of corrupt boroughs, the freeholder seemed to hold out the obvious solution. The first borough to lose its franchise, New Shoreham in 1771, gave way to a constituency based on the rape of Bramber. An electorate which had consisted of about a hundred scot and lot voters was replaced by one comprising eight hundred forty-shilling freeholders, the same men who voted in county elections. The result was the election of a succession of landed families, Gorings, Peacheys, Bishopps, Wyndhams, Shelleys, and Burrells. A similar formula was to be adopted at Cricklade in 1782 and Aylesbury in 1804 but it was not applied more widely. At Hindon in 1775 and 1776 the Commons came close to redistributing the franchise among the neighbouring hundreds, but eventually drew back, when it became obvious that 'the influence of different gentlemen of property in the neighbourhood of the place would have been more or less increased, or diminished, according as the freeholders of one, two, or more hundreds should have been admitted to a participation of the right of election'.[283] Oldfield thought the example of New Shoreham proved that objections to parliamentary reform were frivolous. When constitutional decorum, in the shape of the peaceful election of country gentlemen was its first consequence, how could it be objected to?[284] But not all reformers wanted to turn boroughs into county divisions. Opponents of parliamentary reform exploited the tensions of town and country in this context. When he was elected for Peterborough

[282] E. Milner, *Records of the Lumleys of Lumley Castle* (London, 1904), p. 257.

[283] T. H. B. Oldfield, *The Representative History of Great Britain and Ireland* (6 vols., London, 1816), v. 137; also, see below, p. 321.

[284] *The Representative History*, v. 26.

in 1796, French Laurence warned his constituents against the designs of 'restless innovators', who 'to purify you, as they call it, would pour in upon you half the Soke, which for centuries has depended, and is still willing to depend, upon its proper Capital'.[285] In fact the realities of rural life were more complicated. In the case of New Shoreham itself one effect of reform was to bring the market town of Horsham into the parliamentary constituency, along with the agrarian communities surrounding it. The constable of Shoreham was as contemptuous of the 'barbers, shopkeepers etc., of Horsham' as he was of his country cousins of rural Sussex.[286] One lesson was clear, however. Any attempt to 'improve' the existing structure by broadening access to the franchise would bring resentment and feuding in its wake.

A PARCEL OF MEAN FELLOWS

It was generally agreed that a qualification of more than £20, perhaps £40 or £50, would have been required to restore the respectability of the county electorate. If anything these were conservative estimates. The scheme for social insurance proposed for Devon in 1768 assumed that any freeholder worth less than £30 was too close to poverty not to need assistance.[287] An adequate rental income from land, sufficient to ensure 'yeoman' status, would certainly have had to approach £50. In practice cries for a higher qualification were unlikely to be heeded. The venerable forty-shilling freehold had a symbolic significance which made it sacrosanct. Even the reformers of 1832 did not dare do away with it. But some ingenuity went into devising alternatives. One was the possibility of permitting multiple votes in proportion to landed property. By this means a great landowner would be enabled to deploy block votes which would dwarf even combined voting by his inferiors. It could be argued that this was merely extending a principle implicit in the existing system. 'So closely is the Right of Representation, connected with that of Property, that one Man if his Property be dispersed may have several Votes.'[288]

If the forty-shilling freehold was sacrosanct, at least it could be made as restrictive as the letter of the law allowed. In counties where copyhold and leasehold property prevailed, there were sometimes local conventions which permitted their possessors to vote along with freeholders. Before the multiplication of parliamentary election scrutinies and printed pollbooks, these customary votes could be preserved without undue difficulty. In Leicestershire the antiquarian Browne Willis was informed that copy-

---

[285] *Gentleman's Magazine* (1796), 1048–9.
[286] W. S. Blunt, 'Extracts from John Baker's Horsham Diary', *Sussex Arch. Colls.* 52 (1909), 70.
[287] A. Warne, *Church and Society in Eighteenth-Century Devon* (Newton Abbot, 1969), p. 161.
[288] *The Constitutional Advocate* (London, 1776), p. 12.

holders voted by prescription.[289] In Breconshire in 1696 the Commons discovered that leaseholders for lives voted.[290] In Anglesey in 1725 the 356 'freeholders' who voted included leaseholders for lives of tenements and houses. Significantly the objection made to the Commons extended only to leaseholders for years.[291] To reformers the enfranchisement of copy-holders and leaseholders of suitable standing seemed the obvious way of remedying the absurdities of electoral law. Lord Carysfort, a member of the Society for Constitutional Information, argued in his *Thoughts on the Constitution* in 1783 that they had every right to consider themselves propertied Englishmen worthy of a parliamentary franchise.[292]

Parliament's hypocrisy was revealed in its treatment of copyholders and leaseholders. When superior landed qualifications were under consideration there was no requirement of freehold tenure. It was taken as axiomatic that a copyholder of £300 had as good a claim as a freeholder to be an MP.[293] Similarly, the qualification for a county magistrate could include land held by any tenure; a statute of 1745 went out of its way to extend the categories of land-holding permitted, and included reversionary interests as well as customary tenures. This meant in effect that a lord of the manor or granter of beneficial leases could sit on the bench alongside his own tenants or lessees, and do so by virtue of the same landed property which qualified them.[294] This extraordinary latitude violated the fundamental principle of a propertied polity. It gave the dependent the same rights as those on whom they depended, and created the manifest absurdity of two equal, distinct, and irreconcilable rights in the same 'absolute' property. But this kind of logic was not applied to smaller men. Parliament actually restricted the rights of copyholders in this respect. When the Oxfordshire election of 1754 revealed the existence of a class of freeholders of ancient demesne whose tenure was strictly that of copyholder, the result was an act specific-ally reinforcing the prohibition against their voting.[295]

Similar points were argued in the debate about juries. The case for extending the freehold jury qualification had been considered in detail in 1670. There were strong protests from some country gentlemen in Parliament. It was claimed that leaseholders who sat as jurors would be tempted to use their power to the prejudice of their landlords. Conversely, 'a gentlemen, by his influence upon them, may put them upon unjust things'. The danger of creating an electoral precedent was also cited. 'If

[289] Bodleian Library, GA fo. A 226: Samuel Carte, 'Some Account of the Town of Leicester'.

[290] *Commons Journals*, xi. 463.

[291] H. Owen, *The Life and Works of Lewis Morris (Llewelyn Ddu Fôn) 1701–1765*, (Anglesey, 1951), p. 147; *Commons Journals*, xx. 440.

[292] (London, 1783), p. 38.

[293] H. E. Witmer, *The Property Qualification of Members of Parliament* (New York, 1943), p. 41.

[294] 18 Geo. II, c. 20.

[295] 28 Geo. II, c. 18.

they should be Jurors, it is reasonable they should have voices in chusing Knights and Burgess of Parliament; and what an intolerable change that will be, when the number shall be so multiplied?'[296] However, these objections were eventually overcome. In 1692 £10 copyholders were subjected to jury service, and in 1730 so were lessees of £20.[297] The argument of precedent turned out to have little force. It was not until 1832 that copyholders and substantial leaseholders were admitted to the parliamentary franchise. Jury service was not popular. One of the attractive features of copyhold tenure in the seventeenth century was said to be its exemption from empannelment; it was even claimed that some owners resisted enfranchisement or sought conversion to leasehold on lives to take advantage of it. The anomalies created by tenurial distinctions could certainly seem bizarre. In towns there was a personal estate qualification for jurymen, but it was resisted in the countryside. As a result a farmer with ample personalty to qualify as a turnpike trustee, a judge in a court of conscience, or an improvement commissioner, might find himself incompetent to sit on a petty jury. This appeared unjust. As a critic put it in 1765, 'why should a tradesman owning a piece of land or two or three cottages be called 20 or 30 miles from home, on that duty at much expense and loss of time, when an ingrossing farmer with thousands and his brace of grey hounds at this heels, should not be called upon?'[298] In fact the small copyholder or leaseholder for lives had the worst of all worlds, jury liability without the consolation of a parliamentary vote and a say in their own government. What Parliament granted as an onerous obligation it would not concede as an electoral privilege.

So far as the freehold franchise was concerned, Parliament's dilemma was that by doing nothing it permitted inflation to render its electorate increasingly contemptible. However, by indirect means, it succeeded in restricting its growth. Three acts of 1712, 1745, and 1780, which in theory merely reinforced the forty-shilling freehold qualification, in reality remodelled it.[299] The principle of all three was to reduce fraud and remove uncertainty by associating the qualification with the payment of taxes. The first act specified that forty-shilling freeholders must be liable to a local rate; that of 1745 laid down that they must be assessed to the land tax. Both were ambiguously worded and diversely interpreted. The act of 1712 caused much mystification. The unsuccessful candidate for North-

---

[296] *Debates of the House of Commons, from the Year 1667 to the year 1694: Collected by the Honourable Anchitell Grey, Esq.* (10 vols., London, 1969), i. 230.

[297] Whether, in practice, leaseholders were enrolled in numbers, is questionable. It would not have been easy for petty constables, making their returns of jurors, to value their holdings; see 'The Jurors' Book of 1784', *Colls. Hist. Staffs.* (1947), 73–100.

[298] *London Magazine* (1765), 402.

[299] 10 Anne, c. 23 (amended 12 Anne Stat. 1, c. 5); 18 Geo. II, c. 18; 20 Geo. III, c. 13.

amptonshire in 1730 publicly pleaded its obscurity as his reason for not pursuing a claim of malpractice against his opponents in the courts.[300] The act of 1745 encountered intense resistance from the returning officers who had to enforce it. It was reckoned that sheriffs treated both acts as general statements of intent and permitted freeholders to vote without insisting on the statutory restriction.

Some of this confusion was dispelled in 1780, by an act providing for the deposit of land tax assessments with the county clerk of the peace. This amounted to electoral registration. It also discriminated against electors. The lawyer Samuel Heywood, who specialized in electoral law, considered it a 'law of disfranchisement', particularly where independent freeholders were concerned. They were unlikely to bother to check their assessment, whereas landlords and party men had an interest in doing so. Moreover, many freeholders were exempted by local convention from payment of the land tax on grounds of poverty; others owned freeholds which were free of land tax by private conveyance. Heywood reckoned in 1790 that there were forty thousand freeholds in Lancashire, thirty thousand of them created by the splitting of property for commercial purposes in the space of less than a hundred years. In 1790 he thought only 400 of these were properly assessed and registered.[301] A similar situation prevailed in Yorkshire. It was estimated in 1789 that the North Riding contained twelve thousand freeholders. Yet this was double the number polled at the next contested election in 1807.[302]

There was sufficient concern about the anomalies created by the statute of 1780 to generate further legislation in 1788. The bill of that year was the fifth attempt of its kind, its immediate predecessors having been passed by the Commons but defeated in the Lords. It replaced the land tax assessment with a genuine electoral register. This cure was widely considered worse than the disease, not least because the cost, in the form of a county rate, would be shared by copyholders and others who had no right to vote. It was also calculated that every freeholder would have to pay at least a shilling a year for the privilege of maintaining his right to vote.[303] The act had been conceived as a device to propitiate the county electorate, but its effect was quite the reverse. The campaign against it seems to have begun in Cheshire where there were fears that the leaseholders for lives who by convention voted in parliamentary elections could not properly be registered as freeholders. This suggested what a Pandora's box would be

---

[300] William Hanbury's circular of 16 Jan. 1731, printed in the Bodleian Library's copy of the Northamptonshire pollbook for 1730, Vet A 4 e 2192.

[301] Samuel Heywood, *A Digest of the Law Respecting County Elections* (London, 1790), pp. 102, 124.

[302] North Yorkshire RO, QDE (M) 468/8/2: estimated total in response to circular of HM's Printers, 30 June 1788.

[303] Ibid. 8/22: G. White to Clerk of Peace, 24 Feb. 1789.

opened when the legislature started seriously scrutinizing the customs which actually regulated county elections. Similar outrage was expressed elsewhere, in Yorkshire and Lancashire, and eventually in twenty-two counties.[304] The act was hastily withdrawn before the general election of 1790 could give voters a chance to punish their MPs for voting it on to the statute book.[305] In consequence that of 1780 remained the determining law for county freeholds until 1832. Then, when the act was repealed, the result was a positive inundation of new freehold voters.[306]

Similar considerations applied in the boroughs, but there it was generally believed that the dangers created by numerous, poor voters were still greater. According to Lord George Germain, MPs found it repulsive even to have to face ordinary voters at a Commons enquiry into a contested election. 'A parcel of mean fellows' such as gave evidence to parliamentary election committees provided distressing evidence of the absurdity of the borough franchise.[307] The obvious equivalent of the poor freeholder was the poor freeman. There were ninety-two boroughs in which the franchise was vested in those who enjoyed the freedom and the general assumption was that they created problems even more chronic than their county brethren. Freemen themselves often lamented their lack of independence, as at Rochester in 1722, when they explained their inability to support their preferred candidate: 'Fear of Want, and Dependencies forced them to act against him.'[308] In large cities freemen were notoriously vulnerable to manipulation and intimidation. Coventry elections repeatedly brought allegations of men dismissed by their employers for voting against their instructions, and, still more oppressively, of men expelled from their friendly societies and insurance clubs, for refusing to toe the party line.[309] Mass creations of lowly freemen who were no more than pawns of the corporations which selected them were a feature of many small and not a few large towns. Where the franchise was in ratepayers whose rating was artificially contrived to give them a vote, or even in inhabitant householders, the electorate was equally numerous and equally contemptible. Raising the qualification seemed as high a priority as in the counties. Hume suggested a franchise of householders worth £500, close to the level laid down for many statutory commissions. It would have transformed the parliamentary electorate.[310]

[304] Ibid. 8/12: J. Taylor to J. Bird, 22 Sept. 1788; G. M. Ditchfield, 'The House of Lords and Parliamentary Reform in the 1780s', *Bulletin of the Institute of Historical Research*, 54 (1981), 207–25.
[305] 28 Geo. III, c. 36; see E. Porritt, *The Unreformed House of Commons: Parliamentary Representation before 1832* (2 vols., repr. New York, 1963), i. 26–7.
[306] N. Gash, *Politics in the Age of Peel* (2nd edn., Hassocks, 1977), p. 91.
[307] *London Magazine* (1774), 578.
[308] *Post-Boy*, 24 Mar. 1722.
[309] William Reader's 'Chronicle', e.g. 644, 647.
[310] *Essays Moral, Political, and Literary* (Oxford, 1963), p. 502.

Parliament was no more ready to revise the borough franchise than it was to interfere in municipal corporations, though in practice it was frequently forced to consider individual cases. Borough voting was regulated by charter and local custom: many of the resulting disputes were decided by the law courts in so far as they arose from the rights and wrongs of municipal government, but where they resulted in a controverted parliamentary election they were determined by the House of Commons itself. The Commons got so bogged down in the morass of local constitutions that it twice bound itself to abide by its last adjudication rather than reopen the franchise in the same borough in different Parliaments. These 'last determination' clauses of 1696 and 1729 left further room for argument on increasingly minute points. Whether they significantly affected the overall development of the franchise depends on the consistency with which the House of Commons acted in these election cases. The eighteenth-century belief was that on balance it tended to enlarge the electorate.[311] The modern view is that on the contrary it operated in oligarchical fashion, consistently reducing the size of the electorate.[312] It is difficult to endorse either claim. The Commons was rarely presented with a simple choice between a wide and a narrow franchise. Nor did it pursue a constant policy in these matters. In many cases it conscientiously sought to establish what was justified by local custom. In still more it was moved by party preference, what one boroughmonger defeated at a Cornish poll in 1727 euphemistically described as 'justice in a better place'.[313] This was a matter of scandal at the time, but it did not work in a particularly consistent way. Whether it suited the Whig governments of George I and George II, for instance, to prefer a large or small electorate was entirely a matter of local circumstance. In the lengthy and tedious deliberations of the Commons and its elections committees only two broad principles can be clearly discerned, and then somewhat uncertainly through a dense mist of more immediate considerations.

One object was the elimination of the authentically poor voter. Every argument seemed to point in this direction. Enlightenment philosophers as well as traditionally-minded patriots accepted, as Montesquieu expressed it, that all should have a vote 'except such as are in so mean a situation as to be deemed to have no will of their own'.[314] The eighteenth century inherited from the seventeenth a powerful prejudice against poor voters. It was put trenchantly by Sir William Jones in 1680. 'By the Argument I have heard, we shall have Alms-men to have Voices in Elections. Whoever has the misfortune to be a *Pauper*, must bear that, and be he not able to

---

[311] Heywood, *A Digest of the Law Respecting County Elections*, p. 72.
[312] J. Cannon, *Parliamentary Reform 1640–1832* (Cambridge, 1973), pp. 33–4.
[313] PRO, S P Dom. George II, 1/3 fos. 32–3: Richard Edgcumbe to unknown, 27 Aug. 1727.
[314] *The Spirit of the Laws*, p. 155.

pay towards the Charge of the Government, he ought not to have liberty of Choice of Representative. You will have beggars, at this rate, come to have Voice, and what Choice they will make, you know.'[315] The notion that the poor might vote in a body without reference to their individual interest, that is their immediate profit, was simply incredible. Stories about their predictability in this respect were legion at election time. Even acts of independence looked like dependence in another form. The High Churchman George Horne told with particular pride the story of William Lynch's election for Canterbury in 1768. He attributed it to the gratitude of the poorest freemen, who recalled the benevolence of Lynch's father, a former Dean of Canterbury. 'You had a right to command our votes; *your father fed us*, and *your mother clothed us*.'[316] Horne was impressed by Dean Lynch's philanthropy, but he did not reflect that the voters' conduct merely amounted to payment for services rendered. Nor did he mention that their remembrance was short-lived: at the next general election in 1774 Lynch lost his seat. Occasionally, indeed, it was possible to publicize authentic disinterestedness on the part of destitute voters, but the results merely proved what pressures they were subject to. The report in 1780 that paupers had been ejected from the Norwich workhouse for voting against one of the parliamentary candidates was entirely in line with contemporary assumptions about the vulnerability of the poor.[317]

Such assumptions acted as a powerful antidote to prescriptions of reform, for they countered one of the more plausible arguments of reformers, namely that large, democratic constituencies would prove difficult to corrupt. On the contrary, it was said, since a large electorate could only be created by enfranchising the poor, it must necessarily engender corruption. In 1782 Thomas Pitt pointed out that open, populous boroughs were 'the rotten boroughs of the constitution in the most eminent degree'.[318] The riposte was to urge that corruption was not monopolized by the poor. General Burgoyne, MP for Preston, which vied with Coventry for the title of most unruly of all provincial electorates, boasted that his poorest voters were the least corrupted.[319] Capel Lofft asserted that 'the dependents are not those chiefly who seek their bread by industry'.[320] But claims such as these challenged the most sacred of all eighteenth-century beliefs; accordingly they went largely unheeded.

Like most simple principles, exclusion of the poor could prove com-

[315] *Grey's Debates*, viii. 127: 11 Dec. 1680.

[316] William Jones, *The Works of the Right Reverend George Horne* (8 vols., London, 1818), i. 349.

[317] *Narrative of the Proceedings at the Contested Election for Two Members to Represent the City and County of Norwich* (3rd edn., Norwich, 1780), p. 45.

[318] *A Letter to the Author of the Lucubrations* (London, 1782), p. 25.

[319] *A Letter from Lieutenant General Burgoyne to His Constituents* (London, 1779), p. 19.

[320] *Observations* (London, 1783), p. 21.

plicated in practice. Was it a conclusive proof of poverty to be excused payment of poor rates? There was considerable uncertainty on this point.[321] Receipt of poor relief or charity was taken to be a criterion of poverty. But what constituted charity? In many places there were ancient bequests which were employed to provide benefits more in the nature of bonuses and perks than charities. At Westbury in 1748 it was argued that receipt of Smith's charity, which provided linen fabric, was not at all a sign of poverty since it could only be awarded to men and women who were not on poor relief.[322] Since such endowments were frequently used for purposes of bribery, they were controversial. At Coventry the corporation's use of its right to make loans to tradesmen from the great bequest of Sir Thomas White was described roundly as 'the Prostitution of the Charity Estate'.[323] This was an exceedingly complicated matter. At Taunton in 1790 the returning officer's counsel opined that an improper grant from a charitable trust could not disfranchise the recipient, because the donor would be liable to an action for recovery on the grounds that the grant had been made on false pretences.[324] This ingenious argument seems not to have been tested in Parliament. As far as possible the Commons was inclined to treat any charitable benefit as evidence of poverty. It also took every opportunity to disfranchise those affected, and arbitrarily prohibited voting by the poor even when the parties in dispute had not raised the subject and made it no part of their argument. The theory was that when the House of Commons adjudicated a controverted election it was acting judicially and interpreting existing law. But interference of this kind, evidently considered uncontroversial at the time, was in effect revising the law of charter and custom on the authority of a mere resolution of one branch of the legislature.

The second, related principle was that in favour of a ratepayers' franchise. When the alternative was a poll of every inhabitant there was little doubt about where the ordinary MP's preference would fall. In the case of Honiton in 1710 it was pointed out that this had been the constant tendency of the Commons.

it was held, That a Usage of such Poor Persons Voting for Representatives in Parliament, was in itself unreasonable, and that it would be of dangerous Consequence to commit such Poor Persons the Election of Members to serve in Parliament, as Guardians of the Laws and Liberties of the Kingdom.[325]

---

[321] H. Baring, ed., *The Diary of the Right Hon. William Windham 1784 to 1810* (London, 1866), p. 168.

[322] *Commons Journals*, xxv. 571–9.

[323] William Reader's 'Chronicle', 357.

[324] *The History of the Town of Taunton*, p. 52.

[325] Bodleian Library, Parliamentary Papers of William Bromley, i. 74: 'The Case of James Sheppard'.

Ironically Honiton did not retain its scot and lot franchise. In 1724 a Whig Commons supported 'potwallopers' in their claim to vote, on partisan grounds. This was subsequently treated as the last determination, and for the remainder of the unreformed parliament Honiton had a wide electorate. It was also considered shamelessly corrupt, a standing example of the unwisdom of entrusting voting power to the poor.

A still greater threat to the supremacy of the ratepayer was occasional voting. In freemen boroughs it was easy for corporations to manufacture votes, sometimes by electing to the freedom men who were not even resident locally. At the beginning of George III's reign, when there were hopes that a patriot King would inaugurate a new era of reform, particular interest was taken in this problem. The result was the Durham Act, named after the borough which had recently provided sensational evidence of electoral gerrymandering, but the concern was actually an old one. The solution, to require that honorary freemen be prevented from voting until they had enjoyed the honour for a year, made little difference.[326] There were subsequent scandals to match the case of Durham. In 1769 the corporation of Bedford quintupled its electorate by creating more than six hundred honorary freemen in the space of a year. Reformers were much vexed by such practices. Gloucester, repeatedly the victim of artificial creations, petitioned against them in 1779.[327] Daniel Coke's abortive bills of 1779 and 1780 would have prevented honorary freemen voting altogether or alternatively have allowed them to vote provided they paid a stamp duty for the privilege of their enrolment as freemen.[328] A similar proposal in 1787 was rejected on the grounds that it 'tended to disfranchise many thousand voters'.[329]

Further attempts at reform were made on a local basis. Coventry, a notoriously violent constituency, was the subject of an act to regulate voting by freemen in 1781.[330] From time to time legislation was also proposed to prevent occasional voters in inhabitant boroughs. Nominal householding by non-residents was a common electoral fraud. In 1708 a bill to outlaw it was defeated in a well-attended division.[331] It was revived long after, at another time when country gentlemen with reforming tendencies were active in the Commons, in 1773. On this occasion, with a general election in prospect, its opponents were evidently reluctant to have their views and votes recorded. The bill was killed by repeated adjournments which carried it safely beyond the prorogation of Parliament.[332] Significantly the Reform

---

[326] 3 Geo. III, c. 15.
[327] *Commons Journals*, xxxvii. 391.
[328] Ibid., xxxvii. 424, 920.
[329] *Morning Herald*, 1 May 1787.
[330] *Commons Journals*, xxxviii. 233; 21 Geo. III, c. 54.
[331] Ibid., xv. 557.
[332] Ibid., xxxiv. 119, 234–5, 284, 298, 309, 311, 323, 338.

Act of 1832 disfranchised freemen who were receiving poor relief or non-resident. In this respect as in others it did not so much overturn the eighteenth-century electoral system as bring to a successful conclusion some of its most characteristic and consistent concerns.

5

Real and Personal

TRADITIONAL wisdom dictated the superiority of real over personal property, and associated civic virtue with possession of land. In certain cases Parliament persevered with its faith in this wisdom. But the results were not impressive. By statute MPs were required to be landed proprietors; in practice the law was easily evaded. Attempts to keep control of the militia in the hands of landed proprietors also proved futile; militia officers at all but the highest levels were increasingly drawn from outside and below landed society. For political and parliamentary purposes land was losing both its special identity and its unique status. The old obsession with the conflict of the landed and moneyed interests seemed anachronistic. Party politics ceased to reflect it and much rhetorical energy was devoted to the supposed harmony of hitherto irreconcilable forces. When the champions of agriculture appealed to sectional interest they were notably unsuccessful, not least in the continuing but unavailing battle of graziers against the cloth industry. Landowners shared too many preoccupations with other proprietors and entrepreneurs and were themselves too divided to present a united front. The resulting priorities were clearly reflected in fiscal policy. The land tax, which had never been a simple tax on land, became relatively insignificant, in both its yield to the Exchequer and its impact on landlords. The legislature and the Treasury turned to taxing middle-class incomes and property in their attempts to cope with the tide of wartime borrowing. From the 1740s budgetary ingenuity was directed to tapping the surplus income of ordinary householders. By the end of the century when impending bankruptcy and the threat of revolution forced Pitt to turn to a formal income tax, there was general agreement that the burden of supporting the State lay where its political control had increasingly come to rest, among middle-class Englishman.

THE PRIVILEGE OF BECOMING A LEGISLATOR

It was a common claim that Parliament, including that portion of it charged with representing the community at large, the House of Commons, was pre-eminently a legislature of landowners, whose vested interests as a class it was frequently tempted and sometimes induced to advance. In fact this was not so much an admitted vice as a boasted virtue of 'the landed gentlemen', as Hume put it, 'in whose hands our legislature is chiefly lodged'.[1] The campaign to make property-ownership a statutory requirement for a seat in the Commons had begun in earnest soon after the Restoration, was carried on with vigour after the Revolution, and finally triumphed with the election of an aggressively Tory Parliament in 1710. It was based on the familiar premiss that only men with a landed stake in their country were fit to act as its senators. Both the level and the nature of the parliamentary qualification remained matters of enduring interest and importance throughout the century, and indeed beyond.

The act passed in 1711 stipulated lands worth £600 in the case of county members, £300 in that of burgesses. This was higher than the £500 and £200, respectively, specified in the act which would have been passed earlier, in 1696, but for the veto of William III.[2] One of the first historians of the working class, Gravenor Henson, indignantly calculated that it confined 'the privilege of becoming a legislator to less than ten thousand persons'.[3] Earlier, in 1740, a total of seventeen thousand had been suggested.[4] Henson may well have been closer to the mark. In the 1780s counties of moderate size, such as Derbyshire, Leicestershire, Warwickshire, Buckinghamshire, Oxfordshire, had perhaps 150 estates each big enough to support a £300 rental. In the smaller and less gentrified Worcestershire there were barely a hundred properties of this size. Even in a county where the peculiar distribution of property favoured a broader base, such as Surrey, scarcely 200 landowners would have qualified. In a large county, for example Essex, the figure cannot have much exceeded 300. At this rate it is unlikely that the national total amounted to more than ten or twelve thousand, even allowing for those who held land in several counties.[5]

By the 1780s price inflation and the corresponding growth of rentals had substantially eroded the values of 1711. Discussion of the land qualification was directed more to adjusting for this inflation than challenging the principle involved. In 1747 there was talk of doubling the figures set in 1711.[6] In 1780, at a time of intense interest in the theory and practice of

---

[1] This occurs in some, but not all editions of Hume's essay 'On Taxes'; see D. Forbes, *Hume's Philosophical Politics* (Cambridge, 1975), p. 178.

[2] H. E. Witmer, *The Property Qualification of Members of Parliament* (New York, 1943), p. 21.

[3] S. D. Chapman, ed., *Henson's History of the Framework Knitters* (Newton Abbot, 1970), pp. 228–9.

[4] Witmer, *The Property Qualification of Members of Parliament*, p. 45.

[5] These figures are based on land tax assessments for 1784 (or nearest available year), in the appropriate county record office. They are necessarily approximate, given the difficulty of calculating the actual rental values of properties listed in the assessments. They would have to be reduced further if allowance were made for the considerable numbers of estates held by minors and women, neither class entitled to sit in the Commons, though occasionally some of the former succeeded in doing so. A small reduction should also be made for peers, but it would be offset by the provision which permitted their heirs, and incidentally the heirs to £600, to sit.

[6] *Westminster Journal*, 8 Aug. 1747.

parliamentary representation, John Strutt presented a bill raising the county qualification to £1,000 and the borough qualification to £600. Strutt was the very type of a back-bench independent. The *English Chronicle* discerned in him 'those principles that have been the hereditary characteristics of a country "squire", namely considerable ignorance, under the guidance and direction of strong prejudice, without any mixture of deliberate malignity whatever'.[7] Strutt's bill was received unenthusiastically by the Commons. Opponents seem hardly to have bothered to argue its demerits. The only speech recorded was that of James Luttrell, a member of a prominent Anglo-Irish landed family. The bill, he claimed, embodied 'a doctrine over and over again exploded in parliament, that the landed interest was the only constitutional mode of representation'. It 'affected the virtue of reformation, while it was striking at the root of the constitution'. It 'was undoubtedly a partial prosecution of professional men, annuitants upon landed security, monied men, and persons who reside in this country, and spend the whole income of their estates situated in parts of the British empire, though not in England'.[8]

Such sentiments from an Irishman were not surprising. But it would have startled landed gentlemen in an earlier age that his view went virtually unchallenged. On the other hand there was no attempt at this time to permit the alternative of a qualification by personal estate. The second bill of 1696, lost in the Lords, had initially included a qualification by virtue of personal wealth of £5,000, in effect opening the legislature to men of business.[9] But statutory acceptance of this principle had to wait until 1838. In the mean time the principle of the land qualification remained relatively uncontroversial. Even Cartwright in his tract *Take Your Choice* accepted the need for a substantial estate of £400 in the case of county representatives, and £300 at least as an alternative to personal property for borough members outside London.[10]

When first proposed the land qualification had been more divisive. Towns which feared that they would lose direct representation through members of their own community protested strongly against the early qualification bills. There was understandable suspicion, in London itself, and in provincial cities such as Exeter, Nottingham, and Plymouth, that neighbouring country gentlemen would not make an appropriate mouthpiece for their views.[11] Yet they did not maintain their protest for very long, once the act had been passed. The last general election in which the

[7] Quoted in Sir L. Namier and J. Brooke, *The History of Parliament: The House of Commons 1754–1790* (3 vols., London, 1964), iii. 495.

[8] Cobbett's *Parliamentary History*, xxi. 625–6.

[9] A. S. Turberville, *The House of Lords in the Reign of William III* (Oxford, 1913), p. 180.

[10] (London, 1776), p. 69.

[11] *Commons Journals*, xi. 590, 598, 599, 614.

issue was a real one seems to have been that of 1722. Even then it was thought prudent to emphasize the short-sightedness of the landed classes rather than their oligarchical tendencies. Opposition propaganda urged electors to require the recipients of their votes 'to restore you the Liberty your former Representatives have taken from you of choosing such as you know are Men of good Substance and Understanding Traders, or at least understand and are for promoting Trade and Navigation, and Men of unblemish'd Characters, though they may not happen to be Owners of so much Land as some of their Neighbours, who have no other Qualification for so great a Trust. The Trade of the Nation, and consequently the Landed Interest having suffer'd very much of late Years for want of proper Representation for that part of your Interest'.[12] Thereafter the matter was rarely raised.

There were a number of reasons for this, but not the least was the ease with which it proved possible to evade the terms of the act. Candidates were liable to swear an oath to their ownership of a sufficient estate. The sanction of a legal prosecution for perjury was stern enough, but subsequent enquiry was directed only to the property owned by the candidate at the time he had taken his oath. Despite the manifest fraudulence of swearing to property which had been acquired only for the duration of an election and then restored to its donor, this legalistic protection provided cover for all but the most tender of political consciences. The second Duke of Richmond thought it absurd in 1743 when a Sussex friend declined to stand for Parliament 'meerly from a nice point of honor, which was that he would not swear to a borrow'd qualification'.[13] His colleague the Duke of Bedford also considered the requirement a technicality, offering to add £200 worth to the property of his brother-in-law, Richard Lyttelton, when he stood for the borough of Brackley in 1747 'as there may be 2 or 3 litigious men in the corporation'.[14] Dukes had good reasons for promoting collusive transfers. It is no coincidence that the House of Lords did its best over a century and more to obstruct land qualifications for Parliament. The act of 1711 was itself only carried by the marginal Tory majority which procured the Peace and the Occasional Conformity Act. Even then it included special provision for the sons of peers, to ensure that the heirs to great estates would be treated as if they already possessed them, though this principle was not applied to lesser landowners.

Country gentlemen detested collusive transfers for the same reasons that peers approved of them: they promoted oligarchical control of the Lower House. The belief that the Commons had become merely a tool of

---

[12] *Flying-Post*, 20 Mar. 1722.

[13] T. J. McCann, ed., *The Correspondence of the Dukes of Richmond and Newcastle, 1724–1750* (Sussex, Rec. Soc. 73, 1984), p. 123.

[14] M. Wyndham, *Chronicles of the Eighteenth Century* (2 vols., London, 1924), i. 249–50.

aristocracy was widespread in the late eighteenth century. It could be used in opposition to reform as well as in favour of it. In 1783 one of the more intriguing arguments against proposals for a hundred new parliamentary seats, mainly representing the counties, was the prediction that they would be filled with the dependants and relations of peers. Those who advocated additional county members believed they would strengthen the landed interest. On the contrary, it was replied, it would amount to 'excluding one hundred men of the first property in the kingdom'.[15] The collusive transfer was crucial in this argument.

At the time of the general election of 1768, when much concern was expressed about the incidence of corruption, transfers were condemned as being even worse than bribery conducted by the wealthy. By definition they benefited the man of inadequate means: 'Wholly without property, what is it to him if his country is loaded with oppressions?'[16] There were serious attempts to make collusive transfers illegal. One of the elder Pitt's devices for conciliating the Tory party was the passage of an amending act in 1760. A later critic remarked that it had been 'carried by surprise at the latter end of a session to court the landed interest'.[17] In one of its main objects it was probably successful. The original legislation required a candidate to swear to his lands only when challenged by his rival in front of a returning officer. Where both candidates lacked the necessary qualification there was no means of compelling them to reveal the fact. After 1760 all MPs took the oath of qualification in Parliament itself. This was thought to have had some marginal effect.[18] But in a second respect the act of 1760 was notably deficient. The Tories sought a procedure which would expose an MP whose property fell below the minimum requirement at any point during his parliamentary career. This would have ruled out transfers for the space of a few days at election time. But as modified by its opponents the act merely specified an oath which must be taken when an MP took his seat at the commencement of a new Parliament.[19] This had no more effect than the oath taken before a returning officer, and made the act of 1760 a hollow victory for the country gentlemen.

In theory the Commons itself might have done more to enforce the land qualification. In practice it showed little enthusiasm for doing so. The instances of its intervention occurred for the most part in the decade or so

[15] *A Letter to Mr Debrett, being an Answer to 'Lucubrations during a Short Recess'* (London, 1783), p. 25.

[16] *London Magazine* (1769), 12.

[17] *Parliamentary History*, xxi. 624: James Luttrell, 23 May 1780.

[18] *Remarks upon Certain Illusory Qualifications of Members of the House of Commons* (London, 1818), p. 9.

[19] P. D. Brown and K. W. Schweitzer, eds., *The Devonshire Diary* (Camden Soc., Fourth Ser. 27, 1982), pp. 35, 37.

following the passage of the act of 1711.[20] They suggested two conclusions. One was that a petitioner in an election case would have to be confident of his own credentials before assailing a sitting MP. The law permitted the latter to question his challenger's qualification, a provision which was strengthened by standing orders of 1717 and 1735 confirming this right even where the petitioning parties were a body of electors rather than a defeated opponent.[21] The object was plainly to deter potential challengers. Secondly, it became clear how very difficult it was to prove a deficiency. In 1717 a sustained Whig campaign against the Tory MP for Great Marlow, George Bruere, provided something of a test case in this respect. Bruere had sat for Marlow since 1710 on the basis of local connections and an estate there. But the estate could not be valued at more than £290 and Bruere found himself embarrassingly underqualified as a result of the act passed by his own party in 1711. His solution was to acquire a farm valued at £44 per annum near Worth in Sussex for the suspiciously round figure of £1,000 from his friend Leonard Gale. This had every appearance of a collusive transfer. But in the Commons Bruere was able to prove his conveyance. Faced with evidence that the rent for the farm was still being paid to Gale, he insisted that this was merely an arrangement between friends; living more than fifty miles from Worth as he did, it was easier to permit its former owner to act as rent collector. Even an aggressively Whig Commons declined to press the case further against him.[22] No doubt there were not a few Whig MPs in Bruere's position.

Successful proceedings against an unqualified MP were very rare. They required elaborate detective work, irrefragable proof, and political support in the House of Commons. John Bird, MP for Coventry, fell victim to this combination in 1737, but he strenuously denied that his want of a full qualification was the real issue and the fact that he was granted an office by Walpole to permit a dignified withdrawal suggest that he may have been right.[23] Champions of the landed interest made various suggestions for improving the procedure from time to time. One of the arguments offered in favour of a general land registry was the assistance which it would provide in electoral investigations.[24] It is unlikely that the courts would have taken a sterner view. When Mansfield was trying a case in which the Marshal of the King's Bench was challenged for acting as a land tax commissioner in Surrey, he not only considered the Marshal well qualified by the profits of his office, but also pointed out that a former Master of St

---

[20] Commons Journals, xvii. 578–80; xviii. 71, 141; xix. 101–2, 130.
[21] Ibid., xxii. 355–6.
[22] Ibid., xviii. 572.
[23] A Letter from John Bird, Esq. (London, 1741).
[24] London Magazine (1737), 263.

Catharine's had sat in Parliament by virtue of his office.[25]

The consequences are well known. Though it is impossible precisely to categorize the eighteenth-century House of Commons in terms of the source of members' wealth, there is no doubt that substantial numbers of MPs should be classified as professional and businessmen rather than landowners. By the 1790s every general election was producing approximately sixty merchants, bankers, and industrialists, seventy officers in the armed forces, fifty practising lawyers, and one hundred placemen or servants of government. Authentic country gentlemen who depended almost entirely on their estates for their living were in a minority in the House of Commons as a whole, and an increasingly small one as the century advanced. The proportion of MPs who were businessmen rose from about a tenth under George II to a sixth at the end of the century.[26] By no means all these men would have failed the test of a rigorous land qualification, however. A modest stake in land was desirable for all kinds of reasons. Such were the social and political rewards of landownership, not to say its value as a safe investment, that many for whom it was not the original source of their livelihood were perfectly content to invest in it.

In one respect this was not a state of affairs to which the champions of landed qualifications could readily object. The rational case for the statute of 1711 was not that only bona fide, bone-headed country gentlemen should figure in the Commons but that everyone who presumed to legislate for his country should be compelled to take a stake in its husbandry; he was not required to have made his money in it, or even to derive his principal income from it while he held a parliamentary seat. The Commons was composed not of two classes, landowners and their adversaries, but three: landowners born and bred, men of commercial or other background who had purchased land, and adventurers who had neither land nor interest in land. There is no means of knowing exactly how many of the second category lacked a legally valid property qualification, though the likelihood is that as inflation rendered the burgess qualification of £300 increasingly insignificant a great number of them would have qualified. But it was the third category which remained deficient throughout. The adventurers merely obtained a conveyance of property for long enough to satisfy the returning officer as the law stood before 1760, or the House of Commons as it stood after 1760. In point of logic the landed squire should have objected most strenuously to this last category. But many of those in it were the younger sons of landed gentlemen or the dependants of respectable families. They shared the objectives, interests, and preoccupations of the

[25] 3 Burrow 1288–90: *Sone* v. *Ashton* (1762).

[26] See Namier and Brooke, *History of Parliament*, i, Introductory Survey iii, and R. Sedgwick, *History of Parliament: House of Commons, 1715–54* (2 vols., London, 1970), Introduction, Appendix vii.

class from which they had sprung and the class on which they depended.

It was the second category, properly qualified though its members might be, which often aroused most irritation. Moneyed men, Turkey merchants, naturalized Jewish financiers, 'sugarcanes', commissaries, 'nabobs', and contractors enraged successive generations of the country gentlemen into whose boroughs they intruded themselves; yet they were very likely to have purchased, as much for social as political reasons, a substantial country estate sufficient to qualify them as MPs. In many cases, indeed, they sought nothing more than full acceptance as squires. Certainly this was true of the Pinneys, simultaneously West Indian planters and Dorset landowners. John Frederick Pinney, MP for Bridport from 1747 to 1761, was the quintessential Tory squire. His successor John Pinney explained the family strategy in 1778: 'My greatest pride is to be considered as a private country gentleman, therefore am resolved to content myself with a little and avoid even the name of a West-Indian.'[27] The most execrated of all this class, the nabobs of the reign of George III, frequently adopted a similar attitude. Oriental adventurers such as Francis Sykes, Thomas Rumbold, and Hans Winthrop Mortimer aroused intense irritation by their electoral activities and encountered much hostility in landed society. Yet in their anxiety to join the landowners' club they were in effect accepting the values of the men who had framed the Qualification Act. The real objection to them was not that they did not have a stake in their country, but that they were not considered suitable members of the club. Tightening up the enforcement of the qualification, or raising the level of property required, would not have hurt them at all. On younger sons it would have made more impact. It would also have created a different kind of legislature. Not everybody was impressed by the credentials of the landowner as legislator. 'I thank God,' wrote Lord Lansdowne in 1792, 'the King has nobody about him cunning and wicked enough to advise him to meet the desire of reform, and compose a parliament of qualified men. I mean in the strict legal sense, for I verily believe a more corrupt, ignorant, and tyrannical assembly, would not be found upon the face of the earth.'[28]

UNQUALIFIED OFFICERS

The difficulties which attended the policing of the parliamentary property qualification did not inhibit the country gentlemen from one last attempt to give landownership a commanding place in the State. The most demanding of all qualifications were applied not to civil but to military office. As Lord North reminded the House of Commons in 1775, its own members

---

[27] R. Pares, *A West-India Fortune* (London, 1950), p. 141.

[28] *Memoirs of the Life of Sir Samuel Romilly, Written by Himself; With a Selection from his Correspondence* (3 vols., London, 1840), ii. 14.

were inferior to militia officers in this respect.[29] Received wisdom dictated that the militia should be officered by men of broad acres, veritable Cincinnati prepared to beat their ploughshares into swords. By comparison the standing army was led by mercenary men who had no interest beyond obedience to the will of their master, be he a king or a Cromwell. Practical experience of the standing army as it was in effect established by the Revolution of 1688 and the requirements of warfare made the received wisdom insecure in one respect. Officers' commissions were obtained by purchase rather than by slavish submission to royalty. In that sense the purchase price of a commission was itself a form of property qualification, guaranteeing that the army would be led by men of fortune if not gentility. On the other hand it was the most objectionable kind of property qualification: mere cash. 'It brings men of property into the service, but it deprives them of their integrity. It is too much to demand that men should pay for the privilege of serving their country at the hazard of their lives.'[30] In short it strengthened the case for a higher view of the responsibilities of militia officers, rather than weakening it.

Militia reform at the onset of the Seven Years War provided the ideal opportunity to apply such arguments. The act of 1757 incorporated Tory values at the very moment, as it transpired, that the old Tory party was about to lose its distinctive identity. But it was the first inheritance of an ideologically confused regime as much as the last legacy of the old Tory party, being strongly supported by the elder Pitt and most ardently championed by George Townshend, a choleric Whig whose service in the Hanoverian standing army had given him a jaundiced view of the men who commanded it. More conventional Whigs, Newcastle, Hardwicke, and Devonshire, disliked it. They did their best to prevent its implementation in 1756–7 and would have put a period to its existence at the end of the Seven Years War but for George III.[31]

A property qualification in land was one of the central principles of the Militia Act. It would have been higher but for the opposition of the Lord Chancellor, Lord Hardwicke, to the unsuccessful Militia Bill of 1756.[32] For deputy-lieutenants, charged with raising the militia, and for colonels, it was set at £400 per annum, with a reduction to £300 for small counties and towns with county status, and £200 in the case of the Isle of Ely. A £400 qualification was higher than that for an MP, higher, too, than the

[29] *London Chronicle*, 18 Nov. 1775.

[30] Charles Michell, *Principles of Legislation* (London, 1796), p. 464. Attempts by the Crown to reduce the proprietary rights and entrepreneurial activities of officers are examined by A. J. Guy, *Oeconomy and Discipline: Officership and Administration in the British Army 1714–63* (Manchester, 1985).

[31] *The Devonshire Diary*, pp. 39–41, 54–6, 61, 58.

[32] J. R. Western, *The English Militia in the Eighteenth Century: The Story of a Political Issue 1660–1802* (London, 1965), pp. 135–6.

£300 which Tories thought desirable for magistrates. In a midland county
of average size it would have defined the authentic county community
of substantial gentry and magnates, a handful of landed families whose
representatives could comfortably be assembled in one room. Even so it was
at the lower levels that the qualifications were found to be too demanding. In
an ordinary English county lieutenant-colonels and majors needed £300,
captains £200, lieutenants £100, and ensigns £50. Elaborate arrangements
were made to encourage the service of young men as subalterns but only
where they had roots in the landowning class. Thus a captain might be
either the owner of £200 or the heir to an estate of £400, or the younger
son of a landowner worth £600. These nice gradations, with further
variations for the smaller counties, for Ely, and for the towns with county
status, were calculated to balance the requirements of the service with the
necessity to preserve the respectability and gentility of the officer class. Any
form of land tenure which implied an enduring interest was comprehended,
including not only copyholds and customary tenures, but leases for lives.
Rigorously excluded were tenancies at will, and more particularly the
qualifications by means of personal estate which were becoming commonplace for most purposes of 'improving' legislation. An exception was
made for boroughs which had their own lieutenancies. There a personal
qualification ranging from £5,000 for a field officer to £400 for an ensign
recognized the absurdity of requiring large landed estates in urban districts.[33]

The deficiencies of this system of qualifications were soon recognized.
The ensign's qualification was lowered to £20 in 1762. Seven years later
a general review took place. For colonels and lieutenant-colonels, the
qualification was actually increased, to the £1,000 and £600 respectively
envisaged in 1756. But colonelcies were few in number, and prized for
their political influence and prestige. Perhaps it was reflection on the case
of John Wilkes, who had contrived to achieve a colonelcy under the old
qualification, and had to be dismissed for his temerity in libelling the
Crown, which emboldened the country gentlemen to insist on a still
more restrictive qualification. Wilkes was unimpressed. In old age he was
regularly to be seen walking from his home in Kensington to the City,
dressed in scarlet and buff, a cocked hat, and military boots.[34] Paradoxically
the prestige of a colonelcy made it a particular target for men of newly
acquired opulence. Denis O'Kelly, who made his fortune by purchasing
the horse Eclipse from the Duke of Cumberland, and putting it out to
stud, was inordinately proud of his senior office in the Middlesex militia.

---

[33] Ibid. 340.
[34] J. H. Leigh Hunt, *The Old Court Suburb; Or, Memorials of Kensington Regal, Critical, and Anecdotical* (2 vols., London, 1902), i. 25.

Fortunately for defenders of the traditional character of the militia it was possible to be dismissive about the militia of the metropolitan county, as it was about its magistracy. When Kelly died in 1787 his obituarist witheringly observed that 'no such appointment can ever disgrace the county more'.[35]

The enhanced requirements of colonels were in any case exceptional. For junior officers, a different approach was adopted. The lieutenant's qualification was lowered to £50. More importantly, both lieutenants and ensigns were permitted to qualify with personal estate, held either by themselves or their fathers. The level set was not demanding, and when the ultimate test was applied in the War of American Independence, the results proved embarrassing. In 1779 Edmund Burke remarked on the revival of 'the old Arguments of unqualified Officers in the Present Militia which are notorious'.[36] Lord Rochford was reduced to advertising commissions in the West Essex militia in the newspapers.[37] Even in peacetime it was regretted that, for the gentry, militia service 'restrains their amusements, or disturbs their indolence, and it offers no object to their ambition or vanity'.[38] In wartime the threat of permanent embodiment had a still more depressing influence. When she saw the 'amazing fatigue' of an officer's life at first hand in 1779 Fanny Burney was astonished that anyone would serve 'without compulsion of interest to spur them'.[39] One of the officers of the Huntingdonshire militia, a future Irish patriot, Archibald Rowan Hamilton, recorded how when the American war broke out, the local lords retired. There had been five peers serving at its commencement; by 1779 only the colonel and lieutenant-colonel were noblemen. Hamilton himself was promoted to the command of a company, but resigned because he lacked the landed qualification in the county requisite for a captain.[40]

Hamilton's judgement was matched by the experience of other counties. In neighbouring Cambridgeshire the want of quality was notorious both among junior and senior officers.[41] But gentry were always thin on the ground in Cambridgeshire, and the difficulty it suffered in this respect was hardly surprising. More telling was the example of nearby Buckinghamshire. There the militia offered a decidedly motley appearance, at any rate below the highest ranks. The colonel, Coulson Skottowe, held land in several counties, and his major, Thomas Hampden, was both an MP and

---

[35] *Whitehall Evening-Post*, 3 Jan. 1788.

[36] Western, *The English Militia in the Eighteenth Century*, pp. 340, 309 ff.; J. A. Woods, ed., *The Correspondence of Edmund Burke*, vol. iv: *1778–82* (Cambridge, 1963), p. 109.

[37] D. M. Little and G. M. Kahrl, eds., *The Letters of David Garrick* (3 vols., London, 1963), iii. 1221.

[38] Michell, *Principles of Legislation*, p. 447.

[39] C. Barrett, ed., *Diary and Letters of Madame D'Arblay* (4 vols., London, 1876), i. 144.

[40] *Autobiography of Archibald Hamilton Rowan, Esq.* (Dublin, 1840), pp. 31, 79.

[41] Western, *The English Militia in the Eighteenth Century*, pp. 312–17.

a JP as well as scion of a famous family. But the lieutenant-colonel, Lovel Badcock, represented recent wealth. He did not serve as sheriff, the first requirement of a rising county family, until 1795, and the estate for which he qualified, at Bledlow, had been purchased by his father only in 1749. Of the six captains one, Edmund Waller of Beaconsfield, bore a well-known county name. The others were at best newcomers, like John Osborn, whose father had purchased a small estate at Turville in 1753 and who had served as sheriff in 1759, and Henry Tompkins, a successful Aylesbury lawyer who purchased a small property at Weston Turville in 1764. Tompkins was easily the senior but had long resisted promotion to major. As he had explained to Lord le Despenser, the Lord-Lieutenant in 1766, he lacked the landed qualification. 'Besides a man that cannot afford to keep either a horse or servant will cut a most despicable appearance in the field as Major.' In fact by 1781 Tompkins was either propertied enough or the county desperate enough to make his elevation practicable. But his plight exemplified the difficulty of recruiting reliable officers who were also county gentry. Below the level of captain full advantage had to be taken of the provision of 1769 which permitted qualifications by personal estate. Of the fifteen junior officers, one, Matthew Knapp, was head of a wealthy county family which had established itself at Shenley at the end of the seventeenth century. Another, Matthew Hensbrugh of Hambledon, came of a line of minor squires who had produced one JP, a Whig hack, in the course of the eighteenth century. Two others were thought worthy of inclusion in the land tax commission, the lowest common denominator of county life. The remainder were nonentities.[42]

Buckinghamshire seems to have been typical. In Derbyshire only three of the hundred wealthiest landed families were represented in the officer class in 1779, one of them the wealthiest of all, the Duke of Devonshire, the others being Tristram Revell and Thomas Leacroft, whose estates were relatively small. Revell was induced to serve on the grounds of his experience as a former army officer; his health was so poor he had difficulty taking the salute at Coxheath in 1778.[43] In Oxfordshire the captains and their superiors were respectable enough, but of the subalterns only two or three aspired to modest squirearchical status. The same was true in Leicestershire, Warwickshire, Worcestershire, Surrey, and for the most part in Essex. There, the exception proved the rule. A small group of subalterns with real property, albeit of modest affluence, were prominent

---

[42] The names of militia officers in 1779 are taken from *A List of the Officers of the Militia of England and Wales* (London, 1779), their credentials in the county from the sources listed below, Chapter 6, n. 137; also Bodleian Library, Dashwood MSS, 8–1/11: 15 Feb. 1766.

[43] Earl of Bessborough, *Georgiana: Extracts from the Correspondence of Georgiana, Duchess of Devonshire* (London, 1955), p. 36.

in the mess of the East Essex battalion.[44] But significantly they were almost all resident in Colchester, and formed a cohesive urban interest rather than a rural squirearchy. The overwhelming impression is that the formula reluctantly accepted in 1769 was a judicious recognition of realities. According to the Earl of Radnor in 1780 Lords-Lieutenant had themselves long since abandoned the attempt to enforce property qualifications.[45] Matters certainly did not improve during the next great war, in the 1790s. In 1796, the position was summed up in terms which would have been equally true at any time since the Seven Years War. Field officers were sometimes men of weight, but 'often belong to the lowest class of independent gentry'. Captains were 'men of small fortunes, or relations and dependents of the colonel'. Subalterns were 'sons of farmers and tradesmen, who are tempted by a red coat, ... and apparent equality with gentlemen'.[46]

Where the original militia qualifications survive they reinforce scepticism about the landed worth of the reformed militia.[47] In Dorset, as elsewhere, the crucial test concerned captains, for whom Parliament was reluctant to abandon the landed requirement. At Blandford the young John Bastard, member of a family which included a reputable architect but lacked genteel status, had no difficulty certifying that he owned £50 of personal estate needed to become a lieutenant in 1776, but was hard put to it to produce evidence of £200 worth of land when he was promoted to the rank of captain in 1783. He listed ten separate properties, all houses or tenements, some held on leasehold tenure, and most plainly provided for the purpose by his relations. In the North Riding of Yorkshire there was also difficulty in finding captains of suitable standing. John Burton of Ripon was accounted an acquisition in 1778 because he had formerly served as a lieutenant in the 7th Dragoons. He registered £84 of landed income in the West Riding, £120 in the North. But the land tax assessments reveal that the latter was actually owned by George Allanson, Esq. It had evidently been conveyed to Burton for the purpose of qualifying, in the same way that some MPs were fraudulently qualified. J. W. Wardell's qualification in 1793 may not have been fraudulent, but it was not very impressive. Wardell proudly stated that 'My Estate which gives me the Qualification' exceeded the sum required. But in his signed certificate the word 'My' is deleted in his own hand and 'The' substituted. No doubt it was embarrassing for a captain in the militia to have to admit that the land which qualified him was in fact the only land he possessed. The qualification

---

[44] The militia officers are identified in *A List of the Officers of the Militia of England and Wales*; their property is ascertained from the land tax assessments in the respective county record offices.

[45] *Parliamentary Register* (1802 edn.), xiv. 192: 1 Mar. 1780.

[46] Michell, *Principles of Legislation*, pp. 447-8.

[47] The following examples are drawn from Dorset RO, QDA (M), and North Yorkshire RO, QDA (M).

certificates also reveal that officers took full advantage of the lowest hurdles presented by the legislation. J. C. Foulis, who qualified as a captain in 1789, was the younger son of a deceased baronet. The principle that the heir to property should be granted the privileges of a proprietor was well established. But conceding the principle in the case of a younger son who had no prospect of inheriting, and in this instance was better described as a younger brother, pushed the doctrine of the primacy of land to its limits. The assumption was that it was not necessary to own property, merely to be brought up in close contact with those who did. It is difficult to see that such a qualification was superior to the personal estate required of the subalterns. This, too, meant little in real terms. In 1778 John Haslop of Richmond swore to 'such an Estate in Money as qualifies me to Act as a Lieutenant'. Qualification by money was the nightmare of the political Cassandras of the early eighteenth century. In the late eighteenth century it was sanctified by statute.

In 1779 much effort was devoted to making the militia the focus of national pride. The great encampments set up to meet the threat of invasion, particularly those at Warley and Coxheath, were the subject of the most intense interest. But as with so many aspects of provincial life, there was a theatrical flavour to these activities. Paintings in militia uniform, and more particularly those of ladies wearing their husbands' regimental colours, became fashionable. The noblemen, gentry, and their ladies who paraded ostentatiously at the camps treated them much as they did county races and assemblies, with the advantage that they mustered numbers more reminiscent of the London season than a merely county affair. The landed friends of militia officers, visiting them to dine and dance, seem to have been unembarrassed by their own want of martial spirit. Those not involved in the ritual and festivities of militia life were less than impressed by it. In peacetime, averting a visit by the militia was a favour comparable to fending off a garrison of regular troops. A prebendary of Winchester, John Butler, pleaded on behalf of Farnham in 1766 that the arrival of the Surrey militia would be considered by the hop merchants of the town a uniquely horrible plague: 'the most adverse Weather could not be a greater Calamity to us'.[48] Even in war there were problems. In 1759 at the height of an invasion scare, the colonel of the Surrey militia found controlling the conduct of his men sent to stations on the Thames estuary his principal anxiety.[49] In a similar exigency twenty years later the Bluestocking Elizabeth Carter was dismayed by the news that the Essex militia were to be quartered at Dover and Deal. 'I think that we shall find them but troublesome guests, but it is better to be troubled with our own people, than with the French. Though

[48] Surrey RO (Guildford), Butler to Onslow 28 Aug. 1766.
[49] R. Michell, *The Carews of Beddington* (Sutton, 1981).

our own, to say truth, are bad enough in all reason.'[50] Her contemporary William Cowper, albeit from an Evangelical perspective, had grave doubts about the moral effects of the militia, which he revealed publicly in *The Task*.[51]

Complaints of this kind were to some extent based on observation of the ordinary militiamen, most of whom seemed far below the model yeomen beloved of militia enthusiasts. But they also reflected the composition of the officer class. Part of the cherished myth of a militia was the integrity associated with the leadership of landed men. The reality seemed to be different. A serious-minded young man like the diarist John Dawson, who served in the Northumberland militia during the Seven Years War, was shocked by the immoral company which he had to keep.[52] The contamination brought by the militia was more than moral. Colonels and Lords-Lieutenant had a low opinion of their own officers. At Berwick in 1783 it was remarked that Lord Darlington, commandant of the Durham militia, 'show'd his own Contempt and the Low Origin of his Officers by the Ball Rooms in which he entertain'd Company being nothing better than the Landing Places of the Barrack Staircase'.[53] There was a price to be paid for this inferiority. In Norfolk landowners were dismayed by the irresponsible conduct of the visiting officers, arriving 'with Dogs etc of all sorts as if the Manors were their own'.[54] In this as in other respects, the militia seemed to resemble the regulars. In Wiltshire in 1779 the Earl of Pembroke gave authority for the cavalry encamped on Salisbury Plain to hunt ten of his manors. Instead they 'took the liberty to ride over, and destroy the Game upon every Manor they could force themselves into'.[55] If junior officers could not be trusted to respect game rights, how could they be fit to defend their country?

The militia retained a certain cachet, evoking images which exerted a powerful pull on public allegiance. But some cherished assumptions were being challenged. Soame Jenyns described the 'false principles' on which the militia was based—'that those who are possessed of most property will fight best in its defence'. He claimed 'all poor countries, that is those who have the least property, have always been the most valiant, and most successful in war; and, in rich countries, property has been ever best defended by those who have none'.[56] By the late eighteenth century high

---

[50] *A Series of Letters between Mrs Elizabeth Carter and Miss Catherine Talbot, from the Year 1741 to 1770*, ed. M. Pennington (4 vols., London, 1809), iv. 239.

[51] H. S. Milford, ed., *Cowper: Poetical Works* (4th edn., London, 1967), p. 195.

[52] 'North Country Diaries', *Surtees Soc.* 124 (1914), 255.

[53] Gloucestershire RO, D2227/30: Journal of Revd Samuel Viner.

[54] Sir J. Fortescue, ed., *Correspondence of George III* (6 vols., 1927–8), iv. 191.

[55] Lord Herbert, ed., *The Pembroke Papers (1734–1780): Letters and Diaries of Henry, Tenth Earl of Pembroke and His Circle* (London, 1939, reissued 1942), p. 354.

[56] C. N. Cole, ed., *The Works of Soame Jenyns* (4 vols., London, 1970), ii. 226.

priority was being attached to enlisting men of modest, commercial property in the defence of their country. This assumed particular importance in London where the militia had lapsed into a state of embarrassing decrepitude; particularly after the Gordon Riots in 1780 there was much interest in devising means to galvanize the civic spirit and martial ardour of Londoners. Volunteering in the following decade invoked a similar spirit. The advertisers for the Artillery Company in 1794 emphasized that 'the attendance required for discipline will be found perfectly compatible with the avocations of men of business'.[57] City clerks served in it with an eye on the social, sexual, and commercial advantages which it bestowed. 'Who knows', asked one such in 1797, 'what profit may arise from wearing a red coat?'[58]

Conditions in the metropolis had always been exceptional. Nobody supposed that it was possible to appeal to the landed mentality which applied in the counties. Even so, traditionally the emphasis had been on substantial property. In this respect the change wrought in the late eighteenth century was considerable. The playwright Benjamin Victor recalled having gone to great lengths to qualify himself for service in 1745. To Lord Perceval he had written 'As having been in business might be an objection to the rank of gentlemen in commission, I have the pleasure of telling your lordship, that I gave it up three weeks ago, and that the remaining stock is to be sold off before the 18th of December next, when my house will be restored to its first form, though it will remain mine these three years. As I was not bred to business, this resignation is no small pleasure to me.'[59] By the time that Victor was writing, in 1776, it would have seemed superfluous to dissociate oneself from trade in order to qualify for a junior commission.

In the counties the perceived decline in the standing of the militia was irreversible. The rage for volunteering in the 1790s, under the pressure of revolutionary war abroad and a revolutionary threat at home, made it clearer than ever. The legislation of 1794 which provided a statutory basis for local defence forces made no mention of qualifications. That of 1798 did, but only in the form of £50 in land or £1,000 in personalty for commanders of the small, armed associations which proliferated under the threat of invasion. The preservation of property was often avowed as the principal object of the volunteers, but the social status of volunteers depended much on place and circumstance.[60] In many rural areas at least, it sometimes

---

[57] *An Address to the Inhabitants of London from the Court of Assistants of the Hon. Artillery Company (1794)*, p.16.

[58] A. W. Rumney, ed., *From the Old South-Sea House Being Thomas Rumney's Letter Book 1796–1798* (London, 1914), p. 129.

[59] *Original Letters, Dramatic Pieces, and Poems* (3 vols., London, 1776), i. 114.

[60] M. Montgomery-Campbell, ed., *Records of Stirring Times* (London, 1908), pp. 307–8; see A. Gee, 'The British Volunteer Movement 1793–1807' (Oxford Univ. D.Phil. thesis, 1989), ch. 3.

enlisted the enthusiastic support of the gentry. In the East Midlands where the yeomanry made its first appearance the county communities gave strong support. In Sussex volunteering was described as 'a very harmless amusement for the Country Gentlemen'.[61] In Wiltshire the names to be found in the yeomanry in 1797 compared very favourably with those present in the militia twenty years before. It was a common complaint that in the militia officers were the creatures of the noblemen who frequently commanded regiments. The country gentlemen of Wiltshire were celebrated for their independence. Their patriotic instincts were not in doubt, but they were not likely to be enlisted if a Herbert of Wilton was placed at their head.[62] Senior officers were well aware of the resulting discrepancies. In 1798 the Duke of Gloucester strongly criticized militia officers, compared with the yeomanry.[63] Not least they seemed all too conscious of their own incapacity; such a want of confidence would be catastrophic in battle. This was not merely the perception of a prince and a general. At the same time a Staffordshire squire lamented that it was 'not a Situation for *a Gentleman now* to remain in a Militia Corps'.[64]

One of the marked features of the volunteering movement was a paradoxically democratic tendency, which made those who served equals in a cause rather than slaves to rank and hierarchy. To be a trooper in the yeomanry might be more prestigious than to be an officer in the militia. This logic was as much a feature of middle-class attitudes as of genteel snobbery, and helped mobilize the petty bourgeoisie of town and country alike.[65] It was not new. When volunteers had called for at the time of the Forty-Five, independent tradesmen and craftsmen were reluctant to serve in the same units as their social inferiors, who were induced to volunteer by bounties and the prospect of pay. Acrimonious disputes resulted, sometimes with politically divisive consequences, as at Exeter.[66] But when the principle of volunteering was fully extended in the 1790s the influence of this mentality became much more obvious. In a sense it would have been reassuring to traditional champions of the militia, for it revealed the readiness of ordinary men of property to defend their heritage against assault from without and subversion within. But it had nothing to do with

    [61] A. Hudson, 'Volunteer Soldiers in Sussex during the Revolutionary and Napoleonic Wars, 1793–1815', *Sussex Arch. Colls.* 122 (1984), 168.

    [62] *A List of the Wiltshire Regiment of Yeomanry Cavalry* (Salisbury, 1799); *A List of the Officers of the Militia of England and Wales*, p. 26.

    [63] *The Windham Papers* (2 vols., London, 1913), ii. 81–2.

    [64] Castalia Countess Granville, ed., *Lord Granville Leveson Gower (First Earl Granville) Private Correspondence 1781 to 1821* (2 vols., London, 1916), i. 269.

    [65] J. E. Cookson, 'Patriotism and Social Structure: the Ely Volunteers, 1798–1808', unpublished paper; Gee, 'The British Volunteer Movement', ch. 6.

    [66] *The Disbanded Volunteers Appeal to Their Fellow Citizens* (Exeter, 1746).

property qualifications in a formal sense and not very much to do with land.

A NATURAL ANTIPATHY

The last battle to preserve landed qualifications was virtually lost before it was begun. But there were other battle grounds on which beleaguered defenders of land might hope to regroup their forces. One of the preoccupations that the late eighteenth century inherited was the supposed conflict between land and its meretricious rival the moneyed interest. The bitterness with which this battle had been waged in the decades immediately following the Revolution of 1688 was long remembered. In retrospect it is easy to see that the 1690s and 1700s were somewhat untypical in this respect, producing conditions which were bound to exaggerate a perceived conflict of interest. High wartime taxation, much of it levied on income from land, served to heighten the resentment of country gentlemen against urban, commercial interests which seemed to profit by war and the demands which it made without sharing the burdens which it brought. A continuing agrarian depression kept rents low at a time when consumer spending was rising and the life-style expected of genteel families becoming ever more expensive. The gentry's retreat from Puritanism intensified its resentment of a mercantile and money-making class which seemed to include a high proportion of Dissenters and foreign immigrants within its ranks. The resulting frustration spilled over in the Tory party's victory of 1710 and the subsequent pressure for measures which would preserve the landed gentleman against those who seemed to threaten his ancient hegemony; financial speculators and religious dissenters.

It is also easy to grasp with the advantage of hindsight that there was much illusion, some hypocrisy, and not a little self-serving in the way the defence of the landed interest was employed for political purposes. The impression was given that any income which did not derive from land was suspect and that only the bona fide country squire dependent on his rents was to be trusted with a say in his nation's affairs. But the politicians who exploited this mentality, including Bolingbroke, its most articulate mouthpiece, knew well that the argument against the moneyed interest applied only to a small number of speculators. He also knew that the honest trade which even landed men lauded as one of the foundations of England's greatness was so enmeshed in the structure of credit and capital that it was impossible to identify legitimate targets in a way which would not have endangered more important objectives. Above all he knew that the simplistic vision of Tory squires was highly impracticable.

No Tory minister with an eye to the future could neglect the interests of commerce and turn the clock back to some imagined age of bucolic bliss.

Much that was done by the Oxford ministry of 1710–14 was plainly designed to appease the anger of its squirearchical supporters. The Land Qualification Act embodied the country gentleman's vision of legislative life. Peace offered the still more welcome prospect of heavily reducing the hated land tax. The Occasional Conformity and Schism Acts directed the coercive power of the State where Tories believed the root of the contemporary evil lay, among men who were as subversive in their religious views as they were in their commercial practices and political activities. But there were limits to humouring back-bench Tory susceptibilities, and further concessions to the anti-commercial mentality would have undermined the propertied consensus on which all governments ultimately depended. In this as in other respects the death of Queen Anne and the succession crisis of 1714–15 rescued leading Tories from a considerable dilemma, albeit at the cost of landing them in an even worse plight, eventually consigning them to the political wilderness. It was left to their enemies to make the transition to a politics which throve on the management rather than the entrenchment of interests.

By the middle of the century the common view was that the awesome clashing of interests which had marked the years following the Revolution was a thing of the past. The great wars of 1739–48, 1756–63, and 1775–83 occasionally caught echoes of the old debate, but they never awakened comparable passions. What had happened to quiet, if not to lay the ghosts of Sir Roger de Coverley and Sir Andrew Freeport?

Probably the most important achievement was to separate the sensibilities of the landowner from party politics. This was not easily accomplished. The psychological importance of the landed mentality remained considerable. Opportunities frequently presented themselves for reviving its appeal, and commercial development put stresses on the susceptibilities of country gentlemen which made it easy to reactivate old prejudices. In this sense the early years of Whig rule were crucial, contributing as they did to an easing of previous tensions. They are, of course, closely associated with the supremacy of Robert Walpole. Walpole was unusual in his generation for his determination to show that land was safe with the Whig party, and he drew handsome political dividends from it. His constant emphasis on the desirability of keeping the land tax down caused considerable disarray among his opponents. The *Craftsman* found itself having to argue that a low land tax was not necessarily in the interest of landowners. Still more remarkably, the leaders of the Tory party were driven to stating their preference for a high land tax over the indirect taxes which Walpole preferred.[67] Such contentions were not altogether

---

[67] *Craftsman*, 4 Aug. 1733; *Parliamentary History*, viii. 1211–12: Sir William Wyndham, 23 Feb. 1733.

1 (*a*) The Liberty of the Subject

1 (*b*) Old England, Great Britain

The eighteenth century was marked by widespread fears that the proud inheritance of the freeborn Englishman was being prostituted. Above, his alleged enslavement by government; below, the loss of his independence as an elector.

Special Pleaders in the Court of Requests.

2 (*a*) Special Pleaders in the Court of Requests

Not everyone was impressed by the new forms of justice on offer in the eighteenth century. Above, a court of conscience in session; right, a clerical magistrate.

THE COUNTRY JUSTICE.

2 (*b*) The Country Justice

3 The Inside of a Newly Reformed Workhouse with all Abuses Removed

Alleged 'improvement' of local institutions was greeted with some scepticism; the new-style workhouse is pictured here.

4 (a) Tax on Receipts

4 (b) The Income Tax

All parties found themselves blamed for taxing the middle class. Here both the Fox-North Coalition
and the younger Pitt are pilloried.

5 (*a*) Public Influence or a Scramble for Coronets

5 (*b*) The New Peerage

It was a common claim in the 1780s that the peerage was losing its dignity and status. These cartoons display the causes and consequences of Pitt's ennoblements.

6 (a) The Couch of Adultery

5 (b) The Two Patriotic Duchesses

Aristocratic women were increasingly exposed to public scrutiny. Left, the adultress Lady Grosvenor with her royal lover the Duke of Cumberland in 1770; right, the Duchesses of Devonshire and Portland canvassing for Fox at the Westminster election of 1784.

" —— off, off, ye lendings."

The NOBLE SANS-CULOTTE — *Lord Stanhope*

Pub.d May 3 1794. by H. Humphry. N.º 18 Old Bond Street.

7 The Noble Sans Culotte

The French Revolution naturally stimulated interest in aristocratic radicalism in England. Here the reforming peer Lord Stanhope is derided for his egalitarian views.

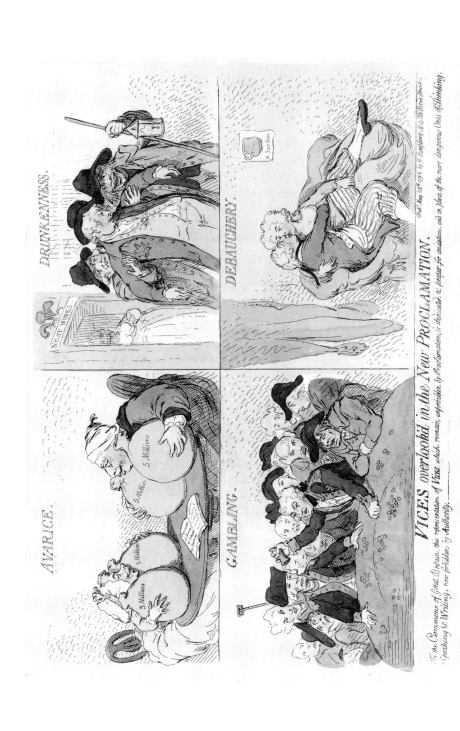

8 Vices overlooked in the New Proclamation

The Revolution also provoked criticism of the government's identification with aristocratic values; the court, appealing for support against sedition and revolution, is here reminded of the threat to public virtue posed by upper-class vice.

incompatible with Tory tradition. There was a high paternalist vein of argument which stressed the responsibility of the landowner to his country and his inferiors, if necessary at the expense of his own fortune. But while this position preserved the ideological purity of the Tory party it gravely threatened the coherence of the interests which traditionally underpinned it.

There remained an obvious association between the Tory party and land. As the Tory party lost its court, careerist wing and became the preserve of country gentlemen, dominated by county MPs and supported most consistently by rural voters, this process of identification sometimes seemed to gather force. Notwithstanding Whig fiscal policy, contemporaries continued to think of the Hanoverian Tory party as more peculiarly the guardian of the landed interest. Even so, changing conditions made caution necessary in this respect. Not all Tories were hidebound fox-hunters, nor did all Tory MPs sit for county constituencies or market towns. In some places populism and parliamentary opposition came together to produce a highly commercial Toryism which had its roots in the resentment of the urban middle and lower class.[68] Whether this was authentic Toryism is a moot point. The most prominent new Tory of the 1750s, William Beckford, for all his Wiltshire lands, was emphatically not a mere country squire, and his concerns, imperial and commercial as they were, might have been thought more appropriate for a Sir Andrew Freeport than a Sir Roger de Coverly. The very use of the term Tory by men like Beckford diluted its Augustan connotation with the countryside.

By the 1750s the Tory party was on the point of disintegrating, and the possibility that party politics might reflect the peculiar anxieties of landowners fast disappearing. But by then even the country gentlemen were finding it difficult to pose as the defenders of an ancient inheritance. The requirements of agrarian improvement put a strain on their credentials as friends of the poor and defenders of the proprietor. Tory landowners were not noticeably less ready than Whigs to take advantage of parliamentary enclosure procedures. Lord Denbigh, for instance, was the very type of the mid-eighteenth-century Tory, a former Jacobite and a hard drinking, hard swearing, fox-hunting booby at the court of George III. He was also an enthusiast for commercial farming and relished the title of improver.[69] If the testimony of tourists is to be accepted, it is possible that some of the Welsh Tory gentry, 'undisturbed with the spirit of enterprise and ambition', lagged behind their English brethren in this respect.[70] But this probably had less to do with their innate conservatism than with the

[68] L. Colley, 'Eighteenth-Century Radicalism before Wilkes', *Trans. Roy. Hist. Soc.*, 5th ser. 31 (1981), 5 ff.

[69] Warwickshire RO, Denbigh MSS, Letterbook, Denbigh to Aylesford, 9 Dec. 1767.

[70] Joseph Cradock, *Letters from Snowdon* (London, 1770), pp. 97–100.

restricted scope for profitable investment in North Wales.

The sixties and seventies were marked by growing anger at the cynicism and uncaringness which seemed to mark the conduct of landlords and their tenants. If there had been any correlation with the politics of those involved it is inconceivable that it would not have been seized upon. In fact the impression gained was that the Jacobite squirearchy had thrown in their lot with their antagonists once they were granted a place in local administration and a share of parliamentary patronage. Lord Shelburne commented bitterly on the 'alienation of all the landed Interest from the ancient Plan of Freedom; Every landed Man setting up a little Tyranny, and, armed with Magistracy, and oppressive Laws, spreading a Waste of Spirit and creating an intellectual Darkness around him. Thus employed the country gentlemen were willing, instead of controlling the abuse of Power, to take their Choice with that Government under which their own peculiar Tyrannies were maintained.'[71]

Agricultural improvement was only one example of developments which could complicate the old, simple assumptions about the line of demarcation between land and commerce. The intermingling of the supposedly distinct worlds of finance, trade, and agriculture did much to promote the sense of a broad commercial consensus in the age of Walpole and Pelham. Partly this was a matter of commonplace observation and commonsensical reflection on economic trends. The readiness of landowners to invest in paper securities, the anxiety of merchants to acquire a share in the land market, the rapid growth of credit and assurance facilities for all sections of propertied society, made traditional notions of the specialized nature of commercial enterprise manifestly untenable. Consequent blurring of ideological edges was demonstrated in many of the political debates of the period, especially where the fiscal policies of the State were concerned. The excise crisis of 1733 gave rise to elaborate calculations concerning the relative burdens of the tradesman, the manufacturer, and the landowner. Walpole appealed simultaneously to the fair trader and the country gentleman. So did his enemies. It was they who won, but in no sense was it a victory for a class or an interest-group.[72] Four years later, in 1737, Sir John Barnard's proposal to reduce the interest rate on the National Debt could be portrayed as relief for long-suffering landowners at the expense of pampered stockholders. But the truth was more complicated. Opponents of the measure insisted that many of those who had invested in the Debt were landowners. Would they and their sons and daughters, whose settlements, incomes, and

---

[71] W. L. Clements Library, Shelburne MSS, 165: 221.

[72] P. Langford, *The Excise Crisis: Society and Politics in the Age of Walpole* (Oxford, 1975), pp. 156 ff.; W. J. Hausman and J. L. Neufeld, 'Excise Anatomised: the Political Economy of Walpole's 1733 Tax Scheme', *Jnl. Econ. Hist.* 10 (1981), 131–44, argue, perversely in view of the parliamentary and electoral evidence, that the landed gentry supported the excise.

reversions often consisted of government stock, benefit more by a reduction of taxation or by maintaining interest rates? Walpole shrewdly exploited this uncertainty, arguing that Barnard's proposal would endanger the dynastic strategy of landed families, for whom the National Debt had become an invaluable prop. Reducing the official interest rate must inevitably lower rates generally. The younger children of the gentry, perhaps the principal beneficiaries of a secure banking and credit system, would need considerably larger cash settlements to maintain their income. The consequence would be still higher mortgages for their parents, and a greater burden on the land.[73]

The irony of such debates in this era was perhaps best exemplified in the controversy provoked by Walpole's notorious raid on the Sinking Fund in 1733. His first biographer presented this as a victory for a patriotic consensus over faction. 'The influence of the minister, aided by the co-operation of the landed, monied, and popular interests, triumphed over opposition.'[74] Yet the institution of the Fund had traditionally been represented as a blow struck on behalf of the landed interest against the speculators. Walpole himself had introduced the original legislation in 1717, on the very day of his resignation in protest at the conduct of affairs at George I's court. In a phrase often recalled he observed on that occasion that he brought in the bill not as a minister but as a country gentleman. His old enemy Shippen relished the opportunity to point out his inconsistency in 1733. It must pain many, he reflected, to 'see a minister of state endeavour to tear down any monument, that was erected by a country-gentleman'.[75] Personalities aside, debates of this kind confirmed what most contemporaries understood well, that it was no longer rational to assume hard lines of distinction between the diverse enterprises of Hanoverian England.

The South Sea Bubble had something to do with changing perceptions of the importance of the moneyed interest. In certain respects it seemed positively to have heightened contemporary anxiety on this score. Not only was it followed by escape from justice for men whose guilt was obvious, it penalized many innocent landholders who had borrowed to invest in stock. But these appearances were rather misleading. Walpole certainly succeeded in screening some highly placed criminals at court and in Parliament. But sufficient of the guilty suffered to gratify the demand for scapegoats. Men like Sir Theodore Janssen were prime examples of the moneyed interest. They were largely new men, and not a few of foreign extraction. Their fortunes had been made as a direct result of those novel developments

---

[73] *London Magazine* (1736), 527.

[74] W. Coxe, *Memoirs of the Life and Administration of Sir Robert Walpole, Earl of Orford* (3 vols., London, 1798), i. 368–9.

[75] *Parliamentary History*, vii. 442–3; viii. 1219.

which were thought to have disfigured post-Revolution society. Janssen was deprived of four-fifths of the estate which he had accumulated before the South Sea scheme, expelled from Parliament, and disqualified from holding public office, though nothing corrupt was proved against him. Moreover, the fact that some landed men suffered along with the Directors of the South Sea Company did not necessarily inhibit the process of healing. Landowners who had succumbed to the attractions of stock were in no position to appeal to the superior virtue of land; those who had not could smugly reflect that virtue was its own reward and speculating vice an ultimately unprofitable investment.

There was also the unceasing propaganda to the effect that the overall interests of land and trade were indeed identical. It was hardly a new contention, but the climate of opinion in which it was made proved increasingly favourable as the century wore on. Defoe's stridency and repetitiveness on the point—'Multitudes of People make Trade, Trade makes Wealth, wealth builds Cities, Cities enrich the Land around them, Land Enrich'd rises in Value, the Value of Lands Enriches the Government'—partly reflects the controversial nature of such arguments in an age of intense party political polemic.[76] Later on they came to seem uncontentious. Some of the most brilliant and critical minds of the middle and late eighteenth century examined them and found them convincing. Hume and Paley both urged that the interests of land and trade were indistinguishable.[77] Trade in this sense was not narrowly defined. It was increasingly assumed to include that moneyed interest once thought inimical to commerce as well as land. Corbyn Morris, a fervent supporter of Walpole, lived to see widespread recognition of the beneficent effects of the National Debt and its associated penumbra of paper. 'Nothing being more certain, than that the *Landed* and *Monied* Interests in this Kingdom must stand and fall together and that their Union and Welfare, upon all Occasions, is *inseparable*.'[78]

By the end of the eighteenth century it seemed difficult to appreciate the bitterness which had once marked relations between landed and moneyed men. Reading Archdeacon Coxe's life of Walpole, the literary memoirist Thomas Green was moved to reflect on the transformation which had occurred in this respect. 'What a change has been effected in the relative weight and ascendancy of the Landed and Monied Interests of this Country, since the period of that administration.'[79] The very term

---

[76] See M. Byrd, *London Transformed: Images of the City in the Eighteenth Century* (New Haven, Conn., 1978), p. 17.

[77] *Essays Moral, Political and Literary* (Oxford, 1963), p. 58; *Paley's Works* (London, 1860), 'Moral and Political Philosophy', p. 186.

[78] *Remarks upon Mr Mill's Proposal* (London, 1771), p. 7.

[79] *Extracts from the Diary of a Lover of Literature* (Ipswich, 1810), p. 98.

'monied interest' gradually lost its pejorative overtones. Its defenders even felt emboldened from time to time to go on the offensive, arguing the patriotic priority of their cause. When the price of government stock collapsed to unprecedented levels in 1780, North was accused by one pamphleteer of having nurtured a Machiavellian scheme to destroy national credit and thereby promote a rush into land.[80] When stock recovered suddenly in 1782, North's successor, Lord Rockingham was duly credited with rescuing the moneyed men.[81] Significantly, their enemies were increasingly circumspect in attack. In the early eighteenth century it was a standard tactic to associate all paper investment with the methods and moral failings of fraudulent speculators. Thereafter it proved prudent to identify the objectionable activities more precisely. Periodic assaults on speculators stressed the peculiarly offensive practices which they employed. There were campaigns against stock-jobbing, notably in the early 1730s and the early 1770s, when reports of financial scandals and anxieties about impending bankruptcy focused attention on the seamy side of City life. But to the extent that the campaigns had a clear objective, it was to eliminate fraud. Trafficking in securities which were not in fact in the vendor's possession at the time of a transaction was repeatedly the target for public and parliamentary criticism. This was considered in effect the 'unacceptable face' of City capitalism. It did not imply widespread doubts about the necessity for a money market and money management.

Appeals to old prejudices were made from time to time, but the object was to encourage a union of interests rather than a narrowly squirearchical rallying of forces. This tendency became marked during the American war, under the combined pressure of economic recession, fiscal strain, and military disaster. The Essex country gentleman Carew Harvey Mildmay lamented the fate of his class, almost 'rooted out, by Foreign wars and taxes'. But he did not think that the moneyed interest would fare much better; it 'has near devoured the Land—and will soon devour Itself'.[82] Moneyed men might well have agreed him. It was at this time that Henry Hoare, head of a famous banking house, decided that its fortunes must be separated from the no less famous estate at Stourhead. Having 'seen for some time past the progress of this nation's ruin', he deeded Stourhead to his grandson Richard Colt Hoare, on condition that he left the banking business for good.[83] The desperation induced in some by the American war did not lead them to denounce one particular form of wealth, let alone to outlaw its possessors. Allan Ramsay, who argued that in almost all

[80] Nathaniel Buckington, *Serious Considerations on the Political Conduct of Lord North, Since His First Entry into the Ministry* (London, 1783), pp. 51 ff.

[81] Denis O'Bryen, *A Word at Parting to the Earl of Shelburne* (London, 1782), p. 32.

[82] North Yorkshire RO, Worsley MSS, 3/235: to Thomas Worsley, 2 Nov. 1777.

[83] *Stourhead* (National Trust guidebook, 1981), p. 45.

eighteenth-century wars the organized interference of businessmen had in effect subverted both the particular interest of land and the general interest of the nation, went out of his way to explain that he had no complaint against the merchants and financiers as such but on the contrary considered them essential to the welfare of the State.[84] Another self-appointed champion of the landowner explained that the true enemy was that combination of professional men, businessmen, and landowners with financial interests who shared in the corrupt concerns of a war-making government.[85] This was much the safest line to take from every standpoint. Its utility was demonstrated when the petitioning and association movement of 1779–80 sought to mobilize public opinion against the Crown, its ministers, and the system of influence on which the war was said to depend. The executive as an enemy united the true authors of national regeneration; 'While the Landholder, Merchants and every other Description of Independent Men in this Country, are every Day feeling the Distresses of this unfortunate War, the Placemen and the Pensioner are the only Persons exempted from the general Calamity.'[86]

In the early 1780s opposition Whigs and reformers sought to exploit this sentiment in much the way that Tory critics of the Whig Junto had done three-quarters of a century earlier. They were given a further chance to do so when war, and war-profiteering, returned in the 1790s. They naturally argued that the malaise was another consequence of the disastrous politics initiated at the accession of George III. Since 1760, 'the Government co-operating with the spirit of enterprise, has matured a new feature in the Constitution, I mean the *monied interest*, which may now be said to form a *fourth estate*'.[87] Such propaganda was guaranteed a sympathetic hearing at times of fiscal and political crisis, in 1779–80, in 1796–7, in 1810–11. It was an important element in the radical tradition inherited by the nineteenth century, and in its most splenetic form, that conveyed in the writings of Cobbett, has permanently affected the judgement of posterity. But as a matter of practical politics, it was not easy to harness its power. Parliamentarians were most ready to take action where they could clearly identify the villains, in the House of Commons itself. Passions of this kind subsided as readily as they had risen. Even at the high point of the agitation against war contractors in the early 1780s, not everyone was ready to subscribe to the old prejudices. It was less easy to summon up faith in a large class of patriotic and independent gentlemen, who might save the constitution, than it had been in the days of Swift and Bolingbroke.

[84] *Letters on the Present Disturbances in Great Britain and Her American Provinces* (London, 1777), p. 32.

[85] *A Prospect of the Consequences of the Present Constitution of Great Britain towards America* (London, 1776), pp. 62–76.

[86] *Commons Journals*, xxxvii. 587: Bedfordshire petition of 1780.

[87] *A Crying Epistle from Britannia to Colonel Mack* (London, n.d.), p. 50.

As Lord Wentworth put it in 1784, 'as to a great influx of monied men into Parliament, I must think they are full as good as Broken Gamesters and penniless younger Brothers'.[88]

By mid-century it had become conventional if not quite unchallengeable wisdom that the interests of land, finance, and trade were well served by a political system which broadly accepted their mutual dependence. Hanoverian Whigs complacently proclaimed the harmony and prosperity enjoyed under Whig rule. Patriot politicians, while they denied the harmony and prosperity, took every care to appeal to as wide a political audience as possible. Here was a conspiracy to treat every issue as if it were not possible to divorce the concerns of commerce and agriculture. War with Spain in the 1730s was opposed by Walpole and urged by his opponents on the same grounds, namely that these interests would jointly suffer or benefit by it. In this respect nothing changed with the political turmoil of the early years of George III's reign. War with America was supported by North and denounced by his opponents similarly on premises which supposed a mingling of interests. In the 1790s loyalists toasted the unity of the landed and commercial interests, as if it could be bracketed with that of Church and King.[89] But there was nothing about this cause which would have distinguished them from their sworn enemies. No politician with an eye on power could afford to appeal to sectional interests.

This is not to say that suspicions of undue influence on the part of one interest or another did not persist. Country gentlemen nurtured a feeling that harmony had been achieved at their expense. Their seeming pusillanimity by comparison with their ferocity in an earlier era brought from Walpole the famous observation 'that a minister might shear the country gentlemen when he would and the landed interest would always produce him a rich fleece in silence; but that the trading interest resembled a hog whom if you attempt to touch, though you was only to pluck a bristle, he would certainly cry out loud enough to alarm all the neighbours'.[90] Walpole, victim of more than one brush with the 'sturdy beggars' of trade, was not an impartial authority, but a similar metaphor was employed and the same verdict recorded later by Soame Jenyns, an MP with long experience at the Board of Trade. The landed interest 'like the silly and defenceless sheep, in silence offers its throat to the butchery of every administration, and is eat up by any ravenous profession; while the trading interest, like the hungry and unmanly hog, devours everything, and if a finger is but laid upon it, the whole country is distracted with the outcry'.[91] No doubt

---

[88] M. Elwin, ed., *The Noels and the Milbankes: Their Letters for Twenty-Five Years 1767–1792* (London, 1967), p. 236.

[89] *Ipswich Journal*, 9 June 1792.

[90] E. Hughes, *Studies in Administration and Finance 1558–1825* (Manchester, 1934), p. 304.

[91] Cole, ed., *The Works of Soame Jenyns*, ii. 217.

both Walpole and Jenyns were thinking of the hated land tax, and the difficulty experienced by ministers intent on a fairer system of taxation. But it was easy to give the view more general application. William Shenstone, indubitably a country gentleman, if an unusually sophisticated one, expressed doubts about the supposed connection between commerce and agriculture, at least where the effects of warfare were concerned. 'The war may suit the *mercantile* world,' he wrote in 1762; 'and the City of London has generally the art to represent the *landed* and *trading* interest as *precisely* the same thing—But I think there is a very material difference.'[92] Certainly merchants and traders were always the first to emphasize their common cause with landowners when they sought support for some specific object. In fact in the stylized art of petitioning this was an almost obligatory stroke. It applied in matters as small as the plea for a duty on wrought silks at the end of the War of the Spanish Succession in 1711—'It is an undoubted Maxim, and constantly verify'd by Experience, That the Value of the Lands of *England* varys as Trade either flourishes or decays'—and as big as the mercantile campaign against the American War in 1775—'so very alarming to the Interest of the Trading Part of these Kingdoms, and in its Consequences to the Landed Interest, ever dependant on each other'.[93]

Occasionally the country gentlemen proved restive on the subject of mercantile influence, especially when circumstances were trying. In the last stages of the American War, with land prices plummeting, Edmund Burke pointed out that there was some potential for a revival of the politics of interest here. Landowners, he noted, had a certain 'natural antipathy' to moneyed men, based on jealousy of inordinate gain in any body of men other than themselves. This made them 'disposed to the censure of abuses among Trading people'.[94] The strains of the 1790s created scope for similar resentments, which, but for the relative buoyancy of land values, might have been more serious still. On the other hand the opponents of land were also capable of challenging the happy consensus when it suited them. Parliament's standing as a landowning legislature made it vulnerable to criticism, whatever its actual record of humouring the moneyed interest. At the very least it lent weight to demands that MPs in general should make themselves better acquainted with the requirements of trade and industry. Malachy Postlethwayt made this one of his principal objectives in his famous *Dictionary*. 'Are not the capital debates in parliament mostly upon matters that have relation to commerce, and the money-affairs and public credit of the nation.'[95]

Postlethwayt's modest appeal could be put less gently. It might even

[92] *The Works in Verse and Prose of William Shenstone* (3 vols., London, 1764–9), iii. 386–7.
[93] Bodleian Library, Parliamentary Papers of William Bromley, ii. 197; *Commons Journals*, xxxv. 73.
[94] Woods, ed., *Correspondence of Edmund Burke*, iv. 219.
[95] *The Universal Dictionary of Trade and Commerce* (4th edn., London, 1774), *sub* 'Landed Interest'.

extend to government itself. The dire subsistence crises of the period made this clear, particularly when, as in 1766–7, a general election was in prospect. 'Why should the landed interest engross the attention of the ministry by the neglect of the mannufactories of our land?' it was asked.[96] This was hardly fair at the end of a Parliament which had gone out of its way to listen to the voice, some would say the artificially amplified voice, of the manufacturing and trading lobbies during the Grenville and Rockingham Ministries. If ever the country gentlemen as represented in Parliament sacrificed a favourite objective, it was when they were induced by ministers to support the repeal of the Stamp Act in the face of fierce resistance from Lord Bute and the 'King's Friends' in 1766. The propaganda which persuaded them relied on the shared interests of landowners, merchants, and manufacturers. As those who deployed it pointed out, rising poor rates provided evidence of the strains which industrial unemployment could inflict even on rural areas. The agent for Massachusetts, Dennys De Berdt, warned that the workmen who lost their work as a result of the disruption of Anglo-American trade would 'fall on the Lands of the Nobility and Gentry'.[97] But American taxation raised untypical issues so far as the everyday business of ministers and MPs was concerned. There was an impression that in other respects administrations were not anxious to take on landlords as a class. As one critic put it, government considered it a maxim to avoid 'doing any thing that may oblige our landholders to lower the high rents, to which they have been enabled of late years to raise the rents of their land estates, by the monopoly that has for so many years been established in their favour'.[98]

THE LANDLORDS OF THIS GREAT EMPIRE

Three of the most prominent features of the mid-eighteenth century, war, improvement, and inflation, posed awkward questions about the relative contributions made by different groups to the national good. War brought immense financial burdens. Under Walpole the main problem had been how to distribute tax savings; now it was how to apportion new taxes. Improvement was diverse, and its implications debatable. But some of it was initiated by agricultural interests, and much of what was not affected agriculture. A good deal of it, in the shape of enclosure, required the specific approval of the legislature. Historians have perhaps paid more attention to parliamentary enclosure than it strictly deserves, but if nothing else it is a reminder of the close and potentially controversial relationship

---

[96] *London Magazine* (1767), 489.

[97] 'Letters of Dennys De Berdt, 1757–70', ed. A. Matthews, *Publications of the Colonial Society of Massachusetts*, 13, Transactions (1910–11), 429.

[98] *London Magazine* (1768), 67.

between economic enterprise and the parliamentary process. Price inflation and the short-lived but severe subsistence crises which made its incidence more noticeable also placed agriculture in a position of special sensitivity, even vulnerability.

Two criticisms came to be made in the course of the resulting disputes, neither of them new but each voiced with a new stridency and heard with a new anxiety. One alleged that the privileges enjoyed by the landed interest were incommensurate with its real worth, and impeded economic progress. The other specifically charged Parliament with expressing the collective interest of landlords rather than the national will. The controversies which gave rise to these accusations had their starting-point in a long-standing debate about export subsidies. The bounty on grain exports, like the land tax and the malt tax, was, in its prevailing form, a product of the years following the Revolution of 1688 and was seen as compensation to the landed interest for the burdens which it had then assumed. Those who demanded a reduction in the land tax, such as the landlords and freeholders of Northamptonshire in 1766, were reminded of this by opponents who thought landowners well treated on balance.[99] For their part champions of the landed interest sought to invest it with the same superior status which attached to much of the Revolution Settlement. The act of 1 William and Mary authorizing the bounty was described by them as 'the Magna Charta of English agriculture'.[100]

By the 1740s and 1750s it was proving a costly Magna Carta. Corn exports rose startlingly from the mid-1730s. The quinquennium 1748–53 recorded the export of 3.2 million quarters, more than the twelve years before 1748 put together, and as much as the total for the thirty years following the accession of Queen Anne in 1702.[101] It was calculated that the cost to the exchequer was by this time £250,000 per annum, equivalent to 6d. on the land tax.[102] In 1752 the sums set aside for payment of the bounty proved inadequate to meet the demands on them in the eastern ports, and special arrangements had to be made to pay interest on the customs debentures issued to exporters. The result was an increasingly tense debate about the merits of the bounty. Advocates of the trading and manufacturing interests took the opportunity to call in question the central assumptions of the preceding years. The bounty was represented as fundamentally selfish. It raised the price of domestic labour and thereby

---

[99] Ibid. 390.

[100] *Monthly Review* (1766), 317.

[101] D. G. Barnes, *A History of the English Corn Laws from 1660–1846* (London, 1930), p. 299; see also D. Ormrod, *English Grain Exports and the Structure of Agrarian Capitalism 1700–1760* (Hull, 1985), p. 25, where exports of 'bread-grain' and barley products are disaggregated to reveal an even more striking increase in the latter during the 1730s and 1740s.

[102] 'Considerations concerning Taking off the Bounty on Corn Exported', 1753, PRO, T. 1. 350, fo. 53.

undermined the competitive position of English goods; simultaneously, it presented foreign manufacturers with subsidized food and thus reduced their own costs. As the highly respected Sir Matthew Decker warned, bounties 'only serve to feed the French cheaper than our own people, and enable them to undersell our manufacturers in the silk, wool, and linen markets'.[103] This was also short-sighted selfishness. Since land depended on trade, anything which stimulated manufactures must ultimately benefit it.

In retrospect these arguments have more than a hint of nineteenth-century controversy about them, particularly when they appealed to the superior commercial and moral credentials of free trade. 'Restraints on Industry destroy the industrious Disposition of the People', declared one furious opponent of the bounty.[104] The debate did not cease with the grain glut of the early 1750s; on the contrary the shortages of the following two decades gave it additional point. Attention switched from the bounty to the whole structure of agrarian protectionism of which it was a part. Farmers and their landlords found themselves attacked, not for mulcting the taxpayer when food prices were low, but for starving the poor when they were high. In each instance it was their claim to special treatment that was at issue, for it was the State which gave them bounties in the export market and the State which protected them against foreign competition at home. In practical terms Parliament was not unresponsive to demands for flexibility. In the conditions of dearth which arose repeatedly between the mid-1750s and the mid-1770s, it regularly authorized temporary suspensions of the laws governing the trade in foodstuffs. Cereal exports were prohibited, foreign and Irish imports permitted, domestic distilling forbidden. Such concessions did not, however, satisfy the critics; rather they stimulated discussion of the underlying principle of the laws thus suspended and promoted a more general onslaught on the entrenched privileges of agriculture.

One consequence of the new climate of controversy was the defensive air which advocates of agriculture increasingly came to acquire. Even Arthur Young's outrage may be better seen as testimony to the heightened vulnerability of his cause than to its latent strength. 'None but a fool can imagine, that the landlords of this great empire, of above fourscore millions of acres, are to yield to the transitory sons of trade and manufacture.'[105] This was unlikely to convince even the landowners themselves, who were, after all, well aware of the economic importance of manufacturing.

---

[103] See R. M. Garnier, *History of The English Landed Interest* (2 vols., London, 1908), ii. 145, where the debate on this point is summarized.

[104] Durham RO, Strathmore MSS, *Considerations Concerning the Taking off the Bounty on Corn Exports* (1743).

[105] *The Farmer's Tour through the East of England* (4 vols., London, 1771), iv. 362.

Moreover, the growing suspicion that agricultural protectionism was the primary cause of a steep rise in prices was a source of concern for them as for others. Inevitably, it was those aspects of this protectionism which could most clearly be shown to be counter-productive and even anti-social which led to the most bitter skirmishes of the 1750s and 1760s.

Among the outworks which attackers saw as easier targets than the central citadel of the corn laws, the distillery had always been one of the most exposed. British spirits brought substantial profits to many farmers. No doubt for this reason they had survived the famous campaign against gin under George II. Distilling was also preserved by appeals to expediency: it was easy to show that a ban on home-produced spirits would be a gift to the smugglers of French brandy. 'Give a new Spring to the Life of Trade, and put a Damp on our crafty Neighbours, who at present flatter themselves we can't live without their luxurious Liquors,' urged a Yorkshire enthusiast for home distilling in 1743.[106] It was also supported with more exceptionable arguments. Lord Bathurst, a staunch Tory and defender of the landed interest, shocked the bishops in the debates of 1743 when he claimed that spirits were essential to the health of the inhabitants of a foggy isle, especially those who lived in fenny and marshy regions.[107] Such claims seemed a flimsy cover for the vested interests of land even when paraded by Tories who prided themselves on their paternalism. Pelham's uneasy compromises in the statutes of 1743, 1747, and 1751, aiming at duties high enough to mollify the humanitarians but low enough to pacify landowners and distillers, saved the situation for a while. But in the late 1750s, the threat of starvation provided an argument more compelling than the dangers of alcoholic intoxication. Prohibitions of distilling were introduced more readily and discontinued more reluctantly than either the restrictions on cereal exports or the licensing of corn imports. The relaxation of the prohibition in 1760 was achieved only with difficulty and after major concessions by the distillers. It was the occasion for a chorus of protest, stressing the damage which they inflicted on the nation's health, on its stock of manpower, and generally on the morals and well-being of 'the lower class of people'.[108]

Another decaying redoubt of the landed position was the bastion erected against Irish competition. This suffered both from the growing effectiveness of the Irish lobby in Parliament and the tendency in the middle decades of the century to question the value of practices which had once seemed indisputably in the interest of a mercantilist-minded nation. A notable instance of the latter occurred in 1747 when Parliament engaged in one of

---

[106] *London Magazine* (1743), 79.
[107] *Parliamentary History*, xii. 1202.
[108] *London Magazine* (1760), 451–4, 505–6.

its periodic debates about the wisdom of permitting British firms to insure
French shipping during wartime. On this occasion there were some heated,
and apparently uncoordinated denunciations of the monopolies, restrictions, and privileges constantly being demanded of the legislature. The
rising lawyer William Murray selected Anglo-Irish trade as a classic case
of the numberless complications and ramifications which resulted from
such special pleading. The prohibition on Irish food imports, he pointed
out, had been conceded to the clamour of 'our landed gentlemen, especially
those in the West'. Designed to secure the interests of home producers, it
had diverted Irish farmers to wool production. This, combined with the
English ban on Irish cloth, had flooded the English market with Irish wool,
and compelled English wool producers to export their own product to the
Continent. In turn this had provoked a prohibition of wool exports,
promoted ever more ingenious and effective wool smuggling, and raised
up a French woollen industry which was visibly overhauling its English
rivals in their traditional markets. Hence the agonized laments of the
clothiers of the West Country and Yorkshire, of which so much had been
heard in Parliament since the mid-1730s. Two other speakers, Theodore
Janssen and Dudley Ryder, agreed with Murray's devastating indictment
of the fatal chain of consequences which flowed from narrow self-interest.
The restrictions on Irish provisions had been the work of a 'provincial'
Parliament, devoted to 'particular considerations' against the national interest. No Parliament of George II could be guilty of such partiality.[109]

Irish provisions were admitted during the Seven Years War; but as in
other matters, such flexibility gave rise to renewed recrimination. In 1761,
though it was the provision merchants who petitioned Parliament to restore
the pre-war prohibition, as was observed in the press, 'The private interest
of some of our landholders was ... at bottom the true cause of these
complaints'.[110] Exceptions and exemptions did not propitiate the critically-
minded. When the navy was permitted to purchase Irish produce free of
duty, it was asked why the manufacturing labour force should not be given
similar privileges. Nobody expected the rich to eat salted Irish provisions,
but for the poor and their paymasters they would have been a boon.[111]
Again, in 1763, when woollen manufacturers were permitted to import
sub-standard Irish butter as industrial grease for a trial period of five years,
it was noticed that imports were subjected to the opinion of two reputable
butter dealers before two JPs. Such butter would have to be 'stale and
dirty indeed', if butter dealers bent on keeping up their prices and rural
magistrates mindful of the interest of dairy producers permitted it to pass

---

[109] *Parliamentary History*, xiv. 108–33: 18 Dec. 1747.
[110] *London Magazine* (1762), 683.
[111] Ibid. 684–5.

their inspection. 'From this act,' commented the parliamentary reporter, 'the reader may see how cautious we are of admitting the free importation of anything that may lessen the price of any land produce, however necessary that importation may be, for the subsistence of the poor, or for enabling us to work up any manufacture at such a cheap rate as to have it in our power to export and sell it at a foreign market.'[112]

It was a common claim in the first half of George III's reign that the landed interest was by and large enhancing its privileged position, whatever tactical adjustments it might make when matters as relatively insignificant as Irish butter imports were concerned. The evidence cited is not very impressive in retrospect, though behind it there lay an understandable concern that landowners as MPs seemed more united and better co-ordinated than had been the case under George I and George II. Especial interest attached to what were seen as conscious attempts to strengthen the political influence of country gentlemen and the rural voters whom many of them represented. The last session or so of every Parliament between 1754 and 1790, with the exception of that of 1780, dissolved in untimely fashion after only four years, witnessed some testimony to the concern of the Commons to appeal to its independent electors, especially to the forty-shilling freeholders. In 1760 it was the Qualification Act; in 1767 a reduction in the land tax; in 1774 the perpetuation of Grenville's Election Act, originally passed on a temporary basis in the wake of the Middlesex Election controversy, in 1770; in 1780 the County Elections Act and the Commons resolutions denouncing the influence of the Crown; in 1788–9 further legislation to safeguard the county franchise.

Most of these measures were opposed by the ministers of the Crown. But with the possible exception of Grenville's Act, which brought the processes of electoral corruption under closer scrutiny, none had a lasting impact on the balance of forces in Parliament. Their interest is rather as evidence of a broad strategy designed to strengthen the propertied community in its traditional, landed sense against the inroads made by commercialism and corruption. Much of the appeal which parliamentary reform enjoyed in the counties derived from its potential in this respect, promising a strengthening of the independent element in Parliament. The extension of the county representation and the elimination of the rotten boroughs had obvious attractions. Indeed, it was one of the strongest arguments against reform that it would bring Parliament more completely under the control of the landed gentry. Equally, part of the case for extending the franchise to large, unrepresented cities was to compensate for the enhanced influence of the country gentlemen in a reformed House of Commons.[113]

---

[112] Ibid. (1764), 126–7.
[113] *The Inadequacy of Parliamentary Representation Fully Stated* (London, 1783), pp. 68–9.

The structural reforms which seemed at hand when the Association movement was at its height in the early 1780s were to be long delayed. In the meantime more concrete results were obtained from the country gentlemen's war on electoral corruption. Whether the victories obtained in this war were of much consequence is none the less doubtful. Their significance is primarily rhetorical. The successful prosecution of corrupt, moneyed men, especially the 'nabobs', for their invasion of parliamentary boroughs was interpreted as a notable triumph. Thanks partly to the labours of the committees set up to adjudicate controverted elections as a result of Grenville's Act, and partly to the support given by judges and juries, there were some sensational cases. That of Shaftesbury, which culminated in bribery convictions at the Dorchester Assizes both in 1775 and 1776, was hailed in the press as 'the most decisive cause ever yet determined in favour of the independency of the landed interest'.[114] But significantly, when the country gentlemen demanded that parliamentary punishment be added to judicial conviction, Lord North was reluctant to oblige. The culprits, Thomas Rumbold and Francis Sykes, were effectively exonerated, and the electors of Shaftesbury suffered no lasting penalty, such as the disfranchisement which some country gentlemen had demanded.[115]

In 1771 New Shoreham had been disfranchised for corruption, following one of the first hearings by a committee appointed under Grenville's Act. In the constituency which replaced it the franchise was vested in all the forty-shilling freeholders of the Rape of Bramber. This was a county electorate under another name, or rather, in later terms, a divisional county electorate. It offered exciting new opportunities to those who had faith in the county electorate, and especially to those who had faith in county MPs. In effect Shoreham was being recovered from Bengal and restored to its ancient situation in Sussex.[116] A similar remedy was applied when Cricklade was convicted of systematic corruption in 1782 and its franchise transferred to the neighbouring district of Wiltshire. But there were doubts about this strategy. Transferring the votes of delinquent boroughs to blocks of quiescent countryside could be portrayed as a gift to rural landlords. It could be argued that the forty-shilling freeholder was just as vulnerable to bribery and intimidation as his borough counterpart, albeit in less mercenary or at least less blatantly monetary fashion. At the very least some allowance had to be made for the tenurial deference of country areas. Conceivably it was this which had held back the Commons from taking similar action, significantly in some of the same boroughs, in the 1690s, at another time when the country gentlemen as a class had made a relatively

---

[114] *London Magazine* (1775), 435; (1776), 443.
[115] *Parliamentary History*, xviii. 1455.
[116] See p. 277.

unified and cohesive attempt to reform the constitution of Parliament. The disfranchisement of Stockbridge had been opposed in 1689 on the grounds that it might lead to a general conversion of borough seats. As Sir William Williams, himself a knight of the shire, for Caernarvon, expressed it, 'you break the ice by this, and give a handle to throw boroughs into Counties'. Such proposals were reminiscent of Cromwell's reform in 1654, and threatened the traditional 'mixture of this House' particularly with regard to the representation of trade.[117] In any event this revolution by stealth remained substantially unachieved. The net effect of the agitation to strengthen the representation of the county squirearchy was to secure four additional seats at the expense of the inhabitants of two insignificant towns. Between 1804 and 1828 this less than impressive gain was increased to ten by matching arrangements in three other delinquent boroughs.[118]

What proved difficult to accomplish in terms of constitutional change was not more readily achieved in point of economic interest. There was continuing controversy about the laws which enabled landowners and their tenants to enjoy a monopoly of the home market for agricultural products. Two statutes of the 1770s, passed at a time when Parliament and government were considered peculiarly vulnerable to the pressures exerted by country gentlemen, sought to provide a permanent solution to the problems which had been met with temporary expedients since the first serious interruption of food supplies in the 1750s. But they could hardly be considered victories for the landed interest. Pownall's Act of 1773 altered the price levels at which bounties were paid, exports prohibited, and imports permitted. A further statute of 1776 provided for the final repeal of the Irish Cattle and Provision Acts. The latter was a manifest defeat from the English landowner's standpoint, terminating a century of discrimination against Irish agriculture. The former in effect made perpetual the concessions which had been granted on a short-term basis during the preceding years. It treated 44s. per quarter as the price at which producers might reasonably expect subsidy from the consumer and taxpayer. Above that level export ceased and some degree of importation was encouraged. This represented a reduction of 4s. on the previous price of 48s., though in practice the higher figure had applied only intermittently during recent years.

Pownall's Act was seen as a retreat by the country gentlemen, in the eyes of many an excessive one.[119] In 1791 a little of the ground conceded

---

[117] *Debates of the House of Commons, from the Year 1667 to the Year 1694: Collected by the Honourable Anchitell Grey, Esq.* (10 vols., London, 1969), ix. 423.

[118] E. Porritt, *The Unreformed House of Commons; Parliamentary Representation before 1832* (2 vols., repr. New York, 1963), i. 16.

[119] *Considerations of the Corn Laws, with Remarks on the Observations of Lord Sheffield on the Corn Bill* (London, 1791).

was won back. The act of that year adopted a complicated combination of price levels and sliding scales which effectively retained the bounty at 44s. but provided some degree of protection against foreign competition above 46s.[120] Prices had generally risen in the 1780s, though without causing chronic shortages. It was obvious to cereal growers that their generosity in 1773 had been rendered more liberal by subsequent events than had been the intention. But 1791 represented an adjustment to inflationary pressures, not a dramatic victory for the agrarian producer. The outcome in both 1773 and 1791 was a compromise, negotiated in the same spirit as other conflicts of interest. There is no comparison with the early nineteenth-century corn laws, which were maintained against a background of rapidly changing ideas about the desirability of freer trade. Eighteenth-century manufacturers, who themselves benefited by a vast, complex system of export bounties and import restrictions, could hardly argue that agriculture should be uniquely exposed to the bracing winds of unlimited foreign competition.

Reform of the corn laws was a matter of fine tuning. More fundamental, and certainly more sensitive questions arose when the restrictions on the wool trade were considered. The traditional strategy was to maximize the benefit to the woollen manufacture, at the cost of the wool producer. In 1662 all exports of wool had been prohibited. Irish wool production for the English market was boosted by the ban on cattle imports, and by the prohibition on Irish woollen manufacturing. In short everything was done to provide the English clothier with cheap raw material, at the expense of graziers who were expected to compete with their Irish rivals in a home market without the option of a legal sale abroad. This highly discriminatory code was partly the product of those 'provincial biases' discerned by enlightened observers, partly a reflection of long-standing deference to the woollen manufacture. It was reckoned in 1787 that woollens accounted for fully a third of the value of home production.[121] The economic importance of the cloth industry over a period of centuries was legendary. It was accepted, or rather assumed not merely by those who had a vested interest in it but by many in government, Parliament, and beyond, who did not. It went with a generally held view of history, with the Englishman's sense of what made his country powerful, wealthy, industrious, even virtuous.

Challenges to this impressive consensus were none the less attempted from time to time. The *Grazier's Complaint* of 1726 offered a disarmingly precise calculation of the comparative advantages of wool production and woollen manufacturing. The final balance sheet, so it calculated, showed that wool growing supported 3,400,000 Englishmen, whereas the working

---

[120] Barnes, *A History of the English Corn Laws*, pp. 57–63.
[121] *Morning Herald*, 7 Feb. 1787.

of wool employed at most 1,000,000. 'It would be an affront to common sense to ask, which of these two is the most valuable and important national interest.'[122] For practical purposes it was an affront which could not be removed without careful negotiation. Prudent campaigners for the wool growers concentrated on the injustice of artificially low price levels. Hence the debate between the Lincolnshire clergyman John Smith and the Trowbridge clothier William Temple concerning the relative quality and price of domestic and foreign wools.[123] Even so Parliament was unresponsive. In 1743 it rejected an application to restrain Irish competition.[124] It even failed to implement a registration scheme, which would have provided accurate information as to the sale of home-grown wool compared with its Irish, Scottish, and Spanish rivals. The defensiveness of the wool lobby at this time is striking. It took pains to reassure parliamentary opinion that it offered no fundamental challenge to traditional assumptions. The merchants and graziers of Grantham distanced themselves from demands for the right to export, 'the illicit Exportation of Wool being stopped, as in all reason it ought to be'.[125] Lincolnshire's plea for registration was put in conciliatory terms. Smith's proposals, offered to the Commons in 1744, were described by their author as paying regard 'to the several different lawful Interests, as nearly as possible, of the Grower, the Manufacturer and the rest of the People'.[126] Such deference made no difference.

Still more humiliating was the defeat suffered in 1753. Since 1696 Irish wool had been legally importable only into west-coast ports. The intention had been to restrict opportunities for smuggling to France and the Low Countries, but the effect was to make Irish wool more expensive than it need have been in the eastern counties where much of the cloth industry was concentrated. When the Commons debated a bill throwing open this trade to all English ports in 1753 only 26 votes could be found against it, though domestic wool growers were bitterly opposed to a measure which significantly favoured their Irish rivals.[127] Only on one occasion did the wool lobby achieve a modest victory, and then by way of preserving the status quo rather than making any advance on it. In 1739 the woollen manufacturers and merchants were denied the repeal of the remaining customs duties on Irish wool imports. On this occasion, at least, the graziers made no attempt to conceal their resentment of 'a few Master Workmen,

[122] J. Bischoff, *A Comprehensive History of the Woollen and Worsted Manufactures* (2 vols., London, 1842), i. 121–2.
[123] J. Smith, *Chronicon Rusticum Commerciale; Or, Memoirs of Wool* (2 vols., London, 1747); W. Temple, *A Refutation of One of the Principal Arguments in the Rev. Mr Smith's Memoirs of Wool* (London, 1750).
[124] *Commons Journals*, xxiv. 447, 457–8, 465–6.
[125] Ibid., xxiv. 457–8.
[126] Ibid. 542.
[127] Ibid., xxvi. 718.

Merchants, and Factors, who, under the Pretence of a publick Good, seek only to amass to themselves great Estates, by oppressing the Body of the People, whose Labours are the Foundation of the Trade itself, and the Support of the Nobility and Gentry of the Kingdom'.[128]

The same animus was displayed forty years later. One of the features of the renewed campaign to open the wool trade was the concern of those involved to identify their cause with the interests of agriculture as a whole. The War of American Independence put a temporary stop to the agrarian prosperity of the early years of George III's reign, bringing a reduction in parliamentary enclosure, and eventually, in 1779–80, a collapse in land values. In the resulting agitation, some notable names were involved: Lord Sheffield, Sir Joseph Banks, Arthur Young, Thomas Day, Thomas Pownall. They made much of the grower's plight in the context of a general erosion of the landowner's standing. They also exploited the contemporary tendency to connect commercial monopoly with moral malpractice. Thomas Day, the opponent of the slave trade, observed that 'the same merciful spirit which inspires the Liverpool traders in their visits to Africa, seems to animate the woollen manufacturers in their treatment of the farmers'.[129] Sir John Thorold, on behalf of his Lincolnshire constituents, denounced the 'mean and rapacious spirit of avarice and monopoly ... consequently producing acts of injustice and oppression'.[130]

For all their influence and fame these voices proved no more successful than the more narrowly based campaigns of earlier years. A judicious scheme to regulate the wool trade in the same manner as the grain trade, permitting exports only at certain price levels, and with appropriate duties, foundered in 1782. Six years later, after an acrimonious debate between the advocates of land and the representatives of the Yorkshire and West Country clothiers, Parliament not only declined to open foreign markets to British wool, but agreed to intensify the war on wool smugglers. Manufacturing was said to be 'the idol of this bill'.[131] Opposition was intense and the bitterness of the debate, which was not in any sense a contest of political parties, very marked. On the second reading it elicited from Pitt an extraordinarily complacent remark, but one which indicates something of the anxiety of a minister confronted with the alarming possibility of a major conflict of interests. He was 'glad to find that there was not likely to be any difference between the commercial and the landed interest on the present occasion; but that at the bottom, every gentleman, let him have

---

[128] Ibid., xxiii. 358.

[129] *A Letter to Arthur Young, Esq. on the Bill Now Depending in Parliament to Prevent the Exportation of Wool* (London, 1788), p. 10.

[130] *Parliamentary History*, xxvii. 389.

[131] *Observations on a Bill, for Explaining, Amending, and Rendering into One Act, the Several Laws now in Being for Preventing the Export of Live Sheep, Wool, and Other Commodities* [1787].

taken which side of the question he would, had wished to preserve those
interests, as they ever ought undoubtedly to be considered, as one and the
same'.[132] Considering the acrimony which the wool growers displayed in
their endeavours to create open war between the commercial and landed
interests, this was Prime Ministerial fudging of a high order. But fudging
helped landowners console themselves in defeat. Arthur Young himself
claimed a kind of victory in 1788. 'The manufacturers experienced so
determined and vigorous an opposition that they would hardly engage,
again in any similar attack upon the landed interest.'[133] This was, to say
the least, an optimistic view of the outcome.

THE LANDED INTEREST

The failure of the graziers provides a clue to the fundamental weakness of
the so-called landed interest. It represented not a unified mass of families
and communities with closely matching concerns, but rather a loose con-
geries of interests, often unconnected, and sometimes competing. The
agitation on behalf of the wool growers was effectively local. *The Grazier's
Complaint* of 1726 significantly appealed to 'the landed interest in general,
and the county of Lincoln in particular'. It struggled to erase the impression
that 'two or three grazing counties' were the only parties involved.[134] Half
a century later the centre of the campaign was still Lincoln. One of its
shrewdest opponents, the poet and merchant Richard Glover, emphasized
its parochialism, threatening Lincolnshire with the 'odium of the three
kingdoms'.[135] Arthur Young got up a petition from Suffolk to demonstrate
that a wider body of opinion was involved, but the result was not impressive.
Lincolnshire men themselves blamed their landed compatriots for treachery
or pusillanimity, not least in the House of Commons. Sir Joseph Banks
asserted that 'the country gentlemen must outnumber the manufacturers
in the House whenever they are sufficiently pinched, but like lions they
want a great proportion of hunger to excite them'. He and his colleagues
found manufacturers conducting themselves as 'an orderly and collected
body' while landowners seemed 'incapable of union or organisation'.[136]

The truth was that most country gentlemen saw no connection between
the cause of the grazing counties and their own. Landlords and their tenants
worked largely within a local economy which might make them remote
from landed men elsewhere. It was not realistic to expect West Riding

---

[132] *Parliamentary History*, xxvii. 382.
[133] M. Betham-Edwards, ed., *The Autobiography of Arthur Young* (London, 1898), p. 165.
[134] M. Bischoff, *A Comparative History of the Woollen and Worsted Manufactures*, i. 115, 120.
[135] Ibid., i. 207.
[136] *Morning Herald*, 14 Mar. 1787; Sir F. Hill, *Georgian Lincoln* (Cambridge, 1966), p. 109; Day,
A Letter to Arthur Young, p. 27.

landowners to sacrifice their community of interest with local manufacturing in favour of a less obvious connection with the landowners of the
East Riding and Lincolnshire. As a great Yorkshire landowner and knight
of the shire, Sir George Savile, pointed out, the manufacturing towns of
the West Riding 'cloathed the hills of Lincolnshire'.[137] Graziers themselves
might hesitate before endangering such relationships. Cotswold sheep-
farmers were not disposed to imperil their links with West Country clothiers
for the common cause which they were supposed to share with their
northern counterparts. Enthusiasts for arable agriculture suspected that in
grazing counties there was too much sympathy for manufacturers,
sufficient, at any rate, to make them reluctant allies in defending the corn
laws.[138]

There were many examples of landowners collaborating with businessmen for regional benefits. The great navigation projects repeatedly
brought such combination to public attention. In the north-west for
example, the prolonged campaign for a Weaver navigation in the early
eighteenth century, and the still more celebrated project for the Trent and
Mersey canal in the 1760s, mixed the interests of agriculture with those
of salt producers and refiners, pottery manufacturers, coal owners, and
ironmasters. One of the paradoxical consequences of a market increasingly
organized on national lines was the stimulus it gave to provincial rivalries,
as different regions strove to transmit their products, agricultural or industrial, to the widest possible body of consumers. The premium thereby
placed on local co-operation was high indeed.

It seemed that the landed interest was becoming ever more fragmentary,
not least in matters of taxation. The distinction between malt counties and
cider counties was especially revealing in this respect. A proposal to tax
cider in 1744 was only defeated after a pitched parliamentary battle between
West Country MPs and their counterparts in the east and north.[139] Twenty
years later when Bute succeeded in imposing a cider excise, the result was
a prolonged controversy. MPs for eastern counties who had the temerity
to oppose the excise on constitutional grounds found their constituents
unappreciative of their altruism. Sir Thomas Cave, MP for Leicestershire,
made himself unpopular by voting for the repeal of the cider tax, 'tho' the
Representative of a Malt County'.[140] The repeal of the excise in 1766 did
not end the war of cider and malt. It broke out again whenever renewed
taxation of either was in prospect. In 1780 Sir Charles Bunbury, MP for
Suffolk, bitterly attacked the malt tax increase of that year and demanded

---

[137] *Parliamentary History*, xxvii. 382.

[138] Northumberland RO, Delaval MSS, 2DE/49/4/7: Sir John Delaval, 'recollections of my speech',
28 Mar. 1770.

[139] G. Hardinge, *Biographical Memoirs of The Rev. Sneyd Davies* (London, [1816]), p. 63.

[140] Warwickshire RO, Denbigh MSS, Letterbrook, Denbigh to Wentworth, 3 Jan. 1768.

matching impositions on cider. There followed a collision of squirearchical Titans, in which the knights of the shire for Gloucester and Devon, Sir William Guise and John Rolle, 'wished the hon. baronet, instead of interfering with other counties and attempting to disturb their peace, would content himself with endeavouring to preserve the peace of his own county'. They also suggested a tax on horse-racing, having in mind, no doubt, Bunbury's passion for the turf and his prominence in the affairs of the Jockey Club.[141]

It was not only regional and local interests that divided landowners. The diverse forms of landed property recognized by English law made it unwise to assume that even at the lowest level of the parish the agreement of landlords was easily reached. In the politics of enclosure manorial rights and tithes played a large part. The tithe question, especially, raised awkward questions of principle, rendering relations between rural property-owners less harmonious than they were sometimes assumed to be. It was also an example of the unpredictable manner in which Parliament could give more than adequate representation to interests in some respects vulnerable to encroachment and erosion. The clergy were excluded by their profession from membership of the House of Commons, an exclusion tested and ultimately reasserted by statute in 1802 after the radical clergyman John Horne Tooke took his seat for Old Sarum in 1801. But their champions in that House had allies. There were lay rectors aware of their own vulnerability, and there were patrons who unsentimentally considered their advowsons a form of property, the value of which could be raised by improvement. When the hop-growers appealed in 1791 for the united support of the landed interest against tithes, on the model recently adopted in revolutionary France, they were not only taking a naïve view of the value of French parallels, they were neglecting the extent to which landowners and tithe-farmers themselves had an interest in the existing structure.[142]

It was argued by some that rectorial consent was a necessary precondition of commutation.[143] Failing that there was still in the Upper House a bench of bishops prepared to deploy its collective voting power against legislation which did not make full allowance for the claims of the Church and the interests of the parochial clergy. Without the assent of the appropriate bishop, whose duty it was to protect future generations of parochial incumbents, a parliamentary enclosure was a perilous speculation. Bishops had something very close to a veto for practical purposes, as Charles Amcotts, MP for Boston, told a Lincolnshire encloser in 1773 when he revealed that the Bishop of Lincoln 'would not Consent' to certain pro-

---

[141] *Parliamentary History*, xxi. 393–4, where these remarks are reported as Rolle's; in the alternative report (*London Magazine* (1780), 270), they are attributed to Guise.

[142] *Whitehall Evening-Post*, 21 Apr. 1791.

[143] *The Speeches in Parliament of Samuel Horsley* (Dundee, 1813), p. 88.

visions in a bill for Brinkhill.[144] In this instance the Bishop's reservations
were made clear, and adopted, not when the bill was before the Lords but
while it was under consideration by a Commons committee. The prospect
of his intervening in the Upper House, if necessary with the collaboration
of his brethren, the spiritual peers, was kept in the background, but it was
quite sufficient to ensure that his wishes were observed.

The result in the great age of enclosure was a formula for tithe commutation and glebe allocation which was manifestly favourable to the
Church. Self-appointed champions of agrarian improvement and the
landed interest fumed against the vested rights of the tithe-owner, representing, so it was said, a standing disincentive to enterprise and investment
on the part of ordinary landlords. But the arguments were not all on one
side. Defenders of the tithe were quite ready to argue that their special
interest worked for the public good. One of the more ingenious claims on
behalf of tithe of agistment, a matter of peculiar complexity and much
controversy, was that it deterred conversion from tillage to grazing. This
was urged by a Fenland incumbent, Cecil Willis, against the clamour, as
he termed it, of his grazier countrymen. His cause, he insisted, was not
merely the cause of a country clergyman, it was 'absolutely necessary to
the Welfare of this commercial Kingdom'.[145] Complications such as this
made nonsense of simple appeals to the united cause of landowners.

Still more problematic was the great divide which separated the dependent from their masters, tenant from landlord, lessee from lessor, copyholder from lord of the manor. The terms and extent of dependency
involved in such relationships varied greatly. Contemporary debate concentrated on the most straightforward of these relationships, that of the
freehold landowner and his rack-rent tenants, but many of the arguments
also applied to less clear-cut divisions of interest in the land. Economic
theorists distinguished the profits of rent from those of husbandry. The
distinction was one which the partisans of agriculture were keen to soften.
Just at the time when Adam Smith was enunciating it so lucidly, they were
stressing the bond which united landlord and tenant, and advocating a
blurring of those lines which separated the fixed capital represented by the
land from the movable capital provided by the farmer.[146] Landlords,
especially great magnates, who took farming seriously as a science were
held up as exemplars of a new class who could render the farmyard or at
least the breeding book an object of interest to polite society and thereby

[144] Lincolnshire Archives Office, Massingberd Mundy MSS, MM.11.3: C. Amcotts to W. Massingberd, 22 Feb. 1773.
[145] Cecil Willis, *The Matter of Agistment Tithe of Unprofitable Stock in the Case of the Vicar of
Holbeach* (London, [1777]), p. 23.
[146] *An Inquiry into the Nature and Causes of the Wealth of Nations*, ed. R. H. Campbell, A. S.
Skinner, and W. B. Todd (2 vols., Oxford, 1976), i. 160 ff.

demonstrate to the humble farmer his dependence on the intelligent co-operation of his landlord. Along with such potent image-making went attention to those improving leases and ever more complicated legal arrangements which were designed to make landlord and tenant genuinely joint investors in their land. The question of what length of lease provided the most productive relationship was much ventilated.[147] The prevailing tendency was to eliminate, wherever practicable, forms of tenure which gave the tenant a degree of independence. The conversion of copyholds to leaseholds, or leases on lives to short tenancies, was of obvious value to a landlord, since it permitted regular rent increases, and gave him a freer hand for agricultural investment or other forms of development. The agricultural experts often accepted the desirability of this process, but denied that rack-rent tenancies, terminable at six months or a year, were profitable. The ideal farmer was not a harassed peasant, milking the maximum immediate advantage from his land, but an enlightened capitalist, investing substantial sums of money over a period of time to the enrichment of himself and his landlord. The advantages of long leases were increasingly accepted on this basis, that they brought greater profit to landowners. But they incidentally strengthened the stake of tenants as a class, and gave them a form of property not to be despised. Leases were not treated for legal purposes as if they were annuities derived from rent charges, but they bestowed a comparable degree of security. Coke of Norfolk was one of those prepared to accept the full implications, arguing for liberal and long leases on grounds of the political independence which they promoted as well as their economic utility.[148]

Educating the landlord in rural science, and strengthening the lease-holder, were meant to profit and unify the landed interest. Whether this design succeeded is open to question. It is not clear that the *rentier* class of the early nineteenth century was better integrated into agrarian life than its eighteenth-century predecessor, though it is possible that the professional stewards which it increasingly employed did bring a more collaborative approach to the farming at least of the great estates. Nor is it easy to gauge the impact of the gentleman, capitalist, engrossing farmer, by whatever name he is known, on tenurial relationships. The contemporary impression seems to have been that precisely because he usurped the economic function and social role of the small country gentleman, reducing his landlord to a glorified rent-collector, the new-style farmer was driving a considerable wedge through the middle of the landed interest.

Such complications could not but affect legislation. In so far as they

---

[147] William Marshall, *The Review and Abstract of the County Reports to the Board of Agriculture*, sub 'Species of Tenure', and 'Tenure'.

[148] A. M. W. Stirling, *Coke of Norfolk and His Friends* (2 vols., London, 1907), i. 267 ff.

were representative of the landed interest, both Houses of Parliament were composed of landowners. But many of them were elected by tenants, and in some measure all owed their well-being to tenants. It was almost impossible to consider any of the great questions which affected rural society without encountering uncomfortable consequences of this fundamental fact. Debates about dearth, unemployment, and poverty gave rise to all kinds of distinctions between the interests of proprietor and occupier. Some of the conclusions drawn from them were and are open to challenge, and at best they provide a caricature rather than a portrait of the tenurial relationship. Yet they plainly contained sufficient truth to affect the politics of the legislative process.

Farmers were assumed to be the monopolists who exacerbated the plight of the poor consumer, landlords benevolently minded protectors of the rural community. Farmers staffed the lower offices of local administration, and as churchwardens and overseers were responsible both for rating their parishes and allocating relief; whether they erred on the side of the ratepayer's pocket or the poorhouse budget it was easy to allege that their landlords, operating at the higher levels of the magistracy in petty and quarter sessions, would have a stronger sense both of the communal consequences and the political implications of poverty. Farmers frequently had only a temporary commitment to the society in which they lived; at the end of their lease, or if rack-renting, in a year, even six months, they might depart for ever. Their landlords, by contrast, possessed that supposedly permanent stake in their country or county (the two terms were significantly synonymous for many purposes) which gave them a superior concern in its well-being, order, and stability. In many places farmers actually bore the burden of the poor rates; for them it was a vital part of the fluctuating annual fortunes of the rural economy. Landlords could, by and large, afford to take a longer view. Most of these stereotypes pointed up the higher humanity and responsibilities of the landowner and the lower nature and duties of the tenant. Whether this was at all fair is debatable. What is undeniable is that it revealed a social and political gulf in the rural landscape which belied the smooth contours and gentle undulations painted by the agriculturalists.

Perhaps it is not surprising that it was left to a reformed Parliament to introduce, for instance, mandatory poor law reform. This is not to say that Georgian Parliaments always balked at offending the tenantry as a class. But the price of doing so could be high, as the history of the game laws reveals. Here, indeed, was a great body of legislation which found the landowners uninhibitedly pursuing their own interest. It is difficult not to view the game laws in the context which they increasingly acquired in the early nineteenth century, despoiling the rural proletariat's inheritance. But in the eighteenth century the class against which this complex code seemed obviously to be aimed was the great mass of prosperous, pretentious tenants. These were the men who found themselves the victims of laws entitling sportsmen to hunt over their farms while excluding them from all sporting rights themselves. The resulting tensions featured much in parliamentary debates and in the controversial press; they also had serious implications for the protection of property and the pursuit of political co-operation at local level. Farmers were enthusiastic supporters of the multiplying associations for the prosecution of felons; they were nothing of the kind in respect of game preservation societies. The drive mounted by the National Game Preservation Association to harry offenders in the 1750s aroused particular irritation, some of which was transmitted to a wider public through the resulting controversy in the press.[149]

It was not only the laws of Nimrod that gave rise to strife. Turnpike legislation brought parish, hundred, and county into conflict, and set different classes of society against each other. The war of broad versus narrow wheel which occupied so much parliamentary time in the mid-eighteenth century had awkward repercussions for those who thought of the land and its exploitation as promoting rural harmony. The poet and amateur surveyor John Scott was outraged when the double toll on narrow wheels, intended to take effect in 1776, was suspended for two years 'in Consequence of the Clamours of a few ignorant and avaricious Farmers'. Farmers, he pointed out, invariably opposed progress in such matters, with the cry that 'the Farmer will be ruined'.[150] Farmers were among the main users of the new road system, and carting costs a critical item in their profit and loss accounts. The damage which their vehicles did to the roads, and the disproportionate expense which they inflicted on other road users, were greatly resented. Landowners found themselves awkwardly placed. Their rent-rolls were all the fatter for giving their tenants a free hand. But the polite classes, of which landowners constituted a large part, were themselves the most enthusiastic travellers on wheels. It was natural to accuse them of concentrating on fast and fashionable transport, by carriage and chaise to London, Bath, and Brighton, at the expense of more essential and socially worthwhile users. Nor did they find it easy to control the activities of their inferiors. At an early stage in the turnpike legislation Parliament permitted qualification for road trustees by means of personal, as an alternative to landed estate. In some places it proved a dangerous innovation. When it suited them, farmers had a disconcerting way of qualifying as trustees and outvoting their betters. The resulting neglect of

[149] P. B. Munsche, *Gentlemen and Poachers: The English Game Laws, 1671–1831* (London, 1981), pp. 56–62, 109–15.

[150] *Digests of the General Highway and Turnpike Laws* (London, 1778), pp. 262, 264.

what was called the landed interest but was actually the landowners' interest caused indignation.[151]

Even in enclosure questions, where attention was concentrated on the activities of landlords, there were worries about the role of farmers. Enclosure commissioners, it was said, as at North Leigh in Oxfordshire in 1761, were all too frequently 'only farmers, or of lower degree'.[152] They often lacked the proprietor's alleged sense of social responsibility and natural integrity; they also, still more alarmingly, had a habit of feathering their own nests at the expense of parochial proprietors. This too was to prove an enduring problem for Parliament.

It is hard to gauge the political importance of tensions between landowners as a class and their tenants as a class, particularly when the electoral complexities of the tenurial relationship, itself a matter of much uncertainty and controversy, have to be taken into account. For political purposes it sometimes suited even magnates to bring tenants within the charmed circle of genteel society. But knowing where to draw the line was tricky. When the second Duke of Richmond asked his Sussex neighbour the Duke of Newcastle if he might bring 'some of our top farmers, that wee call yeomanly men' to an election treat, Newcastle nervously assented provided only 'very topping Farmers' were invited, 'or it will be laid at my door'. What constituted a topping farmer and how he should be distinguished from his inferiors was one of the most pressing questions of country politics.[153]

Thomas Paine shrewdly sought to shatter the alleged harmony of the rural community by placing the interests of occupiers firmly alongside those of other oppressed classes. 'It is difficult to discover', he wrote, 'what is meant by the *landed interest*, if it does not mean a combination of aristocratical land-holders, opposing their own pecuniary interest to that of the farmer, and every branch of trade, commerce and manufacture.'[154] This was going a good deal too far. On many questions farmers shared a common position with their landlords. But they also had distinct interests of their own and a long rhetorical tradition which portrayed them as the long-suffering milch cows of society. A popular ballad like 'The Farmer', sold by travelling chapmen to rural customers, depicted them as perpetually victimized by other classes. 'The poor farmers have all to maintain.'[155] This was the plebeian counterpart to the image of landowners as sheep for shearing, with the difference that farmers could also see themselves as victims of their own landlords. Arthur Young, who devoted much of his

---

[151] W. A. Albert, *The Turnpike Road System in England, 1663–1840* (Cambridge, 1972), p. 58.
[152] *Commons Journals*, xxviii. 880–1.
[153] *The Correspondence of the Dukes of Richmond and Newcastle, 1724–1750*, pp. 36, 80.
[154] *Rights of Man*, ed. H. Collins (London, 1969), p. 248.
[155] Bodleian Library, Douce ballads.

energy to lecturing farmers, was not above championing their interests against a selfish class of proprietors, often quite gratuitously. It would not have occurred to many to blame a supposedly landowning Parliament for subsidizing the British fishery. But Young saw it as improperly favouring one food-producing industry at the expense of another. Moreover the money which financed the scheme came from the rural taxpayer as much as anyone. 'Country farmers payed their shares of grants, to enable their landlords to eat fish cheap at the capital.'[156]

Occasionally the farmer's sense of grievance disturbed the calm surface of county politics. In Essex in the early years of George III there was much discussion of the possibility of setting up a candidate for the county in the farmers' interest. Perhaps significantly, some of the game prosecutions which gave rise to controversy in the national press had commenced in Essex. The sitting county MPs also blotted their copy-book by failing to assist in the reduction of the land tax in 1767, an occasion when most knights of the shire had a very clear idea of their duty. Sir Lewis Namier describes the Essex squire Peter Muilman as 'spinning fantastic plans to rouse the farmers and make them demand from their landlords freedom to choose one Member truly to represent them and their interest'.[157] Yet these plans may not have been altogether fantastic. When, in December 1769, Muilman organized a lobby to press for revision of a road bill the results were striking. Muilman himself claimed full credit, 'The Farmers having succeeded through my Endeavours, so early and expeditiously, in the Repeal of that Part of the Law allowing them only Three Horses in Bye-ways'. The county's MPs indignantly repudiated his claim but the alacrity with which they responded to Muilman's propaganda suggests that they took his threats, and his presumed power base, seriously.[158]

The game laws provide a clear example of landlords united as a class against their inferiors. To the extent that enclosure involved exploitation of the lower reaches of rural society by the upper the same could be said. The claim was made very early in the history of parliamentary enclosure. 'Many of our late Members,' one newspaper noted, 'having considerable landed property, and having chiefly their own interest in view, have greatly contributed to the depopulating the country, and exceedingly distressing the lower class of people, by getting Acts made for enclosing lands, and by putting many farms into one.'[159] This preoccupation with agricultural improvement as the work of an oppressive class of landlords working through their parliamentary predominance has remained one of the principal features of a large and ever-growing body of historiography. But such

---

[156] *The Farmer's Letters to the People of England* (2nd edn., 1768), p. 185.
[157] Namier and Brooke, *History of Parliament*, i. 276.
[158] Essex RO, D/DBe Z2.
[159] *Cambridge Chronicle*, 4 Mar. 1769.

landlord-unity was not at all what propagandists for the landed interest sought in the late eighteenth century. On the contrary it embarrassed them. Many were dismayed by the divisiveness of the game laws. Many too were anxious to explain that enclosure did not cause suffering, or alternatively that its procedures should be improved so as to eliminate such injustice as occurred. Their true aim was to unite agricultural producers against other producers or against consumers, and they employed the ancient rhetorical stock of the 'landed interest' to do so.

This distinction is crucial. Licensing men of property to control or exploit men with little or no property was a favourite activity, frequently encouraged by a Parliament which overwhelmingly represented propertied interests. Even when it remembered its social responsibilities, it interpreted them within the framework of a propertied society. But this had little to do with landownership as such. Most of the criminal law was concerned with the protection of commercial and personal property, as was much improvement legislation. Georgian Parliaments have never been accused of championing the urban poor against merchants, tradesmen, and shop-keepers; or of rescuing the inferior clergy from their perpetual sufferings at the hands of complacent pluralists and a negligent episcopacy; or of securing the welfare of serving soldiers and sailors against arbitrary con-scription and brutal military discipline; or of protecting the collective rights of industrial workers against the exploitation of their employers. In all these matters Parliament was sometimes moved to action by pleas of injustice and hardship; in most, for most of the time, it consulted the interests of property and authority, complacently reflecting, no doubt, that what it did was ultimately for the good of the whole. Controversy was most intense when it drew the line between large and small property in a way which offended significant interests. This was precisely the offence of the game laws. A £100 land qualification was not very high, but by excluding those who possessed personal estate in the form of a tenancy, it militated against a valuable form of property. This kind of conflict was always more likely in rural than in urban society. In an urban context attempts to discriminate in favour of freehold ownership were rare and rendered impracticable by economic conditions. Instead it was possible to calculate a hierarchy of property which made it easy to select qualifications broadly acceptable to the local community. In the countryside the tenurial dis-tinction always mattered more, the landlords who claimed to govern rural society were more entrenched in power, and the possibilities of protest by men of lesser property were limited. But the balance was delicate and the game laws came close to upsetting it, demonstrating in the process that the vaunted unity of the landed interest was largely imaginary.

For practical purposes landlords achieved most when their aims were limited and their potential victims local. This was the essence of the enclosure procedure. It also applied in the rare cases where special demands were made on behalf of individual landowners. In the 1790s canal legislation came to include a clause reserving the right of landowners to a certain proportion of stock in navigation companies in their locality.[160] But they do not seem to have used it to acquire a greater share of canal stock than their property would have naturally implied. Canals were also affected by provisions which ensured that the proud owners of handsome seats and expansive estates did not suffer from the blight inflicted by some navigations. In 1766 the Duke of Bridgwater was induced to make concessions to one such owner, Sir Richard Brook, which he came to regret. But his application to Parliament to cancel Brook's statutory protection in 1770 met with a stony reception.[161] The traveller Thomas Pennant ingenuously considered this a form of public service. Navigation promoters, he wrote of the Trent and Mersey, 'frequently, when the canal passed in sight of any gentleman's seat, have politely given it a breadth, or curvature, to improve the beauty of the prospect'.[162] Such politeness hardly required a legislative stimulus. It was notorious that turnpikes wended hither and thither to suit the purposes of country gentlemen, not by virtue of Parliament's interposition, but simply as a result of the property-owner's influence on his neighbours. In any case these were modest achievements to set beside failures like the repeated and conclusive defeat of the grazing lobby, or the erosion of the old corn laws. The truth was that when the landed interest set out to challenge other interests on a broad basis in defence of rural society as a whole it was quickly made aware either of its internal divisions or its corporate weakness. And even then its instinctive reaction was to emphasize its immersion in a commercial society which made no special allowances for land.

A recurrent debate which exposed the nature of the change taking place concerned the legal status of hawkers and pedlars, described in the Commons by Edmund Burke as 'an humble, but industrious and laborious set of chapmen, against whom the vengeance of your House has sometimes been levelled'.[163] They certainly provoked very different responses. In the countryside they provided a useful service; but by the shopkeepers of countless market towns they were regarded with extreme jealousy. Twice they were subjected to taxation, by an act of William III which required travelling retailers to purchase a license, and nearly a century later, in 1785,

---

[160] J. R. Ward, *The Finance of Canal Building in Eighteenth-Century England* (Oxford, 1974), pp. 153-7.

[161] *Commons Journals*, xxxii. 768.

[162] *The Journey from Chester to London* (London, 1782), p. 52.

[163] *The Works of the Right Honourable Edmund Burke* (Bohn's edn., 8 vols., London, 1854), v. 347; see also Hoh-cheung and L. H. Mui, *Shops and Shopkeeping in Eighteenth Century England* (Kingston, 1989), ch. 4.

when Pitt introduced his shop tax, and imposed a matching increase in the licence fee. In between there were many campaigns to prohibit hawkers and pedlars altogether. It was pointed out that shopkeepers were burdened with the capital investment and overheads of a permanent business; they also paid local rates and taxes, and served their often time-consuming share of parochial offices. Hawkers and pedlars suffered none of these disadvantages and had the advantage of being able to offer smuggled commodities with minimal risk of detection. They were difficult to distinguish from vagrants, and, so it was said, many of them were Scotsmen to boot.

Most MPs sat for borough seats, and were thereby vulnerable to the lobbying of the shopkeeping class. But the country gentlemen who often represented these trading communities were all too aware that travelling tradesmen played a large part in sustaining the commercial life of the countryside. In the well-recorded debates of 1692 and 1693, they approved the sentiments, even if they did not all have the temerity to speak themselves, of those who sat for less exposed constituencies, men like Sir Christopher Musgrave, knight of the shire for Westmorland, and Sir Robert Sawyer, MP for Cambridge University. These speakers bitterly denounced the interest of 'some few tradesmen in corporations'. They made no attempt to conceal the concern of landed families and their tenants. Prohibition would put 'it into the inhabitants of corporations to exact upon the country gentlemen as they please'. Servants would be corrupted in the process of expeditions to market towns to purchase their masters' requirements.[164] The arguments were necessarily complicated. Hawkers could be supported on principles of free trade and, less nobly, by the vested interest of great wholesalers who pointed out that the 'greatest part of their Estate is in the hands of Pedlars'.[165] On the other side there was a certain authoritarian bias against 'a sort of people that pay no taxes to the government nor contribute to any parish charges, that carry about libels against the government'.[166] But at bottom, like many other questions of the late seventeenth century, this was a conflict of town and country, money and land. In the crucial division of 2 February 1693, when the Commons finally passed the licensing bill, no less than 360 MPs cast their votes.[167]

By the mid-eighteenth century the emphasis had shifted on both sides of the argument. Alderman Slingsby Bethel of the City did his best to prove to the landed interest that its prosperity was inseparable from that

---

[164] H. Horwitz, ed., *The Parliamentary Diary of Narcissus Luttrell, 1691–1693* (Oxford, 1972), pp. 132–4, 395–7.

[165] Leicestershire RO, Finch MSS, PP 159: 'Reasons humbly offered to the Lords in Parliament against a Bill entituled, An Act for the better Suppressing of Pedlars, Hawkers etc.', n.d.

[166] *The Parliamentary Diary of Narcissus Luttrell*, p. 396.

[167] Ibid., 397.

of the beleaguered shopkeepers. 'The beauty and magnificence of our great cities will evanish, and by their decay the value of most of the farms in England will be diminished.'[168] Corbyn Morris turned the argument from luxury and vice on its head to show that rural society was the sufferer by the low morals of the travellers. They were 'a set of *unmeriting* People, who carry *Luxury* into all Corners; and sollicit and enflame the Pride of every *Farmer's Wife* and *Daughter* in the Kingdom.'[169] Significantly, the defenders of the hawkers now avoided appeals to the self-interest of landowning, servant-employing families. Robert Vyner, a country gentleman, and, incidentally, a tireless champion of the Lincolnshire wool growers, argued instead for their value to manufacturers and craftsmen, quoting Locke in support. 'I must observe, with the great Mr. Locke, that our merchants and working tradesmen deserve much more the care of the legislature than our shopkeepers, who are, he says, but a sort of brokers between the manufacturer and consumer.'[170] There plainly remained real differences of interest between town and country; yet in changed circumstances it suited nobody to dwell on them. And in its substantive demand, to do away with penalties on hawkers and pedlars, the country was notably unsuccessful.

Interest in the eighteenth century was an ambiguous term, as indeed it is today. But the term landed interest was more than usually ambiguous and the nature of its ambiguity changed with time. For many traditionalists, no doubt, it remained expressive of the true interest of the country as a whole, the timeless repository of national values in an age of transitory commercial prosperity. But this no longer represented the realities of parliamentary politics by the late eighteenth century. Even the enthusiasts for agricultural enterprise, who sought to revive and build on such sentiment, were in truth urging something quite different, not indeed a lost cause, but a more restricted one. There is a certain paradox about this. The campaign for a Board of Agriculture, beginning with Young, Rack, and Donaldson in the early years of George III, eventually triumphed, to commission, in the famous reports on county agriculture, a lasting testament to their efforts. Yet there is a sense in which this success was an indication of weakness, not strength. Donaldson's eloquent plea for a board in 1775 was defensive in tone, and made in terms designed to make the farmer and landowner collaborators in an essentially commercial venture. It was to be a 'Board of Reformation', a 'temple dedicated to industry'.[171] Others saw such an institution more narrowly as a means of supporting

---

[168] *Parliamentary History*, xiv. 247.

[169] *Observations on the Past Growth and Present State of the City of London* (London, 1751), p. 25.

[170] *Parliamentary History*, xiv. 255.

[171] William Donaldson, *Agriculture Considered as a Moral and Political Duty* (London, 1775), pp. 170 ff., 194.

the agriculturalist in his ceaseless struggle with manufacturers and merchants. This was more realistic, but it also reflected the diminishing weight which landowners and their tenants as a body carried. When agriculture had become an interest, not *the* national interest, and when the best that could be hoped for was a powerful lobby capable of influencing government and appealing to Parliament, then indeed the landowner as sole legislator for his country was a figure of the past.

AN ABSOLUTE LAND TAX

If taxation is the touchstone of social policy, the history of the land tax provides a means of assessing eighteenth-century conceptions of the State and its functions. The land tax was a direct result of the Revolution of 1688 and the foreign policy which it necessitated. In the form finally adopted in 1697, it was in theory an income tax set at a uniform rate on both land rents and personal income. In practice it rather resembled a contribution made by landowners on the basis of fixed quotas. The theoretical rates of taxation varied according to budgetary needs, between 1s. in the pound and 4s. in the pound. But these were nominal. Raising the rate from 1s. to 4s., for instance, was achieved by multiplying every quota by a factor of four. The quotas were determined by Parliament as between the counties and by local tradition as between different parishes or districts. Both the principle of the tax and the quotas set remained largely unchanged for more than a century. This was not the original intention. As an embittered petition of 1760 observed, the assessments had been expected to terminate with the end of King William's War. However, 'there being an End of the War but not of the Tax', posterity had been burdened permanently.[172] In fact it was not until a very different war added further burdens in 1798 that the land tax was replaced, or rather supplemented by a more sophisticated tax on incomes.

The land tax was considered something of a phenomenon. Foreigners praised the unselfishness of a landed class which taxed itself unstintingly for the benefit of the nation, without seeking exemptions of the kind which marked continental tax regimes. Even within the British empire, the English position was anomalous. Colonial assemblies either avoided direct taxation, in preference for consumer taxes, or adopted it in a form, the poll tax, which was highly regressive.[173] The Irish Parliament also eschewed a property tax, though a duty on absentee landlords had considerable appeal at a time of mounting patriotic distaste for the magnates who spent their

[172] Lincolnshire Archives Office, Fane MSS, 6/2/12–14.
[173] See R. A. Becker, 'Revolution and Reform: An Interpretation of Southern Taxation 1763 to 1783', *William and Mary Quarterly*, 32 (1975), 417–42.

lives and the produce of their Irish estates in London. What prevented its adoption, when it was seriously considered in 1773, was the fear that it would lead to a general land tax on all Irish property.[174] Scotland paid a land tax but at such a low, fixed rate, that it was regarded as virtual exemption. One of the arguments used against the otherwise attractive scheme for a Scottish militia in 1776 was the threat that it would entail an additional property tax. As in Ireland the cost of patriotism was too high if it meant adopting an English-style land tax.[175]

Historians have been less impressed by the self-sacrifice of the English landlord. Comparisons with the burdens of the French estate have been employed to make it seem less sacrificial.[176] Moreover if the tax burden as a whole is calculated over a period of time, it is clear that the place of the land tax was diminishing.[177] Essentially this was because the State turned increasingly to taxation by indirect rather than direct means. The classification used in the great enquiry of 1868–9, the first which offered a coherent analysis of public revenue from the establishment of parliamentary government, clearly reveals the nature of the changing relationship between indirect and direct taxes. The contribution made to net revenue by the latter fell steadily from 38 per cent in 1710, to 30 per cent in 1750, 26 per cent in 1760, 20 per cent in 1780, and 18 per cent in 1790.[178] Pitt's decision in 1798 to redress the balance somewhat by reintroducing a significant measure of direct taxation was evidently long overdue.

A selfish desire on the part of landowning MPs in a landowning legislature to protect their own income might seem easy to substantiate. Walpole made the elimination of the land tax the central part of his fiscal policy. He got it down to 2s. in the pound in 1730 and to 1s. a year later. The main object of his notorious excise scheme of 1733 was to make possible its final disappearance. Only the extreme unpopularity of the excise, and the belief that he intended applying it to a wide range of commodities including basic foodstuffs, removed this prospect. As it turned out Walpole was the last minister consciously to pursue this policy. His successors lived through recurrent warfare with France, and were much too desperate for revenue to contemplate doing away with a tax which, for all its inequity, provided a reliable form of revenue. Even so, it was obvious that the land tax had many enemies. The last reduction of the land tax in 1767, from 4s.

[174] E. W. Harcourt, ed., *The Harcourt Papers* (14 vols., Oxford, 1876–1905), ix. 94.

[175] *Critical Review*, xlv. 137.

[176] C. B. Behrens, 'Nobles, Privileges and Taxes in France at the End of the Ancien Regime', *Econ. Hist. Rev.*, 2nd ser. 15 (1962–3), 451–75.

[177] P. Mathias and P. O'Brien, 'Taxation in Britain and France, 1715–1810: A Comparison of the Social and Economic Incidence of Taxes Collected for the Central Governments', *Jnl. Eur. Econ. Hist.* 5 (1976), 601–50.

[178] The figures are calculated from the statistics recorded at PP. 1868–9. xxxv; a fuller series based on 5-year averages, but starting in 1715, is in Mathias and O'Brien, 'Taxation in Britain and France, 1715–1810'.

to 3s. in the pound, was carried in the teeth of strong opposition from the Chatham Ministry and its Chancellor of the Exchequer, Charles Townshend, by back-bench country gentlemen conscious of the approaching general election and anxious to propitiate their constituents. From time to time there were proposals to update the land tax, by ordering a general reassessment which would eradicate the anomalies. The brewer Samuel Whitbread pointed out to the House of Commons in 1777 that on two estates of similar value in neighbouring counties he paid totally different taxes, £16 in Lincolnshire, £50 in Leicestershire. His solution was a new assessment which would take full account of the actual value of estates, at least for additional shillings in the pound.[179] It was not well received. Indeed one of the strongest arguments against the idea of abolishing the land tax altogether was the contention that it would thereby be easier to introduce a more efficient and onerous property tax at a later date. This had been used against Walpole, when he held out to the country gentlemen the enticing prospect of replacing the land tax with excises.[180]

Landed self-serving seemed all the more plausible in the light of other changes which took place during the second half of the century. A four shilling rate of land tax in theory represented a tax of twenty per cent on landed income. But the unrealistic assessments adopted in 1697 ensured that very few landowners, and those only in the highly rated counties of East Anglia and the south-east, actually paid such a proportion of their receipts, even during the War of the Spanish Succession when the land tax was at its most burdensome. Economic trends after 1750 made it still more notional. The rapid rise of prices and rents allowed both farmer and landlord to thrive on quotas which remained unchanged, while their profits rose. The regional and local variations both of the tax incidence and the agrarian pattern were so marked that it is impossible to generalize about rates.[181] But there is no doubt that the real incidence of the land tax fell steadily, even dramatically. By the 1780s a 4s. rate would commonly amount to something between one and two shillings even in highly rated counties. In favoured areas of the north, it was reckoned in pence rather than shillings and was accounted much less of a burden than some other taxes, for instance the poor rate.

This erosion of the land tax to the point at which it became a relatively minor burden, was slightly offset by the higher rates set in the second half

---

[179] *Parliamentary Register*, viii. 64.

[180] Langford, *The Excise Crisis: Society and Politics in the Age of Walpole*, p. 158.

[181] Land tax assessments do not generally record real rentals, though some impression of the relation between the tax charged and the rent on which it was based can be gained from the few which do and from estate records. But the ratio between rent and tax varied from parish to parish, according to circumstance. Even the original basis of assessment, used in the 1690s, is far from clear. A simple acreage equivalent does not seem to have been employed consistently; see M. Turner and D. Mills, eds., *Land and Property: The English Land Tax 1692–1832* (Gloucester, 1986), *passim*.

of the century. Governments of the early Hanoverian period did their best
to keep the land tax low in peacetime. Between 1714 and 1756 the tax was
set at 4s. in only twelve years. Between 1756 and 1798 it applied at this
level in thirty-seven years. As a result the average annual rate was 2s. 9d.
before 1756 compared with 3s. 10d. after 1756. Even so the increase in
taxation which this represented was far outweighed by rising agricultural
productivity. Since Parliament not only controlled the rates of taxation,
but also took an enthusiastic part in the promotion of agricultural improvement, it was easy for critics to draw the lesson. The same country gentlemen
who rode roughshod over common rights with the aid of enclosure bills,
protected themselves and their tenants against effective taxation of their
profits. Every argument pointed to class selfishness and aggrandizement
by men employing their legislative influence to advance their own interests.

Although this line of argument has appealed to posterity, it is not very
impressive. The tax was never simply a tax on land, though it is true that
in many places it took that form. The formula for rating personal property,
especially tradesman's stock, was widely applied and in some instances
made a significant contribution to the total collected. Particularly in the
first half of the century, before inflation reduced the real impact of the tax,
it was complained that such personal taxation was excessive. This was
especially the case where any change in local circumstances made it impracticable to load the rating of real property further. The City parish of St
Dunstan's in the West had a large quota which included the contribution
made by customs officials, whose salaries were taxable. When, near the end
of Queen Anne's reign, the customs establishment was transferred to
Westminster, the parish found itself having to make up the difference. The
result, at a time when peace made possible a reduction from 4s. to 2s. in
the pound, was a swingeing rise in the real incidence of the land tax, which
was met by raising the assessments of stock. Land tax commissioners were
also accused of underrating themselves and making up the deficiency from
the taxation of stock.[182]

In places like St Dunstan's the shorthand description of the tax as a
'land tax' was in any case somewhat misleading, since it was in the nature
of a duty on houses and tenements. Indeed, the extent to which it was a
tax on urban property is easily forgotten. For instance, the county of
Middlesex paid a quota exceeding £326,000 with the rate at 4s. This had
almost no relation to land in its conventional, agrarian sense, and vastly
exceeded the quota of any other county.[183] Moreover it concealed major

---

[182] *An Historical Account of the Conduct of the Vestry of the Parish of St Dunstan's in the West*
(London, 1714), pp. 39–40.

[183] Rural, or at any rate agricultural Middlesex was to be found in the five hundreds of Edmonton,
Elthorne, Gore, Isleworth, and Spelthorne; together these paid £20,812 to the land tax, leaving
£305,334 in 1784 to be collected from the strictly metropolitan portion of the county.

differences within the metropolitan area. An acre in the City bore 11s. when the land tax stood at 4s. in the pound. In Middlesex as a whole this figure dropped to 3s. 7d. In rural Buckinghamshire, thirty miles away, the equivalent payment per acre was in the region of 1s. 11d., and three hundred miles off, in the equally rural but notoriously underrated Lancashire, it was 4d.[184] It could be argued that this represented some form of distributive justice. It could not be said that it reflected a consistently applied tax on agricultural land. Inhabitants of London were well aware of their burden. At the end of William III's reign, Brixton and Southwark were complaining that a 3s. rate amounted locally to 4s. 6d. or even 5s. 6d.[185] Subsequent easing of the real burden of the tax did not affect the argument from relative injustice. In 1783 the parliamentary reformers of Tower Hamlets pointed out that they paid more to the land tax than several counties which had their own representatives in Parliament.[186]

Provincial towns and cities also made a substantial contribution in their own right. In some instances this was fixed by Parliament in the same way as the county quotas. For the rest the assessment was a matter of local convention and negotiation. The urban burden was considerable. Lancashire as a county was not heavily taxed, but a large portion of what it paid came from town rather than country. Liverpool and the three manufacturing parishes of Manchester, Salford, and Ashton together paid more than a fifth of the total for the county. Substantial towns already well developed in the 1690s, when quotas were fixed, could certainly claim to be contributing their fair share. Coventry paid 6 per cent of Warwickshire's total, Worcester 7 per cent of Worcestershire's, Oxford 9 per cent of Oxfordshire's.[187] These fractions probably reflected the relative wealth and population of the towns concerned not inaccurately. Those who paid them were at least entitled to argue, however, that they were as much the beasts of burden as the rural squirearchy whose voice was more stridently heard in protest.

This is not to say that town dwellers did not protest. Indeed some of the most determined objections to the land tax came from corporate towns which considered that they were victimized. Great Yarmouth complained in 1699 that the assessment levied in 1692 could not be sustained in the light of property values. A 3s. rate currently levied actually amounted to

---

[184] These figures represent the total tax payable, divided by the total acreage; the actual tax per acre varied within the same county, within the same hundred, and even within the same parish.

[185] *Commons Journals*, xiii. 219.

[186] Ibid., xxxix. 406.

[187] The percentage figures are calculated from actual land tax paid in 1784: Liverpool paid £1,999, the three other parishes £2,631 out of a county total of £22,321; Coventry paid £2,464 out of a county total of £39,679; Worcester paid £2,407 out of a county total of £33,363; Oxford paid £3,282 out of a county total of £38,443.

3s. 7d. in real terms.[188] It was argued in 1732, at a time when Walpole was pleading for the relief of landed squires, that inland trading towns were among the worst sufferers, having been heavily rated to the land tax in the 1690s and in many instances experiencing economic recession as a result.[189] Ely, the only cathedral city not represented directly in the Commons, petitioned unsuccessfully to have its proportion reduced in 1727.[190] Lyme Regis was still protesting at its own share at the beginning of George III's reign. Like other decaying towns it suffered from the imposition of a fixed quota at a time when its wealth was actually contracting. In 1760 it foresaw the 'utter ruine' of the town, as householders left to avoid high taxes and their landlords pulled down houses to escape assessment. It was claimed at this time that the real incidence of a 4s. rate amounted to 5s. in the pound.[191] Twelve years later the process had accelerated to the point at which the true rate could be stated at 6s.[192] Parliament generally ignored such pleas. No doubt MPs could envisage the consequences of creating a precedent. But the belief that many towns were unfairly burdened was certainly common.

Inequity and anomaly were inevitable in a system which had begun on a demonstrably irrational basis. It was not a tax which discriminated against moneyed Englishmen by comparison with landed Englishmen, so much as a tax which discriminated against particular regions and localities. The county quotas set under William III remained unchanged in the eighteenth century, and themselves reflected disparities which went back to earlier assessments. But they were accepted, partly because the political priority was so pressing. The time for putting them right never seemed ripe. In 1666 the Suffolk MP Sir John Holland bemoaned the burden of his own county but admitted that 'it is no time now to go about to rectify the inequality of the rate'.[193] Debate on the rates after the Revolution of 1688 mirrored the same concerns as those after the Restoration. In 1691 the grievances of the old 'associated counties' were again cited, but the representatives of East Anglia were outvoted by those of the west and north.[194] Political exigencies, the extreme difficulty of negotiating new relativities, and the likelihood that failure to agree would make necessary an even more unpopular general excise all contributed. If anything the quotas eventually petrified by the land tax of 1697 positively worsened the discrepancy

---

[188] *Commons Journals*, xii. 607.
[189] *Free Briton*, 27 Apr. 1732.
[190] *Commons Journals*, xx. 731–2.
[191] Lincolnshire Archives Office, Fane MSS, 6/2/12–14.
[192] *Commons Journals*, xxxiii. 468.
[193] C. Robbins, ed., *The Diary of John Milward September 1666 to May 1668* (Cambridge, 1938), p. 311.
[194] *The Parliamentary Diary of Narcissus Luttrell*, pp. 61–2.

between the favoured north, and the south and east.[195] It was suggested that this had represented a kind of tax on political loyalty. London, East Anglia, and the south-east generally shouldered a burden which was essential if the Revolution were to be preserved. Walpole later talked of it being 'differently laid according to the disposition of the counties for the government'.[196] At county level the Dissenter Joshua Toulmin reckoned that in Somerset Taunton paid more than the three other towns of Bath, Wells, and Bridgwater combined, and attributed this to its greater enthusiasm for William of Orange.[197] Perhaps such claims gave greater rationality to the process than it deserved. But they doubtless reflected an appreciation that raising the assessments of regions remote from central government and prone to disaffection would have caused turmoil.

In any event the effect was to perpetuate regional distinctions which the economic changes of the eighteenth century rendered ever more anachronistic. Even at local level the parish and hundred quotas fixed in the 1690s remained largely unaltered. In 1698 a clause which would have made them formally unalterable was only narrowly defeated in the Commons.[198] Sometimes, especially in the very early days of this system, land tax commissioners ventured to modify the apportionments marginally, as, for example, they increased the burden on Woodbridge, in Loes Hundred in Suffolk.[199] But such action remained in the collective mind, causing irritation to the aggrieved long after the offence. In 1798 one of the objections to Pitt's scheme for the redemption of the land tax was that it would petrify for ever the injustices perpetrated by local commissioners over a period of a century.[200] But it was at regional level that the inequities seemed most difficult to justify. The resulting anomalies pitted county against county and province against province. Norfolk and Suffolk alone paid the equivalent of 1d. in every shilling of the land tax, Essex, Cambridgeshire, and Hertfordshire another 1d., Kent, Sussex, and Surrey $1\frac{1}{2}d.$, London and its environs 2d. Yet all seven northern counties put together, with a quarter of the population of England and Wales by the late eighteenth century, paid only a 1d. between them.

The most farcical of all the quotas were those for Cumberland and Westmorland where the real rate of the land tax at 4s. in the pound was reckoned to be less than 6d. in the pound. It was not to be expected that landowners thus privileged would take the same view either of the land tax

[195] J. V. Beckett, 'Land Tax Administration at the Local Level 1693–1798', in Turner and Mills, eds., *Land and Property*, p. 169.

[196] Hughes, *Studies in Administration and Finance*, p. 301.

[197] *The History of the Town of Taunton*, p. 190.

[198] Historical Manuscripts Commission, *Le Fleming MSS*, p. 350.

[199] Robert Loder, *The History of Framlingham, in the County of Suffolk* (Woodbridge, 1798), p. 417.

[200] Somerset RO, DD/DRU/1/4: Notes for a speech by 1st Earl of Carnarvon.

or attempts to reform it as their southern brethren. When the question was debated in the 1760s defenders of the north-west admitted that the quotas amounted to an 'exemption from the land tax', which had been granted 'on the faith of Parliament' at the Revolution and shared in its peculiar sanctity. They also urged regional differences by way of justification. So advantageous was the land tax rate that the capital value of land in the Lake District had risen far faster than elsewhere, with forty years' rental being paid for estates which in other counties would have fetched between twenty-five and thirty-five. This was said to be compensation for the poor land and unforgiving climate of Cumbria, an argument unlikely to impress the equally disadvantaged but highly rated marshlands of Essex and heath-lands of Surrey. It was also claimed that the class of small farmers who worked the land filled the function of exporting a sturdy and numerous labour force to cities in the Midlands and south.[201] This contention, too, can hardly have convinced counties which were already sliding into the overpopulation and unemployment of the rural south in the late eighteenth century. If nothing else, such analyses revealed what most contemporaries knew all to well, that the land tax, in so far as it was indeed a tax on agriculture, was actually a tax on some agriculturalists to the advantage of others.

This sense that expediency rather than class interest dictated the inci-dence of the land tax is confirmed by the urban experience. If town dwellers shared the burden of the land tax, they also shared its gross inequities. The disparity between London and the provinces was noticeable in this as in other respects. Orator Henley, intent on raising a spirit of disaffection among Londoners, pointed out that the populous but impoverished parish of St Giles in the Fields, notorious for its degradation, paid more to the land tax than the cities of York and Bristol.[202] But even in the capital the impact of economic growth on inflexible tax structures was marked. Newly enriched parishes on London's northern and western perimeter paid quotas fixed in the 1690s. The result was a real rate as low as 6d. in some parts of Westminster.[203] On average, it was said, in Marylebone in 1796, it had fallen to 1¼d. in the pound.[204] Marylebone was the classic case of a parish which had been largely agricultural when its quota was fixed under William III, but which, a century later, was overwhelmingly urban. An incidental effect was further to erode any sense of balance between land and stock. Westminster's favourable position could be used, as Adam Smith pointed

[201] *London Magazine* (1766), 642–3.
[202] Lincolnshire Archives Office, Monson MSS, 31/1: Journal of Thomas Thistlewood, 18 Aug. 1748.
[203] Sir John Sinclair, *The History of the Public Revenue of the British Empire* (3rd edn., 3 vols., London, 1803), ii. 341.
[204] *Gentleman's Magazine* (1796), 436.

out, to remove assessments on stock altogether, whereas in the City shop-keepers and tradesmen were expected to carry a substantial burden.[205]

What prevented rationalization of the land tax? One consideration was the difficulty of predicting the effects of change on so irrational a system. In addition to the many taxpayers who were in effect privileged, and understandably reluctant to surrender their privilege, there were others uncertain of their relative position but certain that it could be worse. Not surprisingly there was some reluctance publicly to discuss the incidence of the land tax. In Newcastle Sir Frederick Eden found a notable disinclination to aid his statistical surveys in this respect. Parishes which were eager to explain the burden of the poor rates were mysteriously secretive about what they paid to the land tax. 'It is a very tender subject, and many (in other respects enlightened) persons have refused to give any information respecting it.'[206] Moreover, fixed quotas gave an incentive to collaborative investment. Land tax assessors were quick to rerate individual improve-ments, if only because by doing so they were able to relieve the rest of their parish. But when the value of land in a parish as a whole rose, as it did after enclosure, the effect was to relieve every landowner. The contrast with the tithe, which was a fixed proportion of produce rather than a fixed sum, was striking, and lent additional force to the propaganda deployed against the deadening commercial impact of tithes. The same logic applied in urban districts. A new house or a new shop in a Westminster parish with a low quota reduced each individual's share of the common burden. Large-scale building automatically benefited everyone. At this game there were losers as well as winners. In unenclosed parishes, or old urban parishes, the temptation was to take flight, thereby worsening the position of those who remained still further. But even losers might doubt whether it was worth recasting the rules of the game. Certainly commissioners of the land tax and Parliament itself preferred to leave them unchanged.

Even if the land tax could justly be viewed as essentially an imposition on the agricultural interest, it would remain difficult to calculate the true effect of taxation on land as a whole. Those who complained on behalf of landed society were prone to include grievances which they shared with others. In 1781 it was said of lands in Norfolk and Essex that they were weighed down with taxation which amounted to 16s. in the pound. But the fiscal horrors listed included the taxes on houses and windows, as well as church rates and tithes, which applied to all kinds of communities.[207] The eccentricities of the tax-collecting system sometimes promoted confusion of this kind. The administration of the land tax was combined at local level

[205] *An Inquiry into the Nature and Causes of the Wealth of Nations*, ii. 850.
[206] *The State of the Poor*, ed. A. G. L. Rogers (London, 1928), p. 268.
[207] *Whitehall Evening-Post*, 8 Dec. 1781.

with that on houses and windows; together with certain other impositions, on carriages, horses, dogs, and servants, they were increasingly lumped together as 'assessed taxes' for official purposes. This practice affected the collecting and classifying of statistics in the nineteenth century and has helped determine the categories employed by historians. The result is thoroughly confusing. Taxes on houses and windows, not to say the other duties, were quite unlike the land tax. They were not assessed in relation to fixed parochial or county quotas, they were repeatedly revised and extended by ministers in search of new revenues, and they in no sense represented a peculiar burden on agricultural landlords and tenants.

Further complicating matters, there were taxes which contemporaries considered especially onerous where the landed interest was concerned, but which were not grouped with the assessed taxes. Pre-eminent among these was the malt duty, generally treated by historians as one of those indirect taxes which in theory swelled the burden of taxation on the ordinary consumer, and more especially the poorer members of society. In 1740 William Pulteney recalled its origins in terms which emphasized its unfairness. 'The Malt-Tax was never introduced till towards the latter End of King William's Reign, and was at first most strenuously opposed, and was looked on as a Tax so burdensome upon the poor Labourers and Manufacturers of this Kingdom, that no Man imagined any Minister would have the Assurance to propose renewing it or continuing it, after the War was over.'[208] Ministers not only renewed it but from time to time increased it, with the result that malt made a large contribution to the product of indirect taxes. In 1787 it was yielding approximately £1,300,000 compared with £1,700,000 from the beer excise and £500,000 from duties on spirits.[209]

Since it was reflected in the price of alcoholic drinks bought in the tavern or the ale-shop it was obviously in some sense paid by the purchaser. But unlike the beer tax the malt duty affected home brewers as well as the retail market. The distinction was important, as Lord Bute and George Grenville discovered when they devised a matching cider excise which bore both on production for the home and production for the market. In the case of malt the distinction also affected arguments about the impact of the excises on alcohol. Champions of the landed interest considered it highly discriminatory. When it was under discussion in the Commons in 1670, the Country Party supporter Sir Nicholas Carew observed: 'Whatever excise you lay upon malt is an absolute Land-Tax.'[210] It continued to be viewed in this light during the following century. Significantly, the malt duty was granted, unlike other excises, for a year at a time, and accordingly

[208] The History and Proceedings of the House of Commons from the Restoration to the Present Time (11 vols., London, 1742), xi. 246–7.

[209] P. Mathias, The Brewing Industry in England 1700–1830 (Cambridge, 1959), pp. 356–7.

[210] Grey's Debates, i. 273.

bracketed with the land tax. But whereas Chancellors of the Exchequer declined to review the operation of the land tax, they periodically increased the malt duty. Larger consumption also improved its yield. In the War of Spanish Succession it raised less than half the product of a 4s. land tax; by the 1780s it was producing almost as much, and by the 1790s considerably more. This made the assumption that it was a burden on agriculture, not the consumer, of particular interest.

There was a circularity about all such arguments which made it difficult to determine the final incidence of taxes. Certainly, whenever the malt duty was increased, the use of malt for brewing diminished, suggesting that consumers, rather than producers, actually paid for it. If so the difference between the malt and beer excises was small. It lay merely in modes of collection, and in the advance commitment of capital required of farmers, maltsters, and brewers. Those who took this view sometimes argued for abolishing the beer tax in favour of a steeper levy still on malt, thereby simplifying the process of assessment and collection. But the premiss was not conceded by landed men. They fully accepted that malt production was sensitive to the consumers' response to the final price of alcoholic products. Indeed it was precisely their complaint that high malt duties, by reducing the eventual market, forced down the production of malt. Every penny on malt rather than beer was thereby an additional burden on agriculture and an element in the complex calculations which ruled the farmers' choice of cereal crops.[211] Not surprisingly, politicians found it difficult to choose between these arguments. The malt duty climbed steadily, but so did almost every other kind of excise, including the beer tax. Nor was it only malt which gave rise to such complications. The salt tax controversy in 1732, which seemed a clear enough confrontation between the poor consumer and the landed interest, produced a claim that small landowners and even moderately substantial ones suffered more by the salt excise than by the land tax. The same was said of the soap and candle duties.[212] A similar debate in 1767 produced even more convoluted calculations. Then it was reckoned that a middling landowner with a rental of £100 to £400 would benefit by the abolition of the salt tax, but that farmers who owned £50–£100 of their own, like great landlords, would do better if the land tax were reduced. Most legislators could cope with the distinction between the rich and the poor. Legislating for a threefold division in this way was altogether more of a puzzle.[213]

[211] G. R. Porter, *The Progress of the Nation* (new edn., London, 1851), pp. 554–5.
[212] *London Magazine* (1737), 66.
[213] Ibid. (1767), 163–4.

THE REAL PROPERTY OF INDIVIDUALS

From the middle of the seventeenth century to the 1740s arguments about
taxation tended to resolve themselves into a choice between two stark
alternatives: taxes on income, more especially property rents; and taxes on
consumption, more especially objects of mass consumption.[214] Successive
Parliaments under Charles II, William III, and Anne agonized about this
choice, turning sometimes one way, sometimes another, and exploring new
means of refining one or the other so as to lessen its horrors. Thanks to
the warfare of the post-Revolution years the result was not, however, a
choice, but the worst of both worlds, a land tax which was required even
in peacetime to maintain armed forces at a realistic level, and numerous
excises without which the National Debt could not be serviced. However,
the long years of peace in the Walpole era somewhat arrested this process.
Walpole had the luxury, as it seemed, of presenting a choice. Once again
it became possible to think in terms of eliminating the objectionable land
tax, or alternatively of reducing, if not abolishing the most reviled of the
excises. Walpole himself made no bones about preferring the former. His
was an unapologetic appeal to the interests of landowners and their tenants,
at the expense of the consumer in general. Though he failed in his
endeavour permanently to change the direction of fiscal policy, the arguments which developed at this time, both political and social, were to cast
a long shadow over the future.

It was none the less a somewhat distorted shadow. The debate about
social justice implied the continuing viability of a choice between taxes
which favoured the poor and taxes which favoured the rich. But that
debate did not reflect a significant division of opinion in government or in
Parliament. All ministers after Walpole at least paid lip-service to the
principle that further taxation of the basic necessities of life was undesirable.
They displayed genuine restraint at least in respect of the four duties,
on soap, salt, candles, and leather, which were considered particularly
burdensome to the poor. All four owed their origin to the heroic age of
fiscal policy during the wars of William and Anne, when unprecedentedly
high levels of expenditure forced Parliament to impose regressive taxation.
Salt was first taxed in 1694, candles in 1709, soap in 1712, leather, after a
brief and controversial experiment between 1697 and 1700, in 1710. The
rates were increased in the course of the century, but not in proportion to
the rise in taxation generally, nor ever in relation to inflation. In 1718 they
yielded fractionally below £1 million per annum, equivalent to 2s. on the
land tax; at this level they produced 23 per cent of receipts from all
indirect taxation, and with direct taxes at peacetime levels, 16 per cent of

---

[214] J. Brewer, *The Sinews of Power: War, Money and the English State, 1688–1783* (London, 1989),
pp. 145 ff.

government revenue from all sources. Nearly sixty years later, on the threshold of the American War, they were producing an almost identical sum, but as a proportion of indirect taxes only 13 per cent. During the mid-century wars no minister had proposed extending them and even during the American War, North tried to avoid doing so. His general levy of an additional 5 per cent on all customs and excises in 1779 and 1782 specifically excluded the four duties. But the pressures exerted in the final stages of the war proved too much. First salt in 1780, then soap in 1782, and finally (under Pitt) candles in 1784, were subjected to additional excise duties. Even so they constituted only 7 per cent of new taxes granted to meet the demands of an exceptionally expensive war. When the final accounts were cast in 1785 it was found that the four duties produced about £1.25 million per annum; this was 11 per cent of indirect tax income, and 6 per cent of total revenue, in each case far less than the equivalents in 1718.[215]

Ministers could also point to their reluctance to lay completely new taxes on lower-class income. From time to time there were scares about the prospects of taxes on housing, fuel, and foodstuffs. But the temptation was resisted. The Land Tax Acts specifically exempted houses worth less than 20s. per annum, and in practice, particularly in rural areas where convention sometimes dictated that only land itself was assessed, many homes worth more were probably excused. Poor rating procedures depended to some extent on local practice but exemptions were extensive; in urban areas unrated houses often outnumbered rated. The window tax, even after Dowdeswell increased the yield from it in 1766, exempted far more houses than its Stuart predecessor, the hearth tax. It was the resulting under-registration of housing in the tax statistics that misled demographers into supposing that the population had declined since the late seventeenth century. Richard Price's jeremiads on this subject came to look ridiculous when this was appreciated, as Price's first biographer admitted.[216] The great expansion of middle-class housing in the large cities inevitably attracted the interest of government, but North's house tax of 1778, the most determined attempt to bring it within the tax net, went to considerable lengths to exclude low rental homes, with the result that revenue failed to meet his estimates.[217] Even the excise on bricks, a predictable response to the building boom which began during the Seven Years War, was delayed

[215] These calculations are based on the information in *Calendar of Treasury Board Papers January–December 1718*, xxxii (London, 1962), and *House of Commons Sessional Papers of the Eighteenth Century*, ed. S. Lambert (Wilmington, Del., 1975–6), l, *Finance 1784–7*.

[216] D. V. Glass, *Numbering the People: The Eighteenth-Century Population Controversy and the Development of Census and Vital Statistics in Britain* (Farnborough, 1973), pp. 47 ff; William Morgan, *Memoirs of the Life of the Rev. Richard Price* (London, 1815), pp. 86–7.

[217] *Parliamentary History*, xix. 872.

from 1758 to 1784 by fears that it might raise the cost of lower-class housing.

Food taxes were one of the great dreads of the English mind. Fear of them had much to do with the fury which greeted Walpole's otherwise relatively innocuous proposals to excise tobacco and wine in 1733. A 'general excise' meant an excise on bread, meat, and milk. Neither Walpole nor any other minister seems actually to have contemplated taxing the Englishman's diet. Fuel was in greater danger. The closest call came in 1784 when Pitt proposed a tax on coal levied at the pithead. Strictly speaking there was already a coal excise, first imposed under Charles II, and extended thereafter. By the late 1780s it was producing more than half a million a year. But it applied only to coal carried coastwise, or sold in London, and was raised partly for local purposes, including the financing of new churches in the capital.[218] Elsewhere statutory improvement schemes sometimes permitted a local coal duty, as at Canterbury and Gainsborough.[219] Pitt presumably felt that what could be taxed by paving commissioners to beautify their towns could also be employed by the Treasury for more essential services. In any event the volume of protest aroused by his proposal vanquished all thoughts of proceeding with it. Cheap coal was one of the great boons of the age to the ordinary householder, as the extension of the canal network generated low transport costs. A tax would have been both productive and oppressive.

Burke's belief that 'our taxes, for the far greater portion, fly over the heads of the lowest classes' reflected a widely held view by the last years of the century.[220] But by then the terms of fiscal debate had changed radically since mid-century. Walpole would have found it difficult to comprehend speeches made in the Commons Committee of Ways and Means forty years on. Instead of the old argument about direct taxes on land and indirect taxes on popular consumption, the concern was to find some means of tapping the nation's wealth where it was concentrated most solidly, and where it seemed to be expanding most dramatically, among the broad mass of property-owners, regardless of the source of their wealth. There was a long-standing theory, based on the proposition that all wealth ultimately derived from agriculture, that in the last analysis every kind of tax fell on the land. This doctrine did not survive changing commercial conditions. Malachy Postlethwayt, a formidable champion of the interests of trade and manufacturing, and an enthusiast for the land tax, admitted

---

[218] David Hardies, *Taxation of Coals* (London, 1792). The produce of the duty had been in effect appropriated for national purposes since 1731.

[219] *Commons Journals*, xxxii. 138; 9 Geo. III, c. 21; F. H. Pantin, 'Turnpike Roads in the Canterbury Area', *Archaeologiana Cantiana*, 102 (1985), 179.

[220] *The Works of the Right Honourable Edmund Burke*, v. 314.

that it was untenable.[221] Arthur Young's disbelief in it was more predictable, but expressed the general view of the 1770s.[222]

Young was one of those who tried to calculate what an equitable tax on all kinds of incomes might produce. He reckoned in his *Political Arithmetic* during the American War that landowners received roughly a quarter of national income.[223] Pitt made a similar calculation when he was preparing his income tax in 1798.[224] How much of what remained was earned by the relatively poor and therefore unavailable to the taxman was a matter for dispute. But it was a reasonable assumption that a vast resource of taxable income, most of it possessed by men other than landlords, was waiting to be tapped by a resourceful minister. The simplest means of doing this would have been a tax on all profits. But the bureaucratic implications of a 'a forced contribution of incomes by forced disclosure' were considered horrendous at least until the emergency of 1797–8 made it unavoidable.[225] Lord Auckland was one of those startled by the relative ease with which Pitt eventually carried it through. In the tracts which made his name as a financier, in 1779, Auckland had remarked that 'a state, and especially a mercantile state, should avoid any severe inquisition into the circumstances of individuals'.[226] Charged, twenty years later, with inconsistency, he replied: 'At the period of which I speak, it never entered into the mind of the most enlightened statesmen ... that it could be practicable to establish a forced and general contribution on the only just and efficient system of a forced disclosure.'[227] This was certainly the conventional wisdom. In no war before the revolutionary peril of the 1790s would Parliament have been permitted to impose an effective income tax.

A tax on capital had alternative attractions. In 1720, against a background of intense concern about the size of the National Debt the Tory MP Archibald Hutcheson proposed a levy on all forms of wealth, personal as well as real, rendering the land tax unnecessary and eventually eliminating the Debt entirely. Sixty years later, at a time of comparable anxiety, caused by the rocketing expenditure of the American War, William Pulteney suggested a similar tax.[228] But there were powerful objections. Taxing capital could look very like progressive expropriation by the State. Pitt's legacy duty of 1796 aroused some alarm on this score. Assurances had to be given that it would take eleven deaths over a period of 220 years to eat

---

[221] *The Universal Dictionary of Trade and Commerce*, sub 'Landed Interest'.

[222] (London, 1774), pp. 209–18.

[223] Ibid., Part II (London, 1779), pp. 32 ff.

[224] S. Dowell, *A History of Taxation and Taxes* (4 vols., London, 1884), iv. 361–72.

[225] R. Coupland, *William Wilberforce: A Narrative* (Oxford, 1923), p. 260.

[226] *Four Letters to the Earl of Carlisle, from William Eden, Esq.* (Edinburgh, 1779), p. 47.

[227] *The Substance of a Speech Made by Lord Auckland: in the House of Peers, on Tuesday, the 8th Day of January, 1799* (London, 1799), p. 4.

[228] E. L. Hargreaves, *The National Debt* (London, 1930), pp. 31–6, 82.

up the capital to which it applied.[229] Theorists reasoned that any loss in this respect would be made up by the enormous gains resulting from the elimination of other forms of taxation. But it required considerable faith as well as reason to be sure that this would happen. Moreover, experience of capital taxes was not very reassuring. In a sense some of the taxes on luxuries were in the nature of capital or wealth taxes. This was true of the plate duty of 1756 for example, since it entailed an annual levy assessed on the quantity of plate owned. Even if silver maintained its value the owner might eventually expect to pay the entire capital value of his plate. In practice the tax reduced the market value of silver plate, and panic selling followed. Within five years the product of the plate duty had fallen by more than half, completely wrecking the funding calculations of those who had introduced it. North eventually repealed it as a manifest failure.[230] Predicting the consequences of more extensive levies was a statistical nightmare.

The experience of the plate tax was unencouraging, but even if it had proved more successful it would not have provided grounds for further action. It was acceptable essentially because plate was an unproductive luxury. Taxing it seemed morally justifiable, and, as the new porcelain manufacturers discovered, profitable from the standpoint of encouraging indigenous manufactures. But extending the principle to productive assets would have been far more controversial. In the case of the land tax, the assessment of trading stock was practised erratically, by means of a formula which opted for simplicity rather than social justice. In the case of the poor rate it gave rise to endless dispute in those places where it was customary. Mansfield was confronted with a particularly sensitive instance in 1770 when the blanket-manufacturers of Witney claimed exemption for their stock-in-trade. They were opposed by the Oxfordshire magistracy, a body not known for its representation of the clothiers' interest.[231] Mansfield prudently declined to rule on the general question, but he plainly sympathized with the manufacturers. Five years later he quashed a ruling of the Hampshire Quarter Sessions rating the stock in trade of a brewer, 'declaring it to be his sense, that it was not only impracticable to rate stock in trade with any degree of justice, but that an attempt towards it should be avoided by the common consent of mankind, in order to prevent the innumerable inconveniences and great confusion that must ensue if it was enforced'.[232] Even where Parliament had directed the taxation of stock the consequences were awkward. At Exeter in 1748 it was said that since the local act passed in 1698 'no Proportion between the landed and personal

[229] *Gentleman's Magazine* (1796), 927.
[230] PRO, T. 47. 5.
[231] 1 Black. W. 709: *Rex* v. *Inhabitants of Witney*.
[232] *London Chronicle*, 4 July 1775.

Estates hath been possible to be settled'.[233] In theory it seemed to offer the most equitable of all means of assessing diverse incomes. 'Is there a Tax that goes more generally, or more constantly to Mens Properties, than that founded on the Poors Laws?' one commentator asked in 1744.[234] But it would have been a bold minister who made the most execrated tax of all the basis of a general levy.

It was a maxim of commercial theory that trade and manufactures should not be directly taxed. Champions of home production repeatedly returned to it. Samuel Garbett, one of the spokesmen of the newly vociferous manufacturing lobby in the 1780s, observed that 'property acquired by trade and manufacture is a fit object of taxation, but not the manufactures themselves'.[235] Pitt's most comprehensive defeats followed from his attempt to challenge this assumption. The proposed coal tax of 1784 had to be dropped, and the fustian tax of the same year repealed in 1785 because of the opposition which they provoked from mining and manufacturing interests. Experience did not teach Pitt the error of his ways. In 1797 he laid a duty on clocks and watches. It was perhaps the most disastrous of all fiscal experiments. The duty had to be repealed after one year because it halved the production of the domestic manufacture. The longer-term consequences in terms of talent exiled and advantage gained by foreign manufacturers were incalculable.[236] Taxes on production were agreed to be highly regressive. The tithe itself was one such, and from time to time an even worse evil, the tithe on personal estate, in effect abolished at the Reformation, was remembered: 'the most grievous Tax upon Industry, the Lust of Power ever suggested'.[237]

Where, then, did the ministers who had to finance the recurrent wars of the middle and late eighteenth century turn for funds on which to secure their vast borrowing requirements?[238] One recourse was the expansion of the so-called assessed taxes. Like the excises these were in essence taxes on consumption. But they were assessed on the individual and his life-style, rather than commodities offered for retail sale. North put their rationale clearly in 1778, when increasing the house tax. 'That it was not easy to come at the real property of individuals; but that one ground of judging of this, which prevailed in all nations, was by the expence at which they

---

[233] *Commons Journals*, xxv. 513.

[234] *A Short View of the Frauds, Abuses and Impositions of Parish Officers, with the Laws Relating to the Poor* (London, 1744), p. 32.

[235] J. Thomas, *The Rise of the Staffordshire Potteries* (Bath, 1971), p. 151.

[236] Sinclair, *The History of the Public Revenue*, ii. 258–60.

[237] Sir Michael Foster, *An Examination of the Scheme of Church-Power, Laid down in the Codex Juris Ecclesiastici Anglicani* (2nd edn., London, 1735), p. 157.

[238] The clearest account of 18th-cent. taxation remains Dowell, *A History of Taxation and Taxes*; the resulting pattern, especially as it prevailed at the end of the century, is analysed by P. K. O'Brien, 'The Political Economy of British Taxation, 1660–1815', *Econ. Hist. Rev.*, 2nd ser. 41 (1988), 1–32.

lived.'[239] Like the excises they could be considered voluntary, in the sense that a tax-payer aggrieved by them could dispose of the assets involved and live more frugally. But some of them were carefully calculated to fall on the well-off. From 1747 the window tax was regulated so as to apply a higher rate of duty to houses with numerous windows. The rich man thereby paid more per window than his poorer neighbour, as well as paying for a greater number of windows. This was thought a novelty, and one with much potential for other taxes.[240] In 1778 the house tax itself was graduated so that occupiers of a house worth more than £50 not only paid on the poundage, but paid at a steeper rate per pound than those worth less than £50. Pitt was a great admirer of this principle. In 1789 he applied it to the carriage duty. The first carriage would cost its owner £8 per annum, the second £9, the third £10. Progressive taxation of this kind was to have a considerable future. Tom Paine's self-consciously radical proposals in Part Two of *The Rights of Man* merely enlisted in the cause of social justice a device whose fiscal value was well appreciated at the Treasury.[241]

The most favoured taxes were those on luxuries, what Lord North called 'the elegant conveniencies of life'.[242] His examples included newspapers, cards, and dice, above all the same carriage tax which Pitt was to remodel. North was particularly enthusiastic about carriages, 'because none kept them but such as were really or nominally rich'. Ownership of a carriage was almost a definition of comfortably middle-class status or pretensions. Taxing it involved a minimum of bureaucracy and vitiated the need for prying into an individual's accounts. The introduction of the carriage tax in 1747 was a landmark in the history of taxation, for the principle which it embodied remained central to budgetary policy for half a century. Some highly controversial war taxes, including the plate duty of 1756, the post-chaise duty of 1778, and the servant duty of 1780 were expressions of it. In 1797 when Pitt was desperate for new sources of revenue in the face of a rampant French Republic he pushed the principle to its limit with his 'triple assessment'. A year later he finally gave up the attempt to work within the fiscal framework bequeathed by Pelham, Newcastle, and North, and introduced his income tax. The object, taxing the income of the propertied classes, was the same, the method very different, and one which could not have been contemplated in less desperate times.

[239] *Parliamentary History*, xix. 872.
[240] *London Magazine* (1747), 123.
[241] p. 251.
[242] *Parliamentary Register*, iii. 479, paginated incorrectly, appears after 502. The phrase may have been that of his Secretary of the Treasury, Charles Jenkinson, who employed it in the Budget debate of the following year. It was in this debate that Burke, not blind to linguistic points, accused Jenkinson of being the real minister; see *Parliamentary History*, xix. 251–2.

Another productive category of taxation was that applying to certain legal and professional transactions. The stamp duty went back to the reign of Charles II, and in its late eighteenth-century form could be traced directly to the Stamp Act of 1694. By 1789, *Kearsley's Six-Penny Tax Tables*, a popular tax guide described in 1786 as 'a new fashion in reading', was able to record more than 150 distinct stamp taxes.[243] Their appeal resembled that of the assessed taxes. A stamp duty was in some sense voluntary, in that it affected only those who chose to use the services in question, and it did not directly impinge on the life of the poor. The related license duties also had considerable potential. So far as retailers of wines, spirits, and ales were concerned, they could be seen as combining social regulation with fiscal gain. They were an important part of the legislature's strategy for reducing the consumption of gin. Similar arguments could be maintained with regard to taxes on attorneys in 1785 and 1794, on auctioneers in 1777, and on pawnbrokers in 1785. North's auction tax was the least unpopular of his wartime impositions, because it affected 'a sort of trade, which thrives by the distress of others', as Burke expressed it.[244] Pitt's tax on attorneys of 1794 was also guaranteed to give 'general Satisfaction'.[245] But these were in effect taxes on professions. As the history of the shop tax of 1785 demonstrated, there was a limit to the possibilities of such duties.

The new strategy had its origin in an emerging consensus about the proper targets for progressive taxation. Even while Walpole was unfolding his plans to reduce the land tax and increase excises, his opponents were suggesting another approach, concentrating on luxury items of a kind purchased exclusively by the middle and upper classes: plate, lace, carpets, ribbons, wines, foreign fabrics, servants, carriages.[246] Some, notably wines and spirits, were foreign imports and already subject to customs duties. Of the remainder carriages probably came first because they could be considered peculiarly useless. Their purpose was pleasure or at least convenience, their stimulating effect on English manufactures was marginal, and by increasing the need for horses and horse feed they diverted valuable agricultural produce to the requirements of conspicuous consumption. The contrast with the taxes on soap, candles, and leather, which raised the price of basic necessities for the industrious poor, was obvious. But they were only the most compelling examples of a large category.

Josiah Tucker provided a characteristically neat justification for the new trend in 1753. Society could be divided into four classes: producers of

---

[243] p. 144; *Morning Herald*, 9 Aug. 1786.
[244] *The Works of the Right Honourable Edmund Burke*, v. 347.
[245] Castalia, Countess Granville, ed., *Lord Granville Leveson Gower Private Correspondence*, i. 80.
[246] *Fog's Weekly Journal*, 3 Mar. 1733.

necessities, producers of superfluities, consumers of necessities, consumers of superfluities. Only the last should be taxed. In theory this could be made the basis of an entire fiscal policy. Tucker reviewed this possibility in some detail. He listed thirty-one luxuries to be rated at $1\frac{1}{2}d$. in the pound according to arbitrary assessments of the level of income which might be associated with specific luxuries. A family which kept two coaches and six, for example, would be presumed to enjoy an income of £8,000 per annum. The nominal income equivalents were nicely graduated. Use of a silver service was reckoned to be worth £4,000 a year, a china service £250, china tea dishes £50. Wearing jewels was rated at £100, possessing pictures at £50, and requiring more than one looking-glass at £50. Families of any consequence would be liable for a number of luxuries. A middle-class man with a wife and four children, on an income of £250, would probably be assessed on fourteen luxuries and would find himself paying £21. 17s. 6d. At this rate all existing duties could be dispensed with.[247] Tucker admitted that this scheme was unlikely to be adopted, but its principle was one which every Chancellor in the second half of the century recognized.

The new policy developed markedly during the War of the Austrian Succession and the Seven Years War, but its full potential was revealed in the War of American Independence. In 1775 the annual product of indirect taxation was about £7.7 million. Some of the taxes involved were centuries old, and most went back decades, though the rates at which they were levied had increased steadily in the course of the century. Then, in the space of eight years, North and his successors as Chancellor of the Exchequer, Lord John Cavendish and Pitt, were compelled to find a further £3.5 million per annum from indirect taxes, almost half as much again as the existing burden. Yet they did so without dramatically extending the incidence of the hated excise. By 1785 around 40 per cent of total revenue was derived from excises, rather less than in the middle of the century (53 per cent before the Seven Years War), and almost precisely the proportion of 1718. The house and window duty, increased by North in a deliberate attempt to tax the propertied householder who did not contribute to the land tax, and raised again by Pitt, produced a fifth of the additional sum required. Additional luxury taxes on coaches, post-chaises, male servants, and glassware, all produced small but significant revenues which for the moment at least warded off the threat of additional taxes on necessities. Most impressive of all, North loaded licence duties and the stamp tax, partly by increasing the rates of duty, partly by adding to the range of transactions affected.

The result was that a war to preserve the principle of parliamentary

---

[247] *A Brief Essay on the Advantages and Disadvantages Which Respectively Attend France and Great Britain, with Regard to Trade* (London, 1753), pp. 150 ff.

taxation, the principle first fully asserted in the American Stamp Act of 1765, cost Englishmen a staggering increase in stamp duties at home, the yield rising from about £350,000 in 1775 to £1,216,826 in 1785.[248] This was equivalent to 2s. 6d. on the land tax and almost as much as the product of the salt, soap, candle, and leather taxes put together. The change is sufficiently striking to give some credence to North's claim that he was seeking to maintain a balanced system of taxation, falling where possible on propertied people. Stamp duty rose in terms of duty yielded per head of population from 6d. in 1718 to 4s. 6d. in 1785. In the same period the four taxes on necessities fell from 3s. 9d. to 2s. 9d. These foundations proved sound enough for some imaginative fiscal engineering. Pitt's commutation of the tea duty in 1785 heavily reduced taxation of what had increasingly come to be seen as a necessity rather than a luxury. In its stead the window tax was raised. The tea commutation aroused expert admiration chiefly because it demonstrated how smuggling could be tackled and revenue loss minimized. It was also a prime example of the social policy of the age, reducing the burden on poor consumers, transferring it to householders, and benefiting both trade and the Exchequer in the process.

Crudely interpreted, these changes could be seen as an exercise in mass tax evasion by landowners. The banker Thomas Coutts pleaded instead for a double tax on the country gentlemen on the grounds that 'these trifling taxes produce nothing but vexation'.[249] Henry Fox, who knew more of the difficulties of managing the House of Commons, argued after the introduction of the carriage tax that government was constrained by its unwillingness to pay. He too calculated that a genuine 4s. land tax, assessed at real values since 1689, would have met all the needs of the State.[250] But the land tax had never been intended as a straightforward tax on land, and even as it operated it was far from being that. Nor could Fox's logic have been employed in subsequent wars. The most generous estimate of the income of the landlord class, and the most Draconian project for taxing it, would not have financed the enormous war expenditure of the 1770s and 1790s. By then the framework of debate within which Fox operated had vanished. The landed interest was merely one of many competing interests within a complicated and constantly changing pattern. Pitt's redemption of the land tax in 1798 had great symbolic importance in this respect. It recognized that the utility of fairly taxing landed wealth distinct from other forms of property had gone.

In a sense the decision not to modernize the land tax followed naturally from the policy initiated in 1747. That policy did not exempt landowners

---

[248] Sources as n. 215, above.
[249] E. H. Coleridge, *The Life of Thomas Coutts Banker* (2 vols., London, 1920), i. 176.
[250] *London Magazine* (1748), 398.

from taxation, it merely treated them like other property-owners, though the effects of the window and carriage duties were naturally felt most by those who suffered little or not at all by the land tax. Taxing light and travel rather than land suggested a psychologically important shift of emphasis away from the historic conception of the landed man as the ultimate supporter of the commonwealth. It also irritated those thus enfranchised by taxation. The wife of a Norfolk clergyman confessed herself dismayed equally by the threat to her windows and her 'chariot'. "Tis a sad thing to pay for going a broad and staying at home too if we have any light.'[251] If the object of the new taxes was to search out new sources of wealth, it was highly successful. In the mid-1760s some pains were taken to establish precisely who paid the carriage tax. Even in the countryside, where it might have been supposed that ownership of land went naturally with conspicuous consumption generally, it became obvious that there was a great quantity of non-landed opulence available for tax purposes. In Buckinghamshire, slightly more than a third of carriage and plate taxpayers in the mid-1760s had estates which justified their inclusion in the land tax commission.[252] The rest were either not landowners at all or possessed so little real property that they would certainly not have been accounted gentry if their other forms of wealth had not been taken into account.

In rural areas, the success of these novel 'assessed duties' was something of a bonus. It was urban property which ministers were particularly anxious to identify and charge. Their object was to seek out the wealth of the opulent élite which had little or nothing in common with landed society, and largely evaded the burden of direct taxation. With the new taxes they found themselves close to doing so. In England and Wales as a whole about one in thirty-five of all households was affected by the carriage or plate duty between 1757 and 1766. But in a provincial town of some consequence such as Leicester this rose to one in fourteen. And in London it reached one in ten.[253] The detailed returns preserved for the plate duty reveal the extent to which this impinged on families of modest means. Visions of the enormous quantities of plate possessed by magnate families proved fanciful. In 1757 there were only 101 payers of the duty at its highest rate, including 9 Oxford and Cambridge colleges, in a total of 28,453. The vast majority were prosperous business and professional people with a small quantity of plate. Fully 11,530 of them lived in the London area, and a large proportion

---

[251] A. Hartshorne, *Memoirs of a Royal Chaplain, 1729–1763* (London, 1905), p. 56.

[252] 49 out of 141; carriage-duty payers 1764–6 from PRO, T. 47.4, compared with land tax commissions.

[253] These are necessarily rough estimates based on the maximum numbers paying the plate duty, in 1757, at T. 47. 5, and numbers paying carriage duty in 1764–6, excluding those who also paid plate duty and also excluding carriages for hire, at T. 47. 4.

of the remainder in provincial towns. The explosion of urban growth in the eighteenth century was amply reflected in the yield from such taxes. But those involved paid as individuals, rather than as 'interests', and they paid on the basis of their consumption. Short of a genuine property tax administered by a central bureaucracy this was as close as the eighteenth century could come to equal taxation. It was, doubtless, very rough justice. But it seemed more just than the old taxes on land and excises on necessities.[254]

This is not to say that taxation did not remain a subject of acute disagreement. The controversies of the late eighteenth century sometimes revealed ancient preoccupations. As late as 1790 worries about the legal and constitutional implications of the excise laws surfaced with the opposition to Pitt's tobacco excise. But more consistently they reflected new concerns. No tax was popular and the expedients to which ministers were driven in the later stages of a great war, or in the first stages of a subsequent peace, were often unpopular. It is significant that the taxes which met with the most violent response were not necessarily those which had to be withdrawn. Pelham's bottle tax and Pitt's beer excise, like the turnpikes which provoked popular rioting and the militia which was a tax in all but name, were maintained in the face of fierce opposition. Taxes were dropped either because they offended powerful propertied interests or because they violated the prevailing sense of what constituted a legitimate subject for taxation. The fustian duty of 1784, for instance, did both, and had the shortest history of all new duties.

There was also a fortuitous element in the failure of some taxes. The cider excise certainly alienated important interests in the West Country. But its value as a stick with which to beat the Bute Ministry and the unpredictable return to power of the Rockingham Whigs in 1765–6 had more to do with its repeal.[255] More significant of the changing climate of opinion was the response to the shop tax of 1785, which pressed to the limit the principle of taxing a non-productive and frequently unpopular profession. It had been suggested on these grounds under Pelham. In fact the retailers themselves had been prepared to contemplate such a tax in return for stringent measures against their peripatetic rivals, the hawkers and pedlars. 'Our shop-keepers turned projectors in order to tax themselves,' a parliamentary reporter observed. 'In some future session the petitioners may, perhaps, obtain something of what they pray for.'[256] This prophecy came close to fulfilment in 1759, when the elder Pitt was desperate for funds with which to fight the Seven Years War. It was left to his son,

[254] T. 47. 5.
[255] For the definitive account, see P. T. M. Woodland, 'The Cider Excise, 1763–1766' (Oxford Univ. D.Phil. thesis, 1982).
[256] London Magazine (1748), 460.

equally desperate to underwrite the debt left by a less successful war, to introduce it in 1785. By then the attitude of the shopkeepers had changed. Their opposition was furious. The objection was essentially that shop-keepers paid as ordinary individuals a range of taxes including high shop rates in city centres, a house tax based on rents, and a receipt tax on their business transactions.[257] The shop tax was an example of the limitations of the current philosophy of taxation as tea commutation was of its strengths. Window tax payers included every propertied family. Shopkeepers were a powerful interest who saw no reason why they should be singled out. Pitt repealed the duty in 1789 rather than face a general election with it still on the statute-book.

Pitt's experience in the 1780s also revealed the difficulties which could occur when the principle of assessment by consumption reached deep into Parliament's social constituency. As applied in mid-century it had been meant to search out wealth below the landed class. But after the American War it penetrated much further, in the process exploiting a large gap in the fiscal resources of the State. Payers of the carriage and plate duty represented the upper middle class, perhaps only 3 or 4 per cent of the population as a whole, and even in urban centres less than 10 per cent. Below them lay the much larger proportion of the population, perhaps a third, which bore the burden of poor rates and window taxes. It was this body which found itself being drawn further into the tax net in the final decades of the century. North's additional house duty, and Pitt's taxes on servants, shops, and horses were principally responsible. The effect is revealed in the rare instances where the returns of taxpayers still survive, as at Shrewsbury—they were probably copied and stored as evidence for the campaign of opposition which was mounted against Pitt's budgets.[258] In the main business district of Shrewsbury, Castle Ward within and Castle Forgate, in 1785, there were 240 houses which paid to the house and window tax. These were overwhelmingly the residences of merchants, tradesmen, and shopkeepers. For all of them the land tax was negligible, and most escaped the luxury duties levied by successive wartime govern-ments. Only 5 paid the carriage or chaise tax, and just 30 North's tax on male servants. The story was very different with Pitt's new impositions in the wake of the American War. 79 paid the horse tax, 89 the maid-servant tax, 95 the shop tax. The incidence of the assessed taxes in the ward changed with alarming suddenness. Taxation of servants and transport as it remained in 1783 had affected 33 households. As extended by Pitt in 1784 and 1785 it affected a further 132. The distinction in terms of social status was crucial, not least in the matter of servants. Employing male

[257] Sinclair, *The History of the Public Revenue*, ii. 257–8.
[258] Shropshire RO, Shrewsbury borough records, 274, 298: assessments 1784–6.

servants was expensive and itself the mark of fashionable living. In 1780 there were about 50,000 registered in some 25,000 households.[259] Female servants were cheaper and essential for any family which aspired to a degree of middle-class politeness. They probably outnumbered their male counterparts by eight to one.[260] Perhaps it is not surprising that Pitt was forced to withdraw his tax on them not long after his retreat from the shop tax, in 1792.[261]

Continued peace would doubtless have relieved the pressure exerted by the exigencies of the American War and made possible a relaxation of the unpopular measures which North and Pitt, following enthusiastically where Pelham and Newcastle had been able to tread more cautiously, had adopted. There was always the hope of identifying more luxuries which could be taxed without provoking rebellion. Pitt had fastened on one of these with his hair powder duty of 1786. Though it was hardly popular, it was difficult to oppose. It did not threaten a domestic manufacture of any consequence, and the use of hair powder could scarcely be deemed a necessity. Even in rural areas it found out a gratifyingly large number of men and women prepared to pay for their vanity. In North Yorkshire about 300 had been assessed to the plate duty in 1757; in 1795 1,587 paid for hair powder licences.[262] But the yield from luxury taxes of this kind was necessarily limited and could not serve more than a marginal purpose during periods of war. The Revolutionary War of the 1790s inevitably brought to the fore once again the central problem: how to tax propertied people without destroying that underlying political consensus which it was the purpose of the war to preserve against revolution abroad and subversion at home. There was an obvious solution, one which was certainly not palatable, but which could not reasonably be resisted by any particular group. It lay in Schedules IV and V of the income tax of 1799, as remodelled by Addington, and soon after translated into the dreaded Schedules D and E which continue in the terminology of the modern income tax. Schedule D comprised profits from 'every description of property' or from a profession, trade, or vocation, and not otherwise taxed under the heading of land, tenancy, or dividend. Schedule E originally consisted of salaries earned by public office-holders.

The income tax was a novelty, but less of a novelty than it has sometimes

---

[259] My count from the lists at PRO, T. 47. 8 is 50,044 in 24,750 households; 13,608 of these, in 5,989 households, were in London, Westminster, and Middlesex.

[260] J. J. Hecht, *The Domestic Servant Class in Eighteenth-Century England* (London, 1956), p. 34.

[261] For evidence that Pitt had broken through to a new and particularly sensitive layer of the taxable with his duties on shops and maidservants, see Hoh-cheung and Mui, *Shops and Shopkeeping in Eighteenth Century England*, p. 110.

[262] Plate duty records at PRO, T. 47. 5; the figure is an estimate because the North Yorkshire excise division did not correspond precisely with the North Riding, on which the hair powder returns were based. The latter are at North Yorkshire RO, QDH: hair powder certificates, 1795–7.

seemed. The sense that taxation was approaching saturation level was nothing new. Every generation is prone to believe itself excessively burdened in this respect. Yet the complaint was so common in the last quarter of the century that it cannot be ignored as a distinctive feature of the period. The sheer multiplicity of taxes which existed in the wake of the American War appalled contemporary commentators, and if the returning prosperity of the late 1780s took the edge off some of this criticism, it was renewed with even more emphasis in the emergencies of the 1790s. The volume of this protest was unprecedented. In character, however, the complaints reflect a trend which had emerged in mid-century and which marked a departure from the grievances of the post-Revolution era. Overwhelmingly they concentrated on the burdens placed on middle-class Englishmen. By mid-century it had become commonplace to claim that 'the middle mass of men' were being undermined by the responsibility for maintaining the State, a claim repeated thereafter during every war.[263]

There were incipient signs of middle-class consciousness in these protests. One objection to the receipt tax of 1783 was that it was in effect taxing the tradesman's equivalent of land with the difference that it was accurately assessed.[264] The legacy duty of 1796 was criticized because it applied to personal but not real property.[265] But there was also much hypocrisy. Middle-class objections to the new taxes frequently emphasized the need for a more steeply graduated system of taxation. Taxing the rich was everyone's aim but few were prepared to admit that they were rich. The great meeting held to protest against the receipt duty in June 1783 observed 'that Favour to the Poor, has been held out as a Popular Topic of the Time in proposing this Tax, and most of the Taxes during the War; We agree most cordially with that Principle, provided the Rich, proportionately, of all Ranks and Descriptions, be impartially and equally taxed, and not Traders oppressively'.[266] Circumspect nobility of this kind was not new. The window tax had been objected to as a tax on the poor and middling. Similar complaints were made about the plate duty.[267] But such sufferers were middling only by comparison with the opulent. Very few of those who protested at the under-taxation of the rich had the strong moral position to do so which John Wesley had when he argued that taxing carriage wheels rather than carriage horses was 'barefaced, shameless partiality'.[268]

---

[263] *London Magazine* (1749), 565.
[264] *Parliamentary History*, xxv. 998.
[265] *Gentleman's Magazine* (1796), 839.
[266] Northumberland RO, Delaval MSS, 2DE/49/2/20.
[267] Richard Graves, *The Spiritual Quixote*, ed. C. Tracy (London, 1967), p. 15.
[268] L. Tyerman, *The Life and Times of the Rev. John Wesley* (3 vols., London, 1870–1), iii. 133.

In this as in other respects the real ground of complaint was precisely that Parliament was too successful in its objective of getting at the wealth of propertied people in general. The contrast with the experience of the seventeenth century is very striking. Even a graduated tax like the so-called poll tax of William III, which was meant to seek out families with more than £50 of real or £600 of personal estate, amounted to a flat rate impost on everyone, including the poor.[269] A hundred years later a complex if often anomalous tax system was impinging heavily on a much increased and vastly more burdened middle class. Objective observers were well aware that this was the case. As Sir John Sinclair, author of the magisterial *History of the Public Revenue of the British Empire*, expressed it in 1795 the middling rank were the 'great pillars of the exchequer'.[270] Widespread recognition of this truth accompanied another, closely connected, that the 'gentlemen of England' had suffered severely in the process. This lament was not made particularly on behalf of landowners, as it had been in the War of the Spanish Succession, nor was it the land tax that was at issue. The Peace of 1748 brought bitter protests at 'great Taxes of all kinds, Duties, Excises etc and the officers of the revenue liveing at full ease, pride and insolence towards the best gentlemen, who are in a manner half beggard through England'.[271] Half a century later Bishop Watson put the same point: Lord North had rendered it difficult for a man of five hundred pounds a year to support the station of a gentleman, and Pitt had rendered it impossible.[272] Another Cambridge academic, the Regius Professor John Symonds, expressed similar anxiety in 1795. 'If we be forced to persist in this war,' he wrote to Arthur Young, 'the middle class of the people, of which you and I form a part, must be driven down to the lower.'[273] It was, of course, one of the central achievements of the eighteenth century to confuse gentility and middle-class status so completely that a large body of Englishmen would claim the one without losing the other. A State as successful as the British State in that period would not have prospered without profiting by such ambiguity, as all but the most benighted squires and tireless champions of landed values must have known. In doing so it implicitly recognized the moral and political credentials of those on whom it relied. The platitudes of any age have an historical significance all their own. It was one such platitude which the clergyman William

---

[269] Out of 660 inhabitants of Melbourne, in Derbyshire, 32 of them with servants, only 3 were rated at the higher level; at Lyme Regis in Dorset, there were 34 higher rate payers out of 1336 (R. E. C Waters, 'A Statutory List of the Inhabitants of Melbourne, Derbyshire, in 1695', *Derbys. Arch. Jnl.* 7 (1885), 1–30; Dorset RO, B7 H2).

[270] (2nd edn., London, 1795), iii. 238.

[271] G. Evans, *Religion and Politics in Mid-Eighteenth Century Anglesey* (Cardiff, 1953), p. 133.

[272] *Anecdotes of the Life of Richard Watson, Bishop of Llandaff* (London, 1817), p. 429.

[273] Betham-Edwards, ed., *The Autobiography of Arthur Young*, pp. 254–5.

Keate expressed in 1784 when he wrote that the middle class was 'the most useful, the most willing, and the most beneficial part of the community'.[274]

[274] *A Sermon, Preached upon the Occasion of the General Thanksgiving, for the Late Peace, July 29th, 1784* (Bath, 1784), p. 24.

6

Rural Duties

THE government of the countryside belonged in the supposedly safe hands of landed proprietors. But there were growing fears in the eighteenth century that this class was opting out of its responsibilities at the very time when commercial farming and the social changes which accompanied it most called for attendance to duty. Sheer absenteeism was a large part of the problem, as the requirements both of parliamentary sessions and the social calendar drew the gentry to London or Bath. The declining prestige of the county magistracy partly reflected this genteel retreat from the countryside. It also had to do with the narrowly partisan fashion in which appointments to the commission of the peace were managed under early Hanoverian rule. By mid-century, control of the counties was effectively in the hands of narrow cliques of relatively lowly men whose only re-commendation was their Whiggism. Under George III serious attempts were made to meet the resulting criticisms. Political considerations ceased to govern the appointment of justices and sheriffs. County families showed somewhat more interest in the government of their localities at least for cosmetic purposes. Widespread resort to clerical magistrates, if it did not altogether restore the propertied standing of the bench, ensured a more conscientious approach to business and growing emphasis on the social responsibilities of rural rule. The clergy proved enthusiastic undertakers of the most mundane tasks of local administration and thereby offered a kind of proxy paternalism by which the values and priorities of landed society were preserved. The Church paid a price for its involvement in secular affairs and the clergy themselves were not always admired by those they ruled; but if nothing else their activities revealed the adaptability of propertied society in its most traditional, agrarian setting.

A SCENE OF DESOLATION

The traditional assumption that land uniquely prepared its owners for the cares of government had its sternest test where their authority was naturally at its strongest, in the countryside. It was a test carried out on principles which landowners themselves found it difficult to pronounce unfair. Since the pretensions of property were, by definition, opposed to equal rights, or even a measure of political consent, on the part of those who had little or no property, the resulting debate was conducted largely within a paternalistic framework. The emphasis was on the sense of responsibility, the benevolence, and the integrity of those involved, rather than their acceptability to those below them, or even their talent and efficiency.

Fears that the English gentry were losing interest in their own communities were often expressed in the late seventeenth and early eighteenth century. Some famous images of traditional country virtue, contrasted with decadent Court and City vice, were the result. The *Spectator's* account of Sir Roger de Coverley, at home, in church, on the bench, even on his deathbed, forever the patriarch, ruling servants, tenants, and neighbours with bluff good humour, an autocratic manner and a ceaseless concern for their welfare, remains the most celebrated of all such appeals to old-fashioned values in the face of an increasingly hostile world. The fact that it was penned by Whigs who shrewdly satirized Sir Roger's prejudices and follies, and were convinced of the commercial advantages and political superiority of all that he hated, merely reinforces the potency of this creation. Readers were meant to prefer Sir Andrew Freeport, a self-made man who eventually retired to the country to exercise a reflective, rational kind of paternalism, to the unthinking, outdated variety inherited and practised by Sir Roger. Most were more likely to hanker after the Coverley model, for all its obsolescence.[1] Its appeal remained real, more especially as the sometimes anguished commercialism of early Hanoverian rule stimulated nostalgic susceptibilities. Party politics were not necessarily relevant. Smollett's Sir Launcelot Greaves was plainly a Tory and Fielding's Squire Allworthy presumably a Whig, but they appealed to similar political values. The essential assumption was that landed gentlemen provided virtuous government which was a matter of heredity at least as much as education.

Sentimental concern, expressed in terms of regret rather than revolt, was eventually replaced by something stronger. In the 1760s there was a perceived crisis, of which rural paternalists themselves were acutely conscious.[2] In origin it was closely identified with changing agricultural practices. Like the earlier anxiety, it was given widespread dissemination in literary form. However, it was meant to arouse more powerful feelings and was accompanied by authentic demands for corrective action. Goldsmith's *Deserted Village* appeared in May 1770, but in his dedication of the poem to Sir Joshua Reynolds, the author was at pains to explain that his haunting picture of rural depopulation and deprivation was based on 'my country excursions, for these four or five years past'. Earlier still, in 1762, he had sketched the social evils involved in an essay published in *Lloyd's*

---

[1] *The Spectator*, especially nos. 2, 106, 108, 109, 112, 113, 116, 117, 122, 383, 517, 549.

[2] For an influential discussion of the concept of such a crisis, with the emphasis on its implications for popular attitudes, see E. P. Thompson, 'Patrician Society, Plebeian Culture', *Jnl. Soc. Hist.* 7 (1973–4), 382–405.

Evening Post.[3] About this time, too, the popular author Frances Brooke sought to bring home to a mass audience the dangers of new agrarian trends in her novel, *Lady Julia Mandeville*:

It is with infinite pain I see Lord T—— pursuing a plan, which has drawn on him the curse of thousands, and made his estate a scene of desolation: his farms are in the hands of a few men, to whom the sons of the old tenants are either forced to be servants, or to leave the country to get their bread elsewhere. The village, large, and once populous, is reduced to about eight families; a dreary silence reigns over their deserted fields; the farm houses, once the seats of cheerful smiling industry, now useless, are falling in ruins around him; his tenants are merchants and ingrossers, proud, lazy, luxurious, insolent, and spurning the hand which feeds them.[4]

Goldsmith and Mrs Brooke were plainly capable of putting these matters on every young lady's dressing-table. But they already had a place in the minds of legislators, political commentators, and many others who took an interest in public affairs. In published tracts, in tours, manuals, and other works which were required to comment on the English countryside, and not least in newspapers, monthlies, and other general vehicles of information, the social consequences of economic change on the land were the subject of growing debate.

Recurrent anxieties about demographic trends were exacerbated in the 1750s by a sharp exchange between self-appointed experts whose differences it was difficult to referee.[5] Parliament's refusal to approve proposals for a national census in 1753 permitted nearly half a century of pessimistic prognosis of population decline. There is no doubt that the pessimists were hopelessly wrong both in their historical analysis and their future projections. None the less, their jeremiads received a sympathetic hearing until the census of 1801 proved their inaccuracy and gave grounds for a very different kind of pessimism, emphasizing the dangers of population growth. It was also in the 1750s that concern about food supplies reached a new level. The distress caused by the shortages of 1756–7 was worse than anything witnessed since 1741, and broke a broad pattern of good harvests and relatively low prices which had obtained for much of the reigns of George I and George II. The reign of the third Hanoverian king was to prove very different. Prices never regained their old stability in the second half of the century, nor did more than a few years pass without recurring grain shortages. Landowners could hardly be blamed for this state of affairs. Parliament was quick to suspend, and eventually amend, the laws encouraging the export and prohibiting the import of corn, in order to

---

[3] R. Lonsdale, ed., *The Poems of Gray, Collins and Goldsmith* (London, 1969), pp. 675, 669.

[4] *The History of Lady Julia Mandeville* (2nd edn., 2 vols., London, 1763), i. 222–3.

[5] D. V. Glass, *Numbering the People: The Eighteenth-Century Population Controversy and the Development of Census and Vital Statistics in Britain* (Farnborough, 1973), chs. 1–2.

maintain supplies of food at tolerable prices. Landlords' anxiety about the
dangers of dearth was much in evidence during periods of crisis. But
harvest conditions were beyond their control, as was the underlying population growth which largely accounted for the pressure on prices in the late
eighteenth century.

Well within their control were the agricultural practices which helped
maintain food production, but gave rise to acute controversy on account of
their immediate consequences. The twin evils of enclosure and engrossing
brought intense criticism to bear on the landowning class, and prepared
the way for a more general indictment of its treatment of the rural
community. Of the two, enclosure has attracted the greater historical
interest, partly, no doubt, because the evidence of its incidence, in the form
of enclosure by statute, is so obvious. The early part of George III's reign
was the first great age of parliamentary enclosure. The twenty-five years
1755–79 saw 1,124 acts passed, compared with only 114 in the preceding
quarter of a century, 1730–54. The pace slackened somewhat in the 1780s
but speeded up again during the Revolutionary and Napoleonic Wars.[6]
For this statutory transformation of the landscape in much of eastern and
midland England it seemed obvious who was to blame. The initiative lay
with proprietors of the soil, lords of the manor, and tithe or glebe owners.
The House of Commons was sufficiently concerned by complaints of
injustice to make some attempts at regulation; its standing orders of 1773
set out a standard procedure for the adoption and passage of enclosure
bills. It included provision for adequate advertisement of the encloser's
intentions and for the consent of those primarily affected. But the emphasis
was on the rights of the proprietors: the legislature's main worry seems to
have been the aggrandizement of a minority of proprietors at the expense
of a majority. Some (generally ineffectual) attempts were made to protect
small yeomen, whose want of capital made it difficult for them either to
fight enclosure before the event or benefit by it afterwards. But little interest
was displayed by Parliament in the fate of commoners whose rights were
based on customary use, or in the plight of rural poor who were most likely
to be affected by dramatic changes in the structure of local farming. Above
all the interests of small tenant farmers, whose holdings might be drastically
remodelled or might vanish altogether as a result of enclosure, were
completely ignored; a tenancy, at least a tenancy at will, was not a propertied
right, and received short shrift from the guardians of the subject's property.

Perhaps because enclosure, as 'improvement', was the subject of so much
favourable publicity, its social costs were not necessarily to the fore in
contemporary debate, except in those cases where large bodies of commoners were affected by the appropriation of waste. The enclosure of

    [6] M. Turner, *English Parliamentary Enclosure* (Folkestone, 1980), p. 68.

commons in places where numbers of town dwellers were affected, and in some parishes around London, was highly controversial. But such enclosure was a sensitive issue even without parliamentary intervention, and had more to do with oligarchical corporations than country gentlemen. At Leicester, in the 1750s, the ruling élite's plans for the town's South Fields were bitterly resisted by poor freemen. There was no suggestion of an Act of Parliament, and the resulting conflict was closely enmeshed with municipal politics.[7] Nottingham had the same problem and a very similar experience.[8] Most parliamentary enclosure in the early years of George III was enclosure of open-field systems, and supported on the grounds that it was technically no more than a redrawing of boundaries. It supposedly invaded no individual's property, even if the land which he eventually received bore little resemblance to his original estate, and even if the expense of the enclosure was such as to force him to sell it to his wealthier neighbour.

'Engrossing' provoked greater hostility, though it did not necessarily involve the legislature in a formal sense at all. Sometimes, indeed, it was a direct consequence of an enclosure act. But a substantial landlord might choose to consolidate the farms on his estate, enclosed or not, and thereby transform the character of village life as suddenly and completely as if he had obtained an act of Parliament to do so. Engrossing was also relatively cheap. It involved none of the legal and parliamentary charges payable in the course of promoting an enclosure bill, and few of the expenses, such as commissioners' fees and fencing costs, which followed its successful passage. Tenants were expected to pay for enclosure in the long run, through higher rents, but the initial capital outlay was the landlord's and could be intimidatingly large. The cost of engrossing was much more evenly shared, providing tenants presented themselves with money to invest in bigger, more intensively farmed units. The volume of contemporary protest at the disappearance of small farms and their replacement by large ones was enormous, but the variable quality of land tax and estate records makes it difficult to substantiate in detail. Like enclosure itself, engrossing probably needs to be placed in the context of related developments over a much longer period of time; like enclosure, too, it was marked by regional variations. None the less, as a cause of concern about the pressures imposed on the structure of rural society its significance is not in doubt. Above all, as evidence that the landlord class was seeking to change the terms on which it exploited the countryside, it was no less damaging than enclosure.

The contemporary emphasis on the consequences for agricultural

----

[7] J. Thompson, *The History of Leicester in the Eighteenth Century* (Leicester, 1871), ch. 7.

[8] M. I. Thomis, *Politics and Society in Nottingham, 1785–1835* (Oxford, 1969), pp. 122 ff.

tenancies is telling. The classics of modern agrarian history, the Ham-
monds' *Village Labourer*, Chambers's *Nottinghamshire*, Hoskins' *Midland
Peasant*, have focused interest on the sufferings of the lowliest members of
the rural community, especially where they were the possessors of vestigial
rights which fell victim to proprietorial power. The result is a tendency to
view the extinction of commoners' rights as the 'crucial blow' which
extinguished an entire rural culture.[9] But at least until the 1790s, and to
some extent thereafter, attention was concentrated as much on the plight
of small farmers, not necessarily in the sense of that yeoman class whose
decline is one of the most significant yet perplexing mysteries of English
history, but in the sense of the whole class of men who in principle were
available to accept a 'bargain', or tenancy at will. There were constant
complaints about the shortage of small farms for letting, and the slump in
opportunities for the sons of respectable farmers who could not afford to
finance a substantial lease, and who lacked funds to send them into trade
or the professions. The author William Donaldson gloomily predicted that
these men would be forced to emigrate, perhaps to form an English brigade
in the army of Louis XV, and serve alongside the Jacobite Irishmen and
Scots who had earlier forsaken their native shores for rather different
reasons.[10] Their supplanters were viewed as vultures who preyed on the
misfortunes of others. One of the main indictments of landlords was that
they had effectively handed the rural community over to men who were
unfitted to exercise the powers and carry out the responsibilities thus
delegated to them. Edmund Rack, founder of the first provincial agricultural society, the Bath and West, described the new breed of farmers as
'men of low and grovelling ideas'.[11] Christopher Anstey attacked them in
his *Speculation*, a popular satire on the spread of the commercial mentality
through all sections of society, as rapacious monopolists who 'Usurp the
Empire of the Plains, And lord it o'er the humble Swains'.[12]

The charge of profiteering was central to the case against the great
farmers. Their sole object was profit; their power was their capital, increasingly derived, it was thought, from country banks, that sinister new engine
of provincial commercialism; their method was monopoly, designed to
force up prices to a level which would both pay for their own borrowing

---

[9] J. L. Hammond and B. Hammond, *The Village Labourer 1760–1832: A Study in the Government
of England before the Reform Bill* (London, 1912), ch. 5; J. D. Chambers, *Nottinghamshire in the
Eighteenth Century: A Study of Life and Labour under the Squirearchy* (2nd edn., London, 1960), ch.
7; W. G. Hoskins, *The Midland Peasant: The Economic and Social History of a Leicestershire Village*
(London, 1965), ch. 10.

[10] William Donaldson, *The Life and Adventures of Sir Bartholomew Sapskull* (2 vols., London, 1768),
ii. 203.

[11] Edmund Rack, *Essays, Letters, and Poems* (Bath, 1781), p. 309.

[12] (London, 1780), p. 46.

and yield a handsome return.[13] It was all too easy to compare such men unfavourably with the squire of old, with his innate patriarchalism, his family inheritance of service to the community, his instinctive sense of belonging in the rural chain of being. Commercial monopoly seemed to go hand in hand with uncaring exploitation. 'In this inattention to their moral duty, they neglect the social duties of life.'[14] But the crucial assumption was that such cynicism derived from the overmighty tenant's want of proprietorial interest in his land. 'There should be no gentlemen farmers, except those who manage their own estates.'[15]

The resulting oppression was thought to take various forms. Poor rates, unlike the land tax, were payable by the occupier, not the owner, of the property on which they were levied. Their actual incidence might vary, according to local practice and the terms of tenancies. Theorists could also point out that rent levels necessarily took account of all such burdens carried by the land. None the less, it was obvious that individual tenants usually had an interest in reducing the numbers of poor and keeping their claim on parish funds to a minimum. Farmers were prime candidates for parochial offices, including that of overseer of the poor. In short they were the 'legislator of every village', or proud 'parish governors'.[16] It was a common complaint that hard-hearted overseers and churchwardens, essentially representing the tenant-class rather than landowners, under-mined the more generous disposition of the gentry. Not only did they strive to keep poor relief at a minimum, they did their best to expel the poor altogether. By demolishing cottages and compelling their occupants to take refuge elsewhere, they were guilty of brutality exceeding even that of West Indian slaveowners. When, as a class, they were permitted a share in governing the poor law incorporations which Parliament authorized in some parts of the country, it seemed that their main interest lay in serving themselves in matters such as the placing of poor apprentices.[17]

Whether this distinction between the attitudes of the rural upper and middle classes was valid is, to say the least, questionable. But it was undeniably central to the prolonged debate which poor relief administration provoked between the 1780s and the 1830s.[18] The arguments with which farmers were defended are in this respect as significant as those with which they were attacked. Arthur Young did not dispute their niggardliness, but viewed it in a quite different light, as a spur to efficient and economical

[13] L. S. Pressnell, *Country Banking in the Industrial Revolution* (Oxford, 1956), pp. 346 ff.
[14] Donaldson, *The Life and Adventures of Sir Bartholomew Sapskull*, ii. 190.
[15] Id., *Agriculture Considered as a Moral and Political Duty* (London, 1775), p. 113.
[16] Ibid. 111.
[17] Suffolk RO (Ipswich), ADA 7/AB1/1: Samford quarterly minutes, e.g. 29 June 1790.
[18] See J. R. Poynter, *Society and Pauperism: English Ideas on Poor Relief, 1795–1834* (London, 1969), esp. ch. 4.

administration. In Somerset he found poor rates being paid by owners
rather than occupiers. The result, he noted, was a decidedly more lavish,
and in his opinion more wasteful provision of relief by officers who could
afford to give free rein to their compassion at the expense of their landlords'
pockets.[19] Another enthusiast for improvement, William Marshall, considered the usual complaints futile railing at the iron laws of political
economy. Confronted with demands that farmers should be urged to build
additional cottages for the industrious poor, he merely observed that it was
absurd to suppose that they would 'prefer political regulations to their own
interest'.[20]

In a sense the farmer could not win. Even acts of benevolence would be
interpreted as mere self-interest. In order to explode what he called 'casu-
istry in political humanity', John Thelwall indignantly told the story of a
Wiltshire farmer who, in a desperately hard winter, gave up his crop of
sheep turnips to feed the poor of his parish. This, according to Thelwall,
had nothing to do with public-spiritedness. It simply reflected the farmer's
desire to keep his labourers off the parish. A field of turnips was cheaper
than a sharp rise in the poor rate and safeguarded those relieved against
the dangerous habit of appealing to the overseers.[21] But it is difficult to see
what evidence would have convinced Thelwall of the good intentions of a
benefactor. There is no doubt, for instance, that in a wide range of rural
charities, farmers were necessarily involved. In the friendly societies which
multiplied rapidly in the 1770s and 1780s, and eventually received the
endorsement of Parliament, they were prominent, as prominent in many
instances as the clergy more commonly credited with leadership in such
matters. At Morcott in Rutland, the society initiated in 1773 was founded
by a well-known farmer, Thomas Pridmore, who appears in the minutes
as its 'Father', and was long remembered in the locality. He was followed
in the office by two of his sons in succession. All three took a close interest
in the society and treated it virtually as a hereditary charge. In an area
where resident landlords were notably wanting, proxy paternalism was the
only kind available. Yet it could easily be dismissed as the mercenary
interest of employers who saw the advantage of an insurance scheme which
might obviate the necessity for poor relief.[22]

Poor rates were only the most sensitive feature of a general process of
immiseration, the blame for which could be laid at the farmers' door. The
sheer scale of the new farming seemed to make its practitioners negligent
of their lowlier neighbours. Traditionally, it was pointed out, the small

---

[19] *The Farmer's Tour through the East of England* (4 vols., London, 1771), iii. 418.
[20] William Marshall, *The Review and Abstract of the County Reports to the Board of Agriculture*
(5 vols., repr., Newton Abbot, 1969), iii. 331.
[21] *The Peripatetic* (London, 1793), i. 144–7.
[22] Leicestershire RO, DE 1702/7: Morcott Friendly Society.

farmer sold eggs, poultry, dairy produce, and so on at little more than cost price, in his own locality. But the novel market conditions of the mid-eighteenth century brought with them a novel selfishness. 'The great farmers sell nothing of this kind, consume all in their own families, live as well or better than their landlords, at their clubs and meetings fix the market-prices, and after a plentiful harvest, when they cannot make those advantages, repine rather than rejoice at the blessings of providence.'[23] Some observers thought they had seen in their lifetime a decisive shift in the pattern of relations between employer and employee. 'A sort of open war between farmers and the working hand' was described.[24] The old rhythm of the agricultural calendar, and the old reliance on a fixed quantity of labour, was thought to be giving way to less regular employment and more ruthless use of casual labour. Particularly where the new methods gave rise to intensive cereal production it was easy to claim that farmers preferred a large pool of labour available for short periods of the year to a small pool employed all the year around. The social pretentiousness of the new breed of tenant, expressed in his family's desire for greater privacy, and its imitation of an urban lifestyle, was also criticized. Young men and women who would formerly have been found accommodation in the farmhouse, under the benign supervision of their employer and his wife, were now expected to live at their own expense. The growing resort to cash in place of bed and board was treated as one of the manifest social horrors of the day, for it prevailed in towns and cities as on the land. Soame Jenyns, known both as man of letters and member of the Board of Trade, thought it 'so conducive to the universal corruption of the lower part of this nation, and so entirely destructive of all family order, decency and economy, that it well deserves the consideration of a legislature, who are not themselves under the influence of their servants'.[25] In the countryside the process seemed peculiarly offensive, for there it collided with the customary image of rural harmony and contradicted a widely held sense of the natural order of things.

By the end of the century the idea of a delinquent rural middle class, ensconced in power by its negligent superiors, was well established. Exceptions were cited, but only to make the prevalence of the general rule more obvious. In the Isle of Wight the tourist might find that 'the people are in general handsome and courteous, the consequence of a conscious dependence upon those who *can* and *will* support them'. But here the readiness of farmers to support their inferiors was considered a lingering example of

---

[23] *The Works of the Right Reverend Thomas Newton, D.D.* (3 vols., London, 1782), vol. i, iii, para. xii (not paginated).

[24] *London Magazine* (1765), 37.

[25] C. N. Cole, ed., *The Works of Soame Jenyns* (4 vols., London, 1970), ii. 123: 'World' 157.

practices which had vanished in less isolated parts.[26] Systematic surveys seemed to confirm the impression. Sir Frederick Eden, whose tours and publications made him the John Howard of the poor law, found ample support for it. In Lincolnshire and Norfolk, he reported,

small shopkeepers, manufacturers, publicans and labouring people complain heavily against those whom they call monopolizers of corn, farming clergymen (who are not rare), and the consolidators of small farms. To the conduct of men of this description, the high price of provisions, the increase in the Poor's Rate, and almost every evil that attends or is likely to attend the nation, are not infrequently attributed.[27]

Still more striking testimony, from hostile witnesses, is to be found in the county agricultural reports. Most of the surveyors who penned them were extremely reluctant to admit the charge. They were the high priests of the religion of agrarian improvement and disposed to make right-thinking farmers their acolytes. The social benefits as well as economic advances brought by intensive farming were essential to their creed. But some of them were prepared to recognize the validity of more traditional beliefs. In the South Hams of Devon, Robert Fraser noted the survival of a yeoman class which exercised 'without parade, that old English hospitality which the refinements of modern manners have banished from many other parts of the kingdom. I observed with much pleasure, the attention they paid to their various dependants around them, and their kindness to the poor.'[28] In Shropshire Joseph Plymley directly criticized landowners for abandoning the countryside to cynical farmers. The magistracy in particular he described as 'a kind of tax' owed by landlords on their rents. The conscientious country gentleman should reside on his estate to 'set an example of scrupulous obedience to the laws in his own person, and endeavour to sustain the tone of Christian morality throughout his neighbourhood'. It is perhaps significant that Plymley was an archdeacon, and independent of the landowners and tenants whose activities he scrutinized. William Marshall, who was charged with summarizing the county reports, was irritated by his scepticism about contemporary trends, and did his best to discredit it with some derisive editorial remarks about the clerical reporter.[29] But as evidence of concern about commercial farming, Plymley's refusal to join in the customary worship of the new practices is peculiarly telling.

It also illuminates the essential grounds of complaint against the ruling class of rural England. Its failure was nothing if not a moral failure, an abandonment of its duty to lead and educate by example. The antiquarian

---

[26] *Trans. Thoroton Soc.* 36 (1932), 56: letter of A. Hawkesworth, 15 Nov. 1772.

[27] A. G. L. Rogers, ed., *The State of the Poor: A History of the Labouring Classes in England, with Parochial Reports* (London, 1928), p. 251.

[28] Marshall, *The Review and Abstract of the County Reports to the Board of Agriculture*, v. 554.

[29] Ibid., ii. 229, 231.

Richard Polwhele put this accusation clearly on behalf of his native Cornwall. 'Its inhabitants (*generally speaking*) are all upon an equality. Unaccustomed to the presence of gentlemen, they have lost their respect for rank.—They are governed solely by inclination; and what repeated improprieties and occasional enormities must arise from the inclinations of unformed minds, may be easily conceived.' Only the clergy earned Polwhele's approval, but without the landlord class, they found themselves in a 'solitary, unsupported state'.[30] Smollett made a similar plea for a vigorous squirearchical presence, adroitly emphasizing the superiority of a class trained in the habits of leadership when compared with one which was expected to govern parishes yet lacked the moral resources to do so on its own. His ideal landlord was a 'bounteous benefactor. He was, in the literal sense of the word, a careful overseer of the poor; for he went from house, to house, industriously inquiring into the distresses of the people'.[31]

The line between formal and informal responsibility was, of course, narrow. Where the relief of the poor was concerned, the landowning class as magistrates were expected to play a part in its management, and, as a result of Georgian legislation, a growing one. Moreover, landlords themselves, regardless of their official standing, had certain legal powers and duties which made them as vulnerable as their tenants. One common allegation was that the act of Elizabeth which made it possible to demolish cottages erected on manorial waste without four acres of land for the support of their inhabitants, was being employed to drive long-standing cottagers out of their dwellings and into destitution. Combined with enclosure of commons this could have a shattering effect on marginal communities dependent on custom and the paternalism of their betters. As was pointed out, landlords with a permanent interest in their land were differently placed from farmers who, with the best intentions, enjoyed only a temporary interest in it. All the more did it become them to exercise their manorial rights in a way which would safeguard the livelihood of their poorest neighbours.[32]

LITTLE SOVEREIGNS

All arguments ultimately led back to the landowners themselves. The strongest charge against them, from which most of the subsidiary indictments flowed, was that of mass desertion of their posts. This was levelled at the relatively lowly as well as the magnate class. In Cumberland for instance, in 1792, they were accused of having 'fled to the crowded Haunts

[30] *Poems* (5 vols., Truro, 1810), iv. 98–9.
[31] *The Life and Adventures of Sir Launcelot Greaves*, ed. D. Evans (London, 1973), p. 21.
[32] Nathaniel Kent, *Hints to Gentlemen of Landed Property* (London, 1775), pp. 238–40.

of Commerce and left the Fields to be cultivated by Farmers'.[33] But most
interest naturally focused on their more genteel betters. As Rack remarked,
if whole village communities were left to the mercy of uneducated, insen-
sitive, even inhuman profiteers, the explanation was to be found in 'the
almost general desertion of country villages by our gentry'.[34] George
Lyttelton spoke of this as an imitation of the French practice.[35] But in
one respect it was peculiarly English. The paradox of a parliamentary
constitution as it had been established by the Revolution of 1688, was that
it removed the natural governors of the provinces to a remote capital. From
1689 Parliament met every year for long, and lengthening sessions, not
infrequently extending to seven months of the calendar. In this respect
Parliament proved far more of a metropolitan magnet than the court of the
Tudors and Stuarts had. MPs, from being occasional lodgers in London,
became genuine residents. The *Craftsman*, in 1743, wistfully looked back
to an age, barely fifty years earlier, when they had taken lodgings on the
second floor of a house in the Strand or Covent Garden.[36] Now they were
the tenants, and not infrequently the owners, of a home in Westminster.

The legislator's duties were as much social as legislative. As the eighteenth century wore on, actual attendance in both Houses seems to have
declined. In the Upper House, debates in the Walpole era mustered as
many as 150 or even 160 peers. Under Lord North the total rarely exceeded
130.[37] Divisions in the Commons in the early 1740s occasionally found
more than 500 MPs voting, nine-tenths of its membership. In the 1760s
and 1780s, periods of comparable political excitement, divisions involving
more than 400 were rare indeed.[38] John Robinson, as Secretary of the
Treasury, calculated in 1772 that just under 500 MPs were in town.
Yet the contentious Royal Marriage Bill, the occasion of his calculation,
generated only one division of more than 400; hardly 300 presented themselves for most of the important votes.[39] The sheer regularity of parliamentary sessions had doubtless helped stimulate the development of the
London season; it was hardly necessary to sustain it.

Peers, MPs, their friends and families, did not customarily hasten from
the tedium of a long session and the dust of London streets to rediscover
their rural roots. There were some enticing alternatives to the countryside.
It was remarked in 1778 that by running from spa to bathing place, and

---

[33] G. Smith and F. Benger, *The Oldest London Bookshop: A History of Two Hundred Years* (London,
1928), p. 139: I. Denton to J. Robson, 25 May 1792.
[34] *Essays, Letters and Poems*, p. 308.
[35] *Letters from a Persian in England, to His Friend at Ispahan* (4th edn., Dublin, 1735), p. 115.
[36] 14 May 1743.
[37] See division numbers as recorded in narrative portions of A. S. Turberville, *The House of Lords
in the Eighteenth Century* (Oxford, 1927).
[38] P. D. G. Thomas, *The House of Commons in the Eighteenth Century* (Oxford, 1971), p. 125.
[39] Ibid. 114–15.

from horse-race to bathing place again, 'they may continue to fill up their time tolerably well'.[40] Bath quickly established itself as a gigantic pleasure garden for propertied society. The development of other spa towns, and, especially after 1760, seaside resorts, provided comparable diversions, as did the expensive, but increasingly popular foreign tour. Even the lesser gentry, those accustomed to live on their estates during the London season, frequently found the temptation of a trip to the capital too much for them. They also resorted as readily to fashionable centres of entertainment in spring, summer, and autumn. The baths, assemblies, theatres and races of many country towns provided a humbler but no less appealing version of the pleasures of Bath or Aachen. Malachy Postlethwayt was surprised, in mid-century, by the number of Derbyshire gentry who left their estates to spend much of the year in Derby.[41] He attributed this to the inclemency of the Peak District climate but it is difficult to believe that he could not have made similar observations at Wakefield, Lincoln, and Salisbury. Many towns which missed out on the commercial and industrial growth of the eighteenth century cashed in on the gregariousness of an increasingly class-conscious society. They profited from politeness as others profited from production.[42]

The magnetic effect of provincial towns could almost match the more spectacular attractive power exerted by London. Lady Mountstuart, for all her family's wealth, was appalled by the prospect of her son being summoned to London with a view to a parliamentary career. 'When one can't afford to live in London, one must do the best one can.'[43] The country gentleman Carew Harvey Mildmay also thought the charms of the capital could be exaggerated. In 1771 he described the prevailing notion of genteel emigration to London as a vulgar error. 'How it will appear on a strict survey of the North, I know not; But in the West, except Members of both Houses, Lawyers, and Creolians (who may rather be called Lodgers) there are scarce three Familys in either of the Five Western Countys, who repair to Town for any Time—and their Wives and Daughters are contented with a Months Run at Bath, or some of the Water drinking Places.'[44] Perhaps this was true, but it did not exclude the possibility that many families found the season in Exeter, Plymouth, Taunton or Salisbury preferable to the *longueurs* of continuous country residence.

Wherever they went, the gentry took their money with them. The surviving estate correspondence of landowners is often dominated by the

[40] *The Travels of Hildebrand Bowman, Esquire* (London, 1778), p. 359.

[41] *The Universal Dictionary of Trade and Commerce* (4th edn., London, 1774), vol. i, *sub* 'Derbyshire'.

[42] See P. Borsay, *The English Urban Renaissance: Culture and Society in the Provincial Town 1660–1770* (Oxford, 1989), esp. ch. 5.

[43] E. H. Coleridge, *The Life of Thomas Coutts Banker* (2 vols., London, 1920), i. 151–2.

[44] North Yorkshire RO, C. H. Mildmay to T. Worsley, 1 Dec. 1771.

problem of maintaining the consistent cash flow needed to sustain a polite urban life from an agrarian economy with unpredictable habits.[45] The money market and the evolution of an ever more complex structure of credit transactions had much to do with this. It was easy to assume as a result that a non-resident landlord was a rapacious one. As Robert Bage's honest country gentlemen, James Paradyne, summarized it to his nephew, 'Never rack'd a tenant, George,—no occasion;—never went to court.'[46] It also seemed certain that little of what the land produced would be returned to those who lived on it, except in unusual circumstances—a contested parliamentary election, a spate of country house building and gardening, or a surge of capital investment in agricultural 'improvement'. Modern economic historians, however impressed by the efficiency of estates owned by absentee landlords, do not deny that the profits were spent elsewhere. This was well understood at the time. George Dyer calculated in 1793 that fully half of the income from land found its way to London.[47] Money which might have been spent at home where it would do most good was, so it was forever being alleged, squandered on urban luxury and vice. Elaborate calculations were made of the sums expended on claret, polite suppers, and Italian musicians, and the quantity of village hospitality which they might have financed.[48] How, it was asked, could the leaders of rural society fulfil their manifold social functions—the evenings spent with tenant and parson, the entertainment of farmers' wives in the parlour, the laborious treated and the poor succoured—when they were simply not full-time members of that society? Even Christmas, traditionally a season of 'open house', was now often passed in London or elsewhere. In one of his contributions to the *World* in December 1754, the wit and occasional country gentleman Richard Owen Cambridge lamented the demise of the old Christmas. 'The most fatal revolution, and what principally concerns this season, is the too general desertion of the country, that great scene of hospitality.'[49]

Here was a political issue which could be exploited by government and opposition alike. Sir Robert Walpole justified his policy of reducing the land tax and expanding the excise by pointing out that it would enable the nobility and gentry to revive their reputation for hospitality.[50] Annual parliamentary elections, which Walpole strongly deprecated, were advo-

[45] R. A. C. Parker, *Coke of Norfolk: A Financial and Agricultural Study 1707–1842* (Oxford, 1975), p. 34.

[46] *Man As He Is* (2nd edn., 4 vols., London, 1796), i. 59.

[47] J. V. Beckett, 'Absentee Landownership in the Late Seventeenth and Early Eighteenth Centuries: The Case of Cumbria', *Northern History*, 19 (1983), 87–107; George Dyer, *The Complaint of the Poor People of England* (2nd edn., London, 1793), p. 74.

[48] James Burgh, *Political Disquisitions* (3 vols., London, 1774–5), iii. 45.

[49] G. O. Cambridge, *Works of Richard Owen Cambridge, Esq.* (London, 1803), p. 448.

[50] *London Magazine* (1732), 382.

cated on the grounds that they would compel MPs to display their benevolence at home, 'living chiefly in your own Counties, within the Compass
of your paternal Estates'.[51] Later in the century there were suggestions that
Parliament itself should intervene to encourage such dutifulness. The
agricultural improver David Young advocated a law compelling landlords
who did not reside on their estate to forfeit 10 per cent of their rent, at
real values, to their tenants.[52]

What was meant by residence varied. It was easy to deride the occasional
visit to the country as adding insult to injury. In high summer, when the
heat and stench of London were intolerable, and other diversions exhausted,
the gentry returned to their estates for an intense but theatrical resumption
of their local duties. Their enthusiasm for this role was not always marked.
The young Lord Stanhope, better known to posterity as the fourth Earl of
Chesterfield, likened a summer spent at his family's mansion in Derbyshire
in 1725 to living in hell.[53] There was a distinctly self-congratulatory air
about such excursions. The diarist Caroline Girle, arriving at Weasenham
Hall, Norfolk, with its owners, the Jacksons, was moved to complacent
reflection on the significance of the occasion. 'In however high a stile a
man lives in town, which he certainly does, real benevolence is more
distinguishable in a family at their country-seat.'[54] Sir Egerton Brydges
considered the summer brigade in East Kent superior to the resident
gentry. But Brydges was a great snob and more interested in blue blood
than 'real benevolence'.[55] Others were not convinced. Even the worldly
Lady Mary Coke thought the nineteen-day visit planned by Lord and
Lady Hertford to Ragley, their Warwickshire seat, in August 1770 less
than impressive: 'I don't think they will have time to be tired of the
Country.' A silver lining in this cloud was the possibility that summers
spent with more conviction, but even less conscientiousness, in recreation,
could provide an opportunity for a substitute form of paternalism. The
first Marquis of Salisbury identified Aldeburgh as a pleasant place for
annual retreats, built a great house there, The Cassino, and in due course
found himself celebrated for his 'constant hospitalities'.[56]

The novelist John Cleland painted a sombre picture of the nobleman's
expedition to his country house, as something resembling an annual 'funeral
procession' through a deserted countryside. His account of such a visit to

[51] Ibid. (1740), 334.

[52] David Young, *Agriculture, The Primary Interest of Great Britain* (Edinburgh, 1788), p. 363.

[53] J. W. Croker, ed., *Letters to and from Henrietta, Countess of Suffolk*, (2 vols., London, 1824), i.
197–8.

[54] E. J. Climenson, ed., *Passages from the Diaries of Mrs Philip Lybbe Powys of Hardwick House,
Oxon. A. D. 1756 to 1808* (London, 1899), p. 4.

[55] *The Autobiography, Times, Opinions, and Contemporaries of Sir Egerton Brydges* (2 vols., London,
1834), i. 46 ff.

[56] *The Letters and Journals of Lady Mary Coke* (4 vols., London, repr. 1970), iii. 278; *Gentleman's
Magazine* (1823), 563–4, obituary by James Ford.

his estate by a great Warwickshire magnate, who might well have been
Hertford, was put in terms tellingly perceptive about the relationship
between men only nominally connected with the land. Country seats, he
noted, were temples of dullness, so far as their owners were concerned.
Visiting them was the result of 'a duty to cultivate, at certain seasons, the
old *English* hospitality, if but to give the mine-workers of agriculture their
just encouragement, in their share in the circulation of the revenues
produced by them'. In effect this ritual was a 'kind of land tax'.[57] Cleland
might have added that the form which the annual land tax took was not
necessarily conducive to communal well-being. The principal activities of
the summer—assizes, races, music-meetings, theatres, and assemblies—
were usually concentrated in the county town or similar regional centre.
One high-born convert to paternalism found this out for himself. Lord
Jersey was a young man about town who discovered the joys of country
living at his seat at Middleton Stoney while awaiting the birth of an heir
in 1770. To a correspondent he boasted that 'nobody ever led a country
life more'. He also apologized 'for not sending you Politics, histories etc.
for I really am out of the way of them all and having just sent for the
last Edition of Burne's Justice, you will be convinced that parish rates,
Settlements etc. are now more my objects, and while they last so well and
good; it is only an Amusement the more'. But Jersey was startled to find
how little of his time was actually spent at his seat. The races at Northampton required his presence at Wakefield Lodge with the Duke of
Grafton; those at Oxford brought him to Lord Harcourt's house at
Nuneham Courtenay.[58] A summer in the country was a decidedly peripatetic affair.

Activities of this kind certainly created the visibility lacking at other
times in the year, but the viewers were unlikely to include that rural lower
class generally considered the worst sufferer by upper-class absenteeism.
Occasional tenants' dances kept up a semblance of landlordly amiability,
though Mrs Lybbe Powys's account of one such near her own Oxfordshire
home, at Fawley Court, is not reassuring in this respect. 'The young people
all as usual danced with the tenants six or eight dances; then we came up
to cards and supper. The day always passes very agreeably, as it gives
pleasure to see so many people all so happy.'[59] Condescension was evidently
a marked feature of such occasions. Sunday sports and parochial wakes,
which in theory brought high and low together for traditional festivities,
were in decline. In his lesser role as a Whig squarson Dr Parr made a point
of encouraging May Day celebrations to highlight the deficiencies of

---

[57] *Memoirs of a Coxcomb* (London, 1751), pp. 345–6.
[58] BL, Althorp Papers, F 104: Jersey to Lady Spencer, 17 July 1770.
[59] Climenson, ed., *Passages from the Diaries of Mrs Philip Lybbe Powys*, p. 237.

Warwickshire's Tory gentry in this respect.[60] Private theatricals, a fashionable if perilous exercise in the limits of upper-class display, were welcomed
on the grounds that they encouraged genteel Thespians to return to
their country houses for the Christmas season. The playwright Richard
Cumberland penned a prologue concerning London luxury for one such
performance at Kelmarsh Hall in Leicestershire, in 1774, in which the
moral was made plain.

> Such is the scene: if then we fetch you down
> Amusements which endear the smoky town,
> And through the peasants' poor but useful hands,
> We circulate the produce of your lands,
> In this voluptuous dissipated age,
> Sure there's some merit in our rural stage,
> Happy the call, nor wholly vain the play
> Which weds you to your acres for a day.[61]

Country house drama may have helped restore rental income to the land
whence it came, but like most rural recreations it was conducted behind
closed doors or within carefully selected company. In fact there were very
few occasions which brought the landlord class face to face with its subjects.
As critics were quick to point out, the main effect of a month in the country,
from the standpoint of the ordinary villager, was not a heartening handshake
with the local lord of all, or a heart-warming glimpse of his lady, but
a regrettable acquaintance with their servants, bringing insubordinate
manners, demoralizing habits, and debilitating diseases from town to
country.[62]

At issue, of course, was not merely the remediable sin of absenteeism,
but the less familiar effect of class. Contemporaries believed that they were
witnessing a fundamental shift in social behaviour. As Boswell's friend
William Temple put it in 1779, 'it is the opinion of many excellent and
observing persons, that the manners of the opulent land-proprietor, of the
country gentleman (now a term of reproach) have undergone a considerable
change, within these sixty or seventy years past'.[63] The county was a group
of people rather than a physical location. It was plainly desirable that some
of its activities should be carried out where they naturally belonged, and
where those not directly included could play a vicarious part in the
proceedings. But the mobility of the eighteenth-century county community

---

[60] W. Derry, *Dr Parr* (Oxford, 1966), p. 272; R. W. Malcolmson, *Popular Recreations in English Society 1700–1850* (Cambridge, 1973), pp. 146–9, 162, 169–70.

[61] Joseph Cradock, *Literary and Miscellaneous Memoirs* (4 vols., London, 1828), iv. 262.

[62] J. J. Hecht, *The Domestic Servant Class in Eighteenth-Century England*, (London, 1956), pp. 226–7.

[63] W. J. Temple, *Moral and Historical Memoirs* (London, 1779), pp. 31–2.

made the exercise highly artificial. In fact it could seem almost as remote
as noblemen, like the Earl of Derby or the Duke of Devonshire, who were
virtually unknown in the counties which gave them their titles. The
difference was that the county community away from its own county tended
to behave as if distance in no way diminished its local authority.

During the London season it was common for county societies to meet
and dine in the capital. Something of the same kind also happened in Bath
and even Bristol. The original intention had been to provide aid for poor
provincials marooned far from home. Up to a point, and especially at
Bristol, this design was not forgotten.[64] But in the case of London, these
societies conducted important business. County affairs were transacted
rather as if the counties were colonies administered from a distant metropolis. It is unlikely to be coincidence that the revival of these 'assemblies
long discontinued' occurred in the wake of the Revolution of 1688 when
parliamentary sessions became an annual occurrence.[65] For a knight of the
shire like Edward Popham to have missed the Wiltshire Feast, held regularly towards the end of the session, and in 1754 on the brink of a
dissolution, would have been unthinkable.[66] It was doubtless a tribute to
the care taken to include the leaders of propertied opinion in these assemblies, and also to the communications which they maintained with their
localities, that this system operated as efficiently as it did. But it could
create tension between the leaders of county society, and the less mobile
classes of minor gentry, businessmen, and professionals who remained
behind to supervise the everyday running of the county. In Lincolnshire,
a large county with many non-resident landowners, not only was there an
annual feast in the capital, but the Lord Lieutenant was accustomed to
summon his countrymen to formal meetings.[67] The scheme of 1744 for a
county hospital was prepared in London, with lordly directives to those at
home to take soundings and transmit the news of what was being done by
their betters.[68] Perhaps it was not surprising that Lincoln did not get its
hospital for another twenty years. Yet this was only an extreme example
of a common tendency. If, as is often said, 1688 entrenched the power of
landowning oligarchies against central government, it is worth adding that
these oligarchies were London-based and London-minded.

---

[64] See e.g. Matthew Frampton, *A Sermon Preached at the Anniversary Meeting of Natives of the
County of Wilts., in St. Augustine's Church, Bristol, August viii. 1796* (Marlborough, n.d.), H. R.
Plomer, *The Kentish Feast* (Canterbury, 1910).

[65] *Notes and Queries for Somerset and Dorset*, 8 (1902–3), 265.

[66] Wiltshire RO, 39/10: Popham's diary, 1 Mar. 1754.

[67] Lincolnshire Archives Office, Monson MSS, 11. 29, 65: summons to Sir John Newton and
William Archer, from Duke of Ancaster, 26 June 1727; 'The Family Memoirs of the Rev. William
Stukeley, i', *Surtees Society*, 73 (1880), 59, 63.

[68] *Statutes and Constitutions for the Government of an Infirmary or Hospital, to be Established at
Lincoln* (Lincoln, 1745), p. iv.

The evils of non-residence were widely deplored. The author of a challenging tract of 1764 inveighed against them thus.'Oh what a fine estate, not a cottage or scarce an inhabitant in the parish, no poor and the distiller or merchant takes off the whole crop together. . . . The Nobles and gentlemen of large landed possessions, are, or ought to be the fathers and counsellors of society, not in national assemblies only, but each in his private character.'[69] From a very different standpoint Jonas Hanway, a pious and conventionally conservative commentator pleaded with the gentry to recognize the superior political attractions of the country scene: 'they might live like little sovereigns on their own domain, blessed, and blessing their dependents round them'.[70] A contemporary of both, Laurence Sterne, had Tristram Shandy's father point up the patriarchal catastrophe of the 'current of men and money towards the metropolis'. Were he an absolute prince, he announced, his ambition would be 'that the meadows and corn-fields, of my dominions, should laugh and sing;—that good cheer and hospitality flourish once more;—and that such weight and influence be put thereby into the hands of the Squirality of my kingdom, as should counterpoise what I perceive my Nobility are now taking from them'. He deeply admired Sir Robert Filmer's 'admirable pattern and prototype of this household and paternal power;—which, for a century, he said, and more, had gradually been degenerating away into a mixed government', thereby subverting 'the monarchical system of domestic government established in the first creation of things by God'. Sadly, Shandy's father was not the absolute prince of his dreams. He did, none the less, strike a blow for paternalism by insisting that his wife's lying-in took place at Shandy Hall, instead of in London. Significantly, he could do so only by exploiting a loophole in his marriage contract, the expression of a consensual, rather than patriarchal approach to family life.[71]

Readers were meant to relish the absurdity of this reasoning, but the premises on which it was based were as commonplace in 1759 as they had been in the heyday of divine right theory half a century or more earlier. Paradoxically, at the very time that such values were under threat, they were also at a premium. Land, for purposes of social status, was more desirable than ever in the late eighteenth century, and the patriarchal image which went with it seemed all the more necessary to men who had not earned it by hereditary right. The rural fantasy of the prospective or parvenu country gentleman made the countryside a stage on which he expected to play the part of 'little sovereign', preferably without the real-life labour which went with it. There were many prepared to encourage

---

[69] *A View of the Internal Policy of Great Britain* (London, 1764), p. 286.
[70] *A Comprehensive View of Sunday Schools* (London, 1786), p. i.
[71] *The Life and Opinions of Tristram Shandy Gentleman*, ed. G. Petrie (London, 1967), pp. 73–5.

him in this role, not least the architects and landscape gardeners who
sought to exaggerate his share of the landscape. Just as Capability Brown
and the ha-ha contrived to create the illusion of boundless property for
country house owners, so new model villages and rococo cottages presented
a matching image of benevolent landlordship. The same men who extended
parks, uprooted cottages, enclosed waste, consolidated farms, and moved
villages, also planned new human environments to set off the splendour of
their homes. Shenstone, an influential landscape gardener in his own right,
and an enthusiast for the architectural merits of the well-situated cottage,
argued that neat, pretty, but humble dwellings lent variety and tranquillity
to the rural scene; he also admitted regretfully that pride was involved.[72]
Repton was less bashful on this point, as befitted a self-made man, and
one who made his living from the new taste. If cottages of the poor 'can
be made a subordinate part of the general scenery, they will, so far from
disgracing it, add to the dignity that wealth can derive from the exercise
of benevolence'.[73]

Lest the public be unaware of the correct solution to the deficiencies of
rural rule, it was assailed with ideal stereotypes. Whether it was the
urgency of the crisis which developed from the 1760s, or the vogue for
sentimentalism, the fictitious models of the reign of George III had a
somewhat different flavour from the rational benevolence of Fielding's Mr
Allworthy, or the whimsical chivalry of Smollett's Sir Launcelot Greaves.
There was a new emphasis on feeling, rather than wisdom, and also a desire
to portray the reciprocal relationship which little sovereigns enjoyed with
their subjects. Sir Robert Harold, who made his appearance in Hugh
Kelly's *Memoirs of a Magdalen* in 1767, was an authentic patriarch. It was
said that peasants who lived within twenty miles of his Devon seat were
to a man ready to venture their lives for him.[74] A competitor, Sarah Scott's
George Ellison, was offered in the guise of a Solomon-like magistrate. His
constant concern was the welfare of the poor. He kept the richer people of
his parish firmly in check, managed to reconcile the vicar to his flock, and
failed only in his over-ambitious plan to put an end to drinking and feasting
at harvest time.[75]

These became stock types in the last decades of the century though they
were subject to some significant changes. One was the growing tendency
to present them in a nostalgic, unrealistic light, especially where commercial
pressures were concerned. That a philanthropic squire could also be a

---

[72] *The Works in Verse and Prose of William Shenstone, Esq.* (3 vols., London, 1764–9), ii. 132.
[73] G. Carter, P. Goode, and K. Laurie, *Humphry Repton: Landscape Gardener, 1752–1818* (Norwich, 1982), p. 116.
[74] H. Kelly, *Memoirs of a Magdalen; Or, the History of Louisa Mildmay* (2 vols., London, 1784 (1st edn. 1767)), i. 12.
[75] Sarah Scott, *The History of Sir George Ellison* (2 vols., London, 1766), i. 179–95.

prosperous landlord came to seem implausible. Increasingly, the ideal paternalist was placed safely in a Celtic setting, where agricultural practice was notoriously backward. Mrs Bennett displayed her Welsh baronet, Sir Arthur Meredith of Code Gwyn, as the victim of his own old-world chivalry. 'The family lived precisely in the same style, from generation to generation; the same number of domestics, the same mode of living, and the same rental from their farms; and having neglected to raise their tenants, equivalent to the advances of every necessary of life, these had grown rich into opulence, as their generous landlord had, insensibly, become involved in difficulties.' Meredith was eventually driven from his estate by his mortgage-holder, and compelled to take refuge in the parsonage.[76] Robert Bage's Sir Howell Henneth, who was also beggared by his eccentric generosity to tenants and workmen, enjoyed his decaying splendour at Mount Henneth on the remote Cardiganshire coast.[77] Richard Polwhele took the additional precaution of placing his 'Old English Gentleman', Sir Humphrey de Andarton, in the Jacobite past. Sir Humphrey 'hated Hanoverian stuff', including turnips, preferred pewter to Delft or Wedgwood, celebrated Christmas in feudal manner, refused to take on tenants with white hands, bemoaned the loss of the Cornish breed of 'small sweet mutton' to the commercially approved Leicester, and would have nothing to do with ha-has and hurdles. 'Attacht to farming on its ancient plan, Sir Humphrey brook'd not a reforming man.' His house was a 'patriarchal tent, sustain'd by love'.[78]

More satisfactory than idealized portraits were the living models which sometimes presented themselves. Polwhele paraded not only his anachronistic Sir Humphrey, but also the very contemporary Sir John St Aubyn, one of the county's greatest landowners; not, 'for all the charms of the picturesque, would he disturb one humble habitation'.[79] St Aubyn, father of fifteen illegitimate children and a spendthrift, was hardly a model in all respects. Significantly, more impressive real-life examples seemed to come from the recent past rather than the present. The memoirist Catherine Cappe recalled Sir Rowland Winn of Nostell in Yorkshire, who in 1763 was still maintaining the manner of life of 'an English baron, in ancient times'. He had an establishment of sixty to seventy servants, kept open house for his farmers and cottagers at Christmas, distributed food to the poor, faithfully performed his duties as a magistrate, and took a close interest in the Ackworth Foundling Hospital, an offshoot of the celebrated London orphanage.[80] In Berkshire there were similarly fond memories of

---

[76] *Ellen, Countess of Castle Howel* (4 vols., London, 1794), i. 9–10, 233–4.
[77] *Mount Henneth* (2 vols., repr. New York, 1979, orig. 1782), i. 112.
[78] *Poems*, iii. 76, 99–100, 104, 105, 106.
[79] *The History of Cornwall* (Truro, 1806), p. 3.
[80] *Memoirs of the Life of the Late Mrs Catherine Cappe* (London, 1822), pp. 80–4.

the Cherry family. Their story had all the heavily didactic elements required
for a late eighteenth-century morality play. Francis Cherry of Shottesbrook
had been the embodiment of pious humanity. His household was filled
with happy and industrious servants. One of them, the future scholar
Thomas Hearne, owed his education and subsequent fame to his master's
generosity. His parish was known for its harmony. Cottagers were provided
with orchards and commons to sustain themselves, and the low poor rates
were the envy of the district. But Cherry died and in 1717 his estate was
purchased by Arthur Vansittart, 'a very amiable man but, bred a Dutch
merchant, he entered not into the oeconomy for the poor, took away all
their orchards to make a garden of thirty acres, pulled down several of the
farm-houses and many of the cottages'.[81] The poor rates rocketed, and
Shottesbrook became indistinguishable from other parishes immiserated
by improvement.

Nostalgia, even moralizing nostalgia, was no substitute for living
example. The newspapers were quick to praise individual examples of
traditional benevolence. John Blachford's munificence at Northaw in Hertfordshire in the dearth of 1757 displayed 'a true English Hospitality,
annually observed by all Gentlemen of Fortune in this Kingdom, 'till
foreign Fashions and foreign Attachments so vitiated the Palate, as to reject
the Appearance of Freeborn Britons'.[82] The growing resort to published
obituaries made for many such reflections. The death of Arthur Blaney,
the 'Father of Montgomeryshire', at the advanced age of 81, stimulated a
review of his life in which the traditionally paternalistic and the modishly
progressive were happily mixed. On the one hand he had refused to raise
his rents for forty years and acted as 'the common friend of the poor and
distressed'. On the other hand he had used his weight to promote the
building of roads, canals, and churchs. 'By his unremitting exertions
and most liberal assistance he had given a new face to the surrounding
countryside.'[83] 1795, when Blaney died, was a year of exceptional hardship,
marked in the press by a crop of such homilies. It was not necessary to die
to have one's paternalistic virtues trumpeted. The story of the Lancashire
Collier Girl told of a sick child who slaved in a coal-mine to bring up her
orphaned family. Her integrity, piety, and chastity were respected even in
the rough, masculine environment of a colliery. Her health eventually
broken, she applied in desperation for a position in a neighbouring house,
and was taken in. Here she found a veritable Hospitality Hall, 'where
domestics are treated as "humble friends"', and where she happily dwelled
as 'an example of industry, humility, and kindheartedness'. No names

[81] *Gentleman's Magazine* (1795), 824–6.
[82] W. S. Lewis and P. M. Williams, *Private Charity in England, 1747–1757* (New Haven, 1938),
pp. 20–1.
[83] *Gentleman's Magazine* (1795), 881.

appeared in the first version of this 'true story', but before very long it was
revealed that the paragon of paternalism was William Bankes of Winstanley,
near Wigan.[84] It all went to show how closely Hannah More's 'Tales for
the Common People' resembled real life.

The top awards went to landowners who not only carried out their social
responsibilities, but also managed their estates profitably. This was a high
priority: to reconcile the perceived need for patriarchal benevolence, with
the harsh requirements of commerical farming. Arthur Young and Nathan-
ial Kent, two persistent enthusiasts for agricultural improvement in the
1760s and 1770s, obliged with numerous examples. Young described the
transformation wrought by Charles Turner on his Kirkleatham estate in
Cleveland. Far from destroying cottages, he replaced the hovels of his
villagers with neat brick houses, and provided a new shop and workshop
to stimulate local trade. To displace the traditional smuggling, he erected
two handsome inns, and by 'fixing in them creditable people and annexing
a farm to each, the low mischievous practices of the former houses are
destroyed'. The morally cleansing effect as well as commercial viability of
such a policy ensured that paternalism could be salvaged from the wreckage
of the old agriculture. Turner was an exponent of the new methods: his
cattle breeding and crop rotation were innovative, and at Coatham he even
installed a boarding house and bathing machine to divert tourists from the
rival delights of Scarborough. The population on his estates had actually
increased and the poor rate had diminished. All this he achieved in three
years, contracting 'the business of a dreaming life, into the spirited period
of a few months!'[85] There seem to have been two views of Turner, for in
1783 the banker John King bitterly assailed him as a 'tyrant among his
immediate dependents', and accused him of 'racking and oppressing his
tenants'.[86] But Young's object was always propaganda rather than por-
traiture.

Perhaps Young's favourite instance was that of Nicholas Styleman at
Snettisham in Norfolk. Styleman had been a party to the potential crime
of a parliamentary enclosure, but not, as it turned out, to the disadvantage
of his parish. Forty-one houses with right of commonage, 'which totally
prevented the use of turnips and clover', lost their privileges; but in return
each was provided with three acres and a share in a common reserved for
the cattle of the poor. The cottagers' unlawful depredations on the hedges
and fields of the farmers gave way to a legally secure grant of one hundred
acres for turf cutting. The population rose from 500 to 600, the poor rate

[84] Ibid., 197–9, 486.
[85] *A Six Months Tour through the North of England* (2nd edn., 4 vols., London, 1771), ii. 98–154.
[86] John King, *Thoughts on the Difficulties and Distresses in which the Peace of 1783, Has Involved the People of England* (London, 1783), p. 47.

fell from 1s. 6d. to less than 1s.[87] This was enlightened enclosing. Not far away at Felbrigg, Kent found the Wyndham family practising a policy of enlightened engrossing. The last freeholder in the parish was bought out, and the land divided into a number of small farms of eight to twelve acres to support the poorer tenantry. Kent advocated a carefully graduated leasing policy to provide a variety of farm sizes for the rural community.[88] Both Kent and Young emphasized that paternal supervision and profitability were perfectly compatible. Young was particularly excited by Abraham Dixon of Belford in Northumberland, who, 'daring and comprehensive in his ideas', succeeded in a brilliant mixture of agricultural and manufacturing enterprise. On the land his tenants were encouraged to use new and more efficient machinery. At the same time a tannery and woollen mill were constructed and new coalpits dug to replace exhausted ones. The population of Belford increased sixfold in thirteen years.[89] When names did not have to be named, still more impressive achievements could be claimed. In 1790 the press reported a rural fête held regularly by a northern landowner. It featured ploughing matches, bounties for women supporting aged parents or numerous children, country sports, dancing, and a tenants' dinner. 'The consequence was that while the estates of many gentlemen were depopulated by emigration, his has flourished in such a degree, that by the increase of people he has been able to plant the valuable manufactures of cotton and trimming, to erect four considerable villages, and to take in and cultivate several thousand acres of waste land, to the improvement of his rental, with the blessing of his tenants.'[90]

THE GUARDIAN MAGISTRATE

Non-residence and its attendant evils were associated with a presumed lapse from civic virtue on the part of propertied families. The High Churchman William Jones of Nayland spoke in 1782 of 'that want of *public spirit*, and that aversion to *business*, which has prevailed of late years amongst *our gentry*'.[91] A more worldly clergyman, Sir Henry Bate Dudley, made the same complaint, based on personal experience of county administration.[92] One common element in appeals to the enlightened self-interest of the rural ruling class was recognition of the part to be played by the magistracy. It was highly satisfying when the exemplars of commercial agriculture were also models of judicial wisdom. Turner was an active and

---

[87] *The Farmer's Tour through the East of England*, ii. 24–6.
[88] *Hints to Gentlemen of Landed Property*, pp. 217–18.
[89] *A Six Months Tour*, iii. 38–40.
[90] *Whitehall Evening-Post*, 24 Aug. 1790.
[91] *The Theological, Philosophical and Miscellaneous Works of the Rev. William Jones* (12 vols., London, 1801), vi. 239.
[92] Rogers, ed., *The State of the Poor*, p. 82.

influential JP at Kirkleatham. In John Holroyd of Sheffield Place, Sussex, Young found a particularly impressive example of a watchful magistrate, whose zeal for detecting and extirpating abuses in the administration of the poor law was not less admirable than his commitment to commercial husbandry. Holroyd's major achievement was to reverse the policy of local farmers, who used the poor rate to subsidize healthy labourers while neglecting the children, the elderly, and the sick. Instead he provided apprenticeships for the young, and care for the old and infirm. Parish feasts were abolished, wasteful wage supplements eliminated, and the rates dramatically reduced. Holroyd himself served the office of overseer of the poor to show that he could practise what he preached.[93] The emphasis on controlling the practices of farmers was common to such examples. In Norfolk at the end of the century Samuel Jackson Pratt found another exemplar in Sir Martin Folkes. Folkes's great merit was that he was 'a man remarkably good at Justizeing'. Justizeing, it transpired, meant rectifying the injustices committed by his tenants. ''Tis in vain for a Farmer to *down* with a poor man, because Sir Martin, if he deserves it, will as surely *up* him again.'[94]

The declining conscientiousness of magistrates was one of the most discussed consequences of the collapse of traditional paternalism. Complaints about the shortage of JPs prepared to carry out their duties were not new but swelled notably in mid-century. In Oxfordshire, as early as 1740, a prominent local Whig was complaining to the Lord-Lieutenant, the Duke of Marlborough, that 'there is not one acting justice between Oxford and Banbury (twenty long miles) to the great detriment of All People'.[95] By the 1750s such complaints were endemic; in 1754 Lord Chief Justice Lee was moved to recall the old practice of indicting magistrates who refused to act.[96] As in other matters parliamentary sessions and the London season took a share of the blame. In the 1730s criticism of common attorneys was reinforced by the observation that 'winter justices', 'a Term used by them for the Justices residing in the Country when many of the Men of Figure are generally in Town', were frequently 'through Ignorance, Poverty or Avarice, in the Hands of an Attorney'.[97] But in time absenteeism came to be associated with the more general malaise identified in the social life of the propertied classes. Novelists noticed a growing gulf between generations in this respect. Mrs Bennett not only portrayed the inherited wisdom of Sir Arthur Meredith, but also highlighted the modern follies of the younger generation. Her new Squire Melmoth ignored the precedent

[93] *The Farmer's Tour through the East of England*, iii. 143–7.
[94] Samuel Jackson Pratt, *Gleanings in England* (2nd edn., 3 vols., London, 1801–3), i. 173–7.
[95] R. J. Robson, *The Oxfordshire Election of 1754* (London, 1949), p. 42.
[96] BL, Add. MS 35592, fo. 278: Leeds to Hardwicke, 2 Mar. 1754.
[97] *Fog's Weekly Journal*, 1 Sept. 1733.

set by his father: 'instead of minding the justice business, as old Squire
did, and Quorum meetings, he must go to Helmstone a bathing'.[98] The
poet John Langhorne, himself an assiduous magistrate in his own county
of Somerset, wrote *The Country Justice* to recall a delinquent class to its
duty:

> Lost are those Days, and Fashion's boundless Sway
> Has borne the Guardian Magistrate away.
> Save in Augusta's streets, and on Gallia's shore,
> The Rural Patron is beheld no more,
>
> Forgone the social, hospitable Days,
> When wider Vales echoed with their Owner's Praise,
> Of all that *ancient Consequence* bereft,
> What has the *modern Man of Fashion* left?[99]

The emphasis on competing social attractions was doubtless right. The
antiquarian William Stukeley was not one to haunt the fleshpots of London,
but when he retreated to Grantham and became a magistrate he could not
help admitting the tedium of his new life. 'A country justice has but a very
silly part to act.'[100]

Parliament could not ignore this problem. MPs were certainly well aware
of it. Thomas Gilbert, a keen student of local government and promoter
of a series of poor law reforms, including the statute of 1782 associated
with his name, deplored the reluctance of so many magistrates 'of Fortune
and Ability' to attend to their duties.[101] In the wake of the Gordon Riots,
such was the concern about the shortage of qualified magistrates that a bill
was proposed to enable JPs who had not qualified themselves as magistrates
to act in cases of riot. The bill was lost in the House of Lords, but the
Commons displayed its anxiety on the point by calling for lists of the
commission of the peace which distinguished those who acted from those
who did not.[102]

How justified was concern about this particular form of genteel delinquency? In the case of the one county which has been exhaustively studied
in this respect the answer for the reigns of George I and George II is
striking. Between the early and mid-eighteenth century the proportion of
Kentish magistrates who qualified themselves to act within five years of
appointment fell from 53 per cent to 35 per cent.[103] Attendance at quarter

---

[98] Agnes Maria Bennett, *Anna: Or, Memoirs of a Welch Heiress* (2nd edn., 4 vols., London,
1786), i. 44.

[99] *Part the Second* (London, 1775), pp. 19, 20.

[100] 'The Family Memoirs of the Rev. William Stukeley, ii', *Surtees Soc.* 76 (1883), 341.

[101] *Plan for the Better Relief and Employment of the Poor* (London, 1781), p. 28.

[102] *Lords Journals*, xxxvi. 253; *Commons Journals*, xxxviii. 449.

[103] N. Landau, *The Justices of the Peace, 1679–1760* (Berkeley, Calif., 1984), p. 320.

sessions, simultaneously the judiciary, legislature, and executive of county life, diminished to much the same extent.[104] Kent was not untypical. Lord Hardwicke's correspondence as Lord Chancellor suggests that in the 1750s, attendance at quarter sessions sank to rock bottom. In small counties it became difficult to obtain a quorum. In Rutland in 1755–6, two sessions had to be abandoned on this account. In Huntingdonshire at this time the bare minimum of two justices was maintained, but no more.[105] In Dorset the clerk of the peace was driven to desperate expedients to secure the presence of sufficient magistrates for a quorum.[106]

The reasons for this state of affairs are not difficult to find. Commissions of the peace, appointed by the Crown and its ministers, were always subject to party political bias. The proscription of Tories under George I was selective rather than savage. Its object was a preponderance, not a monopoly. None the less, this was sufficient to ensure that Whigs had unbreakable majorities on the county benches.[107] The effect was predictable. Moderate Tories who were permitted to retain their places increasingly ceased to attend in what, from a party standpoint, was a hopeless and also a somewhat compromising cause. Ironically, Whigs too found it difficult to work up enthusiasm for their duties. The very abstention of the Tories, and the certainty that the Crown would never allow anything but a Whig hegemony of county government, removed one of the main reasons for Whigs to attend to their duties, unless they were unusually public-spirited, or had some obvious personal interest in so doing. The necessity for new recruits was widely recognized. But while relations between the parties at local level remained so bad, every nomination was likely to be the cause of renewed recrimination.

In the 1720s and 1730s a crucial change of policy occurred, though it is unlikely that it was the result of a conscious decision at any particular moment. Before that time the removal of magistrates for political reasons was commonplace. Henceforward it became virtually unknown. Though it is often described as 'oligarchical' Walpole's regime was notably reluctant to use the extreme methods adopted by the Whig government during the

---

[104] Ibid., 322. Landau is at pains to point out the importance of petty sessions, compared with quarter sessions (pp. 262–5), thereby casting doubt on quarter sessions attendance as a measure of the magistrates' conscientiousness. But Kent, a large county of two distinct divisions, may be untypical in this respect. The Cambridgeshire evidence which she also cites is not conclusive, nor is the argument supported, in so far as it is possible to trace petty sessional activities, by the experience of Berkshire, Buckinghamshire, and Oxfordshire.

[105] Returns of quarter sessions at PRO, E. 362. The accuracy of the returns is open to question, but I have used them with circumspection and checked samples against quarter session records in county archives.

[106] See S. J. and B. Webb *English Local Government from the Revolution to the Municipal Corporations Act* (9 vols., London, 1906–29), vol. i: *The Parish and the County* (1906), pp. 422–3.

[107] L. K. J. Glassey, *Politics and the Appointment of Justices of the Peace 1675–1720* (Oxford, 1979), ch. 8; see also Landau, *The Justices of the Peace, 1679–1760*, pp. 86–95.

early years of George I's reign. The proscription of George II's reign was proscription by omission rather than commission. Hardwicke, Lord Chancellor from 1734 to 1757, refused to accept Whig demands for the dismissal of Tory magistrates, even when the demands came from magnates as powerful and as respected as the Archbishop of York. The Archbishop's regretful admission that 'he is Sensible this Political Consideration cannot properly be alleged as an Objection in Form' would have startled Whigs of the previous generation.[108] Paradoxically, Hardwicke's stance made him reluctant to add to the commission as well as determined not to subtract from it. Thus he urged the Whig Earl of Coventry of the need not 'hastily to do that which afterwards could not be safely set right'.[109] He frequently preferred to leave the commission of the peace well alone rather than risk a divisive revision.

Some modifications to the plan of Whig oligarchy were permitted. In 1744–5 Pelham's Broad Bottom experiment induced ministers to concede Tory demands for restoration to the commissions of the peace. But only half-a-dozen counties were involved, the negotiations proved difficult, and the end result did not meet the expectations of the Tories.[110] Thereafter, as the hard lines of demarcation between Whig and Tory began to break down, Tories were able to profit by Whig divisions. Sir Thomas Prendergast lectured the Lord Chancellor on this subject in 1752 when Lord Powys vetoed the introduction of Tory justices in Caernarvonshire: 'Family Picques and private quarrels, in which the publick has no kind of interest, are so prevalent In our parts, that I must humbly intreat your Lordship to require clear and strong reasons, where any gentleman of large property is objected to.'[111] It was by no means only in remote North Wales that Whig factionalism gave Tories their chance. In Huntingdonshire Lord Sandwich described the Duke of Manchester in 1756 as having 'thrown himself entirely into the hands of the Tories'.[112] When Pitt finally broke the mould of Hanoverian politics in 1756–7 there followed a spate of new commissions in which the admission of Tories, albeit on Whig terms, continued.[113]

This process of Tory rehabilitation was completed, with a triumphal flourish, on the accession of George III. Great numbers of new magistrates were appointed in the first two years of the new reign, in what amounted

---

[108] BL, Add. MS 35586, fo. 23: T. Hayter to Hardwicke, 11 June 1737.

[109] Ibid., fo. 372: 23 July 1741.

[110] J. B. Owen, *The Rise of the Pelhams* (London, 1957), pp. 262–3; L. Colley, *In Defiance of Oligarchy: The Tory Party 1714–60* (Cambridge, 1982), pp. 248–50; Landau, *The Justices of the Peace, 1675–1760*, pp. 109–24.

[111] BL, Add. MS 35591, fos. 389–90: Sir Thomas Prendergast to Hardwicke, 10 Aug. 1752.

[112] PRO, 30/29, Granville MSS, 1. 49: Sandwich to Lord Gower, 21 Nov. [1756].

[113] In 1757–8 large numbers of justices were added to the commission in Essex, Lincolnshire, Somerset, Staffordshire, and Suffolk; see PRO, C 234.

to a complete reconstruction of the commission of the peace. Tories, excluded in some areas up to the very end of the preceding reign, were finally restored to what they considered their proper place in county government. There was consequently a distinct revival of interest in the magistracy. This was strongly marked in Oxfordshire, one of the counties most severely affected by the partisan approach to local administration during the early Hanoverian reigns.[114] Of the 27 JPs appointed in 1727, only 3 had subsequently attended quarter sessions; of the 59 newcomers in 1745, only 13 had done so; and of 89 added in 1755, only 17. Active magistrates thus represented less than 19 per cent of George II's nominations to the bench, virtually all of them reliable Whigs, appointed to keep Oxfordshire safe for Whiggism and the House of Hanover. The county was one of those included in the Broad Bottom experiment, yet the Tory gains of 1745 were so grudgingly conceded and so easily offset by Whig counterclaims that they made little difference. The contrast presented by the experience of 1761 was very striking. The 26 additions of that year, including Tory families whose restoration was trumpeted as such in the local press, yielded a much higher proportion of conscientious magistrates: 14 subsequently appeared at quarter sessions.[115] The improvement was short-lived, however. Only 13 of the 90 names added in 1769 are to be found in the quarter sessions minutes. This pattern proved to be typical. In most counties there was a modest revival of interest in county business in the first half of George III's reign, but one which reflected increased commitment on the part of limited numbers rather than widespread enthusiasm. Attendance at quarter sessions rarely fell to the exceptionally low levels of George II's reign, but neither did it rise readily to the high levels of the early eighteenth century.[116]

A place on the commission of the peace had certain attractions. The fluctuating fortunes of the parties between 1689 and 1714 not only heightened its political and electoral value, but also stimulated interest and activity on the part of ordinary magistrates. Under George I and George II, though it was monopolized by one party, contested county elections were increasingly rare, and the incentive even for Whigs to attend to their duties slight. After 1760 a new set of conditions obtained again. Nonpartisan appointments to the magistracy were the rule under George III, not merely because the reign had begun with conscious appeals to a spirit of patriotic harmony, but because government rarely had a direct electoral interest in county elections. Moreover, county society discovered a certain

---

[114] The following calculations are made on the basis of new magistrates named at PRO, C 234, and attendance at quarter sessions recorded in the minutes in Oxfordshire RO.

[115] *An Alphabetical List of His Majesty's Justices of the Peace, for the County of Oxfordshire* (1761).

[116] Landau, *The Justices of the Peace, 1675–1760*, pp. 263–5; see also E. Moir, *Local Government in Gloucestershire 1775–1800* (Pubs. Bristol and Gloucestershire Arch. Soc. 8, 1969), pp. 163–71.

disinclination to revive the earlier 'rage of party'. County elections were not uncommon, but they were increasingly fought according to rules and conventions designed to protect propertied society from the damage inflicted in earlier times. Quarter sessions ceased to be blatantly political.

Complaints about 'justice power', frequent in the electoral conflicts of the early eighteenth century, were much less so in the late eighteenth century. Occasional exceptions tended to prove the rule. The ferocious electoral warfare provoked by the ambition of Sir James Lowther in Westmorland and Cumberland in the 1760s was accompanied by political manipulation of the magistracy in the north-west. But it was not allowed to continue for long. Five JPs removed from the Cumberland bench in January 1767 were restored two years later.[117] Lowther was up to his tricks again a few years later, in 1775, but although he was a strong supporter of administration, the Lord Chancellor of the day, Lord Apsley, refused to be hurried into the promulgation of a partisan commission. To Lowther's great enemy and leading opposition magnate the Duke of Portland he wrote, 'I shall not indulge Sir James with such Expedition. If Your Grace will look over the List, in case you see any Gentleman of fortune omitted you will oblige me by sending their Names and I will take care to have them added.'[118] The net effect of these anachronistic manoeuvres, suggesting the first quarter of the century rather than the third, was merely to underline their futility.

With party politics a minor consideration in the management of the bench, the interest of the magistracy for most families of consequence revolved around its status. This could readily be divorced from the judicial and administrative duties involved. The prime objective of admission to the commission of the peace was social. To *be* in it was a point of pride for the great families, and of ambition for aspiring gentry. To *act* in it was merely onerous. Under Hardwicke, the judges on circuit had been instructed to 'Exhort and Encourage Gentlemen in the Commission of the peace to act as Justices'. Lord Chief Justice Lee, 'as an old Fellow in the Last act of the Farce of Life', pointed out to his Lord Chancellor that 'the Language is Polite, But I am afraid in these times Exhortation from the Judges will signifye Little more than from the Pulpit'.[119] Hardwicke's successors sometimes threatened to accept only those who made it clear that they were prepared to act. But it was not easy to enforce this policy. Lords-Lieutenant came under intense pressure from their countrymen to propose them for what amounted to honorary membership of the bench. The size of the county magistracy steadily increased, and the proportion executing its duties correspondingly fell.

[117] PRO, C 234. 7.
[118] Nottingham University Library, Portland MSS, PwF 292: 14 Aug. 1775.
[119] BL, Add. MS 35592, fo. 278: 2 Mar. 1754.

For some, appointment to the commission of the peace was in the nature of a precautionary tactic. It represented a form of power which did not need to be used until occasion required. This was how General William A'Court, MP for Heytesbury, interpreted it in 1766. When the Wiltshire magistrates declined to assist the sufferers by a costly fire in Heytesbury, A'Court took out his dedimus as a justice solely to enable him to attend the ensuing quarter sessions in favour of his constituents, and with no intention of acting subsequently.[120] Others valued the status of the magistracy while lacking the industry or inclination to participate in its judicial or executive functions. It was said that fear of making enemies and alienating friends was a common motive.[121] In this matter of non-attendance on duty the bench was much like other governing bodies, both official and unofficial. As the Governors of the Shropshire Infirmary put it, an active part was always attended 'with the disagreeable circumstance of being thought officious and assuming, and a certainty of blame and censure for every cross accident or miscarriage that happens'.[122]

There was, above all, the question of rank. However much they wished to appear in the commission of the peace, individuals did not always want to hob-nob with others in it. A common argument for not acting was the snobbish but compelling contention that in point of dignity and property, the acting magistrates were not worthy of respect. Complaints about lowly justices were almost as old as the office itself. But Hanoverian rule certainly exacerbated them. After 1714 quarter sessions no longer seemed to resemble roll-calls of the county families. With the Tory leaders of local society excluded, whether by the Crown or by their own desire to boycott a predominantly Whig institution, and their Whig counterparts increasingly uninterested in a burdensome judicial and administrative office, government was driven to new sources of recruitment. The result was what the Bishop of St Asaph described to Hardwicke as the appointment of men with 'much more Zeal than property'.[123] This tendency had been glimpsed even before 1714, particularly during Harley's ministry, when the Tories were desperate to entrench themselves in power before the death of the Queen. The long Whig supremacy inevitably strengthened it. Probably it would have occurred whichever party had found itself in office for a prolonged period. The results were none the less highly controversial.

---

[120] Wiltshire RO, 1553/37: H. Wyndham to H. P. Wyndham, 5 Aug. 1766.
[121] *Memoirs, Anecdotes, Facts, and Opinions, Collected and Preserved by Laetitia-Matilda Hawkins* (2 vols., London, 1824), i. 16.
[122] Shropshire RO, 3909/6/2: printed report of Salop Infirmary for 1773.
[123] BL, Add. MS 35601, fos. 116–17: received 9 Aug. 1742.

ZEAL OR PROPERTY

No doubt the requirements of Whig oligarchy made it necessary to go
beyond the gentry of broad acres to landowners of the second and even
third rank in county society. In Glamorgan what was involved was 'a much
wider section of the landed community'.[124] But the Bishop of St Asaph's
complaint went much further than this. The commonest charge against
those with more zeal than property was that they were barely landowners
at all, men of low birth, with a background in trade or the dregs of one of
the professions, and dependants of Whig magnates, incapable of standing
on their own feet. Smollett's sketch of a justice who 'had been a pettifogger,
and was a sycophant to a nobleman in the neighbourhood, who had a post
at court', was the most famous of many such parodies of the type.[125] In his
version Charles Johnstone sharpened the satire by having his Justice Guttle,
agent to Squire Bribe'em, defraud his patron of his estate and drive him
into penury in the south of France.[126]

   The selection of lawyers as suitable targets doubtless ensured an appreciative readership. Attorneys, and, somewhat less objectionably, barristers,
had an obvious entrée to a judicial career. They were prohibited from
practising while acting as justices, though the prohibition was flouted by
some of their number. The antiquary William Cole noted that the
Buckinghamshire JP, Walden Hanmer, continued his legal practice after
his appointment to the bench in 1757, 'by which, it is said, he makes as
much or more than suits the Character of a Gentleman'. Hanmer was a
fair example of the breed which had prospered under Hanoverian rule,
especially as there is no evidence, apart from Cole's malicious remarks,
that he was regarded as unusual or especially offensive. His maternal
grandfather had been a Coventry merchant, or as Cole put it, 'a little
trading Presbyterian', who had purchased the Buckinghamshire manor of
Simpson.[127] The manor passed by marriage to Hanmer's father, also a
lawyer and an assiduous Whig magistrate between 1727 and 1739. Hanmer
himself attended quarter sessions religiously from 1757 until he became an
MP in 1768; he subsequently acquired a baronetcy, and on his death in
1783, left an heir, like him and his own father a barrister of Lincoln's
Inn. The family had the luck to inherit estates in Flintshire, but in
Buckinghamshire they were regarded as parvenus, and not very opulent
ones at that. In 1784 they paid only £32 land tax on the Simpson estate;

   [124] P. Jenkins, *The Making of a Ruling Class: The Glamorgan Gentry 1640–1790* (Cambridge, 1983),
pp. 84–7.
   [125] *The Life and Adventures of Sir Launcelot Greaves*, p. 49.
   [126] *The Adventures of Anthony Varnish; Or, a Peep of the Manners of Society* (3 vols., London, 1786),
i. 236–8.
   [127] F. G. Stokes, ed., *A Journal of My Journey to Paris in the Year 1765, by the Rev. William Cole*
(London, 1931), pp. 377, 385.

at that time there were at least one hundred and fifty landowners in the
county who paid more.[128]

It was not necessary to be a lawyer to make hay while the Whig sun
shone. Cole was equally contemptuous of John Shipton, who owed his
prosperity, and his place on the bench, to his years of service as steward
to the Earl Spencer.[129] Nor need one turn to a jaundiced High Church
clergyman for an unflattering estimate of the social credentials of mid-
eighteenth-century magistrates. Hardwicke's voluminous correspondence
as Lord Chancellor is rich in insulting descriptions of the magistrates for
whom he was ultimately responsible. One nominee for Anglesea was plainly
below the salt: 'in his younger year's He was so low as not to be admitted
to Gentlemen's Tables, but used to take his meals among the Upper
Servants'.[130] In his own county of Cambridgeshire, notoriously short of
gentry, Hardwicke was subjected to a stream of correspondence about the
unsuitability of proposed and acting JPs.[131]

Whig peers were effective exposers of each other's preference for lick-
spittles. In Norfolk in 1747, Lord Orford denounced one of Lord Townshend's nominations as a common brewer who had once drawn ale in a
London tavern and had married his widowed mistress; another of Townshend's was described by Lord Leicester as 'a farmer and little trafficker a
fellow whose utmost ambition could aim no higher than high constable'.[132]
Hardwicke sometimes heeded such warnings, but in many instances he
ignored them. It is difficult not to believe that his primary criterion was
party allegiance. Townshend was certainly a Whig peer but a wayward one
accused by his enemies of bringing in Tory magistrates; accordingly his
proposals were treated with considerable caution. Elsewhere it was a
different story. In Gloucestershire Hardwicke accepted the highly controversial nomination of Thomas Bush, an apothecary who, he was assured
in 1740, was giving up his profession to live off his property. Bush was a
Whig stalwart in a district, Cirencester, where the Tories were well established. His abandonment of his profession took longer than his friends had
predicted. In 1741 he was insisting, while describing himself as 'a little
squire that may be thoroughly depended on', that he intended to leave off
his business as an apothecary in order to practise as a physician. Five years
later he was still an apothecary. By then he had evidently served his party
purpose well, for Lord Bathurst, a Tory peer and owner of Cirencester

---

[128] Buckinghamshire RO, land tax assessments.
[129] F. G. Stokes, ed., *The Blecheley Diary of the Rev. William Cole, 1765–67* (London, 1931),
p. 112.
[130] BL, Add. MS 35604, fo. 315: O. Meyrick to Hardwicke, 8 May 1756.
[131] BL, Add. MS 35679, fos. 41, 114, 116, 129, 244, 253, 285.
[132] BL, Add. MS 35602, fo. 293: Orford to Hardwicke, 25 July 1747; fo. 313: Leicester to Hardwicke,
5 Sept. 1747.

Park, was reduced to taking out his dedimus as a justice in order to overawe
him on the bench.[133]

It is not easy to reach a balanced judgement about the changing social
complexion of the magistracy under the first two Hanovarians. There is
some corroborative evidence to support the criticisms of the regime's
opponents. That there were justices in straitened circumstances is not in
doubt. One such was William Hunt of Wiltshire, who left a detailed record
of his doings and incidentally recorded the expenses which he had to bear.
He laboriously calculated that over nine years as a land tax commissioner
between 1738 and 1747 he was out of pocket to the tune of £8. 13s. 1d.,
and over four years as a justice £16. 2s. 3d. This may be impressive as
evidence of his integrity, but it is also suggestive of his financial anxieties
as a small landowner at a time of agricultural depression.[134] For a proprietor
of any consequence such sums would have been trivial. Another magistrate
of Hunt's day who kept a diary was Robert Lee of Berkshire. Lee was a
poor relation of the fifth Earl of Stirling, a Whig landowner in Berkshire
and Somerset. He acted as rent-collector and general factotum to his noble
relative. In the latter years of the Walpole ministry, he was a conscientious
attender at petty and quarter sessions and a vigorous dispenser of local
justice. There is no suggestion that he was a particularly scandalous abuser
of his office, but the diary makes it clear how far his family and public
obligations coincided. Stirling even asked him to become a magistrate in
Somerset, in order to facilitate the management of his estate; Lee's main
business there consisted of reducing his patron's poor rate.[135]

A case as clear as Lee's testifies to the ease with which the commission
of the peace could be used for the private purposes of Whig magnates. But
professional men were not necessarily corrupt self-servers and party hacks.
By virtue of their position in society and their commercial vulnerability
they might well find themselves compelled to accept an appointment which
had no great attractions for them, essentially for negative reasons. Irksome
though he found the business of the rural bench Stukeley had no doubt
that it was incumbent on him to engage in it. His decision to move from
London to Lincolnshire was taken with a view to establishing himself as a
physician. At Grantham he had the patronage of local noblemen and every
prospect of success. But prudence strongly suggested that he safeguard
himself by taking his place in the management of local affairs. 'Here I was

---

[133] BL, Add. MSS 35586, fos. 154, 225: Sir John Dutton to Hardwicke, 14 Mar. 1739, 1 Mar. 1740;
35600, fo. 297: T. Bush to Sir John Dutton, 10 Nov. 1741, fos. 301–2: Dutton to Hardwicke, 14 Nov.
1741; 35603, fo. 237: Bush to Ducie, 12 Dec. 1746.
[134] E. Critall, ed., *The Justicing Notebook of William Hunt 1744–1749* (Wilts. Rec. Soc. 37, 1981),
p. 25.
[135] Berkshire RO, D/EZ 30 F1: Lee Diaries, 1735–7, 1742; D/ED C51, 52–5: Lee correspondence
with Stirling; D/ED F441, 2: Stirling's memorandum book.

in all the public Commissions of peace, tax, Sewers, etc, and I knew the use of being arm'd with power when one lives in the country; where one must be sure to meet with abundance of brutal treatment.'[136] He shared this sense with many attorneys, land agents, and clergy, whose professional dealings made it difficult if not impossible to place themselves beyond the reach of local politics. To Smollett and Johnstone this was doubtless corruption. But to the men involved it was self-defence, part of a continuing need to demonstrate their influence and preserve their livelihood.

Not all JPs were Lees, or even Bushes, Hanmers, Hunts, or Stukeleys. Determining just how representative such men were is complicated by the varying attitudes of the justices themselves. Most magistrates after 1714 were so only in name, by their presence in the commission of the peace. Many of those who did act on their commission were at best casual in carrying out their duties. In Buckinghamshire, twenty years after the Hanoverian Accession, there were 116 magistrates. Of these 65 never presented themselves at quarter sessions. A further 37 attended very occasionally, or had ceased regular attendance some years previously, as a result either of infirmity or disillusionment. There remained 14 who were present at the sessions year in, year out, dispensing local justice, rough or otherwise, for the multiplicity of purposes within the power of ordinary magistrates. In most counties, for most of the Georgian period, there was such a group of committed, conscientious men, on whom the everyday business of parish, hundred, and county, as well as the administration of justice, depended.[137] It was this group which contemporaries generally had in mind when they referred to the magistracy, whether in critical or complimentary terms.

In Buckinghamshire in 1735 it was a decidedly mixed group. It was not composed entirely of Whig camp followers. Four of the fourteen were actually Tory squires, including one of the knights of the shire, Richard Lowndes, an indefatigable student of county affairs.[138] Four others were Whigs of some standing. Alexander Croke of Marsh Gibbon was the representative of an old royalist family which had turned Whig in the late seventeenth century. He would have made a respectable Squire Western but for his politics; according to his descendant, 'by his hounds and other

---

[136] 'The Family Memoirs of the Rev. William Stukeley', i. 105.

[137] These and the subsequent conclusions are based on the land tax assessments, the quarter sessions records, and the printed and MS pollbooks, all in Buckinghamshire RO, the diocesan records in Oxfordshire RO, Assize papers in PRO, Assi, and the manorial histories in the Victoria County History volumes for Buckinghamshire. Counties for which there are published studies reveal the same prominence of a small corps of active justices; see G. Welby, 'Rulers of the Countryside: The Justices of the Peace in Nottinghamshire, 1775–1800', *Trans. Thoroton Soc.* 78 (1974), 75–87; Moir, *Local Government in Gloucestershire 1775–1800*.

[138] Henry Crosse of Bledlow, Richard Saunders of North Marston, Bernard Turney of Cublington.

gaieties, [he] had at least not increased his property'.[139] Francis Lygoe of
North Marston was an old war-horse of a Whig country gentleman, who
had been expelled from the commission by the Tories in 1712, and, on his
readmission in 1714, proved a faithful servant of government. Francis
Tyrringham of Nether Winchendon, in the Whig heartland of the Vale of
Aylesbury, had been George II's first Sheriff of Buckinghamshire, as his
father had been George I's. Charles Lowndes was a cousin of Richard's,
though his politics were of a very different kind; he eventually became
Secretary to the Treasury.

It is among the remaining six that the Whig *arrivistes*, if such there were,
must be found. All six might be made to fit this description, though none
altogether convincingly. One was Job Hanmer of Simpson, father of Cole's
Hanmer; he depended on a fortunate marriage and his profession for a
living. Another was Charles Pilsworth, an adroit Whig lawyer, and son of
a Gloucestershire clergyman. Having settled at Oving, he made a marriage
with Francis Tyrringham's sister, which eventually brought him the considerable Tyrringham estate. He became an MP, aspired to a judgeship,
and much impressed the local justices by his knowledgeable chairmanship
of quarter sessions. John Revett owed his estate at Chequers in Elles-
borough, later bequeathed in perpetuity to the country comfort of British
Prime Ministers, to a fortunate marriage by his father, a professional
soldier. Samuel Wells was the second of his name to own the Rectory of
Chipping Wycombe; his father had been a land tax commissioner, he was
himself described as Gentleman rather than Esquire, and he doubtless
relied on his Whiggism, in a parliamentary borough, to carry him a notch
higher into the commission of the peace. There remain two genuine
newcomers, both in the Chiltern south, Thomas Parr of Datchet and
George Stehn of Woburn. Neither seems to have had any previous connection with the county and neither left a mark on it, though Parr reserved
himself a vault in Datchet church in 1741. Both were presumably men who
had purchased their way into Buckinghamshire society.

This was hardly the stuff to feed Tory paranoia. On the other hand it
does not suggest, either, that the county community was functioning in
the ideal manner envisaged by the traditionalists. There was a good deal
of alien blood on the active bench, whether introduced by marriage, by
time-serving, or by professional success. There was also a shortage of
propertied substance. Apart from Richard Lowndes, none ranked among
the top fifty landowners in the county. By no means all came within the
top hundred. One professed Tory objective under George II was to confine
the magistracy to propertied men of £200 or even £300 a year. Success in
this would have cut a considerable swathe through the Buckinghamshire

---

[139] Sir A. Croke, *The Genealogical History of the Croke Family* (2 vols., Oxford, 1823), i. 704.

bench. Ironically, two of Lowndes's Tory colleagues would have fallen victim to it. Richard Saunders of North Marston held an estate which had been in his family since the sixteenth century, but it was certainly worth less than £200 per annum. Henry Crosse owned land at Bledlow which his own father had obtained by marriage, and which was later to go by marriage to Samuel Whitbread the brewer; it is doubtful whether in Crosse's lifetime it produced more than £200. Among the Whigs, probably only Croke and Tyrringham would have qualified. The contrast with Queen Anne's reign, when the flower of the county's gentry had regularly appeared at quarter sessions, is marked. So is the contrast with the turn-out at assizes. In the late 1730s when a succession of Tories held the office of sheriff, the grand jurymen who presented themselves before the assize judges provided an impressive showing of baronets and great landowners.[140] Many of the Tories, and not a few of the Whigs who paraded on these occasions, were themselves magistrates, and could have addressed themselves to the duties of the ordinary justice, had they so desired. That they preferred not to do so was partly owing to the futility of partisan contests within the bench at a time of confirmed Whig supremacy, partly, no doubt, the result of the burdens and inconveniences attending active participation.

Complaints about the declining commitment of the rural ruling class under George III have to be set against the background of his predecessor's reign. Whether they were justified by the actual record of the magistracy in the late eighteenth century is another matter. In some areas there was a continuing tendency for the lesser men, those below the first rank of county families, to dominate local administration. But in others their superiors were also active. Though the gentry never returned to their duty in force, there is evidence that they were still capable of taking their responsibilities seriously. This involved the county benches in conscientious oversight of the poor law, frequently with a view to that paternalistic intervention against the rural middle class which was so much urged on them.[141] It also found them pioneering new policies, not least in penal and police matters.[142]

Evidently, the pressure generated by the public debate about the passing of old-style paternalism created a certain sense of urgency which in its turn helped promote a new spirit of vigour in social policy and local administration. It was a two-way process, with men who had gained their practical experience in local affairs not infrequently playing a leading part in national campaigns. Buckinghamshire produced one of the most influential of the philanthropical agitators fired by the plight of the rural poor in Thomas Bernard. Bernard's career embraced an extraordinary

[140] PRO, Assi 35: 176.12, 177.14, 179.15.
[141] P. Dunkley, 'Paternalism, The Magistracy and Poor Relief in England, 1795–1834', *International Rev. Soc. Hist.* 24 (1979), 371–97.
[142] Moir, *Local Government in Gloucestershire 1775–1800*, ch. 3.

variety of good causes. He was Treasurer of the Foundling Hospital, a member of the Society for Bettering the Condition of the Poor, promoter of Count Rumford's schemes for improving lower-class household management, and founder of the Royal Institution. He was also a tireless writer, whose concerns ranged from encouraging infant education to increasing the consumption of fish and reducing the salt duty. In short he was typical of the new breed of concerned, evangelical reformers who flourished in the last decades of the century. Yet his formative experience was in the Vale of Aylesbury, where his father Sir Francis Bernard, a former Governor of Massachusetts, had an estate and highly placed friends. As a young man Thomas was a firm believer in the need to restore a sense of responsibility and social commitment to the county's rulers. In 1775 he wrote to a like-minded country gentleman, Sir William Lee, 'I am so far an errant Leveller in my Principles, that I think the first Attention of every State should be paid to the multitude; to give a Spring to their Industry, and Comfort to their domestic life; ... the evil might in a great measure be remedied, if Gentlemen would reside more on their Estates, pay more attention to the consideration of the poor, instead of turning their Eyes to the Capital in search of objects of ambition or pleasure'.[143] Ironically Bernard was to spend his life in the capital, but his concerns sprang naturally from the new interests of county families in the 1770s.

In Parliament the new spirit was expressed in the regularity with which problems of social regulation were discussed. Admittedly it did not always produce a dramatic legislative return. But it was precisely the nature of policy-making in the late eighteenth century that it depended essentially on the community. Most of the social legislation of the 1770s and 1780s was either difficult to enforce, or enforceable only at the desire of local authorities. Pownall's new Corn Law of 1773, which somewhat reduced the market preference given to home-produced cereals, with a view to easing recurrent food shortages, Popham's Acts of 1774, designed to improve prison management at a time when John Howard had directed attention to its deficiencies, Gilbert's Act of 1782, offering the possibility of parochial union to promote more efficient poor law administration, and the Friendly Societies Act of 1793, promoting the formation of parochial insurance clubs under suitable supervision, could not be claimed as spectacular achievements when set in the context of contemporary social criticism. Debates which ranged far and wide over the entire field of poor relief, criminal law jurisdiction, employer–employee relations, and basic economic regulation created expectations which were left largely unsatisfied by concrete action at the centre. But they had a more stimulating effect locally. County rates soared in the late eighteenth century, and the most celebrated,

---

[143] Buckinghamshire RO, Hartwell MSS, Bernard to Lee, 2 July 1775.

and one of the most applauded 'improvements' of the day, the prison reconstruction programme, was very much the work of the county benches, led by the celebrated examples of Gloucestershire and Sussex.[144] The innovative nature of county government in the 1780s and 1790s, a development which increasingly led both Parliament and government to encourage local initiatives, would scarcely have been possible in the bitter and divisive atmosphere of George II's reign. Where party had reigned supreme, the change was particularly striking. In North Wales, novel policies, including the building of gaols and systematic provision for the poor, were associated with the activities of a new breed of magistrates appointed when the barriers against Tory advancement were thrown down during the Seven Years War. Their opponents naturally blamed these expensive innovations on the folly of relaxing the rigour of Whig rule.[145]

The county magistracies displayed increasing confidence in the last decades of the century, nourished partly by the sense that they represented a certain consensus of propertied opinion in the face of growing social problems, partly by the leadership which at least some elements among the county gentry displayed. Analysis of the composition of the bench in Buckinghamshire in 1780, twenty years after the accession of George III, yields decidedly different results from the same exercise conducted for 1735. By 1780 the total size of the commission of the peace had increased somewhat, to about 130. Of these, 87 never attended quarter sessions, and 14 appeared only irregularly. In 1735 the group prepared to play an occasional part had been larger. On the other hand the men who appeared regularly were more numerous in 1780, 26 compared with 14 in 1735. But 12 of these were clergy; the lay element was numerically what it had been forty-five years before. However, among these laymen, there was a much stronger representation of the county's senior figures. Buckinghamshire MPs seem hardly to have troubled with county government in the 1730s; they took quite a different view in the late 1770s and early 1780s. Of the 14 laymen who appeared frequently at quarter sessions in this period, no less than 9 were either serving in the Commons or had done so. Some of them bore well-known county names: Aubrey, Drake, Grenville, Lowndes, Waller. They also included Lord Le Despenser, current representative of the Dashwoods of West Wycombe, and a conscientious Lord-Lieutenant.[146] In point of property they could have bought out their predecessors of

[144] S. J. and B. Webb, *English Local Government from the Revolution to the Municipal Corporations Act* (9 vols., London, 1906–29), vol. v: *English Prisons under Local Government* (1922), pp. 54–62; J. R. S. Whiting, *Prison Reform in Gloucestershire, 1776–1820: A Study of the Work of Sir George Onesiphorus Paul* (London, 1975).

[145] G. N. Evans, *Religion and Politics in Mid-Eighteenth Century Anglesea* (Cardiff, 1953), pp. 232–5.

[146] John Aubrey, Joseph Bullock, William Drake, George Grenville, Thomas Grenville, Walden Hanmer, Charles Lowndes, Edmund Waller, Lord Le Despenser.

1735 many times over. Their colleagues without parliamentary experience comprised two newcomers, one who had married into the county, another who had bought his way into it, and two representatives of substantial families.[147] Only one was an authentic hanger-on; Henry Tompkins had little property and owed his position to his service in the militia and the patronage of the Temples. Broadly speaking, the prominent element in county government in the 1730s had consisted of moneyed newcomers and older families of the second or third rank; in the 1780s it boasted a considerable sprinkling of the county élite. A similar comparison between the 1730s and 1780s in Dorset reveals a similar pattern; an increase in numbers of reliable attenders, due primarily to the appearance of a body of clergy, and a distinct assertion of leadership by prominent county families.[148]

The 1770s and 1780s produced some stirring times in county politics. The interest of the county community in the relationship between local and national affairs was stimulated by the embodiment of the militia, renewed election contests, and the economical and parliamentary reform agitation. But it would be unwise to separate these considerations from a more general readiness on the part of propertied society to reintegrate itself in county life. Fashionable ladies even felt the tendency had gone too far. In 1778 Thomas Hampden was thought 'odder than ever as he talk'd of nothing but The Militia, Farming and Justice business all day long'.[149] But such oddity should not be exaggerated. The bench was only the uppermost layer of local government. The complaints of those who believed that the gentry as a class had deserted their implied duties as landlords, squires, and friends of the poor could not be met simply by pointing to the presence at sessions time of Grenvilles, Dashwoods, and Wallers in Aylesbury, and Brownes, Draxes, and Sturts at Dorchester. On the other hand, that presence betokens a change of attitude on the part of leading families, and at least suggests a desire to be seen to be playing a part in the formal business of the county. This tendency seems to have developed simultaneously in counties other than Buckinghamshire and Dorset. Parliamentary families became notably more attentive to their judicial duties. In Berkshire in 1735 one MP was present at quarter sessions; in 1780 there were four. Between 1736 and 1745, only one MP attended quarter sessions for the first time; between 1745 and 1756, two; between 1776 and 1785, four.[150] In

---

[147] T. H. Gott, John Fremantle, Sir John Russell, Matthew Knapp.

[148] Dorset RO, quarter session order books; the periods compared are 1730–9 and 1777–86. The attendance of MPs was poor in both periods, doubtless because the county was more remote from London than Buckinghamshire was.

[149] M. Elwin, ed., *The Noels and the Milbankes: Their Letters for Twenty-Five Years 1767–1792* (London, 1967), p. 103.

[150] Berkshire RO, quarter sessions minutes.

Gloucestershire the contrast is less marked, but this was because the decline in the social quality of the local magistracy was also less marked than in Buckinghamshire. Gloucestershire was notably more reluctant than its neighbours Somerset and Wiltshire to admit clothiers to the bench under George II, though its clothiers were thought both more numerous and more opulent than their rivals elsewhere. It also hung on to its MPs as magistrates longer than Buckinghamshire and Berkshire. There was still a smattering of them in the 1730s; they had vanished by the 1750s, but reappeared under George III.[151]

Corroborative evidence of a reawakening of upper-class interest in county government, at least for the purposes of electoral management and political theatre, is provided by the history of the shrievalty. The unpopularity of the office in the seventeenth century had stimulated evasion by the upper gentry and progressively reduced the social status of those occupying it.[152] Under the early Hanoverians it sank further. It was a peculiarly thankless task at the best of times, involving much expense and a cumbersome procedure of accounting before the Exchequer, quite apart from the official duties involved in serving and returning legal writs. The annual ritual of pricking for sheriffs was a farce which did not conceal the fact that the real appointment lay with government on the advice of its local supporters. Perhaps no office produced more anguished pleas for exemption from those threatened with appointment, or more bitter protests from those selected. Hardwicke, as Lord Chancellor, received and preserved numerous letters on the subject.[153] In some places the gentry contributed to insurance schemes designed to mitigate the financial consequences of an unexpected spell as sheriff.[154] In county business they constituted a club of considerable importance in its own right.[155]

Whig governments used the shrievalty in a manner which deprived it of what remaining prestige it had. As returning officer at county elections, the sheriff enjoyed considerable influence, at least in close contests. In election years the government ensured that only reliable Whigs, usually of low rank and unable to defy their fate, were nominated. In other years, especially in mid-Parliament, Tories were generally appointed. Lord Powys put the point candidly to Lord Hardwicke, when recommending Tories as sheriff of Shropshire in 1751, four years after one general election, and three before another, 'I wou'd wish to ease the Whigs of bearing the

---

[151] J. de L. Mann, *The Cloth Industry in the West of England from 1640 to 1880* (Oxford, 1971), pp. 117–18; Gloucestershire RO, quarter sessions minutes.

[152] J. A. Sharpe, *Crime in Seventeenth-Century England: A County Study* (Cambridge, 1983), p. 33.

[153] BL, Add. MSS 35600–4.

[154] G. Eland, ed., *Purefoy Letters 1735–1753* (2 vols., London, 1931), ii. 363 ff; L. G. Mitchell, ed., *The Purefoy Letters 1735–1753* (London, 1973), pp. 53–6.

[155] Huntington Library, Stowe MSS, 366: T. Price to G. Grenville, 7 Feb. 1748.

Trouble and Expence of that Office, at this Juncture.'[156] Closer proximity
to a general election made for some testing calculations. Lord Ducie tried
to get a good Whig off for Gloucestershire in December 1746, on the
grounds that he 'will be content to serve, in order to make things easy; but
we wish to keep him for a more proper Occasion'. Ducie was a reliable
Whig Lord-Lieutenant, but seems to have been notably reluctant to avoid
using the word he meant: 'election'. Instead he speculated what would
ensue 'if anything extraordinary were to happen during his year'.[157] As was
later made clear, 1747 was to witness a snap general election, called a full
year prematurely in order to give Pelham's ministry an electoral advantage.
But there were some secrets known to Lord Chancellors which were not
even to be entrusted to loyal Lords-Lieutenant.

This blatantly partisan use of the office aroused intense anger and
contributed to the catastrophic fall in the standing of the sheriff. After
1760 the decline was arrested, and even reversed, though political manipulation did not cease overnight. Some old Tories tried to take their revenge
in the early years of the new regime. Lord Denbigh protested to Lord
Chancellor Northington in 1767 against the appointment of Thomas Grace
of Showell for Leicestershire: 'a very good sort of half Gentleman Grazier,
but by no means fit to be Sheriff, particularly in this Election year'.[158] He
discovered that a fellow court peer, Lord Gower, had already acted to
prevent Grace's elevation. Another partisan of the court, Sir James
Lowther, engaged in scandalous manoeuvres in his campaign to achieve
electoral mastery of the north-west. The shameless partisanship which his
supporter the Sheriff of Cumberland displayed in the general election of
1768 resulted in his humiliation before a thoroughly irritated House of
Commons.[159] His fate was itself a sign that things were changing. In a
Whig sheriff his antics would not in the least have shocked one of George
II's Parliaments, let alone provoked censure. Indeed the only case of
consequence in which one had been prosecuted occurred in 1742 when the
fall of Sir Robert Walpole permitted his enemies to take action against
the shrieval opponent of Sir Watkin Williams Wynn in Denbighshire.[160]
Sheriffs under George III were increasingly expected to umpire according
to the rules, and even grew accustomed to boast of their independence. It
was said of the Sheriff of Essex in the contested election of 1763 that
'no Sheriff ever acted on such an occasion with greater Candour and
Impartiality'.[161]

[156] BL, Add. MS 35603, fo. 318: 28 Oct. 1751.
[157] BL, Add. MS 35602, fo. 240: 17 Dec. 1746, fo. 249: 31 Dec. 1746.
[158] Warwickshire RO, Denbigh MSS, Letter Book, 99: 13 Dec. 1767.
[159] J. Wright, ed., *Debates of the House of Commons* (2 vols., London, 1840), i. 339–45, 356–60,
401–4.
[160] R. Sedgwick, *History of Parliament: House of Commons, 1715–54* (2 vols., London, 1970), i. 375.
[161] *Suffolk Notes from the Year 1729* (Ipswich, 1883–4), p. 55.

The Crown's loss of interest in the politics of its sheriffs eventually became something of a handicap in more than an electoral sense. In the summoning of county meetings, the sheriff had an important role to play. When the reformers demanded such assemblies to consider a reform programme in 1780, the political views of the sheriffs took on an unexpected significance. The resulting crop of petitions hostile to the ministry was blamed on sheriffs friendly to the opposition.[162] In Cambridgeshire the second Earl of Hardwicke, as Lord-Lieutenant and opponent of the 'Associators', urged 'Government this Year to look after their Sheriffs'.[163] His father would have recognized this language, but it had long ceased to be relevant to party politics.

With impartiality came respect. The shrievalty began to seem once again a dignified, even desirable office. In Buckinghamshire it continued to be used as an initiation rite for new landowners, but one which was offered only to those who were genuinely men of wealth and property. Alongside them the old gentry of the county took their full turn. What had been a punishment for Tories and an unthinkable burden for Whigs of rank became an uncontroversial and acceptable part of county life once again. The readiness to serve of men who could easily have escaped the obligation, if they had chosen, was a feature of the 1770s and 1780s. No Lee of Hartwell or Lovett of Soulbury would have deigned to serve while their Whig friends dominated government in the early Hanoverian period. But Sir William Lee did so in 1772, as did Sir Jonathan Lovett in 1782.[164] The reappearance of titled names in the shrieval rolls was notable in many places. In Suffolk, three baronets served between 1785 and 1791, as many as had served in the previous forty-five years.[165] In Norfolk four served in seven years between 1778 and 1784, compared with three in the preceding eighty-five.[166] Cambridgeshire and Huntingdonshire were notoriously short of gentlemen, let alone titles; yet they did muster three shrieval baronets in the first twenty-five years of George III's reign, compared with none in the previous reigns, and two under Anne and George I.[167] Across the

---

[162] *The Sense of the People: A Letter to Edmund Burke, Esq.* (London, 1780), p. 10.

[163] BL, Add. MS 35379, fo. 7: Hardwicke to P. Yorke, 11 Jan. 1780.

[164] E. Viney, *The Sheriffs of Buckinghamshire* (Aylesbury, 1965), p. 53.

[165] A. Suckling, *The History and Antiquities of the County of Suffolk* (2 vols., London, 1846), pp. xlv–xlvii; Sir Thomas Gooch (1785), Sir Thomas Charles Bunbury (1788), Sir William Rowley (1791); cf. Sir John Barker (1743), Sir John Rous (1759), Sir John Blois (1764).

[166] *Vicecomites Norfolciae* (Stow Bardolph, 1843): Sir Henry Peyton (1778), Sir Thomas Beauchamp Proctor (1780), Sir Martin Browne Ffolkes (1783), Sir Thomas Durrant (1784); cf. Sir Horatio Pettus (1745), Sir Edward Astley (1763), Sir Hanson Berney (1761).

[167] *High Sheriffs for the Counties of Cambridge and Huntingdon, 1509–1905*: Sir Philip Vavasor (1760), Sir Charles Cope (1773), Sir John Chrisloe Turner (1785); cf. Sir John Conyers (1715), Sir Thomas Hatton (1725).

country as a whole this change seems to have occurred about 1750.[168] Revolution monarchs were much more cautious about creating baronets than their predecessors.[169] Accordingly a baronetcy became a more highly esteemed honour. The readiness of those who enjoyed it to serve as sheriffs was accordingly all the more striking. Under George III a baronet who refused the office would have been thought unworthy; his father might have considered it an indignity even to have been offered it. The shrievalty came to be considered a genuine honour by those on the margin of attaining it. Joseph Cradock, a propertied poetaster, was plainly delighted to be able to remark in his memoirs that he had been compelled to accept it in 1778 'having no shelter in a profession'. This was a way of revealing that for all his metropolitan sophistication he was a genuine Leicestershire landowner. He manifestly revelled in his experience, so much that he deputized for his cousin Sir Edmund Cradock Hartopp in 1781 when the latter went to Devon for the summer.[170]

PRIEST AND JUSTICE

There was a decidedly theatrical quality about the sheriff's office in late eighteenth-century England, and more than a hint of tinsel about the interest of parliamentary families in the doings of the bench. Both went with the elaborate ritual of summer visits, and county subscription lists, whether for balls, hospitals, or topographical poems, which seemed to some contemporaries to provide the thinnest of coverings for the widespread abandonment of rural life by people of great property. So far as most magistrates were concerned, there was none the less a vast amount of ordinary, everyday work to be done. The eighteenth century witnessed a marked expansion of 'justice business', as Parliament increasingly entrusted powers of summary jurisdiction and administrative supervision to the county magistracy. This expansion contrasted with the experience of the seventeenth century and was much noticed by contemporaries.[171] It had obvious political complications. The Jacobite historian Thomas Carte commented bitterly on the electoral influence which JPs derived from their

---

[168] The numbers of baronets appointed, by quinquennium, were as follows; they are calculated from the lists of sheriffs published annually, in Dec. or Jan., in the *London Gazette*. All English and Welsh counties were treated in the same way, except that Cambridgeshire and Huntingdonshire were treated as one unit for this purpose, the Sheriff of Cornwall was appointed by the Prince of Wales as Duke of Cornwall, not the Crown, and Middlesex came under the shrieval authority of the elected Sheriffs of London. 1735–9: 6; 1740–4: 11; 1745–9: 11; 1750–4: 22; 1755–9: 11; 1760–4: 17; 1765–9: 14; 1770–4: 20; 1775–9: 10; 1780–4: 20; 1785–9: 19; 1790–4: 12.

[169] Creations were as follows, annual average in brackets: Charles II, 429 (11.9); James II, 19 (6.3); William III, 36 (2.8); Anne, 28 (2.3); George I, 41 (3.2); George II, 27 (0.8).

[170] *Literary and Miscellaneous Memoirs*, i. 71, 89.

[171] Sharpe, *Crime in Seventeenth-Century England*, p. 28.

growing control of poor law administration.[172] Even a Whig House of
Lords pointed in 1757 to the demands 'laid in almost every Session of
Parliament, by new Acts, upon them'.[173] At the very least this tendency
made the office of magistrate more burdensome. It also made failure to
execute it more noticeable.

Work of this kind needed workhorses. In the early part of George II's
reign they were found among hackneyed Whigs bent on making a profit
from their office, whether in financial or political terms. Later they were
discovered elsewhere. The twenty-six Buckinghamshire magistrates who
attended regularly at quarter sessions in the late 1770s included twelve
clergy. This represented a revolution in provincial life. In 1735 there were
only four clergy on the Buckinghamshire bench, two of them successive
Provosts of Eton, the others very senior churchmen. None attended quarter
sessions regularly. Like some other counties Buckinghamshire went some
years before further clerical magistrates were appointed. In 1755, a few
parochial clergy appeared, and six years later a dozen more.[174] The experience was common. Clergy were introduced in numbers into most counties
at some point in the latter part of George II's reign. In 1761 there were
nearly a thousand of them, compared with barely fifty at the beginning of
the century.[175] Thereafter their place in the commission of the peace was
consolidated, and by the 1780s, the clerical justice, to be a prominent figure
in rural England in the nineteenth century, was firmly established.

The appointment of clerical justices, in due course a commonplace of
rural government, was not completely new. It had been briefly essayed in
the distant past, before the Civil Wars of the 1640s, and it commenced
again after the Revolution of 1689. As the Church Party, the Tories saw
an obvious advantage in enlisting the local services of clerical supporters.
Under the House of Hanover, the Whigs retaliated. In Gloucestershire, in
1714, there were four magistrates in holy orders; by 1716 one had died,
and the three others had been ignominiously expelled. In their place were
appointed six Whig clergy.[176] A similar experiment took place in Glamorgan
between 1710 and 1717.[177] It was not adopted everywhere. In Buckinghamshire, for instance, it had been resisted at this stage. In 1717 a
clerical friend of Lord Fermanagh, Tory MP for Amersham and a faithful
churchman, told him 'You won't suffer a Parson to come into the Commission of Peace, much more into the House of Commons.'[178]

---

[172] *A Full Answer to the Letter from a By-Stander* (London, 1742), p. 193.

[173] *Commons Journals*, xxvii. 919.

[174] PRO, C 234. 3.

[175] Landau, *The Justices of the Peace, 1679–1760*, p. 143.

[176] PRO, C 234. 13.

[177] Jenkins, *The Making of a Ruling Class*, p. 89.

[178] M. M. Verney, *Verney Letters of the Eighteenth Century from the MSS at Claydon House* (2 vols., London, 1930), i. 395.

More interesting than the local variations is the fact that in the first
decades of Whig rule the initiative of the last Stuart reign was not systematically followed up. Whig anti-clericalism may have been partly
responsible. An alternative possibility is that the available pool of Whig-
gishly inclined parochial clergy was simply not big enough. After 1714 the
plums of ecclesiastical patronage were reserved for Whigs: those who
possessed property or talent were guaranteed advancement. Where there
were inferior Whig clergy worthy of nomination to the bench without
scandal or controversy, they were often appointed; but in point of numbers
they made little impact until the 1740s and 1750s. By then conditions had
changed. The stormy relationship between Whig churchmen and Whig
politicians which had prevailed in the 1730s was a thing of the past.
Moreover, the very permanence of the Whig regime had encouraged the
development of an all too healthy body of Whig clergy, positively pleading
for every crumb of preferment available.

It is not difficult to grasp who gained by the appointment of clerical
justices. Individual clergy plainly did so, however debatable the benefits
to their order. As one Kentish clergyman ingenuously put it in 1749, 'it
might be a considerable Convenience to my Affairs to have my Name
inserted in the Commission'.[179] The impotence of Church courts to defend
the propertied rights of the clergy was notorious in the mid-eighteenth
century, and was underlined by the attempts of Gibson and his supporters
to defend them. In tithe disputes incumbents could only be strengthened
by direct access to the brotherhood of the bench, regardless of whether
such cases were formally brought to its judicial determination. Quakers
had fought hard to secure and extend summary jurisdiction by magistrates
in tithe litigation. The Church staunchly defended the rights of its courts.
But if its ministers could officiate as justices the involvement of petty
sessions took on a different complexion. Nor was the pastoral and political
influence of the clergy likely to be lessened by an awareness, on the part
of its flock, of the judicial power of clerical magistrates. It transformed the
position of a particularly turbulent priest, John Walter of Bingham in
Nottinghamshire. From his installation as Rector in 1764 he was perpetually
at odds with his parishioners and found himself involved in a punishing
series of lawsuits. As incumbent of the most lucrative living in the county,
he was an obvious candidate for inclusion in the first batch of Nottinghamshire clergy to join the bench, in 1793, and it was this that decisively
strengthened his hand against his persecutors.[180]

This is not to say that the clergy always had sinister motives for seeking

[179] BL, Add. MS 35603, fo. 137: J. Tunstall to Hardwicke, 11 Feb. 1749.
[180] A. Henstock, 'A Parish Divided: Bingham and the Rev. John Walter, 1764–1810', Trans. Thoroton
Soc. 85 (1981), 90–101.

office. Clerical diaries like that of Edward Jackson, Vicar of Colton in Lancashire, reveal the extent to which a country incumbent's social life might centre on the recreational opportunities offered by regular meetings for the purposes of local administration.[181] The attractions of the magistracy helped keep the parish clergy where they belonged, in their parishes. Non residence did not, after all, always, or even usually go with idleness. An interesting case in this respect is that of a Nottinghamshire clergyman of the generation which preceded John Walter. Charles Allen became Rector of Sutton Bonington in 1753, but served his cure for only three years. Thereafter he put in a curate and took himself off to Leicester where he happily served as a curate to others. Allen was a convivial and not uncultured man who took his place in the town's élite, and involved himself in hunting, card assemblies, and book clubs. At that time Nottinghamshire was firmly closed to clerical justices, and social acceptance in neighbouring Leicester must have seemed particularly appealing. Thirty years later, when a rectorship would automatically have entailed a place on the bench for a resident priest, he might have made a different choice.[182]

The growing tendency for propertied families to employ their Church patronage as a means of supporting younger sons made it tempting to exploit the potential influence of the magistracy. But perhaps still more blatantly cynical was the conduct of the noblemen who often nominated clerical justices. Magnates had an obvious interest in acquiring reliable friends on the county bench. Even party strife took second place to this priority. When the Duke of Beaufort's gamekeeper travelled fifteen miles to find a magistrate who would sustain his master's game rights in 1741, Hardwicke admitted that the practice of seeking out sympathetic justices was 'not a thing to be commended', but declined to provide a remedy.[183] Considering that Beaufort was a prominent Jacobite and an implacable opponent of Whiggism in a county where Hardwicke himself had property and political friends, the Lord Chancellor's judicial impartiality was impressive. The Church was something of a haven for aristocratic power. Certainly, the clergyman as the tool of oligarchy was one of the more conventional images of the age. *The Modern Justice, in Imitation of the Man of Taste* announced 'I'm priest and Justice in our upright Land', and went on to portray a clergyman who held three livings and owed his place in the commission to his lordly patron; constant attention to his commands ensured that he could rule the district in company with his master's steward, earned him valuable fees, a rich variety of illicit perks, and not a

[181] T. E. Casson, 'The Diary of Edward Jackson, Vicar of Colton, for the Year 1775', *Trans. Cumbs. and Westmor. Ant. and Arch. Soc.*, NS 40 (1940), 1–45.

[182] W. Buckland, 'Some Account of the Rev. Charles Allen', *Trans. Thoroton Soc.*, 29 (1925), 170–8.

[183] 2 Atkyns 192: *Roy* v. *The Duke of Beaufort* (1741).

few 'genteel presents'.[184] In the immensely popular novel *Hermsprong*, the vicious Lord Grondale rightly assumed that he could rely on the local clergyman, the Rev. Dr Blick, to misuse his judicial powers against an unwelcome suitor of his daughter. The unfortunate Hermsprong was arrested and tried on a trumped-up charge as a French spy and a revolutionary agitator.[185] Satirical exaggeration of this kind seems pardonable. A letter of Lord Ailesbury to Hardwicke in 1743 provides all too credible confirmation of its thrust. Ailesbury was anxious to make two amendments to a list of new justices which he had recently submitted. One involved omitting a cleric who had blotted his copy-book by protecting a younger brother guilty of clandestine marriage to an heiress. Aristocratic fathers were even more determined to protect their daughters from an imprudent marriage than to obtain complaisant local magistrates. The second proposed the addition of another clergyman, 'as a particular convenience to myself, he being situated in the middle of my Estates, where we are very thin of Justices, and besides the trouble of it, it would be improper in me, who does act sometimes, to be trying my own causes, and your Lordship may depend upon his being one much valued and regarded by all sorts of people and is one of a good extraction'.[186] Ailesbury's idea of propriety evidently had more to do with public appearances than principle. His nominee was duly appointed.

The appointment of clergymen as magistrates was not to everyone's liking. The growing reluctance of lay justices to act sometimes reflected their distaste for working with clerical colleagues. According to the third Duke of Bolton, Lord-Lieutenant of Hampshire in 1752, this was a critical question. 'I have promised the Gentlemen of the County not to recommend any of the Clergy, for they being resolved not to attend whilst any Parsons are in the Commission, is the reason that they are so slack in doing their Duty, and therefore I am determined to recommend none of the Clergy, but those who are dignified.'[187] This feeling seems to have been widely entertained. In Cambridgeshire in 1754, one magistrate thought that 'Clergymen never appear to so much advantage in a Lay dress or office, as in their Canonicals, and discharging the Duties of their Spiritual Function; and I think it a pity they should be call'd off, without absolute necessity, from the business of their profession, till they are got above it.'[188] In Norfolk, Lord Buckinghamshire fobbed off clerical applicants by assuring

---

[184] (London, 1755).

[185] Robert Bage, *Hermsprong; Or, Man As He Is Not* (3 vols., London, 1796), iii. 155ff. Blick shared his name with a controversial clergyman in Bage's home town of Birmingham, Francis Blick; see his *Sermon on John vii. 17 Delivered in the Parish Church of Sutton Coldfield: January 30, 1791* (Birmingham, 1791).

[186] BL, Add. MS 35601, fo. 201: 3 June 1743.

[187] BL, Add. MS 35604, fo. 40: Bolton to Hardwicke, 1 Oct. 1752.

[188] BL, Add. MS 35679, fo. 129: E. Leeds to Hardwicke, 23 July 1754.

them that if any others of their cloth were admitted, apart from senior, 'dignified' clergy, their own names would be added.[189] The easiest answer to such arguments was that the clergy were approached only when laymen had conspicuously failed in their duty. Ferdinand Warner urged Hardwicke to appoint his own brother, incumbent of a Berkshire parish, while admitting that he personally disapproved of clerical magistrates. In this case, he observed, the parish was anxious to secure its priest's services, and gentlemen in the commission were very few.[190]

Proof positive of any of these contentions is difficult to obtain. The experience of the three neighbouring counties of Oxfordshire, Buckinghamshire, and Berkshire was markedly different, but not in ways which make it easier to resolve the problem. Superficially, the case of Oxfordshire suggests that clerical magistrates were responsible for driving their lay colleagues from the bench. The clerical presence was marked from the 1740s, and by the 1770s and 1780s was dominant; a sessions at which lay magistrates were in the majority was almost unknown in the late eighteenth century. On the other hand many of the clergy concerned were senior members of the university. It would be but a slight exaggeration to say of Oxfordshire at times in this period that its governing class consisted largely of Heads of House. In the Qualification Act of 1732 the House of Lords had inserted a clause exempting Oxford and Cambridge heads in Oxfordshire, Berkshire, and Cambridgeshire from the requirement that JPs be owners of real estates.[191] Half the justices attending quarter sessions in 1751 were Doctors of Divinity.[192] Dignified clergy of this kind were not objected to anywhere; the ordinary country gentleman may well have been overawed by them, but he was in no position to accuse them of social inferiority.

Berkshire should have been an example of what the gentry could do when left to their own devices and their snobbish preferences. Very few clergy were introduced in the latter part of George II's reign or the early part of his successor's. Those appointed were either genuinely dignified clergy, like William Dodwell, a Canon of Salisbury, or members of prominent county families, like Warner's brother and John Craven, a relative of Lord Craven.[193] But the conscientiousness of the laity was not very impressive. At no quarter sessions between 1770 and 1780 were more than ten magistrates present. In this respect the reign of George III was not superior to the bad old party days of George II. By 1782 the struggle to keep the clergy out had to be abandoned. In that year, nineteen were appointed to the bench. They duly turned out in force. Paradoxically, laymen seem to

---

[189] A. Hartshorne, ed., *Memoirs of a Royal Chaplain, 1729–1763* (London, 1905), p. 177.

[190] BL, Add. MS 35604, fos. 313–14: 4 May 1756.

[191] *Commons Journals*, xxi. 5.

[192] Oxfordshire RO, quarter sessions minutes.

[193] PRO, C 234. 2.

have been stimulated to attend in greater numbers too in the late 1780s.[194]
Buckinghamshire's experience lay between that of its two neighbours. The
clergy were a regular and increasing presence from the 1750s. Laymen who
carried out the duties of the magistracy under George III were somewhat
higher in social status than their predecessors of the 1750s, but not more
numerous.[195]

What is incontestable is that the pressures to elevate clergy to the bench
were so strong as to be almost irresistible. For all the Duke of Bolton's
obstinacy, Hampshire capitulated quickly under his successor, the Duke
of Chandos. In 1761 there were 23 clergy out of a total of 258 JPs; in 1764
a further 104 names were added, 27 of them belonging to clergy; in 1769
an additional 91 included 18 clergy.[196] Most counties were in much the
same position, and the greater propensity of the clergy to act as magistrates
made their presence still more marked. In Kesteven under George II one
in four of newly appointed justices acting were clergymen; under George
III one in two.[197] By 1832 there were six counties in which the clergy
constituted more than 40 per cent of the qualified commission of the peace,
and one, Lincolnshire, in which they were in a clear majority.[198] Only two
counties proved immune to this remarkable contagion beyond the first half
of George III's reign, Nottinghamshire, which surrendered in 1793, and
Sussex, which was still untouched in 1832. It can hardly be coincidence
that these were bastions of early Hanoverian Whiggism, with a high
incidence of Whig magnates (dukes were notably thick on the ground in
Nottinghamshire and Sussex). One of them, the famous Duke of Newcastle,
was for many years Lord-Lieutenant of both. Presumably a combination
of anti-clericalism and patronage made it possible both to shun the clergy,
and secure the fidelity of the gentry. Having survived the difficult years of
the mid-eighteenth century, both counties were able to proceed thereafter
without resorting to the Church.

The simplest explanation of the clerical appearance at the helm of local
government is perhaps the most appealing. Families with an investment in
the Church and propertied men with clerical clients at their command had
a vital interest in admitting the clergy to places on the bench. Once
conceded to some this claim could not but be conceded to others. The
second Duke of Richmond, resisting the introduction of the clergy in
Sussex in 1744, remarked that appointing one would provoke the jealous
displeasure of a hundred others, an argument for which he claimed the

[194] Berkshire RO, quarter sessions minutes.
[195] See below, p. 418.
[196] PRO, C 234. 14.
[197] Lincolnshire Archives Office, Fane MSS, 6/11/3/7.
[198] Bedfordshire, Cambridgeshire, Cornwall, Lincolnshire, Northamptonshire, Westmorland;
PP. 1831–2, xxxv. 231–72.

support of the Archdeacon and Dean of Chichester.[199] In Norfolk Lord
Buckinghamshire's instinct was sound. It was a question of all or none.
Norfolk held out for longer than most. One or two clergy were infiltrated
in the 1780s, but only at the very end of the century was there a substantial
incursion. It quickly turned into a mass invasion.[200] There seems to have
been only one exception to this rule. Uniquely, Derbyshire succeeded in
reversing the process. Six per cent of its commission was clerical in 1761,
but thereafter it reverted to lay control. In 1832 it had no qualified clerical
magistrates. It is worth noting that Derbyshire, like Nottinghamshire,
Sussex, and Norfolk, had a long history of subjection to the rule of
Whig peers under George I and George II, and a continuing tradition of
influential Whig opposition under George III.[201]

The clerical magistrate inevitably had an effect on public perceptions of
the bench. One important consideration was that the most respected and
wealthy clergy were not necessarily those most conscientious in attending
to their duties. The obvious candidates for elevation were, of course,
precisely those with these qualifications. It was recognized that owners of
temporal estates who happened to have been ordained had an incontestable
claim to join their brothers and cousins in the commission of the peace.
Accidents of descent not infrequently brought landed estates into the hands
of younger sons who had been meant for a career in the Church. Even in
Sussex the well endowed clerical baronet, Sir Thomas Broughton, was
granted the unique distinction for a clergyman of nomination to the
bench.[202] Elsewhere the category of the peculiarly eligible could readily be
extended. Men of good family, men who owned their own advowsons, men
who occupied particularly profitable livings, men of independent income,
all seemed equipped for a full share in county government. Unfortunately,
such men were subject to the same competing diversions and distractions
as other suitably qualified governors. One of the standard justifications for
the inequality of clerical incomes was the social utility of gradations which
permitted each class of laymen to be served by clergy with whom it was
comfortable. But the consequence was that upper-class clergy had much
the same inclinations and disinclinations as upper-class laymen. Even clergy
of relatively lowly status might doubt the advantages of judicial office.
Joseph Greene, Rector of Welford in Warwickshire and a protégé of the
Duke of Dorset, 'declin'd that honourable distinction, as some reckon it,

[199] T. J. McCann, ed., *The Correspondence of the Dukes of Richmond and Newcastle, 1724–1750*
(Sussex Rec. Soc. 73, 1984), p. 144.

[200] PRO, C 234. 26.

[201] There has been some confusion on this point. The Webbs, *The Parish and the County*, p. 384,
specify Derbyshire, Kent, and Sussex as counties resisting clerical justices; B. Keith-Lucas, *The
Unreformed Local Government System* (London, 1980), p. 50, observes that Derbyshire and Sussex
never included them.

[202] BL, Add. MS 5071, fo. 203: Sussex JPs, 1781.

knowing such a feather in my cap could be no counterbalance for the weighty business I must then undertake to manage'.[203]

The Buckinghamshire clergy who were prominent on the bench in the early 1780s included one or two representatives of well established county families, notably G. H. J. Purefoy of Shalston, the fortunate cousin of a family which had held the manor of Shalston since the fifteenth century, and Thomas Willis, grandson of the antiquarian Browne Willis, and Rector of Bletchley by appointment of his family's trustees. But most genteel clergymen of this type simply failed to act. Primatt Knapp, Rector of Shenley, and Thomas Lowndes, Vicar of Astwood, both bore important names in the county, but neither troubled to execute his commission. Those who did act tended to be careerist clergy, often the nominees of highly-placed patrons. Henry De Salis was presented to the Vicarage of Wing by the fifth Earl of Chesterfield, in succession to that William Dodd who was sent to the gallows after forging a bond of the same Earl; he eventually became Count De Salis in the peerage, but carried little weight in terms of local property or connections. William Cleaver, later Bishop of Chester, was the son of a lowly Master of Buckingham School, but owed his flying ecclesiastical start to the Temples of Stowe. Most of his active colleagues were the possessors of substantial livings but hardly the kind of figures who would be associated with the governing élite of the county. John Cleobury was one of the earliest clergy in the Buckinghamshire commission, in 1756, and held two incumbencies, one of them, Great Marlow, in a parliamentary borough. When he died in 1801 at the age of 83, he earned a suitably flattering monument in Great Marlow church: '49 years the pious practical Minister of this Church: 40 years an active, upright Magistrate for this County: ever studiously promoting the honour of God, and the peace and comfort of his neighbours'.[204] His assiduousness and integrity seem not to have been in doubt, but he was manifestly not one of the county community as traditionally interpreted. Nor were the remaining clerical justices, most of them parochial incumbents of moderate standing.[205]

A similar if slightly less depressing situation obtained in Gloucestershire. Some of the clergy appointed as representatives of the better known county families displayed an interest in their duties as magistrates. The Leighs, Selwyns, and Coxes could all boast clerical younger sons who at least qualified themselves. But clergy from other leading families, men like William Somerville, Henry Berners, and Kinnard Baghott, among the

---

[203] L. Fox, ed., *Correspondence of the Reverend Joseph Greene* (London, 1965), pp. 109–10.

[204] G. Lipscomb, *The History and Antiquities of the County of Buckingham* (4 vols., London, 1847), iii. 604.

[205] Lilly Butler (not beneficed), William Ellis, Vicar of Caversfield; John Lord, Rector of Drayton Parslow; John Millward, Rector of Middle Claydon; John Pettingall, Rector of Stoke Hammond.

wealthiest incumbents in the archdeaconry of Gloucester, showed the same
lack of interest as their lay brethren. A striking feature of the clerical
magistracy, strongly exemplified in Gloucestershire, was its professional
appearance and origins. The sons of clergy were much more likely to prove
active magistrates than the sons of laymen. In most instances, they were
not from local families at all but rather owed their position to the patronage
of government or noblemen. In the populous deanery of Stonehouse three
of the acting justices of the 1760s and 1770s were in this category; none
was particularly wealthy, all were themselves sons of clergy, all three owed
their preferment to the Crown, together with, in one case, Lord Ducie, in
another Lord Bathurst.[206]

Clergy of this kind often made honest judges and sound administrators,
but it was difficult to present them as genuine patriarchs, men brought up
in a family tradition of gracious benevolence. Significantly, celebrations of
the clergy as exemplars of propertied paternalism were generally confined
to those of them who were essentially landed gentry. The Rector of Kirkby
Clayworth was praised in 1788 for his ingenious variation on the clerical
tithe, when he paid for the upkeep and education of the tenth child in three
families in his parish. But the Rector was the Reverend Sir Richard Kaye,
Dean of Lincoln and a clerical baronet. His cloth was almost incidental to
his estate.[207] Again, the Reverend John Granville was eulogized for his
benevolent leadership in Staffordshire. But Granville was a proprietor in
his own right and a clerical 'improver' at that.[208] Compared with men of
this kind the clergy who manned the bench were only one degree above
the attorneys, apothecaries, and estate managers who had allegedly disfigured the bench under George II. In the eyes of those they ruled they
lacked a certain credibility. This was particularly true of those who fancied
themselves their equals in ordinary rural life. 'The great requisite', wrote
Vicesimus Knox, 'is, to give the clergyman of the parish authority. But the
rustic esquire and purse proud yeoman are often jealous of his influence,
and, instead of augmenting, are usually ready to diminish his power by
vexatious opposition.'[209] The opposition to Walter at Bingham was perhaps
not vexatious, for even by the bishop's official he was accused of trampling
on his parishioners when he should have been leading them. But his
opponents were of just the class described by Knox, and not a little resentful

---

[206] Stephen Philips, Vicar of Bisley (Crown); James Benson, Rector of Sapperton (Lord Bathurst)
and Canon of Gloucester; George Hayward, Vicar of Frocester (Lord Ducie) and Rector of Nymphsfield
(Crown).

[207] *Whitehall Evening-Post*, 3 Jan. 1788.

[208] John Gisborne, *The Vales of Wever, a Loco-Descriptive Poem, Inscribed to the Reverend John
Granville, of Calwich, Staffordshire* (London, 1797), pp. 60–2.

[209] *The Works of Vicesimus Knox* (7 vols., London, 1824), ii. 519.

of a 'squarson' who could claim none of the 'natural' authority of a true squire.[210]

QUALIFIED FOR A REFORMER

Concern about the declining respectability of the magistracy as a class produced periodic demands for property qualifications to protect its prestige. The political manipulation of the commission of the peace during the years of party strife between 1689 and 1721 intensified this agitation. A series of bills was proposed in Parliament during these years.[211] Eventually, in 1732, an act was passed requiring magistrates to possess to least £100 worth of land, freehold, copyhold, or long leasehold.[212] The country gentlemen who pressed for this statute envisaged a sum twice or three times as high. Under George I, the Whig Lord Chancellor Cowper had applied his own criterion of 'a brace off hundreds a year'.[213] But in the Walpole era the Whig government would have blocked any qualification at all rather than have one at a higher level. The fact that it was the House of Lords which inserted the lower sum suggests that aristocratic preference as well as political calculation was involved.[214] Slightly modified by a statute of 1745, which qualified customary freeholds and reversionary interests in land worth £300, this remained the only requirement throughout the rest of the eighteenth century.[215] It was woefully inadequate for its purpose. £100 had been set at the Restoration as the minimum qualification for the right to kill game, and was thought by many landed men too low even for that purpose. To put magistrates on the same footing seemed outrageous. As a justice's manual of 1771 pointed out, there were many mere, illiterate game destroyers who were useful in the war against vermin, but were highly unsuitable as JPs.[216]

What was worse, the machinery created to catch unqualified justices was grossly defective. A magistrate who qualified himself to act by taking the appropriate oath had to submit a schedule of the lands which entitled him to do so. But there was little to stop him subsequently disposing of them. The act of 1745 did not help at all in this respect. It permitted a justice who had sold his sworn qualification, if challenged at law, to cite any other qualification which he had since obtained. His challenger, in such a case, was required to bear the legal costs. In these circumstances even a well-

---

[210] Henstock, 'A Parish Divided: Bingham and the Rev. John Walter, 1764–1810', p. 98.

[211] Landau, *The Justices of the Peace, 1675–1760*, pp. 150–4.

[212] 5 Geo. II, c. 18.

[213] 'The Letters of Henry Liddell to William Cotesworth', ed. J. M. Ellis, *Surtees Soc.* 197 (1985), 149.

[214] Landau, *The Justices of the Peace, 1675–1760*, pp. 159–60.

[215] 18 Geo. II, c. 20.

[216] *The Justice of the Peace's Manual* (Leicester, 1771), pp. 14–16.

informed opponent, who had knowledge of the sale involved, might find himself defeated by purchases of lands in a distant county of which he knew nothing. This was a delinquent magistrate's charter.[217]

Regardless of the legal complications, £100 was certainly not enough to keep out the Whig hacks of Walpole and his friends. But its longer term significance was that it let in the clergy. In this respect the difference between the £100 and the £300 or £400 preferred by many Tories was crucial. Clerical profits from tithe and glebe quite commonly exceeded the lower figure in the late eighteenth century but were less likely to attain the higher. Moreover, the most conscientious clerical magistrates were precisely those who did not enjoy the most comfortable livings. In the archdeaconry of Gloucester in 1776, when the value of tithes was rising rapidly, and parish incumbents were both absolutely and relatively much wealthier than they had been at the time of the Qualification Act of 1732, most would have been unable to meet a qualification of £300. Of the thirteen justices in orders active in that year only four had landed incomes in excess of £300. Five would have been excluded by a qualification set at £200.[218]

Wherever land qualifications were set low enough, the clergy were quick to respond. They figured prominently in the turnpike trusts, for which the qualification was usually well below £100. They also appeared regularly as land tax commissioners. This was a sensitive office. The land tax was simultaneously the pledge of the landed classes' commitment to the Revolution Settlement and the symbol of their nominal hegemony. Parliament never relaxed its determination to keep its administration out of the hands of the Crown. The tax was assessed and collected by ordinary parishioners, usually those who also served their turn in parochial offices such as churchwarden and overseer of the poor. They were accountable, not to the central revenue boards in London, but to local commissioners appointed by statute and in practice nominated exclusively by the House of Commons. Peers were excluded from the commission. There was even an attempt in 1699 to make the sheriffs, as resident members of the county community, rather than receivers-general appointed by the King, responsible for remitting the funds collected to London. Highly impracticable though such an arrangement would have been, it was defeated in the Commons by the narrow margin of 78 votes to 70.[219] The control of the only substantial property tax by the House of Commons and its administration by country gentlemen were the twin guarantees that it would never fall under the control of monarchy or oligarchy.

The property qualification for commissioners was set at £50 per annum

---

[217] *London Magazine* (1762), 66–7.

[218] Acting clerical magistrates from quarter sessions records, parish values from diocesan archives, both in Gloucestershire RO.

[219] *Commons Journals*, xii. 586.

from land in 1699. Two years later a House of Commons dominated by country party principles and prejudices doubled the requirement.[220] This was below what was generally regarded as suitable for the magistracy in the reign of Queen Anne, but sufficient to ensure that landowners would in effect be taxed by other landowners. In the early eighteenth century the vast majority of the land tax commissioners named by Parliament were described as 'Esquire' or 'Gentleman', at a time when these titles still had meaning. More than taxation was involved. Land tax assessment was vulnerable to political intrigue and personal interest. For practical purposes the quotas paid by individual parishes were fixed under William III and remained unchanged hereafter. But assessors had considerable leeway in charging particular properties. No doubt their misdemeanours were generally better concealed from the historian than those at Moreton Morrell, in Warwickshire, in 1791. There a curate appointed by the Marquis of Buckingham, Thomas Welch, informed his patron's steward: 'As Edward Irvine one of your Tenants will be assessor of Taxes the year ensuing, I am of opinion we can accomplish an alteration in the Land Tax ... you may depend on my steady Support but I must desire you to say nothing of my writing to you on the occasion.'[221] In cases of this kind much depended on the commissioners, whose duty it was to appoint assessors and hear appeals against assessments. In a revealing dispute at Apsley Guise in 1770 the local commissioners unblushingly stated 'that it was the universal practice to appoint such Assessors only as were agreeable to the Commissioners of the Parish, not only as a Compliment to Brother Commissioners, but as supposed chief proprietors and in course principally interested in the Choice'.[222] In this instance the Earl of Salisbury had persuaded one of the commissioners to interfere in the parish of another, thereby disrupting the genteel and all too cosy conventions which usually determined land tax apportionments in Bedfordshire. Commissioners on the make had ample opportunity to underrate themselves and their friends, and overrate their enemies. The West Country physician Claver Morris recorded with pride his success in using his influence as a commissioner to reduce his own assessment.[223] Clergy often had a special interest in such manoeuvres. Under Queen Anne the land tax was much affected by religious conflict. An attempt, in Suffolk, to tax the incomes of Dissenting ministers attracted the attention of the national newspapers.[224] Proposals

---

[220] 10 Will, III, c. 9; 12 and 13 Will. III, c. 10.

[221] Huntington Library, Stowe MSS, Box 488: T. Welch to J. Parrott, 29 Mar. 1791.

[222] E. O. Payne, *Property in Land in South Bedfordshire 1750–1832* (Beds. Hist. Rec. Soc. 23, 1946), pp. 16 ff.

[223] E. Hobhouse, *The Diary of a West Country Physician AD 1684–1726* (London, 1934), pp. 86–7.

[224] *Defoe's Review in 22 Facsimile Books* (New York, 1938), iii. 373–6: 6 Aug. 1706.

to exempt the poorer clergy from taxation also proved controversial.[225] Throughout the eighteenth century the peculiar nature of clerical property and diverse local traditions in rating it gave rise to contention and confusion.

The history of the land tax commission somewhat resembles that of the commission of the peace. It grew rapidly in size. In the early eighteenth century the names of the commissioners were tacked on to the annual land tax bills; from 1758 they were the subject of special acts, passed solely for the purpose of naming them.[226] In 1723 there were nearly thirteen thousand commissioners outside London and Middlesex; by 1775 this figure had almost doubled to more than twenty-five thousand.[227] In the process of expansion, great numbers of landowners on the margin of acceptability were included; so was a considerable body of clergy. Outside the metropolis there were 830 clerical commissioners in 1723, 6 per cent of the total; in 1775, there were 3,838, 15 per cent. As with the magistracy, party considerations had a bearing on the changing composition of the commission. They were, however, somewhat complicated by the fact that land tax commissioners were nominated not by the Crown but by the House of Commons itself, a prerogative which it guarded jealously. The convention was that county MPs took responsibility for the revision of the land tax commission, usually in the first session of a new Parliament and again in mid-Parliament.[228]

The MPs who controlled the appointments were frequently influenced by partisan considerations. At times of political tension the Commons as a whole was forced to divide on the names of individual commissioners. But such blatant rigging in the interests of party was most common in the early eighteenth century, when party disputes were at their most bitter, and generally associated with a hotly contested general election. This was the case, for instance, in 1707, 1710, and 1722.[229] But there were limits to this process. To proscribe gentlemen was a hazardous business which was increasingly avoided. Certainly the Hanoverian regime seems to have been prepared to tolerate a Tory presence on the land tax commission to a much greater extent than on the commission of the peace. Or rather, the Whig majority in the House of Commons was more circumspect than Whig ministers acting on the basis of the royal prerogative. Property taxation was a peculiarly sensitive matter, perhaps more so than any other single issue. To have entrusted it to the care of Whigs in heavily Tory regions would have been asking for trouble. In the eyes of Tories such a land tax would have seemed a form of parliamentary ship-money. Even for a regime

---

[225] *Commons Journals*, xiii. 661.

[226] 31 Geo. II, c. 7.

[227] 9 Geo. I, c. 2; 15 Geo. III, c. 26.

[228] Somerset RO, Dickinson MSS, DD/DN/210: J. H. Coxe to C. Dickinson, 6 Feb. 1753.

[229] *Commons Journals*, xv. 456; xvi. 434; xx. 71.

which was used to being reviled as an alien and oligarchical imposition this price was too high to pay.

In the era of party conflict clerical commissioners were particularly affected. As with the magistracy they were the marginal element, albeit potentially numerous, which could be brought into play for political reasons. In counties where the balance of power was nicely poised, the results were striking. In West Sussex, the electoral balance shifted from Tory to Whig during the early decades of the century. Accordingly Tory clergy were appointed to the commission under Queen Anne, and Whig clergy thereafter. In the Sussex election of 1734, clerical land tax commissioners voted five to one in favour of the Whig candidates against a 'Country' coalition of opposition Whigs and Tories. By contrast the parliamentary representation of Dorset continued to be dominated by Tories; Tory clergy remained prominent in the commission.[230] But even with clerical nominations the trend was toward a less partisan approach. By the middle of the century it was becoming usual to include resident clergy who had the requisite qualification regardless of their politics.

Under George III the land tax commission, like the commission of the peace, was vastly bigger than would once have been envisaged, and far removed from the ideal of the early eighteenth century. Membership in it was also largely honorific. Active commissioners were a very small minority, drawn mostly from the humbler ranks of those nominated. The House of Commons was well aware of this development. Eventually it permitted land tax commissioners paying tax on less than £100 to act. This rectified an obvious anomaly. JPs were merely required to have land worth £100. Land tax commissioners were required to have land taxed on an assessed value of £100 in their own county. But a combination of undervaluation and inflation meant that land assessed at £100 for tax purposes was likely to be worth a great deal more—in some southern counties, as much as £300, by the 1760s. Applied strictly, this requirement would have made the commission truly the preserve of the county gentry. But there was little chance of them acting, and Parliament prudently clarified the requirement so as to permit all those actually owning £100 worth of land, regardless of the tax paid on it, to do so.[231]

This was just as well, since active land tax commissioners were far from being substantial landowners in the late eighteenth century. In this respect the contrast with the beginning of the century was marked, and suggests that the devaluation of the commission either proceeded further than that

---

[230] See P. Langford, 'Convocation and the Tory Clergy, 1717–61', in E. Cruickshanks and J. Black, eds., *The Jacobite Challenge* (Edinburgh, 1988), p. 118.

[231] *Commons Journals*, xxx. 116.

of the commission of the peace, or alternatively that it failed to revive to the same extent under George III. There was at one time a tendency for the classes acting in both commissions to overlap and merge, the same men effectively dominating both.[232] In Buckinghamshire in 1712, all but five of the twenty-two men who carried out the duties of the land tax commissioners were also JPs; fifteen of them were regular attenders at quarter sessions. It evidently suited the party bosses of the county to keep control of both bodies in the same hands. In 1712 this meant Tory hegemony. Only in the Aylesbury Hundreds, where Tories were very thin on the ground, were three of the four land tax commissioners not on the bench. Elsewhere the Tories were strong enough to ensure that magistrates dominated the administration of the land tax.[233] The local policies of Harley's ministry, between 1710 and 1714, were at least as 'oligarchical' as those of its Whig successors, and given a similar tenure of office, would doubtless have become entrenched in the same way. The same pattern, with Whigs rather than Tories prominent, prevailed after 1714. This changed in the middle of the century, sometimes dramatically. In Buckinghamshire in 1784 there was little resemblance to the situation in 1712. Only a few of the active land tax commissioners were also active justices.[234]

By the 1780s the social standing of the land tax commission was notably lower than that of the bench. A smattering of county gentry were generally to be found playing their part, but most of the laymen were of modest property and status. This was not merely the case in the south and around London, where the difficulties of finding resident gentry might have been greater than elsewhere. In Derbyshire in 1784 there were thirty-four land tax commissioners who made themselves available to countersign assessments. Of these only one, J. A. Shuttleworth, could be described as a great proprietor. Another seven might be generously considered county gentry; in the hierarchy of land tax payers they ranked between 75th and 128th in the county as a whole. All the rest were either clergy or minor gentry, according to the debased meaning of the term in the late eighteenth century.[235] Under William III the Welsh gentry had sought and obtained a lower qualification on account of their relative poverty. Accordingly it remained at £50 in the Principality. But they came to be embarrassed by such a lowly requirement. In 1779 it was raised to £100 on the grounds that it was 'degrading the Welsh gentlemen'.[236]

[232] Landau, *The Justices of the Peace, 1675–1760*, p. 219.

[233] The commissioners are named at Bodleian Library, MS Willis 20, fos. 96–7; the justices attending quarter sessions are recorded in Buckinghamshire RO, quarter sessions minutes.

[234] Commissioners from signatures on land tax assessments, justices from quarter sessions minutes, both in Buckinghamshire RO.

[235] The commissioners' names and property are derived from the land tax assessments in Derbyshire RO.

[236] *Parliamentary Register*, xi. 222.

If a man with £100 from land was no longer very impressive, it did not follow that he was lacking in wealth. Gentleman farmers had a place in the land tax commission. As proprietors they might be of little consequence; as occupiers they might be much more opulent. In the St Augustine East division of Kent, every acting land tax commissioner between 1775 and 1784 was tenant as well as landlord; some were occupiers of substantially more land than they owned.[237] They were, after all, more likely to be genuine residents than their broad-acred betters. But to an earlier age some of them would have seemed more suitable as mere assessors and collectors than commissioners. The implications were not restricted to the management of the land tax. There was a tendency to resort to the land tax commissioners for supplementary purposes. In 1747 summary hearings of window tax appeals were transferred to them. One of the objections to the Militia Bill of 1756 was that it gave local commissioners the same powers as deputy lieutenants in the raising of militiamen. Lord Hardwicke, a determined opponent of this provision, considered them 'some of the lowest People of any Kind of Property in this Kingdom'. He also pointed out that when entrusted by Parliament with emergency powers for the control of cattle distemper, the result had been serious abuses in the administration of the law.[238]

TABLE 3   *Clerical Land Tax Commissioners As Percentage of Total Commission*

County	1723		1775	
	No. of Commissioners	Percentage of Total Commission	No. of Commissioners	Percentage of Total Commission
Bedfordshire	7	5	43	20
Berkshire	32	8	111	14
Buckingham-shire	24	6	111	20
Cambridge-shire excl. Ely)	27	19	55	21
Cheshire	25	7	45	11
Cornwall	25	11	33	8

[237] R. T. Grover, 'The Land Tax in East Kent: A Study in Landownership and Occupation with Specific Reference to the Methodical Implications of the Land Tax Assessments' (University of Kent M.Phil. thesis, 1981), ch. 2.

[238] *Two Speeches of a Late Lord Chancellor* (London, 1770), p. 49.

County	1723		1775	
	No. of Commissioners	Percentage of Total Commission	No. of Commissioners	Percentage of Total Commission
Cumberland	16	14	54	18
Derbyshire	0	0	43	10
Devon	22	5	175	18
Dorset	1	1	34	18
Durham	23	9	84	11
Ely	16	11	47	15
Essex	25	4	149	13
Gloucester-shire	31	8	166	18
Hampshire	40	9	119	17
Herefordshire	2	1	137	28
Hertfordshire	24	6	155	14
Huntingdon-shire	6	4	84	26
Kent	42	7	113	11
Lancashire	12	3	66	9
Leicester-shire	41	15	103	24
Lincolnshire	60	10	184	16
Monmouth-shire	21	11	43	14
Norfolk	8	3	208	25
Northampton-shire	6	3	108	28
Northumber-land	15	10	41	10
Nottingham-shire	3	2	0	0
Oxfordshire	29	11	126	25
Rutland	13	22	11	41
Shropshire	15	5	118	18
Somerset	14	4	100	13
Staffordshire	9	5	78	13
Suffolk	13	3	129	19
Surrey	47	7	86	6
Sussex	32	8	132	21
Warwickshire	6	4	53	14
Westmorland	5	9	39	21
Worcester-shire	18	7	74	18
Wiltshire	20	4	114	19

County	1723		1775	
	No. of Commissioners	Percentage of Total Commission	No. of Commissioners	Percentage of Total Commission
Yorkshire ER	14	7	41	13
Yorkshire NR	11	4	80	12
Yorkshire WR	30	7	146	11

Note: Middlesex is not included.
Source: commissioners are listed in 9 Geo. I, c. 2, and 15 Geo. III, c. 26.

Clergy were prominent everywhere in land tax administration by the 1780s. Any parochial incumbent who was resident could expect to be nominated to the land tax commission, even in areas which resisted the introduction of ordained magistrates. In Sussex, for example, clerical commissioners were numerous, and generally those who acted were of moderate fortune; the same was true of Gloucestershire. By 1775 only one county still had none at all: Nottinghamshire. In just three other counties, Lancashire, Cornwall, and Surrey, less than 10 per cent of commissioners were clergy. At the opposite extreme, Rutland headed the list with 41 per cent, and in five other counties, Herefordshire, Northamptonshire, Huntingdonshire, Norfolk, and Oxfordshire, the clergy constituted more than a quarter of the commission. The process by which this had occurred matched what happened to the bench: gradual infiltration in the first half of the century, followed by wholesale invasion after 1750, as greater numbers of clergy were appointed, and a higher than normal proportion of them revealed their readiness to act. Sometimes the change occurred with startling suddenness. In the land tax commissioners' minute-books which survive for the Chiltern Hundreds the names before 1745 are overwhelmingly those of laymen. Only two clergyman, the Rector of Amersham and the Vicar of Aylesbury, were present at the meetings for Burnham Division between 1738 and 1745. But of the nine new names recorded between 1745 and 1757, five belonged to clerics.[239] This was also the period when the clergy appeared in numbers on the Buckinghamshire bench. There was not a necessary connection, however. Buckinghamshire was relatively resistant to clerical land tax commissioners during the first half of George II's reign; in other counties they were nominated in great numbers at an earlier stage. The fact was that wherever the clergy were invited to assume a secular responsibility, they were ready to respond. They were not fastidious. It is less true of the clergy than of the laity that once active in the magistracy, they declined to act as tax commissioners. They were truly jacks of all trades in the government of provincial England.

[239] Buckinghamshire RO, land tax commissioners minute-books 1738–52.

The justice and the land tax commissioner were the most important administrators in the counties and the only ones for whom a qualification as a landed proprietor was essential. All the evidence suggests that by the last quarter of the eighteenth century, the qualification was a minimal safety net rather than a guarantee of proprietary politics. The sacred duty of the great landowners was being shared with parsons and parvenus. But they were not necessarily viewed in the same light as those for whom they deputized, even when their estates were of similar value. To the extent that ordinary farmers had succeeded in infiltrating rural government, there was general agreement that they were ill-fitted to discharge the duties of their betters. Appeals for better treatment of the poor, for instance, were generally addressed over their heads, to their landlords. In this respect the victims of agrarian change retained a touching faith in the paternalistic tradition of the gentry and a commitment to obsolescent political theory which would have heartened philosophers of the Bolingbroke school. In a sense they were the most complete believers in the proposition that property was a stake in the community which bound its possessors as nothing else could. Possibly this was a concomitant of that 'moral economy' which has been said to represent the popular response to the market forces of eighteenth century England.[240] Certainly farmers were a satisfying target for the anger of their inferiors and the irritation of their superiors. For practical purposes they had to be borne with, but they remained an uncomfortably unpopular class. Something of the same was true of others who stood between the traditional patriarchs of the countryside and their traditional subjects. West Country weavers expected the gentry to intervene in their private war with the clothiers, and sometimes found them disposed to do so.[241]

Inevitably, some members of the landlord class itself were suspected of callousness. 'Nabobs' who bought an estate in the country and a seat in Parliament with the proceeds of an oriental adventure were considered unwelcome imports, unworthy of the place which they had purchased in county society. This was usually a short-lived problem. In practice, such men were particularly anxious to qualify themselves for their new role. Acceptability was what they sought above all else, and one of the quicker ways to earn it was to take a full share of their local duties, acting as sheriffs, qualifying as magistrates, and generally demonstrating that they were conscious of having purchased a public trust with their private property. Ironically, they were even criticized for this, on the grounds that men of low birth should refrain from interfering in business for which they were

---

[240] E. P. Thompson, 'The Moral Economy of the English Crowd in the Eighteenth Century', *Past and Present*, 50 (1971), 95–7.

[241] Mann, *The Cloth Industry in the West of England from 1640 to 1880*, pp. 110–12, 117.

manifestly unprepared.[242] But this was merely an incident in the age-old process by which new wealth was combined with ancient estates. Before very long they, or their sons, were indistinguishable from the supposedly indigenous gentry. At that point, of course, they could start behaving like those gentry, abandoning, if they desired, the part in local administration which the need to demonstrate their commitment to genteel life had briefly dictated.

The clergy were altogether more problematical. Their common profession and vocation set them apart from the laity however much, in point of manners, they seemed to resemble them. Even the intrusive nabob seemed to be more acceptable to many villagers than their own parson.[243] Their cloth and their peculiar propertied rights seemed to set them apart. William Cowper lamented the difficulty of finding 'many parishes, where the Laity at large have any society with the Minister at all'.[244] Moreover their very ubiquity made them controversial. In the 1690s they were virtually unknown in the context of local administration; fears about their influence had to do with the propaganda power of the pulpit, the jurisdiction of Church courts, and the clergy's near monopoly of education. Half a century or so later, under George III, it was their place in the secular processes of government which seemed infinitely more threatening to critics with an anti-clerical cast of mind, and which disturbed even friends of the Church.

Commissions of the peace and land tax commissions were by no means the only clerical concerns. Turnpike trusts relied a good deal on them, as did commissions of sewers. At parochial level their new roles caused particular problems. As surveyors of highways, an office which increasingly required a degree of professional and businesslike competence, they were much in demand. Not surprisingly they were readily brought into conflict in that capacity with farmers who paid their tithe as incumbents, and provided statute labour for their road-repairing demands. In one such instance at Blewbury in Berkshire, in 1776, a 'very respectable Special Jury' took pleasure in punishing 'an officious and insolent Informer' for laying charges against a clerical surveyor whose accounts had been approved by the magistrates.[245] In another case, that of the Reverend James Brooke at Over Arly in Worcestershire, enraged parishioners were driven to a public protest: 'If the Lord Lyttelton had sent the devil among us, we could not have a worse enemy than we have of you ... All that you want

---

[242] Joseph Cradock, *Village Memoirs* (London, 1765), p. 82.

[243] Ibid., 115–17.

[244] J. King and C. Ryskamp, eds., *The Letters and Prose Writings of William Cowper* (5 vols., Oxford, 1979–86), ii. 133–4.

[245] J. Townsend, *News of a County Town: Being Extracts from 'Jackson's Oxford Journal' relating to Abingdon, 1753–1835* (London, 1914), p. 85.

is to have a bowling green between Arely and Churchill.' Perhaps it did not help that Brooke was also master of the local grammar school.[246] The clergy were employed as enclosure commissioners, a still more controversial role. One such, Henry Homer, Rector of Birdingbury in Warwickshire, made an important contribution to the literature of agrarian improvement.[247] Very often they appeared in a number of guises, such was their appetite for business. Figures like the Reverend William Lamplugh, Vicar of Deanesley in Yorkshire, a county magistrate, an enclosure commissioner, and a trustee of the Keighley–Wakefield turnpike, were by no means unusual.[248] Even on municipal corporations it was possible to find clergymen as elected co-opted councillors. The appearance of 'reverend mayors, and reverend common council men' eventually provoked protests.[249] The resulting debate can be viewed in various lights. It had obvious implications for the way in which the clergy were treated by their flock. The spiritual functions and pastoral efficiency of the Church were arguably at risk when its ministers involved themselves in judicial and administrative duties. Religious establishment also took on a new meaning when it was employed less to reinforce the moral persuasiveness of Protestant Christianity than to buttress the vested interests of a propertied governing class.[250] The resulting arguments had consequences for the authority of the State as well as the Church.

The case for the clergy as governors and administrators depended on the special qualities which their profession implied. On this basis they could claim a degree of superiority on behalf of the cloth. Dr Johnson's Ashbourne friend John Taylor certainly did so. As a clerical justice he was thoroughly embarrassed when his firm action against food rioters in 1766 earned him a congratulatory letter from the Cheesemongers Company and the award of a silver cup. The cup he declined on the grounds that 'a Magistrate and a Clergyman is rewarded by his own Conscience for all endeavours to discharge his duty'. Moreover he stressed his care of the poor, and urged the cheesemongers to join him in pleading for lenient treatment of the convicted rioters.[251] As paternalists clergymen had some

---

[246] General Evening Post, 20 Jan. 1761; Victoria County History, Worcestershire, iv. 518.

[247] See in DNB, and M. W. Beresford, 'Commissioners of Enclosure', Econ. Hist. Rev. 16 (1946), 131.

[248] G. Firth, 'The Genesis of the Industrial Revolution in Bradford 1760–1830' (University of Bradford Ph.D. thesis, 1974), ch. 1.

[249] Cursory Observations on the Charters Granted to the Inhabitants of Tiverton (Tiverton, 1823), pp. 9–11, 45.

[250] See E. J. Evans, 'Some Reasons for the Growth of English Rural Anti-Clericalism, c1750–c1830', Past and Present, 66 (1975), 84–102.

[251] E. A. Sadler, 'Dr. Johnson's Ashbourne Friend', Derbys. Arch. Jnl. 60 (1939), 6–7. He evidently did receive the cup, however. It was bequeathed in his will to be added to the communion plate in Ashbourne church; see T. Taylor, A Life of John Taylor (London, 1911), p. 77.

natural advantages over lay squires. Pastoral responsibility gave them an understanding of the ordinary parishioner's concerns which was hardly available even to a conscientious country squire. Contemporary opinion stressed not the formal responsibility of local office, but its informal influence. The good magistrate was not one who signed writs, took affidavits, and sat in judgement, but one who, by his wisdom and benevolence, made all these duties, as far as possible, superfluous. In these respects clergy had a head start because it was assumed that their power of example and their opportunities for guidance made them the natural instructors of the rural community. Even without secular office, they enjoyed a certain prestige in this respect. The republican Whig Thomas Hollis went to extraordinary lengths to ensure a good appointment to the living which he controlled in Dorset, on exactly these grounds: 'It is amazing how much even one ingenious worthy man of character can change a country place in a few years.'[252] Parliament needed no instruction on this point. When parochial friendly societies were given encouragement by statute in 1793 it was to the clergy that the legislature turned for support. But the informal practice preceded formal recognition. In rural box clubs which were founded before 1793, clergymen were often patrons and supporters.[253]

With the powers of a JP added, the natural authority enjoyed by the clergy could be commanding indeed. The dramatist Richard Cumberland described its utility in the case of his father, Rector of Stanwick in Northamptonshire, Prebendary of Lincoln, and Archdeacon of Northampton. He was evidently an active magistrate, but activity in the Cumberland sense entailed a constant presence in kitchen and cellar, attending to the grievances of humbler parishioners. 'He never once had occasion during his long residence amongst them to issue his warrant within the precincts of his own happy village.'[254] Jeremiah Harrison, a clerical magistrate in the Yorkshire Dales, acquired a similar reputation, according to his daughter Catherine Cappe; after his retirement, when he returned to his parish for a brief visit, his former neighbours flocked to him for advice. Harrison even sought to remedy the deficiencies of property law, promoting the informal and inexpensive exchange of smallholdings in open fields by setting up his own registry of conveyances.[255] Both Cumberland and Harrison were Whigs, appointed to the bench because they were politically dependable. Cumberland, a supporter of the Whig magnate Lord Halifax, even marched off with the Northamptonshire regiment raised to fight the Pretender in the Forty-Five. Filial judgements of their

[252] F. Blackburne, *Memoirs of Thomas Hollis, Esq.* (2 vols., London, 1780), i. 55.
[253] See e.g. Leicestershire RO, DE 1508/8: Appleby Original Friendly Society, begun 1779.
[254] *Memoirs of Richard Cumberland* (London, 1806), p. 37.
[255] *Memoirs of the Life of Mrs Catherine Cappe*, pp. 76–7.

worthiness are hardly conclusive. But the very terms in which their record was defended are pointers to the qualities valued in magistrates and also to the advantages which the clergy had in supplying them.

Successful clerical magistrates of the late eighteenth century had diverse origins and career patterns. Henry Bate Dudley was for many years a vigorous dispenser of justice in Essex. The memoirist Henry Angelo described him as 'the most useful, as well as the most determined justice, perhaps, that ever sat on the bench. The police of his district, indeed, was the best regulated of any in the county'.[256] Yet Dudley was in many ways the very type of the scandalous Georgian clergyman. As a young 'macaroni parson' he had figured in the notorious Vauxhall affray, in 1773, displaying his talents as a pugilist against a young Irish aristocrat. He subsequently edited one of the most successful and also most provocative journals of the period, the *Morning Post*, and ended up in gaol for a libel on the Duke of Richmond. A fortunate legacy and the purchase of a handsome Essex living brought him relative respectability in the 1780s but not without a subsequent controversy concerning the allegedly simoniacal terms on which he had bought his parish. Dudley's most distinguished contemporary as a clerical magistrate was probably the Yorkshire cleric Henry Zouche. Zouche was a contributor to the debate about the poor law, a promoter of the moral reformation movement in the 1780s, and for most of his life a conscientious JP in the West Riding. But he was a controversial figure in politics, as a supporter of the Rockingham and Fitzwilliam interest, and an advocate of parliamentary reform. In a sense he owed his place on the bench to his hereditary politics. His father Charles Zouche had preceded him in the vicarage of Sandal Magna and had been appointed on party grounds to the West Riding bench in 1734, to the scandal of local opinion which, according to Lord Strafford, considered a former schoolmaster in the neighbourhood a highly improper candidate for the magistracy.[257] Neither Dudley nor Zouche could be said to have been reared in the school of the Vicar of Wakefield.

What was hoped of the clerical magistrate was simply that he would be resident and businesslike, the two desiderata which seemed most to be wanting in the upper reaches of the gentry. This was a sensitive topic even among the clergy. The wealthy and dignified clergy were all too likely to be non-resident pluralists whose lives were conducted much like those of the landed gentry, with the difference that their income was drawn from tithes rather than an estate. Contemporary commentators were acutely aware of the significance of Church livings, as 'annuities for gay and

---

[256] *Reminiscences of Henry Angelo* (2 vols., London, 1828), i. 158.
[257] BL, Add. MS 35600, fo. 89: memorandum by Earl of Strafford.

illiterate youth of great families', in William Paley's phrase.[258] Even the
inferior clergy were increasingly charged with non-residence, either in the
sense that they entrusted their parochial duties to a curate, or in the sense
that they construed their parochial duties as requiring no more than
occasional, Sunday attendance at their church. Like their betters they felt
the pull of polite society, especially polite urban society. The tendency of
the clergy to resort to a neighbouring market town to escape the tedium
of rural life was much deplored. London and Bath might be beyond their
pocket, but there were usually less expensive places to which they might
repair, and which could at least boast a gentleman's club and a regular
assembly.

The consequent dilemma is well displayed in the correspondence of the
young Richard Cumberland, a cousin of the dramatist, and like him a
descendant of the famous Bishop Cumberland of Peterborough. Appointed
to a Gloucestershire vicarage, he found himself tempted by the attractions
of Cirencester, with winter lodgings at seven shillings a week. The decision
to migrate was painful. 'Had I the smallest circle of social neighbours near
me or a better Constitution to bear the severity of this Climate at all hours
and seasons, nothing would tempt me to quit a Situation in every other
Respect desirable.' The situation included three servants, a good horse,
two faithful spaniels, and books; 'add to this abundant Power of doing
good both public and private and thus innocently gratifying even Vanity
and ambition as well as the benevolent affections.' But, as he remarked,
'every Man is not qualified for a Reformer'.[259]

Resident clergy prepared to take upon themselves the full range of
squirearchical duties seemed all the more admirable. Their status vis-à-vis
the landed gentry was, however, somewhat ambivalent. The defender of
the clerical magistrates, John Disney, argued that they were sufficiently
similar to the landlord class in point of education, background, and breeding
to make them natural proxies for it in local affairs. But he also implied,
like Taylor of Ashbourne, that they brought a more serious, high-minded
attitude to the execution of their duties.[260] The ambiguity, even tension in
this argument remains in retrospect. To describe county magistrates as
'simply the local squires putting into force their own ideas and policy' is
at least inaccurate to the extent that many of those involved were not
squires, and were parsons.[261] On the other hand there is not much doubt
that many parsons were faithful servants of squires. It was not necessary

[258] Paley's Works (London, 1860), 'Moral and Political Philosophy', p. 52.
[259] C. Black, ed., The Cumberland Letters, 1771–1784 (London, 1912), pp. 275, 333.
[260] Considerations on the Propriety and Expediency of the Clergy Acting in the Commission of the Peace
(London, 1781), pp. 7, 14.
[261] Hammond and Hammond, The Village Labourer 1760–1832, p. 20.

for the first rank of the county élites actually to officiate in order to secure its interests. They might be like Sir William Williams and Watkin Williams, who in George II's Denbighshire 'rarely ever will be troubled with the common business of a Justice yet they never fail to show their Authority where they themselves are concerned'.[262] There is no evidence that the clergy and their less elevated colleagues on the bench neglected the interests of those who nominated them, and much that they went out of their way to serve them, sometimes in highly controversial matters, like the enforcement of the game laws. Defenders of this intermediary power even urged its servility as one of its virtues. In her characteristically condescending tract, *Black Giles the Poacher*, Hannah More had Mr Wilson, the Upright Magistrate, significantly a clergyman, decline to justify the system which he was appointed to defend. 'It is not your business nor mine, John, to settle whether the game laws are good or bad. Till they are repealed, we must obey them.'[263]

The suitability of the Mr Wilsons for incorporation in a governing class was a matter of dispute. One real life example was the Reverend Harry Place, the incumbent of Marnhull in Dorset from 1778 to 1828. As Rector he was preceded by his father and succeeded by his son. In Hutchins's *History of Dorset* he appears as a paragon of virtue, employing his hegemony in parish life to combat poverty, vice, and debauchery. What the poor, the vicious, and the debauched thought of him is not recorded, but the judgement of at least one Dorset yeoman is. In the diary of a local farmer, Henry Kaines, Place earned an unsolicited obituary. 'He was a tormenting rector of that place for about 50 years, he was also a Commissioner of Taxes and a Justice of Peace, in each capacity he was feared, dreaded, and universally disliked by almost all his neighbours, many of whom he ruined and brought to poverty, and their families for years to come.'[264] Adjudicating such diverse verdicts is difficult in the case of individuals, impossible in that of a class. What is not in doubt is that without the beneficed clergy it would have been necessary to descend lower down the rural hierarchy and to resort still more widely to tenant farmers, country attorneys, and humble curates. If they revealed the failure of rural paternalism in its traditional, idealized form, they simultaneously demonstrated its flexibility and resourcefulness. They were also indisputably novel. In the 1580s they would have been unthinkable, in the 1680s astonishing. That is a measure of the extent to which the landowning gentlemen of England had been forced to amend their practice and policy, even in their own undisputed

---

[262] A. L. Cust, *Chronicles of Erthig on the Dyke* (2 vols., London, 1914), i. 231.

[263] *The Works of Hannah More* (6 vols., London, 1833–4), ii. 191.

[264] *The History and Antiquities of the County of Dorset* (4 vols., repr. London, 1973), iv. 325–6; Dorset RO, D 391/1: diary of Henry Kaines.

domain of rural society. It is not, however, a sign that they had lost interest in it. The campaign to revive the cause of rural paternalism helped restore respectability to county government and revive the morale of the class responsible for it. The clergy were junior partners in an enterprise which had seemed about to collapse in the middle of the century, but which by its end gave every appearance of enduring.

7

Just Authority

I T was generally recognized that law and authority were confronted with the most difficult problems in urban, industrial, and semi-rural areas. There were numerous 'country' districts as well as towns which lay outside the control of the landed gentry and its machinery of county government. Moreover, economic growth and the consequent social change seemed positively to be conspiring to remove the urban masses from the super-intendance of their natural masters, the bourgeoisie. Contemporary wisdom emphasized both the commercial value of a labouring class properly super-vised, and the political danger of leaving it to its own devices. Time-honoured assumptions about the sacred rights of all Englishmen were prudently modified when propertied people reflected on the need to indoc-trinate and discipline their inferiors. But there was growing awareness that these tasks could not be left to the titled, the genteel, and the opulent. Much attention was devoted to making middle-class men and women understand their fitness and duty in this respect. The desired mentality was prominently displayed in informal, especially philanthropic concerns, in which the governing capacity and patronage rights of ordinary house-holders were to the fore. In the resulting institutions and practices there could be seen a major commitment to novel forms of public life and political activity by small property-owners. In responding to this call, they could have had no difficulty in grasping that it was part of a larger mission, led by a morally inspired monarchy pursuing objects as safely authoritarian as they were public-spirited. It also fitted well with the mundane anxieties of men for whom the management of family and household was the highest of all priorities.

SPECIAL JURISDICTIONS

If the country justice featured as a figure in, or missing from, a rural landscape, his alleged irresponsibility had the worst effects in those numer-ous areas where economic growth and industrial innovation were trans-forming the face of the countryside. These were not the favourite places in which to build a country seat or found a landed dynasty. Moreover, because the burdens of office were particularly heavy in industrial districts, landowners who did reside locally were unlikely to be enthusiastic about assuming them. At Manchester, by the 1770s, it was reckoned that the volume of local business cried out for a regular system of magistrates sitting by rotation.[1] Like some other great cities Manchester was dependent on the goodwill of individual county magistrates. Thomas Butterworth Bayley, chairman of the Lancashire quarter sessions for more than thirty years, and champion of reforming county government, was Manchester's 'enlightened monarch'.[2] He and his colleagues were congratulated on the 'Plan of Arrangement' which they devised, in anticipation of statutory requirements, for the regulation of fees, the supervision of clerks, and the availability of magistrates.[3] Birmingham also had what amounted to its own JP, Joseph Carles, by the 1780s.[4] Carles was said to have beggared himself by his exertions on behalf of the public. His friends' campaign to raise funds for his support in effect made him a stipendiary magistrate, before such posts had formally been established by statute. It was obvious that in the long run provision of a kind quite different from the rural pattern would have to be made for such places. Outside opulent cities the position was still worse. In the West Riding of Yorkshire, in Lancashire, in parts of the Midlands, there was an excess of population, and a deficiency of volunteers for the onerous task of social control. In many places it could be said, as it was said of Oldham in 1758, that the entire community consisted merely of 'a few rich traders amongst the numerous, half-starved, half-clothed poor weavers'.[5] The shortage of active JPs in manufacturing districts, for example those of West Yorkshire, was marked.[6]

Even a uniformly dutiful county magistracy would not have been all-powerful. Incorporated boroughs usually had their own magistrates, not appointed by the Crown but owing their commission to local election or co-option. As was observed in 1771 'the *civil government of cities* is a kind of small independent policy of itself'.[7] The survey of active magistrates conducted for Parliament in 1831 found 184 of these jurisdictions in England and Wales.[8] They included some important places which were entitled to consider themselves the equals of the counties: such were London itself, Bristol, Liverpool, and Newcastle. But they also included

[1] Daniel Defoe, *A Tour through the Island of Great Britain* (8th edn., London, 1778), iii. 274.
[2] L. S. Marshall, *The Development of Public Opinion in Manchester, 1780–1820* (Syracuse, 1946), pp. 37–8; *The Works of Thomas Percival* (new edn., 4 vols., 1807), iv. 290.
[3] Thomas Gisborne, *An Enquiry into the Duties of Men in the Higher and Middle Classes of Society in Great Britain, Resulting from Their Respective Stations, Professions, and Employments* (3rd edn., 2 vols., London, 1795), i. 449–50.
[4] J. Money, *Experience and Identity: Birmingham and the West Midlands, 1760–1800* (Manchester, 1977), pp. 12–14.
[5] Quoted by J. Foster, *Class Struggle and the Industrial Revolution* (London, 1974), p. 23.
[6] J. Styles, 'Our Traiterous Money Makers: The Yorkshire Coiners and the Law, 1760–83', in J. Brewer and J. Styles, eds., *An Ungovernable People: The English and Their Law in the Seventeenth and Eighteenth Centuries* (London, 1980), pp. 206–7.
[7] *London Magazine* (1771), 21.
[8] PP. 1831–2, xxxv. 231–72.

many market towns and glorified villages: Wallingford, Wokingham, Andover, and Lydd were thus dignified. In Cornwall, notorious for its decayed parliamentary boroughs, there were 15 corporations with their own magistracy, in Kent, 16. In such counties these municipal judges constituted a considerable proportion of the county's complement of qualified magistrates. In Cornwall there were 46 compared with 90 for the rest of the county; in Kent 119 compared with 174.[9] Nor was the authority of borough justices confined to town-dwellers. The liberty of Shrewsbury embraced a great tract of Shropshire countryside. So did that of Wenlock, though the town which gave it its name was utterly insignificant.[10] Visitors to Peterborough were intrigued to find the 'Burrough Soke' in which 32 'towns' were subject to the magistracy of the borough.[11] In rural Lincolnshire Grantham boasted its sovereignty over 13 'towns', and in Kent the justices of the beggarly town of Romney ruled 2 townships and 19 parishes.[12] In such areas the peasantry were governed not by their natural rulers, the country gentry, but by townsmen.

The value of these jurisdictions was well-known. Gloucester had lost its 'inshire hundreds' in 1662 by way of punishment for its part in the rebellion against Charles I. It was meant as a lasting mark of infamy. Conversely county government was often conducted from towns not subject to its control. In these instances the shire hall and gaol were in effect outposts in enemy territory. When Christopher Musgrave, MP for Carlisle, had the effrontery to assault an alderman of the city in 1692, and found himself promptly disfranchised by the corporation, the argument put on his behalf was that he had done so in the castle, which was not technically within the liberty.[13] In their own jurisdiction municipal magistrates could be difficult to deal with. Stories were legion of the defiance which they might offer not merely to their county brethren but to the judges of the high courts. One such concerned what happened at Newcastle in 1792 when an assize judge ruled against the corporation in a case concerning local tolls. By tradition the corporation and the judge were required to take a pleasure trip by barge to Tynemouth. In this instance there were acrimonious exchanges on board and the judge was provoked to threaten the mayor with imprisonment. The mayor responded by offering to commit the judge on the grounds that the Tyne was within his own jurisdiction. Not surprisingly,

[9] Ibid. 237–9, 247–9.

[10] This continues to give rise to confusion. In J. de Vries, *European Urbanization 1500–1800* (London, 1984), p. 271, Wenlock appears as a major city of more than 10,000 inhabitants.

[11] Suffolk RO (Ipswich), HA/21/B1/1: William Kirby, 'Journey to Peterborough', 1759.

[12] M. Evans, ed., *Letters of Richard Radcliffe and John James of Queen's College, Oxford, 1755–83* (Oxford, 1888), p. 10; J. J. Cartwright, ed., *The Travels through England of Dr Richard Pococke*, vol. ii (Camden Soc. 44, 1888), 97.

[13] J. A. Downie, 'The Disfranchisement of Christopher Musgrave, M.P., by Carlisle Corporation in 1692', *Trans. Cumbs. and Westmor. Ant. and Arch. Soc.*, NS 75 (1975), 174–87.

the twice-yearly voyage to Tynemouth was suspended for a while.[14]

The social status of borough justices varied. In most cases they were senior members of the corporation, those who held aldermanic office, or had served as mayor. In great cities this made them men of substance, the oligarchs and plutocrats of urban life. But in small towns they might be mere tradesmen, depending for their power on political skulduggery or religious prejudice. In 1750 they were described as 'the most ignorant, illiterate, groveling-minded, self-ended Tradesmen, and sometimes Labourers'.[15] The most notorious of such cases perhaps occurred in the Cinque Ports where the jurats were elected from the freemen and exercised powers matching those of the King's judges. At Hastings in 1784 'sailors, smugglers, tailors, barbers, and the lowest mechanics' found themselves elevated; Winchelsea was said to boast an illiterate thatcher as mayor.[16] Such claims were presumably exaggerated, but there seems no reason to discredit the sober observation in 1744 that less than 1 per cent of all corporation JPs would have qualified if the act of 1732 requiring county magistrates to own land worth £100 per annum had applied in the boroughs. As was pointed out, their potential responsibility was more onerous. In many corporations 'a greater Number of People is collected within the Compass of a few Acres, than within several Miles wherein a Country Justice shall act'.[17]

The burden placed on borough justices by Georgian Parliaments was still heavier than that laid on their country brethren.[18] It was also controversial. Corporations were feared more for the powers wielded by their magistrates, than for any which the corporation as a whole might have. The right to appoint overseers of the poor seemed, more especially in an urban context, a right 'to swallow Mens Properties'.[19] Its electoral significance in boroughs represented in Parliament was obvious. But any question of extending the influence of borough justices was still more divisive. Statutory schemes to involve them in municipal improvement raised this question in acute form. The bitterly contested Bristol Watch Bill of 1755 was designed to give rating and watching powers to the oligarchical rulers of the city. The fact

[14] J. Sykes, *Local Records; Or, Historical Register of Remarkable Events, Which Have Occurred in Northumberland and Durham, Newcastle-upon-Tyne, and Berwick-Upon-Tweed* (2 vols., Newcastle, 1866), i. 146.

[15] G. S. Green, *The Life of Mr. John Van, A Clergyman's Son, of Woody, in Hampshire* (2 vols., London, [1750]), ii. 102–3.

[16] T. H. B. Oldfield, *The Representative History of Great Britain and Ireland* (6 vols., London, 1816), v. 357–9; J. Russell, *The Ancient Liberties and Privileges of the Cinque Ports and Ancient Towns: To Which Is Prefixed an Original Sketch of Constitutional Rights* (London, 1809), p. 62.

[17] *A Short View of the Frauds, Abuses, and Impositions of Parish Officers, with some Considerations on the Laws Relating to the Poor* (London, 1744), p. 30.

[18] R. G. Wilson, *Gentlemen Merchants: The Merchant Community in Leeds 1700–1830* (Manchester, 1971), p. 165.

[19] *London Magazine* (1745), 270.

that the most senior of them were justices made matters much worse. In his satirical novel *Lydia*, John Shebbeare did not hesitate to characterize the opulent aldermen of the country's second city as corrupt and brutal tyrants. Other critics, seeking to make the lesson clear for those unfamiliar with the politics of the boroughs, urged 'how dangerous it would be to the people of any county, to give the justices of peace the sole power of chusing and removing one another'.[20] Even quasi-electoral arrangements could be unavailing in this situation. As was pointed out in Coventry at the end of the century, a bill which bestowed rating authority on a commission composed of eight magistrates and ten elected townsmen gave no lasting security when it was considered that any appeals against rating would be heard by the magistrates. A minority armed with judicial powers could easily intimidate a majority enjoying only administrative powers.[21]

The powers of these justices varied. Sometimes they were virtually autonomous. There were seventeen boroughs which were counties of themselves, and forty more exempt from the interference of the county bench. In other cases there were overlapping jurisdictions, guaranteed to produce friction. In a dispute concerning the relationship between Warwick and Warwickshire in 1734 the standard position was expressed clearly. Where there was nothing in the charter specifically to exclude county justices, the presumption was that they might act. But when they did so they were not to be considered as justices for the borough, nor could they hold sessions for matters arising within it. In this instance the waters were muddied by a private act of 6 William III which had given additional powers to county justices in order to encourage the Warwickshire gentry to reside in the shire town following a particularly devastating fire there.[22] Such complications were not uncommon and gave rise to much confusion. When Helston was granted a new charter in 1774 one of the points contended for was an express provision to prevent the county magistrates from acting within the borough.[23] In an age of intense legislative activity boroughs were required to keep a watchful eye on the incursions of their country neighbours. Sir George Onesiphorus Paul's pioneering gaol bill of 1785 caused a panic among the common councilmen of Tewkesbury. As the corporation minutes recorded, if the statute permitted the building of a county bridewell in Tewkesbury, 'a Jurisdiction of the County Justices will of course be introduced'. Paul was duly warned off with an instruction to include in the bill a clause specifically protecting exempt boroughs.[24] It was only in exceptional circumstances that Parliament overrode borough

[20] *Lydia; Or, Filial Piety* (4 vols., London, 1755), ii. 198 ff.; *London Magazine* (1756), 11.
[21] Bodleian Library, G. A. Warwicks b 1: William Reader's 'Chronicle of the Times', 46.
[22] 2 Barnardiston 424–6: *Rex* v. *Archer et al* (1734).
[23] J. H. S. Toy, *The History of Helston* (London, 1936), p. 242.
[24] Gloucestershire RO, TBR A 1/7: 1 Feb. 1785.

rights. When it authorized the Essex magistrates to act in Colchester in 1742, it did so only because the corporation had in effect dissolved and the want of chartered justice was clear to all.[25]

Exclusive jurisdictions were of obvious concern to a landowning class well represented in Parliament. The difficult debates concerning the incorporation and enfranchisement of Newark in 1675 uncovered some of its sensitivities. Sir William Scroggs, a faithful servant of the royal prerogative and in this case counsel for the aldermen, suggested that the King's right to erect peculiar jurisdictions within a county ensured 'that people may have justice at home for their more trivial occasions'. His opponent, counsel for the freemen, replied that 'The country gentlemen avoid these corporation jurisdictions as they would the plague'.[26] This was also the sense of most MPs who spoke to the question. Here was a tension which Charles II and James II, in their campaign against their municipal opponents, might have exploited more effectively. There was at least one precedent for using county magistrates to curb the independence of their brethren in the boroughs. At Taunton Charles I's charter provided for six county JPs to act in the town. In the late eighteenth century this provision was still being enforced to the advantage of Somerset country gentlemen.[27] Anger at the capricious judgement of borough governors did not diminish. Bishop Pococke, on his travels in the mid-1750s, was appalled by the profligate, lawless justice which Aberystwyth inflicted on 'all strangers, and even on gentlemen of the county who have difference with any persons in ths place'.[28]

Under the early Hanoverians party considerations exacerbated the conflict of county and borough justices. The Crown's control of the county commissions of the peace often gave Whigs hegemony in rural areas where they were numerically weak. But they were powerless to uproot entrenched Tory magistracies in corporations. In politically crucial matters like poor rate assessments this could be frustrating. It was such frustration that brought the West Riding justices to enquire of the Crown's law officers as to the status of Leeds in 1748. When the result proved unfavourable, Sir Rowland Winn pointed out that Leeds was by no means unique. If the privileges of other corporations were equally sacrosanct, it 'will reduce the West Riding Commission into a small compass'.[29] Religious tensions also played their part. There was a bitter complaint about the powers of magistrates in Rye in 1761, culminating in a demand that 'all special

[25] 15 Geo. II, c. 18.
[26] *Debates of the House of Commons, from the Year 1667 to the Year 1694: Collected by the Honourable Anchitell Grey, Esq.* (10 vols., London, 1969), iii. 189–90.
[27] Joshua Toulmin, *The History of the Town of Taunton* (Taunton, 1791), p. 63.
[28] Cartwright, ed., *The Travels through England of Dr Richard Pococke*, ii. 181.
[29] BL, Add. MS 35603, fos. 16–17: Sir R. Winn to Hardwicke, 23 Jan. 1747.

jurisdictions, the common nurseries of barbarism and despotism, be abolished'. In this instance the root cause was animosity between a local
clergyman and so-called 'infidels' among the justices.[30]

It did not require political and religious differences to expose the problems created by exclusive jurisdictions. That summary justice which was
so detested a feature of excise enforcement might be found equally objectionable when it was wielded by tradesmen in corporations. Excise officials
in London were infuriated by their inability to secure a conviction against
Samuel Johnson's father, before his friends the Lichfield magistrates.[31]
Judges were repeatedly called upon to remove civil and criminal cases from
places where the jurisdiction was so narrow as to render impartiality
problematical. Towns enjoying county status, such as Gloucester, Poole,
and Nottingham, were irksome in this respect.[32] As county government
expanded in the late eighteenth century there was resistance from corporations. Colchester protested bitterly against the proposal for a new
Essex gaol in 1769, particularly in so far as it required previously exempt
boroughs to make a financial contribution. Conversely, Shropshire was
irritated by Shrewsbury's attempt to make the county pay for the rebuilding
of its bridge in 1771.[33] Legislation designed with national priorities in view
caused similar problems. The new militia of 1757 was controversial in this
as in other respects. At Nottingham there were objections to a force
effectively chosen by the county, while Lincoln was alarmed by its disproportionate share of taxation levied to support the families of militiamen.[34] These were not merely parish pump politics; they raised
fundamental questions about who governed, and who paid for government,
in populous cities.

With so many MPs representing corporate towns Parliament was unlikely
to act against the boroughs, though it was occasionally induced to treat
them differently from counties. Thus, their power to allow salaries to
surveyors of highways was restricted because there was an obvious danger
of corruption in a small town where the magistrates were likely to be
involved in more than a supervisory role.[35] But in general, attempts by
country gentlemen to steal a march on the boroughs were resisted. In 1772,
when Sir Charles Bunbury, as knight of the shire for Suffolk, sought to
make corporation magistrates subject to the county benches in billeting
cases, he was defeated. His opponent Rose Fuller remarked that it was

[30] *London Magazine* (1761), 316; the original allegations were withdrawn, p. 400.

[31] J. L. Clifford, *Young Samuel Johnson* (London, 1755), p. 60.

[32] 2 Barnardiston 285, 306: *Damon* v. *Jolieffe* (1733); 3 Burrow 1331–5: *Rex* v. *Harris et al* (1762);
1564: *Mylock* v. *Saladine* (1764).

[33] *Commons Journals*, xxxii. 364; xxxiii. 271.

[34] Ibid., xxvii. 755; Sir F. Hill, *Georgian Lincoln* (Cambridge, 1966), p. 149.

[35] John Scott, *Digests of the General Highway and Turnpike Laws* (London, 1778), p. 5.

'what the legislature never has yet done'.[36] The revolutionary threat at the end of the century made it easier to break down this barrier. By a statute of 1803 Nottinghamshire JPs were authorized to act within the county town, a consequence of the riots of 1794 and electoral malpractices in 1802.[37] Reformers advocated a more general system of appeals from corporations to county sessions, but in vain.[38]

The prejudice against borough justices rested in part on the assumption that the county benches, though buttressed only by a £100 qualification, commanded a superior respectability. In the case of one county this was admittedly absurd. Trading justices, who at best depended for their livelihood on the profits of their office and who at worst were indistinguishable from the criminals with whom they dealt, were to be found wherever urbanization created a criminal subculture capable of supporting them.[39] But in Middlesex they were virtually synonymous with the name of magistrate. To the extent that modern scholarship has amended the contemporary image it is in terms of the acutely difficult problems of the western world's largest and least controlled metropolis, especially that portion outside the City itself. The fitness of those faced with solving them remains uncertain.[40]

The conventional image of the typical Middlesex or Westminster justice was slow to change. When Lord North pointed out that Wilkes's cause had not commended itself to the Middlesex magistracy, his opponents were quick to reject the relevance of such a criterion of political weight. John Glynn, knight of the shire for Middlesex, sarcastically observed that 'in speaking of a gentlemen of that county, it would not be thought an additional compliment to say of him, that he was in the commission of the peace'.[41] Most contemporary comment was blunter. In his satire *The Ghost*, another friend of Wilkes, Charles Churchill, paraded the unlikelihood of a justice 'Who takes no *Bribe*, and keeps no *Clerk*'.[42] There were real attempts at reform in the second half of the century. The efforts of the Fielding brothers to levy war on London crime were generally well received, as was the introduction of a regular scheme of rotation, with established public offices, in 1763. The act of 1792 instituting stipendiary magistrates aroused similar approval. Yet the fictitious and satirical types paraded before the

[36] *London Magazine* (1773), 169.

[37] *The History, Antiquities, and Present State of the Town of Nottingham* (Nottingham, 1807), pp. 7–8; M. I. Thomis, *Politics and Society in Nottingham, 1785–1835* (Oxford, 1969), p. 145.

[38] Green, *The Life of Mr. John Van*, ii. 107.

[39] N. Landau, *The Justices of the Peace, 1679–1760* (Berkeley, Calif., 1984), pp. 184–5.

[40] S. J. and B. Webb, *English Local Government from the Revolution to the Municipal Corporations Act* (9 vols., London, 1906–29), vol. i: *The Parish and the County* (1906), pp. 326–7, 558–80; R. Paley, 'The Middlesex Justices Act of 1792: Its Origins and Effects' (Reading Univ. Ph.D. thesis, 1983).

[41] *London Magazine* (1770), 33–4.

[42] D. Grant, ed., *The Poetical Works of Charles Churchill* (Oxford, 1956), p. 91: 'The Ghost', ii. 432.

public at the end of the century are difficult to distinguish from those of Moll Flanders's London, except in one important respect: they were much more likely to be associated specifically with class prejudice. To the charge of common corruption was added that of systematic social injustice. In the age of Godwin's Caleb Williams, it was one which could plausibly be made against the entire apparatus of justice. But it was pressed with particular earnestness against the Middlesex bench. Mrs Bennett's Justice Atwood was an 'inveterate enemy to all rogues *who were poor*' and her Sir Richard Peacock 'affected so tender a heart, that he has been known to shed tears at a sessions, with his spread hands on his heart, in behalf of a petition from a commissioner of turnpikes, and high roads, while his callous heart retreated from the woes of his own blood, and turned a deaf ear to the pleas of the distressed of all denominations'.[43] John Trusler's Justice Fleece'em, a former old-clothes-man who learned to make a profit from dispensing justice to whores, was more crudely drawn, but equally unappealing.[44]

While such pictures remained credible it was difficult for ordinary Londoners to have faith in those entrusted with their supervision. More important, it was difficult for propertied Londoners to take them seriously. Potential justices were dismayed by 'the indignity too frequently offered to the authority of magistrates, by appointing a lower class of people to that important office'.[45] The Middlesex bench as a whole was frequently said to be concerned about its standing. According to the daughter of Sir John Hawkins, who acted as Chairman of Quarter Sessions in the 1770s, there were conscious attempts to improve it. In London's eastern suburbs, justices were 'by prescription ... of the lowest order'. Elsewhere, it was possible for gentlemen to act. But even on this reading, the last quarter of the century witnessed a disastrous decline. Laetitia-Matilda Hawkins attributed this to the political exigencies of government during and after the War of American Independence.[46] It was not only colleagues who were discouraged. Critics often concentrated on the social injustice of courts which brought the full weight of the law to bear on the poor while deferring to the wealthy and well-born. But some of the victims were articulate and moneyed, if not exactly respectable, and found it easy to disparage the justice which they received at such hands. When, in 1799, the banker John King faced a charge that he had 'had an amorous intercourse' with two

---

[43] *Anna; Or, Memoirs of a Welch Heiress*, (4 vols., London, 1785), iii. 231–2.

[44] John Trusler, *Modern Times; Or, The Adventures of Gabriel Outcast* (4th edn., 3 vols., London, 1789), i. 62–5.

[45] William Donaldson, *The Life and Adventures of Sir Bartholomew Sapskull* (2 vols., London, 1768), ii. 42.

[46] *Memoirs, Anecdotes, Facts, and Opinions, Collected and Preserved by Laetitia-Matilda Hawkins* (2 vols., London, 1824), i. 20–4.

prostitutes, and 'had accompanied it with the whim of a scholastic discipline, inflicted with more than customary severity', he published a bitter
attack on the Middlesex justice who had interviewed him. 'His interrog-
ations are extraneous and impertinent, his determinations a sarcasm on
justice, and evince in what profound contempt the magistracy of Middlesex
was held, when such a man was incorporated in it.'[47]

The perceived quality of the borough and trading justices mattered all
the more because urban and suburban society were becoming more central
to Englishmen's experience. A growing proportion of them lived in towns
and cities. The precise figures depend on definitions of what constituted a
town or city. Urban historians tend to employ the widest of eighteenth-
century definitions.[48] A settlement of 2,500 inhabitants might qualify for
this purpose. In the sense that such a place was certainly not regarded at
the time as a mere village, this is not unreasonable. But it does not follow
that it should be treated exactly in the manner of larger places. The
hierarchy of municipal life includes some notable divisions. Market towns
were not readily to be compared with county towns, nor county towns with
regional capitals, nor regional capitals with great conurbations, nor great
conurbations with London. Moreover, even places of similar population
might be diverse in other respects. The most dramatic growth occurred in
those with more than 10,000 inhabitants. They included two naval bases,
with government the main employer, a number of relatively specialized
manufacturing centres on their way to Victorian fame, several ports with
a substantial share of overseas, especially colonial trade, some old provincial
centres with sufficient industrial or commercial vigour to be prospering, a
great leisure centre, whose *raison d'être* was the recreation of the upper and
middle class, and London itself.[49] To complicate the picture further there
were predominantly mining and manufacturing villages which fell below
the minimum criterion of 'urban' settlement. There was no uniformly
urban experience in eighteenth century Britain, only a variety of non-rural
experiences. None the less, one generalization seems safe. The proportion
living in such places, however they are termed, was growing. By the end
of the eighteenth century some 30 per cent of the population lived in
'towns' with more than 2,500 inhabitants, compared with less than 19 per
cent at its beginning.[50]

Most of these men and women would have had difficulty recognizing the
time-honoured model of the rural magistrate. Even in simple administrative
terms the familiar associations of county, hundred, and parish were largely

---

[47] *Mr King's Apology; Or, a Reply to His Calumniators* (London, 1799), p. 5.
[48] See P. J. Corfield, *The Impact of English Towns 1700–1800* (Oxford, 1982), Introduction.
[49] C. W. Chalklin, *The Provincial Towns of Georgian England: A Study of the Building Process 1740–
1820* (London, 1974), ch. 2.
[50] Corfield, *The Impact of English Towns*, p. 9.

irrelevant. Urban government often depended on local customs, charters, and statutes. The bewildering variety of municipal constitutions is well known thanks to the laborious researches of the Webbs.[51] So are the anomalies which they exhibited. At one extreme, some of the greatest cities of early industrial England had no government worthy of the name, and notoriously depended on the ancient structure of manorial and parochial offices, overlain with the more modern but hardly more representative supervision of county magistrates. At the other extreme, some of the most insignificant country villages had an elaborate panoply of chartered self-government.

The capital itself exemplified the eccentric political arrangements to which urban Englishmen were subject. London had a much prized corporate government which outranked some Continental States in complexity and revenue. Its authority was reinforced by successive charters and guaranteed by act of Parliament: that same Convention Parliament which preserved the heritage of all Britons in the Bill of Rights had also reaffirmed the inheritance of Londoners in the act confirming their charters. The twin city of Westminster could hardly claim the same rich tradition of self-government. In so far as it had a corporate structure at all, it was that of a closed ecclesiastical corporation, the Dean and Chapter. But in the eighteenth century most of its effective functions were performed under parochial authority, whether derived from usage or statute. The parishes of Westminster would have been large cities in their own right anywhere else in Britain or indeed Europe as a whole. They presented fearful problems of political organization and social control. The sums which they collected by way of taxation made the politics of local rating a subject of acute sensitivity. The parish of St George's, Hanover Square, paid more to the poor rate in the early 1780s than any other parish in the country. Its annual average of £12,912 between 1783 and 1785 exceeded what County Durham paid to the land tax at its maximum rate of 4s. in the pound and came close to that levied on Northumberland, including the city of Newcastle. Yet by comparison with some of the outer parishes of the metropolis, those which fell neither in Westminster or the City, and had only the county government of Middlesex or Surrey to supervise them, its problems were few. Again, the scale of suburban government, judged by the criterion which eighteenth-century Englishmen thought most relevant, its fiscal arrangements, was startling. The handful of parishes in the Tower Division of Middlesex, divided and subdivided in the course of the eighteenth century as their population soared, paid an average of £102,875 in poor rates between 1783 and 1785. This compared with

---

[51] S. J. and B. Webb, *English Local Government from the Revolution to the Municipal Corporations Act* (9 vols., London, 1906–29), vols. ii and iii: *The Manor and the Borough*.

£80,301 for the whole of Lancashire, and comfortably exceeded what any county, not excluding the three ridings of Yorkshire together, paid to the land tax. The landowners of Yorkshire doubtless thought themselves of more consequence than the householders of Tower Hamlets, but the justices, vestries, and overseers who ruled the eastern suburbs of London were entitled to consider their affairs of comparable significance.[52]

There was ample awareness of the irrational and inefficient character of town government. What was lacking was the political will to change it, at any rate in a systematic way. It would be anachronistic to analyse this in terms of the absence of a reforming impulse. Rather it involved a lack of agreement on what reform would be most desirable, and a sense that absence of government was in many circumstances preferable to its presence. The age had a horror of State intervention in local liberties, and especially of any suggestion that chartered rights should be interfered with, which made it difficult even to contemplate rationalization. But it did not follow that rationalization was much desired in principle.

The continuing debate on the value of chartered government reveals this uncertainty about the virtue of any particular formula. There were many arguments against incorporation for towns which lacked the privilege of a royal charter. They were rehearsed in great detail at Manchester and Birmingham. These were the two largest cities which lacked corporate status, and in both there were periodic attempts to obtain it. In the case of Manchester these provoked some bitter controversies.[53] Incorporation held out the dangerous possibility that the resulting governing body would be monopolized by particular religious affiliations and political interests. It also threatened the vaunted freedom enjoyed in the most dynamic manufacturing centres with the horrors of regulation. Moreover, the visible record of many corporations seemed one of official corruption, political manipulation, and electoral violence. But beyond these propositions there was a more profound rejection of prescriptive models of government, however arrived at. What increasingly united the propertied citizens of towns and cities was a spirit which sought improvement not in political panaceas but in highly specific remedies.

POLLUTED CITIES

One reason for the lack of interest in systematic municipal reform was a recognition that some of the most disturbing aspects of urban growth and change were common to places which in legal and constitutional terms were extremely diverse. They plainly went far beyond deficiencies of

---

[52] *Reports of Committees of the House of Commons* (London, 1803), ix. 615, 628, 630.

[53] E. Redford and I. S. Russell, *The History of Local Government in Manchester* (3 vols., London, 1939), i. 195.

political organization, and were unlikely to be improved by political action. A frequent cause of complaint was the growing neglect of the classes which had traditionally been subject to close control by employers and town governors alike. It was assumed that the ancient pattern of urban life placed rich in proximity to poor and ensured a harmonious hierarchy of social relations. The head of a respectable household supposedly exercised a benevolent dictatorship, comprehending not merely his immediate family but also his apprentices and employees. Unfortunately, it seemed that the economic rationalism and social snobbery which were breaking up the patriarchal estate were also breaking up the patriarchal business. The practice of 'boarding out' servants, with a financial allowance replacing the provision of bed and board, was much deplored. It neatly matched the contemporaneous complaint that farmers and their wives were turning farm servants into day labourers, and thereby abandoning responsibility for their moral welfare. Even apprenticeships, which often carried a quite clear and contractual requirement of paternal care on the part of the master seemed to be losing their traditional character. The entire system of apprenticeship was under intense pressure in the eighteenth century, but the lapsing of direct supervision was not the least of its perceived deficiencies.

Fears of this kind were related to broader changes in the organization of urban life. The social geography of many towns and cities was manifestly changing in the late eighteenth century. The great march to the suburbs had begun. Its effects were naturally most noticeable in London. The development of the West End was to some extent an aristocratic phenomenon, but the dramatic expansion beyond, into rural Middlesex, was much more a middle-class affair. In the early 1770s a building boom in the parish of St Marylebone particularly captured public interest, but Marylebone was by no means unique, for on every side of London there was a spate of development in the last quarter of the eighteenth century. The effects on the City were striking. Portman Square and Portland Place, it was said, were being preferred to 'the polluted and polluting city'.[54] Commuting became commonplace and much remarked on. The merchant who expected to live outside the City and enter it only during business hours was a new but increasingly familiar figure. James Lackington, the enterprising mass bookseller who travelled daily to his famous emporium in Finsbury Square, hoisting a flag above his shop to indicate that he was in residence, was part of a recognizable revolution in middle-class habits. So was the businessman who bought a house in London's eighteenth-century green belt, and spent long weekends out of the smoke and dust of the metropolis altogether. The desirability of a country box in one of the outer ring of villages, Clapham,

---

[54] *The Works of Vicesimus Knox* (7 vols., London, 1824), v. 280.

Fulham, Camberwell, Newington Butts, or Kentish Town, was axiomatic in the 1770s.[55]

A merchant who insisted on living where his forebears had, in the narrow streets of the City, was thought decidedly eccentric. In the early years of George III, Israel Mauduit, partner in a woollen drapery and incidentally a formidable political pamphleteer, was one such. His carriage and livery were impressively opulent, his dress and manners gave him a positively ducal air. Yet he was a resident of the highly unfashionable Clements Lane, at a time when most of his brethren had long since moved to Westminster.[56] Middle-class desertion of the town was thought to have much the same effect as genteel desertion of the countryside. Young clerks and apprentices lost the good example of their betters. 'The lower order of tradesmen, destitute of education and of liberal views' moved into abandoned houses, shops, and corporate offices and found themselves exercising a supervisory role for which they were utterly unfitted.[57] Special significance was attached to the sexual imbalance which resulted. Middle-class women were blamed for inducing their husbands to seek a polite residence in the suburbs or the country, and castigated for abandoning their own share in the management of the City as a community. The immorality and insubordination of male employees and servants could be laid at their door.[58]

The corollary of middle-class migration was the entrenchment of lower-class poverty. Slum parishes in which the propertied presence was slight were an obvious feature of the metropolitan landscape. Jonas Hanway's enquiry into infant mortality in the 1760s was one of the first attempts to chart the geography of urban privation. In identifying the black spots of London, it incidentally revealed the effects of class. Burials exceeded christenings by 17 per cent in Westminster, 26 per cent in outer London, 43 per cent in the City itself, and a horrifying 58 per cent in the slum parishes along the Surrey riverside and in Holborn. The difference, as he pointed out, was essentially one of opulence. Mortality and poverty were closely related.[59] Nor did the emigrants necessarily carry a sense of social responsibility to their new surroundings. The squalor which they had left behind they had no intention of tolerating where they arrived. In the new districts south of the Thames John Thelwall noticed practices which resembled what was happening in the countryside, not least when they were designed to uproot undesirable residents. Cottages in Surrey's villa

[55] *London Magazine* (1772), 578.

[56] *Anecdotes, Biographical Sketches and Memoirs; Collected by Laetitia-Matilda Hawkins* (London, 1827), p. 166.

[57] *Works of Vicesimus Knox*, i. 43.

[58] Thomas Gisborne, *An Enquiry into the Duties of the Female Sex* (London, 1797), pp. 332–5.

[59] *Serious Considerations on the Salutary Design of the Act of Parliament for a Regular, Uniform Register of the Parish-Poor in All the Parishes within the Bills of Mortality* (London, 1762), pp. 74–6.

parishes were 'the warts of the landscape, which fastidious opulence is ever anxious to burn away'.[60]

The extent of the change should not be exaggerated. In some old cities such as Gloucester, Norwich, and Lincoln, the inner parishes were still, in the third quarter of the eighteenth century, the location of the most opulent classes. But in many other provincial towns the pattern was evolving, as inner cities became increasingly places of low income and outer suburbs became centres of respectable propertied life. The social zoning of New-castle developed in the early eighteenth century.[61] Leeds, Birmingham, and Sheffield were all acquiring new suburbs of superior merchant housing in the late eighteenth century.[62] Some ambitious solutions were proposed. One belief was that the problem was primarily one of planning, even of bricks and mortar. It seemed a simple matter to provide for a proper social balance in future building schemes. Such plans were designed to avoid any suggestion of interference with the requirements of bourgeois taste. A scheme for a new town at Shooter's Hill outside London, envisaged that 'The houses, though intended to be built with the greatest and most exact uniformity, will be adapted suitably to the persons by whom they are to be inhabited; some for trade, others private; small tenements will also be built at easy rents in proper places (not to destroy the uniformity of the two) for the reception of persons of inferior rank.'[63] With a similar object in view, the surveyor John Gwynn offered a corrective to the huge expan-sion of middle- and upper-class housing in Westminster. He envisaged, alongside the richer streets, 'smaller spaces contiguous for the habitations of useful and laborious people, whose dependence on their superiors requires such a distribution; and by adhering to this principal political advantage would result to the nation; as this intercourse stimulates their industry, improves their morals by example, and prevents any particular part from being the habitation of the indigent alone, to the great detriment of private property.' Gwynn even hoped to reintroduce this pattern in the City itself. 'The merchants are the opulent people of the city, and the greatest part of its inhabitants are entirely dependent upon them, indeed their dependence is mutual, for which reason it is plain their residence ought to be in the city.'[64] A tract of 1800, *Domestic Union, Or, London as it Should Be!!* sought to make the provision of mansions for the wealthy in the City an urgent social priority.[65] Such expectations were hopelessly

[60] *The Peripatetic* (3 vols., Southwark, 1793), i. 138.
[61] J. Ellis, 'A Dynamic Society: Social Relations in Newcastle-upon-Tyne 1660–1760', in P. Clark, ed., *The Transformation of English Provincial Towns* (London, 1984), pp. 198–9.
[62] Wilson, *Gentlemen Merchants*, p. 198.
[63] *London Magazine* (1767), 100.
[64] *London and Westminster Improved, Illustrated by Plans* (London, 1766), pp. viii, 15.
[65] Pp. 19–20.

naïve. Few developers had an interest in promoting balanced development: when the City sought to create a 'respectable neighbourhood' on the Finsbury estate, it got no support from the Prebendary of Finsbury, who owned the freehold: he was said to have remarked that their scheme 'was no advantage to him'.[66]

Social differentiation had consequences for local finances. The flight of the businessman deprived the oldest urban parishes of invaluable rates, at exactly the point when the influx of poorer residents increased the strain on local budgets. This vicious circle operated in small as well as large towns. At Whitby the tendency for better-off families to congregate in the suburb of Ruswarp, with its distinct apparatus of poor relief administration, gave rise to bitter complaints about the resulting immiseration of the town. Middle-class emigrants were replaced by lowlier immigrants who lacked the ability to pay the poor rate and were all too likely to become a burden on it.[67] The temptation for relatively wealthy parishes was to barricade themselves in, resisting the influx of the poor, providing themselves with superior amenities which their rateable values could finance, and generally driving the wedge between opulent and populous localities still deeper. Again, there was a parallel with rural developments. In the countryside landlord and farmer alike sought to create or maintain 'closed' parishes. The priority was to keep the population small in proportion to propertied values: the settlement laws were employed to hold immigration to a minimum. Typically such parishes had only a few landowners, perhaps only one who was also lord of the manor, and a tiny population. They often lived cheek by jowl with open parishes in which freeholders were numerous, the manorial courts powerless, and economic activity sufficiently diverse to stimulate immigration. The closed parish might owe more to the open parish than it liked to suppose, directly in the sense that its market for agricultural produce might depend on it, indirectly in the sense that the national market itself depended on the vigorous but undisciplined growth of such places. In an urban context similar situations could easily arise. It often suited a wealthy city parish to maintain its own superior character while a neighbouring, less favoured parish provided the labour on which it ultimately depended.

The ruses employed by ratepayers in town and country could be strikingly similar. Haugh in Lincolnshire succeeded in appointing its own overseers of the poor in 1762, and obtained the endorsement of the Lindsey Quarter Sessions for doing so. On appeal to Westminster Hall it was finally defeated. It transpired that Haugh comprised only one farm, with four

---

[66] Henry Ellis, *The History and Architecture of the Parish of St Leonard Shoreditch* (London, 1798), p. 249.

[67] G. Young, *A History of Whitby, and Streoneshalh Abbey* (2 vols., Whitby, 1817), ii. 596.

houses, all rented from the farmer; it had not previously been treated as a separate vill for poor law purposes. As the court observed, 'it may probably be an Attempt by the Farmer, who has no Poor of his own to provide for, to exempt himself from contributing to any Poor's Rate, by making *Haugh* Farm, a separate Vill; which it never yet has been, for the Purpose of maintaining the Poor'.[68] A similar case arose in County Durham in 1765 when the Court of King's Bench ruled on an attempt to divide the parish of Stanhope into four parts for the purpose of poor relief. As Alexander Wedderburn observed, 'The truth is, that the rich part of the parish want to separate themselves from the poor part, and throw the burthen upon them.' In this instance the division went back to 1723; none the less the judges pronounced against it.[69]

Similar tactics were employed in an urban setting. Gray's Inn and Lincoln's Inn not only claimed exemption from parochial taxes, but in 1774 sought parliamentary legislation to enforce it. The bill was narrowly defeated in the Commons. As one of its opponents pointed out, the precedent would have been dangerous. 'They would receive petitions from every square and rich street in London, desiring to be exempt from contributing to the support of the poorer part of the parish.'[70] Parliament was indeed wide open to such applications. Legislative procedure made it possible for almost any community to apply for statutes safeguarding its own position. The rampant particularism of the age concealed differences of class as much as locality. The creation of new urban parishes by act of Parliament could often be defended on seemingly strong grounds at a time when rapid population growth was rendering ancient parochial divisions manifestly absurd. But the object might be the protection of the rich rather than the welfare of the poor. When St George the Martyr sought complete separation from St Andrew Holborn in 1767 it provoked a remonstrance from its twin. The Commons was told that 'the said parish of *Saint George the Martyr* chiefly consists of well-built Houses, inhabited by Persons of Fortune; and that a great Part of the Parish of *Saint Andrew, Holborn*, which lies above the Bars, consists of small Houses, and are for the most Part inhabited by the lower Sort of People, who are not of Ability to contribute to the Rates necessary for relieving the Poor, repairing the Highways, and cleansing the Streets'.[71] Four years later a similar confrontation occurred between opulent St John Clerkenwell and impoverished St James Clerkenwell.[72]

Some of the most blatant attempts to create secure fortresses of property

[68] 1 Black. W. 419–20: *Rex* v. *Showler et al* (1763); 3 Burrow 1391–3.
[69] 3 Burrow 1610–15: *Peart and another* v. *Westgarth and another.*
[70] *London Magazine* (1774), 521.
[71] *Commons Journals*, xxxi. 161.
[72] Ibid., xxxiii. 151–2.

and snobbery occurred in connection with plans for the improvement of Westminster. There had always been a tendency for wealthy parishes, and even wealthy portions of parishes, to seek legislation authorizing a rate for the adornment of the locality. This amounted to a declaration of independence on the part of rich parishioners. The Pall Mall Bill of 1751 was opposed by the parent parish of St James on the grounds that 'it would remove a Burden from those upon whom the Legislature has hitherto laid it, and who are best able to bear it, and would lay it upon those who are less able'.[73] Sometimes the object was literally to keep out the lower classes. When the residents of Charterhouse Square obtained statutory permission to enclose and beautify their surroundings in 1743, their reasons were duly recorded in the preamble of the bill. The danger was that the square would become a receptacle for rubbish, dirt, and dunghills, frequented by beggars, vagabonds, and other disorderly persons. Without defensive measures, it would be rendered 'unfit for the habitation of Persons of Character and Condition'.[74] As the West End expanded, similar fears were entertained there. When Berkeley Square sought a bill to promote 'inclosing, paving, cleansing, enlightening, and adorning' the square in 1766, it was reported that it had 'become a Receptacle for disorderly Persons, to the great Annoyance of the Inhabitants, and to the danger of their Lives and Properties'.[75] Poor areas could not hope to match such projects: the expense of obtaining an act of Parliament and the impossibility of raising adequate funds by rating alike militated against them. Only by organizing improvement in areas large enough to make possible the equalization of the tax burden could Parliament solve this problem.

The Westminster Paving Commission, created at the beginning of George III's reign, represented one limited, eventually unsuccessful attempt to pursue such a policy. Much of its early life was spent in running warfare with the parishes which it was intended to administer. In 1771 it was forced to concede the establishment of district committees of commissioners. Eleven years later St George's, Hanover Square, in the words of the Westminster commissioners, 'one of the largest and most opulent' of its parishes, managed to obtain a distinct commission of its own.[76] Other parishes followed. The commission was not more successful in resisting separatist movements of a still narrower kind. In 1774 Grosvenor Square, and in 1775 Piccadilly, requested and obtained their own street improvement authorities. Significantly, a similar demand in 1775 by Stratford Place, not in Westminster but in the parish of St Marylebone, where it was opposed by the largest landowner in the parish, the Duke of Portland,

---

[73] Ibid., xxvi. 279.
[74] 16 Geo. II, c. 6.
[75] *Commons Journals*, xxx. 632.
[76] 11 Geo. III, c. 22; *Commons Journals*, xxxviii. 947; 22 Geo. III, c. 84.

was denied.[77] The essential impression given was that when the propertied rulers of a wealthy Westminster parish were determined to assert their power and privileges, there was little that Parliament would do to stop them. Selfishness and irresponsibility were not the exclusive prerogatives of an increasingly cynical class of rural landlords and their capitalist tenants.

SUPPORTERS OF SOCIETY

The needs of town and country alike were seen not merely in relation to the visible failings of their rulers, but also in terms of the evolving needs of the classes with whose care they were charged. Once again, there is a sense in which the realities of lower-class life were irrelevant. It was the propertied Englishman's understanding of the requirements of his unpropertied countryman, soundly based or not, which shaped his response. In some respects contemporary assessments closely match those of posterity: in others they are worlds apart. One of the most enduring worries was the material well-being of the lower classes. Historians have yet to construct a reliable index of real living standards, let alone agree on the incidence of hardship and poverty. An index of propertied anxiety on this score would be equally difficult to compile. What is not in doubt is that the marked economic changes of the mid-eighteenth century intensified such concern. The contrast with the second quarter of the century is striking. Then, slow population growth and a series of good harvests combined to keep real wages high and provisions plentiful. Interest in reform of the poor law was erratic. It depended on unpredictable occurrences of dearth, as in 1740–1, or on unusual conditions, as during the 'crime wave' which followed the War of Austrian Succession. The second half of the century brought new conditions. There were recurrent shortages, associated with poor harvests and rocketing prices, culminating in the disastrous year of 1795. Population growth outstripped even the capacity of an expanding economy to cope with the demand for necessities. The price inflation which affected almost everything in the reign of George III had a particularly detrimental effect on foodstuffs, including bread, dairy produce, and meat. The differential effects of inflation loaded its social consequences on the poorest classes. No doubt there were some middle-class families on fixed or relatively inflexible incomes, for example those of army officers and clergy unable to benefit by the rising value of tithes. But if one thing is clear about income trends it is that wage labourers, especially in the countryside, were vulnerable to price rises. The volume of contemporary comment on their plight, especially in periods of stress,

---

[77] 14 Geo. III, c. 52; 15 Geo. III, c. 57; *Commons Journals*, xxxv. 323.

for instance, the 1760s and early 1770s, and the mid-1790s, is testimony
to its perceived importance.

Recognition of worsening conditions did not entail the adoption of one
solution, or even one analysis of the problem. The most prominent issues
which required a public stance on the part of the State were the management
of grain supplies, regulation of prices, control of wages, provision of poor
relief, and implementation of the settlement laws. All commanded close
attention and all found self-appointed experts and legislators alike profoundly divided about the correct course of action. Only one thing united
them: a conviction that there was a problem which needed the closest
attention of propertied society. One obvious sign of the growth of this
conviction was the changing terminology of the day. 'Poverty' in the first
half of the eighteenth century tended to signify a state of destitution likely
to afflict those unable or unwilling to earn their own bread. The extent to
which the poor were held responsible for their own plight varied, but it
was the general assumption that only the unemployed and the infirm, or
those rendered unemployable or infirm by their sex or age, qualified in
normal times for the title of the poor. Concern focused on the poverty of
degradation rather than immiseration, its expression the obsession with the
luxury and vice which supposedly afflicted London's lowest class in the
age of Hogarth. This attitude was quite compatible with an understanding
that in exceptional times more prosperous people could be driven into
poverty; but for the most part dearth was sufficiently rare and sufficiently
temporary not to shake the general proposition. Later it became increasingly
obvious that poverty was not only consistent with a regular wage but in
some occupations almost inseparable from it. Careful students of the living
standards of the ordinary labourer's family showed with alarming precision
that it was simply not possible to live on an agricultural worker's earnings.
The evidence which the Berkshire clergyman David Davies presented to
this effect was published in the disastrous year of 1795, but much of it had
been collected in 1787, at a time when the economic climate was notably
less forbidding than it became in the 1790s.[78]

The expressions 'industrious poor' and 'labouring poor' were increasingly used in the late eighteenth century. It is tempting to attribute this
changing vocabulary to an emerging sense, in a consumer society, that
poverty was strictly relative. Certainly there were many who believed that
the poorer classes were far better off than their predecessors in real terms,
if only because housing and diet had improved in the course of the
eighteenth century. At the same time that Davies was conducting his
researches, his Hampshire colleague, Gilbert White, was complacently
recording the comfort enjoyed by sober and industrious cottagers in

[78] *The Case of the Labourers in Husbandry Stated and Considered* (London, 1795).

Selborne.[79] But such optimism was rare. Moreover, even those who believed that it was possible to stay alive on an ordinary wage were well aware that it provided nothing like security. A sudden rise in prices or a temporary shortage of work pushed the most prudent workman into debt and deprivation.

Regardless of living conditions there was evidently a need, on the part of propertied society, to place all those who lacked property on the same level. This was one of the obvious advantages of a term such as 'labouring poor'. It was virtually synonymous with the 'lower class', a term which obtained common currency at about the same time. When the two were conflated to describe a labouring or working class at the end of the century, the process of lumping together all those who depended for a living only on the property which they had in their labour was effectively complete. It was, none the less, something of a fiction. In the late eighteenth century as earlier there were many respectable artisans, small tradesmen, and modest farmers who did not fit readily into so simple a definition of two nations. But the depression of real wages helped to create the impression that one vast class of wage-earners was evolving. Defoe had argued that 'the Dearness of Wages forms our People into more Classes than other Nations can shew'.[80] This was not the perception of the late eighteenth century. Managing unpropertied Englishmen was never seen as an easy task: but it was obviously a much simpler one if nice gradations and confusing distinctions within their ranks were eradicated or ignored.

The need for a clear-sighted policy did not depend exclusively on sympathy for a vast, vulnerable class of the perpetually poor. It derived equally from a belief that the same class was vital to the well-being of the nation as a whole. This was hardly a novel claim, but rather one which had traditionally competed with alternative views. There was a long-standing notion that the lowest ranks of society diminished the nation's wealth, not merely in the sense that they often drew poor relief but in the sense that they took more out of the common stock than they contributed. Gregory King's well-known distinction between those who added to the national income and those who diminished it was an expression of a commonplace view.[81] King's table of occupations and classes, devised in 1688, was considered viable, with some modifications, for a century and more afterwards. But his way of distinguishing their productivity gradually lost its attraction, as the full economic importance of the labouring classes in their broadest sense was appreciated. The mounting recognition that

---

[79] *The Natural History of Selborne*, ed. R. Mabey (London, 1977), pp. 201–2.

[80] *Defoe's Review in 22 Facsimile Books* (New York, 1938), ii. 69: 14 Apr. 1705.

[81] The limitations of King's analysis in a number of respects are explained by G. S. Holmes, 'Gregory King and the Social Structure of Pre-Industrial England', *Trans. Roy. Hist. Soc.*, 5th ser. 27 (1977), 41–68.

manpower was crucial to the accumulation of wealth as well as to military mobilization helped alter attitudes towards emigration: what had once been viewed primarily as a healthy safety-valve, directing those who were a drag at home to more profitable employment abroad, increasingly came to be considered a dangerous drain of labour and talent. The notion that a prudent State should actually encourage emigration seemed horrifying to many in the late eighteenth century, at any rate before Malthus and the economists brought new perspectives to bear on the relationship between commercial expansion and population growth.

Part of the concern about the poor derived from the belief, mistaken as it turned out, that Britain was afflicted by a chronic shortage of manpower. From the 1740s until the census of 1801, successive generations lived with the fear that the population was in numerical decline. The population controversy naturally made the physical condition of the labouring poor a subject of added concern. Much charitable endeavour was sustained on the principle stated simply by the philanthropist Jonas Hanway: 'The Blood of a Nation the first Object in true Politics'.[82] But even without this stimulus, all the evidence is that educated subjects of George III were disposed to accept the overwhelming importance of breeding up a healthy stock of manual labourers. The poor were described as 'the nation's strength', 'the most considerable and useful, part of the community', or simply the 'supporters of society'.[83] At bottom what was involved was an assumption that labour was indeed the basis of wealth, a position which commanded support long before Adam Smith gave it decisive intellectual legitimacy.

From this assumption derived a readiness to concede how much the rich owed the poor. 'There is nothing more clear, than that we owe all to the labour of the lower class of people; it is this that supports all that deem themselves above work.'[84] The enthusiasm with which the defenders of property reminded themselves of the source of their prosperity verged on the masochistic. 'This valuable class of the creation', wrote the Birmingham businessman William Hutton, 'are the props of the remainder. They are the rise and support of our commerce. From this fountain we draw our luxuries and our pleasures.'[85] The clergy were quick to use this argument when appealing to the benevolence of the better-off. Charity sermons were studded with references to the debt owed by rich to poor, and bishops not

---

[82] *Serious Considerations on the Salutary Design*, p. 9.

[83] A. Young, *The Farmer's Tour through the East of England* (4 vols., London, 1771), iv. 311; Francis Spilsbury, *Free Thoughts on Quacks and their Medicines, Occasioned by the Deaths of Dr Goldsmith and Mr Scawen* (London, 1776), p. 127; John Throsby, *The Memoirs of the Town and County of Leicester* (6 vols., Leicester, 1777), v. 136.

[84] *London Magazine* (1760), 32.

[85] *An History of Birmingham* (3rd edn., Birmingham, 1795), p. 99.

backward in reminding the debtors of their dependence. Richard Terrick as Bishop of Peterborough recommended the London Hospital on the grounds that the industry of the poor was essential to the higher ranks.[86] The Bishop of Llandaff, John Ewer, sought assistance for the same institution with the assertion that this was 'an allowed maxim'.[87]

The argument became almost obligatory as a means of reinforcing the duty of riches to relieve poverty. It had perilous implications which were discussed with surprising freedom. One was the manifest unfairness of a world in which the most valuable class was the worst treated. No doubt it could be justified, either on the grounds of a divine plan for humanity which included social inequality along with original sin, or by reference to the iron laws of political economy. Even so it was potentially awkward. As Samuel Johnson observed, keeping wages down was essential to the commercial welfare of the country. 'Here then is a problem for politicians. It is not reasonable that the most useful body of men should be the worst paid; yet it does not appear how it can be ordered otherwise.'[88] There was also the possibility that the poor themselves might seek more adequate recognition of their value. A fashionable cleric on his way to a bishopric, John Warren, had the courage in 1776 to urge their failure to do so as additional grounds for the exertion of propertied philanthropy. 'Of all the circumstances attending Civil Society, there is no one more remarkable than the patience, with which the Poor, in general, are observed to bear the greatest hardship, and the alacrity they show in undertaking the most servile offices; that the few Proprietors of the World may live in peace and plenty.'[89] This was, to say the least, a hazardous admission to make. It is doubtful if he would have made it twenty years later when revolution was in the air.

In this respect as in others the attitudes of the propertied were marked by certain ambiguities, even contradictions. These complicated the task of supervising the unpropertied classes. In no way, however, did they render that task less necessary. On the contrary, they made it all the more crucial to ensure that supervision was provided in the correct quantity and the most suitable form. One concerned the social mobility on which visiting foreigners so frequently remarked, when comparing English society with its Continental counterparts. This was a source of some pride to Englishmen themselves. Partly, no doubt, it seemed the natural complement to legal

---

[86] *A Sermon Preached before His Grace William Duke of Devonshire, President, and the Governors of the London Hospital* (London, 1761), p. 5.

[87] *A Sermon Preached at St Lawrence Jewry, on Thursday, April 10, 1766* (London, 1766), p. 15.

[88] R. W. Chapman, ed., *Johnson's Journey to the Western Isles of Scotland and Boswell's Journal of a Tour to the Hebrides with Samuel Johnson, LL.D.* (Oxford, 1970), p. 338.

[89] *A Sermon Preached before the Governors of Addenbrooke's Hospital, on Thursday, June 27, 1776* (Cambridge, 1776), p. 11.

rights and political liberties which were the special heritage of a uniquely favoured race. Perhaps, too, it eased the sense of guilt sometimes felt by those who enjoyed plenty in the midst of poverty, when they were able to reflect that with a suitable spirit of enterprise the most wretched of their fellow countrymen might aspire to better things. 'Rags to riches' stories featured in numerous plays and novels. Actual instances of low birth leading to high life were much commented on. Some of the most celebrated examples were men of letters. Plebeian poets abounded. Cases like those of Stephen Duck, the labourer whose verses won the patronage of Queen Caroline, and Robert Dodsley, the footman turned playwright who became one of the shrewdest and most influential publishers of his day, were much applauded under George II. But by the time of James Woodhouse, the poetical shoemaker who enjoyed the support of some distinguished lit-terateurs, including William Shenstone and Mrs Montagu, some misgivings were being expressed. Woodhouse descended into embittered poverty. The tragic case of Thomas Chatterton also pointed up the dangers of encouraging mechanics and artisans in their literary aspirations. Moralists advised more prudent use of time away from the counter or the lathe, and began to voice doubts about the wisdom of encouraging the poor and unprivileged to pursue fame and fortune.

Yet the pretensions and aspirations of the low-born could not be alto-gether discouraged while more respectable men boasted of the peculiar freedom which English laws permitted. Nor could they be crushed without endangering that aggressive commercial spirit which explained so much of Britain's success in the markets of the world. It was readily assumed that such success was closely linked with the pursuit of property in an open society. Reluctance to labour was identified as the characteristic of primitive peoples. Even the Irish, uncomfortably close to home, and 'enemies to labour as all uncivilized people are', were treated as a cautionary case-study for Englishmen doubtful of the true basis of their prosperity.[90] Adam Smith offered the most complete and coherent account of the relationship between the division of labour and economic growth. He also stressed, in terms which illuminate the contemporary interest in challenging the justification for plantation slavery, the crucial part played by the accumulation of property. 'A person who can acquire no property, can have no other interest but to eat as much, and to labour as little as possible.'[91] In the context of discussions of the treatment of the English poor, this was elevated into an axiom. 'To abstract the idea of property is to root out every principle of industry.'[92]

[90] *A View of the Internal Policy of Great Britain* (London, 1764), p. 77.
[91] R. Anstey, *The Atlantic Slave Trade and British Abolition 1760–1818* (London, 1975), p. 117.
[92] *Gentleman's Magazine* (1796), 190.

This, at least, was the theory; in practice, particularly as population growth gathered pace and the social problems engendered by it multiplied, there were some doubts about the details of nature's grand design for free-born Britons. For one thing the poor did not always seem to appreciate the alluring prospect held out to them. In their lack of enthusiasm for the delights and rewards of labour, they almost resembled the despised Irish peasant, if not still more barbarous people. There were, of course, ancient attitudes, sanctified by tradition, and supported by generations of poor law planning, which emphasized the unregenerate idleness and wickedness of the undeserving poor. But this line of argument, attractive though it remained to some, clashed with some cherished beliefs. Why, if the magic of property provided such a stimulus to honest endeavour, were so many labourers unstimulated? In desperation Richard Lloyd, a vigorous champion of poor law reform under George II, turned to a programme of systematic indoctrination as the answer. 'The enormous height to which the wickedness of the present poor is arrived is entirely owing to their not being enurd to industry when young.' Lloyd envisaged the establishment of institutions in which great numbers of poor children would receive suitable preparation for a lifetime of labour. 'If the plan succeeds the other sorts will all dye away (one way or other) by degrees, and the laws about them will grow useless and repeal themselves.'[93]

Not all commentators were so heartless, but the debate never died. Some argued that a combination of mistaken strategies in the past and artificial interference in the labour market in the present condemned the labourer to an inadequate reward for all his efforts. Others who believed they knew the labour force best were sceptical about this. They had recourse to the original sin of indolence rather than the failings of contemporary wisdom. William Temple, a Trowbridge woollen manufacturer, celebrated both for his defence of the textile industry and his whole-hearted championship of Wilkes, had little faith in the acquisitive instincts of his workmen. In his copy of a tract which asserted that the labourer could not save, there is a characteristically furious note in his own hand: 'False! he will not.'[94] Temple's scepticism was shared by many who believed that if the English worker was not by nature idle, he was at least as idle as the requirements of subsistence and three days a week in the ale-house permitted. Modern economists label this the 'leisure preference'. In the eighteenth century it was a very old chestnut, roasted time and again by successive generations of self-appointed authorities.

Employers who sought greater productivity from their employees were naturally enthusiasts for Temple's view. Arthur Young went to some

[93] Cambridge University Library, Cholmondeley (Houghton) MSS, 51: 68.
[94] *A View of the Internal Policy*, p. 35, in the British Library.

trouble to investigate their claims at Manchester. Like Temple's Trowbridge, it was a textile centre, but one with a more promising future. In
Lancashire a cotton industry with a seemingly limitless capacity for soaking
up labour complained constantly that it needed more hands. High wages,
it was argued, merely drew the labourer to the tavern, and deprived his
employer of many hours of work. Young, who saw the degradation as well
as the wealth of industrial expansion, and was by no means friendly to
manufacturers, was not completely convinced. Even the employers, he
noted, would not presume to specify the level of wages required to stimulate
the workforce without starving their families: 'the line of separation is too
delicate to attempt the drawing'.[95]

Young's own analysis was somewhat different. He censured the poor not
for their idleness but for their acquisitiveness, albeit their propensity to
acquire the wrong things. Like many others he considered the consumption
of tea, for instance, a dangerous as well as expensive luxury.[96] Yet there
was a certain difficulty in condemning the lower class for aspiring to
share the tastes of their betters. The Mandevillian argument that luxury
promoted economic growth was implicitly accepted by many, though few
of its advocates would have wished to be associated with the name of its
author, and fewer still were prepared to follow it through to its logical
conclusion. Even more platitudinous was the assertion of a fundamental
freedom to labour and to purchase freely with the fruits of one's labour.
Why should the workman not have the same liberty in these respects as
his middle-class fellow countrymen?

An escape from this dilemma was provided by the suggestion that at the
lower levels of society luxury lost its power to stimulate but retained its
capacity to enervate. Among polite and propertied people it furthered trade
and production, and promoted cultural refinement. The educated and
wealthy could cope with its moral dangers. Among the poor it merely
encouraged vicious and improvident habits. Here was a most promising
line of argument, exactly fitting the bourgeois need to treat the requirements
of their inferiors, ennobled by labour or not, quite differently from their
own and their betters'. It allowed them to abandon the notion that a
commercially viable society must be an open, flexible one. Instead the
emphasis might be shifted to discipline and subordination. Every man's
right to labour and prosper became every man's duty to work and be
prudent. In this the element of class discrimination was prominent. Part
of the objection to creating unlimited access to a consumer market was that
it unleashed 'such an emulation in fashionable follies, such an emulation
for power, and pre-eminence, as renders the lowest orders impatient of

---

[95] *A Six Months Tour through the North of England* (2nd edn., 4 vols., London, 1971), iii. 193.
[96] *The Farmer's Letters* (3rd edn., 2 vols., London, 1771), i. 296–300.

controul'.[97] The fact that middle class imitation of upper-class follies was still more marked was frequently ignored in this argument. None the less the requirement was clear. 'The true policy of a commercial nation is to train up the people as much as possible in their proper rank.'[98]

How was this to be achieved? A fall in real wages could do wonders. In Herefordshire, the reporter for the Board of Agriculture observed, 'the spirit of honest independence amongst the peasantry is damped into the sullen submission of slaves'.[99] The process of technological innovation also seemed to point to a more regimented labour force. Adam Smith, in a well-known premonition, hinted at the emergence of a class of wage-labourers who would be mere drudges.[100] John Millar was clearer on the point. 'Is there not reason to apprehend, that the common people, instead of sharing the advantages of national prosperity, are thus in danger of losing their importance, of becoming the drudges of their superiors, and of being degraded from the rank which they hold in the scale of society?'[101] From a political standpoint this might be considered reassurng. John Moir paid homage to the prevailing view of human aspirations when he remarked that 'the prospect of power and property is the great origin and ligament of all human associations or political institutions'. But he also considered that in the majority of cases the ordinary conditions of life dictated acceptance of authority. 'A servile and vulgar predilection for subordination is the common effect of that mechanical bias we receive from the settled forms or modes of society under which we are born.'[102]

There were, in any case, other means. Moral reformation was concentrated on changing the habits of the poor rather than the rich. When the rich were urged to amend their own conduct it was more on the grounds that their example would influence their inferiors than with a view to their personal improvement. Moral education, for example that offered by the Sunday schools, had obvious implications for the generation of sound working habits. It is ironic that Sunday schools were frequently opposed by employers who feared that they would lift the gaze of those who attended them beyond the horizons of mundane employment. In fact, as their defenders pointed out, the inculcation of a submissive and disciplined approach to work was one of their aims.[103] Nor could it readily be supposed that they concentrated the minds of their pupils on worldly advancement.

---

[97] *London Magazine* (1770), 212.

[98] Jonas Hanway, *Moral and Religious Instructions* (London, 1767), p. xiv.

[99] J. Duncombe, *General View of the Agriculture of the County of Hereford* (London, 1805), p. 137.

[100] *An Inquiry into the Nature and Causes of the Wealth of Nations*, ed. R. H. Campbell, A. S. Skinner, and W. B. Todd (2 vols., Oxford, 1976), ii. 781–2.

[101] W. C. Lehmann, *John Millar of Glasgow, 1735–1801* (Cambridge, 1960), p. 281.

[102] *Gleanings; Or, Fugitive Pieces* (London, 1777), i. 125.

[103] T. W. Laqueur, *Religion and Respectability: Sunday Schools and Working Class Culture 1780–1850* (New Haven, Conn., 1976), pp. 124–34.

The 'solace of religious hope' was one of their priorities: its effect would be to make them *'labour more abundantly'*.[104] Not least it was always comforting to reflect that the poor were free of the burdens of propertied life, and thereby released to concentrate on sobriety and salvation. 'It is one of the circumstances which soften the lot of the poor, that they are exempt from the solicitude attendant on the disposal of property.'[105]

SEDITION AND TUMULT

Interest in the subordination of the lower class cannot be separated from concern about its rebelliousness. The belief that the ordinary Englishman was peculiarly independent in his political views was far from new. Foreigners had long observed his want of respect for rank. A Danish tourist in the early eighteenth century shrewdly remarked that 'The French respect their superiors, the English respect themselves.'[106] For French visitors a comment on the irreverence of the lower classes was almost *de rigueur*.[107] Their hosts were generally disposed to consider it a compliment, but there was growing uncertainty on this point. Royalty itself was at risk. Lord Bute was shocked in 1761 at the clamour to which the King was subjected by a playhouse audience after an increase in the beer tax.[108] Before long George III and Queen Charlotte became accustomed to the sullen ungraciousness of theatre pits which declined to doff their hats in the royal presence, but when their brother-in-law the King of Denmark was besieged by crowds following his progress with a mixture of vulgar fascination and downright ill manners it seemed time to apologize on behalf of the 'natural, but embarrassing curiosity of the English'.[109] It is most unlikely that the disrespect shown to national leaders in the 1770s and 1780s exceeded that displayed in the presence of George II and Sir Robert Walpole half a century earlier. But the very concern of newspapers to report popular insults suggests a heightened sensitivity in this respect. In 1776 Lord and Lady North were even followed to the Three Choirs Meeting at Worcester for an account of their ill treatment by 'an ignorant and insolent populace'.[110]

Popular interest in politics was also much noticed by foreigners.[111] It

---

[104] *Works of Vicesimus Knox*, vi. 424.

[105] *Works of Thomas Percival*, iv. 376.

[106] S. E. Fraser, ed., *Ludvig Holberg's Memoirs: An Eighteenth Century Danish Contribution to International Understanding* (Leiden, 1970), p. 232.

[107] e.g. P. J. Grosley, *A Tour to London*, trans. T. Nugent (2 vols., London, 1772), i. 88–9.

[108] J. Carswell and L. A. Dralle, eds., *The Political Journal of George Bubb Dodington* (Oxford, 1965), p. 417.

[109] *London Magazine* (1768), 441.

[110] *London Chronicle*, 21 Sept. 1776.

[111] e. g. J. Marchant, ed., *A Frenchman in England 1784* (Cambridge, 1933), p. 112.

was freely admitted by the English themselves, often as a concomitant of English pride and independence. 'We hear nothing but politics, we see nothing but politics, we feel nothing but politics, we eat nothing else.'[112] Oliver Goldsmith described a 'universal passion for politics', which among the lowest mechanics at least, went with haughty language and disrespectful manners.[113] The early years of George III's reign constituted something of a watershed in this respect. The rhetoric of liberty, especially as exploited by the Wilkesites, was much blamed. Smollett attacked the 'artisans, inferiour tradesmen, and the lower class of plebeians, such as those who now presume to direct the wheels of government'.[114] Dr Johnson characteristically remarked that 'the *garrulosity* of the people about their rights did infinite harm, and is injurious to good government and morality'.[115] Smollett and Johnson were *parti pris* in these matters, but their belief that popular insubordination had risen sharply with the reign of George III reflected a widely held view. In the 1760s there was mounting anxiety on this score. One sign was the subtle redirection of the propaganda associated with State occasions. The sermons delivered on 30 January to mark the execution of Charles I traditionally concentrated on the wickedness of his political opponents, especially those who could conveniently be accused of religious fanaticism as well as republican sentiments. But increasingly they were used to highlight the threat of plebeian disorder. George Stinton similarly commended the commemoration of 1688 as a means of educating in their political duties 'the vulgar, who are always the great instrument in disturbing and subverting governments'.[116]

An obvious cause for concern was the turbulence associated with popular politics. Pride in the establishment of parliamentary supremacy since the Revolution of 1688 had to be reconciled with several disquieting features of the 'happy constitution' then inaugurated. One was the colossal corruption seemingly inseparable from a form of government which rendered the executive dependent on a majority at Westminster. Another was the indiscipline of the populace. Perhaps there was an increased propensity to riot in the late seventeenth and early eighteenth century.[117] Contemporaries thought they saw the most striking effects in politics. In retrospect it is generally assumed that the elections of the late eighteenth century were sedate and disciplined compared with their predecessors. But in some

---

[112] *The Literary Fly*, 27 Mar. 1779.

[113] *Collected Works of Oliver Goldsmith*, ed. A. Friedman (4 vols., London, 1766), ii. 28–9.

[114] R. D. Spector, *English Literary Periodicals and the Climate of Opinion during the Seven Years' War* (The Hague, 1966), p. 144.

[115] Prince Hoare, *Memoirs of Granville Sharp* (London, 1820), p. 463.

[116] *A Sermon Preached before the Honourable House of Commons, on Saturday, 30 January, 1768* (London, 1768), p. 17.

[117] R. B. Schoemaker, 'The London "Mob" in the Early Eighteenth Century', *Jnl. of British Studies*, 26 (1987), 273–304.

respects this is a rather misleading appearance.[118] The incidence of contested elections certainly diminished in the course of the period. Moreover
techniques of management and control became notably more sophisticated
and successful. But the triumph of Georgian electioneers was essentially
the conquest of the small boroughs. Larger constituencies were never
mastered. Indeed, contests in counties and large boroughs multiplied in
the late eighteenth century. In such places the franchise was frequently
widely distributed. The counties had big electorates in which small freeholders predominated. Borough franchises gave the vote to large numbers
of relatively humble freemen or ratepayers. The public visibility of popular
voting was not in the least affected by the growth of oligarchy in smaller
constituencies.[119]

Historians have paid so much attention to the growth of the parliamentary reform movement that it is easy to neglect the swelling tide of
opinion which favoured curbing the populism associated with the existing
franchise. This included a considerable number of the reformers
themselves. The leader of the Gloucestershire Association, Sir George
Onesiphorus Paul, and his compatriot Sir William Codrington, MP for
Tewkesbury, sought 'a superior class of Electors, persons capable of
judging, and above the reach of personal corruption'.[120] Inflation had long
since rendered the forty-shilling freehold a derisory property qualification
and particularly at general election time there were demands that it should
be raised. 'We are not, in spite of the shocking scene of a county poll, as
yet roused to the necessity of raising the qualification of the voters, in
proportion to the change of property,' it was said in 1775, after a sharp
increase in the incidence of county contests.[121] Views of this kind were not
the monopoly of the gentry. The ignorance and corruptibility of the small
freeholder were despised by many of only slightly higher status themselves.
The Sussex shopkeeper Thomas Turner was disgusted by the riot and
tumult which occurred at the public entertainments organized by the Duke
of Newcastle with a view to Sussex elections.[122] A more restricted franchise
would have compelled the gentry to take more notice of the opinions and
importance of the middling freeholder. It would also have appealed to the
moral and aesthetic susceptibilities of the 'sober and rational part of the
kingdom ... Such is the mean and corrupted state of the People, that

[118] G. Holmes, *The Electorate and the National Will in the First Age of Party* (Lancaster, 1976),
pp. 12–13.
[119] For a spirited defence of the vitality of the borough electorate, see. J. A. Phillips, *Electoral
Behaviour in Unreformed England* (Princeton, NJ, 1982).
[120] E. Moir, *Local Government in Gloucestershire 1775–1800* (Pubs. Bristol and Gloucestershire Arch.
Soc., Records Section, 8, 1969), p. 71.
[121] *London Chronicle*, 5 Dec. 1775.
[122] D. Vaisey, ed., *The Diary of Thomas Turner, 1754–1765* (Oxford, 1984), pp. 107, 188.

there is an universal expectation on these occasions of riotous mirth and intemperate feasting.'[123]

The violence of borough elections in places of any size was particularly notorious. It was also more offensive in that non-voters had a way of intervening in what was not regarded as their business. 'In these Parliamentary times, even persons who are not qualified to vote can scarcely avoid mixing in the political brangle,' it was said at Shrewsbury in 1774.[124] It was for this reason that many respectable inhabitants of unrepresented cities were opposed to demands for their enfranchisement. Good working habits might be endangered by the licence and luxury of an electoral contest.[125] Opponents of parliamentary reform urged rejection of an 'honour which would be attended with serious mischiefs to their loom and manufactures'.[126] It was even suggested that legislation should be introduced to prevent the unenfranchised appearing in the vicinity of polls. Since there was a statutory ban on the presence of troops at election time, why should not the poor be similarly excluded from what was essentially a rite of property? Those who resisted removal could be taken up as vagabonds, placed in a house of correction, and flogged.[127]

It seems unlikely that late eighteenth-century elections were more disruptive than their Augustan predecessors. In retrospect it is the continuity which seems most striking. Coventry, with arguably the most violent of all urban electorates, had a long-standing reputation for head-breaking and blood-letting. Defoe's account of 'a set Battle in the Streets of Coventry' at the election of 1705 closely resembles the reports made to the House of Commons on that of 1780.[128] The mid-century riots at Leicester, particularly in 1754, during a period of supposed political calm, left behind a desolation which long remained in the memory of those who witnessed it.[129] What does seem clear is that public attention increasingly focused on the problem of electoral disorder after 1760. Earlier, it had been possible to treat it lightly. One commentator of 1740 likened election tumults to the 'kindly, tho' troublesome *Eruptions* in the *Spring*, [which] carry off much *greater Evils* than *they occasion*'.[130] The circumstances of George III's reign suggested to some that they might be symptoms of a more

---

[123] *An Address to the People of England, on the Inexpedience of Dissolving the Present Parliament* (London, 1770), p. 17.

[124] *The Shrewsbury Jubilee* (Shrewsbury, n.d.), p. 105.

[125] Sir John Sinclair, *Lucubrations during a Short Recess* (London, 1782), p. 11.

[126] *A Dialogue on the Actual State of Parliament* (London, 1783), p. 33.

[127] *The Works of the Right Reverend Thomas Newton D.D.* (3 vols., London, 1782), vol. i., App. iii, 'A Letter to the New Parliament', para. viii (not paginated).

[128] *Defoe's Review*, ii. 113–6: 10 May 1705; iii. 506: 24 Oct. 1706; *Commons Journals*, xxxviii. 54–8. The subsequent proceedings in 1780 were prolonged and culminated in a bill to regulate the conduct of elections at Coventry.

[129] Throsby, *The Memoirs of the Town and County of Leicester*, v. 89.

[130] *The Livery-Man; Or, Plain Thoughts on Publick Affairs* (London, 1740), p. 10.

deep-seated disease. The Middlesex election of 1768 and the talk of parliamentary reform which it stimulated provided the basis for continuing public interest in electoral matters. A new system of select committees for the adjudication of controverted elections coincided with the beginnings of extended newspaper reporting of parliamentary debates. In this climate revelations of electoral corruption and disorder before the committees attracted immense publicity. The corruption and disorder were not new; the publicity was.

The press was crucial. It was believed that the public at large was being involved in political controversy as never before. Between 1689 and 1760 it had been possible for the authorities to treat criticism of government as tantamount to disaffection. Under George III, at least before the onset of the Revolutionary Wars in the 1790s, this ploy was unavailable. The abolition of general warrants also removed a valuable means of combating opposition propaganda. The ferocity of the press in the era of Wilkes and Junius was much condemned, not always by friends of the court. Moreover, the first war fought in this era, the War of American Independence, raised awkward questions of principle. It was tempting to blame it for the frenzy of political debate which occurred in the late 1770s. 'Englishmen are naturally politicians, from the freedom they enjoy; but, since the beginning of these troubles, Englishmen have been politicians in the fullest sense of the words. Nerone neronior. They have outdone themselves. Our very women and children have scribbled pamphlets, proposed plans of reconciliation, and obligingly come forward to settle the affairs of the nation.'[131] In theory the court had weapons of its own, as the prosecution of John Horne and the proscription of the notorious *Crisis* in 1776 revealed. But spectators at the public burning of the *Crisis*, achieved before a crowd of 5,000 only with the help of 50 constables, were unlikely to consider it a triumph for government, and public burnings were not resumed.[132] The truth was that Lord North and his successors did not command the legal advantages enjoyed by Walpole and Pelham. The younger Pitt was forced to call in Parliament and the power of statute when he reinforced the government's position in this respect in the mid-1790s.

An increasingly uninhibited press was thought to hold special dangers where the ignorant and undiscriminating masses were concerned. In 1733 the satirist Samuel Madden had predicted the emergence of a nation of prime ministers.[133] Late eighteenth-century Prime Ministers had reason to fear that his prophecy had come true. What Allan Ramsay described as 'a studied train of insult pointed at all Persons in authority' threatened to

[131] *Critical Review*, xiv. 145.
[132] C. Black, ed., *The Cumberland Letters, 1771–1784* (London, 1912), pp. 77–9.
[133] Samuel Madden, *Memoirs of the Twentieth Century* (London, 1733), p. 133.

remove all restraints on popular participation in politics.[134] Samuel Horsley directly linked popular insubordination with the Crown's inability to control the press. Since the time of Wilkes's *North Briton*, he thought, the pillory had become a stepping-stone to glory. 'Has not a great change in the demeanour of the lower orders actually been produced?'[135] The charge was considered damning where moderate opinion was concerned, and the opponents of government went to some lengths to distance themselves from demagogic populism. Their publications, it was urged on their behalf in 1779, were 'intended for the Freeholders and middle class of People'.[136] It was because the contamination of the lowest class was particularly feared that so much attention was paid to the polemical use of graphic satire. Cartoons which ridiculed authority in a form appreciated by the most untutored mind were much criticized. This was not the paranoia of court politicians. The essayist Vicesimus Knox, a Foxite Whig, wrote some of his most penetrating pieces against the licence accorded the caricaturist. He even believed that the Gordon Riots of 1780 could be attributed to 'the contempt thrown on the higher orders by various methods, and among others, by ludicrous representations on the copper-plate'.[137]

Propertied apprehension of popular politics cannot be separated from wider anxieties. Traditionally, there was a sense that the riot expressed a rugged English liking for direct, libertarian action, which, while it operated within clearly defined limits, might be bearable. It became increasingly difficult to sustain this view. Partly, the change had to do with the extinction of party, at least in its old form. Whigs had always deplored High Church and 'Jacobite' mobbing; Tories had equally detested its Low Church equivalent. Yet both resorted to the use of popular violence, not least in elections. The junction of the Tory party with their old enemies in 1760 in effect cut the Tory leadership off from its popular base in many towns.[138] The new Whig opposition which commenced soon afterwards was hesitant about appealing beyond the propertied public to a genuinely popular constituency. To the extent that the latter was permitted a voice, it was increasingly heard in favour of radicals who had little in common with any of the parliamentary factions. Not until the 1790s, under the stress of a revolutionary conflict, did respectable politicians again resort to authentically populist tactics, and only then at arm's length, through the likes of John Reeves. Nor were they always happy about the resulting loyalist excesses. There were doubtless supporters of Church and King who

[134] *Letters on the Present Disturbances in Great Britain and Her American Provinces* (London, 1777), p. 32.
[135] *The Speeches in Parliament of Samuel Horsley* (Dundee, 1813), pp. 178–9.
[136] *The Englishman*, 27 Mar. 1779.
[137] *Works of Vicesimus Knox*, ii. 416.
[138] L. Colley, *In Defiance of Oligarchy: The Tory Party 1714–60* (London, 1982), pp. 162–74.

considered that Priestley deserved his fate in the Birmingham riots of 1791, but few of them gloried in it. Increasingly the assumption was that 'assembly' and 'commotion' were synonymous terms. As the Norfolk country gentleman Sir Mordaunt Martin put it, the Birmingham riots should 'shew those who mean well how injudicious it is to draw together a set of wretches, whose collected force is more difficult to direct than that of gunpowder or steam'.[139]

If there was a time when sympathy for popular violence was widespread, it was probably during the Pelhamite era. Then a narrowly based regime faced a nation which, if it had little enthusiasm for a Catholic Pretender, was not much enamoured of its Hanoverian ruler. Supposedly Jacobite activity in Oxford in 1747 was violent enough to make the ministry contemplate statutory intervention in the universities, yet there was much support for its opponents, and the plan was prudently dropped.[140] The Jewish Naturalisation Act of 1753 brought vigorous opposition which forced the repeal of the measure. The same Parliament, that of 1747–54, witnessed a violent outburst against bawdy-houses in 1749 in which there were political elements associated with a contested election at Westminster. Even in this case, the mob was defended on the grounds that they were 'proceeding in their summary way, to do the Work of a Number of fruitless presentments'.

As hot-headed, wild and impetuous, as an English Mob, when it is up, appears to be, there is, generally speaking, such a Bottom of natural good sense diffus'd through the common people of England, that the least Exertion of legal Authority, will serve to check their Fury, or, of itself, set Bounds to it, as it mixes with their Management and Spirit of Equity, Moderation, and even good Nature, unknown to the like popular Insurrection in other Countries, and is perhaps one of the best Proofs of the peculiar art of Liberty to inspire gentle and governable Sentiments.

The very idea of Draconian action was ruled out:

It is but too sensible a Complaint, that the Spirit of the *English* is already too much broke, sunk, and declin'd from its ancient Manliness; so that such a farther Subdual of it might lower and deaden it, so as to leave inanimate the Body of the People, and bury it in universal Indolence, Stupidity, and Carelessness.[141]

In this defence of an English mob, penned by the novelist John Cleland, there was a tribute to the Duke of Newcastle, who had made 'his first public Entry into Power at the Head of one'. It was a boast which Newcastle

[139] The process is described by R. R. Dozier, *For King, Constitution and Country: The English Loyalists and the French Revolution* (Lexington, Ky., 1983). The quotations are from *Observations on the Conduct of the Protestant Dissenters, Part II* (London, 1790), p. 15, and T. J. Pettigrew, *Memoirs of the Life and Writings of the Late John Coakley Lettsom* (3 vols., London, 1817), ii. 59.

[140] L. S. Sutherland and L. G. Mitchell, eds., *The History of the University of Oxford*, vol. v: *The Eighteenth Century* (Oxford, 1986), pp. 121–5.

[141] J. Cleland, *The Case of the Unfortunate Bosavern Penlez* (London, 1749), p. 46.

himself, recalling his part in the tumultuous accession of George I, was in the habit of making. On his death in 1768 newspapers relished repeating it: 'I love a mob (said he) I headed a mob once myself. We owe the Hanover succession to a mob.'[142] No doubt Newcastle was somewhat glamourizing his youthful activities, but his pride in his populist credentials fitted well with a Whig tradition which emphasized the ordinary Englishman's rejection of popery and absolutism. Its appeal did not die readily. In the disorders which followed the Forty-Five there was a certain readiness to tolerate appropriately partisan demonstrations of mob power. 'People rising in this Manner, with a View to support the Government, are not to be blamed.'[143] This was the pronouncement of a Lord Chief Justice, Sir William Lee, confronted with violence against person and property in a good Hanoverian cause at Wigan in 1749. Nor, indeed was this exclusively a ploy of Whig ministerialists. Tories implicitly approved rioting High Church mobs, and were capable of considering popular violence as the last and legitimate resort of a community intolerably provoked by Whig oligarchy and corruption. Even in Parliament it was sometimes defended, particularly when military matters were under consideration. A standard argument for the standing army was its utility in the control of the lower orders. One opponent of Walpole in 1737 remarked in reply that mobs were 'represented as most hideous Things. I confess they ought not to be encouraged; but they have been sometimes useful.'[144]

Such attitudes did not survive long. Even in the early 1750s Henry Fielding was warning that the mobility threatened to 'shake the Balance of our Constitution'.[145] The following years witnessed serious outbreaks of popular protest, against food shortages in 1756–7, and against the Militia Act of 1757. The authorities came down heavily on both, but especially on the militia riots. Significantly the Militia Act was more a Tory than a Whig measure, and its passage the price of the Tory party's support for William Pitt. Tory country gentlemen saw themselves as the patriarchal champions of a people systematically cheated by cynical Whig government. But they were as quick to condemn resistance to compulsory enlistment as their Whig colleagues. Sympathy for the plight of starving rural rioters was accompanied by growing resistance to anything which suggested real violence. The notion that mobbing might be a sign of health in the body politic, let alone a means of enforcing laws which the authorities had neglected to implement, became unthinkable. 'What can be more fierce and tremendous than popular commotions?' enquired a tremulous reactionary in 1796, at a time when severe shortages raised the spectre of

[142] Ibid.; *London Magazine* (1768), 329.
[143] 1 Black. W. 47–8: *Rex* v. *Inhabitants of Wigan* (1749).
[144] *London Magazine* (1737), 480.
[145] M. C. Battestin, *Henry Fielding: A Life* (London, 1989), p. 546.

widespread rioting.[146] The undertones of class conflict also became increasingly prominent. The 'Advice to the Poor' offered at Norwich in the midst
of the disturbances of 1766 stands in sharp contrast to the tolerance of
earlier years:

Remember that the security of every man's property is absolutely necessary to the
good of society: All rioting, and tumults tend to undermine and over-turn society;
And whatever has this tendency, threatens ruin and destruction to the poor as well
as to the rich. The welfare and happiness of both are inseparable: Destroy the
poor, and the rich must fall with them: Ruin the rich, and what becomes of the
poor? The very nature of society requires different orders and degrees of men.—
Suppose all were reduced to the same level: Suppose,—if you can without horror
suppose this large and flourishing city to be laid in ashes, and all distinctions thus
finally removed: What, then, would be the condition of the poor? Where would
be your trade? Where would the strong and healthy manufacturer meet with
employment—the infirm and aged with relief and support?—Where would your
wives and children hide their heads, or procure a morsel of bread to satisfy their
hunger?[147]

It was understood that urbanization and industrialization were imposing
new strains. Manufacturers were at pains to emphasize that the powers
which they sought over their workforce were those taken for granted in
landed society. As the Gloucestershire clothiers put it in explaining their
attitude towards some embarrassing upheavals among the weavers in 1757,
they did not desire 'to have it in their power to oppress the weavers, but
only to be enabled to keep up that due subordination amongst their own
servants, which ought always to be religiously preserved in all communities
of men'.[148] Landed men did not always sympathize with such claims, as
the clothiers well knew. But as the century wore on there was a tendency
to suppress doubts about the motives of employers, or at least to accept
that industrial expansion was creating social and political ills which could
not be cured by traditional means. It certainly seemed difficult to deny
that the concentration of labour in itself constituted a public order problem.
Bentham called manufacturing towns the natural seminaries of riot, and
the Whig 'Dr Johnson', Samuel Parr, told a congregation at Birmingham
that the effect of industrialization on the masses was to stimulate 'an
uncommon violence in all their passions'.[149] An account of life in the
Yorkshire woollen manufactory described the 'very large Buildings which

---

[146] John Moir, *Preventive Policy; Or, the Worth of Each, the Safety of All* (London, 1796), p. 123.
[147] *London Magazine* (1766), 581.
[148] *A State of the Case, and a Narrative of Facts, Relating to the Late Commotions, and Rising of the Weavers in the County of Gloucester* (London, 1757), p. iv.
[149] *The Correspondence of Jeremy Bentham*, vol. iv, ed. A. T. Milne (London, 1982), 487: to Evan Nepean, 10 Nov. 1793; W. Derry, *Dr Parr* (Oxford, 1966), p. 129. For a county study substantiating such fears, see M. Thomas, 'The Rioting Crowd in Derbyshire in the Eighteenth Century', *Derbys. Arch. Jnl.* 95 (1975), 44.

are called Factories' and pointed to the 'Immorality which is always produced by the Association of large Bodies of People'.[150] John Thelwall admitted that the charge had some force, but took an optimistic view of the likely outcome. 'Whatever presses men together ... , though it may generate some vices, is favourable to the diffusion of knowledge, and ultimately promotive of human liberty. Hence, every large workshop and manufactory is a sort of political society which no Act of Parliament can silence and no magistrate disperse.'[151]

What gave Thelwall comfort was likely to have the opposite effect on most propertied people. Whether in town or country it was believed that lower-class manners were changing for the worse. Politics and public morality were closely related. Riots could be connected with a decline in religious observance, according to a Leeds Dissenter, Joseph Ryder, when he witnessed the Yorkshire turnpike riots of 1753.[152] The agitation against popular recreations, especially wakes and feasts, owed much to a conviction that 'the profligacy and insolence of the lower class are risen to a very alarming pitch'.[153] Some onlookers were intrigued to note the mixture of fear and condescension with which prosperous townsfolk were coming to view their inferiors. The Durham clergyman Samuel Viner was impressed by the grandeur of the Mayor of Newcastle's Feast in 1783, but dismayed by the precautions which had to be taken on the occasion. 'The Iron barrier to prevent even in the Dining Room of the Chief Magistrate the rude intrusion of Servants seems to shew the tumultuous and ungovernable state of the lower Class of people.'[154] The growing readiness of corporate bodies to act firmly when confronted with rowdiness was a source of comfort. At Whitby the refusal of Quakers to join in public rejoicings by illuminating their windows was traditionally the occasion of much broken glass. But during the coronation festivities of 1761, one of their number, Isaac Richardson, recorded a remarkable change in this respect. 'The rulers of the town took more care to keep the rabble in subjection than they had ever done before, and my neighbours, who aforetime had been ready to laugh at me, and to make light of my sufferings, showed me kindness, and assisted in dispersing the rude people, so that through the mercy of Providence, I suffered little damage.'[155]

There were losses as well as gains. The antiquarian John Brand lamented the passing of an urban culture which had permitted high and low to

---

[150] York Minster Library, Hailstone MSS., KK 14: Case of Woollen Manufactures, 1794.

[151] C. Cestre, *John Thelwall: A Pioneer of Democracy and Social Reform in England during the French Revolution* (London, 1906), p. 187.

[152] H. McLachlan, 'Diary of a Leeds Layman, 1733–1768', *Trans. Unitarian Soc.* 4 (1927–30), 261.

[153] *British Chronicle*, 15 July 1779.

[154] Gloucestershire RO, D 2227/30: Journal of Revd Samuel Viner.

[155] *Records of a Quaker Family: The Richardsons of Cleveland* (London, 1889), p. 17.

mingle without any sense of threat to either. There had been a time in
Newcastle when the corporation 'used to unbend the brow of Authority
and partake, with their happy and contented People, the puerile pleasures
of the festal Season'.[156] Sentiment aside, it was inconvenient not to have
dependable means of expressing popular loyalty to the powers that be. In
the 1790s loyalist societies and Volunteer troops were mustered to mount
suitably convincing demonstrations. Before that the militia, when it happened to be embodied, had its ceremonial uses. George III's new-found
enthusiasm for holidaying in Dorset in the 1780s created some problems
in this respect. *In extremis*, it was necessary to resort to the ubiquitous
mutual benefit clubs, some of which had undesirable associations in the
minds of employers. At Sherborne in August 1789 the King and Queen
were greeted by the local friendly and union societies, parading with colours
and music. The newspaper report on the occasion was tinged with relief.
'Their appearance seemed to give general satisfaction, and they conducted
themselves with the utmost regularity and decorum.'[157] No doubt one of
the reasons for the friendly society legislation of 1793 was the desirability
of legitimizing forms of association which were adequately supervised.

Some observers accepted that the lower sort might find it harder to bear
the social injustices to which they were subjected. Nottingham's address
to its MPs during the riots of 1766 observed that 'the luxurious profusion
of the great, and the comfortable way of life enjoyed by those of middle
rank, gives a keen edge to the real calamities of the poor, and pushes them
into acts of destructive violence. They think there is no law, divine or
human, to oblige them to starve in the midst of plenty.'[158] Historians have
been reluctant to discern an authentically levelling spirit in the food riot
of the eighteenth century, but propertied people at the time were not
always so charitable. According to Hannah Darby, the daughter of a great
Shropshire ironmaster, the colliers who rose in protest against bread prices
in 1756 made no attempt to conceal their intentions. 'The mob gave
themselves the title of levelers, and so they were indeed.'[159] The 'levelling'
which went on in enclosure riots, for instance near Banbury in 1765,
doubtless had a deliberate ambiguity about it.[160]

In one sense what matters is not the real intention of rioters, but the
propensity of their betters to glimpse an anti-propertied impulse in any
form of popular protest. These apprehensions were often expressed by

---

[156] *Observations on Popular Antiquities* (Newcastle-upon-Tyne, 1777), pp. 252–3.
[157] *Notes and Queries for Somerset and Dorset*, 4 (1894–5), 156–7.
[158] *London Magazine* (1766), 589.
[159] E. P. Thompson, 'The Moral Economy of the English Crowd in the Eighteenth Century', *Past and Present*, 50 (1971), 127–8; E. Greg, *Reynolds–Rathbone Diaries and Letters 1753–1839* (London, 1905), p. 185.
[160] *London Magazine* (1765), 486.

middle-class men and women as much as by authentic representatives of the gentry. This, on its own, was sufficient to inaugurate a new era of tension in class relations. There is no doubting the signs of disintegration in the old, comfortable concept of a natural hierarchy, in which fatherly authority could readily take the strain of occasional, child-like tantrums on the part of the lower orders. Here indeed was no hierarchy, but two nations divided by property, as John Brown put it in 1765.[161] Few illusions were entertained about the mentality of the unpropertied. Thus William Smith, physician and prison reformer expressed it: 'The indigent are fitted in all respects for sedition and tumult; they are conscious of their low estates, and hope to better themselves in the scramble.'[162] Such anxieties drew on well-established fears, including the belief that even educated people without property were a public danger. Generations of Jacobites had been warned against the blandishments of Jesuit priests with the argument that men who were permitted to own nothing of their own would be only too glad to ruin what others enjoyed.[163] It was not reasonable to expect a superior sense of responsibility from the uneducated, and even the time-honoured slogan 'Liberty and Property' lost its plausibility in the mouths of a mob. Part of the peculiar importance of the Gordon Riots was that they demonstrated this with such force. It was suggested in the press that 'no property' would have been a more suitable cry for the Protestant Association than 'no popery'. 'Never did property seem less safe than while the Country has been for some days governed by an English mob.'[164] Had he lived twelve years longer to witness the events of 1780 the old Duke of Newcastle would surely have regretted his boast.

Yet the rhetoric of rights continued to unite the two nations. It was thereby a source of endless embarrassment to the propertied class. The liberty of the propertied subject was not at all the same as the liberty of the unpropertied subject. Naval impressment, a notoriously sensitive issue, applied only to the latter. When accidentally used to enlist the former, it produced an awkward kind of outrage. Yet there was little interest in conceding genuine equality of treatment. Indeed the very claim to equality was viewed with extreme misgivings, not least in the context of the poor law. There was no status lower than that of poor men and women compelled to enter a workhouse. Yet they often behaved as if they too had the full rights of their compatriots. This was particularly true of those who, in conformity with approved doctrine, helped support themselves in parish care with their own earnings. The vestry clerk of South Mimms in

---

[161] *Thoughts on Civil Liberty, on Licentiousness and Faction* (Newcastle, 1765), pp. 108–15.

[162] William Smith, *The Student's Vade Mecum* (London, 1770), p. 67.

[163] W. Beaumont, ed., *The Jacobite Trials at Manchester in 1694* (Chetham Soc. 28, 1853), p. 103.

[164] *Whitehall Evening-Post*, 29 June 1780; E. W. Harcourt, ed., *The Harcourt Papers* (14 vols., Oxford, 1876–1905), xi. 261.

Middlesex complained bitterly of his charges in 1760. 'No Person is Able to Do any thin' with them—for to say any thing to them is All in Vain— for they all Earne their Own Living and Thinck that the Parish is behouden to them and Divers of the Weemen Thinck that they are very hard done by to be Confined to their Spining.'[165] The idea that workhouse inmates might decline to think of themselves as prisoners was shocking. Henry Fielding, defending his proposed Middlesex county workhouse, equated the liberty of the 'lowest people' with that of 'begging and stealing, of robbing and cutting Throats', and described criticisms of the restraints on their freedom as 'enthusiastical' and inconsistent with all order and government.[166] Arthur Young, appalled by the refusal of the incarcerated poor to spend their slender earnings prudently, was even more dismayed to find that they insisted on their right to exercise. At Nacton in Suffolk, he noted, they were unreasonably disgusted by their confinement. 'They are not allowed constant liberty without the yards (which indeed would be impossible) and this they dislike.'[167]

A high priority was to redefine the liberty of those whose social status condemned them to second-class treatment, whether in the form of impressment in the navy or immurement in a poorhouse. Richard Watson, in his day a reformer of some renown, was dismayed at the lack of understanding which they displayed. 'The common people were, in every village, talking about liberty and equality without understanding the terms.'[168] Jonas Hanway was more specific.

The sons of Britons are all born to liberty; but I am sorry to say, they do not understand what liberty means. If it were the liberty of doing mischief to each other, the *poor* against the rich, it would be full as bad as the *rich* against the poor; for then we should all become miserably poor indeed, and a den of savages. True liberty consists in doing well; in obeying parents, masters, and superiors, who have a title to command us.[169]

Watson and Hanway counted themselves Whigs but the situation which they deplored could be linked with the triumph of Whig ideology, an ethic which taught every member of the community to think in terms of his own rights rather than his social duties. The Jacobite Thomas Carte considered that he had seen in his lifetime a decisive change in this respect, as the traditional bonds of unity and hierarchy dissolved in a corrosive mixture of individualism and commercialism. The people, he remarked in 1742, had become a 'loose Multitude, a Rope of Sand, and are to be considered

---

[165] F. Brittain, *South Mymms* (Cambridge, 1931), p. 59.
[166] Battestin, *Henry Fielding: A Life*, p. 568.
[167] *The Farmer's Tour through the East of England*, ii. 181.
[168] *Anecdotes of the Life of Richard Watson, Bishop of Llandaff* (London, 1817), p. 270.
[169] *Moral and Religious Instructions*, p. xliii.

only as so many Individuals, or single persons'.[170] It was this that made them so difficult to direct and unify, not least for the Tory gentlemen who might have led them in a heroic mission to restore the Stuarts. Carte was particularly concerned by the destruction of military tenures and the failure of the State to replace them with an alternative social cement, but his argument had more general application. In the late eighteenth century it came to be something of a commonplace, which commercially minded Whigs could adopt as readily as patriarchal Tories. It seemed the characteristic of a multitude corrupted by the growth of luxury, that it would come to describe its lusts as its liberties.[171] The political consequences must be grave indeed.

THE MIDDLE STATE

In a modern society fears of a mounting crisis in social relations, not to say an impending loss of political stability, would result in demands for action by the State. But the eighteenth century had no models for such action acceptable to a libertarian tradition inherently suspicious of all government. There was, however, a growing conviction that the remedy, whatever it might be, lay with the broad mass of property-owners. It was an old idea that true virtue began and perhaps ended with the middle ranks of society. As Swift expressed it, they were neither lured from the path of virtue by ambition, nor driven from it by poverty.[172] Moralists who subscribed to a more optimistic view of human nature than Swift could accept the same conclusion from different premises. Bishop Butler considered them the repositary of 'natural morality', 'free from the Vices of the highest and the lowest Part of Mankind'.[173] He shared this position, if little else, with Mary Wollstonecraft, who considered middle-class men and women the most 'natural', that is the least spoiled of the human race.[174] Long-standing faith in the golden mean and the virtues of moderation could be summoned up in support. There was also much emphasis on the material sufficiency which guaranteed an independence not attainable by the poor. As John Brown put it, 'Their *imaginary* Wants are *fewer* than those of the *Poor*: Hence Their Appetites are less inflamed to Evil.'[175] The resulting faith in middle-class merit was an almost unchallengeable platitude. William Whitehead, as Poet Laureate in the early years of George III a fitting

---

[170] *A Full Answer to the Letter from a By-Stander* (London, 1742), p. 200.

[171] Thomas Bedford, *The Origin of Our Grievances: A Sermon* (London, 1770), p. 18.

[172] In the *Drapier Letters*, quoted by I. Ehrenpreis, *Swift: The Man, His Works, and the Age*, vol. iii: Dean Swift (London, 1983), pp. 290–1.

[173] *Fifteen Sermons Preached at the Rolls Chapel* (London, 1749), p. 349.

[174] B. R. Pollin, *Education and Enlightenment in the Works of William Godwin* (New York, 1962), p170.

[175] *Thoughts on Civil Liberty, on Licentiousness and Faction*, p. 112.

mouthpiece for all that was most banal in contemporary thought, solemnly advised his readers: 'One rule remains. Nor shun nor court the great, Your truest center is the middle state.'[176] The rage for politeness, a code of manners designed for a commercial society, perfectly fitted the aspirations of the middle state and was closely identified with it. John Harris, author of a tract on the function of the code, put the point clearly: politeness 'beholds the monarch without trembling, its superiors without servility, and looks upon its inferiors without contempt'.[177]

Intriguing comparisons were made with the bourgeoisie abroad. Travellers in eastern Europe gloomily reported the absence of 'that respectable, intelligent, and opulent part of a nation, a middle class, the pride and glory of an Empire'. When they did find it they noted that it was 'less prejudiced, more liberal, and more intelligent than the landed gentry'.[178] But in Britain, not only was it virtuous: it was increasingly powerful. 'The dignity and honour of this kingdom is now entirely supported by the *middling class* of people', it was argued on the eve of the War of American Independence.[179] Above all, if used in a properly co-ordinated way, nothing would withstand it. As Robert Wallace put it, 'in Britain the voice of the middle ranks among the people has a mighty influence. These are always the last to be corrupted. In their integrity and activity there is a grand resource.'[180] In such claims, there could be discerned the pretensions of a new ruling class, equipped with a sense of its moral superiority and confidence in its strength. The path to power was not easy, however. It was a recognized paradox that the forces which were extending the influence of the middle-class Englishman also threatened his moral welfare. That same luxury which had sapped the virtue of the landed classes held dangers for those who claimed the right to replace them as natural rulers. The political turbulence of the 1760s seemed to suggest that this was precisely what was happening. Advocates of commercialism were anxious to defend its record in this respect; the poet William Julius Mickle argued that the probity of the middle class was itself evidence that commerce had an ennobling effect.

Mankind, it may be said, are liable to be corrupted, and wealth affords the opportunity. But this axiom will greatly mislead us from the line of truth if taken in a general sense. The middle rank of men is infinitely more virtuous than the lowest. Profligacy of manners is not therefore the natural consequence of affluence, it is the accident which attends the vulgar mind in whatever external situation. And when vulgar minds are preferred to the high offices of church and state, it is

---

[176] *A Charge to the Poets* (London, 1762), p. 22.
[177] John Harris, *An Essay on Politeness* (Dublin, 1776), p. 21.
[178] Pollin, *Education and Enlightenment in the Works of William Godwin*, p. 171; Pettigrew, *Memoirs of the Life and Writings of the Late John Coakley Lettsom*, ii. 311.
[179] *London Magazine* (1774), 568.
[180] *Characteristics of the Present Political State of Great Britain* (London, 1758), p. 232.

the negligence, or wickedness of government, and not the increase of wealth, which is the source of national corruption.[181]

Mickle's faith in middle-class virtue was certainly impressive, surviving as it did a searching investigation of that most tarnished of commercial concerns, the East India Company, on which he was an expert. It was shared by others. In 1779 when commercialism was being blamed for the disasters which beset Britain during the American War William Temple had the temerity to insist, on the contrary, that without luxury, 'All the knowledge, principle, activity, industry, that enlighten and dignify the middle class of people, would presently disappear and be supplanted by ignorance, servility and sloth.'[182] But not everyone was reassured. Hannah More warned of the consequences of prosperity: 'This rapid revolution of manners of the middle class has so far altered the character of the age, as to be in danger of rendering obsolete the heretofore common saying, "that most worth and virtue are to be found in the middle station".'[183] Here was a great mission: the middle-class Englishman must save society from the evils which beset it, and redeem himself at the same time. What more was needed to inspire the crusade for regeneration of a failing social system?

Cleansing middle-class life of its vestigial impurities was a pre-condition of victory in this cause. Standard assumptions about the nature of virtue more or less excluded demeaning vocations and trades. Landed property traditionally owed much of its prestige to the safeguard which it provided against the narrow concerns of a tradesman's life. In the early eighteenth century it remained politically profitable, at least in some contexts, to exploit propertied distaste for the covetousness and corruption 'unalterably chain'd to tradesmen'.[184] Thereafter it became necessary to exercise caution. In terms of snobbery the prejudice against trade remained powerful. On the other hand it had to be reconciled with lip-service to the acknowledged value of commerce. In 1770 Charles Jenner gently satirized the resulting ambivalence in a conversation between two genteel ladies. 'To be sure one is apt to talk in that way of one's tradesfolks; and yet trade is a very good thing ... only let them keep their own places; particularly the lower class.'[185]

For purposes of State it was not so easy to declare the utility of keeping tradesmen in their places. Even the most passionate defenders of Harrington's Utopia drew a distinction between legitimate commerce and

---

[181] *The Lusiad; Or, the Discovery of India* (Oxford, 1771), p. civ.

[182] W. J. Temple, *Moral and Historical Memoirs* (London, 1779), p. 36.

[183] *The Works of Hannah More* (8 vols., London, 1801), vii. 75: 'Strictures on the Modern System of Female Education'.

[184] *A Preface to the History of the Ale Sellers at Boston in Lincolnshire* (London, 1721), p. 4. For an interpretation of attitudes towards trade and tradesmen which differs radically from what follows, arguing for a marked shift from favourable to hostile tendencies in mid-century, see J. McVeagh, *Tradefull Merchants: The Portrayal of the Capitalist in Literature* (London, 1981).

[185] *The Placid Man; Or, Memoirs of Sir Charles Beville* (2nd edn., 2 vols., London, 1773), ii. 130.

illegitimate money-jobbing, between honest trade and ignoble usury. None the less there remained a certain amount of adapting to be done. It was a task which the writers of the sentimental school of the 1760s and 1770s were very ready to undertake. They found appreciative readers when they emphasized the compatibility, indeed the harmony, between trade as a vocation and virtue in its practitioners. Edmund Rack, a faithful weather-vane of propertied opinion, spoke freely of 'men of refined taste and sentiment, who are engaged in the bustle of commercial life'.[186] At Bristol James Thistlethwaite offered as a model of virtue 'a tradesman, a member of society, an honest man and a christian'.[187] The new vogue for sentiment provided an appropriate vehicle for such arguments: sentiment carried with it a concept of gentility accessible to all who had wealth enough to aspire to politeness. The code of honour was assimilated to the cult of feeling.

Even sentiment had its dangers. Like old-fashioned virtue it could be contaminated by the pursuit of material goods, certainly by a life spent in buying and selling them. One contemporary of Rack and Thistlethwaite, and like them a literary hack living off a middle-class readership, fell headlong into this trap. William Combe came from impeccably honourable, if not quite landed origins. But he frittered away a substantial patrimony and by his later twenties had only his upbringing and education (Eton and Oxford) to boast. Perhaps it was this which impelled him to argue that the benefits of sentiment could be enjoyed only by men of leisure. He had the temerity to make this claim during a period of residence in Thistlethwaite's Bristol, the second city of the empire, and a home of commercial vigour and mercantile snobbery alike. Combe publicly blessed Heaven that he was not a man of merchandise, a blessing which he was subsequently compelled to retract in favour of a plea that he had meant only to condemn those who unworthily allowed gross materialism to overcome their finer feelings. 'I know many who are engaged in the trading and gainful professions ... on whom nature has written gentleman in such legible characters.'[188]

Combe's blunder would not have been perpetrated by a native Bristolian. In his *Bristollia* of 1749 the antiquarian Andrew Hooke had staunchly insisted that "'tis the Merchant that is the true practical Philosopher'.[189] Yet it was precisely in great cities such as Bristol that educated outsiders were likely to be most disturbed by the unenlightened attitudes of those engaged in business. An Oxonian poet marooned in Newcastle confessed to disgust at the frenzy, ambition, and party which prevailed on a 'commercial

---

[186] *Essays, Letters, and Poems* (Bath, 1781), p. 401.

[187] Henry Burgum, *A Narrative of Facts* (Bristol, 1775), p. 6.

[188] H. W. Hamilton, *Doctor Syntax: A Silhouette of William Combe, Esq. (1742–1823)* (London, 1969), pp. 39, 42.

[189] (London, 1749), p. 4.

Tyne'.[190] Trailing around the towns of the Midlands, the actor Samuel Ryley felt compelled to subscribe to the impression that trade 'is a grand enemy to the social and moral virtues'. Like Combe, Ryley was prepared to make exceptions, but exceptions which proved the rule. 'I would not, by this philippic, infer, that *all* men of business are thus depraved—God forbid! There are, to my narrow knowledge, men in trade who are an honor to their country and themselves; but they are as one to a thousand.'[191] Yet the challenge had to be faced, not least because the readership available in such places brought writers their bread. At Manchester in 1777 Thomas Bancroft somewhat rhetorically enquired whether 'the gross breath of Commerce has tinctur'd the gale?' only to conclude reassuringly that in fact tradesmen were perfect patriots.[192]

The previous generation had paid much attention to this matter. In *The Romance of a Night* John Cleland had his hero, son of a clergyman and clerk in a Lisbon trading house, succeed to a peerage, thanks to an unlikely sequence of deaths in his family. Most readers would have expected the Lord Veramore who thus stepped forth in ermine to make an inappropriate peer of the realm. On the contrary, wrote Cleland, 'his commercial employment had, instead of contracting his views, greatly inlarged them. He had in that noble factory personally learnt how compatible the profession of a merchant is with the greatest, and even the politest life.'[193] Veramore's training was significant. It was not uncommon for merchants, particularly those engaged in overseas trade, to rise to great office in a corporation, or even to present themselves as legislators. But there remained an assumption that the mere occupation of a businessman, however necessary, and however compatible with Christian living, placed its practitioners at a considerable disadvantage when virtuous statesmen were called for.

This view was often adopted by men who themselves were at best on a par with wealthy traders. Professional men—clergymen, army officers, even in some cases lawyers and physicians—liked to think that they were unsullied by the materialism of life in a middle station. Humbug of this kind was all the easier to indulge in when, as so often, they mixed with families of rank. The patina of gentility rubbed off on them, it seemed, in a way impossible for tradesmen who dealt only indirectly with the great. This notion, too, had to be combated if propertied Englishmen as a class were to be made fit to govern. Like John Cleland, Edward Kimber had his hero Joe Thomson set out on a life of trade. His father had rejected the Church, the army, and the law as careers, not for want of money and openings, but because they were less compatible with integrity and

[190] John Brand, *On Illicit Love* (Newcastle, 1775), p. 4.
[191] S. W. Ryley, *The Itinerant* (9 vols., London, 1808–27), i. 269–70.
[192] *The Poetical Correspondent* (Manchester, 1777), p. 5.
[193] *The Surprises of Love* (2nd edn., London, 1765), pp. 79–81.

enlightenment. 'I have the utmost veneration for merchants and traders, who diffuse the blessings of commerce and traffick to every individual, and are the upholders and supports of the interest and independency of this nation. In all other callings I have mentioned, there is a degree of servility and meanness, necessary to a man who would be eminent, that I, by no means, would make necessary to you. By trade, you will preserve a generous independency, if you act wisely and prudently; and will become a useful and valuable member of the common-wealth, and an advantage to your friends and relations.'[194]

This emphasis on independence, normally associated with the landed proprietor, and the reference to friends and relations, usually the bene-ficiaries of men with patronage at their disposal, would have surprised many readers and pleased not a few. Cleland did not hesitate to stress the relationship between businesslike habits and independence. 'Remember that Independence is the beautiful and legitimate Daughter of Industry and Oeconomy. The first shall procure, the second preserve thee an honourable Property.'[195] The point was hardly profound. Countless self-made men knew the power bestowed by wealth. 'If you have it,' as a harassed young insurance clerk remarked, 'you are out of its power.'[196] But it was not just a question of riches. It was possible to argue that the complexity of modern society had created ever more opportunities for the exercise of authentic independence. As John Millar pointed out, moneyed men, for all their unpopularity, lived off their interest and depended on nobody for their welfare. Merchants and traders were no less self-reliant; they had so many customers that none was in position to extract a favour or enforce his will. Even farmers, in theory the pawns of their landlords, were in practice the masters of great capital: many of them were able to insist on long leases which gave them effective independence. All such men were enfranchised by the economic conditions of the day. 'In proportion as they have less need of the favour and patronage of the great, they are at less pains to procure it.'[197]

The social consequences were not necessarily pleasing. Deference to betters was replaced by arrogance and defiance. More telling still, inferiors could be treated with condescension and insolence. Millar was no sen-timentalist, and he had a shrewd eye for the new abrasiveness which marked middle-class attitudes. Others, less plausibly, sought comfort in the mutual dependence of commercial society. As the educationalist John Ash put it, 'Labour and traffic may ... be considered as the common, and, perhaps,

---

[194] *The Life and Adventures of Joe Thompson: A Narrative Founded in Fact* (London, 1783, originally 1750), p. 23.
[195] *The Oeconomy of a Winter's Day* (London, n.d.), p. 8.
[196] Black, ed., *The Cumberland Letters*, p. 147.
[197] *Observations Concerning the Distinction of Ranks in Society* (London, 1771) p. 185.

the most indissoluble band of civil society. It unites the high to the low, the great and the small, the rich and the poor together, and renders them all, in a manner, dependent on each other. My tailor, my shoemaker, my chimney sweeper, my most menial servant, is not more dependent on me than I on him.' It was the function of Ash, of coure, like Cleland and Kimber before him, to provide the patriarchs of urban society with an image of themselves which flattered if it did not deceive. Like the landed paternalist he needed to be congratulated on his benevolence, not merely acknowledged for his power.[198]

Perhaps he also needed reassuring about the stability of the world in which he lived. Most enthusiasts for trade preferred to ignore its less comfortable consequences, and concentrate on the benefits. It was easy to assume that success in business life required a certain minimum of integrity, if only because a reputation for dishonesty or unreliability would drive away customers. William Hickey remarked almost casually that his acquaintance James Grant could be trusted in view of 'his situation in life as a merchant, a West India agent, and citizen of London, of course everything depending upon his moral character and conduct in life'.[199] In this respect expectations of landed men might be much lower. Commerce also commanded a degree of politeness. In the Potteries Bishop Pococke was delighted by the civility which he encountered and associated it with the manners of people who depended for their livelihood on salesmanship. 'There is such a face of industry in all ages and degrees of people, and so much civility and obliging behaviour, as they look on all that come among them as customers.' In Aldeburgh, James Ford thought the tradesmen of the town 'fair, civil and obliging, without any of that wretched and obsequious servility, too frequently met with in what is called *genteel life*'.[200] Others confessed to unreasoning faith in the creed of commerce. Henry Brooke's celebrated encomium in *The Fool of Quality* entailed no serious argument. It was simply an appeal to industry and commerce as 'the natural, the living, the never-failing fountains, from whence the wealth of this world can alone be taught to flow'.[201] The international possibilities of unfettered commerce were also beginning to feature in complacent reflections on its benign influence. The Dissenting divine William Wood described it in 1781 as a 'social chain which surrounds the globe, and was intended to bind all its inhabitants into one harmonious body'.[202] Wood's lifetime unhappily

[198] *Sentiments on Education, Collected from the Best Writers* (2 vols., London, 1777), i. 222.

[199] A. Spencer, ed., *Memoirs of William Hickey* (10th edn., 4 vols., London, 1948), ii. 355.

[200] Cartwright, ed., *The Travels through England of Dr Richard Pococke*, i. 8; *Aldborough Described* (Ipswich, [1820]), p. 61.

[201] Ed. E. A. Baker (London, 1906), pp. 25–7.

[202] Charles Wellbeloved, *Memoirs of the Life and Writings of the Rev. W. Wood* (London, 1809), pp. 22–3.

coincided with a series of devastating world wars, in which commercial ambitions were prominent. His explanation was that the spirit of commerce had been abused and prostituted. William Hazeland, a Tottenham school-master and winner of a Cambridge essay prize on the subject in 1756, ignored the difficulties and credited commerce with achieving economic progress while ensuring social stability. The contrast which he drew with the effects of primogeniture in land inheritance was particularly ingenious. Commerce, it seemed, was a kind of gavelkind. 'A free and open trade operates, like a Kentish yeomanry, distributing the patrimony alike among all its children, enriches a whole posterity, and gives none of them an opportunity to oppress and ruin the rest.'[203]

Not everyone was reassured. It was possible to have too much even of so good a thing as independence, especially if there was a danger of commercial growth liberating everyone from the bonds of an older eco-nomic system. Some commentators were not afraid to link the most prized of all political values with disorder and even anarchy. 'Nothing', wrote William Smith in the wake of the Wilkesite disturbances, 'makes man break out into greater irregularities than supposed equality or independency, which licentious supposition tends to eradicate society, to introduce con-fusion and anarchy, to justify rapaciousness and brutal force.'[204] It was not simply because it was so platitudinous, even vacuous an ideal, that independence could be given an egalitarian turn. Employed in natural rights theory as the expression of every man's liberty rather than some men's property it took on a disquieting significance. It was, after all, the advocate of equal rights for women, who described it as the 'grand blessing of life, the basis of every virtue'.[205]

Hence, no doubt, the anxiety to rediscover the silver lining in the cloud of dependence. Oliver Goldsmith thought a life without independence debased, but 'I would not be thought to include those natural or political subordinations which subsist in every society, for in such, tho' dependance is exacted from the inferior, yet the obligation on either side is mutual'.[206] Hence, too, the assertion that a commercial society offered a form of distributive justice more satisfying than primitive forms of social organ-ization. Slavery, for instance, was condemned on precisely these grounds—not because it represented an outmoded, patriarchal system, but because it conflicted with the commercial chain of being. Thus Peter Wilkins recommended to King Georigetti of Sass Doorpt Swangeanti the intro-duction of western arts and manufactures. 'Those who were before your

[203] William Hazeland, *A View of the Manner in Which Trade and Civil Liberty Support Each Other* (London, 1756), p. 13.

[204] *The Student's Vade Mecum*, p. 61.

[205] Quoted by K. M. Rogers, *Feminism in Eighteenth-Century England* (Brighton, 1982), p. 184.

[206] *Collected Works of Oliver Goldsmith*, ii. 397.

slaves shall then take it as an honour to be employed by you, and at the same time shall employ others dependent on them; so as the great and small shall be under mutual obligations to each other, and both to the truly industrious artificer; and yet everyone content only with what he merits.'[207] Behind this comforting camouflage lay a simple truth. Independence, having ceased to be the exclusive prerogative of the landed gentry, was none the less to be restricted to men of substance. How could it be otherwise? If social relations were ultimately about the exercise of power, the eighteenth century was not squeamish in acknowledging the nature of such power. The same men who cried up the virtues of independence ruthlessly enforced the dependence of others. The first gave them self-respect, no doubt; the second gave them authority in the eyes of their equals. In practice very few, even among the propertied, were truly free of all obligations: but this merely intensified the scramble to make dependants of others. Such was the solace of countless middle-class men, whether in trade or the professions, who recognized yet resented their limited liberty in a hierarchical society. Tightening the chains of those who depended on them was a natural response. But the ambiguity of their own position could be painful.

The clergy who were called upon to deputize for gentry well understood this agonizing dilemma. They frequently owed their preferment to a lay patron; yet 'they expected and were expected in some measure to assume the role of parochial potentate. Unfortunately, if landed gentlemen were often glad to delegate their power, they did not always wish to abdicate it altogether. The result could be frustrating for those caught between lordly patrons and truculent parishioners. Such was the well-recorded plight of the young clergyman Richard Cumberland, who found himself in possession of two small Cotswold livings. His patron Thomas Smith was absent a good deal in London and Bath, and Cumberland fancied himself viceroy of this little realm. Not only did he set about 'improving' the tithes of his parish in line with the true value of land: he also demanded deference from tenants and their labourers alike. But neither his tithe demands nor his patronizing ways went down well, and he found himself engaged in some embarrassing tussles. Secure, as he thought, in Smith's goodwill, Cumberland was staggered by Smith's enraged reaction in front of his farmers. 'Mr Smith's change of sentiments and treatment of me before men, by whom I once wished to be respected and was till *then*, affected me beyond description and in spight of my Pride I found it difficult to restrain my Tears.' In a fearful scene at dinner in a neighbour's house, 'he flew into the most violent passion and before a Company of 8 or 9 people called me to the most severe

---

[207] Robert Paltock, *The Life and Adventures of Peter Wilkins, a Cornish Man* (London, 1783, originally 1750), p. 164.

Account and abused me in Terms of authority, mixed with such looks as I shall never forget.' Smith subsequently admitted that the demand for higher tithes was reasonable. What could explain his strange conduct? wondered Cumberland. 'I comforted myself after all with the Hope that Mr Smith's behaviour was only meant to humble me a little and make me feel my Dependence.' Eventually he was allowed to enjoy a little brief authority on Smith's terms. It did not prove an altogether gratifying experience. 'Feasting my farmers', planning a school of industry, and suchlike parochial concerns occupied his time, but the sheer tedium of parish government proved irksome. Ironically Smith himself, despite his landowner's pedigree, was actually a surgeon at St Thomas's Hospital in London, and rarely mixed in Gloucestershire society. Smith and Cumberland were collaborators and competitors in a society where the relationship between property and power was undeniable but complex. Calming the resulting tensions could be painful.[208]

The main consolation for a man in Cumberland's position was the pleasure of patronizing inferiors. Parish clergy were well placed to relish it. The antiquarian William Cole, who was the incumbent of a Buckinghamshire living, saw himself as the benevolent despot of his community, and like Cumberland was infuriated when his will was challenged. Cole was a High Churchman and a Tory, Cumberland a convinced Whig. But in this respect there was little to choose between them. Lecturing the farmers on their duties, dining them in condescending style on Sundays, meticulously enforcing their tithe obligations, all formed part of the duties of one who was more patriarch than pastor. The resulting authority could be paraded to impress one's superiors as well as deployed against one's inferiors. When the Chancellor of Lincoln, a great dignitary in Cole's diocese, called on him, 'I chose to be among my Hay People, it being a particular Pleasure and Amusement to me'.[209] Tactics of this kind naturally varied according to personality and position. Richard Hind, a clerical bully whose career was marked by persistent controversy, systematically snubbed the self-made manufacturers who were so prominent among his Rochdale parishioners in the 1780s. If he got away with his overbearing manners, it was because Rochdale was large and denominational life diverse. It was only in his own mind that he was the uncrowned sovereign of the town.[210] More typically, clergy dreaded having to deal with propertied congregations. To be the incumbent of a parish with none above the rank of a petty constable was a blessing.[211]

[208] Black, ed., *The Cumberland Letters*, pp. 197, 198, 200.

[209] F. G. Stokes, ed., *The Blecheley Diary of the Rev. William Cole, 1765–67* (London, 1931), p. 68.

[210] H. Howorth, ed., *The Vicars of Rochdale by Rev. Canon Raines*, vol. ii (Chetham Soc., NS 2, 1883), p. 242.

[211] Evans, ed., *Letters of Richard Radcliffe and John James of Queen's College, Oxford, 1755–83*, p. 40; the parish in this case was Holwell in Dorset.

Even the lowest clergy felt fitted by education and vocation to exercise a measure of authority. Country gentlemen were expected to do so almost by hereditary instinct. But neither training nor tradition was essential. Early industrialists were aware of the extent to which production depended on wise government of the workforce. A few of them even had the opportunity to create new communities, and seized it with enthusiasm. Richard Arkwright's celebrated establishment at Cromford was an experiment in industrial paternalism as well as in technological innovation. It involved elaborate plans for tied houses and cottage gardens, provision of food and services, and indeed everything required to create an orderly society dedicated to efficient management. It was intended to give the impression of more than mere production. Arkwright's elaborate festivals suggested a complete community in which social ease and recreation were to take their place alongside pious industry.[212] Samuel Greg's only slightly less famous works at Styal were inspired by similar ideas, as were William Strutt's at Belper.[213] The thinking was not new. It represented the transfer to a manufacturing environment of concepts taken for granted in settled agricultural communities. The Scottish historian John Ramsay of Ochertyre recorded the mangement of the Leadhills Mining Company by the mathematician James Stirling in terms which almost looked forward to Owenism. Stirling not only gave every encouragement to the intellectual development of his charges, but even attempted to provide them with a system of welfare in some measure controlled by themselves. 'Nowhere, from every account, did strict discipline and subordination appear less burdensome and grievous than at Leadhills where the gentleman presided with dignity and benignity.'[214] Further back still the great Crowley ironworks at Sunderland had been run on the basis of an elaborate rule book which codified the best practices of the most paternalistic employer.[215]

The need for industrial paternalism seemed obvious. For Ramsay, Stirling was an honourable exception. 'I have lived in times when all ranks of men have been changing their modes and manners and sentiments, some for the better, and others for the worse. During my course there have been new maxims laid down by proprietors and men of business which sounded to me harsh, precipitate and unpolitic.'[216] Ramsay was not alone in this belief. Dr Parr was dismayed by the attitudes which he found at Birmingham and urged his hearers there to make their workers 'connect the

[212] R. S. Fitton, *The Arkwrights: Spinners of Fortune* (Manchester, 1989), p. 189.

[213] F. Collier, *The Family Economy of the Working Classes in the Cotton Industry 1784–1833*, ed. R. S. Fitton (Manchester, 1964), ch. 5; C. L. Hacker, 'William Strutt of Derby (1756–1830)', *Derbys. Arch. Jnl.* 80 (1960), 49–70.

[214] A. Allardyce, *Scotland and Scotsmen in the Eighteenth Century* (2 vols., Edinburgh, 1888), ii. 306–16.

[215] M. W. Flinn, ed., *The Law Book of the Crowley Ironworks*, Surtees Soc. 167 (1952).

[216] Allardyce, *Scotland and Scotsmen in the Eighteenth Century*, ii. 384.

idea of a benefactor with that of an employer'.[217] Christopher Anstey satirized what he thought the prevailing mentality in 1780:

> Ah! Well they know that if the Poor
> Were cloth'd and fed, they'd work no more,
> That nothing makes Mankind so good,
> So tractable, as Want of Food,
> And like those frugal Politicans
> Who take their Maxims from Physicians,
> Think Starving is the best Foundation
> Of popular Subordination.[218]

This was certainly not the way the new paternalists saw themselves. Nor would it have been prudent of them if they had. In an urban setting as in the countryside, it was advantageous to cultivate a suitably patriarchal image. In electoral literature the benevolent businessman was an increasingly familiar figure, regardless of his political views. The reformer Major Cartwright, who owned the Revolution Mill in Retford, was presented to electors as 'The Man of the Mill' in terms which could equally well have applied to the arch Tory Arkwright.[219] Some candidates came with testimonials from their workforce. When Thomas Nash contested Coventry in 1768 he published the approval of his employees at his linen factory at Lambeth.

It is impossible to express his kindness to us all. Our wives and children work under him, as well as ourselves. He purchases coal and other necessaries for us in large quantities, and lets us have them at the cost price, which is a great benefit to us. He cloathes our children once a year; in the last year he cloathed above fifty of them from top to toe, and has given many of them shoes and stockings since.

Nash's workers were evidently well informed. They were able to report that when he had been fined by the Merchant Taylors Company for refusing to serve as Master, he explained:

he did not grudge to pay the fine, but he did not like it should be spent in eating and drinking as had been the custom, but he would willingly give them one hundred pounds instead of fifty, if they would divide it amongst the poor members of the company, which was accepted and distributed accordingly.[220]

Nash's opponent, Sir Richard Glyn, a London Alderman, replied in kind, parading his philanthropy in his own ward. He also somewhat lessened the effect of Nash's propaganda by alleging that Nash had been an exporter of

---

[217] Derry, *Dr Parr*, p. 129.

[218] *Speculation; Or, a Defence of Mankind: A Poem* (London, 1780), pp. 48–9.

[219] G. Cartwright, 'Some Cartwright Records', *Trans. Thoroton Soc.* 13 (1909), 131; Cartwright withdrew before the poll in June 1790.

[220] William Reader's 'Chronicle', III: 12 Nov. 1768.

corn, indeed one of those monopolists who had promoted depopulation in the countryside and dearth in the towns.[221] Nash was defeated on the poll.

The paternalism of the employer was not just a weapon in electoral politics. It was patriotic in a more fundamental sense, strengthening the sinews of a nation and breeding a hardy, dependable people. The ultimate object was a transformation of working habits. At Swinton in the North Riding, Arthur Young recorded one ingenious experiment in enlightened patriarchy. The colliers and lead-miners, it was said, were notoriously insolent, ill-disciplined, and 'sturdy' people, who often changed their jobs, drank away their money, and generally proved almost impossible to organize. William Danby, the Swinton landlord and colliery owner, had the idea of 'rendering them more dependant, though at the same time more happy. "If," said he, "I can give these fellows a better notion of a local property and happiness, I shall gain a power over them, which I can easily turn to their good, and the benefit of their families, as well as to my own convenience."' The essence of his scheme was to offer each family a small plot of land for the cultivation of corn and the pasturing of cattle. The results were thought spectacular, not least in emptying the local alehouse.

Those young fellows, who formerly were riotous and debauched, now marry, settle, and become the honest fathers of a laborious and valuable race of children. Nothing is so much desired as a little farm; which, being a reward for industry and sobriety, becomes an incitement to a continued good behaviour: And by this well-concerted conduct, the whole colliery, from being a scene of idleness, insolence, and riot, is converted into a well-ordered and decently-cultivated colony: It is become a seminary of industry; and a source of population.—Great is the merit of being so offended at vicious habits as to determine their eradication,— to project a scheme of reformation, as beneficial to the public as himself,—to conduct it through all the difficulties of overcoming and changing human nature herself—to convert a den of thieves and rascals into honest and industrious subjects;—this was effected by Mr. *Danby*, and without the violence of a *Sixtus*:—he planned with the sagacity of a *Machiavel*, and executed with the humanity of a *Trajan*.[222]

Changing human nature was a high ambition indeed. Young held up for applause the example of James Crofts, who, with Danby's help, was enabled to work twenty out of twenty-four hours. At the colliery he was occupied from midnight to noon. There followed eight hours labour in one of the fields donated by his employer, before a brief respite at 8 p.m. 'The greatest and indeed the only object of his thought was the improvement of the wilds that surround him.' A public subscription was launched for Crofts, Young's publisher helpfully providing a list of correspondents with whom donations might be lodged. Paradoxically, the object of the subscription

---

[221] Ibid. 118, 121.
[222] *A Six Months Tour through the North of England*, ii. 261–4.

was to buy Crofts out of Danby's mine, and enable him to set up on his own. No doubt a paragon who had so strikingly justified his master's confidence deserved the ultimate reward of true rather than false independence.[223]

FRIENDS AND BENEFACTORS

Few employers had the resources to imitate Arkwright and Darby, or even Glyn and Nash. Nor did the evidence of crisis in the countryside necessarily impel the complacent town dweller to do more than reflect on the inadequacies of the landed gentry. Yet at his own door he was likely to be witnessing something of a similar emergency. Defenders of cities in the late eighteenth century were not wanting, but the most enthusiastic of them admitted that they generated major problems. At the very least, 'it cannot be denied that where men congregate in large bodies, it gives more scope to the passions than in smaller societies'.[224] It needed no new Hogarth to publicize the manifold vices of life in London, or in the bigger provincial towns. Here, if the challenge was to be met, it must be by a mixture of collective action and individual enterprise. The class which had clearly failed in the country could hardly be expected to succeed in the town. William Moss, a Liverpool surgeon who wrote in 1774 in favour of measures for improving public health, had no illusions on this score. 'The middle (active especially) station of life, is that which seems to assume the more immediate guardianship and protection of the more inferior orders.' The titled and opulent, he thought, had not been educated with the moral burdens of city life in mind; moreover they expected to spend their lives in pursuit of gaiety. The business community was made of sterner stuff in the latter respect, and was more sensitive to the plight of its dependants in the former. The great

too rarely are found to quit the allurement of the gay and fashionable world, for the dull irksome task of exploring the melancholy haunts of the lowest and most miserable of their fellow creatures. But the man of business, and, particularly, that respectable character, the *British Merchant*, from the daily opportunities he has of being sensible of the value and necessity of their services; of being witness to the toils and hardships they daily submit to, to gain by honest industry a pitiful, and that perhaps inadequate, subsistence for themselves and their helpless, suppliant, craving families; has his affections kept awake to their suffering; voluntarily becomes their adviser and patron; and, in their hour of distress, when beset with calamities which humanity in *every* station is heir to—but which become augmented, and doubly aggravated in theirs—he takes upon himself the benevolent

---

[223] *A Six Months Tour through the North of England*, ii. 269, 271.
[224] James Stuart, *Critical Observations on the Buildings and Improvements of London* (London, 1771), p. 42.

office of their guardian, advocate, and protector; and in him the faithful and industrious of the poor never want a friend and benefactor, whatever may befal them.[225]

The prime expression of middle-class determination to control the forces as well as alleviate the suffering created by the expansion of urban society was organized philanthropy. It was a frequent observation of the late eighteenth century that the age was peculiarly one of charitable endeavour. In this as in many other respects posterity has tended to associate with the Victorian era developments which belong equally with its predecessor. One notable tendency was the rejection of the traditional model of the benevolent man as a wealthy individual who left a great fortune to the perpetuation of his own name and the erection of an institutional charity. The early eighteenth century had witnessed some remarkable examples of this type, including John Radcliffe, a celebrated physician and benefactor to his old university of Oxford, Thomas Guy, a printer who left his estate for the foundation of a famous London hospital, and Edward Colston, a merchant who enriched Bristol and not a few other places by his benefactions. There were various objections to the pattern of charity which such men had helped create. One, put with particular disgust by the poet and reformer Thomas Day, was the element of self-glorification which was involved in great benefactions of this kind. 'Proud and ostentatious Charity', designed to immortalize the benefactor, seemed only one remove from the despised pre-Reformation mentality of donations for prayers to save the donor's soul.[226] A second was the suspicion with which corporate and chartered bodies were commonly regarded. One of the reasons for the parliamentary enquiry of 1786 into parish charities was the belief that well-meant money had found its way into unworthy pockets. A third was the limited impact of such bequests. They were likely to be contested by those, especially relations, who thought they had a better claim to benefit. Elizabeth Godolphin's will of 1726, establishing the Godolphin School at Salisbury, was not implemented until 1783 thanks to the obstruction of her family.[227] Most such bequests were made by wealthy men who had no family of their own, and whose altruism was not always appreciated. Colston was criticized for omitting from his will eight nephews and nieces. Of Guy it was said that if he had returned his gains from the sale of South Sea stock to the families who were ruined speculating in it, 'he had raised a monument as much to his glory as the hospital, and added justice to his mercy'.[228] Above

---

[225] *A Familiar Medical Survey of Liverpool: Addressed to the Inhabitants at Large* (Liverpool, 1784), pp. 63–6.

[226] *Select Miscellaneous Productions, of Mrs Day, and Thomas Day, Esq., in verse and Prose* (London, 1805), p. 89.

[227] M. A. Douglas and C. R. Ash, *The Godolphin School 1726–1926* (London, 1928).

[228] *London Magazine* (1752), 514–5.

all the sheer scale of social deprivation required a better co-oidinated campaign and less untypical family circumstances.

It is tempting to associate the unpopularity of the old pattern with conscious change, embodied, for instance, in the Mortmain Act of 1736. The act was designed to make deathbed legacies, more particularly of landed property, virtually impossible. Part of its rationale was the supposedly natural right which sons and daughters were thought to have to the property of their parents. Its effect remains uncertain, but it seems likely that it was itself a product of changing attitudes rather than the cause of them. Perhaps the last great instance of the traditional model of philanthropy occurred a little later when the severe winter of 1740 brought a mass demonstration of charity, in which the well-publicized giving of individuals predominated. *The Open Heart and Purse; Or, British Liberality Display'd* recorded the campaign in detail. It was certainly not lacking in ostentation. For obvious reasons the Prince of Wales's visits to the poor had to be made incognito. But Sir John Chardin, Baronet, 'walked from St Paul's to the Tower, and distributed Money to the Poor all the Way'. Displays of this kind were not repeated in the food shortages of the 1750s and 1760s. The mentality of public giving, the sense of what was appropriate in the charitable manners adopted by polite people was changing markedly. The model was that described in the epitaph of a Dean of Durham, William Digby: 'his charities not ostentatious, but judiciously arranged: a liberal subscriber to everything that tended to publick advantage'.[229]

Liberal subscription was the watchword of the new philanthropists. 'It is an age of charity, and there are already an incredible number of things supported by voluntary subscriptions', declared the advocate of a national academy of music, John Potter, in 1762.[230] The principle had been used extensively by the charity schools and the associated SPG and SPCK. But the mid-eighteenth century was both more secular-minded and more adventurous in this respect. The great London institutions, the Foundling and the Madgalen, as well as the provincial hospital movement, were outstanding instances of a new mode of philanthropy based on the widest possible body of donors. Their founders were not men of great wealth, but relatively humble, if idiosyncratic figures, like Thomas Coram, the champion of the Foundling, and Jonas Hanway, the friend of the infant chimney-sweeps and advocate of many other good causes. They were organizers, not givers.

Certain features of improvement by subscription had a particular bearing

---

[229] L. Digby, *My Ancestors Being the History of the Digby and Strutt Families* (London, 1928), p. 88.

[230] *Observations on the Present State of Music and Musicians* (London, 1762), p. 102.

on the role of the middle class as a governing class. One was a profound disinclination to seek aid from the State. When it did get involved, as in the case of the grants made by the Irish Parliament to the famous Dublin Society, accusations of malversation and corruption were apt to follow.[231] Government was not usually expected to play a part, though individual governors, including the royal family itself, were increasingly required to act as patrons of public charities. The distinction was crucial. Even the judges were in effect deprived of what might have been a reforming role. Charity commissions authorized by the Lord Chancellor virtually ceased. The judiciary was evidently reluctant to engage in what might have been construed as intrusion.[232] The Crown had residual powers, through the Attorney-General, to review and regulate trusts, but showed little interest in employing them. Parliament itself was kept out of charitable activity as far as possible. Because of its exceptional éclat and importance the Foundling Hospital for a while received financial support from the legislature: the experiment proved disastrous and had to be abandoned in the 1760s. Most hospitals were founded without recourse to a parliamentary charter. Only in matters where the State's responsibility had long been acknowledged, notably poor relief, was legislation resorted to. Even in this case Parliament did its best to conform to the approved model of public subscription. Local poor law acts involved the setting up of boards of guardians who as far as possible were meant to remove poor relief from the control of parish officers and place them firmly in the hands of propertied people. They were uncontrolled by central authority and rather resembled a joint-stock company than an agency of government.

The desired features of organized charity were defined clearly by John Hey, a Fellow of Sidney Sussex College, Cambridge, in 1777: 'What we want is some contrivance which shall answer all the following purposes:— shall leave property secure, or even add to its security; shall leave men unconfined by civil Laws as to providing any thing for the poor beyond mere necessaries; shall keep alive and nourish the natural power of benevolence, and yet prevent its being thrown away unthinkingly or abused ungratefully.'[233] The particular institution being recommended by Hey was Addenbrooke's Hospital at Cambridge. Addenbrooke's had been endowed by legacy in 1719 but lacked adequate funds until public support was forthcoming in 1767. Like many other hospitals established both in London and the provinces between the reign of George I and the end of the century, it was an example of the new pattern of philanthropy, simultaneously

---

[231] *The Miscellaneous Works, in Verse and Prose, of Gorges Edmond Howard, Esq.* (3 vols., Dublin, 1782), iii. 263 ff.

[232] G. Jones, *History of the Laws of Charity 1532–1827* (Cambridge, 1969), ch. 11.

[233] John Hey, *A Sermon Preached before the Governors of Addenbrooke's Hospital, on Thursday, June 26, 1777* (Cambridge, 1777), p. 8.

meeting a perceived need, while ensuring accountability to members of the public who contributed to it. Annual subscription, which could be cancelled at short notice, was characteristic of such charities. Occasional legacies and larger benefactions apart, the great majority of them depended on small, annual donations. In that sense they could not survive without a broad basis of support among the propertied class of the areas which they served. Typically a school needed some tens of subscribers, and a hospital some hundreds, drawn from a wide range of occupations and embracing men and women of small property. The landed gentry appeared prominently in subscription lists, but the massed support of their inferiors was of far greater financial consequence.

The fact that bodies of this kind were not dependent on the State did not lessen their political significance. In functional terms they looked very similar. George Dyer, who offered a systematic analysis of contemporary philanthropy in 1795, gave a warning on this subject. 'The state of society in a country may be so corrupt, that charitable as well as political institutions may be little more than publick exhibitions of mistakes, sources of vice, or nurseries of misery.'[234] In practice this warning was not likely to be heeded, nor did Dyer seriously expect it to be. The object of the comparison was to emphasize the greater potential of voluntary bodies. At the very least it was presumed in their favour that they would be less vulnerable to inefficiency, self-serving, and corruption than government. Viewed more positively, they held out the prospect of solving fundamental problems in such a way that posterity would be entirely relieved of their burden. Robert Young, founder of the Philanthropic Society for the support of orphaned children in 1788, went on to outline a more ambitious scheme called the Social Union. Based on the Science of Society, it proposed to 'disseminate through all orders a knowledge of the social science'. The result would be to promote subordination, enforce the laws, strengthen government, and secure all those liberties defensible in an orderly society. The Social Union held no terrors for the rich.

It proposes to create a new fund of happiness for the poor, by a judicious direction of their own exertions; and instead of calling upon the rich to sacrifice any part of their luxuries or comforts in donations to the indigent, it will on the contrary give them an increase, in the natural course of things, from the augmentation that will be made in the primary springs of wealth, the labour and happiness of the poor. The association designs no absurd and visionary reforms which the nature and condition of men forbid it to expect.[235]

Young sought a minimum subscription of half a guinea for this venture.
    In essence the subscribing association was an appeal to a different kind

---

[234] *A Dissertation on the Theory and Practice of Benevolence* (London, 1795), p. 36.
[235] Robert Young, *Transactions of the Social Union* (London, 1790), pp. 4–5.

of State, one not confined to the formal machinery of executive, judiciary, and legislature, but open to all men and even women of property, and effective in the treatment of any social problems. Bishop John Butler of Oxford boasted of 'associated charity' as a 'sublime invention ... reserved for the present century'.[236] It almost defined progress. Surveying his native county of Cumberland in 1792 Jonathan Boucher was appalled to find it 'at least a century behind every other county in the Kingdom', for here was one community which had completely failed to engage in improvement by voluntary contribution. Boucher listed the institutions supported by other counties and absent in Cumberland: poorhouses and workhouses, infirmaries and hospitals, agricultural and manufacturing societies, public libraries and institutes for the promotion of arts and science. His suggested solution was the immediate creation of a county association, empowered to take in subscriptions and loans, governed by every subscriber worth £100, and devoted to an immense range of good causes.[237]

What Boucher had in mind was in effect a political programme based on local initiative, but untainted by electoral or parliamentary connections. 'Politics' was indeed involved both in a conventional and a much broader sense. The means by which charities were set up included the customary techniques of parliamentary politics: intensive propaganda, determined lobbying, and the patronage of important people. Moreover, the actual management of charities was itself an elaborate and rapidly multiplying form of participatory politics. As a means of enlisting relatively humble people in the processes of government, it was controversial. In the early eighteenth century lowly managers of charity schools came in for severe criticism. 'There is a Melodious Sound in the word Governor that is charming to mean People'; 'if there be the least satisfaction in governing children, it must be ravishing to govern the Schoolmaster himself'.[238] But the link between property and power was crucial. At Shoreditch the school set up in 1709 was a parish responsibility, supported by door to door collections. In 1793 a new scheme was adopted, securing larger sub-scriptions from the well-to-do and making it unnecessary 'to visit the habitations of the indigent'. But it followed that only those who contributed should share in the management of the school, and its constitution was duly changed. The resulting oligarchy of 'the more opulent part of the parishioners' was described as 'the best and cheapest system of government that experience can suggest'.[239]

---

[236] *A Sermon Preached at St Mary's Church in Oxford, on Thursday, July 2, 1778* (Oxford, 1778), p. 15.

[237] 'A Cumberland Man', in C. M. L. Boucher, 'Jonathan Boucher', *Trans. Cumbs. and Westmor. Ant. and Arch. Soc.*, NS 28 (1927), 147 ff.

[238] Quoted in I. Pinchbeck and M. Hewitt, *Children in English Society* (2 vols., London, 1969), i. 291.

[239] *An Account of the Rise, Progress, and Present State, of the Charity School for the Education of Boys in the Parish of St Leonard, Shoreditch, in the County of Middlesex* (London, 1793), pp. 10–11.

Governing was certainly one of the duties and pleasures of the middle-class subscriber. In the case of the hospitals it was the prerogative of all subscribers of a given sum. Initially it was argued that the sum should be substantial. At Winchester, one of the earliest hospitals, 'the management of our Affairs is entrusted to a select number of Such, as are for the most part the greatest Contributors, and consequently the most interested in our success. And *wherever* these Charities shall be established, Nothing ought to be more studiously avoided, than placing the Government of them in many hands, which will always be attended with great confusion, and will, in the end, prove fatal to the whole Design.'[240] These were the words of Alured Clarke, a founding father of the provincial infirmary movement. The Winchester formula envisaged a governing body of fifty, composed of subscribers of £2 per annum or more. This, or more commonly two guineas, became the standard qualification for a Governor in most places, even when, as at Hereford, there was a shortage of potential candidates. Oxford was unusual in asking three guineas, and Lincoln still more so with a requirement of five.[241]

In the early days of the hospital a small core of governors seems to have been envisaged and found acceptable. At Northampton the statutes stipulated a threefold division: five-guinea subscribers who were automatically members of the standing committee which managed the hospital, two-guinea subscribers who were full governors, and thereby eligible for service on the committee as well as entitled to attend general meetings, and one-guinea subscribers who had only the right to recommend patients. In 1747 there were 51 in the first category, 55 in the second, and 181 in the third.[242] But while the structure remained broadly the same in most places, ordinary subscribers seem to have been increasingly ready to pay for the privilege of becoming governors. As a result, if the intention was an oligarchy, it was not a very exclusive one. At Leicester, between 1766 when the hospital was mooted and 1774, by which time it was firmly established, only 19 of the 220 subscriptions fell below the two guineas needed to qualify. Some of the northern infirmaries, for example those of Manchester, Leeds, and Newcastle, considered it desirable to formalize this effective identification of subscribers with governors by making the minimum subscription for the nomination of in-patients two guineas, the same sum

[240] Alured Clarke, *A Sermon Preached in the Cathedral Church of Winchester, before the Governors of the County Hospital* (2nd edn., London, 1737), pp. vii–viii.

[241] *Rules and Orders for the Government of the General Infirmary at Hereford* (Hereford, 1775); printed *Rules* (Oxford, 1770), and *Statutes* (Lincoln, 1745).

[242] Richard Grey, *A Sermon Preached in the Parish Church of All Saints in Northampton, March 29, 1744* (Northampton, 1744), p. 18.

which they required of governors.[243] At Shrewsbury the distinction was blurred by a provision in the rules which made two-guinea subscribers governors but permitted additional governors to be chosen from the one-guinea subscribers. Subscribers were more or less equally divided between these two categories.[244] Multiple votes on the joint stock analogy were not the rule. Again Lincoln was untypical in permitting five-guinea subscribers double the vote of their two-guinea colleagues.

The work of establishing and running an infirmary was a potentially onerous responsibility. For those prepared to attend more than quarterly meetings, it entailed weekly boards for the admission and discharge of patients, and the supervision of the wards. At Lincoln, established in 1768, those who regularly attended to such duties were drawn from a stock of twenty to thirty subscribers who were usually resident in the city and had both time and inclination to meet. They included a considerable sprinkling of clergy, a number of professional men, and substantial citizens of Lincoln as well as a few landed gentry. The county élite turned out only for annual meetings or special occasions. A typical weekly board in the first decade might involve less than a dozen governors.[245] The minutes of the infirmaries at Gloucester and Leicester reveal a similar pattern.[246] In fact at Leicester weekly committees were sometimes inquorate, and the hospital physicians and surgeons compelled to take temporary responsibility. But government was not merely about regular attendance. As in other branches of the eighteenth-century polity, the right to attend was treasured, however weak the will to exercise it on a regular basis. The theory was that a large body of potential governors was a guarantee of honest and efficient admin-istration. At Shrewsbury in 1754 it was argued that 'Misapplication, which is the general objection to publick Charities, is here impossible, from the nature of the thing. The hands which give, are the same that distribute this Charity.'[247] When need required, governors would attend. A hint of a scandal, a major policy decision about buildings or medical practice, a controversy among professional advisers or employees, would stimulate a sudden interest in management. At Leicester in 1772 a dispute between two physicians, in which the weekly committee sided with one of them, was eventually terminated by a general meeting which overrode its com-mittee and ordered all references to the affair to be expunged from the minute-book.[248] The men who met regularly in a club-like atmosphere were

---

[243] Printed statutes and rules published for Manchester, 1769, Newcastle, 1752, and Leeds, 1806; Leicestershire RO, 13 D 54/13.

[244] Shropshire RO, 3909/6/2: printed report of 1746.

[245] Lincolnshire Archives Office, HOSP. 1.

[246] Gloucestershire RO (Shirehall), HO 19/1/1–5; Leicestershire RO, 13 D 54/1.

[247] Shropshire RO, 3909/6/2: 'Some Further Considerations'.

[248] Leicestershire RO, 13 D 54/1: 18 June 1772.

always aware that they could be called to account by a wider constituency.

Chartered bodies with a fixed number of trustees, often co-opted, carried no such safeguard, and without it, the hope of raising new funds from a sceptical and well-informed public was slender indeed. This was advanced as one of the main reasons for founding a new mental hospital in London, when an older establishment, Bethlehem, catered for the same need. In defence of St Luke's, 'the being under the immediate Inspection and Government of its own Patrons and Supporters' was urged as a decisive consideration.[249] Adaptability, in what was rightly considered an age of rapid change, was also important. The report of the select committee which investigated Bridewell and Bethlehem in 1792 was critical of their hide-bound constitution, devised 'in Times less enlightened', and impossible to change since they were governed by charter.[250] Subscribers could change the rules of voluntary bodies whenever there was a majority for doing so.

Governing was not the only prospective delight for subscribers. Richard Grey, the clergyman who gave the first sermon on behalf of the North-ampton infirmary in 1744, pointed out that 'Private Persons, may be *Real* Gainers, in point of Interest, by contributing to this Work'.[251] Ser-monizers on these occasions were not always quite so candid, but it required little imagination to grasp what kind of interest was concerned. Subscription carried with it the right to nominate to a hospital bed. Admission tickets, both for in-patients and out-patients, were obtainable on a graduated scale to match the generosity of the donors. The details varied but the minimum subscription for one in-patient per annum was in the order of a guinea. Here was a particularly gratifying form of patronage which provided the relatively humble subscriber with the means of benefiting his inferiors or dependants. As the author of the *Salisbury Guide* ingenuously put it, 'The pleasing Reflection of having it in one's power, at a small expence, of having numbers of poor, indigent persons cured, must be very great to a good mind.'[252] This pleasure was not confined to men. In most cases women had to act as governors by proxy; but in the recommendation of patients, and in the visiting of hospitals, their sex was irrelevant. (In the case of the so-called ladies' charities, it was, of course, the men who were excluded.)

At most infirmaries there was nothing to stop a patron using hospital facilities for his own servants, a useful perk in a household where a sick servant was certainly a liability and perhaps a source of infection. Bishops who gave charity sermons were not squeamish about this. Isaac Maddox,

---

[249] *Reasons for the Establishing, and Further Encouragement of St. Luke's Hospital for Lunaticks* (1763), p. 5.

[250] *Report of the Select Committee of Enquiry* (1792), p. 9.

[251] Printed list of subscribers at Bodleian Library, Gough Northants 15 (7).

[252] (Salisbury, 1769), p. 46.

Bishop of Worcester, pointed out that in the case of smallpox, 'to keep a Servant in such a Condition, is, generally speaking, exceedingly inconvenient: To thrust them out of Doors under such Circumstances, always inhuman, commonly fatal.'[253] Thomas Secker publicly conceded, without recrimination, that some 'had Servants, Dependents, or Neighbours, under Cure in the Infirmary, of whom they would else have taken the Charge themselves'.[254] Strictly speaking, some hospitals frowned on the admission of servants, for the excellent reason that surgeons and physicans considered themselves thereby deprived of valuable fees for home attendance. But only rarely were there rules excluding them, and it is difficult to believe even in these cases, given the problems experienced by most infirmaries in controlling their admissions, that they were enforceable.[255]

Charitable institutions understood the importance of patronage. They kept elaborate records and devised complicated procedures to ensure that subscribers got what they paid for and no more. Hospitals could hardly penalize a patient once admitted, on account of his patron's misdeeds, but schools were quite capable of expelling pupils whose original proposer had ceased subscribing.[256] There was little danger that rights of patronage would lie unused. The privilege of recommending could be delegated. Peers, gentry, and others who were unlikely to be resident in the town where they had purchased this privilege nominated proxies who reinforced their influence or could be expected to return the favour. A subscriber without suitable patients of his own to put forward could offer his turn to a friend or colleague. The demeaning art of obtaining a subscriber's recommendation, required of successful applicants for charity well into the twentieth century, was widely established in the eighteenth.[257] Public bodies, such as vestries, themselves appealed for such recommendations on behalf of their poor; in such cases the subscriber was not only relieving the unfortunate, but laying his parish under an obligation to him.[258] Where records of nominations survive, as they do for the Devon and Exeter Infirmary, they suggest that virtually all subscribers found one reason or

---

[253] *A Sermon Preached before His Grace Charles Duke of Marlborough, President, the Vice-President and Governors of the Hospital for the Small-Pox* (London, 1760), p. 25.

[254] *A Sermon Preached before the Governors of the London Hospital* (London, 1754), p. 25.

[255] *The Statutes and Rules, for the Government of the General Infirmary, at the City of Salisbury* (Salisbury, 1767), p. 26. However, J. Woodward, *To Do The Sick No Harm: A Study of the British Voluntary Hospital System to 1875* (London, 1974), pp. 40–2, is more optimistic about the success of infirmaries in restricting the admission of servants.

[256] See e.g. H. Stone, 'The Ipswich Charity Schools of Grey Coat Boys and Blue Coat Girls', *Proc. Suffolk Inst. Arch.* 25 (1952), 172–8.

[257] The process is memorably described in W. H. Davies, *The Autobiography of a Super-Tramp* (London, 1942), ch. 22.

[258] See e.g. F. M. Cowe, ed., *Wimbledon Vestry Minutes, 1736, 1743–1788* (Surrey Rec. Soc. 25, 1964), pp. 10, 13: 24 Jul. 1748, 26 Feb. 1749. In due course it became common for parishes to subscribe on their own behalf.

another for using their entitlement.[259] From the beginning some scepticism was expressed about the motives of those involved. As one of the sceptics in the Lords put it in 1736, when only a handful of the subscription infirmaries had been established, 'rich Men get in to be Governors of Hospitals, not with the pious View of making an Interest in the next World by Works of Charity, but with the ambitious View of making an Interest in this, by having so many Posts or Preferments at their Disposal. This last View, I am apt to suspect, is the true Source of that Spirit which has been lately raised for erecting and endowing Hospitals.'[260] In this respect the distinction between subscribing and governing was particularly significant. Mere subscribers could only nominate patients. Governors were entitled to join in the appointment and election of hospital staff, a potentially profitable field for the cultivation of interest and the exertion of influence. For the self-important there were obvious attractions. Not many governors would have had the courage that the Quaker Richard Chester displayed at St Thomas's when he delivered a stinging rebuke to the famous physician and poet Mark Akenside, on account of his unsympathetic treatment of patients, but the pleasure to be derived from sitting in judgement was doubtless considerable.[261]

THE FIFTH COMMANDMENT

The new philanthropy provided ample opportunities to display authority combined with benevolence. It could also be linked with the exercise of enlightened patriarchalism in a strictly domestic sphere, completing the symmetry which governed the public and private life of the middle class. Sermons delivered on behalf of charity, accompanied by a touching demonstration of the recipients' gratitude, with processions of orphanage children or hospital patients, are rich sources for this theme. Typical was the address which John Penrose, himself a clergyman, heard at Bath Abbey in 1766. It was largely devoted to extolling the merits of the Centurion, whose zeal for religion was matched by kindness to his servants and a regular family life. These virtues were indissolubly joined, all of a piece.[262]

By its very nature philanthropy was often devoted to providing the advantages of a family to those who had none of their own. Moss of Liverpool pointed out that the poor in cities frequently owed their plight to 'the chilling blights of parental inclemency'. His appeal to the sentimental values associated with family life verged on the mawkish. It included a

---

[259] Devon RO (Exeter), 1260 F/HR/ 11–12.

[260] *London Magazine* (1736), 710.

[261] Pettigrew, *Memoirs of the Life and Writings of the Late John Coakley Lettsom*, i. 23.

[262] B. Mitchell and H. Penrose, *Letters from Bath 1766–1767 by the Rev. John Penrose* (Gloucester, 1983), p. 59.

pathetic prose portrait of a scene all too common in Liverpool, the arrival
of a vessel after a long voyage, the welcoming presence on the quayside of
wives long separated from their husbands, the tragic revelation of a husband's death in a distant clime, the domestic catastrophe of a family without
its ruler and breadwinner.[263] But family was a metaphor as well as a material
and moral community. Medical men were expected to treat the poor like
children. As Thomas Percival told them, 'greater *authority* and greater
condescension will be found requisite in domestic attendance on the poor'.[264]
Wherever children were the beneficiaries the analogy was explicit. No
conflict was envisaged between the interests of those thus aided and the
wider social purpose to which their upbringing was usually directed.
The luminaries of the Evangelical Revival gave enthusiastic support to
enterprises in which the two were considered coincident. Mrs Trimmer,
for instance, was an advocate of the schools of industry, which were
designed to provide education and material support for infant children,
while training them in industrious habits and incidentally manufacturing
goods to make the process self-financing. She and her friends took particular
pleasure in the invention of a spinning-wheel allowing eighteen small
children to spin at one time.[265]

Capitalists who pursued the same objective in their business concerns
gained similar approval. The use of child labour in regimented manufacturing establishments was much applauded initially. Stratwell's silk
manufactory at Basingstoke employed 140 children together with a further
50 who were maintained until they were of an age to work. It featured in
Richard Sullivan's published *Tour* of 1780 as an object of interest to the
benevolently minded tourist.[266] Later the use of child labour and the social
consequences of factory discipline were to become highly controversial,
but in the last quarter of the eighteenth century doubts were rare. So
plainly did the moral advantage lie with those who combined commercial
enterprise with communal responsibility that at least some of their
opponents were forced to defend traditional forms of economic organization
by emphasizing their superior credentials in this respect. Thus the Yorkshire woollen trade somewhat desperately defended itself in 1792. 'Every
Family might be said to be a distinct Factory, consisting of the Master,
his Wife, and Children; and in this little Community the Labour of making
a Piece of Cloth is happily divided, so that every Individual takes a part in
Proportion to their Ability; and the Master, whilst providing a comfortable
Maintenance for himself and his Family, superintends and directs their

---

[263] *A Familiar Medical Survey of Liverpool: Addressed to the Inhabitants at Large*, pp. 59, 11–16.

[264] *Works of Thomas Percival*, iv. 385.

[265] *Some Account of the Life and Writings of Mrs Trimmer* (2nd edn., London, 1816), i. 182.

[266] [R. J. Sullivan], *Observations Made during a Tour through Parts of England, Scotland, and Wales*
(London, 1780), pp. 87–8.

Conduct.'[267] This anxiety to claim for the family the virtues of the factory
is at least evidence of the public credit enjoyed by the first industrialists.
A cotton-manufacturer like Arkwright could set his record in housing
artisans against the callousness of country gentlemen who drove cottagers
from their manors. An ironmaster like Reynolds could boast of designing
pleasant 'Workmen's Walks', with seats which 'commanded beautiful
views' at a time when many landowners were bent on excluding parishioners
from their parks and prospects.[268] Moralists attached great significance to
evidence of a paternalistic concern in a novel setting. In his treatise on the
duties of the upper and middle classes, Thomas Gisborne made much of
Josiah Wedgwood's example in providing poor relief, schooling, library
facilities, and sexually segregated accommodation for his workers.[269]

Middle-class Englishmen needed no reminder of the relevance of the
ordinary man's domestic life to the wider concerns of economic management and political control. 'Hear me, ye Heads and Rulers of Families',
began the author of a philippic denouncing luxury, vice, and popery in
1750.[270] The priority of the family in the Aristotelian sense, somewhat
adapted to different conditions, remained axiomatic. '*Private and familiar
intercourse* forms a kind of separate republic, which has laws of its own,
distinct from those of the state, tho' influenc'd by them.'[271] It remained a
common conception of the period that the family, as the 'natural society
of wife and children', was the fundamental form of political organization.
'Every family', as Vicesimus Knox put it, 'is a little community; and who
governs it well, supports a very noble character, that of the *pater familias*,
or the patriarch.'[272] It also seemed likely that it promoted certain political
tendencies in a party sense. Family life, it was observed in 1779, 'makes
Tories of us all ... see if any Whig wishes to see the beautiful Utopian
expansion of power within his own walls'.[273] The radical Whigs of the
1770s were certainly not family men for the most part. 'Honest Whigs'
such as Richard Price, John Cartwright, James Burgh, Thomas Day, John
Jebb, William Jones, Thomas Paine, Andrew Kippis, and Granville Sharp,
were either unmarried or married without children. The corollary did not
follow, as the examples of John Wesley and Samuel Johnson, among
their most influential opponents, reveal. Yet many, including the bachelor

---

[267] York Minster Library, Hailstone MSS, KK 14.

[268] H. M. Rathbone, ed., *Letters of Richard Reynolds* (London, 1852), p. 43.

[269] *An Enquiry into the Duties of Men in the Higher and Middle Classes of Society in Great Britain*,
ii. 370ff.

[270] *A Letter from a Citizen of London to His Fellow Citizens* (London, 1750), p. 26.

[271] John Mainwaring, *A Sermon Preached at St Mary's Church, in Cambridge, at the Lent Assizes,
1766* (London, 1766), p. 18.

[272] *Works of Vicesimus Knox*, i. 182.

[273] *London Magazine* (1779), 178.

philanthropist Jonas Hanway, felt that isolation in private life promoted, and even demanded dedication in public.[274]

Speculations about the relationship between the control of family relations and the conduct of public affairs were made all the more interesting by what were seen to be some sinister trends in the development of the western family. Hester Chapone described the family as a form of commonwealth which was growing ever more difficult to govern.[275] The point was as obvious to a humble yeoman, leaving directions to his widow for the mangement of their children, as it was to more sophisticated mothers and fathers: 'we give them our Authority by submission to their wills'.[276] The place of daughters especially was a matter of anxious debate. In the 1740s *Pamela* initiated a discussion of the role of women which found refined blue-stockings ready to question if not defy received wisdom. By the 1770s, the defenders of masculine superiority were becoming genuinely concerned about the threat to their cause. Everything in contemporary life which seemed to magnify the independence and irresponsiblity of women was subjected to criticism. Pin money and the female dower, the supposed preoccupation of women with luxury and even vice, the iniquity of ladies' boarding schools, the extreme frivolity and immorality of female fashions, all became hackneyed horrors of the age. A torrent of sermons, letters, and essays denounced the freedom which women enjoyed to desert domesticity in favour of dangerous diversions. The lesson, reiterated with an intensity out of all proportion to the menace which it was meant to eradicate, was clear: good wives stayed at home, wore homespun clothes, and attended to good works and infants; good daughters learned to cook and sew, practised unvarying modesty and submission, and confined their reading to improving homilies. This was not what many wives and daughters actually wanted; nor was it truly what many fathers with a realistic view and a desire to marry their daughters profitably could seriously expect. But it was certainly evidence of the perceived threat to long-established rules of domestic relations and bourgeois life. Artistic licence as well as literary merit was devoted to fending off the challenge. Boydell's collaboration with Robert Smirke on the subject produced an emblematic print 'intended to represent conjugal and domestic happiness, as the result of prudence, industry, and a well-regulated life'.[277] Family, business, and politics went together.

Wives and daughters made the life of the paterfamilias far from easy. Servants of either sex were a still greater worry. The indiscipline of the servant class was a perennial problem. The law continued to treat the

---

[274] *Virtue in Humble Life*, i. 251–2.

[275] *The Works of Mrs. Chapone* (4 vols., London, 1807), ii. 143.

[276] Lincolnshire Archives Office, Misc. Don. 464/1: John Greswell, Directions to Wife, 28 Aug. 1772.

[277] *Proposals for Engraving by Subscription, Five Prints* (London, 1795), p. 10.

master–servant relationship as a special one, not to be compared with any other strictly contractual arrangement.[278] Employers much valued justices like those described by Fielding, who 'would commit a servant to bridewell, at any time when a master or mistress desir'd it'.[279] Even Whiggish Englishmen did not shrink from the claim that service involved a sacrifice of freedom. John Armstrong, physician and poet, stressed the dependence of those 'whose Liberty in some degree you have purchased for a certain Term'.[280] The 'some degree' doubtless distinguished servants from that state of slavery which all Englishmen despised. But it none the less placed the liberties of some Englishmen far below those of their masters. Perhaps this was all the easier because so many of this numerous class were actually women. By the end of the eighteenth century it was reckoned that there were approaching a million servants of both sexes.[281] It is unsurprising that there were periodic attempts to improve their reliability and integrity as a class. The same men who lectured wives and daughters, also lectured servants. The popularity of the subject doubtless attests more to the anxieties of employers than the sensibility of employees. Employment agencies were justified on grounds of their valuable part in raising the standards attained by servants as well as in terms of their convenience. Inevitably the vogue for voluntary improvement societies in the late eighteenth century produced in 1789 a Society for the Encouragement of Good Servants.

A notable feature of the debate about servants was the desire to assert the rights of the small employer. A high proportion of females, especially, were employed by families of modest means. They could not match the wages and living conditions provided by wealthier employers. Nor could they be anything but alarmed by the independence and indiscipline associated with the servants of the great. The causes of complaint varied. Masters and mistresses who gave their cast-offs to their servants aroused the ire of those who could not afford such finery for themselves, let alone their employees. 'As the case stands at present,' it was claimed in 1758, 'the servant who applies for a place, resembles rather a visitor to the person she applies to, than one solliciting employment.'[282] Employees of the great were accused of boorish behaviour in public places, not least the theatre; much dread was expressed of the smart manners and loose morals of dissolute

---

[278] See R. Trumbach, *The Rise of the Egalitarian Family: Aristocratic Kinship and Domestic Relations in Eighteenth-Century England* (New York, 1978), ch. 3, where it is argued that the changing status of servants promoted 'domesticity' in place of 'partriarchy' within the family itself; this is debatable, but the perceived danger represented by servants is not.

[279] *Tom Jones* ed. R. P. C. Mutter (London, 1969), p. 327.

[280] *Lancelot Temple: A Short Ramble through Some Parts of France and Italy* (London, 1771), p. 95.

[281] J. J. Hecht, *The Domestic Servant Class in Eighteenth-Century England* (London, 1956), p. 34.

[282] Saunders Welch, *A Proposal to Render Effectual a Plan, to Remove the Nuisance of Common Prostitutes from the Streets of this Metropolis* (London, 1758), p. 5.

West End servants who contaminated their provincial counterparts whenever they came into contact with them.

The best-publicized assault on the rights of servants as a class was the campaign against vails, or tips, which developed in the 1760s. Vails were an important source of income to many employees, but one which exposed the social differences between their masters. The sums payable to footmen before access could be gained to politically influential employers were much complained of. So was the expense of being entertained by anyone of rank. It was said that no ordinary gentlemen could afford to dine with a lord, and no poor curate to sup with a bishop without paying a ransom which would have kept their family in dinners for a week. The war on vails proved highly successful. It was plainly not merely a question of servants' gratuities. The object was to render all servants one class, and all masters another. Just as countless middle-class men and women sought to attain a life of gentility which made them morally if not materially the equals of the first gentlemen in the land, so they sought to employ their inferiors on the same terms. It was not an altogether realistic ambition. The upper servants in an aristocratic household could hardly be put on a par with the humble maidservants of a tradesman. There remained vestiges of a tradition which had once made it possible for a gentleman to serve in a noble family. There were also the functional requirements of houses which required skilled, almost professional services to maintain them and a measure of deference as well as high remuneration for those who provided them. Above all, there was the snobbery which separated establishments of widely differing wealth. None the less a certain agreement on common standards of remuneration and treatment was plainly desirable: vails fell victim to this desire.

So what was left of the notion of genuine warmth and interdependence, of shared experience and candid communication? Literature continued to celebrate the fidelity of good servants but in muted terms. The good servant of the late eighteenth century was sober, honest, orderly. Less was constantly feared, generally expected, and severely chastised. More was hardly asked. Class solidarity was of supreme importance. 'Caballing with servants' was considered 'a most flagrant breach of everything honourable', particularly when it set friends against each other, as it did in the case of two famous authors, John Hawkesworth and Sir John Hawkins.[283] True friendship with a servant was inconceivable except, perhaps, quixotically in picaresque novels. The danger of permitting children to mix with servants was much emphasized. Just as servants must be trained in habits of deference and respect, so must children be brought up to be austere and unapproachable employers. Deplorable scenes of undue and even indecent

[283] *Anecdotes, Biographical Sketches and Memoirs, Collected by Laetitia-Matilda Hawkins*, p. 15.

familiarity were set in servants' kitchens or the servants' 'hall'. But it is difficult not to believe that the real anxiety was the proximity of family and domestics in much smaller establishments. One advantage of resort to law was that it would make it possible to relieve this anxiety. Thomas Newton's scheme for a 'reform' to preserve domestic peace and happiness included a tax on servants' wages in place of the servant taxes which employers were expected to pay, and a regulating statute which would grant 'masters a just authority over them, that the head may no longer be as the tail, nor the tail preposterously as the head'.[284] Significantly, masters who violated the approved code of magisterial conduct themselves were considered unrepresentative in their irresponsibility. Such were aristocratic young bachelors, who, without a household of their own, could afford to treat their valets with deplorable familiarity. Such too were the irreverent intellectuals who enjoyed a bogus equality with their servants, for instance the Whig wit Samuel Parr, who joked about having 'the misfortune to differ in politics' with his servant.[285] Few employers would have tolerated such a misfortune for long.

It would be claiming a great deal to claim that family life did indeed make Tories of middle-class Englishmen. It is possible, none the less, that the supposed threats to the domestic life of families of modest means corresponded with their political worries. The inclinations of middle-class men gave rise to many misgivings among opponents of government in the late eighteenth century. It was a long established maxim of country ideology that the middle ranks, the smaller freeholders and tradesmen, were well disposed to the cause of liberty, and innately more resistant to authority than their superiors and inferiors alike. Noblemen could be considered the tools of princes. The lower classes were inherently dependent on power and patronage. Civic as well as moral virtue belonged with the golden mean. But in the early years of George III's reign it was becoming increasingly plain that the old 'middling sort' could not be depended upon when its 'patriot' instincts were appealed to. The simplest explanation was the spread of luxury. At the beginning of the American War, when so much was expected by America of her British friends, and so little received, it was claimed that the court had deliberately promoted a spirit of luxury to ruin and finally annihilate the middle rank of people, as 'the grand cement of the community'.[286] There were variations on this theme. One was the contention that the middle class, appalled by the spectre of social revolution, sought oblivion in the gross materialism and voluptuousness of the age. 'Even the middle ranks are terrified into a tame and silent

[284] *Works of Thomas Newton*, vol. i, Appendix iii, 'A Letter to the New Parliament', paragraph xiii (not paginated).
[285] Derry, *Dr Parr*, p. 55.
[286] *London Magazine* (1774), 412; (1775), 272.

acquiesecence. They learn to consider politics as a dangerous subject, not to be trusted without hazard of liberty or life.'[287]

In these speculations the opposition did not have everything its own way. Opponents of George III were asked 'if you would wish to carry your notions of independence into private life, and introduce them into all families, and orders of people, on this side, as well as across the Atlantic'.[288] It was said that 'in a republic, men grow selfishly lazy in the consciousness of their independence. Whereas in a monarchy there is a reciprocation of active benevolence from the highest to the lowest.'[289] This contrast between the generous humanity of a hierarchical society with a King at its head, and the frigid austerity of a republic of equals, corresponded well with the characteristic concerns of a patriarchal yet philanthropic middle class. Kingship was crucial in many ways: one was its appeal to those resentful of aristocratic arrogance and oligarchical corruption. This was endlessly stressed by champions of George III, with some force, as even a Whig like Laurence Sterne conceded.[290] Oliver Goldsmith employed it in his appeal to the monarchism which existed in the broad mass of propertied opinion. 'Every jewel plucked from the crown of majesty would only be made use of as a bribe to corruption; it might enrich the few who shared it among them, but would in fact impoverish the public.' Chided by his Whig friends for his royalism, Goldsmith insisted: 'I'm for Monarchy to keep us equal.'[291]

There was also the moral credit which accrued to the monarchy under George III. Its value was enhanced by the contrast between the King and his brothers first, his sons second. The domestic purity, even puritanism, of the royal household of King George and Queen Charlotte, not to say their interest in the good causes which attracted so many of their respectable subjects, stood out as a beacon of probity to a nation which increasingly expected moral guidance where it had long since ceased to tolerate political dictatorship. It is tempting to associate this popularity with the latter part of George III's reign, when the threat of revolution put an additional premium on his leadership.[292] But its origins go back to the beginning of the reign, and suggest that there was a monarchical constituency for the winning long before, if George II had been able or willing to cultivate it. A large part of the case against the Whig regime of the 1750s had been its ethical failings. John Shebbeare made this explicit in his satirical *History of the Sumatrans*, linking political corruption with moral decay. The con-

[287] *Works of Vicesimus Knox*, v. 207.

[288] *Dramatic Conversation* (London, 1782), p. 60.

[289] *London Magazine* (1779), 178.

[290] L. P. Curtis, *Letters of Lawrence Sterne* (Oxford, 1975), p. 126.

[291] *Collected Works of Oliver Goldsmith*, i. 213; H. J. Bell, 'The Deserted Village and Goldsmith's Social Doctrines', *Proc. Mod. Lang. Assoc.*, 59 (1944), 760.

[292] See L. Colley, 'The Apotheosis of George III: Loyalty, Royalty and the British Nation 1760–1820', *Past and Present*, 102 (1984), 94–129.

troversial Marriage Act of 1753 even allowed him to blame oligarchical ambition for sexual catastrophe and to paint the consequences of Pelhamite politics in startling terms: 'the Streets were crowded with Prostitutes, the brothels with Riot, and the Hospitals with the Remains of Beauty expiring in the Putrescence of Concubinage'. Shebbeare looked to 'Amurath III' to restore personal purity as well as patriotic unity to Sumatra.[293]

Whether the new reign brought order and decency to the streets of London was debatable. What was not in doubt was George III's determination to seize the moral initiative in politics. At the outset of the reign, with his adoption of the patriot programme of his father, Frederick Prince of Wales, he began to cultivate the image of a public-spirited monarch. At the time much significance was attached to his decision to make the judges independent of the Crown by promoting legislation which gave them life tenure. The propaganda possibilities were to be fully exploited for posterity in James Barry's monumental designs for the Royal Academy. Barry was the protégé of the King's critic, Edmund Burke. But his portrayal of George III depicted him as a bountiful patriarch, and incidentally included an image of the Queen dispensing her own bounty.[294] Popular representations of the royal family were deeply loyal long before the turmoil of the 1790s brought a rush of sentimental enthusiasm to its aid. The exhibit in Cox's Museum in 1772, which included pictures by Zoffany, a throne, and music playing God Save the King, was typical in this respect.[295] Celebration of the King as the true father of his people was commonplace in the 1760s and 1770s, for all the bitterness with which Whigs and Wilkesites assailed him.

None of this was particularly surprising, though it is easy to understand why some contemporaries were mystified by the support of propertied people at large for the Crown. Conventional theory taught that a society dedicated to the protection of property was naturally republican. But in the limited monarchy created in 1688 and consolidated by the Hanoverian Succession, it was easy to reconcile property and the royal prerogative. As philosophers observed, monarchy and property had a natural connection at least in the sense that the most respected accounts of the history of human society gave them a common origin in the heroic age of tribal kingship.[296] It was equally a connection which made sense in the philanthropic climate of the late eighteenth century. Benevolence, property, and paternalism were bound up in a nexus of values which predisposed

[293] The History of the Excellence and Decline of the Constitution, Religion, Laws, Manners and Genius of the Sumatrans (2 vols., London, n.d.), i. 273.

[294] W. L. Pressly, James Barry: The Artist as Hero (London, 1983), p. 90.

[295] A Descriptive Catalogue of the Several Superb and Magnificent Pieces of Mechanism and Jewellery, Exhibited in the Museum in the Spring Gardens, Charing Cross (London, 1772), pp. 22–3.

[296] A View of the Internal Policy of Great Britain, pp. 176–7.

many middle-class people in favour of monarchy and the conservatism with which it was associated. It was not necessary to subscribe to the entire range of prejudices and principles implied by traditional divine right theory. When the author of *Peter Wilkins* explained the death of his father, he placed it not in 1688, but in 1685, in Monmouth's rebellion, when there was no doubt of the impropriety of rebellion. In 1751 this represented a safe option, combining moderate Whig sentiments with patriarchal theory. Peter was lectured as to the lesson. 'Your father, Peter, rose against the lawful magistrate, to deprive him (it matters not that he was a mad one) of his lawful power.'[297]

The Hanoverian monarchy derived its title from the Revolution of 1688, but it took no great pleasure in the fact. And as time wore on, the advantages of claiming something of the mystique of its predecessors became more pronounced. From an aristocratic standpoint there was little to be gained by this tactic. Whig magnates thought of themselves as more or less equals of the Dukes of Brunswick, and showed little enthusiasm for investing them with a superior, hereditary legitimacy. From a bourgeois perspective, by contrast, there was much to be said for granting Revolution monarchs the rights which they claimed in a variety of contexts, for themselves. Significantly, the philanthropists of the late eighteenth century, consciously or not, often exploited this perception. As Hanway, like so many others of the new breed of philanthropists a pronounced authoritarian, put it, it was essential to bear in mind the fifth commandment: obedience was 'not to be restrained to your *natural parents* alone ... but also the *king*, and all that are put in *authority* under him'.[298] For those with a propertied stake in society as it was currently organized, with families to rule and employees to keep in order, this lesson needed no reinforcing. In the 1790s what Hannah More called 'this revolutionary spirit in families' and the constitutional war on kings coincided.[299] But the resulting response of bourgeois Englishmen had its roots in views and values which needed no foreign revolution to entrench them.

[297] Robert Paltock, *The Life and Adventures of Peter Wilkins* (Everyman edn.), p. 17.

[298] *The Soldier's Faithful Friend* (3rd edn., London, 1778), p. 85.

[299] *Works of Hannah More*, vii. 173. See also S. Deane, *The French Revolution and Enlightenment in England 1789–1832* (Cambridge, Mass., 1988), ch. 2.

8

Personal Nobility

IT is common to contrast the so-called English aristocracy with its Continental neighbours. Peers as such enjoyed few legal immunities and possessed only a portion of the propertied wealth which determined the
distribution of power. None the less the existence of a titled class was a
genuine threat to the perceived well-being of a society in which the human
priorities of social rising and snobbery competed with the ideological
requirements of self-help and egalitarianism. Titles were numerous and
regarded with a jealous eye. The formal privileges of peers were the subject
of continual controversy. In a relatively open, rapidly changing society,
nobility was exposed to constant criticism and challenge. Its political
influence was kept within bound partly by the divided loyalties of peers
themselves, partly by the success of the Crown in aligning middle-class
opinion behind it. Combating the immorality and irresponsibility associated
with peers was a more demanding task. Propertied society imposed on
aristocratic behaviour its own patterns of conduct. Peers were compelled
to present an image of openness and accessibility in their relations with
inferiors. They were also expected to provide leadership rather than authority, as patrons of philanthropic association and commercial improvement. Public divergence from the ethical and religious standards expected
of them was severely punished by a new tribunal, that of public opinion.
Individual peers became conscious of the need to justify their privileges,
in the process evolving a rhetoric of public service. Generalizations about
the aristocratic and élitist nature of Georgian society assume that the
prominence of the nobility signifies its unchallengeable hegemony. A more
subtle appreciation of its role rather suggests the extent to which it was
made the tool of an increasingly dictatorial bourgeoisie.

CHILDISH TITLES

English opinion was supposed to be hostile to the pretensions of an
aristocracy. 'Titles', observed the poet Shenstone 'make a greater distinction than is almost tolerable to a British spirit.'[1] Tourists like the Dane
Ludvig Holberg, visiting England in 1706–8, found a marked distaste for
honours, titles, and dignities among the Englishmen with whom they

---

[1] *The Works in Verse and Prose of William Shenstone, Esq.* (3 vols., London, 1764–9), ii. 229.

mixed.[2] Popular myth and story abounded with tales of stout-hearted commoners unimpressed by aristocratic grandeur, forming part of an anecdotal tradition which was still being enriched with further examples in the eighteenth century. One concerned the physician John Radcliffe's rebuke to the 'proud' Duke of Somerset, when the latter as Lord-Lieutenant of Ireland was kept waiting for his medical attendance: 'The King can make any man a *Duke*, and any man a viceroy, but God, only can make a *Radcliffe*.[3] The continual retelling of such stories constantly reinforced the ordinary Englishman's faith in his own contempt for rank.

Dislike of titles was related by some to the progress of civilized values. In England, it was thought, wealth alone impressed, and the 'beggarly nobility' were despised or at best pitied.[4] The laws of primogeniture not infrequently resulted in the separation of estates from titles, and thereby created a class of impoverished peers whose plight was a suitable subject for sentimental moralizing but not for practical assistance. They were among the sacrificial victims of economic growth and could not be permitted to hold up the progress of commerce. It was observed that more primitive nations, including the neighbouring Scots and Irish, retained an almost superstitious reverence for heredity. The Irish especially were thought regrettably 'aristocratical' in their prejudices. English pride was merely purse pride.[5] Coleridge, even in his radical phase, was concerned to make title a matter of no consequence, in order to concentrate on the more serious question of the property and power it carried. 'Do the childish titles of aristocracy detract from my domestic comforts, or prevent my intellectual acquisitions?'[6] But his very anxiety to dismiss them revealed his understanding that his brother reformers were not always so clear-headed. Wordworth's bitterness about 'the baleful influence of aristocracy and nobility upon honour, happiness and virtue' was much more typical.[7]

Sensitivity on this point was periodically augmented by the fear that titles were multiplying at an excessive rate. Even before the wave of Pittite creations in the 1780s and 1790s, there were worries about an undue increase in the size of the peerage, worries which are obscured in retrospect by its demonstrable stability. Historians of the nobility point out that new creations were offset by extinctions due to death and shortage of heirs and

---

[2] S. E. Fraser, ed., *Ludvig Holberg's Memoirs: An Eighteenth Century Danish Contribution to International Understanding* (Leiden, 1970), p. 209.

[3] *Memoirs of the Life of the Rev. Dr. Trusler* (Bath, 1806), p. 32.

[4] *The Dramatic and Poetical Works of the Late Lieut.-Gen. J. Burgoyne* (2 vols., London, 1807), ii. 81; John Shebbeare, *The Marriage Act* (2 vols., London, 1754), ii. 107.

[5] G. Cannon, ed., *The Letters of Sir William Jones* (Oxford, 1970), ii. 479; *Memoirs of the Life of the Rev. Dr. Trusler*, pp. 27–8.

[6] *The Collected Works of Samuel Taylor Coleridge: Lectures 1795 on Politics and Religion*, ed. L. Patton and P. Mann (London, 1971), p. 11.

[7] S. Gill, *William Wordsworth: A Life* (Oxford, 1989), p. 35.

that many creations were in reality promotions within the peerage. The House of Lords grew from 153 in 1688 to 187 in 1707 and thereafter fluctuated very little in size during the first seventy years of Hanoverian rule. By 1780 it had reached 224, only three more than it had been in 1728.[8] But this did not stop contemporaries receiving and spreading the impression that titles were being squandered on the undeserving. George I's numerous creations certainly had this reputation, which it took his more miserly successor some years to erase. In 1733 the satirical seer Samuel Madden helpfully provided a list of tradesmen, time-servers, and political hacks who might expect future ennoblement from such a meretricious regime. He took particular pleasure in identifying opposition Whigs and Tories who would surely be bought in due course. Some on the list were meant to be ludicrous, such as Edmund Halsey, 'Duke of Preston', a brewer who had succeeded in marrying his daughter to the Whig peer Lord Cobham. Others were truer than perhaps even Madden expected. The Tory Grosvenors, Gowers, Windhams, and Pitts whom he named were all to gain noble preferments under Hanoverian Kings.[9]

George II was notoriously 'odd about titles', as George Bubb Dodington put it.[10] His oddity seems not to have extended to Irish peerages. For a while at least, this category of ennoblement was relatively uncontroversial. Not only did it make no difference to the British House of Lords, it added nothing to the burden of the Irish pension list and had no effect on the Irish Parliament. As the Duke of Newcastle observed of one candidate, Lord Bracoe, in 1759, 'he is not an Irishman, has no interest there; never was nor ever will be in Ireland as I apprehend: and therefore his Promotion is very indifferent to the Peers of Ireland'.[11] The titles which he took, Viscount MacDuff and Earl Fife, were nominally in the Irish peerage, but clearly revealed their Scottish pedigree. George III pursued a similar policy at first.

Irish peerages had English consequences. English peers and their families frequently expressed contempt for an Irish title. Henry Fane, a cousin of the Earl of Westmorland, claimed that he 'should be as much ashamed of an Irish Title as of a Red Ribbon'.[12] One of George I's few recorded *mots* concerned an Irish peerage and the same comparison with a red ribbon. He was said to have bestowed one on William Bateman, son of a Lord Mayor of London, in preference to installing him as a Knight of the Bath,

---

[8] A. S. Turberville, *The House of Lords in the Eighteenth Century* (Oxford, 1927), ch. 15 and Appendix A.

[9] *Memoirs of the Twentieth Century* (London, 1733), pp. 271-7.

[10] J. Carswell and L. A. Dralle, eds., *The Political Journal of George Bubb Dodington* (Oxford, 1965), p. 275.

[11] E. Milner, *Records of the Lumleys of Lumley Castle* (London, 1904), p. 191.

[12] Lincolnshire Archives Office, Fane MSS, 6/13/11: Henry Fane to Thomas Fane, 13 May 1762.

on the grounds that while he could make him a lord, he could not make him a gentleman.[13] But untitled gentlemen were not so discriminating. A request for an Irish peerage was a natural first step for an MP who had served King and minister well and was expected to remain in the Lower House. Since a large proportion of the successful applicants were in fact Englishmen with only a nominal Irish connection at best, George II and George III in his early years did more to boost the number of resident noblemen than might be supposed. When Charles Jenner talked of 'this peer-making age' shortly after the death of George II, it was in the context of an Irish peerage.[14] The crucial change occurred in this respect in the 1770s when North began expressing alarm about 'English and Scotch gentlemen on this side of the water, who solicit for seats in the House of Lords in Ireland, which the greatest part of them will never see'.[15] He did so in the context of an Irish patriot movement which was increasingly sensitive to the colonial status of Irish society. The award of Irish titles to Englishmen fitted with other grievances such as British misuse of the Irish pension list, absentee landlordship, and parliamentary interference in Irish taxation and legislation. The major constitutional revision of Anglo-Irish relations in 1782 made this question even more delicate. One forgotten reason for the new policy as to British creations under the younger Pitt is that Irish creations became less practicable after the granting of Irish parliamentary independence in 1782. The Crown's prerogative in Ireland was theoretically unaffected but the political climate in which it was exercised changed dramatically in Dublin if not in London.

George III's British creations were controversial even before they multiplied spectacularly in the 1780s. His reign began with sixteen new peerages in two years, sufficient to provoke comparisons with the occasion in 1712 when Queen Anne had made twelve peers in order to obtain a Tory majority in the Upper House. The ministerial instability of the 1760s brought further creations, which markedly expanded the House of Lords and, but for greater caution in the following decade, would have made Pitt's later generosity seem less remarkable. Even during the more stable North regime there was a flurry of anxiety in 1776, when thirteen new titles were awarded in a batch.[16] North gazetted another seven in 1780 and eight in 1782. None the less, Pitt's creations were on a new scale and generated an entire mythology. Historians have sought to disperse the

---

[13] W. S. Lewis, ed., *Horace Walpole's Correspondence* (48 vols., New Haven, Conn., 1937–83), xxiv. 227.

[14] *The Placid Man; Or, Memoirs of Sir Charles Beville* (2nd ed., 2 vols., London, 1773), ii. 177.

[15] E. W. Harcourt, ed., *The Harcourt Papers* (14 vols., Oxford, 1876–1905), x. 158: North to Harcourt, 29 May 1776.

[16] *Serious Considerations on the Measures of the Present Administration* (2nd edn., London, 1763), p. 5; *Horace Walpole's Correspondence*, xxiv. 205; Turberville, *The House of Lords in the Eighteenth Century*, p. 417.

myth, pointing out that most of them were either of men closely related to peers, or essentially political appointments for professional politicians, lawyers, and service officers.[17] But appointments of this kind were not necessarily uncontroversial, especially if the services for which they were received were manifestly partisan. Contemporaries talked openly of the purchase of peerages when they considered the position of families which were 'well with all administrations' in the common phrase.[18] Moreover, the fact that they were prepared to believe the myth of Pitt's *novi homines* has a significance which statistical correction cannot remove. There was plainly an assumption that the extension of the peerage by government in the circumstances of the late eighteenth century was threatening traditional values pre-eminently embodied in the system of hereditary honours. The genealogist Sir Egerton Brydges was shocked 'by his palpable preference of mercantile wealth, and by his in born hatred of the old aristocracy'.[19] The Whig Lady Spencer concurred: 'Pitt's whole object was to raise Commercial men and to lower landowners and old families.'[20] Her friend Coke of Norfolk was much praised for refusing ennoblement in such company, possessing, it was said, 'a dignity of mind above all heraldry'.[21] But he could not resist taking an earldom in 1837. No doubt he was sacrificing his personal preference in the cause of bolstering the hereditary principle.

When the peerage expanded rapidly, the first-generation element was naturally prominent; at any one time a large proportion of the power and patronage was enjoyed by noblemen belonged to it. To the extent that proposals for restricting the royal prerogative of making peers had any support, at least before the Peerage Bill of 1719 ruined this cause by associating it with the oligarchical aspirations of Whig magnates, it was on the grounds that the unworthy element was far too visible. Soon after the Revolution there had been attempts to legislate against 'reckless' creations, or at least to make them dependent on a qualification in property which would subsequently be inalienable from the peerage.[22] The belief that an aristocratic class was not viable without a secure landed base was a recurrent one. It was still defensible in the late eighteenth century and to some extent influenced the distribution of peerages. Public grants to famous servants of the public were based on the assumption that while service might merit a title, it needed property to support it. But new peers did not generally

---

[17] M. W. McCahill, 'Peerage Creations and the Changing Character of the British Nobility, 1750–1830', *Eng. Hist. Rev.* 96 (1981), 259–84.

[18] *The Dramatic and Poetical Works of the Late Lieut.-Gen. J. Burgoyne*, ii. 142.

[19] *The Autobiography, Times, Opinions, and Contemporaries of Sir Egerton Brydges* (2 vols., London, 1834), i. 196.

[20] A. M. W. Stirling, *Coke of Norfolk and His Friends* (2 vols., London, 1907), ii. 338.

[21] Ibid., ii. 48.

[22] A. S. Turberville, *The House of Lords in the Reign of William III* (Oxford, 1913), p. 168.

lack resources and for practical purposes most of the animus against them related to their origins rather than their wealth.

Parvenu noblemen were understandably defensive about their origins. This made them more inclined to assert their own pretensions in ways which struck their inferiors as arrogant, extravagant, and bizarre. It also made them critical of peers with better pedigrees. The human emotions which gave rise to this behaviour did not make for consistency. The same men who gloried in their new found dignity were quite capable of enlisting anti-aristocratic sentiment in their private war with new colleagues. But the effect was to impair the coherence of the peerage as a corps, not least because it helped focus attention on the less attractive aspects of noble life. Newly ennobled politicians were subjected to much abuse, especially when they had previously identified themselves with the cause of the 'commons'. The extraordinary bitterness encountered by Pulteney in 1742, and Pitt in 1766, manifested genuine horror at the hypocrisy of two self-proclaimed patriots. Even a lawyer whose promotion was predictable but who had based his political career on populism, as John Dunning had, was 'tarnished, by his descent into a peerage'.[23] The unaristocratic manners of some new peers were so notorious that they became the butt of public derision on that account. Lord Thurlow, George III's favourite Lord Chancellor, was an instance. Richard Tickell, in his *English Green Box*, had him mistakenly taken up by a press gang ('the first man a press gang would pitch upon for a sailor, and the last they could suspect of being a gentleman') and then joining cheerfully in their roisterings.[24]

It was gratifying when *nouveau riche* noblemen failed to behave nobly. In the nature of things the newly ennobled were more likely to be exposed to temptation since most were in one sense or another politicians. But perhaps the envy of others made it more likely, too, that they would be caught out when tempted. The last two impeachments of English ministers were in this category. Lord Macclesfield, impeached as Lord Chancellor for the sale of judicial offices in 1726, had been made a peer on account of his legal and political services. He was abandoned even by the Whigs who served with him in a regime not known for its spotless integrity. It is difficult to believe that he would have suffered quite as he did if he had been a Cavendish or a Russell. Lord Melville, the former Henry Dundas, was impeached for his direction of the Admiralty in 1806. As a friend of Pitt and a long-serving supporter of George III, his humiliation was particularly embarrassing. Whig opponents emphasized the disgrace he had bought to his order. 'A noble lord had been detected in peculation, malversation and every species of conduct that could degrade him.'[25] This

---

[23] Joseph Towers, *A Letter to the Right Honourable the Earl of Shelburne* (London, 1782), p. 25.

[24] (London, 1779), pp. 101-2.

[25] Stirling, *Coke of Norfolk and His Friends*, ii. 43-4.

was humbug but shrewdly expressed humbug. It depended for its force on the unexpressed assumption that the nobility in this case was recent and ill-deserved.

The distinction between new blood in the process of turning blue and old blood of the true shade was not without political and parliamentary importance. Chatham, long an exploiter of anti-aristocratic feeling among younger sons in the Commons and among more patriarchal commoners in the City of London, did not altogether change his tactics when he entered the Lords. Perhaps the very unpopularity which he incurred by taking a title made him more sensitive in this respect. 'He should be prouder to be an alderman than a peer,' he had told the Lower House in 1758.[26] In the Lords he was not allowed to forget such boasts, nor indeed did he desire to do so. There were some characteristically theatrical confrontations with peers of longer standing, as in 1777, when Lord Gower told him that 'the Nobility of this country were not to be borne down by the popular harangues, which that Lord had dealt out these forty years'.[27] But the newly titled did not have to be neurotic on the subject of their status, as Chatham plainly was, to encounter difficulties on this score. No body of legislators had more influence in the legislative process than the law lords, most of them newly ennobled. They lacked the inborn sense of responsibility of a hereditary caste, nor were they subject to the electoral discipline which MPs had to answer to. Yet when the House of Lords used its right of veto, it was frequently they who induced it to do so. Champions of debt reform were quick to point out their lack of representative standing in this respect, and in the 1780s when the Upper House repeatedly blocked Insolvency Acts, it was they who were blamed.[28] Enthusiasts for the peerage sometimes drew the line at the law lords. When William Playfair penned his defence of the Lords in 1809 he was careful to except the baleful influence of the lawyers and pleaded for other peers to assert their right to intervene even in so-called legal questions.[29]

Titles were not, in any case, simply a matter of peerages. Baronetcies, having languished in the mid-eighteenth century, were created in some numbers subsequently. The 39 years between the Revolution and the death of George I saw the creation of 105; George II made only 27 in 33 years; but in the first 40 years of his successor's reign 233 were added. In the 1760s concern was expressed both as to quantity and quality.[30] Half a century later the most famous of all fictitious baronets, Sir Walter Elliot

---

[26] Turberville, *The House of Lords in the Eighteenth Century*, p. 304.
[27] Surrey RO (Guilford), Onslow MSS, J. Butler to Lord Onslow, 6 Dec. 1777.
[28] *The Plenipotentiary* (London, 1787), p. 9.
[29] *A Fair and Candid Address to the Nobility and Baronets of the United Kingdom* (London, 1809), pp. 31–2.
[30] *The Letters and Journals of Lady Mary Coke* (4 vols., London, repr. 1970), i. 90.

of Kellynch-Hall in Somerset, who traced his own family's elevation to Charles II, would have been well aware that the great majority of his order were of recent standing.[31]

Courtesy titles were even more noticed than baronetcies. Younger sons of dukes and marquesses bore the title of 'lord', unlike the sons of their juniors, who were merely 'honourable'. The eldest sons of peers automatically enjoyed a courtesy title. It caused irritation in some quarters that many of these thought themselves justified in attaching a courtesy title in turn to their own sons. This produced eccentric results when one of these so-called lords survived his father but not his grandfather, as Lord Robert Manners, a famous naval officer in the American War, did. In this instance the family cited their right by virtue of a private estate act in which the title had been accidentally permitted to stand, and the King's acceptance of Lord Robert's title at a royal levee.[32] Another such title, that of the Marquis of Carmarthen, heir to the Dukedom of Leeds and Baron Osborne in his own right, was the subject of a formal protest in the Upper House in 1779.[33] Titles were meant to embody certain historic principles of hereditary honour. But if the rules of protocol which governed their conveyance came to seem erratic or unfair, the underlying sense of legitimacy was weakened.

Similar principles applied to females, but title-bearing women always outnumbered title-bearing men. Their life-span was on average longer. Moreover, a woman who married a titled man thereby acquired a title herself; the converse did not apply. Also, the daughters even of the lower ranks of the peerage were addressed as 'Lady', while their brothers could claim only the appellation 'honourable'. These women retained their title even when they married commoners from whom they took their married name. Part of the horror that greeted the elopement of an aristocratic woman with a man of inferior rank had to do with the resulting incongruity. Spectacular instances included the sister of the second Marquis of Rockingham, who became, by her marriage to her footman, Lady Henrietta Alicia Sturgeon. Even without such vexing social complications, the practice by which titled women retained their title on marriage caused understandable confusion. In 1776 Joseph Edmondson helpfully published the names of 169 ladies in this class, conveniently printed in the same format as Collins's *Peerage*, for binding with it. Fifty-five of these women derived their title from Scottish peerages, and seventeen from Irish, making their

---

[31] It should be said that Jane Austen herself took a more than passing interest in the titled families to which she was distantly related. Most of the fictitious titles which occur in her novels were derived from them; D. J. Greene, 'Jane Austen and the Peerage', *Proc. Mod. Lang. Assoc.* 68 (1953), 1017–31.

[32] *Memoirs of the Life of the Rev. Dr. Trusler*, p. 13.

[33] *Lords Journals*, xxxv. 708–9.

status a still more sensitive matter from an English standpoint.[34] It also considerably augmented the recognizably blue-blooded. Many sons and daughters, grandsons and granddaughters, not to say relations by marriage, were able to boast of an authentic 'lady' in the family by this route. Such status could be crucial in arguments about preferment. Peter Ludlow's campaign for an Irish earldom in the last years of George II's reign depended on it. His wife was Lady Frances Lumley Saunderson, daughter of the Earl of Scarborough. Her precedence before her marriage, as an earl's daughter, ranked with that of a viscountess. When she married a commoner she retained it. But when her husband acquired an Irish barony in 1755 she found herself demoted to the level of a baroness. Princess Amelia, unmarried daughter of George II and an expert on questions of rank, enquired maliciously of Lady Scarborough why 'I would let her loose her Rank'.[35] This humiliation proved unbearable. In 1760, against the strong advice of the Duke of Bedford as Lord-Lieutenant of Ireland, Ludlow was made an earl and his wife rescued from her ignominy.

Women did better out of titles than men. The wife of every baronet, not a few of whom were notoriously impoverished, was her 'ladyship' to the same extent as the wife or daughter of a duke. So was the wife of the much despised knight. It was assumed that wives rather than husbands were generally behind an expressed desire for a knighthood. When told by Lord Sandwich that he ought to accept one for his wife's sake, the uncourtierlike Admiral Campbell replied 'Then let the King knight *her*.'[36] In literary lore the 'City knight' was the extreme example of the devalued currency of titled snobbery, since senior citizens of London who had a share in the presentation of addresses to the Crown could claim a knighthood, and occasions for such addresses, for example on the birth of a prince or princess, were frequent. But the custom of addressing the King became more popular under George III and there was ample opportunity for provincial men and women to obtain similar honours. Enthusiasm for addressing sometimes aroused scepticism on this account. One instance was the less than menacing attempt on the life of the King in 1786 by the crazy Margaret Nicholson, which provoked numerous loyal addresses. The knights of the order of Madge Nicholson became a laughing stock. One of them was the manufacturer Richard Arkwright, whose address from the Derbyshire hundred of Wirksworth was presented after long delay in consequence of the difficulty of obtaining signatures in a county dominated

---

[34] *A Companion to the Peerage of Great-Britain and Ireland* (London, 1776).
[35] Milner, *Records of the Lumleys of Lumley Castle*, p. 187.
[36] *Memoirs, Anecdotes, Facts, and Opinions, Collected and Preserved by Laetitia-Matilda Hawkins* (2 vols., London, 1824), ii. 76.

by the Whig Cavendishes.[37] George III was more generous than his predecessor with knighthoods. It was he, in 1777, who for the first time authorized grants by letters patent, in this case to the Indian judge Robert Chambers, to obviate the necessity for personal attendance and 'dubbing'.[38]

The only exception to the rule that women did well out of honour acquired by marriage was the unadorned state of a bishop's wife. Although her husband sat in the House of Lords and was entitled to be addressed as 'my lord', she remained a humble Mrs, below the most vulgar wife of the most ludicrous City knight. Since bishops' wives were sometimes known for their fashionable life style and pretentious manners, this gave rise to anguish in episcopal palaces and mirth elsewhere. Thomas Gisborne observed that at least the ladies of the bench did not, like their predecessors under Queen Elizabeth, publicly seek the honours and privileges of their husbands' rank.[39] But their discomfort was well known. The satirist William Combe mocked their humiliation in his poem *The Fast-Day: A Lambeth Eclogue*. In his dedication to Mrs Cornwallis, the Archbishop of Canterbury's lady, he observed that wives must be accounted among a bishop's temporalities, yet they were not permitted to share his temporal privileges. 'There are few situations in superior life, which are attended with circumstances of greater mortification, than that wherein Yourself, and the other Ladies of the Right Reverend Bench, are unluckily placed. You share the wealth, and some of you, without doubt, the power of your Lords; but the Titles which adorn their names are not communicated to yours, and their Rank will not convey to you the pretensions which are claimed by Spouses of City Knighthood. You are at the very entrance of the temple of Honours, and are excluded from it.'[40]

It was often said that titled women were more snobbish than titled men, and accordingly provoked greater resentment on the part of the untitled. Novelists exploited this assumption to some effect; Henry Siddons did so by describing the consequences for family life. Mrs Mainfort's 'insatiable rage for the countenance and acquaintance of persons of high rank, often rendered her manners offensive to indifferent people, and disgusting even to her husband and her daughter'. John Potter went further: his Miss Southern was seduced by a peer in her youth but none the less sought to compel her niece to make an unloving, titled marriage.[41] Real life seemed

---

[37] *Morning Herald*, 2 Jan. 1787; their number was greatly exaggerated. Between Aug. and Dec. 1786 the *London Gazette* recorded only thirteen such knighthoods. However, the impression was given, in the context of the numerous addresses printed in full by the *Gazette*, of a considerable addition to the knighthood; for Arkwright, see *London Gazette*, 23 Dec. 1786.

[38] W. A. Shaw, *The Knights of England* (2 vols., London, 1906), vol. i, p. lii.

[39] *An Enquiry into the Duties of the Female Sex* (London, 1797), p. 346.

[40] (London, 1780), pp. viii, iii–iv.

[41] Henry Siddons, *The Maid, Wife and Widow* (3 vols., London, 1806), ii. 228; John Potter, *The Curate of Coventry: A Tale* (2 vols., London, 1771), ii. 45.

to provide supporting evidence. Pulteney's disastrous decision to go to the
Lords in 1742 was explained in terms of 'a Right Honourable Name To
call his Vixen by'. In this as in other matters women were subjected to a
double standard. When the widowed Duchess of Manchester chose an
Irish adventurer for a husband in 1743, it was observed that at least she
had not disgraced her title by taking her lover to her bed before she married
him, as was the case with others of her rank. But simultaneously she was
accused of sullying her title by such an alliance. Matters were not improved
by her success in obtaining first a barony and eventually an earldom for
her newly acred husband.[42] Mary Wollstonecraft accepted the claim that
women were particularly prone to snobbery and used it to bolster her
argument that they were compelled by a bitterly unjust society to adopt
unpleasant and unworthy prejudices.[43] Certainly the anomalies and ambiguities of rank and precedence gave rise to particular animosity among
women. The diaries of a court lady such as Lady Mary Coke are alive with
the empty rivalries and rumpuses of titled life. Ironically Lady Mary's own
title was something of an oddity. As daughter of a duke, she had been Lady
Mary Campbell in her unmarried state. By her marriage to the heir of the
Earl of Leicester, she became a Coke. However, the marriage was never
consummated and her entitlement to the name seemed far from clear. Her
own ambition, a source of merriment to her court contemporaries, was to
acquire a better title by marrying George III's brother, the Duke of York.
Instead she was fated to bear her nominal husband's name into an old age
which stretched far into the nineteenth century.[44]

The premium carried by titles in the marriage market enhanced the
significance which contemporaries attached to them. No doubt it was
distressing that they should become mere commodities. Satirizing the love
of the *nouveaux riches* for a lordly name was an innocent enough occupation
widely engaged in by novelists, who pitted the romantic love of the young
against the cynical snobbery of their parents. But a title was a valuable
asset in its own right. This was made clear in the case of those broken
down families which had nothing left to offer but their honour. One such
was the house of St Albans, descended from kings but virtually penniless
by the reign of George III. The hard-headed Yorkshire baronet Sir
Henry Etherington pronounced himself unimpressed when the question of
marrying his niece into such a family was broached in 1788. 'In point of
real property they have nothing, but of rank too much without a proper
future to support it. But ladies like high rank, though it's a shadow without
a substance!' Yet when negotiations nearly broke down it was Sir Henry

---

[42] *An Ode Addressed to the Author of the Conquered Duchess* (London, 1746).
[43] *A Vindication of the Rights of Woman* (2nd edn., London, 1792), pp. 329, 337, 340.
[44] *The Letters and Journals of Lady Mary Coke.*

who revived them, confessing that the prospect of his niece mothering a
duke 'would make a vast difference, at least in regard to me'. His Miss
Moses duly married her lord.[45]

In matters of this kind there was a subtle but significant shift in the
course of the mid-eighteenth century. Country gentlemen and their families
had sometimes resisted incorporation in the social milieu and cultural world
of noblemen. In 1722 the Durham clergyman John Thomlinson thought
it a distinct disadvantage to marry into the family of Lord Chesterfield, to
be offset in part only if 'I shall not live among his relations'.[46] Circumstances
in the early eighteenth century often militated against close connections of
this kind. The politics of the period tended to distance Whig lords from
Tory gentlemen. Moreover there was still a strong sense of ranks and
orders, of the gulf between peers and commoners. It might produce in the
latter a kind of obstinate pride which matched the patronizing condescension of the former. Also, with squirearchical incomes under pressure,
the sheer cost of keeping up with aristocratic cousins and in-laws was likely
to be intimidating. By the late eighteenth century things had changed.
Political differences rarely set families at odds and could be kept well within
the bounds of polite intercourse when they did. The belief that peers were
a race apart had been eroded, though in a way which made wealth the
determinant of power and title an auxiliary expression of status. Above all
men of property found themselves in an increasingly bourgeois society
which paradoxically placed growing emphasis on impressing one's inferiors.
Pulling up the drawbridge of squirearchical status and retreating into
country life was still an option but one that savoured of desperate defensiveness, and gained nothing. In the social war connections were more, not
less important and aristocratic connections especially so. Not infrequently
it was people of rank who dreaded the expense of fashionable living, and
people of riches who cheerfully accepted whatever incidental disadvantages
a title might bring.

Measuring public awareness of the distinctiveness of titles is an impossible task. What is not in doubt is that it was considerable at a time when
men and women bearing the title of lord or lady ran into some thousands.
Literary sources exaggerate the significance of title but in doing so say
much about the contemporary mentality. Critics were irritated by the
fascination of the novel-reading public with titled life. As the *Critical
Review* put it in September 1776, reviewing Fanny Burney's *Evelina*, 'we
wish, to see one novel in which there is no lord'.[47] Such a book became
something to boast of. Gregory Way proclaimed on behalf of his *Learning*

---

[45] A. M. W. Stirling, *Annals of a Yorkshire House* (2 vols., London, 1911), ii. 206–15.
[46] 'Six North Country Diaries', *Surtees Soc.* 118 (1910), 165.
[47] xlvi. 204.

at a Loss; Or, the Amours of Mrs Pedant and Miss Hartley, that there were
no peers to be found in his pages. 'A mere simple baronet or two, and
those but small ones, are my most dignified Male Characters; and as to my
females, they are all Commoners.'[48] Conscious attempts in the 1780s to get
away from the obsession with rank in such literature were only partially
successful.[49] No doubt a *Complete Peerage* drawn from the pages of contemporary fiction would be an impressive tome, far outweighing its factual
counterpart. Even so the chances of encountering or at least having a sight
of a lord or lady in polite life were higher than might be supposed given
the small size of the peerage strictly defined. Perhaps it was this that
enabled impostors to impose on the gullible. Famous confidence tricksters
like 'Lord Rosehill', who cheated a succession of East Anglian women in
1773, and 'Lord Massey', who relieved a London jeweller of gems worth
£760 in 1791, were exploiting the assumption that peers were not as
uncommon as the rules of primogeniture might suggest.[50]

Titles mattered most, no doubt, in seemingly trivial matters. It was
widely believed that the carriage tax of 1747 hurt the pockets of bourgeois
citizens who were not liable to more traditional forms of taxation, especially
the land tax. In general this was true, but carriages customarily bore the
arms and accoutrements of their owners. With the traditional art of carriage
decoration in decay, armorial display became all the more noticeable.
Where titled residence was concentrated, in London, the prominence of
such symbols of superiority was striking. In the London excise division,
in 1766, 527 titled carriage owners were listed, from the Dissenting brewing
magnate and City knight Sir Benjamin Truman at the bottom, up to the
owner of five carriages in St James, King George, entered by the local
excise officer under the letter 'K', at the top. They constituted one in ten
of all London carriage owners. But titled families typically owned two or
more vehicles, and more than one in five of private conveyances seen on
the streets of the capital, often bearing the wives, children, employees, or
friends of the titled person himself, were identifiably carriers of rank. In
Westminster the proportion might in some seasons be much higher. In a
society which greatly valued private travel, it is unsurprising that visitors
were often overwhelmed by this impression of aristocratic opulence.[51]

---

[48] (2 vols., London, 1778), i. 12.

[49] J. M. S. Tompkins, *The Popular Novel in England 1770–1800* (London, 1932), pp. 175 ff.

[50] *Ipswich Journal*, 21 Aug. 1773; N. Drallor, *The Life and Adventures of James Molesworth Hobart*
(2 vols., London, 1794), ii. 135.

[51] PRO, T. 47. 4: I have calculated the average tax paid by titled and non-titled payers whose names
begin with A and applied the resulting differential to all. There were 4,811 payers in London as a
whole, 9,098 in the rest of the country. These figures do not include carriages for hire, of which there
were 1,989 in London, 3,684 elsewhere.

COMMONERS WITH CORONETS ON THEIR COATS OF ARMS

Titles doubtless had a resonance which was felt more powerfully the closer one approached them. Plebeian irreverence in the face of rank was much commented on by the same tourists who were startled by the wealth and status of the English élite. It is possible that it became more evident in the late eighteenth century. There was an unmistakably anti-aristocratic element in the Wilkesite movement, partly reflecting innate hostility to privilege, partly associated with specific grievances.[52] In Catherine Macaulay's assault on the Rockingham Whigs it was expressed to some effect by way of denouncing 'Aristocratic faction and party'.[53] More damaging, however, was the encouragement which the political language fashionable in the last decades of the century gave to an egalitarian trend increasingly marked amongst the well-to-do, those who were close enough to nobility to feel the injustice. Even among broad-acred country gentlemen there was a long-standing dislike of nobility which manifested itself in a kind of inverted snobbery well known to those who depicted the manners of the squirearchy. It was at its height during the reign of George II, when the close identification between Whiggism and the hereditary peerage made the natural prejudices of Tory country gentleman all the stronger. Some of them expressed contempt for the notion of ennoblement. Samuel Foote gently mocked the type in the boasted pedigree of his Mr Cadwallader in 1757: 'There's *Welch* Princes, and Ambassadors, and Kings of *Scotland*. and Members of Parliament: Hold, hold, ecod, I do no more mind an Earl or a Lord in my Pedigree, hold, hold, than *Kouli Khan* wou'd a Serjeant in the Train'd Bands.'[54] Some Tories changed their tune in the 1760s and 1770s. What would have been offensive from the hand of George II was evidently welcome from that of George III, at least to a family like the Curzons, who were all the more delighted to appear at court at the moment when their over-mighty Derbyshire neighbours the Cavendishes were departing from it. But the underlying attitude lingered on in some quarters, and was exploited from time to time by electioneers urging the minor gentry and freeholders to resist the power of the great families.

It was given a sharper edge by the popularity of natural rights theory. Many young men who read Rousseau in the 1760s and 1770s were of a class and education to feel the injustice of privilege. The young William Jones, a distinguished orientalist and a tireless reformer, confessed that he could not stomach the arrogance of nobles. His formal position, that rank

[52] J. Brewer, 'English Radicalism in the Age of George III', p. 348, in J. G. A. Pocock, *Three British Revolutions: 1641, 1688, 1776* (Princeton, 1980).

[53] *Observations on a Pamphlet, Entitled, Thoughts on the Cause of the Present Discontents* (3rd edn., London, 1770), p. 7.

[54] *The Author: A Comedy of Two Acts* (Dublin, 1757), p. 28.

could never be admitted as a substitute for virtue, in Rousseau's classical, republican sense, was shared by many who joined the Society of Supporters of the Bill of Rights, the county associations, and the Society for Constitutional Information, and looked forward to the aggressive egalitarianism of the 1790s.[55] Attitudes of this kind were particularly common where some other circumstance, a Dissenting education, for example, predisposed the young to challenge conventional ideas. The Victorian author Mrs Schimmelpenninck, brought up as a Quaker in a Birmingham household where Joseph Priestley and his friends were familiar faces, recalled the constant harping on 'the injustice of the law of primogeniture, and of scandalum magnatum, the privileges of the higher orders'.[56]

In this context the propensity of public education to throw commoners and nobles together had a marked effect. In some respects it may have served to ease the tensions of rank. In others it exacerbated them, especially when the institutions involved went out of their way to make life easier for the privileged. As an Oxford graduate and Fellow of University College, Oxford, Jones knew something of this. There was a growing tendency in his lifetime to question and criticize the concessions made by the universities to rank. Oxford's fashionably laudable attempt to discourage the keeping of servants, in 1772, as part of its campaign against extravagance and dissipation, was marred by its exemption of noblemen; the result was some unexpectedly unfavourable publicity.[57] In the critical, even radical climate of university life in the 1770s practices which seemed unexceptionable earlier were becoming controversial. When the Regius professor of Modern History at Cambridge advertised his lectures in 1774, he asked heads of colleges to send him the names of those they appointed to attend his lectures, but requested noblemen who 'designed' to attend to inform him personally. A critic commented that this 'plainly suggests to their young minds a notion, against which every wise friend would anxiously guard them, that they are not, like Persons of inferior ranks, to be under the direction of their Governors'.[58] Again, what was involved was a subtle change of attitude: assumptions of deference could no longer be taken for granted.

It was a common supposition that the peerage as a class did not enjoy formal privileges of any consequence. This was the basis of Lord Bolingbroke's famous observation that in England peers were 'commoners with coronets on their coats of arms'.[59] If this was true, it was the result of

---

[55] *The Letters of Sir William Jones*, i. 167, 200.

[56] C. C. Hankin, ed., *Life of Mary Anne Schimmelpenninck* (2 vols., London, 1858), i. 222.

[57] *London Magazine* (1772), 367.

[58] *An Observation on the Design of Establishing Annual Examinations at Cambridge* (14 Nov., 1774), p. 16.

[59] *The Works of Lord Bolingbroke* (4 vols., London, 1844), ii. 149.

unceasing vigilance and that extreme sensitivity to rank which was so characteristic of English attitudes. Arguments about privilege were by no means unknown. There were some notable tussles in the years following the Revolution. The struggle to obtain a Treason Act which would provide a fairer chance of justice for the accused was complicated by the determination of peers to assert their superior rights. It was a claim which the House of Commons was equally bent on resisting. In conference with the Lords in 1692, it roundly told them, 'The Peerage is in no Danger; the Peers have Power enough.' A succession of bills between 1689 and 1695 foundered on the Lords' insistence that peers must be tried for treason before a court to which all their brethren had been summoned, regardless of their relationship with the accused.[60] This was one tussle which the Upper House won, when it became clear that the Lords preferred to go without a bill rather than surrender their privileges. Their resistance was stiffened by their belief that in other matters they were having to make considerable concessions.

The most important of these concerned taxation. During the Cavalier Parliament peers had complained bitterly of their loss of standing in such matters.[61] By the end of the century the Commons won control of money bills for practical purposes; more remarkable still was its success in keeping peers entirely out of land tax assessment and collection, a victory of symbolic as well as material significance. Parliamentary assessments from the time of the Interregnum and land tax assessments from the 1690s were controlled by commissioners named by act of Parliament. These statutory commissions never included peers. Yet in some counties the proportion of tax which they paid could be as much as a fifth, and in particular districts still more.[62] Small squires and even humble yeomen might find themselves fixing the quota, approving assessments, and hearing appeals on property whose owners were peers disfranchised in this way.[63] In the early years of the land tax, one peer, Lord Ashburnham, was appalled to find the commissioners with whom he dealt invulnerable to his influence and pronounced them as 'terrible and absolute as any Basha'. The tendency of commissioners to shift the burden of taxation on to great landlords he

---

[60] *Commons Journals*, x. 622; Turberville, *The House of Lords in the Reign of William III*, pp. 106–12.

[61] *Debates of the House of Commons, from the Year 1667 to the Year 1694: Collected by the Honourable Anchitell Grey, Esq.* (10 vols., London, 1969), i. 263: 4 Apr. 1670.

[62] Derbyshire 17%, Buckinghamshire 18%, Warwickshire 22%; calculated from land tax assessments for 1784 in Derbyshire, Buckinghamshire, and Warwickshire Record Offices.

[63] I have calculated the proportion for 206 hundreds or land tax divisions in 25 counties scattered through every region of England in or about 1784; the highest proportions paid by peers are as follows: 41%: Kirby division, War. and Ashendon hundred, second division, Bucks.; 40%: Kenilworth division, War. 39%: Kiftsgate hundred, Glos., Corby hundred, Northants., and Nassaburgh hundred, Northants.; 38%: Buckingham hundred, first division, Bucks.; 35%: Framland hundred, Leics. and Burton Dassett division, War.

attributed to the power of the House of Commons.[64] Not only members of the House of Lords were excluded, but also their eldest sons.

From time to time this convention was challenged. In the bill of 1693 the House of Lords inserted a clause which would have permitted peers to be rated on their personal estate and office only by other peers and the money thus levied paid only to collectors appointed by themselves. By the Commons this was considered the thin end of an alarmingly thick wedge, opening the way to a separate system of taxation for nobles. 'If you had passed it there had been an end of this House,' Charles Montagu observed.[65] The amendment was rejected *nem. con.* In 1742 the name of the Marquis of Carnarvon, heir to the Duke of Chandos, was inserted in the land tax commission for Bath, where Chandos was a major landholder. If this was the first fruit of the defeat of Walpole and the triumph of Pulteney, it was singularly unpalatable. Carnarvon's name was removed by 168 votes to 112, in a division which aroused the interest of the Tory country gentlemen.[66] In time the Commons went further and sought to extend the role of land tax commissioners, with predictable opposition from the Lords. Commissioners were permitted to administer recruiting for the army, but an attempt to employ them in the embodiment of the militia caused uproar. The Militia Bill of 1756 was defeated in the Upper House in part because of this clause. That of the following year passed only when the Commons agreed to accept JPs in place of the commissioners.[67] Perhaps the most daring instance of this kind occurred in 1760 when an act concerning the Weaver Navigation empowered the Lancashire land tax commissioners to determine property disputes resulting from damage inflicted by waterway improvement.[68] Perhaps it is not surprising that this was the first and last clause of its kind. In effect it put the nobleman's land at the mercy of his inferiors.

There was nothing to stop peers sitting and acting on the bench either in counties or incorporated boroughs. But the ambience of a quarter sessions was not always very congenial, nor did magistrates take kindly to lordly condescension displayed in such a setting. Attempts by right honourable justices to assert their authority met with firm resistance. The fifth Lord Willoughby de Broke caused mayhem in Staffordshire by claiming a superior authority as a peer and informing the people of

---

[64] C. Brookes, 'John, 1st Baron Ashburnham and the State, c. 1688–1710', *Hist. Res.* 60 (1987), 69, 70, 73.

[65] *Commons Journals*, x. 780; H. Horwitz, ed., *The Parliamentary Diary of Narcissus Luttrell, 1691–1693* (Oxford, 1972), pp. 369–71.

[66] *Commons Journals*, xxiv. 167. The tellers for the year were Thomas Prowse and Thomas Gore, Somerset Tories.

[67] J. R. Western, *The English Militia in the Eighteenth Century* (London, 1965), pp. 138–40.

[68] T. S. Willan, *The Navigation of the River Weaver in the Eighteenth Century* (Chetham Soc., 3rd ser. 3, 1951), p. 69.

Uttoxeter that he was empowered to grant alehouse licences refused by other magistrates. 'You cannot conceive', the Lord Chancellor was told, 'the confusion He makes in the Country, for the Parish Officers, many of whom are ignorant People, think themselves obliged to obey his precepts, and the Justices, if they doe their duty, will have more business than they can doe, in levying penalties on the People whom He makes to attend.' By the 1740s it was unusual for a magistrate to be struck out of the commission of the peace, and for a peer to be removed was unheard of. This was Willoughby de Broke's unique distinction. Hardwicke's response to the complaint about his conduct was to issue a fiat directing his exclusion.[69]

Equality was a matter partly of symbol, partly of substance. Nothing impressed foreigners more in this respect than the fact that peers and commoners had to pay the same highway tolls and had the same access to post horses and carriages.[70] But constant vigilance had to be exercised as to the claims made by the high-born. Where money was involved they were quick to exploit whatever advantages they had or thought they had. The Earl of Suffolk in 1757 was dismayed to find that his copper-miners in Cumberland could not claim the legal immunities enjoyed by his personal servants when they trespassed on the property of others. 'All that can be done is, to proclaim the Miners are my Lords Labourers and let who will touch them at their Peril.'[71] One of the advantages of a press which served a wide public was that it was able both to exploit and reinforce resentment of such arrogance. Court cases were reported in appropriately angry terms, however trivial the issue. One such in 1764 involved a shopkeeper in Covent Garden who refused to accept the apology of a buck on the rampage, made a speech to the jury in which he declared that 'he came there as an Englishmen', and obtained a verdict of £200.[72] Macaroni outrages were not the only target for honest bourgeois indignation. A matter of growing concern was the deference accorded titled persons in the theatre. In 1768 this produced some bitter class polemic, claiming that ordinary theatre-goers in England paid more for their seats than elsewhere in Europe and objecting to noble patrons whose servants reserved their seats in advance, and who expected the audience to rise when they entered. The 'tame humility' of the 'middling classes of the British people' in the face of such oppression was strongly criticized. There was also anger when aristocratic women claimed legal protection for the gaming clubs which some of them

---

[69] BL, Add. MS 35601, fo. 63: W. Cotton to Mr Justice Parker, 19 June 1742; see also fos. 118, 122, for Willoughby de Broke's own attempts to influence Hardwicke.

[70] P. J. Grosley, *A Tour to London; Or, New Observations on England, and its Inhabitants*, trans. T. Nugent (2 vols., London, 1772), i. 15; J. Marchand, ed., *A Frenchman in England 1784* (Cambridge, 1933), p. 6.

[71] O. R. Bagot, ed., 'The Letters of Catharine, Countess of Suffolk and Berkshire, Relating to Levens Estates', *Trans. Cumbs. and Westmor. Ant. and Arch. Soc.*, NS 47 (1948), 56: 10 Jan. 1757.

[72] *London Magazine* (1764), 325.

ran. This was particularly provoking when it was reflected that they above all others had a duty to set an example to their inferiors.[73]

Even when peers had undoubted rights it was becoming difficult to use them. Parliamentary privilege was shared by Lords and MPs alike and was not objectionable as a mark of aristocratic privilege, however annoying it was on other grounds. But the peer's right to give his word of honour instead of taking an oath was especially prized by the peers themselves and shared with none. As a badge of status it caused great irritation. In a much noticed concession, the fifth Earl of Chesterfield's readiness to waive his right when he testified against his tutor William Dodd in 1776 revealed at least his awareness of what additional unpopularity he might incur in controversial circumstances. Two years later the incident was recalled when the House of Commons inserted into the House Tax Bill a clause making all householders swear on oath when appealing against assessment. In the Upper House Lord Effingham strenuously but vainly opposed what he considered an invasion of privilege.[74] There was a parallel here with the peer's right to invoke the *scandalum magnatum* procedure against commoners who libelled him. It featured in radical denunciations of lordly privilege, but Sandwich, who positively relished his role as aristocratic Aunt Sally, and used it against a printer in 1773, was the only peer to do so in the second half of the century. Others preferred to employ the ordinary law of libel. Reliance on privilege could be expensive and counter-productive. The Countess of Huntingdon assumed that her clergy were immune to legal sanctions against preaching without episcopal licence. Her right to appoint personal chaplains was not in dispute. But their public preaching was another matter. Significantly their status was tested not by a bishop enraged by an aristocratic challenge to his authority but by a parish incumbent who believed that he was losing revenue when the faithful heard a Methodist preacher in a chapel beyond his own control. The result was a comprehensive defeat for the Countess and one which had the effect of rendering her famous connection a Dissenting sect.[75]

In matters of privilege there was a crucial difference between what could be associated with title and what could be attributed to wealth. Some of the most difficult debates had to do with practices which were aristocratic in the broad sense employed by historians but not in the accurate use of the term employed by contemporaries. Duelling, for instance, though it represented a code of honour which belonged pre-eminently with the peerage, had spread far beyond it. In fact the most inveterate duellists were

[73] Ibid. (1768), 452; E. J. Burford, *Wits, Wenchers and Wantons: London's Low Life: Covent Garden in the Eighteenth Century* (London, 1986), ch. 9.

[74] *London Magazine* (1778), 220.

[75] A. C. H. Seymour, *The Life and Times of Selina, Countess of Huntingdon* (2 vols., London, 1839), ii. 307–11.

more likely to be army officers with only their 'honour' to defend, than peers with a larger stake in society. Similarly, nobody pretended that the game laws were the special responsibility of the peerage. Nor was upper-class indebtedness peculiarly an aristocratic activity. There was indeed a danger that persons of rank might be viewed as the leading examples of vice. But it was precisely as examples that they were coming to be seen. There was a great difference between a privilege which was the unique entitlement of the titled, and a practice which might happen to be identified with them on account of their prominence. The former was becoming indefensible. The latter was redeemable. Not only could it be reformed but in doing so rank could be made the instrument of general improvement.

AN OVERBEARING TYRANNIZING OLIGARCHY

In one crucial arena, that of politics, more was involved than the question of example, good or bad. The fear that peers might encroach on the rights of the community at large seemed well grounded. Noble influence in the House of Commons was extensive and increasing.[76] Reformers naturally denounced it, and from time to time it featured in formal protests against the defects of the representative system. At Norwich in 1768 the electors' instruction to their MPs included a demand that the eldest sons of peers be prevented from sitting in the Commons.[77] The extent to which members of the Upper House in effect nominated members of the Lower was a commonplace complaint, almost as commonplace as the objection to the influence of the Crown. On the other hand here too it was difficult to separate rank from riches. The long-term control of seats in the Lower House constituted much the most powerful argument for obtaining promotion to the Upper, a consideration which renders elaborate statistical demonstrations of the parliamentary power of peers rather pointless. It was money rather than title that commanded rotten boroughs, and moneyed rather than titled men who came in for the most criticism. There were endless appeals on behalf of the 'natural interest' of local landowners against the 'unnatural influence' of nabobs, contractors, and the like. George III, especially, did the peerage a service by his reluctance to ennoble disreputable newcomers. He could hardly object to a barony for Robert Clive, the victor of Plassey and the saviour of British India. But Sir Lawrence Dundas, the 'Nabob of the North', who made a fortune as a commissary in Germany during the Seven Years War and was thereby the leading example of a class much despised in the 1760s, fared differently. He was a formidable borough-monger and for many years placed his parliamentary

[76] J. Cannon, *Aristocratic Century* (Cambridge, 1984), pp. 105 ff.

[77] *A Letter to John Day* (Norwich, 1768), p. 6; this did not appear in the general *Instructions to Representatives to Serve in Parliament, Elected in the Year 1768*, published at this time.

weight behind the government, in pursuit of his campaign for a peerage. But the most the King would grant him was a baronetcy. Like others of his kind, for instance the financier Sampson Gideon, who also constructed a great electoral empire, Dundas would have to die before his family could receive the honorary reward for his services. Time made it possible to remove 'the smell of the shop'.[78] But delayed ennoblement of this kind obstructed the straightforward identification of electoral oligarchy with inherited honours.

For the community at large the most sensitive point in the process by which noblemen as such got themselves or their families represented in the Commons was their intervention in constituencies where the electoral process was outwardly open, though the indignation expressed on this account was often highly synthetic. Some contemporaries felt this them-selves. Richard Gardiner's account of the part taken by Lord Townshend at a public meeting in Norwich in 1768 expressed the absurdity of such a state of affairs very clearly. Townshend was a Norfolk magnate and inci-dentally a talented cartoonist. 'Lord Caricatura spoke a great deal on the occasion, but *said nothing*, it being his Lordship's opinion, "that a Peer ought not to *influence* the election of a commoner:" His Lordship therefore *contented* himself with taking down the names, and *taking off* the *faces* of the whole Company.'[79] But there is an obvious distinction between the cynicism of politicians who manipulated the formal rules of elections to highlight the role of their noble opponents, and the naïvety of less soph-isticated opinion which might genuinely be affronted by a violation of the rules. John Cogan's *John Buncle Junior*, a repository of commonplace middle-class sentiments on this as on other matters, included a significant assault on the impropriety which occurred 'when a Peer of the Realm engages, directly, or indirectly, in the contest. This is such an insolent infringement upon the common rights of mankind as ought never to pass without exemplary punishment.... When I behold the *Right Honourables* sport with the liberties of mankind, and aim at grasping all the power and influence in the kingdom to themselves, I cannot forbear in the warmth of my resentment.'[80] Feelings of this kind made it possible for wealthy commoners to join with their inferiors in denouncing noble impudence. It is one of many ways in which the assumption that the landed class can be treated as a unit is highly misleading.

The Commons resolution forbidding peers from voting in elections was provoked by the Earl of Manchester, who had cast his vote in the Maldon election of 1699. It was shortly followed by a general ruling against

---

[78] *The Autobiography, Times, Opinions, and Contemporaries of Sir Egerton Brydges*, i. 280.

[79] *Memoirs of the Life and Writings (Prose and Verse) of R–ch–d G–rd–n–r, Esq. Alias Dick Merry-Fellow, of Serious and Facetious Memory!* (London, 1782), p. 119.

[80] (London, 1776), pp. 210–1.

interference.[81] Formal protests were common during the years of party strife. They involved the Earl of Peterborough at Malmesbury in 1701 and the Duke of Beaufort at Salisbury in 1714; the offence was not less when the peers were bishops, as in the case of the Bishop of Worcester in 1705 and the Bishop of Carlisle in 1711.[82] The Cathedral Act of 1708, which gave the patronage of cathedral chapters subject to customary statutes to their bishops, aroused anger on this score, since as Robert Harley put it, it placed the nomination of twenty-eight MPs in the hands of spiritual peers.[83] These controversies were recalled in the 1770s when there was a marked recurrence of hostility to the electoral activities of noblemen. The break-up of the Tory party in the 1760s permitted the reopening of electoral warfare in counties which had slumbered in some instances for decades. In a succession of electoral contests, many of them by-elections, Whig magnates took advantage of the death or retirement of Tory knights of the shire to reassert their influence. They were not very successful, but their activities were sufficient to arouse the cry of commoners' rights, and even to provoke formal charges of aristocratic intervention such as had figured in the party conflict of Queen Anne's reign. The Duke of Chandos, as Lord-Lieutenant of Hampshire, found himself arraigned for his interference in the county election of 1779, when he injudiciously signed a circular to the freeholders.[84] Chandos's friends retaliated by accusing his rival the Duke of Bolton of a similar breach of privilege. At one level this was a ritual form of political warfare which deceived nobody. At another it expressed views about the proper roles of noble and commoner which could influence opinions and affect votes. A hostile pamphleteer linked the Chandos affair with the conduct of Lord Derby in Lancashire and prophesied dire consequences if such offences were not punished. 'If the Influence of the Peerage is suffered to prevail in popular Elections, the Constitution of England is gone for ever, and an overbearing, tyrannizing Oligarchy, will rise upon its Ruins.'[85]

Concern about the growth of the nobleman's patronage also increased, again, not so much because there was an aristocratic revival, as because changing conditions and attitudes made aristocratic influence more

[81] *Commons Journals*, xiii. 63–4, 648. Some peers continued, unavailingly, to claim the right to poll. One such was the Duke of Norfolk in the Westminster election of 1796; see K. Garlick and A. Macintyre, eds., *The Diary of Joseph Farington* (New Haven, Conn., 1978–), ii. 579.

[82] *Commons Journals*, xiii. 711–12; xvii. 481; xvi. 548; G. Holmes, *British Politics in the Age of Anne* (London, 1967), p. 29.

[83] C. Jones and G. Holmes, *The London Diaries of William Nicolson, Bishop of Carlisle 1702–1718* (Oxford, 1985), p. 456. See also G. V. Bennett, *The Tory Crisis in Church and State 1688–1730* (Oxford, 1975), pp. 89–97.

[84] *A Collection of All the Hand-Bills, Squibs, Songs, Essays, etc. Published during the Late Contested Election for the County of Hants* (Winchester, 1780), pp. 58 ff.; the first Duke of Chandos, in 1722, had been more cautious: see Cannon, *Aristocratic Century* , p. 104.

[85] *An Address to the Gentlemen, Clergy, and Freeholders of Lancashire* (London, 1780), p. 42.

prominent. The changing condition was the improvement in the vital statistics of noble life, which after 1750 placed larger numbers of younger sons on the job market. It needed only a relatively small expansion of demand for employment to have a disproportionate effect, particularly when it is remembered that the same demographic forces were having the same effect lower down. Noblemen were well placed to get more than their fair share at all times. The novel feature of the late eighteenth century was the need to allocate their share to their own families rather than to their friends, dependants, and clients. Contemporary wisdom, pledged to that openness of English society which was supposedly such a feature of the Englishman's inheritance, boasted that noble families preferred to place their younger sons in trade than in the army, the navy, the Church or the Bar.[86] This was utterly untrue, but it evidently represented a belief too fondly held to be lightly abandoned. In practice a mercantile career was expensive, demanding in terms of talent and application, and ungenteel. The professions offered more attractive prospects in every respect. The results were seen widely. In the armed forces, indeed, blue blood was already commonplace. Even so the incursion of noblemen at times of increased mobilization, for example at the height of the War of American Independence, gave rise to much grumbling from those supposedly elbowed out, not least in Parliament itself.

In the Church the appearance of peers and their sons on the bench, in cathedral chapters, and not least in ordinary livings which would earlier have been bestowed on a tutor, a poor cousin, or simply a local boy made good, was the subject of adverse comment. It was not necessary to be a democrat to find cause for concern in such promotions. Vicesimus Knox, the Headmaster of Tonbridge School, was at most a moderate Whig but considered the influence of noble families in the Church a standing rebuke to 'Jesus Christ and the poor fishermen!'[87] Clergymen of modest origins knew that they would have to swim with this tide. Thomas Newton, Bishop of Bristol, reflected that while the apostles had been of low birth, modern circumstances made it desirable that blue-blooded bishops should add to the strength and ornament of the Church, provided at least that there were 'some, who are honorable in themselves, as well as in their families; and whose personal merits and virtues, if they had not been nobly descended, would yet have intitled them justly to the rank and preeminence that they enjoy'.[88]

If there was a danger that the pretensions of the peerage might become a major political issue, it was perhaps at its height in the early Hanoverian

[86] John Moir, *Gleanings, Or, Fugitive Pieces* (London, 1777), p. 144.
[87] 'The Spirit of Despotism', in *The Works of Vicesimus Knox* (7 vols., London, 1824), v. 223.
[88] *The Works of the Right Reverend Thomas Newton, D.D.* (3 vols., London, 1782), ii. 601.

period. The Peerage Bill of 1719 gave the impression of a regime dedicated to the entrenchment of noble power. The extraordinary concentration of offices and influence in the hands of the great Whig clans, veritable 'Duketti', for a prolonged period between the accession of George I and the death of Henry Pelham, enhanced this impression. Above all the near extinction of the Tory peerage, as families with a strong royalist and Tory tradition were coerced or cajoled into Hanoverian Whig conformity, ensured that the nobility as a whole was identified with the cause of Whiggism. Here, surely was material which could be used with effect by a Tory party enjoying strong support both from county squires and the alienated urban middle-class. That it was not so employed appears remarkable.

Appearances were rather misleading. In practice Walpole's regime was not identified with the spirit of resurgent nobility. Walpole himself was considered a parvenu whose attempts to rival the great houses of East Anglia merely confirmed his degrading origins. His long supremacy at the court of successive kings was achieved at the cost of antagonizing powerful magnates, some of them only too ready to employ aristocratic rhetoric against his allegedly plebeian prejudices. The dismissals which followed the excise crisis in 1733, involving courtiers of high birth and long pedigree, was rich in such rhetoric, especially when Walpole had the effrontery to remove noblemen from their commissions in the army, treated by many peers as almost a natural right of nobility. Moreover, Walpole's ministry had a rough ride in the House of Lords. His majority there was rarely secure, and without the reinforcements provided by the bishops and the Scottish peers would have vanished completely. The fact that his enemies in the Upper House were Whigs rather than Tories somewhat complicated the party warfare but also divided the peers as a class. Division of this kind was the normal state of affairs. In the party warfare preceding the Walpole era both the peerage and the House of Lords had been split down the middle. Junto Whiggism may have had the superior forces, but not so obviously that the Whig party could easily be identified with the cause of aristocracy. The notorious influx of Tory peers in 1712, designed to give Harley's ministry mastery in the Upper House, and treated by Whigs as gross misuse of the royal prerogative, actually involved only twelve new creations and demonstrated how evenly matched the parties were.

It suited kings to portray themselves as the victims of would-be oligarchs. The Pelham regime was the outstanding example of an aristocratic government, headed in the Lords by the Duke of Newcastle, heir to a great estate, and in the Commons by his brother Henry Pelham. It commanded the support of most of the great Whig families, and almost all the ducal titles associated with the Revolution and the Hanoverian Succession. When he tried to break its power in 1746 George II complained 'that he was held under the dominion of an aristocracy'.[89] Yet his appeal was made to a peer, Lord Granville, against an overwhelming majority of the House of Commons. The Pelhams' priority, like Walpole's, was always the Lower House, sometimes to the anger and distress of their ducal supporters. The Duke of Newcastle's relationship with his Sussex ally the Duke of Richmond was stretched to breaking-point in 1746 when Henry Fox was made Secretary of War. Fox had eloped with the Duke's daughter in what had been a great public scandal and gave rise to an equally great private enmity between the Lennox and Fox families. Richmond was furious at Fox's promotion and all the more because it reflected ministerial anxiety about the Commons. 'In plain English his pride must be flattered preferable to myne, because he can and would *speak* against you.'[90]

There was no escape for Richmond, but George II possessed the means to break the hold of the Pelhams. Had he enlisted the support of the Tory country gentlemen, he would have found them willing allies in a crusade against the great magnates. Instead he put his prejudices before his liberty. If there was confusion in this it was shared by others. Horace Walpole had no doubt that the years of the mid-century had witnessed a major offensive by oligarchical politicians. 'I have seen ... the House of Lords striding to aristocracy at the end of the last reign', he wrote in 1769.[91] Yet the outstanding example of this alleged tendency was the Lords' rejection in 1758 of a Habeas Corpus Bill which had been pressed hard by William Pitt and had obvious popular support. In this instance it was the King himself who stimulated aristocratic resistance, on the grounds that the royal prerogative would suffer.

For George III as for his predecessor, the propaganda is not a reliable guide to parliamentary politics. George III was portrayed by his champions as the enemy of oligarchy and aristocracy, the saviour of a country which had fallen into the hands of a narrow, noble clique. If so this was a cause which was supported by numerous noblemen, many of whom had previously supported that same narrow clique. In Scotland, admittedly, where the fall of the Argyll interest came to be seen as a crucial stage in removing 'the fetters of aristocratic despotism', the claim has some plausibility.[92] In England, however, dishing the Pelhamites could hardly be put in such grand terms. In some respects the opposition to George III and Bute was more popular than aristocratic. In the tortured politics of the 1760s the only administration which had difficulty carrying its measures in the House of Lords was the avowedly 'Whig', and allegedly 'aristocratic'

[89] *The Works of the Right Reverend Thomas Newton, D.D.*, i. 42.

[90] T. J. McCann, ed., *The Correspondence of the Dukes of Richmond and Newcastle, 1724–1750* (Sussex Rec. Soc. 73, 1984), p. 215.

[91] *Horace Walpole's Correspondence*, xxiii. 164: to Sir Horace Mann, 31 Dec. 1769.

[92] Thomas Somerville, *My Own Life and Times 1741–1814* (Edinburgh, 1861), p. 381.

ministry of Lord Rockingham in 1766. The political instability of the 1760s put a considerable strain on the logic and consistency of anti-aristocratic polemic. Junius, the self-appointed tribune of the people, charged the court of George III with plotting against the English nobility. But his evidence for this conspiracy was oddly inconsequential. It featured Mansfield's direction to the jury in Lord Grosvenor's prosecution of the Duke of Cumberland for misconduct with his wife. Mansfield told the jurors that in assessing damages for the violation of his marriage-bed, Grosvenor could claim no special privilege as a peer. Junius considered this an affront to traditional values. 'Under an arbitrary government, all ranks and distinctions are confounded. The honour of a nobleman is no more considered than the reputation of a peasant.'[93] If this was the strongest evidence he could find of a court conspiracy against nobility his case was thin indeed.

The long-lived North ministry, supposedly representing the triumph of the King's Friends over the Whig aristocracy, was never in difficulty in the Upper House. Yet it combined the support of the peers with shrewd use of anti-peer polemic, accusing the parliamentary opposition of oligarchical designs on the integrity of the State. The *History of a French Louse* in 1779 supposedly revealed the King of France's plan to divide Britain into three viceroyalties, each headed by a Whig magnate. Lord George Germain's elevation to the Lords in February 1782 provoked a debate in which opposition peers found themselves asserting that he might be worthy of a seat in the Lower House but not in the Upper.[94] North, himself the heir to an earldom, proved an adroit operator in this respect. In 1779 Fox discerned in his Militia Act 'the idea of contemning aristocracy' because it did not allow for consulting the Lords-Lieutenant. North, far from denying 'the charge of despising the aristocratic power', insisted that his policy was based 'not on the aristocracy, but on the body of the people'.[95] Significantly, it was during the American War that the term 'aristocracy' began to be used to describe a body of men rather than a system of government.

In the constitutional struggle which followed North's fall, it was the Crown which was able to appeal to anti-aristocratic sentiment. Fox's assertion in 1782 that a Prime Minister must be nominated by the Cabinet was readily interpreted, in the words of the neutral blue-stocking Mrs Carter, as 'an attempt to convert, or pervert, our government into an oligarchy'.[96] The Shelburne ministry which followed seemed to Bentham a kind of sporting encounter with 'the great aristocracy of the country: it

[93] *The Letters of Junius*, ed., J. Cannon (Oxford, 1978), p. 209.
[94] Turberville, *The House of Lords in the Eighteenth Century*, pp. 23–4.
[95] *Parliamentary Register* (1802 edn.), xii. 547–50: 2 July 1779.
[96] *Letters from Mrs Elizabeth Carter, to Mrs Montagu, between the Years 1755 and 1800* (3 vols., London, 1817), iii. 166.

was as they say at Cricket, *Shelburne against England*.[97] The tussle between the King and the Fox–North Coalition could be portrayed similarly, even when the heat of battle had passed and it was possible to state its outcome in unemotional terms. Looking back on the history of 1784 the court peer Lord Harcourt remarked that Fox's success would have meant that 'there would have been neither king nor people in the country; but one commanding aristocracy'.[98] From a very different standpoint Lord Holland was content to portray Fox as seeking to strengthen aristocracy against the Crown.[99] At the time the point had been a commonplace of the propaganda warfare. In the general election of 1784 the opponents of the Coalition made much of its aristocratic character. At York it was described as 'that mighty aristocracy', 'that formidable Aristocracy'.[100] Yet the King's master-move, which led to the unseating of the Coalition and its electoral humiliation, had been to induce the House of Lords to reject the Coalition's major legislative measure, its East India Bill.

It was an odd alignment of forces that laid on the Upper House the burden of defending the Crown against aristocratic assault. Yet there was an increasingly common perception that the court of George III was antithetical towards the values represented by peers of the realm. It was even complained that Queen Charlotte had absorbed this prejudice on her marriage, her treatment of both peers and peeresses being contrasted with that of her predecessor Queen Caroline.[101] Plainly, what constituted the aristocracy was a matter for careful definition. The Duke of Norfolk caused a sensation by publicly describing Pitt's elevations of 1786, notably Sir John Delaval and Charles Jenkinson, as 'persons of a description that he believed the people neither expected nor approved of', and in 1794 the Duke of Portland distinguished what he called the 'natural aristocracy' which he believed George III had set out systematically to debase and vilify.'[102] Presumably Norfolk and Portland thought only Whigs were fully qualified as aristocrats. This was indeed one of the triumphs of George III: to have associated in the minds of most of his subjects the cause of Pelhamite, Rockinghamite, and Foxite Whiggism with overweening aristocracy, even while he enlisted the aid of a majority of the English peerage against them.

The confusion created by ministerial politics was matched elsewhere. Noblemen were prominent in the extra-parliamentary movements of

---

[97] A. T. Milne, ed., *The Correspondence of Jeremy Bentham* (London, 1981), iv. 158: to Lansdowne, 24 Aug. 1790.

[98] *The Harcourt Papers*, vii. 128.

[99] L. Mitchell, *Holland House* (London, 1980), p. 125.

[100] Stirling, *Annals of a Yorkshire House*, ii. 188; York Minster Library, Hailstone MSS, 1.4.4.

[101] A. M. Broadley and L. Melville, *The Beautiful Lady Craven* (2 vols., London, 1914), i. 53.

[102] Northumberland RO, Delaval MSS, 2DE/49/4/17: Delaval's notes; *The Windham Papers* (2 vols., London, 1913), ii. 202.

George III's reign. What they did for the cause of reform is difficult to assess, but they surely served their class. Though their numbers were few, their rank was high. Several were dukes and most were of ancient blood. The Dukes of Richmond and Manchester were bitter opponents of Lord North and vociferous supporters of the parliamentary reform movement. The blood of Revolution Whigs and royalist Tories mingled in the cause of aristocratic radicalism. Lord Abingdon represented a family noted for its loyalty to the Stuarts in the seventeenth century. So did his cousin and friend, Lord Craven. The language which these men employed both in and out of Parliament was considered astonishingly inflammatory. Richmond and Manchester openly accused George III of emulating the despotic designs of his Stuart ancestors, appealing to an alliance of great lords and uncorrupted commoners against a vicious tyranny. Abingdon was a tireless critic of moderate Whiggism, condemning Edmund Burke's party manifestos in terms which could readily match those of the City radicals. Yet he had a high opinion of his rank and fearlessly allied the cause of nobles and people, claiming indeed a special status for the former in point of popular representation. He took particular pleasure in the role of the Lords in 1688. When James II had fled, leaving no possibility of a legally summoned Parliament, 'The Power of the Lords became that of their being *pro Tempore* the actual Representatives of the Nation at large'.[103] Abingdon's origins made him vulnerable to criticism and also mockery, not least because his prose style was easily exposed as vulgar and ungrammatical. 'Unhappy would it be for the English tongue, if Nobility should stamp the fashion on his Lordship's Dialect.'[104]

Champions of the nobility argued that a disaster such as the American War made the case for aristocracy stronger rather than weaker. Matthew Robinson Morris, subsequently elevated to the House of Lords as Lord Rokeby, pointed out that oligarchical, or as he called them aristocratical constitutions, had an excellent record, Venice and Genoa among popish states, Holland and Sweden among Protestant. In England it was the House of Commons that stood in need of reform.[105] On the other hand reforming noblemen were not immune to criticism in this respect. Three of the pontificating ducal Associators enjoyed hereditary sinecures which were prime targets of economical reformers. The Dukes of Grafton, Richmond, and Manchester, the first two descended from bastards of Charles II, had patents entitling them to the proceeds of certain customs duties. The Lords debate of 8 February 1780 on this subject, in the midst of intense agitation in favour of reform, caused them considerable embarrassment. Grafton

---

[103] *Thoughts on the Letter of Edmund Burke, Esq.*: (6th edn., Oxford, 1777), p. xlvii.

[104] *A Dissertation on the Political Abilities of the Earl of Abingdon* (London, 1780), p. 40.

[105] *Peace the Best Policy* (London, 1977), pp. 81–2.

responded by defending his patent as a royal contribution to family life. 'He was happy to be a father of a young family, unprovided for in a great measure, and he could not say but he felt much, and had his struggles, but he had the satisfaction to add that he had resolution to overcome them.' Manchester also pleaded a small fortune for a duke, but announced his readiness to accept sacrifices in the cause of reform. 'In such an event he would seek a residence in some distant clime, where he could live in privacy, and suit his style of living and exterior appearance to means derived from a very scanty income.' Richmond, at least, resisted flabby appeals to sentiment. He simply insisted that a Crown patent was property as good in law as any other form of property. The propaganda value of the ducal patents was frequently exploited by their opponents. In 1793 George Dyer relished pointing out that the 48s. a chaldron paid for coal in London, compared with 30s. in Cambridge, was devoted largely to maintaining the Duke of Richmond in comfort befitting his station.[106] By this time reforming nobles were in shorter supply, though there remained sufficient to generate a lively debate about their standing. One of them, the Duke of Bedford, was made the target of that most devastating of all rebukes to populist peers, Edmund Burke's *Letter to a Noble Lord*. Another, Lord Stanhope, was a perpetual thorn in the side of government. The great ball which he gave at Chevening in honour of the radical Unitarian Jeremiah Joyce, when Joyce was released from Newgate in December 1794, demonstrated the value of blue-blooded support for a republican agitator.[107]

The sheer confusion created by the diversity of noble attitudes was particularly marked in the Association movement during the last stages of the American War. The speeches made by London and Westminster reformers, and the tracts distributed by the London-based Society for Constitutional Information, dwelled a good deal on the sinister pretensions of peers as well as on the more obvious threat presented by the influence of the Crown. Thomas Day pronounced that there had never been an aristocracy, 'from ancient Rome to modern Venice, that was not the universal tyrant and inquisitor of the species'.[108] Provincial reformers exploited the same rhetoric, with chapter and verse as to the baneful effects of aristocratic politics. At Huntingdon Lord Sandwich was accused of inveigling 'a set of ignorant dependants into a renunciation of their rights, and an acquiescence under their grievances'. 'Where, my Lord, was the

---

[106] *Parliamentary Debates* (1802 edn.), xiv. 151, 168, 175–6; *The Complaints of the Poor People of England* (2nd edn., London, 1793), pp. 15–16. Paine also denounced Richmond's coal profits (*Rights of Man*) ed. H. Collins (London, 1969), pp. 228, 247; perhaps his recollections of his days as an exciseman in Sussex, where Richmond was the leading magnate, gave edge to his criticism.

[107] J. Seed, 'Jeremiah Joyce, Unitarianism and the Vicissitudes of the Radical Intelligentsia in the 1790s', *Trans. Unitarian Soc.*, 17 (1979–82), 97 ff.

[108] *Two Speeches of Thomas Day Esq.* (London, 1780), p. 15.

pride of birth? Where was the blush of hereditary honour?' In neighbouring
Hertfordshire the prominent part of the Lord-Lieutenant, Viscount Cranborne, in organizing a Protest in opposition to the local reformers, attracted
equal opprobrium.[109]

Yet similar points could be put on the other side. Noblemen were
prominent in the petitioning, leading one defender of the court to urge
freeholders not to be dazzled by the names of noble families among the
signatures. The same intrigues of which Sandwich and Cranborne were
accused on behalf of the court, were detected in the activities of their
opponents.[110] Some reformers, indeed, saw the advantage of aristocratic
assistance. Thomas Day was notably mute on the subject of blue-blooded
tyranny when he spoke at Cambridge, where the petitioning committee
was dominated by Whig peers.[111] Government peers were accused of
betraying their caste. Cranborne was dismissed on account of 'unfortunate
connections, the tincture of foreign education, the glitter of courts', Sandwich as a placeman, the Earl of Essex as a pensioner, the Duke of Marlborough as a servile courtier.[112] Controversies of this kind made it increasingly
easy to establish the image of George III rescuing bourgeois England from
the horrors of oligarchy. In this context, the hypocrisy of reforming
noblemen made a good debating point long before the French Revolution
produced some devastating examples of the consequences. Leonard Smelt,
who was sub-governor to the eldest sons of the King and had the temerity
to speak against Wyvill in his native county of Yorkshire, made effective
use of this in denouncing Yorkshire magnates like Lord Rockingham
who employed workmen in the mining and textile industries in the most
degrading conditions.

When those who possess, from an hereditary claim only, all the distinctions of
society, and such an excessive disproportion of its benefits, as to have a thousand
of their fellow creatures employed in the hardest work and with the poorest
subsistance to contribute to their ease and luxury.—When such talk of the natural
equality of men and their right to change the government they live under, who
can withhold their astonishment? And yet this has been so long the fashionable
language of this county, that all subordination, and order, all decency is at an end,
and has carried its effects up to the crown, which so far from having too great an
influence, has been deprived of that most essential part of it which a proper

---

[109] *Four Letters from the Country Gentlemen, on the Subject of the Petitions* (London, 1780), pp.
17–21.

[110] *Thoughts on the Present County Petitions* (1780), p. 3.

[111] Day, *Two Speeches of Thomas Day Esq.*

[112] *A Letter to the Right Honourable Viscount Cranborne, Lord-Lieutenant and Custos Rotularum of
the County of Hertford* (London, 1780).

education and early habits formerly implanted in the hearts of men,—a general disposition to respect it even in the warmest political contests.[113]

VARNISHED VICES

If it was difficult to identify the titled with a consistent set of political principles, it was easy to fasten on their supposed moral characteristics. Rank could be seen as innately antithetical to high standards. Those who enjoyed it 'being independent of the lesser cares of life, from their situation, seldom pay a proper regard to their moral duties, which are the very cement and bond of society'.[114] But however predictable, the worry about decadent nobility was that it displayed the viciousness of vice with painful clarity. Very few people expected the rich to behave better than the poor, even when they urged them to do so. But nobility expressed timeless values of virtue and honour; it also commanded respect and deference. When noblemen betrayed their moral duty they were bestowing a dangerous legitimacy on immorality. As William Godwin analysed it, a title had the effect of varnishing, or gilding vice.[115] It was not one of his more original observations. Moralists had long since made the point hackneyed, and reached for ever more horrifying metaphors in their efforts to lend it force. Thomas Hunter described the corruption, degeneracy, and licentiousness engaged in by men of illustrious title 'as the sun and stars converted into blood would strike us only as more signal and horrible portents'.[116] It appealed equally to writers who exploited the cult of feeling and bourgeois honesty. General Burgoyne, who combined play-writing with a military career, and knew well through his marriage into Lord Derby's family the pros and cons of aristocratic connections, would not have surprised the audience for his *Heiress* in 1786 when he told them that a 'title may bring forward merits, but it also places our defects in horrid relief'.[117]

The literary market for criticism of the great proved almost limitless. Teaching the well-born how to behave, or as Robert Bage put it in his novel *Man As He Is*, conducting rich high-blooded young Englishmen to the temple of wisdom, was a stock theme.[118] The 'macaroni' age of the late eighteenth century set records in this respect, as the explosive growth of a

---

[113] *An Account of Some Particulars Relative to the Meeting Held at York, on Thursday the 30th of December, 1779* (London, 1780), p. 21.

[114] Potter, *The Curate of Coventry*, i. 45.

[115] William Godwin, *Enquiry Concerning Political Justice*, ed. I. Kramnick (London, 1796), p. 478. It was Coleridge, criticizing Godwin's view, who used the expression 'gilded vice'; see *The Collected Works of Samuel Taylor Coleridge: Lectures 1795 on Politics and Religion*, p. 11. Godwin spoke of 'vice, deprived of that varnish with which she delighted to gloss her actions'.

[116] T. Hunter, *Reflections Critical and Moral on the Letters of the Late Earl of Chesterfield* (London, 1776), p. 212.

[117] *The Dramatic Works of the Late Lieut.-Gen. J. Burgoyne*, ii. 142.

[118] (2nd edn., 4 vols., London, 1796), iv. 101.

literature devoted to middle-class needs, the revival of evangelical tendencies both in and outside the Church, and the expanding disposable
income of the upper classes combined to create promising conditions.
William Warburton had regretted that Samuel Richardson had not used
his *Pamela* to launch a more systematic critique of 'the follies and extrava-
gancies of high life, which to one of Pamela's station and good sense would
have appeared as absurd and unaccountable as European polite vices and
customs to an Indian'.[119] Had he lived to see the torrent of criticism which
flowed in the last quarter of the century, he would not have thought the
opportunity lost for long.

It is possible to date the new censoriousness with some precision.
Publications which surveyed the peerage in numbers and with identities
clearly revealed or only lightly veiled were a product of the 1770s and
1780s. The techniques varied but what they had in common was an interest
in peers as a class rather than the few who had happened to be prominent
in politics and were on that account naturally exposed to public criticism
and ridicule. One such, published in 1782, was Coleman's *A Satirical
Peerage of England*, which used as its purchase point the mottoes of the
noble families of England. It lost no opportunity to associate nobility with
mercenary attitudes and ignoble sentiments. The Duke of Grafton's motto
'Et decus et pretium recti' was translated 'Peers get rewarded all their
lives'; the Earl Poulett's 'Gardre la Foi' 'What faith you have got you
should keep as a treasure, for Peers always change it for profit or pleasure';
the Earl of Chatham's 'Benigno nomine' 'Hallo—people—neighbours—
hear! By God's blessing—I'm a Peer!'; the Earl of Abercorn's 'Solus
nobilitas virtus' 'The Virtue of Lords—we never shall know it, They keep
it so close—they seldom will show it.' Other publications were more specific
about the failings of peers and their wives. *Miniature Pictures* presented
them as stage figures, unkindly exhibiting Lady Craven's highly public
copulation with the French Ambassador ('Play the French Tune') and the
Earl of Hertford's notorious parsimony ('I own myself of the Company of
Beggars').[120] The political implications were rarely ignored. Some of the
most vitriolic of the mock 'peerages' were those which described peers in
a parliamentary setting. *The Patricians* of 1773 was one such. Lest anyone
suppose that the corruption to be seen in the House of Commons could
be offset by the superior virtue and wisdom of the Upper House, it claimed
to demonstrate in depressing detail 'that *birth* alone has no pretence, To
truth, or honour, dignity, or sense'.[121]

The shorthand for aristocratic delinquency was Chesterfieldism, in

[119] A. W. Evans, *Warburton and the Warburtonians: A Study in Some Eighteenth-Century Controversies* (London, 1932), p. 125.
[120] (3rd edn., London, 1781).
[121] *The Patricians* (London, 1773), p. 4.

honour of the fourth Earl of Chesterfield, whose letters to his illegitimate
son, Philip Stanhope, were posthumously published by Stanhope's widow
in 1774. The letters seemed to embody all that was artificial, vicious, and
cynical in aristocratic mores. The fact that they also contained much
common sense and laudable sentiment made them more rather than less
controversial. Vice paraded under the veil of virtue appeared all the more
provoking. In this respect they might have been less objectionable if they
had been published when they had been penned. Even so, much of the
'politeness' printed under Chesterfield's name commended itself to those
who sought a guide to the canons of contemporary gentility. A succession
of digests and abridgements offered what was considered an anodyne
essence of his prescription for civilized life. But with or without expur-
gation, the cynicism and artificiality of the model of polite manners presented by Chesterfield remained peculiarly offensive to an age which had
learned to cherish innocence and spontaneity as the hallmarks of a 'sensible
people'. Confronted with the man of honour in this shape, the man of
feeling could not but revolt.

It did not need the publication of a satanic gospel to draw attention to
the moral menace of a corrupted nobility. There was evidence of mounting
public awareness of the misdeeds of highly placed men and women. When
Lord Santry was convicted of murdering his running footman in 1739 his
pardon attracted little interest. Twenty years later Lord Ferrers's trial and
execution for the murder of his servant was treated as a great public
sensation. Ferrers had a stronger case for a pardon than Santry, if only on
the grounds of insanity, but the sense that justice must be seen to be done
was overwhelming. The sexual failings of peers and peeresses were also a
continuing source of fascination. The arraignment of Lord Baltimore for
rape in 1768 cast a lurid light on the moral frailty of the nobility and was
followed eagerly in the newspapers. Part of its appeal lay in its resemblance
to the plot of many a popular novel. The victim was a young milliner, a
pious girl whose biblical turn of phrase delighted journalists. Subjected to
a campaign of sexual harassment which would have tried a veritable Pamela
she had seemingly resisted all her noble seducer's blandishments. Baltimore
was said to have lost his patience, removed her to his country house at
Epsom, and accomplished by force what he had not been able to achieve
by persuasion. The consequent trial provoked an avalanche of moral
outrage in the press, but the outcome was disappointing. The jury did not
see the devout Miss Woolnoth as a latter-day Pamela. There was sufficient
evidence of a prior agreement between her father and Baltimore, and also
of her own complicity, to save the peer's neck. It did not, however, save
his face. Rather than live with the publicity which the trial had attracted,
he removed himself to Italy and eventually died there. This aristocratic
flight from public notoriety was the most significant feature of the whole

affair. Trial by the press and punishment by popular prurience was a new experience for the noble rake.

Another aristocrat who preferred exile abroad to ignominy at home was the Duchess of Kingston, the former Miss Chudleigh. Her trial for bigamy in April 1776 was conducted in a blaze of publicity exceeding even that devoted to Baltimore's ordeal. From the standpoint of high society, it ranked with other entertainments of the day. The great event of 1774 had been Lord Stanley's fête champêtre, that of 1775 the Thames Regatta. The Kingston trial took place in the spring at the height of the London season and represented a notable addition to the social calendar. But its peculiar fascination was the spectacle of a duchess, formerly a royal maid of honour, being judged by her peers in full view of the nation. Not only she but her class was on trial, doubly so because the process by which it tried its own crimes was under close scrutiny. The trial took place in the House of Lords at a time when the newspaper-reading public was becoming familiar with the regular reporting of proceedings in both Houses. But even at the trial the attendance was by no means exclusively aristocratic. Every peer was permitted seven tickets, many of which found their way into distinctly ignoble hands. One spectator, the young Samuel Johnson, Sir Joshua Reynolds's nephew, reckoned that there were more than 2,000 people present of whom approximately 370 were peers and peeresses.[122] That the subject of this extraordinary mixture of judicial and popular tribunal was guilty was hardly in doubt. At the time of her marriage to the Duke in 1769, her husband Augustus Hervey, thereafter elevated to the Earldom of Bristol by the premature death of his brother, had still been alive. Her first marriage had been contracted in secrecy and she succeeded in convincing an ecclesiastical court that it was not binding. But the evidence presented in the Lords was damning, both as to the fact of an earlier marriage, and the Duchess's duplicity. Her humiliation was complete when the Attorney-General brutally attributed her conduct to her 'ambition and a lust of lucre' and 'doubted whether to the last she determined in favour of one husband in preference to another, but as the option was likely most to administer to her love of dominion and love of money'.[123]

There was a certain irony about her plight. Miss Chudleigh had been the mistress, successively, of two men who legitimized her position by marriage. Not a few peeresses led respectable lives following a murky past. But the history of her harlotry had been revealed in the most public manner possible, and it was this as much as her bigamy which rendered her position intolerable. Private vice made public must receive exemplary punishment,

---

[122] S. M. Radcliffe, *Sir Joshua's Nephew* (London, 1930), pp. 197–8.

[123] *The True and Secret Account of the Proceedings and Trial of the Duchess of Kingston* (London, 1776), p. 18.

though in this case it was not the formal punishment that was exemplary. On conviction the Duchess pleaded her privilege as a peer. That she was entitled to do so was difficult to deny, since, if she were not legally married to the Duke of Kingston, she must be Countess Dowager of Bristol, and if she had not been legally married to the Earl of Bristol, she must be Duchess of Kingston. The Lord Chancellor, Lord Apsley, 'told her that little or no punishment could be inflicted on her, but that the feelings of her own conscience would supply that defect'.[124] The proper penalty would have been burning in the hand. Lord Mansfield, the legal luminary of the age, concurred in the inappropriateness of such a punishment: 'To the hand of a Lady, this might be very disagreeable.'[125] But he was also disturbed by the whole proceeding. In advance he had warned of the dangers of a public trial in 'the eyes of Great Britain and all Europe'.[126] A trial which focused attention on the Duchess and then gave her immunity from the customary penalties of the law would do little to impress potential offenders among the public at large.

Baltimore and the Duchess of Kingston were both charged with criminal offences. They had noble compatriots whose lapses were less serious, but none the less fascinating to their inferiors. Aristocratic adultery was a persistent theme of moral commentators. Some sensational cases were available for inspection around the time of the Baltimore and Kingston scandals, including that in which the King's brother, the Duke of Cumberland, was dragged into the courts by the husband of his mistress, Lady Grosvenor, in 1770. There was a wealth of embarrassing detail of the liaison, obtained by agents of Lord Grosvenor at an inn where the Duke and Lady Grosvenor had been caught *in flagrante*. This was reported at length in the papers. Cumberland had to pay £10,000 damages, though the bill was actually footed by his unfortunate royal brother. His disgrace was completed by his marriage to Mrs Horton, member of a notoriously libertine family, the Luttrells. The Grosvenor case was only one of many. Like others, too, it led to a formal application for divorce. Such applications seemed to provide objective evidence that aristocratic vice was growing. They increased notably after 1750 and in the 1770s.[127] In theory the procedure was open to all, but in practice most who used it were of high rank, and in many instances titled. Divorce bills customarily originated in the Upper House, where they were scrutinized by the law lords and bishops. Naturally enough, there was a tendency to view divorce as an

---

[124] *The True and Secret Account of the Proceedings and Trial of the Duchess of Kingston* (London, 1966), p. 32.

[125] Cobbett's *Parliamentary History*, xvii. 1109.

[126] Ibid., xviii. 1114.

[127] R. Trumbach, *The Rise of the Egalitarian Family: Aristocratic Kinship and Domestic Relations in Eighteenth-Century England* (New York, 1978), ch. 3; L. Stone, *The Family, Sex and Marriage in England 1500–1800* (London, 1977), p. 39.

aristocratic disease, though one which, like other dangerous infections, would quickly transmit itself to other classes unless it were eradicated at source. It was easy to assume what was not technically true, that divorce legislation was the peculiar privilege of lordly legislators. The author of the satire *The Divorce* in 1779 portrayed lawyers persuading an over scrupulous nobleman to divorce his unfaithful wife.

> Your Lordship is a Man of Fashion;
> And what's the Privilege of *Peer*,
> If laws of God and Man you fear?

The bishops also emphasized the connection between rank and vice. The bills of 1771 and 1779 which they promoted to prevent the remarriage of 'guilty parties' to a divorce presumed that divorce was a device of the opulent and titled to break their vows and legitimize their adulteries. Such perceptions were understandable. In 1779, for instance, the only divorce applications rejected by the Lords were two concerned exclusively with commoners. The cases involving titled men and women were approved, though in one of them, the Marquis of Carmarthen's citation of his wife for adultery, the evidence of 'criminal conversation' was unsatisfactory. The petitions which failed were those of humbler petitioners, a drysalter of Edmonton, and an officer in the Sixth Regiment of Foot.[128] Such divorce proceedings, on the tiny scale permitted by English law, were not necessarily evidence of deteriorating morals. Any judgement as to the changing sexual practices of the peerage would be highly speculative. What is certain is that the public impact of these cases was marked at a time when those involved were being subjected to a more searching inspection by the press and were themselves seemingly more ready to risk such inspection by taking their cause to the law courts and to Parliament. In a sense this was a tribute to the enhanced rights of aristocratic women and the increased freedom of all peers in sexual matters. It also revealed their fidelity to the concept of marriage as a meaningful relationship, especially when an adulterous second marriage entailed excommunication by polite society, as it usually did for women. In this sense they too were rejecting the cynicism of Chesterfieldism, though in the process they were exposing themselves to further public criticism.

All but one of the accusations levelled at men of rank could be levelled at women. Duelling, by its nature, was a masculine vice. But gambling, irreligion, fashionable frivolity (especially in respect of dress), and sexual immorality were all indulged in by women. Satires on noble women matched those on noble men, sometimes with political overtones. It was a

---

[128] *Lords Journals*, xxxv. 549 ff. *passim*.

gift to the caricaturists that the Duchess of Devonshire, a byword for female extravagance in the 1770s and 1780s, was also known for her ventures into party politics, not least in the celebrated Westminster election of 1784. But there were many other examples. The *Picture Gallery* of 1780 presented unflattering thumbnail sketches of numerous peeresses. The *House of Peeresses; Or Female Oratory* portrayed a parliamentary debate between pious peeresses and less suitable models, including readily identifiable adulteresses, and ladies with a reputation for ruling their husbands, such as the Duchess of Bedford.[129] Since it was generally agreed that women were responsible for laying the foundations of family life and youthful virtue, the corruption of womanhood at its highest levels appeared peculiarly dangerous. Forming the manners of the nation's governors was more especially the function of upper-class women, and when they failed their failure was likely to be infectious. *Female Government* in 1777 traced the collapse of patriarchal authority to aristocratic women who preferred to be governed by their admirers, often chaplains or military men, rather than by their husbands.

The question of morals could not be separated from the wider responsibilities of the peerage. Politicians were exposed to a new spirit of prurience under George III. In this respect Lord Bute set an unfortunate and undeserved precedent. The scurrility which he endured in the press on account of his supposed intrigue with the King's mother made it clear that for princesses and prime ministers alike there was now no private domain. Bute's successors did not need to be Scotsmen on the make to suffer similarly. The Duke of Grafton's liking for high-class prostitutes, especially the celebrated Nancy Parsons, became a feature of the hostile propaganda deployed against his ministry, culminating in the diatribes of Junius. It must surely have contributed to Grafton's loss of nerve at the time of his resignation in 1770. Of his successors, Lord North, Lord Shelburne, and the younger Pitt led exemplary lives so far as women were concerned. If Lord Rockingham's character was not spotless the stains had well nigh vanished after a quarter of a century of blameless married life. But there were other senior ministers who found their amours the subject of ridicule and recrimination. The outstanding example was that of Lord Sandwich, First Lord of the Admiralty for many years and a leading member of North's Cabinet. As 'Jemmy Twitcher', who had 'peached' Wilkes and his *Essay on Woman* in 1763, he was an easy target for hostile moralizing. His colleagues under North found him robust, genial, civilized. But in the public mind he remained Jemmy Twitcher. During the last stages of the American war when military prospects dwindled and political animosities intensified it was tempting to charge him with the additional crime of

[129] (London, 1779).

corruption, though the evidence was thin. The sensational murder of his mistress Martha Ray by a crazy clergyman in 1780 completed this picture of blue-blooded vice. Sandwich's career went back to the 1750s, when his political conduct and sexual morals would not have been connected for purposes of public discussion. His misfortune was to live into an age which took a more censorious interest in the personal doings of the great. He perhaps felt something of this himself. In his later years he took pains to disassociate himself from his dissolute days in the Hell Fire Club. If his life with Martha Ray could hardly be portrayed as one of domestic innocence, it lacked the colourful outrageousness of his youth. Those who met him and his mistress were impressed by his sobriety and her modesty.[130] As a musician he helped raise funds for the Leicester Infirmary, and played a prominent part in the great Handel commemorations of the 1780s, the proceeds of which went to charity.[131] Along with other court peers of the 1780s he was identified with various good causes, and was patron of a well-known dispensary for the poor.

By the time of Sandwich's death, in 1792, immorality had come to seem almost the prerogative of the opposition to the court. Royalty had something to do with this development. The Prince of Wales's reputation for womanizing was established at an early stage, as a result of his well-publicized affair with Perdita Robinson in 1780. His association with the Foxite party followed soon after, in the summer of 1783. The contrast with his father and mother was striking. George III, as well as being the father of Prince George, was the cousin of Charles James Fox, and the brother of the Duke of Cumberland. He was the successor of two princes notorious for their marital infidelity, and the only king since Charles I noted for personal continence. His wife seemed a pillar of domestic virtue, all the more when it was recalled that the first Hanoverian Queen, Sophia Dorothea, had been immured in the fortress of Ahlden on account of her infidelity and the second, Caroline of Ansbach, noted for her complaisant attitude towards sexual lapses, as well as her latitudinarian tendencies in theological questions. In the epic struggle of Fox and George III this moral consideration was of great significance. The King needed all its force in 1784.

In this the early 1780s constituted something of a turning-point. In the 1770s it had still been feasible to associate the King with the ruin of the English nobility. The argument was developed in the anonymous *A Letter to Us, from One of Ourselves* of 1777. It offered a bizarre version of the myth of the King's Friends, as applied more particularly to the case of the peers. Bute and the Scots were held forth as 'Bawds and Pimps, to forward

---

[130] Joseph Cradock, *Literary and Miscellaneous Memoirs* (4 vols., London, 1828), i. 117–18.

[131] W. Weber, 'The 1784 Handel Commemoration as Political Ritual', *Journal of British Studies*, 28 (1989), 52–3.

the great Plan of Prostitution. When a Nobleman or Commoner became shook in his Morals, or hurt in his Fortune, which are the Effects of Intemperance or Excess, and began to look out for the Means to support the Continuance of his Pursuits, he was sure to find a fatal Assistance in some treacherous North Briton.' The result had been subservience and dependence. 'The first Class of the Nation threw themselves into Disgrace and Servitude.' St James's became a kind of public warehouse in which the peers could purchase titles and places at the cost of their integrity. 'Our Nobility, placed on an Eminence among the People, instead of supporting the Dignity of their Station, are become a Shame and Disgrace to it. Our young Nobleman are Jockies, Whoremasters, and Spendthrifts, while those advanced in years are repairing the Waste of their Youth, by a shameful Plunder of the Public.'[132] Even in 1777 this was an eccentric line of argument. Many would have accepted the notion of a decline in aristocratic morality and integrity, but few would have attributed it to the court.

ENGAGING CONDESCENSION

More than anything else, what caused anxiety about an aristocracy that was rotten at its core was the example it set and the guidance it provided. Chesterfield had appeared not simply as a cynical analyst of upper-class manners but as an active instructor in them. It was his role as tutor which seemed so exceptionable, as William Johnson Temple put it, 'when nobility acts a part so unworthy of honour and virtue, as to excite to preferment through the medium of hypocrisy and sensuality, without sentiment and sympathy'.[133] Chesterfield's advice had been addressed to his illegitimate son, whose career did not suggest either that he had followed it closely or benefited by it when he did. But some of the odium which his legitimate heir, the fifth Earl, suffered when he insisted on the prosecution of his tutor William Dodd in 1776 surely derived from this source. It seemed appropriate that the name of Chesterfield should be associated with aristocratic callousness of this kind.

Constructing a model of nobility which would act as an effective alternative, even an antidote to Chesterfieldism, was a complex business. It began with a crucial subject, the nobleman's notion of his own nobility. A certain sense of humility, of the need to earn rather than inherit deference was essential. This featured heavily in praise of peers, one of the commonest forms of poetic patronage-seeking. Thus the Bristol poet Henry Jones expressed his admiration for the fifth Baron Berkeley despite rather than because of his inherited titles. 'In him the rank and sterling worth accord,

---

[132] Pp. 16–19.
[133] *Moral and Historical Memoirs* (London, 1779), p. 6.

Intrinsic worth for once hath made *a Lord*.'[134] This notion that hereditary status must be treated by its holder as the least of his accomplishments was also strong among those who sought to make peers fit for heaven. The epitaph which Lady Huntingdon commissioned from Bolingbroke for her husband was appropriate in this respect: 'If he derived his title from a long roll of illustrious ancestors, he reflected back on them superior honour. He ennobled nobility by virtue.'[135] It was outdone by the evangelical preacher John Fletcher in praise of the evangelical peer the young Earl of Buchan: 'Oh! how far below his grace is his nobility.'[136] On a more worldly plane martial worth was also associated with a readiness to sacrifice the advantages of rank. The point was put clearly by Thomas Anbury when he published his account of Burgoyne's disastrous march to Saratoga. His work was dedicated to Lord Petersham, one of Burgoyne's most admired officers. Anbury made Petersham's form of nobility a paradoxical kind of egalitarianism in the common cause. He had apparently delighted 'when out in the field, to forego the pleasure which high rank' and fortune brought him. 'You found the care of your men to be at once the true proportion of your country's service, and a most gratifying enjoyment to your own benevolence; while on their parts, they considered their leader as their best friend and benefactor.'[137]

With equality went openness, the answer to those who charged nobility with stand-offishness. The readiness of country house owners to permit public viewing when they were not in residence and even, on fixed days, when they were, was part of polite proprietorship. Travellers might contrast the 'true politeness of Lord and Lady Strafford in permitting strangers to have open access' with 'the insolent pride of nabobs and contractors, who, accidentally becoming possessed of fine seats, refuse that gratification to all who are not of their *present* acquaintance'.[138] In this respect, though the ordinary Englishman's home might be his castle, the aristocratic Englishman's was not. At Harewood House in Yorkshire in 1794, a visitor found 'His Lordship obliged to leave his own House every Saturday that the Public may view'. He concluded that this would 'shew little people that the possessors of those fine Houses ought to be no objects of Envy'.[139]

---

[134] *Clifton: A Poem, in Two Cantos* (Bristol, 1747), p. 16.
[135] *The Life and Times of Selina, Countess of Huntingdon*, i. 75.
[136] Ibid., ii. 18.
[137] H. Rogers, ed., *Hadden's Journal and Orderly Books* (Albany, NY, 1884), p. 372.
[138] William Bray, *Sketch of a Tour into Derbyshire and Yorkshire* (London, 1778), p. 133.
[139] Gloucestershire RO D 2227/30: Journals of Revd Samuel Viner. See also I. Pears, *The Discovery of Painting: the Growth of Interest in the Arts in England 1680–1768* (New Haven, Conn., 1988), p. 178; Pears points out that art collections were frequently placed in town houses, where the likely audience was to be found, and then moved to the country increasingly in the late 18th cent. But it is not clear that town houses were generally open to the public, and it seems more likely that it was the inconvenience of permitting them to be seen in London which prompted their owners to move them to a country seat often open to visitors. The object was surely display rather than proprietary seclusion.

Weekends imposed a considerable strain. As early as the 1730s the Duke of Richmond's menagerie at Goodwood was attracting up to five hundred visitors on a Sunday. The Duke was undismayed, but his workers complained of being 'much troubled with Rude Company to see the animals'.[140] Even town houses, if not open to the public, could be made less forbiddingly closed to it. Urban palaces designed psychologically as well as physically to exclude passers-by were criticized as indicating a withdrawal from public scrutiny. The front to the streets should 'present something that intimates a relation to the society in which you live'. The political implications were made explicit. Burlington House, it was said, with its screen and its enclosed courtyard, somewhat resembling a gaol, would procure respect in Algier or Tunis but not in London. 'He who thus immures himself in a free country, will hardly obtain consideration or power.'[141]

The debate on the subject of the nobleman's schooling is a clear example of the importance attached to accessibility. Interest in the relative merits of private and public education went back at least to the previous century and remained intense. Growing acceptance of the value of a public school education is attested by the increasing proportion of peers who attended such schools. There is an obvious temptation to interpret this tendency as evidence of a increasing assertion of aristocratic power. It produced a caste with a 'common attitude and a common sense of purpose'.[142] But it might just as readily be interpreted as the reverse, the submission of aristocrats to a code of values in which they had no intrinsic interest and to a form of patron–client relationship in which the power of the client might seem as marked as that of the patron. This was in effect argued by William Gilpin in 1760 during his highly successful schoolmastering career at Cheam school. He considered public schools thoroughly damaging in point of learning, morals, and health. But they were necessary evils. For boys 'suited for acting in a public station, a public school is the most natural and proper introduction'.[143] The titled were destined by their position for a public station and must submit to their educational fate.

The case made on behalf of public schools was not so much their academic quality, since it was difficult to deny the value of an individual tutor in point of scholarship and pedagogical technique, as the service which it performed in bringing together the future governors of society. It taught young noblemen that in certain contexts they were no better than

[140] T. P. Connor, 'Architecture and Planting at Goodwood, 1723–1750', *Sussex Arch. Colls.* 117 (1979), 189–90.

[141] James Stuart, *Critical Observations on the Buildings and Improvements of London* (London, 1771), pp. 26, 34.

[142] Cannon, *Aristocratic Century*, p. 34.

[143] F. J. G. Robinson, 'The Education of an 18th Century Gentleman: George Edward Stanley of Dalegarth and Ponsonby', *Trans. Cumbs. and Westmor. Ant. and Arch. Soc.*, NS 70 (1970), 190.

their fellow mortals. Schools were egalitarian communities where the only hierarchy was that provided by schoolmasters, and their function was precisely to maintain the equality of those in their charge. Competition with commoners who might be cleverer, more industrious, more personable, and not least, physically stronger, could only benefit the high-born. This was the theory. The practice was less certain. The author Percival Stockdale accepted that schoolboys enjoyed displaying their disdain for rank. 'Many young gentlemen of Eaton and Westminster, are eager to make a young lord know that he is their equal by nature.' But there was a snag. 'The good effects, however, of this ardour, soon wear off. Repeated and thorough drubbings, without the walls of the school, will never make one of our young nobility behave like a man for life. In his mature years, he will always treat an inferior as if he was a being of a different species.'[144] Moreover, schoolmasters were not impartial referees in the rivalry of schoolboys rendered equal by their common pursuit of learning, but seekers after preferment who knew the value of preferential treatment for their better-born pupils. At the very least they grasped how important it was to catch and keep a blue-blooded clientele. The Headmaster of Winchester between 1793 and 1809, W. S. Goddard, frankly admitted that 'he owed the prosperity of the school to the influence of a few boys of very high stamp'.[145] Treating such boys as if they were commoners was not very practicable, whatever the views of the boys themselves. One of the most famous of Eton's many schoolboy rebellions, in 1743, gave rise to much rancour when the headmaster, William Cooke, expelled a commoner but pardoned a peer's son on account of his rank.[146]

Parents, of course, were not discouraged by such arguments. It was proximity which they valued in a school, not equality. In a sense they wanted the lordly to maintain their superiority if only because they wanted them to remember their superior responsibilities. In mature years they must recall their connections, including those made during an impressionable time of life, at school. Making connections was the essence of a public education. Criticism of schools focused on their tendency to encourage vicious connections; praise centred on their propensity to promote useful ones. Bourgeois boys who mixed with young aristocrats might look forward to preferment of various kinds. Blue-blooded youths, for their part, might learn qualities of leadership and attract followers with talent and industry, qualities which were not hereditary and not necessarily valued in hereditary aristocrats. The element of hypocrisy in all this is obvious in retrospect but was less so at the time. The promotion of merit and virtue was not

[144] *The Memoirs of the Life and Writings of Percival Stockdale* (2 vols., London, 1809), ii. 416–17.
[145] A. F. Leach, *A History of Winchester College* (London, 1899), p. 411.
[146] 'Letters of Spencer Cowper, Dean of Durham, 1746–74', ed. E. Hughes, *Surtees Soc.* 165 (1950), 28.

only seen as compatible with a system of connections, it was assumed to depend on it. At a time when the State had almost no formal machinery for providing a career open to the talents, aristocratic influence provided the natural alternative. This was not considered corrupt, for corruption was the misuse of patronage, its perversion rather than its underlying principle. Nor was the traffic one way. An aristocracy which was in effect submitting itself to the requirements of a broad propertied society was preserving its influence but at the expense of much of its freedom of action.

What the nobleman needed most to learn at school was the art of attending to those anxious to be impressed by his nobility. Bourgeois snobbery provided a rich resource, but not one which could be taken for granted. The line between resentment and obsequiousness was narrow. As Henry Gabell, himself second master of Winchester, put it, 'more perhaps have been jacobinized by the little galling aristocracies of private life, than by any public grievance whatever'. The corollary was that an affable encounter could turn a potential republican into an enthusiastic advocate of aristocracy. Thus the young clergyman Samuel Viner described his experience at Durham in 1783, when he found himself at close quarters with the Duke of Northumberland, 'this great Peer'. His apprehensions proved unjustified. 'In short in this Visit the prejudice which people in humble Life are too apt to entertain against those of the highest ranks was entirely removed so that I know not which to admire most the magnificence and the Comfort of the Castle, the pleasing and useful attentions of the servants or the engaging Condescension of one of the first peers of the Realm.'[147] No doubt Northumberland was less ecstatic. The poet William Whitehead gently derided the sacrifice made on such occasions when he described the feelings of his friend Lord Harcourt on attending the Mayor's feast at Abingdon in the summer of 1767.

To be the first person in the place; to be addressed with deference, and that deference mixed with a satisfaction at having the honour to address you at all; to see a glow of happiness playing on Mrs Mayoress's plenteous countenance when she gives both hands in the conclusion of the minuet, or receives her fan from some humble relation who can never aspire to equal dignity; to have every black silk gown with pink ribbons in the whole assembly bursting with desire to be taken notice of; to have half a word give pleasure, and a familiar smile raise into rapture even a decayed beauty of three-score; to overhear whispers in every corner of the room 'How charmingly he looks!' 'How delightfully he is dressed!' 'He is certainly the best bred man in England; you know, Madam, I always said it;'— these, my Lord, are gratifications which will repay the little trouble you may be at to gain them.[148]

---

[147] *A Discourse Delivered on the Fast-Day in February 1799* (London, 1799), p. 37; Gloucestershire RO, D 2227/30: Journals of Revd Samuel Viner.
[148] *The Harcourt Papers*, vii, 271: 14 July 1767.

Ultimately this kind of respect was obtained at the cost of some hypocrisy. Those who mixed in the polite world knew that noblemen preferred noble company, and that to see a lord and a 'private gentleman' together at ease was a rare thing. Adept practitioners of the social rules succeeded in preserving their own snobbery while maintaining the duties of rank. One such was the lady who kept one day a week, Sunday, for those of her friends and acquaintances who were not titled. The Sabbath for her was anything but the 'Lord's Day'.[149] The important point was not that lords and ladies should sacrifice their social preferences, only that they should keep them under strict control for purposes of public display. There was an old tradition of bourgeois exclusiveness which doubtless had its roots partly in inverted snobbery, partly in a code of values emphasizing the distinct function of every rank. It was still being expressed in moralistic form where the poor were concerned in the late eighteenth century. And in its more abrasive version it remained in the literature of bourgeois separateness. John Cleland made use of it in *The Oeconomy of a Winter's Day* in a piece of blunt advice to ordinary citizens 'of the middle Condition'. Social intercourse with superiors he strongly deprecated. 'Shun, as thou woudst a Pesthouse, the Table of the Great: ... Leave Lords to Lords, like to like; so shalt thou not to be defiled with their Fooleries.'[150] This vein was still more profitably worked by writers who portrayed the great deliberately humiliating their inferiors even when approached in a suitably deferential manner. S. W. Ryley, in his compendium of contemporary prejudices and commonplaces *The Itinerant*, included a tale of a young nobleman in company at Worcester who not only refused a play-manager's request to command a performance from his troupe, but went out of his way to ridicule him in front of his friends. The result was a stinging lecture from the manager: 'I am aware, my Lord, that superior rank, is not always accompanied by superior abilities, but I should think; that education, the natural consequence of noble birth, would at least, so far enlarge the mind, and liberalise the manners, that the unfortunate would always meet with encouragement and support, sympathy, and not insult.'[151]

Ryley's annoyance was with a peer who would not patronize a play. But at the opposite extreme were those enthusiastic participators in an open society who were even prepared to appear in one. The perils of aristocratic display were clearly on view in private theatricals. In theory they were merely a diversion for country house society, scarcely to be distinguished from the card playing, billiards, and other indoor pursuits with which gentry thrown together indoors at Christmas or in the summer amused

---

[149] Stirling, *Annals of a Yorkshire House*, i. 318–19.
[150] (London, n. d.), pp. 17, 10.
[151] (9 vols., London, 1808–27), i. 277.

themselves. Peers of Lord Sandwich's circle were prominent in musical societies, and not averse to demonstrating their talents to a fee-paying audience on charitable occasions. There seemed little distinction in principle between playing the drums for the public as Sandwich did, and playing the boards, as growing numbers of young noblemen were prepared to do. The spectacle of noblemen acting fictitious noblemen in plays designed to amuse and titillate the bourgeoisie aroused intense interest, and at the height of the vogue in the late 1780s was taken seriously by dramatic critics. At the Richmond House Theatre in June 1788 one such performance was much admired. The play was De Boissy's *Les Dehors trompeurs* translated as *False Appearances* by General Conway, a former Commander-in-Chief of the army. The Prime Minister William Pitt was in the audience, with a galaxy of aristocratic men and women led by the Duke of Bedford and the Marquis of Carmarthen. The principal actors were Lord Derby as the Baron and Lord Henry Fitzwilliam who 'looked and played the character of the Marquis incomparably'. One critic wondered if Fitzwilliam's talents could 'be dedicated to the service of the public, without debasement of his own honour, or diminution of his own fortune'.[152]

Not only smart metropolitan audiences were entertained in this way. It is easy to see how in a rural context what began as a private amusement became a potentially controversial exhibition before the vulgar. This was what happened to Lord Villiers's dramatic ventures at Phyllis Court in Oxfordshire in January 1777. Originally designed for the family, they were thrown open to tenants and local people and eventually presented on three successive nights at formal performances in neighbouring Henley. Mrs Lybbe Powis, who was in the audience, was able to list a remarkable array of titled names present, drawn from the country seats of the Thames Valley and the Chilterns. The players themselves were of similar rank, with support from a professional company where necessary. The whole affair seemed thoroughly respectable, yet Mrs Lybbe Powis could not suppress some doubts about the wisdom of fashionable people appearing in this 'very public nature'. A decade and more later she was still attending such productions, in this case those which Lord Barrymore presented at Wargrave.[153] Barrymore tested this form of aristocratic complaisance virtually to destruction. He was a notorious rake and a not less notorious practical joker. Although he took his theatrical exploits seriously, spending £60,000 to build his own theatre at Wargrave, he relished as much as anything the opportunities for outrageous behaviour which it offered him. He missed no opening for insulting the opulent and befriending the lowly

[152] *Whitehall Evening-Post*, 3 June 1788.
[153] E. J. Climenson, ed., *Passages from the Diaries of Mrs Philip Lybbe Powys of Hardwick House, Oxon, A.D. 1756 to 1808* (London, 1899), pp. 178–94, 238–54.

with a view to enjoying the discomfort he caused to both. The stories of his antics as a doorman at his own theatre were told and retold, especially that of a farmer who bribed him with a shilling into letting him in without a ticket, only to discover that he had been patronizing a peer of the realm: 'Odd's rabbit; if he vanted to be's treated as a gintlemon, vy did he not tal me *he was a gintlemon?*'[154]

Theatricals of this kind did not flourish for long. It did nothing for their standing that the notorious Lady Craven was an organizer of such entertainments.'[155] In time they came to seem immoral as well as indecorous. More importantly, they revealed the difficulty of translating the role of patron into that of performer. This was a truth well known in other arts. As authors, peers found themselves in a particularly difficult position. They belonged naturally in a dedication or in a list of subscribers, not on the title-page. On a scholarly or sacred subject, admittedly, they might risk launching into print. But the great majority of the peers whom Horace Walpole listed in his *Royal and Noble Authors* were men who had published before they were elevated to the Lords. Exceptions tended to prove the rule that authorship ill-became a nobleman. Of the Earl of Suffolk, who published his verses in 1725, Walpole remarked that 'the Executors of this Lord conferred some value on his works, by burning a great number of the copies after his death'.[156] There was always the danger of ridicule, the worst enemy of a ruling class. For a lord to be paraded before the reviewers, the conventional form of torture inflicted on common authors, would seem unthinkable. Perhaps it was for this reason as much as for any other that blue-blooded bishops were so reluctant to appear in print. Professionally they were expected, like other dignified clergy, to sermonize and to publish their sermons. But most confined themselves to the bare minimum, consisting of their ex-officio preaching before the House of Lords and the religious societies, notably the SPG. Lord James Beauclerk, a younger son of the Duke of St Albans, and Bishop of Hereford for forty-one years, got away with publishing just one sermon, that which he delivered before the Lords on 30 January 1752, to mark the martyrdom of Charles I, his great-grandfather.

Lords who were tempted into print frequently regretted it. It was the supreme irony of Chesterfield's literary career, after he had been publicly criticized for the inadequacy of his patronage by Dr Johnson, that the letters which he wrote for his son were published after his death and against the wishes of his family. One cautionary tale told by Walpole was that of Lord Grimston, who at the age of 13 published a novel called *The Lawyer's*

[154] J. R. Robinson, *The Last Earls of Barrymore* (London, 1894), pp. 53–4.

[155] Broadley and Melville, *The Beautiful Lady Craven*, vol. i, pp. xxiii–iv.

[156] *A Catalogue of the Royal and Noble Authors of England* (2 vols., London, 1758), ii. 120.

Fortune, or Love in a Hollow Tree. He subsequently repented and tried to buy up all the copies. But when he stood as a candidate for the borough of St Albans in 1736, his redoubtable enemy the Duchess of Marlborough had an edition printed by way of election propaganda, with a new front-ispiece displaying an elephant dancing on a rope. Grimston even attempted to buy up this edition, only to be outdone when the Duchess commissioned a new issue printed in Holland.[157] On the whole it took reckless flouters of tradition to engage in literary experiments beyond the age of indiscretion. Georgiana, Duchess of Devonshire, wrote a novel called *The Sylph* in 1779 but flouting convention was her speciality.

Dangerous though it might be to indulge in thoroughly modern forms of display, it did not follow that the traditional rites of nobility would be approved at least where middle-class men and women were concerned. Cool analysts of the public pomp associated with rank and title had no doubt about its purpose. Vicesimus Knox summarized the point with characteristic acuity. 'The pageantry of life, considered in a political view, as designed by the grandees to awe the people, and keep them out of the park of selfish happiness, which the grandees have fenced with high pales, and guarded with spring-guns and man-traps, certainly may lay claim to the praise of deep cunning or worldly wisdom.'[158] One of the anxieties about the ritual required by State occasions was that it placed peers in a light which might be brilliant but unflattering. The coronation mania of 1761 provoked the gloomy reflection among the serious-minded that 'under such a Government, not the Nobleman who *thinks* best, but who cuts the *finest figure* will meet with most respect'.[159]

Here was a challenge for the thinking nobleman: to impress the enlightened while spurning the vulgar. One possibility lay with learned clubs and societies. There was a growing tendency for peers to find themselves presiding over such bodies. The Royal Society was a case in point, with two peers successively as Presidents in mid-century, the Earl of Macclesfield and the Earl of Morton. Much the same happened to the Society of Antiquaries. The first President was a well-known antiquarian, Philip Le Neve, but thereafter peers were given an opportunity to show their powers of leadership. Lord Hertford (later Duke of Somerset) was President from 1724 to 1750, and in the 1720s Lord Winchilsea and Lord Burlington were prominent in the Society's affairs. Subsequent Presidents, with only short interruptions by commoners, included the Duke of Richmond, Lord Willoughby of Parham, the Bishop of Carlisle, and Lord de Ferrers. Twenty-eight peers were elected members between 1778 and 1788, and in

---

[157] W. Davis, *A Second Journey round the Library of a Bibliomaniac* (London, 1820), p. 103; *A Catalogue of the Royal and Noble Authors of England*, ii. 214–15.

[158] *Works of Vicesimus Knox*, v. 287: 'Spirit of Despotism'.

[159] *General Evening Post*, 12 Sept. 1761.

1799 the Duke of Clarence even brought the support of royalty.[160] In the printed membership lists of the learned societies the names of peers were printed in capitals. Even for lowlier bodies an aristocratic name or two were almost *de rigueur*. The Natural History Society, founded in 1782, had one from the beginning in Lord Lewisham.

It is easy to see why noblemen felt able to join and lead societies of this kind. In genteel scholarship they could take a polite, even an informed interest without risking their rank or their name. In the nature of things education and family tradition might well make them at home with scholars. Grand Tourists were prominent in such instances. The Earl of Sandwich was first President of the Egyptian Society and figured with other aristocratic names among the Dilettanti. Whether such men really matched the scholarly feats of their fellow members was more doubtful. The Royal Society had regulations going back to 1663 to facilitate the election of nobles, but their prominence in the middle and late eighteenth century gave rise to some disquiet.[161] The same was true of the Society of Antiquaries. As the antiquarian Francis Douce put it, 'though I respect nobility when joined with talent I would prefer talent to nobility on *all* occasions'. Douce had in mind the long presidency of one peer, successively Lord de Ferrers, Earl of Leicester, and Marquess Townshend. Yet within a year of Townshend's death in 1811, the Society proceeded to a contested election in which it rejected the widely respected Englefield in favour of a peer, the Earl of Aberdeen.[162] The fact was that noblemen provided certain useful services. Societies of this kind were innately factious. In internecine squabbling the peers were more likely to be accepted as impartial referees. They were also less liable to the jealousies which existed between members who had their reputation and perhaps their livelihood at stake. When a peer was elevated to the highest post which a society had to bestow all might complain that in point of qualifications the result was a scandal, but all could equally explain their own failure on the grounds that rank had been preferred. Moreover there was satisfaction in hob-nobbing with peers who for these purposes were prepared to be accepted on equal terms. They even had to submit to scrutiny and election. The first contested election for the Presidency of the Society of Antiquaries occurred shortly after the Society had moved to its grand new headquarters in Somerset House, in 1784, when Edward King was defeated on a poll by the same Lord de Ferrers whose rule Douce later deplored.[163]

Patronizing a peer who customarily saw himself as a patron was part of the pleasure of belonging to associations of this kind. Sometimes it was

[160] J. Evans, *A History of the Society of Antiquaries* (Oxford, 1956), p. 187.
[161] C. R. Weld, *A History of the Royal Society* (2 vols., London, 1848), i. 146.
[162] Evans, *A History of The Society of Antiquaries*, pp. 219–20.
[163] Ibid., 182–3.

precisely the men who complained about the creeping influence of aristocracy who were themselves responsible for it. William Jones was one
such. As a member of the Society for Constitutional Information and
champion of parliamentary reform he had strong views about the dangers
of aristocratic hegemony. Yet he was also tutor to the young Lord Althorp,
heir to the Earldom of Spencer. In that capacity he suffered agonies which
he resolved by convincing himself that he was training his charge for an
enlightened part in public life. But he was not above seeking the electoral
support of the Spencer family. He also put up Althorp, 'my best, my only
friend', for the famous Literary Club, to consort with Burke and Reynolds,
calming Althorp's modest doubts about his own suitability and assuring
him that membership was not confined to men of letters.'[164] For a talented,
sensitive parvenu like Jones it helped to be able to show favour to a family
which existed to show men like him favour. Others, of course, would have
nothing to do with such compromises, if compromises they were. The
artist and acquaintance of Jones, James Barry, advised Nollekens not to
enlist noblemen as subscribers. 'If the nobility wanted his works, they
knew where he was to be found, and might come to him.'[165] By and large
the Joneses were more numerous than the Barrys, and there were enough
Lord Althorps to satisfy demand.

THE PROPEREST OF ALL MEN

Leadership was a matter not of authority but of example. Improvers and
projectors were quick to identify those of their superiors who might be
identified as fitting exemplars. This was a delicate yet crucial problem, for
the mixing of commerce, by definition an innovative, progressive concern,
with nobility, by definition a richly traditional concept, was controversial.
It was often said that commercialism had destroyed aristocratic virtue.
Turning land into cash by means of mortgages gave landowners a taste for
luxury while subverting the true basis of their power and prosperity. Even
heavily entailed lands could by one means or another be made the basis
for reckless borrowing if the prospective owner was young enough to
anticipate the day when the entail could be broken. It did not go without
notice that the gambling mania which so disfigured polite society in the
1770s coincided with an almost explosive release of credit and paper money
into the economy. 'It was the facility of obtaining money that drove our
degenerate nobility to the gaming-table', wrote the banker John King.[166]
In Parliament young lords were expected to parade their financial rectitude

---

[164] Cannon, ed., *The Letters of Sir William Jones*, i. 297.
[165] J. T. Smith, *Nollekens and His Times*, ed. W. Whitten (2 vols., London, 1920), i. 9.
[166] *Thoughts on the Difficulties and Distresses in which the Peace of 1783 has Involved the People of England* (London, 1783), p. 14.

and pounce on ministers who misspent a farthing of the public's money, yet it was said that when they did so they were quite likely to have come from a gaming house where they had lost thousands on a throw.[167] Cynicism about the financial motives of peers was common. When the sums spent on the famous Regatta of 1775 seemed to exceed what had been laid out in the way of services and refreshments, critics accused Lord Lyttelton, one of its chief promoters, of profiting personally to the extent of £1,500.[168] Lyttelton was the very embodiment of the aristocratic macaroni, and a favourite target of the censors of the 1770s. No doubt he owed something of his fearsome reputation to the contrast which it suggested with his celebrated predecessor in the title, the friend of Pope, a distinguished writer, and a pious churchman. But the mere fact that he could be accused of pocketing the proceeds of a public banquet revealed the scepticism which obtained about the customary conduct of his class. Even the sins of these grandees seemed lacking in grandeur.

When it came to profit-making of less reprehensible kinds few people expected the nobility to forego the commercial advantages open to them. Yet there remained a feeling that there were limits to the entrepreneurial exploits in which a peer could engage. Lady Bessborough expressed her worries on this score when her brother-in-law the fifth Duke of Devonshire sold off Burlington House for building leases, and in the process evicted his long-standing tenant and cousin the Duke of Portland. Portland himself reacted with an impressive display of icy dignity. Lady Bessborough observed, 'there is something goes against me in all this, yet it is fair for any one to make the most of their property'.[169] The Duke of Devonshire was an exceptionally rich man, albeit one whose expenditure was also spectacular, and the temptations were still stronger for the blue-blooded poor. In 1745 the second Duke of Richmond was attracted by a scheme for a new settlement in America and did his best to argue his friend the Duke of Newcastle into approving it. 'If the thing in it self is right, and that somebody of distinction must be at the head of it, and that it will cost no money, and that some may be gott fairly, honestly, and quite openly, I don't see why I should not have it as soon as any other.' Newcastle, whose faults did not include mercenary self-interest, had a devastating reply: 'the desiring one of your Quality and Condition, to be at the Head of it, does not lessen the Appearance of a Job.'[170] When even peers thought their code violated by the commercialism of their class, it is hardly surprising that their inferiors were sometimes shocked.

[167] *A Letter to a Celebrated Young Nobleman on his Late Nuptials* (London, 1777), p. 2.

[168] *The Boat Race* (London, 1775).

[169] Castalia Countess Granville, ed., *Lord Granville Leveson Gower (First Earl Granville) Private Correspondence 1781 to 1821* (2 vols., London, 1916), ii. 268: 23 July 1807.

[170] McCann, ed., *The Correspondence of the Dukes of Richmond and Newcastle*, p. 169.

Even on a morally safe basis, aristocratic enterprise was not without perils. It involved a readiness to sacrifice rank, both in the sense that the acquisition of knowledge and skills could seem ungenteel, and in the sense that it meant mixing with men who were barely gentlemen at all. The obvious arena in which these difficult compromises might be achieved was that in which the aristocratic estate had a natural interest, agricultural improvement. 'Is it in *Fact*,' enquired the *Westminster Journal* in 1743, 'whatever *Custom* may have made it, any Disgrace to be a *Gentleman*, nay a *Nobleman Grazier*, or a *Nobleman Farmer*?'[171] In the following reign it was amply demonstrated that there was no such disgrace. Joseph Cradock recorded the natural grace which the Duke of Grafton displayed when he found himself among the graziers and cattle-breeders of Northamptonshire. He also noted the Earl of Denbigh's pride in his reputation as an 'economist' and 'improver'.[172]

Arthur Young was an indefatigable searcher after noblemen who could be enlisted in his campaign for improvement. The Marquess of Rockingham, like the Duke of Grafton, was lauded as a Prime Minister who was not too proud to dirty his boots. To the title of statesman and patriot he had added that of farmer.[173] The county reporters of the 1790s needed no instruction in this technique. In Herefordshire, Lord Bateman, who happened to be Lord-Lieutenant of the county, was described as a great farmer, 'an appellation by which he condescends to distinguish himself'.[174] The Duke of Norfolk cultivated the image of 'a good honest Gentleman Farmer'.[175] The term 'gentleman farmer' had come into being to describe a new breed of tenants whose wealth made them genteel, but who lacked the proprietorial standing of the squirearchy. It had exactly the ambiguity to match the pretensions of the former with the condescension of the latter. The crucial requirement was that the great should enter into this alliance with enthusiasm, at least for purposes of display. When the Board of Agriculture was established in 1793 one of its first initiatives was to promote the establishment of farmers' clubs in which magnates such as the Duke of Bedford, the Earl of Egremont, and the Earl of Winchilsea played a leading part.[176] But there was not necessarily anything very forced about such mixing. At the turn of the century two great Whig landlords, the Duke of Bedford and Coke of Norfolk, vied with each other for the

---

[171] *Westminster Journal*, 29 Oct. 1743.

[172] *Literary and Miscellaneous Memoirs*, i. 111.

[173] *A Six Months Tour through the North of England* (2nd edn., 4 vols., London, 1771), vol. i, pp. xvi, 271–316.

[174] J. Clark, *General View of the Agriculture of the County of Hereford* (London, 1794), p. 17.

[175] W. Lefanu, ed., *Betsy Sheridan's Journal: Letters from Sheridan's Sister, 1784–1786 and 1788–1790* (Oxford, 1986), p. 119.

[176] M. Betham-Edwards, *The Autobiography of Arthur Young* (London, 1898), p. 30.

applause of improvers, holding great agricultural fairs in which they were to be seen in the company of their inferiors.

A higher priority still than commercial progress was social amelioration. Noblemen were expected to play a public part wherever philanthropic need dictated. This meant leading others, or more commonly being led by others but lending one's name and weight to their activities. Some peers had the initiative to point the way themselves. Lord Romney, known for his patronage of good causes, personally insisted, in the food shortage of 1795–6, on selling corn by the bushel at Maidstone Market. The advantage of such intervention from on high was that it ensured excellent publicity. Romney was lauded in the *Gentleman's Magazine* as having 'exaltedly taken the lead'.[177] The patriarchal role ideally required of a magnate in his own neighbourhood could be usefully exploited. High marks were awarded the Earl of Leicester because he could be presented as one who admitted the error of his own ways. The story told was that having devoted his life to the building of his Palladian palace at Holkham he looked about him and saw with dismay the consequences of his greed: 'I am Giant of Giant's Castle, and have eat up all my neighbours.' His premature death put a stop to his plan to repopulate the district, but it was taken up later by his eventual heir, Coke of Norfolk.[178] Peers had the standing to override the opposition of lesser gentry and farmers. One who made himself a model in this respect was the eighth Earl of Winchilsea. He was an early advocate of allotments for labourers, arguing strenuously for giving the poor a propertied interest of their own.[179] He proved an active magistrate in Rutland, a small county in which the leadership of a magnate could be decisive. His support for friendly societies was influential, as was his advocacy of parish workhouses for children on what he called the 'Rutland plan'. These 'Schools of Industry' began in Lincolnshire, but it was their importation into Rutland under his direction and at the instigation of the clergyman Thomas Foster that signalled their establishment on a broader basis. In the first report of the Society for Bettering the Condition and Increasing the Comforts of the Poor Winchilsea was selected for public commendation on this account. Young called him 'one of the very best of the nobility, and a really respectable moral character, and benevolent to the poor'.[180]

Winchilsea was not unique but his energy was unusual. A more realistic

[177] *Gentleman's Magazine* (1796), 960.

[178] Robert Potter, *Observations on the Poor Laws, on the Present State of the Poor, and on Houses of Industry* (London, 1775), p. 65.

[179] J. R. Poynter, *Society and Pauperism: English Ideas on Poor Relief, 1795–1834*, p. 99.

[180] Leicestershire RO, Finch MSS, Rut 3–7; *The First Report of the Society for Bettering the Condition and Increasing the Comforts of the Poor* (London, 1797), pp. 28–30; Betham-Edwards, ed., *The Autobiography of Arthur Young*, p. 388.

model was provided by his numerous colleagues who were prepared to give their name to the support of a large association in which the work was done by others. In the diverse causes of Georgian England peers were prominent as subscribers, governors, most of all as figureheads. Medical charities, as the most characteristic and widespread form of voluntary association, resorted extensively to them.[181] In the capital the highest ranks of the peerage were much in demand. Whig dukes almost all played their part under George II, in some instances passing on what was evidently considered an hereditary honour to their heirs. The Duke of Richmond presided over the London Hospital, the Duke of Portland over the British Lying-In, the Duke of Bedford over the Foundling. Successive Dukes of Marlborough were Presidents of the Middlesex Small Pox Hospital. Before very long even dukes were not grand enough. St George's had as its first President the Bishop of Winchester. But when he died in 1734 the Prince of Wales took his place. He was succeeded by his own son, in due course King George III. Thereafter the most fashionable causes aimed high. The Duke of York, George III's brother, took over the London in 1765. The future George IV was only 8 when he found himself President of the Lying-In Charity for Poor Married Women, with two pious courtiers, the Earl of Dartmouth and Earl Harcourt, as his Vice-Presidents. Queen Charlotte's had originally been the General Lying-In Hospital and the Queen also became Patroness of the Magdalen.

There were various means of indicating the support of peers. Of the fifteen wards in St George's in 1744, thirteen were named after noblemen and royalty, the other two being allocated to an opulent commoner, Sir Benet Sherard, and the memory of the famous physician John Radcliffe. Vice-Presidencies assisted in the honouring of nobleman one rank below the highest. In the Magdalen, the Presidency was held by the Earl of Hertford, with Lord Romney as Vice-President. Its sister institution the Female Orphans Asylum had the Earl of Lichfield and Lord North as sucessive Presidents, with Lord Vere beneath them as Vice-President. This device was widely employed in the provinces, where the President might be a bishop, or a great magnate. Vice-presidencies had the advantage that they could be bestowed in whatever numbers were needed to satisfy demand. At its inception the Leicester Infirmary had the patronage of the Duke of Montagu, with a string of peers below him as Vice-Presidents, the Earls of Dartmouth, Huntingdon, and Stamford, and Viscount Wentworth. Another useful device was to distinguish between Patron and President. The Royal Humane Society attracted the formal patronage of George III, but was able to reward its most prominent aristocratic supporter, the Earl of Stamford, with its Presidency. The Society for Bettering the Condition

---

[181] J. Blomfield, *St. George's* (London, 1933), pp. 20–1.

of the Poor also had the King as Patron, with the Bishop of Durham as President. The maximum room for manoeuvre was created by the Salop Infirmary. In Shropshire there was no one family which could claim the leading role, and county politics were notoriously divisive. The solution adopted was to elect a patron annually, with the peers and gentry of the county operating a rota.

Provincial hospitals always mustered an impressive turn-out because at the county level the electoral stakes were high. But the tendency to turn to noblemen for public support was typical of many other charities, both in town and country. Humbler ventures were soon emboldened to seek their assistance. The metropolitan dispensary movement, a creation of the early years of George III's reign, quickly acquired peers as patrons: the Earl of Winchilsea for Armstrong's Dispensary in Red Lion Square, the Earl of Dartmouth for the General Dispensary in Aldersgate Street, and the Earl of Sandwich for the Carey Street Dispensary. The Emmanuel Society, another model for provincial imitation, had an impressive array of peers at its head, the Duke of Montagu, the Earl of Radnor, the Earl of Ashburnham, and Lord Willoughby de Broke. So did the Benevolent Institution for the Sole Purpose of Delivering Poor Married Women in their Own Habitations, in the Duke of Leeds and Lords Malden and Hood. The Society for the Relief of the Ruptured Poor, founded in 1796, had to make do with Henry Dundas, the President of the India Board, though in due course he was elevated to the Lords.

Wherever local connections and local influence operated it became increasingly essential to obtain noble patronage. In the early eighteenth century, despite the popularity of the charity school movement, it would have been unthinkable to approach a peer of the realm for support for so lowly a project as a parochial school. In the late eighteenth century attitudes were quite different. The subscription list for the Bewdley School founded in 1784 was headed by three peers.[182] The same applied to small charities for the poor and infirm. In Rutland the Morcott Hospital, with an income of £160 per annum, supporting six paupers, had seven trustees in 1779 of whom four were peers.[183] The agricultural society instituted at Odiham in 1784 elected Lord Rivers as its President and soon acquired the support of the Earl of Dartmouth, the Earl of Northington, and the Duke of Chandos.[184] Local or at least regional connections sometimes extended to metropolitan bodies. The Scottish Corporation in London naturally required the support of eminent North Britons. It had the Dukes of Buccleuch and Montrose as President in the last years of the century. In

---

[182] William Jesse, *The Importance of Education: A Discourse, Preached in Bewdley Chapel, on Sunday the 27th Day of March, 1785* (Kidderminster, 1785).

[183] Lincolnshire Archives Office, Misc Don 173/1.

[184] See the references to the Odiham society in *Annals of Agriculture*, 1785–8.

the Cymmrodorion the Prince of Wales had long had the place of honour, but opulent and well-born Welshmen were expected to support him. The objects of both societies were charitable as well as recreational and patriotic.

What were the advantages of aristocratic patronage? One was simply the power of example. The traditional model of noble patronage had the philanthropic nobleman founding schools, augmenting livings, establishing almshouses. In 1765 the Evangelical Moses Browne publicly lamented the passing of this type.[185] But the general assumption was that the new model which had the nobleman heading a subscription list could do more good. Even in a strictly local context where the nobleman might have been expected to observe his traditional duties, he was likely increasingly to appear as a fund-raiser rather than funder. The manufacturer Richard Reynolds put the point clearly when he urged the Marquis of Stafford to contribute to a Sunday school in Ketley, 'not only as giving a sanction to the undertaking, and placing his lordship in the most amiable point of view, as the father of the helpless part of his tenants, but exhibiting an example more likely to be followed by the neighbouring gentleman'. Considering that the children who attended it lived in cottages owned by the Marquis, and their parents laboured in works rented from him, it might have been thought that he would see fit to support this enterprise more directly.[186] In part no doubt this was a measure of the selfishness of the Marquis of Stafford. There were still peers who took their personal responsibilities seriously. The pious Lord Spencer maintained his own school on his Northamptonshire estate and closely supervised its running.[187] On the other hand the third Viscount Lonsdale turned Lowther College, founded by the first Viscount, into a textile manufactory.[188] For a nobleman such as Stafford to act as a prominent subscriber was probably as much as could be expected.

The frequently expressed belief that 'the example of the higher classes is necesssary to excite a general spirit' was based on a sober assessment of the snobbery and tight-fistedness of bourgeois society.[189] Men and women who observed that their betters would not fork out were unlikely to do so themselves. Noble subscription was the first link in a chain of giving. At each level of society the principle of keeping up with the Joneses dictated the requirement to give as much and to the same causes as the Joneses. But the process had to be initiated at the top to achieve maximum success.

---

[185] *A Sermon Preached to the Society for Reformation of Manners, on Friday May 17, 1765* (London, 1765), pp. 10–11.

[186] H. M. Rathbone, ed., *Letters of Richard Reynolds* (London, 1852), p. 265.

[187] BL, Althorp Papers, F 133: W. Smith's letter of 21 Feb. 1778.

[188] J. V. Beckett, 'Lowther College 1697–1740: "For None but Gentlemen's Sons" ', *Trans. Cumbs. and Westmor. Ant. and Arch. Soc.*, NS 79 (1979), 103–7.

[189] *An Address to the Inhabitants of London, from the Court of Assistants of the Hon. Artillery-Company* (1794), p. 11.

Realistic appraisals of the prospects for charitable fund-raising took account of this. The anonymous author of *A Sentimental Discourse upon Religion and Morality* in 1776 dwelt heavily upon it. He identified the crucial failing of the great as 'that pride, which is charitable only thro' ostentation'. What would be the result he asked, if one put to the rich and high-born the plight of a poor widow with three or four children and no pension to support them. Surely a cold 'I cannot help it'. On the other hand, 'Could the benefits they would confer be known to all the world, they would not only seize every opportunity of doing good; but even be the first to solicit the benefaction of other friends in favour of the poor. Let a fire burn a town to ashes, let an inundation deprive the inhabitants of several villages of their subsistance, a subscription is presently proposed and filled up: will you know whether humanity or pride has caused so many names to be put upon that ostentatious list?'[190] Publicity opened pockets. One obvious reason for the demise of the charitable brief, aside from the expense of its administration, was the absence of publicity attending it. The danger that a non-giver might be gossiped about in church or at the alehouse was real enough in a parochial setting but held no terrors in the wider world in which middle- and upper-class families moved. A printed statement or list was another matter, especially when it took the form of a black list. At Nottingham during the Forty-Five subscribers to the loyal association who defaulted on their payments once the Jacobite danger had passed found their names in the *Nottingham Courant*. Charities were reluctant to go this far, but after some hesitation the governors of the Salop Infirmary identified subscribers who were in arrears with an asterisk in their published lists. In this instance at least the result was a sudden improvement in punctual giving.[191]

Most of the charities of Georgian England were founded by middle-class men and women. Clergymen were prominent, so were lawyers, doctors, and businessmen. Few of them had great wealth in their own right, and the most celebrated philanthropic busybodies, such as Jonas Hanway and Robert Young, were positively impoverished. All depended on cultivating influential connections, and enlisting the support of powerful families. When they failed they blamed the great. The success of the campaign to establish a hospital in Hereford was long in doubt because it proved so difficult to secure the support of the county's magnates. Thomas Talbot, the clergyman who sought to galvanize them, warned repeatedly and in public that 'If it fails, it must be for want of a Patron among the Noble and Opulent'. Were they, he asked, 'less humane, less bountiful, or

---

[190] Pp. 141–3.
[191] 'The Rebellion of 1745', *Trans. Thoroton Soc.*, 38 (1934), 54–64; Shropshire RO, 3909/6/2: printed reports of Salop Infirmary, 1779–81.

less disposed to alleviate the sufferings of their fellow-creatures and fellow-christians than gentlemen of the same rank and fortune in other parts of the kingdom?' Even the prayers which he required them to join in were to 'the Great Patron of the Poor and Afflicted'. A subscription list with the Deity at its head must surely attract the support of the nobility and gentry of Herefordshire.[192]

At the Three Choirs meeting of 1799 a Gloucestershire country gentle-man described the ostentatious form of submission which circumstances were imposing on the county magnates. 'To show you what grand People we are in Gloucester, no less Personages than the Dukes of Norfolk and Beauford, Bishop of Gloucester, Lords Bathurst and De Clifford stood begging with plates in their hands for the Poor of the Church door, voilla!'[193] Perhaps it was this element of humiliation which sometimes made it difficult to get peers to play their full part at the Three Choirs. At Hereford in 1791 Bishop Butler was infuriated when the Duke of Norfolk expressed reluctance to act as Steward. 'The office is a considerable Charity, and I was in hopes, that a wealthy and popular Character would not have abstained from it.'[194] Responsibilities of this kind belonged with a host of duties which were unavoidable for families hoping to retain a leading place in the affairs of their locality. A dutiful part in charities was an aspect of election management and failure to perform it could be a damaging propaganda gift to one's enemies. Patrons who defaulted could be gently reminded of the danger, as Butler was in effect reminding Norfolk. Norfolk had electoral ambitions in Herefordshire and more especially in Gloucester where he had accepted the office of Lord Mayor. Reluctance to take his appointed place in the sister cathedral was not a light matter. He must have thought better of his decision, for at the Hereford meeting in 1792 he duly appeared as Steward.

Bringing noblemen to heel was a delicate operation. In Lincolnshire in 1768 the establishment of the infirmary found some major figures in the county unwilling to endorse it. One was Lord Monson, a peer with extensive electoral interests. In time his family's alienation from an important charity evidently became a matter of mutual embarrassment. When they broached the subject in 1788 the governors of the hospital proceeded cautiously. Their initial tactic was to approach Lady Monson with a request that she 'hold the plate' after the ensuing annual sermon for the charity. When she politely declined on the grounds that her husband was not a subscriber, they penned an equally polite letter to Lord Monson, observing that they were 'sensible how necessary it is to the true interest of every public

---

[192] *Three Addresses to the Inhabitants of the County of Hereford* (Hereford, 1774), p. 18.

[193] Leicestershire RO, Turville Constable Maxwell MSS, DG 1467: C. B. Mostyn to F. F. Turville, 29 Sept. 1799.

[194] Surrey RO, Onslow MSS, J, Butler to Lord Onslow, 7 Sept. 1791.

Institution to be countenanced by rank and character'. Monson replied in terms which indicated his dilemma: he was not among the initial subscribers for good reasons, was anxious to help, but uncertain how to act. He promised to write further in due course. Three months later his family began enlisting as subscribers.[195] This elaborate minuet was a stately affair, conducted without loss of face on both sides. But its significance is obvious. Monson had been called to order and warned of the consequences of continuing in isolation from a great public cause in his own county. Patronage of this kind was not so much condescension as submission.

Example was not the sole consideration. Peers had connections, not least with other peers in a similar situation. Elaborate networks of favour and patronage might be made accessible. In celebrating the completion of Westminster Bridge, a project of exceptional expense and complexity, the playwright Colley Cibber attributed ultimate success to the ninth Earl of Pembroke: 'the zeal and resolution of a truly noble commissioner, whose distinguish'd importance has broke thro' those narrow artifices, those false and frivolous objections that delay'd it, and has already begun to raise, above the tide, that future monument of his publick spirit'.[196] Horace Walpole also celebrated Pembroke's high-mindedness in a tribute duly recorded in *Collins's Peerage*, one of the ways in which the virtues of the nobility were trumpeted to a mass audience. 'It was more than taste, it was passion for the utility and honour of his country.'[197]

Cibber attached particular significance to Pembroke's part in defeating the corruption which affected a great project like Westminster Bridge: 'private jobs, ... a tedious contention of private interests, and endeavours to impose upon the publick abominable bargains'.[198] The presence of a peer at the head of any organization provided a certain guaranty of standards. This was not necessarily a question of the individual's integrity. Rather the assumption was that a patron of rank would simply not be susceptible to the temptations which beset lesser men. The abuses discovered in the management of the Harpur Charity at Bedford in 1761 were a case in point. The trust had been controlled by the borough of Bedford, with the predictable consequence that it was misused for personal and electoral purposes. By a decree of the Lord Chancellor and with general approval the corporation was left in legal possession but subject to the supervision of the Duke of Bedford, 'a Nobleman, whose Virtues and Abilities add a lustre to his high rank and great fortune, and who is, therefore, the properest of all men to be at the head of such a Trust'.[199]

---

[195] Lincolnshire Archives Office, Hosp. 1, minutes 21 July 1788 and subsequently.
[196] *An Apology for His Life by Colley Cibber* (Everyman ed., London, n.d.), p. 222.
[197] *Collins's Peerage of England* (9 vols., London, 1812), iii. 144.
[198] *An Apology for His Life by Colley Cibber*, p. 222.
[199] *General Evening Post*, 27 June 1761.

Nobody can have supposed that Bedford, an experienced politician and a tireless electioneer, was incapable of corruption. But his status and wealth made it equally inconceivable that he would have let estates to himself or disposed of the charitable funds to his family, as the corporation was accused of doing. In a more important instance, the Three Choirs itself, a similar motive had operated. During the first half century of its existence the Three Choirs had been organized by the choristers and municipal authorities. But by the early 1750s there was sufficient concern about mismanagement by individual stewards and the corporations of the three cathedral cities to make a new strategy advisable, based on the hope that 'gentleman of higher rank than the members of the Choirs would so far countenance it as to undertake the conducting it as Steward'. From 1755 two stewards were appointed annually, one a senior clergyman, the other a layman. Before very long peers of the realm were being nominated. The first, at Worcester in 1761, was Lord Foley, the second, at Hereford in 1765, the Earl of Oxford. Peers served in three successive years between 1771 and 1773 and thereafter it was taken for granted that the titled families of the three counties would assume the mantle when desired.[200]

Collaboration of Church and State, in a strictly informal sense, was a feature of aristocratic patronage. It was not accomplished overnight. Under George II the anticlericalism of Whig oligarchs and the lingering Toryism of many clergy made co-operation difficult. The great London hospitals were patronized by Whig noblemen: the senior clergy, even bishops, were hardly involved. Even the Foundling, the most spectacular philanthropic enterprise of the age, was a heavily secular affair, dominated by the fashionable peers and gentlemen of the court of George II. The clergy were more prominent in the provinces, though it is significant that Whig magnates were sometimes reluctant to support them. Circumstances thereafter were somewhat different. Party tensions eased. The Church itself became a more gentry-dominated body as its value in patronage terms was made more obvious to aristocratic fathers with large families. The critical test case was perhaps that of a clerical charity, the Sons of the Clergy. Before the accession of George III, no titled person acted as a steward. But in 1759 Lord Delamer, a younger son who had gone into the Church, risen to be a Canon of Bristol, and inherited the family title unexpectedly on the death of the third Baron, was appointed. Once the Sons of the Clergy had discovered that they could have the services of a nobleman, they ceased to worry about his status as a layman. In 1761 the Methodist Earl of Dartmouth, the closest thing available to an aristocratic lay preacher, served as Steward. He was followed by the Duke of Richmond and Lord

---

[200] C. L. Williams and H. G. Chance, *Origin and Progress of the Meeting of the Three Choirs* (Gloucester, 1895), pp. 26–7.

Willoughby de Broke in 1762, the Earl of Oxford in 1763, the Earl of Northumberland in 1764. Thereafter every year to the end of the century, with the exception of 1791, saw at least one noble steward.[201]

VIRTUE CONFERS THE CORONET

Bringing together the nobility and clergy was not merely a question of getting them to sit on the same committees. The offence of Chesterfieldism was moral and therefore had obvious religious implications. Converting the peerage to a proper view of its responsibilities meant converting it to Christianity first. Thomas Hunter's *Reflections Critical and Moral on the Letters of the Late Earl of Chesterfield* made the point clear. Chesterfield's want of morality he attributed to his reluctance to admit the existence of a future state, 'where a Peer of Great Britain might possibly rank below peasants and slaves ... Virtue confers the coronet, a crown and kingdom, on him alone who is master of himself, who conquers his passions, who beholds with an undazzled eye superfluous riches, superficial honours, and empty titles, the blandishments of false pleasure, and the eclat of false glory.' A patrician who supported law and virtue, 'would be more than noble; we should hail him as divine'. More specifically, the Evangelical Thomas Gisborne urged on peers their duty to be prominent in the observance of their religious duties. This meant regular attendance at Sunday services, the delinquency of the polite classes being notorious in this respect. It also meant the maintenance of devout household chaplains, since the abuse of noble 'scarfs' for purposes of clerical preferment and even corruption was notorious. Not least it meant the performance of parental duties in one's family, with the emphasis on a concept of family which included every species of servant as well as wives and children.[202]

Peers, and more especially peeresses, in many instances accepted this call. Lady Huntingdon made the second birth of the nobility her particular mission. Her connection included a number of peers and peeresses at its core, and a wider circle of occasional devotees, one of them ironically the wife of the fourth Earl of Chesterfield. Their meetings at her London home and their frequent attendance at the chapels of the great metropolitan charities provoked mirth among the modishly sceptical, but also earned the approval of middle-class Londoners. Whereas Wesley brought evangelism from the bottom up, and often drew a halt before reaching men and women of rank, Lady Huntingdon worked downwards, beginning with West End

---

[201] The stewards were listed with the published sermons from 1778; in 1791 Henry Addington, Speaker of the House of Commons and later Prime Minister, was substituted for a titled steward.

[202] (London, 1776), p. 188, 211, 230; Thomas Gisborne, *An Enquiry into the Duties of Men in the Higher and Middle Classes of Society in Great Britain, resulting from Their Respective Stations, Professions, and Employments* (3rd edn., 2 vols., London, 1795), i. 166–8.

society, and proceeding beyond into the polite congregations of spa and seaside towns. Some of those whom she hoped to catch, including Bolingbroke, Chesterfield himself, and Frederick, Prince of Wales, were surely beyond even her missionary zeal.[203] Others were better long-term bets. The aristocratic women of the Huntingdon connection continued to remind their class of its social duties. Many of the noblemen who patronized the philanthropic causes of the 1780s and 1790s were the husbands or blood relations of these women. Titled families such as the Hertfords, Stamfords, Ancasters, Leeds, Montagus, and Ashburnhams, variously active during the 1790s in the affairs of the Humane Society, the Society for the Relief of Poor Married Women, the Lying In Society, the Emmanuel Society, the Philanthropic Society, and the Society for the Reformation of Manners, all had connections which can be traced back to the heyday of the sect in the 1750s and 1760s.

Lady Huntingdon exploited a manifest need for religion of rank but she did not create it. Lord Dartmouth, the one English peer identified over a long period with Methodism, was in this respect untypical. Among the peers who took an interest in ecclesiastical and moral questions in the late eighteenth century there were not a few who disliked the Methodist mania. Aristocratic piety was not the monopoly of one party. It was tinctured with Anglican Evangelicalism, but also included a colouring of High Churchmanship and even old-fashioned latitudinarianism. Sometimes it simply reflected a strong sense of the social and political importance of retaining religious leadership in an age of revolution. Among court peers, who played an important role in identifying moral causes approved by the middle class with the political values of Lord North, the younger Pitt, and George III, this was very marked. It went beyond the formal business of patronizing fashionable causes. As Lady Stafford, wife of one of the King's most loyal supporters, put it in 1787, 'I think it a great Duty for People in high Life to go to Church, not only on their own account, but to give a good example to inferiors.'[204] Others, no easier to classify in terms of theology or ecclesiastical politics, were perhaps expressing a certain kind of continuity. The third Earl of Hardwicke was 'a great Lord who is not ashamed of praying to God'.[205] The chapel at Wimpole, in which, like a true paterfamilias, he headed family prayers, had been built by Lord Harley, son of a Tory Prime Minister closely identified with the cause of the Church, and designed by James Gibbs in extravagantly baroque style. Its subsequent owners, the first two Earls of Hardwicke, might generously be described as conventionally latitudinarian. Even the third Earl was no

---

[203] G. F. Nuttall, 'Howel Harris and "The Grand Table": A Note on Religion and Politics 1744–50', *Jnl. Eccl. Hist.* 39 (1988), 531–44.

[204] Castalia, Countess Granville, ed., *Lord Granville Leveson Gower Private Correspondence*, i. 7.

[205] Betham-Edwards, *The Autobiography of Arthur Young*, pp. 338–9.

High Churchman. After much agonizing in 1787 he gave his support to the repeal of the Test and Corporation Acts. He and his house fairly represented the catholicity of English upper-class religion.

The contrast with Chesterfield's generation seemed very striking. The religious scepticism of the nobility under George I and George II was not something discovered by Evangelicals under George III. It had been the source of much concern at the time. The antiquarian and clergyman William Stukeley, no Tory or High Churchman, but a pious Low-Church Whig, gave an eccentrically personal turn to his analysis of aristocratic infidelity by blaming another antiquarian, the famous Martin Folkes. Folkes's infidel club of 1720 was alleged to have spread a disastrous infection through the Royal Society and beyond. 'He perverted Duke of Montagu, Richmond, Lord Pembroke, and very many more of the nobility, who had an opinion of his understanding; and this has done an infinite prejudice to Religion in general, made the nobility throw off the mask, and openly deride and discountenance even the appearance of religion, which has brought us into that deplorable situation we are now in, with thieves, and murderers, perjury, forgery, etc. He thinks there is no difference between us and animals; but what is owing to the different structure of our brain, as between man and man.'[206] Stukeley was certainly exaggerating the influence of individuals; yet his concern reflected widespread dismay at the irreligion of the peerage as a body. But for the religious revival of the next generation it would surely have created a dangerous gulf between middle- and upper-class values.

Some aristocratic piety had its origins in middle-class life. This was true of the brand offered by the celebrated Countess Spencer, the examplar of aristocratic female virtue as her contemporary the Duchess of Kingston seemed the embodiment of aristocratic female vice. Of many highly-placed women with an interest in good causes, perhaps none was more respected. Wife and widow of a peer, the first Earl Spencer, himself known for piety and philanthropy, she came from a humble family which had prospered by serving the Hanoverian regime, the Poyntzes. Her career exemplifies some of the contradictions of 'improving' noble life as well its more consistent features. In politics she was a determined Whig. Her daughters married Whig magnates, the Duke of Devonshire and the Earl of Bessborough. On the other hand her son, heir to the earldom and pupil of William Jones, was eventually to become First Lord of the Admiralty during the years in which Pitt was building a new Tory party. In her own family, too, Lady Spencer had to cope with very diverse patterns of aristocratic behaviour. The sexual misconduct of both her daughters was notorious and their life the subject of public interest and obloquy. The Duchess of

---

[206] 'The Family Memoirs of the Rev. William Stukeley', *Surtees Soc.* 73 (1880), 100.

Devonshire was indeed a perpetual source of embarrassment and anxiety to her mother, though one which she coped with in a spirit of patient resignation. Her letters on the subject of the Duchess's indiscretions would not be out of place in a Victorian homily yet they were addressed to a daughter who was to be regarded as the very personification of dissolute Georgian society. Her son was dutiful, austere, principled, a model of respectable, Evangelical living.

Lady Spencer herself was no kill-joy. Like her daughters she delighted in foreign travel and salon society. Yet she was deeply religious, and unflinchingly high-minded. She had her own Sunday school, closely supervising its affairs, and was not inhibited by her sex from taking a large part in the management of poor relief in the parish where she had her country retreat, Wimbledon. There she led a committee of ladies entrusted with oversight of the workhouse, and was the recipient of slavish promises by the parish vestry not to proceed 'till they are favoured with her Ladyship's sentiments'.[207] Her charitable activities were unmatched by any of her contemporaries. Among the Althorp Papers are thirty volumes documenting her work: some thousands of begging letters, carefully arranged and preserved, frequently annotated, and invariably acted upon. Lady Spencer's own note on the first of these files is characteristically modest. 'All the letters Concern Charities of different Kinds which I keep as a Cordial—to remind me of my Lords never failing Generosity and Humanity and of the endeavours with which I executed and sometimes endeavoured to imitate his benevolence.'[208] In fact her husband died in 1783, and it is clear that before his death as well as for twenty years after it she was at least as vigorous a benefactor as he. The letters confirm her leading part in the Society for Charitable Purposes, founded in 1773 by a group of fashionable women for the relief especially of those of their sex who had fallen on hard times. The Society, commonly known as the Ladies Charity, had begun in unassuming manner but quickly came to resemble the humanitarian projects founded by men, supported by numerous subscriptions and imposing on its lady patronesses an arduous round of letter writing, committee meetings, and financial accounting. It created a model for much later philanthropic activity.[209] The titled names which occur in connection with the Society and also with Lady Spencer's other charities crop up frequently in the published reports of philanthropic associations of the period: among Dukes and Duchesses, Northumberland, Leeds, Ancaster, Portland, and Montagu; among Earls and Countesses, Hertford,

---

[207] C. Barrett, ed., *Diary and Letters of Madame D'Arblay* (4 vols., London, 1876), iii. 366 ff.; F. M. Cowe, ed., *Wimbledon Vestry Minutes, 1736, 1744–1788* (Surrey Rec. Soc. 25, 1964), pp. 53–4, 56.

[208] BL, Althorp Papers, F 132.

[209] See F. K. Prochaska, 'Women in English Philanthropy, 1700–1880', *Int. Rev. Soc. Hist.* 19 (1974), 426–45.

Dartmouth, Gower, Bute; among Barons and Baronesses, Gage, Romney, Falmouth, Erskine, Willoughby de Broke, Dartrey.

One not numbered among Lady Spencer's friends was the Earl of Radnor. Yet if there was a titled man to enter in the lists against Baltimore or Lyttelton as Lady Spencer might be pitted against the Duchess of Kingston, it was perhaps Radnor. He too came of respectable rather than grandee background. The family was of Huguenot origin. Radnor's grandfather had been a Tory country gentleman, even a Jacobite, but one engaged in trade and with charitable interests which included the Georgia Trust. His father, Governor of the Levant Company and President both of the French Protestant Hospital in London and the infirmary at Salisbury, was considered a model of domestic virtue. He also had ties with English Nonconformists and was religious in an age not widely identified with noble piety. 'Few such noblemen!' commented the famous Dissenting minister Job Orton on Radnor's death in 1776.[210] The second Earl was an exemplary student at University College, Oxford, a college known for its scholarship and discipline. There he was described as 'very regular' and doing 'as much exercise as a Servitor'.[211] As an MP he was introduced to the House of Commons by his friend Charles Marsham, son of the philanthropist Lord Romney, and quickly made a name as an independent Whig with an unusual interest in ecclesiastical questions. He defended the Church and his university against the agitation to abolish subscription to the Thirty-Nine Articles but supported Dissenting demands for further toleration.[212] He joined the Society for the Propagation of the Gospel as soon as he succeeded his father in the peerage, at a time when for a peer to do so was most unusual, and served as Steward to the Sons of the Clergy soon after. He and his wife acquired a decidedly puritanical reputation, which was put to a severe test when they found themselves having to play host to the Prince of Wales and his mistress Lady Bampfylde in 1785, not being accustomed to 'that kind of politesse'.[213]

Radnor was politically ambitious, in a manner which was too idio-syncratic to bring him preferment, but incidentally reveals some of the characteristic attitudes of principled nobility. He opposed North, supported Pitt, and abhorred the French Revolution, but his politics were truly independent. He never held office, and took a fierce pride in stating his position in isolation, sometimes, as it seemed, quixotically. What motivated

[210] *Letters to a Young Clergyman, from the Late Reverend Mr Job Orton* (2nd edn., Shrewsbury, 1800), ii. 88.

[211] Stirling, *Annals of a Yorkshire House*, i. 197.

[212] Sir L. Namier and J. Brooke, *The History of Parliament; The House of Commons 1754–1790* (3 vols., London, 1964), ii. 302.

[213] M. Elwin, ed., *The Noels and The Milbankes: Their Letters for Twenty-Five Years 1767–1792* (London, 1967), p. 222.

him more than anything else was a burning sense of moral commitment. Like other young men educated in the 1760s he had absorbed that compound of enlightened sentimentality and conservative piety which did so much to influence English public attitudes. Among his private papers there is a collection of notes for speeches which say much about his beliefs. His enthusiasm for his duties as a magistrate was extraordinary. Systematic attendance at quarter sessions for someone of his rank was unusual. But Radnor was a magistrate with a mission. Both in Wiltshire and Berkshire, where his estates were situated, he proved an energetic justice and Chairman of the Bench. In this latter capacity he carefully prepared and in some instances had printed his charges to Grand Juries. His sense of duty was overwhelming, if somewhat egotistical. When appointed Lord-Lieutenant of Berkshire in 1792 he made a point of presiding at quarter sessions, and told a bench somewhat startled to find they were to be chaired by their own Custos Rotulorum that the conferment of the honour by the King 'appears to call upon me for the personal, and active Exercise of Duties, which I therefore purpose to perform as constantly as I can with Convenience'.[214] It was not the view of other Lords Lieutenant that their commission from the Crown was of quite such a personal nature, but Radnor was as good as his word.

In his homilies he showed more interest in general principles than the mysteries of the common law. He worried about popular excesses, such as those arising from an over-enthusiastic prize fight, about the threat of disturbances caused by food shortages, and about the iniquities of corn monopolies. He was shocked by sedition and strove to impress on the people of Berkshire the wickedness of what was occurring across the Channel. This was unsurprising. More intriguing was his readiness to deal head on with questions of equality and privilege. 'It is an obvious objection to us who are seated on this Bench,' he observed at Reading in January 1793, 'that we are interested in maintaining the Distinctions of Rank and fortune.' Obvious though this may have been, chairmen of quarter sessions did not customarily go out of their way to remind a jury of it. His answer to the objection was equally unoriginal but again revealed that he had put thought into it. Property, habits of life, knowledge of the world, education, independence of situation, 'opportunities of improvement which in the inferior ranks is less obtainable', and the demonstrably disastrous consequence of the division of property justified his privileged position. On balance he had no doubt that Englishmen were well served by their ruling class. 'There never was in my Opinion, and it is fairly questionable whether there ever will be a Time, or Country in which the superior orders of the

---

[214] For this and subsequent quotations, see Wiltshire RO, Radnor MSS, 490/1412: Grand Jury Charges at Salisbury, Marlborough, Abingdon, and Reading.

Community have in general acted, or can be expected to act more worthily to their Country, more honourably to themselves, more beneficially, or humanely to those, who stand in need of them, than the present Time is Witness of in this Kingdom.' This was said at Salisbury in April 1793 at the outset of the war with France. Radnor pronounced himself especially satisfied by the harmony which attended relations between governors and subjects. 'Is there in the World a Place, where the superior Classes of the Community enter so much into Communication with those below them as in this Country?'

Neither Lord Radnor nor Lady Spencer was necessarily typical, but in their obsession with what they considered their duty they represented a novel development. This is not to claim that such noblemen and women were more public-spirited or patriotic than their predecessors, rather that they were expected to display their public spirit and patriotism in a new way. Naturally the new model could seem as burdensome as it was novel. Aristocratic leadership was a matter of choice, however much the moralists lectured aristocrats on the subject of duty. Some retreated into country life. Others opted out altogether rather than enjoy the mixed blessing of nobility in a bourgeois society. Such was the third Earl Cowper, grandson of a famous Whig Lord Chancellor, but himself an aesthete with no taste for English politics or society. He spent almost his whole lifetime in Florence.[215] Others flouted the new conventions. Up to a point they did their class a service by reminding it and its inferiors of the abyss which lay beyond moral duty. A few tried to have it both ways. Lord Lyttelton, the very embodiment of aristocratic rakery on the Grand Tour and as a young peer, attempted to make himself more respectable, and in so doing provided the hypocritical tribute which vice played to virtue. He knew well that what was in question was in large degree a matter of presentation, of image: as was said on his behalf 'there is no situation in Life which will admit of an avowed contempt of vulgar prejudices'.[216] Lyttelton's bizarre death in 1779, following his experience with a female apparition, gave rise to speculation that Providence itself had been tried beyond tolerance by his irresponsibility.[217]

Most peers were at least able to find some means of adapting to the approved pattern to the extent of avoiding censure. Moreover it was not as restrictive a pattern as it might seem. If the typical reformed nobleman was a courtier, a Pittite, pious or with pious wife, and dedicated to the promotion of charity and the defeat of revolution, there were others who

---

[215] B. Maloney, *Florence in England; Essays on Cultural Relations in the Second Half of the Eighteenth Century* (Florence, 1969), pp. 47 ff.

[216] *Poems by the Late Thomas Lord Lyttelton* (4th edn., London, 1780), p. ix.

[217] R. Blunt, *Thomas Lord Lyttelton; The Portrait of a Rake, with a Brief Memoir of His Sister* (London, 1936), pp. 186–203.

were able to take some advantage of the vogue for improvement. Arthur Young hated the fifth Duke of Bedford's immorality but admired his agrarian experiments.[218] The Duke of Bridgewater showed no interest in good causes, but his canal enterprises in an age which often equated commercial growth with the social good made him much admired as a source of entrepreneurial inspiration. In the American and Revolutionary Wars no opportunity was lost to applaud blue-blooded heroes. Effeminacy was one of the dreaded consequences of a taste of luxury and the Earl of Dewdrop a standard figure in the gallery of macaroni peers.[219] The Earl of Effingham's refusal to fight in America in 1775 was claimed as a victory for patriotic principle over imperial corruption, but it could also be seen as an example of declining martial spirit in the old English nobility. Lord Percy's exploits in New England in 1775 and Lord Robert Manners's heroic death in the West Indies in 1782 provided valuable evidence on the other side. Perhaps the most spectacular case of martial self-sacrifice was one on which the antiquarian James Ford dwelled in his book *The Suffolk Garland*. Lionel Tollemache, heir to the Earldom of Dysart, was the only British officer killed at the siege of Valenciennes in 1793. His father and two uncles had also perished in the service of their country, albeit in somewhat less gallant fashion. The father died in a duel with a Guards officer at New York; one of the uncles was lost at sea, the other had the misfortune to fall from his post at the masthead. The young Lionel was the last male of a line which traced its ancestry beyond the Norman Conquest. He was interred in the family vault at Helmingham, with a monument by Nollekens, and provoked many poignant reflections on the fluctuating fortunes but immortal glory of English nobility.[220]

Part of the appeal of the new-model nobility was that it could even beguile the temperamentally sceptical. Joseph Priestley, increasingly an opponent of all hereditary honours, argued for an aristocracy which could combat moral corruption by its enlightened influence. Justification by good works entailed, not least, patronage of intelligence and merit. Priestley owed something to his own employer and patron, Lord Shelburne, and to Shelburne's heir, Lord Fitzmaurice he addressed a dedication in 1777, assuring him: 'The only method of *perpetuating* any order of men whatever, is to make it truly *respectable* and *useful*.'[221]

The variety of roles which peers could play was exploited by those responsible for polishing up their image for posterity. Lengthy obituaries and epitaphs were a feature of the late eighteenth century. In 1755, in his

---

[218] Betham-Edwards, *The Autobiography of Arthur Young*, p. 372.

[219] Samuel Hoole, *Modern Manners: In a Series of Familiar Epistles* (London, 1782), p. 87.

[220] *The Suffolk Garland* (Ipswich, 1838), pp. 296–9.

[221] M. Canovan, 'Paternalistic Liberalism; Joseph Priestley on Rank and Inequality', *Enlightenment and Dissent*, 2 (1983), 26.

portrait of the fictional Earl of Liberal, the novelist John Shebbeare pleaded for a new kind of monument, recording not the public honours of the nobleman, but his dealings with his inferiors and dependants. It would feature charity to the poor, generosity to tenants, wisdom in domestic management. In short it would teach the 'mild lessons of Religion, Virtue, and Humanity'.[222] Shebbeare would have been impressed by many memorials of the subsequent age, for instance those celebrating the attributes of aristocratic virtue enjoyed by three successive Dukes of Ancaster, who died within the space of thirty years between 1778 and 1809. The third Duke was connected through his wife with Lady Huntingdon's circle. He was President of the Lock Hospital for venereal diseases, a favourite charity of fashionable society. His obituarist also emphasized his dutiful conduct in 'that county over which he presided, and in which, during the recess of parliament, he lived with hospitable magnificence and liberality'. His heir hardly had time to build such a reputation, dying within a year of his father at the age of 23. The most was made of his travels, on the Grand Tour, and as an officer who fought in the American War. It seemed that he had an 'ambitious desire of real glory', which 'facilitated to this excellent young nobleman the acqusition of every accomplishment, either suited to that exalted station for which he was born, or conducive to his improvement in that most honourable profession in which he chose to follow the splendid example of his renowned ancestors. Indefatigable in this glorious pursuit, he visited foreign, but chiefly northern climes; and with a deep-rooted scorn for all the refinements of enervating luxury, he gloried in the character of a hardy Briton, and enriched it with the study and observation of the most celebrated military establishments.' The fifth Duke, brother of the third, had similar interests. He was a Vice-President both of the Lock and the British Lying-In. As a landlord he was 'regarded as the very best in England. Very few of those who held farms on the extensive domains of the Duke have had their rents advanced during the thirty years in which his Grace was their landlord.' The Duke's monument, by Westmacott, showed him with an angel on one side and Charity on the other.[223]

The church in which the Ancasters were laid to rest was full of family memorials. These included the Berties of royalist fame, and also the first two Dukes, who had particularly grand monuments, the work of two leading sculptors of the day, Scheemakers and Roubiliac.[224] Visitors who gazed on their visible remains were expected to be impressed by their grandeur and take their grace for granted. The notion that they must also be impressed by a statement of their public merits was a more peculiarly

[222] *Lydia; Or, Filial Piety* (4 vols., London, 1755), iv. 249.
[223] *Collins's Peerage*, ii. 25–7; iii. 307; *Gentleman's Magazine* (1809), 189, 276.
[224] The tomb of the fifth Duke is at Swinstead, all the rest at Edenham, neighbouring parish churches in Lincolnshire.

late eighteenth-century one. Stories of benevolent nobility were sought after. In the case of the sixth Lord Digby, who regularly visited the Marshalsea Prison in a plain blue 'alms-giving coat', in order to pay for the release of unfortunate debtors, the public was given a heart-touching account of his philanthropy nearly forty years after his death in 1757, allegedly by a correspondent who had known him well, and doubtless with a view to the social crisis of the 1790s rather than the 1750s.[225]

It was not necessary to be dead for such merits to be recorded. To some extent peers had to be their own propagandists; those who wished to play any part at all in public life had to address themselves to the public. Making speeches which would subsequently be relayed to a wider audience in the press was one of their new duties. In the early eighteenth century, public oratory was not required of peers, for all the emphasis on rhetoric in the classical curriculum. Lord Rockingham survived an entire parliamentary session as Prime Minister in 1765–6 without opening his mouth in the House of Lords. His was the last generation that could expect political advancement without a capacity for public utterance. In the 1770s the Upper House was forced to abandon any serious attempt to prevent the publication of its debates.[226] More importantly, leadership in any form of public association required at least a modicum of oratory. But it was not a demanding requirement. Debating skill and forensic rigour were hardly called for. Rather it was a question of saying a few words suitable to the occasion. A short homily at a charity dinner, a rousing sentence or so at a militia meeting, a cheering toast at an election gathering. If necessary these could be dressed up for the newspapers. It is difficult to believe that the addresses to volunteer troops and subscribers, which became *de rigueur* for peers who engaged in the patriotic defence of their localities in the 1790s and which were widely reported in the press or published as broadsheets, can have been delivered in full or in audible tones in village squares and on windswept hillsides before large numbers of people.[227] What matters is that peers were being forced to engage in a new form of exposure on terms determined by what was publicly acceptable rather than by traditional assumptions about the discreet, dignified, almost invisible might of the landed magnate. Even the King found himself participating in this process, as when he visited Worcester in 1788 and responded to a welcome from the Lord Mayor, in itself something of a departure, by declaring that his reception was 'ample recompense to me for the *public service* of twenty-

---

[225] L. Digby, *My Ancestors Being the History of the Digby and Strutt Families* (London, 1928), p. 81.

[226] W. C. Lowe, 'Peers and Printers; The Beginning of Sustained Press Coverage of the House of Lords in the 1770s', *Parliamentary History*, 7 (1988), 241–56.

[227] See e.g. the rousing speech delivered 25 Aug. 1803 by the Duke of Rutland, recorded by 'a Gentleman then present', and circulated as a broadsheet; Leicestershire RO, DE 836/29.

eight years'.[228] A Continental monarch, even an 'enlightened despot', might assert his credentials as the first servant of the State in a testament to his successors, or perhaps in a graciously candid correspondence with a leading philosopher of the day. An English monarch was apt to find himself doing so before a large gathering of his provincial subjects in the full glare of publicity. And a magnate who actually relished performances of this kind, as Radnor did, had every opportunity to display his talent at it.

Involved, of course, was the creation of a rhetoric of public service. What reality lay behind the rhetoric is not easily determined, but of its functional significance there can be no doubt. A class without confidence in its own status and values has no future. The crisis caused by Chesterfieldism afflicted peers as much as any. The Earl Harcourt's verdict on contemporary lordlings in 1779 was not meant to be humorous: 'From what I have myself observed of the character of our young nobility, I am grown to hate a Lord, as much as if I were a rich citizen or a country Squire.'[229] From a very different vantage-point, Lady Craven had a similarly poor opinion of the young peers of her day, a malaise which she traced to 'cookery and coaches'.[230] Even if they doubted the impact of commercialism on aristocratic manners, noblemen might be perturbed by the public perception of its effects. The Evangelical Lord Bulkeley connected the trial of the Duchess of Kingston with a new disrespect towards persons of rank.[231] In this context the confidence which Lord Radnor and Lady Spencer displayed in their class was bound to bolster morale at a time when the titled were being set a tough, even a revolutionary test.

The way that test was faced was observed with close and anxious attention. In the 1790s the formal arguments against aristocracy, especially against hereditary wealth and power, were put with vigour and persistence. Middle-class opinion was not necessarily shaken by such arguments, carrying as they did uncomfortable implications for the stability of bourgeois life both in the home and the community. But in the resulting debate the record of aristocracy, the moral and material impression which it was able to make on its society, was a matter of great moment. Titled improvement was necessary to provide even men well-disposed to the nobility with grounds for retaining their faith in it. The resulting panegyrics are difficult to take seriously in retrospect. Yet they were taken seriously enough at the time. One such was penned by the writer William Playfair whose nine volumes of *British Family Antiquity* in 1809–11 included a robust defence of titled families. He drew a contrast between the age of Chesterfield when

<hr>

[228] Valentine Green, *The History and Antiquities of the City and Suburbs of Worcester* (2 vols., London, 1796), i. 292.

[229] *The Harcourt Papers*, xi. 23.

[230] Broadley and Melville, *The Beautiful Lady Craven*, ii. 178.

[231] Cannon, ed., *The Letters of William Jones*, i. 200.

peers had been taught to laugh at nobility itself. In his own time, he thought, the peerage exemplified virtue, learning, invention out of all proportion to its numerical strength. He hoped by his work to make it 'known by every class, that a regular authentic record exists, which proves that, both as to virtue and genius, the nobility of the British empire are fully equal to any other rank in society'.[232] Playfair was a crank, though he could at least claim to have experienced the consequences of revolution at first hand, having been present at the fall of the Bastille and a resident of France for a time thereafter. Above all, he and many others thought that the factual evidence on which they could draw was sufficient to answer if not confound the critics.

If England had a kind of voluntary service nobility, it could be forgiven much, even encouraged to take much. John Moir was one who thus confronted the egalitarians. Those who criticized the life-style of the great, he asserted, had no understanding of the intricate nature of aristocratic privilege. 'The detail, of high life, is but little understood, because not much within the notice of such as are confined by fortune or occupation to the humbler sphere of ordinary avocations or manual labours.' Only those who did so understand, as Moir evidently did, knew that the virtue of peers must be sustained by a highly unequal division of property. 'Persons taught from infancy to indulge grand and liberal views, in all their collateral circumstances, and reared amidst the greatest affluence and independence, could hardly exist on what others might deem luxury.'[233] This was unlikely to convince the William Godwins of the world but Moir at least expected it to convince the unbiased.

Yet, more important than assessing the evidence was simply to provide it for others, the public at large, to assess. In introducing a new edition of *Collins's Peerage* in 1812, the editor Sir Egerton Brydges went to some pains to explain its importance. *Collins's Peerage* had first been published in 1709. It went through four editions before Collins himself died, in 1760, and two more in 1767 and 1778. It was respected for its genealogical scholarship but increasingly despised for its fawning flattery. Collins assumed that virtue went with rank and made no attempt to describe precisely what merits this alleged aristocracy possessed. Burke himself 'characterized the pages of Collins as setting up no other tests of merit than honours, and judging equally of all who possess equal titles and places'. Brydges offered a more up-to-date approach. He attacked the 'insolent and haughty of the nobility' and castigated their 'sensual lives'. He insisted that titles did not dazzle him, and that their only valid function was to 'prove incentives to liberal conduct, cultivated pursuits, and honour-

---

[232] Vol. i, p. ix; x. 19.
[233] *Preventive Policy; Or, the Worth of Each, the Safety of All* (London, 1796), p. 193.

able ambition'. His description of the ideal is itself a comment on the demands which Georgian society had come to make of its aristocracy, however perfect or imperfect the record. 'A young British Peer, who cultivates his mind, and refines his manners; who studies the public affairs of his country, and takes a virtuous part in them, is in a situation as desirable as a chastised and enlightened ambition can form a wish for.'[234]

[234] *Collins's Peerage*, vol. i, Preface.

Conclusion

MANY of the developments described in this book continued far beyond the end of the eighteenth century. The success of the landed gentry in preserving their control of the counties, with the aid of co-operative clergy and increasingly quiescent tenantry, was a still more striking feature of Victorian than of Hanoverian society. Middle-class improvers went on ruling many towns and cities beyond the reform of the municipalities, and sometimes even gained by it. 'Governing the kingdom by committees', which seemed at the time a novel feature of George III's reign, positively intensified thereafter, with the continuing multiplication of both statutory and voluntary bodies.[1] Bourgeois models of professional service and bourgeois ideals of public enterprise gained steadily on older traditions of institutional and administrative practice. The roots of patriarchal politics in the home and family were probably strengthened by the cultural and religious forces at work in early industrial society. Voluntary association, the panacea of the mid-eighteenth century, had lost little of its appeal a century later. The honorific role of the nobility developed to the point where it was eventually to be left with almost nothing else. Parliament remained for most purposes a kind of glorified umpire, adjudicating the disputes of propertied interests and liberally interpreting the rules of appropriation. In the mid-nineteenth century the State itself, Carlyle's 'dramatic speciosity', could still be seen in the same, restricted terms that it had been a hundred years earlier.[2] The use of the law to restrain popular rights while paying lip-service to libertarian ideals certainly did not diminish with the social tensions which accompanied early industrialization. Above all that fundamental faith in property and its credentials which underpinned eighteenth-century public life was enhanced by the propaganda victories of the political economists and by the triumph of the market mentality.

Yet, notwithstanding the continuities, there are marked differences about the early nineteenth century. The propertied mentality, for all its resilience, had to be maintained in the face of determined, sometimes demoralizing assaults. Edmund Burke, the apostle of counter-revolution, rightly treated

---

[1] Countess of Ilchester and Lord Stavordale, *Life and Letters of Lady Sarah Lennox, 1745–1826* (London, 1904), p. 613.

[2] *Latter-Day Pamphlets* (London, 1898), 'The New Downing Street', p. 159.

the ideological conflict which commenced in the 1790s as one that centred on its perceived legitimacy. He described Jacobinism as 'the revolt of the enterprising talents of a country against its property', and discerned in revolutionary France 'the dreadful energy of a State, in which the property has nothing to do with the Government.... The conditon of a commonwealth not governed by its property was a combination of things, which the learned and ingenious speculator Harrington, who has tossed about society into all forms, never could imagine to be possible. We have seen it; the world has felt it; and if the world will shut their eyes to this state of things, they will feel it more.' In France, he thought, the public had ceased to exist at all; and in the sense that it existed in England, as the expression of private property unrestrained by the bureaucratic power of the State and even empowered by the legislative force of the State, he may well have been right.[3] The ultimate victory would seem to have been that for which Burke hoped, though he did not live to see it. But it was a costly victory. Never again would it be possible to take Harrington's assumptions for granted. Nor could proprietors continue to depend on implicit veneration for proprietary rights despite the energy put by nineteenth-century Englishmen into inculcating it. To this extent the decade of revolution, the 1790s, wrought changes which could never be reversed. The mental landscape had quaked, and buckled, and if it seemed recognizably the same when the dust of war and revolution settled, remembrance of the convulsion and of the threatened catastrophe was too strong ever to make peace of mind possible.

This sense of a threat which had constantly to be combated was quite alien to earlier generations. It pervaded nineteenth-century life as it had never pervaded eighteenth-century life. It not only put property on the defensive but exposed all kinds of internal divisions and rifts which, if they had never altogether been absent, had been more or less concealed from view. The steady process of extending powers and rights beyond the ranks of the gentry had assumed a certain community of interest between proprietors of very diverse wealth. If England was truly a nation of shopkeepers, they had yet to assert their full potential, let alone identify their distinctive interest. But the status and objectives of the lower middle class were not necessarily compatible with those of their superiors who mixed more freely in genteel life. For most purposes this fluctuating gulf could be narrowed, especially when the priority was bourgeois unity in the face of those either above or below. But in the last years of the eighteenth century there were signs that some issues, for instance the incidence of new taxation, might make it much wider. Perhaps even more disruptive

---

[3] Edmund Burke, 'Letters on a Regicide Peace', in *The Works of the Right Honourable Edmund Burke*, v. 207, 254–6.

was the rediscovery of deep differences between bourgeois and landed society. Partly this had to do with the economic fluctuations caused by a period of warfare longer than any since 1713 and exacerbated by unprecedented industrial and demographic expansion; partly, too, it reflected the growing consensus of commercial interests against the corn laws, and a dawning realization that the protection demanded by agricuturalists was no longer necessary for manufactures. But it was also affected by the rhetoric of a revolutionary decade. There was a growing tendency to identify national survival with the interests of agriculture, the interests of agriculture with the supremacy of the landed gentry, and the supremacy of the landed gentry with the preservation of the constitution. Politicians became accustomed to exploit this logic in the most trivial concerns and undemanding situations. Thus was Samuel Romilly's modest scheme to make freehold estates liable for the debts of their deceased owners described by Canning in 1807 as 'an attempt to sacrifice the landed to the commercial interest, a dangerous attack made upon the aristocracy, and the beginning of something which might end like the French Revolution'.[4]

The struggle between land and trade, and the assertion of middle-class consciousness in terms which favoured ordinary householders and ratepayers, were in due course to disrupt comfortable accommodations that had hitherto made for relative harmony. That harmony obtained in a ruling class which survived in large part because it had not been necessary to define it or its interests too rigorously. What made such definition unavoidable and therefore brought about conflict is a complicated and probably insoluble problem, and doubtless inseparable from the ramifications of revolution and industrialization. It can be said, however, that at least until the 1790s neither the natural rights debate which preceded the former nor the commercial growth which ushered in the latter had suggested that the process would be any but a very prolonged one.

The reforms which demolished the old framework of political life were those which took effect some thirty years after the eighteenth century had closed. The repeal of the Test and Corporation Acts terminated a century and a half of Anglican ascendancy, and the Great Reform Act abolished a century and a half of parliamentary oligarchy. But the rhetoric of the reformers can be misleading and has certainly misled historians. The successful adaptation of public institutions to the requirements of commercial society had not been impeded either by an unreformed Parliament or an unrepealed Clarendon Code. There was, of course, a case both for parliamentary and ecclesiastical reform throughout the eighteenth century. It was often put, sometimes with a good prospect of implementation. But

---

[4] *Memoirs of the Life of Sir Samuel Romilly, Written by Himself; With a Selection from His Correspondence* (3 vols., London, 1840), ii. 181.

in the last analysis what defeated the reformers was the very adaptability of the system which was to seem so inflexible by the 1820s. Parliament became for practical purposes the servant of propertied society after 1688 and the religious establishment which it safeguarded ceased to be a significant check on the co-operation of propertied men. This functional efficiency was taken for granted by many, and even in the turmoil of the 1790s could still be urged against demands for change. By the 1820s, plainly, it was no longer a decisive argument, either because the efficiency had lapsed or because the terms in which it could be advocated were no longer acceptable. Why this happened is a matter of controversy and cannot be answered without detailed consideration of developments in the early nineteenth century. From the standpoint of eighteenth-century life what is significant is that it is only dimly visible in the middle part of George III's reign. The arguments of parliamentary reformers were put with vigour but made little mark on propertied opinion even when, in the 1790s, the appeal of natural rights theory was proving widespread and the evidence of electoral corruption massive. But at the close of the century the balance of advantage was beginning to shift, compelling even arch conservatives to argue their case on ground which would not support them. The Prime Minister himself, William Pitt, was one who had capitulated to the principle but sought to prop up the practice, thereby anticipating many others.

If anything, the assault on the religious establishment was even longer in the making. For all the intellectual rigour and political determination of the Rational Dissenters, it was not until the 1790s, and then only slowly, that the remaining restrictions on the civic rights of religious minorities acquired an importance matching that which they had achieved in the seventeenth century. The tendency of the eighteenth century had been to dilute and break down laws which it hardly seemed worth contesting in point of principle. Just as parliamentary reform depended on acceptance of a novel principle, so ecclesiastical reform depended on raising the theoretical rights of Dissenters to the point where they must override the most convincing evidence of practical benefits. Generations of politicians had learned to treat religion as a matter of private conviction and public indifference. But the evangelical revival and the moral earnestness which became increasingly *de rigueur* for politicians at the close of the century brought a marked change. Wilberforce's *Practical View of the Religious System of Professed Christians in the Higher and Middle Classes of This Country Contrasted with Real Christianity* both expressed and reinforced this tendency. 'The advancement or decline (of religion) in any country, is so intimately connected with the temporal interests of society as to render it the peculiar concern of a political man.'[5] Attitudes which were to inform

---

[5] See R. Coupland, *Wilberforce: A Narrative* (Oxford, 1923), pp. 237–8.

the politics of Gladstone's generation might already be glimpsed. The fact that neither Wilberforce nor Gladstone, in the first instance, were ecclesiastical reformers does not matter. What was changing was the underlying mentality, the way of looking at such questions, which deprived eighteenth-century apathy of its preserving properties.

Wilberforce's tract was published in 1797 during a national crisis which worsened further in 1798. To identify one year in which the characteristic attitudes of decades underwent a sea change would be absurd. But it is certainly a convenient point at which to mark the gradual passing of a mentality. It is similarly a convenient point at which to take stock of a century and more of political evolution. 1798 was a year of crisis beyond anything experienced since 1688. Yet it was also a year of survival. The threats of naval mutiny and national bankruptcy, endangering the most British of Britain's traditional strengths, its wooden walls and its funded debt, receded. Irish insurrection was quelled and French invasion fended off. Soon after, the tax system was overhauled and the laws governing popular association and assembly revised. In brief, a gravely threatened State shored up its defences. Contemporaries thought of this as an ideological victory, a triumph of patriotic spirit, national character, and moral fibre. But at bottom, of course, it had to do with the readiness of politically respectable opinion at many levels to respond to the call for unity. Posterity has associated this response with the preservation of an essentially aristocratic system of government. Yet it extended far beyond aristocratic society, uniting the many for whom liberty and property were perilously vulnerable assets with the few for whom they signified unchallengeable power and privilege. Such a partnership in reaction and repression counted for much when the priority seemed so clearly to defeat revolution abroad and subversion at home. Certainly, without the active collaboration of a broad-based middle class there would have been no question of 'weathering the storm'. And in the adaptability of British public life to the diverse needs of such a class may surely be found the clue to its loyalism and conservatism. In this respect at least the ideological outcome of the 1790s was the natural result of a century of propertied politics.

Index

Aachen 379
Aberdeen, 4th Earl of 557
Aberystwyth 442
Abingdon 178, 341, 552
Abingdon, 4th Earl of 133, 537
A'Court, William 397
Acts and Bills (*see under place for local legislation*)
  Magna Carta 85, 155
  Statute of Winchester 168–9, 223
  Act of Supremacy 85
  Poor Relief Acts 157, 162
  Petition of Right 85, 155
  Statute of Frauds 49, 50
  Registry of Bills and Acts 50–1
  Test and Corporation Acts 71–7, 80–6, 88, 89, 91, 92, 99, 110, 115, 130, 584
  Mutiny Acts 143
  Treason Bills 525
  Indemnity Acts 73–4, 80
  Act of Settlements (1662) 157
  Act of Uniformity (1662) 84, 85, 99
  Bill of Rights (1689) 143, 156
  Bounty Act (1689) 316
  Toleration Act (1689) 78, 80, 85, 87, 93
  Custom of York Act (1693) 46
  Hawkers Act (1693) 337
  Land Tax Bill (1693) 526
  Stamp Act (1694) 357
  Affirmation Act (1696) 106
  Qualification Bill (1696) 289
  second Qualification Bill (1696) 290
  Act of Settlement (1701) 155, 156
  Affirmation Act (1702) 106
  Act amending Statute of Frauds (1706) 49
  Cathedral Act (1708) 531
  Norwich Bill (1711) 76
  Occasional Conformity Act (1711) 73, 76, 306
  Qualification Act (1711) 54, 113, 192, 193, 289–306
  Elections Act (1712) 280–1
  Schism Act (1714) 76, 306
  Catholic Registration Act (1715) 115
  Septennial Act (1716) 154, 155
  Peerage Bill (1719) 54–5, 514, 533
  Relief Act (1719) 73
  Calico Act (1721) 184
  Catholic Taxation Act (1723) 115
  Custom of London Act (1723) 46
  Workhouse Act (1723) 156–7, 240
  Mayoral Elections Bill (1724) 215
  City Elections Act (1725) 215
  Small Debts Bill (1730) 158
  Justices Qualification Act (1732) 415, 420–1, 440
  Small Debts Bill (1734) 158
  Gin Act (1736) 153
  Mortmain Act (1736) 38, 492
  Quaker Tithe Bill (1736) 16
  Smuggling Act (1736) 153
  County Rating Act (1737) 222–3
  Hat Act (1737) 184
  Stuff Button Bill (1738) 203
  Pension Bill (1740) 113
  Foundling Hospital Act (1740) 77
  Act affecting Common Recoveries (1741) 49
  Highway Act (1741) 163
  Small Debts Bill (1741) 158
  Small Debts Bill (1742) 158–9
  Gin Act (1743) 318
  Small Debts Bill (1743) 158
  Elections Act (1745) 280–1
  Justices Qualification Act (1745) 420
  Smuggling Act (1746) 126
  Gin Act (1747) 318
  Heritable Jurisdictions Act (1747) 47
  Iron Act (1750) 184
  Gin Act (1751) 318
  Wills Act (1752) 47
  Game Preservation Act (1753) 6
  Highway Act (1753) 163
  Irish Wool Bill (1753) 324
  Jewish Naturalization Act (1753) 470
  Marriage Act (1753) 3, 6, 17, 508
  American Mutiny Bill (1754) 152
  East India Mutiny Bill (1754) 192
  Militia Bill (1756) 296, 297, 426, 526
  Highway Act (1757) 163
  Militia Act (1757) 296–, 471, 526
  Habeas Corpus Bill (1758) 153, 534
  Qualification Act (1760) 113, 292, 320
  Militia Act (1762) 297
  Annuities Act (1763) 273
  Butter Act (1763) 319–20
  Durham Act (1763) 273, 286
  Highway Bill (1763) 192
  Chancery Act (1764) 49–50

Acts and Bills (*cont.*):
  Fisheries Bill (1765) 192
  Stamp Act (1765) 359
  Declaratory Act (1766) 149–50
  Highway Act (1766) 163
  Quo Warranto Bill (1767) 215
  Militia Act (1769) 297
  Divorce Bill (1771) 545
  Royal Marriage Act (1772) 378
  Grenville's Elections Act (1774) 320
  Dissenters Relief Bill (1772) 88
  Gunpowder Bill (1772) 44
  Quaker Bill (1772) 88
  Royal Marriage Act (1772) 150
  Tithes Bill (1772) 88
  Banking Bill (1773) 44
  Dissenters Relief Bill (1773) 82
  Highway Act (1773) 163, 236
  Pownall's Act (1773) 322–3, 404
  Grenville's Elections Act (1774) 320
  Hop Bag Bill (1774) 174
  London Building Act (1774) 259
  MPs Residence Act (1774) 192
  Popham's Acts (1774) 404
  Quebec Act (1774) 83
  Irish Cattle Act (1776) 322
  Worsted Act (1777) 246
  Catholic Relief Act (1778) 8, 82, 83, 99
  Framework Bill (1778) 204
  Freeman Bill (1778) 286
  House Tax Bill (1778) 528
  Irish Relief Act (1778) 83
  Dissenters Relief Act (1779) 80, 82
  Divorce Bill (1779) 545
  Framework Bill (1779) 204
  Elections Act (1780) 280–2, 320
  Freeman Bill (1780) 286
  Magistracy Bill (1780) 392
  Small Debts Bill (1780) 246
  Gilbert's Act (1782) 157, 392, 404
  Wool Bill (1782) 325
  East India Bill (1783) 536
  London Small Debts Act (1785) 246
  Shop Tax Act (1785) 337
  Small Debts Act (1786) 246, 247
  Freeman Bill (1787) 286
  Freeholders Registration Act (1788) 157, 281–2, 320
  Wool Bill (1788) 325
  Catholic Relief Act (1791) 82, 83, 99
  Corn Act (1791) 322–3
  Friendly Societies Act (1793) 404
  Irish Freeholders Act (1793) 83
  Volunteering Act (1794) 303
  Volunteering Act (1798) 303
  Thelusson Act (1800) 46–7
  Clergy Exclusion Act (1802) 328

  Curwen's Act (1809) 114
  Reform Act (1832) 53, 59, 282, 286–7, 584
Adams, William 130
Addington, Henry 363
Addington, Stephen 94
Addison, Joseph 118
advowsons 18–20
Aikin, Anna 2
Ailesbury, 3rd Earl of 414
Akenside, Mark 500
Alcock, Thomas 108
Aldeburgh 381
Alderton, Thomas 257
Allanson, George 300
Allen, Charles 413
Allen, John 87
Althorp, George, Viscount 558, 571, 572
Amcotts, Charles 328
Amelia, Princess 518
America
  British friends 506
  Congress 43
  manufactures 184
  proposed Test Act 105
  representation 199–200
  taxation of 116, 148, 149–50, 167, 198, 315, 339
  War of Independence 56, 58, 65, 91, 123, 133, 134, 135, 298, 311, 313, 314, 325, 351, 363, 364, 468
Anbury, Thomas 549
Ancaster, 1st Duke of 577
Ancaster, 2nd Duke of 577
Ancaster, 3rd Duke of 577
Ancaster, 4th Duke of 577
Ancaster, 5th Duke of 577
Andover 439
Andrews, John 66–7
Angelo, Henry 433
Anglesey 275, 279, 399
Annesley, James 39
Anstey, Christopher 372, 488
Apsley, 1st Baron 396, 544
Apsley Guise (Beds.) 422
Arkwright, Richard 487, 502, 518–19
Armstrong, John 504
army 20, 105, 296
Artillery Company 303
Arundel, Stephen 273
Arundell, 8th Baron 68
Ash, John 33, 482–3
Ashbourne 431
Ashburnham, 1st Baron 525–6
Ashburnham, 2nd Earl of 563
Ashendon (Bucks.) 169
Ashton under Lyne 181, 343
Aston, Sir Willoughby 134
Atcham 158, 242, 254

Atterbury, Francis 76, 104
Auckland, 1st Baron 353
Audley, Matthew 261
Augusta, Princess of Wales 546
Austen, Jane 517
Avery, Benjamin 74
Aylesbury 23, 179, 277

Badcock, Lovel 299
Bage, Robert 3, 36, 138, 380, 387, 540
Baghott, Kinnard 418
Bagot, Lewis 19, 88
Balguy, Thomas 52–3
Baltimore, 6th Baron 542, 544, 573
Bampfylde, Catherine, Lady 573
Banbury 474
Bancroft, Thomas 481
Bank of England 58, 209
Bankes, William 389
Banks, Sir Joseph 325, 326
Barclay, David 90
Barkham, Suffolk 252
Barnard, Sir John 126, 188, 308–9
Barrington, Shute 88, 563
Barry, James 508, 558
Barrymore, 7th Earl of 554–5
Barwell, Richard 9
Basingstoke 501
Bastard, John 300
Bate Dudley, Sir Henry 390, 433
Bateman, 2nd Viscount 560
Bateman, William 512–13
Bath 214, 231, 238, 259, 345, 379, 384, 500
Bathurst, 3rd Earl 566
Bathurst, 1st Baron 220, 318, 399–400, 419
Bathurst, Henry 55
Bayley, Thomas Butterworth 438
Beadon, Richard, Bishop of Gloucester 566
Beauchamp, Francis, Viscount 190
Beauclerk, Lord James 555
Beauclerk, Lord Vere 178
Beaufort, 2nd Duke of 531
Beaufort, 3rd Duke of 413
Beaufort, 5th Duke of 566
Beckford, William 149, 155, 307
Bedford 286, 567–8
Bedford, 4th Duke of 179, 194, 291, 518, 562, 567
Bedford, 5th Duke of 538, 554, 560, 576
Bedford, Gertrude, Duchess of 546
Bedford Level 213
Bedfordshire 185
Belford (Northumb.) 390
Bell, Hugh Barker 23
Benevolent Institution 563
Bennett, Agnes Maria 22, 387, 391, 445
Bentham, Jeremy 212, 472, 535
Berington, Joseph 79, 100

Berkeley, 5th Baron 548
Berkeley Square 454
Berkshire
    elections 55
    landownership 39–40
    magistracy 400, 406, 407, 414–15
    petitions 56
    quarter sessions 178, 574
    turnpikes 237
Bermondsey 236
Bernard, Thomas 403–4
Berners, Henry 418
Berwick 190
Bessborough, Henrietta, Countess of 136, 559, 571
Bethel, Slingsby 337–8
Beverley 95
Bewdley 182, 215, 563
Bickerstaffe, Isaac 131
Bird, John 293
Birmingham
    bank 255
    canal 201
    disorder 470, 472
    highways 163
    hospital 260
    incorporation 215–16, 260, 448
    local legislation 171, 205
    magistracy 438
    manufacturing 61, 497–8
    parliamentary lobbying 173, 201
    party 126
    poor relief 208
    religion 22, 73, 75, 79, 95
    small debts court 25, 244–5
    social geography 451
    unrepresented 187, 206, 270
Blachford, John 388
Blackburn, Lancelot 394
Blackstone, William 3, 27, 85, 148–9, 152, 154, 166, 271
Blake, William 219
Blaney, Arthur 388
Blewbury (Berks.) 430
Blick, Francis 414
Blount, Thomas 65
Board of Agriculture 338–9, 463, 560
Bodmin 179
Bolingbroke, 1st Viscount 31, 32, 59, 154, 258, 305, 313, 524, 549, 570
Bolton 181, 206
Bolton (Cumbria) 171
Bolton, 3rd Duke of 414
Bolton, 6th Duke of 68, 531
Boston 236
Boston tea party 147
Boswell, James 383

Boucher, Jonathan 116, 495
Bouverie, Sir Jacob 573
Bowles, John 61
Boydell, John 503
Brackley 291
Bradford 172, 177
Brand, John 124, 473-4, 480-1
Braxfield, Lord 59, 211
Brecknock, Timothy 149
Brecon 228
Breconshire 279
Brereton, Thomas 203
bridges 180-2
Bridgewater, 3rd Duke of 336, 576
Bridgwater 345
Bridport 92, 96, 229
Brighton 206
Bristol
    Burke and 189, 190
    corporation 210, 219
    county societies 384
    Dissent 76
    land tax 346
    local legislation 76, 219, 440-1
    magistracy 438
    parliamentary lobbying 173
British Fishery 126
British Lying-In Hospital 562
Brixton 343
Bromley, William 185-6
Brook, Sir Richard 336
Brooke, Frances 8, 369
Brooke, Henry 32, 49, 483
Brooke, James 420
Brosely 234
Broughton, Sir Thomas 417
Brown, John 32, 52, 475, 477
Brown, Lancelot 386
Browne, Moses 564
Browne, Thomas 67
Bruere, George 293
Brydges, Sir Egerton 381, 514, 580-1
Buccleuch, 3rd Duke of 563
Buchan, 11th Earl of 549
Buckham, Mrs 261
Buckingham 179
Buckingham, 1st Marquis of 68, 190, 422
Buckinghamshire
    carriage tax 360
    lace-making 185
    land tax 343
    land tax commission 425, 428
    landownership 39, 289
    local legislation 179, 180
    magistracy 222, 398, 401-3, 405-7, 411, 418
    militia 298-9
    oath taking 104

rivalries 177
shrievalty 409
turnpikes 237, 253
Buckinghamshire, 1st Earl of 414-15, 417
Buckner, John 88
Bulcamp (Suffolk) 252
Bulkeley, 5th Viscount 276
Bulkeley, 7th Viscount 579
Bunbury, Sir Charles 327-8, 443
Burford 61
Burgh, James 6, 7, 502
Burgoyne, John 5, 284, 540, 549
Burke, Edmund
    and Barry 508
    and Catholicism 83
    Civil List reform 55
    in Club 558
    on Dissent 72
    on freeholders 272
    on French Revolution 582-3
    on hawkers 336
    on instructions 189, 190, 198
    on landed interest 314
    and loyalism 93
    on militia 298
    and nobility 538, 580
    and party 124, 136, 537
    and political rights 98
    on poor law 177
    on taxation 117, 352, 358
Burlington, 3rd Earl of 120, 556
Burlington House 550, 559
Burnell, Mary 68
Burnet, Gilbert 28, 85, 122
Burnet, Thomas (1635?-1715) 3
Burnet, Thomas (d. 1750) 28
Burney, Charles 84
Burney, Fanny 83, 298, 521
Burton, John 300
Bury 181
Bury St Edmunds 179
Bush, Thomas 399
butchers 175
Bute, 3rd Earl of 90, 135, 315, 327, 348, 361, 464, 534, 546
Butler, Charles 42, 79, 101
Butler, John 14, 276, 301, 495, 566
Butler, Joseph 88, 477
Buxton 66
Byrom, John 120-1, 203, 210

Caernarvonshire 394
Calne 252
Camberwell 450
Cambridge
    corporation 223, 230
    colleges 360

hospital 493
  improvement 219, 230–1, 232, 239
  peers at 524
Cambridge, Richard Owen 5, 380
Cambridgeshire
  land tax 345
  magistracy 399, 414, 415
  militia 298
  quarter sessions 178
  reformers 539
  representation 188
  shrievalty 409
  turnpike 203
Camden, 1st Baron 149
Campbell, Admiral 518
canals 165, 181, 196, 198, 201, 204, 208, 209, 336
Candler, Anne 166
Canning, George 584
Canterbury 158, 231, 284, 352
Capdock (Suffolk) 257
Cappe, Catherine 66, 387, 432
Carew, Sir Nicholas 348
Carew, Thomas 103, 126
Carles, John 438
Carlisle 137, 212, 439
Carlyle, Thomas 582
Carmarthen, Francis, Marquis of 517, 545, 554
Carnac, John 128
Carnarvon, 1st Earl of 345
Carnarvon, Henry, Marquis of 526
Caroline, Queen 460, 536, 547
Carte, Thomas 410–11, 476–7
Carter, Elizabeth 24, 301, 535
Cartwright, John 290, 488, 502
Carysfort, 1st Earl of 272, 279
Castle Sowerby 148
Cave, Sir Thomas 327
Cavendish, Lord John 358
Cecil, Richard 23
Chambers, J. D. 372
Chambers, Robert 519
Chambers, William 110
Champion, Richard 198
Chandler, Samuel 80, 81
Chandos, 1st Duke of 526
Chandos, 2nd Duke of 416
Chandos, 3rd Duke of 531
Chapone, Hester 503
Chard 238
Chardin, Sir John 492
charity 491–500
Charles I 465
Charles II 149, 442
Charlotte, Queen 464, 507, 536, 547, 562
Charlton, Lionel 197
Charterhouse Square 454
Chatterton, Thomas 460

Chaytor, William 24
Cheltenham 240, 260
Chequers 402
Cherry, Francis 388
Cheshire
  button weavers 203
  petition from 157, 281
  representation 188, 199, 200
  road bill 201
  small debt courts 243
Chester, Richard 500
Chesterfield 93
Chesterfield, 3rd Earl of 521
Chesterfield, 4th Earl of 381, 541–2, 548, 569–70, 579
Chesterfield, 5th Earl of 418, 528, 548
Chesterfield, Melusina, Countess of 569
Chichester 218, 227, 233
Church
  as corporation 210
  and Dissent 71–98
  and elections 268–70
  and nobility 532, 568–9
  and oath taking 110–11
  and Parliament 151–2
  and party 126–7
  and property 14–24, 35
Churchill, Charles 444
Cibber, Colley 131, 567
Cirencester 160, 399, 434
Civil List 55, 143, 146
Clapham 449
Clarence, William, Duke of 557
Clarendon, 2nd Earl of 252
Clark, Alured 128, 496
Clarke, Samuel 109
Cleaver, William 418
Cleghorn, George 268
Cleland, John 5, 381–2, 470, 481, 482, 483, 553
Clement XIV 100
Cleobury, John 418
clergy
  criticism of 430–1
  and Dissent 86–9, 92–3
  and enclosure 328–9, 431
  and land tax commission 422–3, 426–8
  as magistrates 411–20
  and new institutions 242, 243, 262
  and Parliament 151–2
  and paternalism 432, 485–6
  as proprietors 16–18
  and subscription 109
Clerkenwell 171, 236, 269, 453
Cleveland, 3rd Duke of 24
Clitheroe 136, 181
Clive, Robert 529
Coatham 389

Cobbett, William 138, 312
Codrington, Sir William 466
Cogan, John 530
Coke, Daniel 286
Coke, Sir Edward 191
Coke, Lady Mary 381, 520
Coke, Thomas William 21, 55, 136, 198, 275, 330, 514, 560, 561
Colchester 168–9, 442, 443
Cole, William 271, 398, 399, 486
Coleridge, Samuel Taylor 511, 540
College of Physicians 268
Colston, Edward 491
Combe, William 198, 480, 481, 519
Commission of Public Accounts 263
Conduit Mead 40
consumer goods 10
Conswick 60
Conway, Henry Seymour 554
Conybeare, John 121
Cooke, William 551
Coram, Thomas 492
Corfe Castle 171
corn laws 316–18, 322–3, 369–70
Cornwall
    assizes 179
    Convocation of Tinners 213–14
    fishery 191
    land tax commission 428
    magistracy 439
    representation 188, 193, 199
Cornwallis, Caroline 519
corporations 209–32
Coutts, Thomas 117, 359
Coventry
    button manufacture 203
    corporation 218, 441
    Dissent at 89, 92, 97, 131
    elections 282, 285, 286, 467, 488–9
    land tax 343
    local legislation 171
Coventry, 5th Earl of 394
Cowper, 1st Earl 420
Cowper, 3rd Earl 575
Cowper, William 38, 210, 302, 430
Coxe, J. H. 237
Coxe, William 310
Coxheath camp 299, 301
Cradock, Joseph 26, 132, 410, 560
Cranborne Chase 68
Cranborne, James, Viscount 539
Craven 66
Craven, 6th Baron 129, 537
Craven, Elizabeth, Lady 12, 541, 555, 579
Craven, John 415
Crew, Nathaniel, Lord 119
Cricklade 252, 277, 321

Crofts, James 489–90
Croke, Alexander 401–2
Cromford 487
Cromwell, Oliver 196, 322
Crosse, Henry 403
Crowley 487
Cumberland
    land tax 161, 345–6
    landowners 378
    local legislation 161
    magistracy 396
    unimproved 495
Cumberland, Henry Frederick, Duke of 7, 535, 544, 547
Cumberland, Richard, bishop 434
Cumberland, Richard, of Glos. 434, 485–6
Cumberland, Richard, jun. 432
Cumberland, Richard, sen. 432
Cumberland, William Augustus, Duke of 297
Cymmrodorion 564

Danby, William 489–90
Darby, Hannah 474
Darlington, 2nd Earl of 24, 302
Dartmouth, 2nd Earl of 198, 562, 563, 568, 570
Davenant, Charles 42
Davies, David 456
Davies, Sneyd 123
Dawson, John 302
Day, Thomas 273–4, 325, 491, 502, 538, 539
Deal 161, 301
De Berdt, Dennys 315
debt, law of 4, 265
    small debt legislation 43, 131, 158–61, 172, 234, 243–8, 260
Decker, Sir Matthew 317
De Clifford, Baron 566
Defoe, Daniel 3, 5, 26, 29, 36, 145–6, 165, 273, 310, 457, 467
De Grey, Thomas 195
Delamer, 4th Baron 568
De La Rochefoucauld, Duc 170
Delaval, Sir John 189–90, 536
De Lolme, Jean Louis 46
Denbigh, 6th Earl of 109, 129, 307, 408, 560
Derby 229, 249–50, 379
Derby, 10th Earl of 47
Derby, 12th Earl of 531, 540, 554
Derbyshire
    button weavers 203
    land tax commission 425
    land tenures 66
    landownership 62, 235, 289, 379
    local act (1769) 157
    magistracy 417
    militia 299

oath taking 104
representation 188, 196
De Salis, Henry 418
Despenser, Baron le 299, 405
Devon 104, 278, 376
Devonshire, 4th Duke of 296
Devonshire, 5th Duke of 66, 299, 559
Devonshire, Georgiana, Duchess of 546, 556,
    571, 572
Digby, 6th Baron 578
Digby, William 492
Dilettanti 557
Disney, John 109–10, 434
dispensaries 563
Dissenters
    and land tax 422
    legal rights 72–8, 80–90, 98–9, 130
    and moneyed interest 305
    politics 91–6, 135, 268
    and rank 524
Dixon, Abraham 390
Dodd, William 20, 262, 418, 528, 548
Doddridge, Philip 89
Doddsley, Robert 460
Dodington, George Bubb 512
Dodwell, William 415
Dolben, Sir William 134
Donaldson, William 66, 338, 372
Doncaster 205, 218
Dorchester 171, 239
Dorset
    land tax commission 424
    militia 300
    magistracy 393, 406, 435
    representation 196
    turnpikes 235
Dorset, 1st Duke of 417
Douce, Francis 557
Dover 161, 234, 301
Dowdeswell, William 351
Dublin Society 493
Ducie, 2nd Baron 408, 419
Duck, Stephen 460
Dudley 163
Dudley, 1st Viscount 198
Dudley, 2nd Viscount 69
Dundas, Henry 515, 563
Dundas, Sir Lawrence 529–30
Dunning, John 515
Dunstable 253
Durham
    corporation 222
    elections 286
    militia 302
    turnpikes 235
Durham, County 62, 68, 447
Dutch 60

Dyer, George 494, 538
Dyer, John 4, 380

East India Company 34, 45, 148, 184–5, 194,
    209, 210, 214, 479
Eden, Sir Frederick 347, 376
Edmondson, Joseph 517
Effingham, 3rd Earl of 528, 576
Egerton, Francis 243
Egerton, John 198
Egerton, Samuel 194, 273
Egerton, Sir Thomas 198
Egremont, 3rd Earl of 252, 560
Egyptian Society 558
elections
    corruption 128, 221
    dislike of 267–70
    disorder at 465–8
    disputed 52, 468
    franchise 270–87, 466
    humiliation of 273–7
    and magistracy 395–6
    and oaths 113
    and peers 529–31
    and religious divisions 94
    and representative system 187, 270–87
    septennial 155
    and shrievalty 407–8
    and statutory bodies 131, 230–1
Ellesmere 158
Elliot, Sir Gilbert 135
Ellys, Anthony 57
Elwes, John 11, 194
Ely 344
Emmanuel Society 563, 570
enclosure 45, 147, 148, 166, 169, 170, 171, 195–
    6, 258, 307–8, 315–16, 325, 333, 334–6,
    370–1, 431, 474
Englefield, Sir Henry 557
engrossing 370–2
Erskine, James 151
Essex
    elections 275, 334
    land tax 345, 346, 347
    landownership 289
    magistracy 442
    militia 298, 299–300, 301
    representation 193, 196, 197
    rivalries 179–80, 443
    and tolls 183
Essex, 4th Earl of 539
Etherington, Sir Henry 520–1
Evans, Allen 78
Evelyn, John 31, 146
Evesham 198
Ewer, John 459
Excise Board 263, 443

Exeter 93, 111, 217–18, 246, 290, 304, 354, 379, 499–500
Exeter, 8th Earl of 12
Exeter, 9th Earl of 43–4, 247–8
Emden 20
Eynsham (Oxon.) 171

Falkland Islands 144
family 500–9
Fane, Henry 512
farmers 329–35, 371, 429
Farnham 301
Fawley Court 382
Felbrigg (Norfolk) 390
Fellowes, Robert 249
Female Orphans Asylum 562
fen drainage 145, 158, 167, 260
Fenwick, Sir John 104
Ferguson, Adam 31, 33
Fermanagh, 1st Viscount 411
Ferrers, 4th Earl 542
Ferrers, Baron de 556, 557
Fielding, Henry 368, 386, 444, 471, 476, 504
Fielding, Sarah 3
Fife, 1st Earl of 512
Finch, Daniel, Lord 64–5
Finsbury 452
Fitzherbert, Maria Anne 83
Fitzmaurice, Thomas 275
Fitzmaurice, William, Viscount 576
Fitzwilliam, Lord Henry 554
Fleming, John 226
Fletcher, John 123, 200, 549
Flinders, Matthew 247–8
Flint 267
Foley, 2nd Baron 568
Foley, Paul 147
Folkes, Martin 571
Folkestone 161
Foote, Samuel 523
Ford, James 381, 483, 576
Forester, Pulter 17
Forty-Five 116, 304, 432
Foster, Thomas 561
Fothergill, Alexander 173
Fothergill, John 89
Foulis, J. C. 301
Foundling Hospital 77, 129, 387, 404, 562, 568
Fox, Charles James 45, 91, 117, 135, 136, 146, 214, 219, 535, 536, 547
Fox, Henry 105, 359, 534
France 60
Fraser, Robert 376
Frederick, Prince of Wales 126, 214, 492, 508, 562, 570
free-masonry 211
friendly societies 172, 374

Frome 206
Fulham 450
Fuller, John 62
Fuller, Rose 443
Furness 104

Gabell, Henry 552
Gainsborough 182, 352
Gale, Leonard 293
game laws 45, 331–2, 334, 335
Garbett, Samuel 355
gardening 12–13
Gardiner, Richard 530
Garrick, David 132
George, William 53
George I 512
George II 153, 464, 512, 513, 533–4
George III
    as carriage owner 522
    and Catholic Emancipation 83–4, 102
    coronation 189
    and Dissent 89, 90
    and Lord Denbigh 109
    and militia 296
    and mobs 464
    and nobility 513, 518, 529–30, 534–5, 539
    and parliamentary sovereignty 153
    and party 124
    as patron 562, 563
    popularity 507–8, 547–8
    as public speaker 578–9
    and William Dodd 20
George IV 83, 562, 573
Germain, Lord George 282, 535
Gibbons, Sir John 168
Gibbs, James 570
Gibson, Edmund 86, 88, 151–2, 412
Gideon, Sampson 530
Gilbert, Thomas 156, 157, 392
Gilpin, William 127, 550
Girdler, J. S. 263
Girle, Caroline (later Mrs Lybbe Powys) 62, 381, 382, 554
Gisborne, Thomas 93–4, 202, 502, 519, 569
Glamorgan 39, 52, 398, 411
Glanville, John 52
Gloucester
    bridge 182
    corporation 220, 223
    elections 286, 566
    hospital 256, 261, 497
    magistracy 439, 443
    social geography 451
    workhouse 268
Gloucester, William Henry, Duke of 304
Gloucestershire
    clothiers 472

land tax commission 428
    magistracy 399, 407, 411, 418–19, 421
    prison reform 234, 405
    turnpikes 253
Glover, Richard 326
Glyn, Sir Richard 488–9
Glynn, John 444
Goddard, W. S. 551
Godolphin, Elizabeth 491
Godwin, William 34, 35, 110, 233, 274, 445, 540
Goldsmith, Oliver 36, 121, 368–9, 465, 484, 507
Goodricke, Henry 134–5
Goodwood 550
Gordon Riots 101, 229, 303, 392, 469, 475
Gore, Thomas 526
Gosport 216
Gough, Richard 21
Gower, 2nd Earl (later 1st Marquis of
    Stafford) 198, 408, 516, 564
Grace, Thomas 408
Grafton, 3rd Duke of 382, 537–8, 541, 546, 560
Granby, John, Marquis of 133
Grant, James 483
Grantham 120, 324, 392, 400, 439
Granville, 2nd Earl 534
Granville, John 419
Great Marlow 293, 418
Great Yarmouth 69, 343–4
Green, John, Bishop of Lincoln 328–9
Green, Thomas, jun. 97, 310
Green, Thomas, sen. 96, 97
Greene, Joseph 94, 417–18
Greg, Samuel 487
Gregory, George 63
Gregory, John, of Leicester 258
Gregory, John, of Whitchurch 173
Grenville, George 105, 153, 315, 348
Grey, Richard 498
Grimston, 1st Viscount 555–6
Grosvenor, Henrietta, Lady 7, 544
Grosvenor, Richard, 1st Baron 7, 535, 544
Grosvenor Square 454
Guernsey 167
Guise, Sir William 328
Guy, Thomas 491
Gwynn, John 26, 451

Haddington, 6th Earl of 144–5
Halifax 160, 164, 172, 182, 206, 234, 245, 246–
    7, 262
Halifax, 1st Earl of 432
Hallifax, Samuel 88
Halsey, Edmund 512
Hamilton, Archibald Rowan 298
Hammond, J. L., and B. 372
Hampden, Thomas 298–9, 406
Hampshire 94, 237, 354, 414, 416, 531

Hampstead 23
Hanbury, William 131
Handel commemorations 547
Hanmer, Job 402
Hanmer, Walden 398, 402
Hanway, Jonas 123, 166, 195, 385, 440, 458, 476,
    492, 503, 509, 565
Harbord, Sir Harbord 198
Harcourt, 1st Earl 382, 552, 562
Harcourt, 2nd Earl 536, 579
Hardman, James 162
Hardwicke, 1st Earl of
    as judge 50, 74, 151, 152, 179, 269–70
    and magistracy 393, 394, 396, 397, 399, 413,
        414, 415, 527
    and militia 296, 426
    religion 87, 570
    and Scotland 47
    and shrievalty 407–8
Hardwicke, 2nd Earl of 409, 570
Hardwicke, 3rd Earl of 570–1
Hare, Francis 151
Hare, Hugh 4
Harewood, 1st Baron 549
Harewood House 549
Hargrave, Francis 98
Harley, Edward, Lord 570
Harley, Robert 397, 425, 531, 533
Harrington, James 51–4, 57, 58, 479, 583
Harris, Howell 151
Harrison, Jeremiah 432
Hartesmere (Suffolk) 157, 251
Hartopp, Sir Edmund Cradock 201, 410
Haslop, John 301
Hastings 440
Hastings, Warren 148
Haugh (Lincs.) 452–3
Haute Huntre (Lincs.) 148
Havard, Neast 229
Haweis, Thomas 20
Hawkesworth, John 36, 505
Hawkins, Sir John 40, 180, 445, 505
Hawkins, Laetitia-Matilda 40, 225, 445
Hawkshead 21
Hay, William 156
Hazeland, William 484
Hearne, Thomas 388
Helston 215, 441
Henley, John 346
Hensborough, Matthew 299
Henson, Gravenor 17, 289
Hereford 264, 496, 566, 566, 568
Herefordshire 131, 428, 463, 560
Herring, Thomas 86
Hertford, 1st Earl of 381, 382, 541, 562
Hertford, Isabella, Countess of 381
Hertfordshire 345, 539

Hervey, Augustus John 543
Hervey, Frederick Augustus 87
Hervey, John, Lord, 113
Hervey, William 137
Hey, John 110, 493
Heytesbury 397
Heywood, Samuel 281
Hibbert-Ware, Samuel 126
Hickey, William 483
Higgins, Francis 85
High Wycombe 275
Highgate 113
Hildesley, Mark 42
Hill, Aaron 124
Hill, Rowland 22
Hind, Richard 486
Hindon 277
Hitchin 74
Hoadly, Benjamin 53, 109
Hoare, Henry 255, 311
Hoare, Richard Colt 311
Hobbes, Thomas 28, 33, 108
Hogarth, William 274
Hoghton, Sir Henry 90, 134
Holberg, Ludvig 464, 510
Holborn 17, 267, 453
Holkham 561
Holland, Sir John 344
Hollis, Thomas 56, 127, 432
Holroyd, John 391
Homer, Henry 431
Honiton 285
Hood, 1st Baron 563
Hooke, Andrew 480
Hopkins, William 109
Horne, George 87, 88, 284
Horsham 278
Horsley, Samuel 38, 80, 84, 87, 100, 101, 469
Horton, Mrs Anne 544
Hoskins, W. G. 372
hospitals
    contracts 256
    and Dissent 77
    financing 251
    foundation and government 493-500
    offices 259-60, 261, 264, 268
    and party 128-9
    patrons 562-3, 568
    and public domain 212
Howard, John 77-8, 404
Howarth 177
Howlett, John 3
Hull 61, 182, 208, 223
Hume, David 29, 30, 108, 119, 282, 288, 310
Hungerford, John Peachy 94, 125
Hunt, William 400
Hunter, Thomas 540, 569

Huntingdon, 9th Earl of 549
Huntingdon, 10th Earl of 24, 562
Huntingdon, Selina, Countess of 123, 528, 549,
    569-70
Huntingdonshire
    elections 272-3
    land tax commission 428
    militia 298
    magistracy 393, 394
    reformers 538-9
    shrievalty 409
Hurley Priory 38
Hutcheson, Archibald 353
Hutchins, John 435
Hutton, William 22, 33, 61, 126, 201, 244, 245,
    458

Ibbetson, James 167
Ilminster 238
India 31, 34
Inns of Court 166-7
Ipswich 89, 96, 119, 120, 179, 225, 249
Ireland
    commerce 198, 318-19, 322, 323-5
    linen manufacture 184
    peerage 511, 512-13, 517-18
    representation 200
    taxation 339
Irvine, Edward 422

Jackson, Edward 413
Jackson, John 109
Jacobites 60, 102, 103, 116
James I 262
James II 149, 442
James, Samuel 74
Janssen, Sir Theodore 309-10
Janssen, Theodore 319
Jebb, John 1-2, 35, 210, 211, 502
Jenkinson, Charles 536
Jenner, Charles 479, 513
Jenyns, Soame 302, 313, 375
Jephson, Alexander 35
Jersey, 4th Earl of 382
Jesuits 210, 475
Jews 48, 114, 115
John, King 53
Johnson, Maurice 125
Johnson, Samuel 31, 37, 81, 127, 153, 177, 431,
    443, 459, 465, 555
Johnson, Samuel (nephew of Reynolds) 543
Johnstone, Charles 262, 398, 401, 502
Johnstone, Sir James 61
Jones, Henry 548-9
Jones, Sir William, MP 283-4
Jones, William, of Nayland 390

Jones, William (orientalist) 87, 154, 211, 502, 523–4, 558, 571
Jortin, John 109
Joyce, Jeremiah 538
juries 279–80

Kaines, Henry 435
Kaye, Sir Richard 419
Keate, William 365–6
Keck, A. J. 257
Keighley 206
Kelly, Hugh 386
Kelmarsh Hall 383
Kendal 168, 180
Kenrick, Timothy 93
Kent
  county MPs 201
  land tax 345, 426
  local legislation 160–1
  magistracy 392–3, 439
  small debt courts 245
Kent, Nathaniel 389–90
Kentish Town 450
Keppel, Augustus 137
Kerrich, Thomas 86
Kerrick, Walter 42
Ketley 564
Kidderminster 92
Kidgell, John 255
Kimber, Edward 481–2
King, Edward 557
King, Gregory 457
King, John 389, 445, 558
Kingston, 2nd Duke of 543–4
Kingston, Elizabeth Chudleigh, Duchess of 543–4, 571, 573, 579
Kippis, Andrew 2
Kirkleatham 389, 390–1
Kirton 43–4, 247–8
Knapp, Matthew 299
Knapp, Primatt 418
Knight, Richard Payne 13
Knight, Robert 60
Knox, Vicesimus 4, 419, 469, 502, 556

lace-making 185
Lackington, James 449
Lambeth Asylum 262
Lancashire
  bridge bill 181–2
  elections 281, 282, 531
  land tax 162, 343, 428
  small debt courts 243
  turnpike 173
Lancaster 180
landownership 37
  and business 61–3, 479–82

divisions 326–39
as interest 58–64, 305–49
and law 36–51
magistracy 438
and middle class 365
and paternalism 265–7, Chap. 6 passim
and property qualifications 233–4, 237–8, 288–305
registry 50–1, 293
status 211
taxation 448
tenures 65–70, 278–80, 329–30
Langhorne, John 392
Lansdowne, Baron 199
Launceston 179, 220
Laurence, French 278
Law, Edmund 88
Law, John 86
Leacroft, Thomas 299
Le Blanc, Abbé 118, 274
Lee, Sir George 21, 391, 396
Lee, John 214
Lee, Robert 400
Lee, Sir William 404, 409
Lee, Sir William, LCJ 471
Leeds 61, 182, 187, 206, 252, 269, 442, 451, 473, 496
Leeds, 4th Duke of 168
Leeds, 5th Duke of 563
Leeds–Liverpool canal 204, 208
Le Gay, Charles 227
Legh, Thomas 198
Le Grice, Charles 18
Leicester
  corporation 224, 228
  elections 467
  hospital 128, 257–8, 496, 497, 547, 562
  party at 131
  plate tax 360
Leicester, 1st Earl of 399, 561
Leicestershire
  elections 94, 122, 125, 133, 275–6, 278–9
  land tax 341
  landownership 235, 289
  militia 299
  representation 196
  shrievalty 410
  turnpikes 239
Le Neve, Philip 556
Lewes 250
Lewis, John 110
Lewisham 256
Lewisham, George, Viscount 557
Lichfield 443
Lichfield, 3rd Earl of 562
Liddell, Sir Henry 170
Lincoln 277, 379, 443, 451, 496, 497, 566–7

Lincolnshire
  county society 384
  elections 137
  fen drainage 167
  hospital 384
  land tax 162
  land tax 341
  local legislation 160, 175, 234
  magistracy 416
  quarter sessions 178
  wool 324–7
Lindsey, Theophilus 110
linen manufacture 184
Littleton, Edward 105
Liverpool
  corporation 217, 223
  domestic life 501
  elections 95, 130, 170
  hospital 130, 259
  land tax 343
  local legislation 173–4, 175
  magistracy 438
  mock corporation 218–19
  parliamentary lobbying 173
  small debts court 244
Liverpool, 2nd Earl of 205
Llandaff 92
Lloyd, Posthumus 89
Lloyd, Richard 156, 241, 461
Lloyd, William 531
Lock Hospital 577
Locke, John 5, 8, 28–9, 30, 33, 37, 45, 338
Lockier, Francis 51, 105
Lofft, Capel 86, 116, 284
London
  Bethlehem 498
  Bridewell 498
  bridges 180–1
  coal duty 182
  county societies 384
  court of conscience 131
  custom of 46
  land tax 343, 345
  London Hospital 5, 129, 255, 261–2, 562
  plate tax 360–1
  religious life 97
  representation 95, 188, 193, 195, 290
  St Luke's Hospital 498
  St Thomas's Hospital 486, 500
  social geography 449–52
  turnpikes 258–9
  upper-class residence 378–9
London, City of
  corporation 447
  Dissent 78, 263
  Elections Act (1725) 215, 268
  estates 40

finance 311, 314
finances 218
land tax 347
local legislation 175
paving 183, 260
rivalries 180
royal hospitals 217
Lonsdale, 3rd Viscount 564
Lords, House of
  and George III 535–6
  and House of Commons 291–2, 525–6, 529–31
  and legislation 191, 202, 328–9
  and magistracy 420
  and new peers 516
  and party 119
  and press 578
  representative function 196, 198, 537
  size 512
  and Walpole 533
Lort, Michael 84
Lovatt, Sir Jonathan 409
Lowndes, Charles 402
Lowndes, Richard 401
Lowndes, Thomas 418
Lowndes, William 41
Lowth, Robert 86
Lowther College 564
Lowther, Sir James 137, 396, 408
loyalism 91, 135–6, 313, 469
Ludlow, Peter 518
Lumley, Richard 277
Lumley Saunderson, Lady Frances 518
Luttrell, James 290
Lydd 439
Lyddell, Sir Henry 119
Lygoe, Francis 402
Lying-In Charity 562, 570
Lyme Regis 56, 197, 344, 365
Lynch, William 284
Lyttelton, 2nd Baron 559, 573, 575
Lyttelton, Charles 556
Lyttelton, George, 1st Baron 49, 378, 420
Lyttelton, Richard 291

Macaulay, Catherine 26–7, 37, 211, 523
Macaulay, Thomas Babington 134
Macclesfield, 1st Earl of 49, 515
Macclesfield, 2nd Earl of 556
MacDowell, L. C. B. 34
Madden, Samuel 468, 512
Maddox, Isaac 397, 398, 498
Magdalen Hospital 129, 262, 562
magistracy
  borough 440–4
  and butter regulation 319
  compared with freeholders 272

composition and evolution 400–22
and gunpowder making 44
and party 394–5
and paternalism 376, 377, 391–2, 432–3
and property qualifications 234
and turnpikes 237–8
Maidstone 183, 561
Malden, George, Viscount 563
Malthus, Thomas 458
Man, Isle of 43
Manchester
    Dissent at 76, 77
    hospital 496
    incorporation 448
    and Irish linen 184
    land tax 343
    local legislation 77, 203, 204, 206, 236
    magistracy 437–8
    manufactures 2, 462
    mock corporation 218
    parliamentary lobbying 174
    and party 120, 126–7, 131
    representation 187, 198–9, 270
    street improvement 170
Manchester, 3rd Duke of 394
Manchester, 4th Duke of 226, 272, 537–8
Manchester, 4th Earl of 530
Manchester, Isabella, Duchess of 520
Manners, Lord Robert 517, 576
Manningham, Thomas 5
Mansfield, William Murray, 1st Earl of 24–5,
    49, 73, 78, 85–6, 218, 293–4, 319, 354, 535,
    544
Market Harborough 23, 94, 125
Marlborough, 2nd Duke of 274, 391, 562
Marlborough, 3rd Duke of 562
Marlborough, 4th Duke of 539
Marlborough, Sarah, Duchess of 56, 555
Marshall, William 374, 376
Marsham, Charles 573
Martin, John 82
Martin, Sir Mordaunt 470
Mason, William 58, 130
Massingberd, Charles Burrell 12
Mauduit, Israel 90, 450
Mawbey, Sir Joseph 137
Maxwell, Francis Kelly 262
Melbourne (Derbys.) 365
Meredith, Sir William 201
Methodism 35, 123
Mickle, William Julius 478–9
Middlesex
    electors 56, 149–50, 272, 468
    highways 163
    land tax 342–3
    magistracy 222, 258, 444–5
    registry 50

relations with City 180
representation 188, 193
small debt legislation 159
Small Pox Hospital 562
Middleton Stoney 382
Midleton, 4th Viscount 63
Mildmay, Carew Harvey 311, 379
militia 79–80, 266–7, 295–305, 361, 471
Millar, John 30, 463, 482
Milner, John 101
Milton, Lord 47
Misterton (Notts.) 166
Moir, John 97, 124, 262, 269, 580
Monson, 3rd Baron 566–7
Monson, Elizabeth, Baroness 566
Montagu, 1st Duke of 67, 562, 563
Montagu, 2nd Duke of 571
Montagu, Charles 526
Montagu, Lord Charles 226
Montagu, Elizabeth 62, 460
Montesquieu, Charles de Secondat, Baron de 7,
    29, 30, 59–60, 283
Montgomery 158
Montgomeryshire 182, 388
Montrose, 3rd Duke of 563
Moore, Sir Francis 50
Moore, John 58
Morcott (Rutland) 374, 563
More, Hannah 389, 435, 479, 509
Morris, Claver 422
Morris, Corbyn 310, 338
Morris, Lewis 7
Mortimer, H. W. 295
Morton, 14th Earl of 556
Moss, William 490, 500
Mostyn, Charles Browne 79, 80
Muilman, Peter 193, 334
Muir, Thomas 211
Musgrave, Sir Christopher 143, 337, 439

'nabobs' 9, 295, 321, 429–30
Nacton (Suffolk) 252
Nash, Thomas 488–9
National Debt 58, 60, 69, 116, 143, 155, 250–1,
    308–9, 310, 353
Natural History Society 557
navy 263, 271, 319, 475
Naylor, Benjamin 93
New Shoreham 277, 278, 321
Newark 442
Newbury 178
Newcastle
    butter trade 170
    coal industry 204
    corporation 438, 439, 473, 474
    finances 217
    hospital 128, 496

Newcastle (*cont.*):
  land tax 347
  parliamentary lobbying 173
Newcastle, 1st Duke of 176, 296, 333, 356, 363, 416, 466, 470–1, 475, 533, 534, 559
Newington Butts 450
Newmarket 178
Newton, John 270
Newton, Thomas 506, 532
Nicholson, Margaret 518
Nicholson, William 531
Nimmo, William 38
Nollekens, Joseph 21, 558, 576
Norfolk
  and American War 116
  assizes 179
  elections 55
  land tax 345, 347, 428
  local acts 158
  magistracy 391, 414, 417
  militia 302
  shrievalty 409
Norfolk, 11th Duke of 531, 536, 560, 566
North, Anne, Lady 464
North, Frederick, Lord
  and American war 313
  and Church 89
  and corporations 215
  and Dissent 98
  and finance 112, 144, 163, 311, 351, 354, 355–6, 358–9, 362, 363, 365
  and framework knitting 204
  and Ireland 198–9
  on magistracy 444
  on militia 295–6
  and mobs 464
  and nabobs 321
  and party 133, 134
  as patron 562
  and peerage 513, 535
  personal life 546
  and press 468
  and Pynsent 56
  in 1784 91, 135
  as turnpike trustee 238
North Leigh (Oxon.) 333
Northampton 128, 382, 496, 498
Northamptonshire
  elections 128, 131, 200–1, 280–1
  farmers 560
  lace-making 185
  land tax commission 428
  landownership 316
  magistracy 432
  turnpike 202
Northaw (Herts.) 388
Northington, 1st Earl of 408

Northington, 2nd Earl of 563
Northumberland 62, 161, 302, 447
Northumberland, 1st Duke of 552, 569
Northumberland, Elizabeth, Countess of 273
Norton, Lady Dorothy 5
Norwich 179, 217, 236, 246, 249, 284, 451, 472, 529, 530
Nostell 387
Nottingham
  Dissent at 73, 91, 92
  elections 134, 290
  library 137
  magistracy 443, 444
  militia 443
  paving bill 249
  poor 474
  workhouse 236
Nottinghamshire 413, 416, 417, 428
Nowell, Thomas 149
Nugent, Robert 48
Nuneham Courtenay 382

oaths 99–114, 236
Odiham 563
Ogden, James 270
Oglethorpe, James 176
O'Kelly, Denis 297–8
Old Artillery Ground 157
Oldfield, T. H. B. 277
Oldham 438
Oldswinford 234
Onslow, 1st Earl of 276
Onslow, Arthur 104
Onslow, Thomas 137
Orford, 2nd Earl of 399
Orton, Job 91, 130, 573
Osborne, John 299
Oswestry 158
Otley 206
Over Arly (Worcs.) 430
Oxford 202, 343, 382, 496
Oxford, 4th Earl of 568, 569
Oxford University 92, 122, 134, 360, 470, 524, 573
Oxfordshire
  election of 1754 69, 279
  land tax commission 428
  landownership 289
  magistracy 354, 391, 395, 415
  militia 299
  turnpikes 235

Paine, Thomas 115, 161, 333, 356, 502
Paley, William 34, 143, 148, 310, 434
Pall Mall 454
Palmerston, 3rd Viscount 59
Paltock, Robert 484–5, 509

Pardo, Convention of 54
Parkin, Charles 125
Parliament
  authority 148–56
  character of legislation 156–72
  and charity 493
  composition of Commons 294–5
  and copyright law 26
  and highway controversy 163–4
  and interests 176–86, 335
  and land tax commission 423
  and landownership 288–95, 316–29, 334
  and lobbying 172–5
  and local custom 162–3
  and oaths 107
  and property 43–51, 139–40, 156
  reform 205–6, 277–8, 292, 320–2, 467, 529
  and representation 187, 270–87
  sessions 140–5, 147
  see also Acts and Bills; Lords, House of
Parr, Samuel 382–3, 472, 487–8, 506
Parr, Thomas 402
Parsons, Nancy 546
party
  decline of 118–38
  and family 502
  and land tax commission 423–4
  and landownership 306–15
  and local legislation 203
  and magistracy 393–5, 405, 411–12
  and parliamentary sovereignty 152–3, 156
  and patronage 568
  and popular disorder 469–71, 476–7
  terminology 209
  and titles 521, 523, 533
Paul, Sir George Onesiphorus 441, 466
peers
  accessibility 549–51
  chaplains 23–4, 570
  and Commons 530–1
  and land tax commission 421
  and morality 540–9
  patronage 27, 531–2, 551–69
  and politics 532–40
  privileges 523–9, 544
  as public servants 574–81
  and religion 569–74
  as titled class 510–22
  at university 524
Pelham, Charles Anderson 137–8
Pelham, Henry 62, 107, 109, 318, 356, 361, 363, 394, 468, 533
Pelham, Thomas 191
Pembroke, 9th Earl of 567, 571
Pembroke, 10th Earl of 302
Pennant, Thomas 266–7, 336
Penrose, John 500

Penrose, Thomas 267
Perceval, John, Viscount 303
Percival, Thomas 2, 144, 502
Percy, Hugh, Lord 576
Percy, Thomas 35
Pershore 198
Peterborough 278, 439
Peterborough, 3rd Earl of 252, 531
Petersham, Charles, Viscount 549
Petre, 9th Baron 83, 100, 101
Petworth 252
pews 21–3
Philanthropic Society 494, 570
Philips, George 57
Phyllis Court 554
Piccadilly 454
Piers, Henry 5
Pilsworth, Charles 402
Pinney, J. F. 295
Pinney, John 295
Pitt, Thomas 64, 284
Pitt, William, elder 43
  and Habeas Corpus Bill 534
  lobbied 197
  and magistracy 394
  and party 124
  as peer 515, 516
  rewarded with property 56
  and suspending power 149
  and taxation 361
  and Tories 292, 296
Pitt, William, younger
  and lobbying 205
  and party 135
  and peerage 511, 513–14
  personal life 546
  and press 468
  and religion 82, 101
  in 1784 45, 219
  taxation 2, 37, 118, 155, 340, 351, 352, 353, 355–6, 358, 361–2, 363
  at theatre 554
  and wool trade 325–6
Pius V 83
Place, Henry 435
Playfair, William 516, 579
Plymley, Joseph 376
Plymouth 77, 177, 223, 224, 230, 290, 379
Pochin, William 125
Pococke, Richard 442, 483
Pole, Charles 194
Pole, German 121
Polwhele, Richard 377, 387
Pomfret, 2nd Earl of 67
Pontefract 182
Poole 443
Pope, Alexander 123, 258

poor law
  attitudes to poor 456–64
  conduct of poor 475–6
  legislation governing 156–8, 240–1
  poor rate 354, 373–4
  as source of disputes 177
  workhouse bills and incorporations 76, 212,
    213, 236, 240–3, 248–9, 251, 254, 256
Popham, Edward 384
population 369–70
Porteous riots 147
Porteus, Beilby 19, 79, 88
Portland, 3rd Duke of 137, 396, 454, 536, 559,
  562
Portsmouth 96, 216
Postlethwayt, Malachy 314, 352, 379
Potter, John 492, 519
Pownall, Thomas 322–3, 325
Powys, 1st Earl of 394, 407
Pratt, Samuel Jackson 9, 391
Prendergast, Sir Thomas 394
Prentice, Thomas 91
Preston 178, 284
Price, Richard 2, 35, 36, 81, 91, 93, 351, 502
Price, Uvedale 13
Pridmore, Thomas 374
Priestley, Joseph 2, 73, 79, 81, 84, 93, 245, 470,
  502, 524, 576
Privy Council 145, 204–5
property
  and Church 14–24, 265
  and copyright law 25–8
  diversity of 58–70
  English obsession with 1–14
  and legislation 156–8
  of MPs and peers 195–6
  and party 119, 124, 128, 137
  and peerages 514–15
  regulation of 35–51
  and the State 51–7, 139, 145–8
  and theory 28–34
property qualifications
  generally 207–9, 265
  land tax commission 421–2
  magistracy 420–1, 429, 440, 444
  militia 295–305
  parliamentary 54, 64, 113, 192–3, 288–95
  statutory bodies 230, 233–43, 242, 246–7
Prowse, Thomas 163–4, 526
Prussia 184
Pulteney, William, Earl of Bath 348, 515, 520
Pulteney, William 353
Purefoy, G. H. J. 418
Pyle, Edmund 90
Pynsent, Sir William 56

Quakers 16, 73, 90, 92, 103, 105, 106, 473

Queenborough 162

Rack, Edmund 338, 372, 378, 480
Radcliffe, John 491, 511, 562
Radnor, 1st Earl of 573
Radnor, 2nd Earl of 252, 300, 563, 573–5, 579
Ragley 381
Ramsay, Allan 311–12, 468
Ramsay, John 487
Randolph, Thomas 122
Rann, Joseph 97
Ray, Martha 547
Reading 178
Reeves, John 469
Repton, Humphry 12, 55
Revell, Tristram 299
Revolution of 1688 2, 4, 103, 118, 211, 214, 378
Reynolds, George 151
Reynolds, Sir Joshua 368, 558
Reynolds, Richard 502, 564
Rice, John 60
Richard I 53
Richards, John 18
Richardson, Isaac 473
Richardson, Samuel 541
Richardson, Thomas 174
Richardson, William 106
Richmond (Surrey) 249
Richmond (Yorks.) 180
Richmond, 2nd Duke of 120, 176, 291, 333, 416,
    534, 550, 556, 559, 562, 568, 571
Richmond, 3rd Duke of 135, 233, 433, 537–8
Ridley, James 4
riots 469–74
Ritson, Joseph 165
Rivers, 1st Baron 563
Rivington Grammar School 75
Robartes, Francis 143
Robertson, William 55
Robinson, Sir George 125
Robinson, John 378
Robinson Morris, Matthew, 2nd Baron
    Rokeby 537
Robinson, Perdita 547
Rochdale 181, 486
Rochester 161, 224, 282
Rochford, 4th Earl of 135, 298
Rockingham, 2nd Marquis of 132, 166, 311, 315,
    361, 517, 535, 539, 546, 560, 578
Rolle, John 328
Roman Catholics
  legal rights 78–80, 82–4, 93, 98, 99–101, 114
  property rights 8, 37, 48, 51, 99–100
  taxation of 115
Romilly, Samuel 4, 50, 584
Romney 439
Romney, 2nd Baron 562, 573

Romney, 3rd Baron 561
Ross, John 87
Rossendale 181
Rotherhithe 208
Roubiliac, Louis François 577
Rousseau, Jean-Jacques 523-4
Royal Academy 121
Royal Humane Society 562, 570
Royal Institution 404
Royal Society 84, 556, 571
Royston 125, 178
Rugby 129
Rumbold, Thomas 295, 321
Rumford, Count von 404
Russell, James 113
Rutland 393, 428, 561
Rutland, 3rd Duke of 120, 128, 133
Rutland, 5th Duke of 201, 222
Ryder, Dudley 319
Ryder, Joseph 473
Rye 442-3
Ryley, Samuel 22, 553

Sacheverell, Henry 17
St Albans 556
St Albans, 2nd Duke of 178, 274
St Aubyn, Sir John 387
St Bartholomew 253
St Botolph without Aldersgate 217
St Botolph Aldgate 182
St Botolph without Bishopsgate 217, 254
St Dunstan's in the West 342
St Eustatius 35
St George's, Hanover Square 447
St George's Hospital 562
St Giles in the Fields 346
St James Westminster 220-1
St Marylebone 195, 220, 259, 346, 449, 454
St Mawes 190
St Paul, Covent Garden 220, 235
St Sepulchre, Middlesex 169, 229
Salford 343
Salisbury 129, 169, 222, 255, 379
Saltash 215
Sandwich 161, 203
Sandwich, 4th Earl of 203, 255, 272, 273, 394,
    538-9, 546-7, 554, 557, 563
Saunders, Richard 403
Saunders, Robert 256
Savile, Sir George 56, 277, 327
Sawyer, Sir Robert 337
Scarborough 222, 389
Scarborough, Frances, Dowager Countess of 518
Scheemakers, Peter 577
Schimmelpenninck, Mary Anne 79, 524
schools
    charity schools 77, 121, 495, 563

of industry 561
and party 129
public 550-2
Scotland
    and Bute 547-8
    elections 55
    after Forty-Five 47
    Johnson on 31
    linen manufacture 184, 205
    peerage 511, 517-18
    Scottish Corporation 563
    taxation 339-40
    Union of 1707 155
    wool 324
Scott, James 132
Scott, John 197-8, 264, 332
Scott, Sarah 386
Scott, William 134
Scroggs, Sir William 442
Seaford 113
Secker, Thomas 88, 499
Selby-Leeds canal 201
servants 10, 503-6
Seymour, Sir Edward 103
Shaftesbury 321
Shaftesbury, 5th Earl of 68
Sharp, Granville 154, 502
Sharp, John 16
Sharp, Thomas 128
Shebbeare, John 3, 153, 156, 176, 441, 507, 577
Sheffield 187, 451
Sheffield, 1st Baron Sheffield 325
Shelburne, 2nd Earl of, later 1st Marquis of
    Lansdowne 135, 272, 295, 535-6, 546, 576
Shenstone, William 13, 386, 460, 510
Sherard, Sir Benet 562
Sherborne 474
Sherlock, Thomas 261
Shipley, Jonathan 132
Shipmeadow (Suffolk) 255
Shippen, William 309
Shipton, John 399
Shoreditch 269, 495
Shottesbrook (Berks.) 388
Shrewsbury
    bridge 182, 443
    corporation 222, 223, 228
    elections 467
    hospital 129-30, 232, 397, 497, 563
    local institutions 228-9
    local legislation 158, 171, 249
    magistracy 439
    petition 182
    poor law incorporation 241, 242, 248-9, 257
shrievalty 407-10, 421
Shropshire
    landlords 376

Shropshire (*cont.*):
  and party 129–30
  poor law incorporations 241–3, 254
  relations with Shrewsbury 182, 443
Shuttleworth, J. A. 425
Siddons, Henry 519
Sidney, Algernon 149
Sinclair, Sir John 266, 365
Sinking Fund 155
Skelton, Philip 32–3, 40–1
Skottowe, Coulton 298
slavery 7–8, 98, 148, 460
Smalridge, George 76
Smelt, Leonard 539–40
Smirke, Robert 503
Smith, Adam 107, 329, 346, 458, 460, 463
Smith, George 211
Smith, John, author 324
Smith, John, unitarian 93
Smith, Sydney 264
Smith, Thomas 485–6
Smith, William 249, 475, 484
Smollett, Tobias 368, 377, 386, 398, 401, 465
Snettisham, Norfolk 390
Society of Antiquaries 125, 556, 557
Society of Arts 127
Society for Bettering the Condition of the
  Poor 404, 561, 562–3
Society for Charitable Purposes 572
Society for Constitutional Information 210, 524,
  538
Society for the Encouragement of Good
  Servants 504
Society for the Relief of Poor Married
  Women 570
Society for the Relief of the Ruptured Poor 563
Society for the Reformation of Manners 570
Society of Supporters of the Bill of Rights 210,
  524
Somerset
  local legislation 169–70
  magistracy 400, 442
  poor rate 374
  small debts 159
  turnpikes 238, 252
Somerset, 6th Duke of 120, 511, 556
Somerville, Thomas 66, 135
Somerville, William 418
Sons of Clergy 272, 568
Sophia Dorothea 547
South Sea Bubble 42, 60, 309–10, 491
South Mimms (Middx.) 475–6
South Shields 22
Southampton 128, 224, 225–8, 232
Southwark 22, 131, 182, 193, 269, 274, 343
Spain 313, 314, 324
Spalding Society 125

Speed, John 225–7
Spence, Thomas 35
Spencer, 1st Earl 399, 564, 571
Spencer, John 56
Spencer, Margaret Georgiana, Countess 514,
  571–3, 575, 579
Squire, Samuel, Bishop of St David's 5, 52
Stafford, Susanna, Marchioness of 570
Staffordshire
  button weavers 203
  magistracy 526–7
  militia 304
  quarter sessions 178
Stamford, 5th Earl of 562
Stanhope (Durham) 453
Stanhope, 3rd Earl 111, 538
Stanhope, Philip 542, 548
Stanley, Hans 226
Stanley, Thomas 174
Stanwell 168, 170
statutory commissions 75, 77, 127–8, 130, 146,
  208–13, 221–64
Stedman, John 31
Steele, Richard 118
Stehn, George 402
Sterne, Laurence 385, 507
Stewardson, William 106–7, 112
Stinton, George 465
Stirling, 5th Earl of 400
Stirling, James 487
Stirlingshire 38
Stockbridge 322
Stockdale, Percival 275, 551
Stockport 206, 246
Stockton 129
Stoke on Trent 187
Stourhead 311
Stowmarket 257
Strafford, 1st Earl of 131, 202, 433
Strafford, 2nd Earl of 549
Strafford, Anne, Countess of 549
Stratford-upon-Avon 94, 253
street improvement 171, 182–3, 208, 223–32,
  235, 239–40, 249–50, 261
Stroudwater and Thames canal 208
Strutt, John 289
Strutt, William 229, 487
Stuart, James 490
Stukeley, William 87, 125, 392, 400–1, 571
Sturge, John 86
Sturgeon, Lady Henrietta Alicia 517
Styal 487
Styleman, Nicholas 389–90
Sudbury 276
Suffolk
  and American War 116
  assizes 179

Dissent in 74, 95
  elections 276
  land tax 345
  local acts 158, 165
  poor relief incorporations 241–2, 262
  shrievalty 409
  wool 326
Suffolk, 8th Earl of 555
Suffolk, 11th Earl of 67, 527
Sullivan, Richard 502
Sunday Schools 97, 123, 463
Sunderland 187
Surrey
  elections 137, 276
  land tax 345, 346
  land tax commission 428
  landownership 235, 289
  militia 299, 301
  registry 50
  small debt courts 245
  turnpikes 255
Sussex
  county MPs 201
  elections 466
  land tax 345, 424, 428
  magistracy 416, 417
  militia 304
  prison reform 405
  rivalries 176–7
  turnpikes 191, 235, 255
Sutton Coldfield 21, 215–16
Swift, Jonathan 49, 58, 312, 477
Swindon 252
Swinton (Yorks.) 489
Sykes, Francis 295, 321
Symonds, John 365

Talbot, Thomas 565–6
Talbot, Thomas, bishop 82
Taunton 77, 226, 268, 271, 285, 345, 379, 442
taxes
  American stamp tax 43, 359
  attorneys 357
  auctions 357
  beer 43, 348, 361, 464
  bricks 351–2
  candle 349, 350–1
  carriages 348, 356, 357, 358, 359, 360, 362, 364, 522
  cider 43, 327–8, 361
  coal 182, 352, 355
  dogs 348
  excises 144, 308, 340, 352, 357, 361
  fustians 174, 355, 361
  generally 43, 143
  glass 358, 361
  hair powder 363

  hearths 351
  horses 348, 362
  houses 163, 347, 348, 351, 355, 358, 362
  income tax 118, 353, 356, 363–4
  land 143–5, 161–2, 306, 314, 316, 339–47, 351, 352–3, 359–60, 365, 422–3, 525–6
  leather 350–1, 354
  legacies 353–4, 364
  licences 357, 358–9
  local 181, 249–50
  and local custom 161–3
  malt 143–4, 327–8, 348–9
  newspapers 356
  and oaths 106–7
  pawnbrokers 357
  plate 43, 188, 354, 356, 360–1, 362, 364
  poll 375
  receipts 362, 364
  and religious minorities 115
  salt 265, 349, 350–1
  servants 267, 348, 356, 358, 362–3
  shops 361–2
  soap 349, 350–1
  stamps 357, 358–9
  tea 359, 362
  Townshend duties 43
  voluntary 116–18
  windows 347, 348, 351, 356, 358, 360, 362, 364
Taylor, John 431, 434
Tempest, John 134
Temple, William (clothier) 324, 461
Temple, William Johnson 383, 479, 548
Tenison, Thomas 22
Terrick, Richard 459
Tewkesbury 92, 229–30, 232, 250, 441, 466
Thatched House Society 265
theatricals 382, 553–5
Thelusson, Peter 46–7
Thelwall, John 374, 450–1, 473
Thetford 179
Thistlethwaite, James 480
Thomlinson, John 521
Thorold, Sir John 148, 325
Three Choirs 566, 568
Throsby, John 122
Thurlow, 1st Baron 44, 271, 515
Tickell, Richard 515
Tillotson, John 16
tithes 15–16, 17, 328–9, 347, 356, 412, 421
Tollemache, Lionel 576
Tompkins, Henry 299, 406
Tooke, John Horne 41, 150, 195, 328, 468
Tooke, William 195
Topham, John 52
Tories
  and attack on party 121–2

Tories (*cont.*):
  break-up 531
  and courts 119
  and George III 89
  and landownership 48, 58–9, 291, 292, 305–8, 318
  and militia 296
  and oaths 103
  and suicide 5
  and taxation 265–6
  see also party
Totnes 253
Toulmin, Joshua 97–8, 123, 226, 268, 271, 345
Tower Hamlets 245, 447–8
Towers, Joseph 515
Townsend, James 144, 196
Townshend, 3rd Viscount 399
Townshend, George, 4th Viscount 296, 530
Townshend, Charles 108, 341
Trapp, Joseph 17
Treby, Sir George 270
Trent and Mersey Canal 198, 208, 327, 336
Trimmer, Sarah 502
Tring 168
Trowbridge 461–2
Truman, Sir Benjamin 522
Trusler, John 111, 269, 274, 445
Tucker, Josiah 30, 37, 193, 357–8
Tunbridge Wells 124–5
Tunstall, John 412
Tunwell, Francis 219
Turner, Baptist Noel 194–5, 270
Turner, Charles 389, 390–1
Turner, Daniel 211
Turner, Sir Edward 195
Turner, Thomas 466–7
turnpike trusts 131, 163–4, 171, 173, 181, 202, 203, 208, 209, 234, 235, 236–9, 252–3, 258–61, 332, 336, 361, 430
Tyburn tickets 263
Tyrringham, Francis 402, 403

Uxbridge, 1st Earl of 68

Valenciennes 576
Vanneck, Sir Gerard 276
Vansittart, Arthur 388
Venn, Richard 152, 155
Vere, 1st Baron 562
Verney, 2nd Earl 64
Vernon, Edward 241
vestries 195, 217, 220, 221, 223
Victor, Benjamin 303
Vignoles, Charles 227
Villiers, George, Viscount 554
Viner, Samuel 473, 552
Volunteering movement 79–80, 117, 303–4

Vyner, Robert 266, 338

Wake, William 110
Wakefield, Gilbert 92
Wakefield Lodge 382
Wales
  land tax commission 425
  landowners 307
  language 7
  local reforms 405
  MPs 200, 205
  turnpikes 235, 267
Walker, George 92
Walker, Richard 257
Walker, Samuel 19–20
Walker, Thomas 174
Wallace, Robert 478
Waller, Edmund 299
Wallingford 232, 240, 439
Walpole, Horace 534, 555, 567
Walpole, Sir Robert
  and Atterbury Plot 104
  and Catholicism 115
  and Dissent 74
  fall 408
  fiscal policy 43, 144, 155, 265, 306, 309, 313, 315, 340, 344, 352, 358, 380–1
  and instructions 189
  and mobs 464
  and peers 533
  and press 468
  and property 54
  and workhouse bill 204
Walsall 163, 201
Walter, John 412, 413, 419
Wapping 271, 274
Warburton, William 88, 541
Wardell, J. W. 300
Wareham 171
Wargrave 554
Warley camp 83, 301
Warren, John 87, 459
Warrington Academy 2
Warwick 441
Warwickshire
  button weavers 203
  landowners 235, 383
  militia 299
Washington, George 56–7
Westmacott, Sir Richard 577
Williams Wynn, Sir Watkin 408
Watson, Richard 2, 90, 92, 132, 152, 365, 476
Watts, Isaac 74
Way, Gregory 521–2
Weaver navigation 170, 199, 200, 327, 527
Webb, S. J., and B. 447
Wedderburn, Alexander 34, 453

Wedgwood, Josiah 502
Wednesbury 201
Welch, Thomas 422
Weld, Edward 83
Weld, Thomas 83, 101
Wells 345
Welton (Northants.) 169
Wenlock 439
Wentworth, 2nd Viscount 313, 562
Wesley, John 5, 32, 35, 123, 364, 502, 569
West Bromwich 96, 201
West Indies 200
Westbury 285
Westminster
  bridge 567
  elections 470
  government of 447–8
  land tax 346, 347
  paving commission 182, 183, 220–1, 235,
    454–5
Westmorland 161, 345–6
Wetherby 208
Wharton, Charles 56
Wharton, Duke of 275
Whigs
  and attack on party 121–2
  and courts 119
  and landownership 48, 59, 306, 312, 313
  and oaths 103, 110
  Real 2–3
  and suicide 5
  and taxation 265
  see also party
Whitbread, Samuel 192, 341, 403
Whitby 164, 197, 227, 452, 473
Whitchurch 158, 169, 173, 241–2, 254
White, Gilbert 456–7
White, Sir Thomas 285
Whitechapel 183, 208
Whitehead, William 477–8, 552
Wigan 181
Wight, Isle of 375–6
Wilberforce, William 23, 136, 164
Wilkes, John 81, 144, 150, 189, 204, 233, 297,
  469
William III 103, 104
Williams, Watkin 435
Williams, Sir William 322, 435
Williams, William 51
Willis, Browne 278, 418
Willis, Cecil 329
Willis, Richard 562
Willis, Thomas 418
Willoughby de Broke, 13th Baron 526–7
Willoughby de Broke, 14th Baron 563, 569
Willoughby of Parham, 5th Baron 90, 556
Wilson, Thomas 136

Wiltshire
  cavalry in 302
  feast 384
  magistracy 397, 574–5
  militia and volunteering 304
  representation 188, 193
Wimbledon 572
Wimpole 570
Winchelsea 440
Winchester 128, 496, 551, 552
Winchilsea, 5th Earl of 556
Winchilsea, 8th Earl of 13, 560, 561, 563
Windham, William 83, 135, 190
Windsor 178, 274
Winn, Sir Rowland 387
Winterton, 1st Baron 252
Witney 354
Wokingham 439
Wollstonecraft, Mary 7, 477, 520
Wolverhampton 178, 182, 187, 201, 206, 235
Wood, William 483–4
Woodbridge 345
Woodhouse, James 460
Woodstock 216
woollen manufacturers 107, 148, 173, 184, 185,
  323–6
Woolnoth, Miss 542
Worcester 217, 236, 343, 464, 568
Worcestershire 289, 299
Wordsworth, William 511
Workington 206, 511
Wotton Underwood (Bucks.) 169
Wyndham, Sir William 265, 266
Wynne, Sir Watkin Williams 120

Yarmouth 91, 135
Yates, Joseph 3
Yeovil 238
York
  assembly 120
  custom of 46
  elections 536
  land tax 346
  local legislation 169
  library 259
  lunatic asylum 130
  petition 182
York Buildings Company 38
York, Edward Augustus, Duke of 520, 562
Yorke, Charles 178
Yorke, James 88
Yorkshire
  elections 281, 282
  magistracy 438, 442
  militia 300
  reform movement 56, 57, 539–40
  registry 50

Yorkshire (*cont.*):
  taxation 363, 448
  turnpike trusts 259, 431
  wool trade 325–7, 472–3, 501–2
Young, Arthur
  on agriculture 42, 258, 317, 325, 326, 333–4,
    338, 576
  on paternalists 389, 390, 489
  on poor law 374, 476

  on taxation 116, 353, 365
  on turnpikes 237
  on workforce 461–2
  on workhouses 256, 257
Young, Robert 494, 565

Zoffany, Johan 508
Zouche, Henry 433